FROM CONFUCIUS TO ZHU XI

GLOBAL PERSPECTIVES ON MEDIEVAL AND EARLY MODERN HISTORIOGRAPHY

General Editor
Francesco Borghesi, *Università di Modena e Reggio Emilia/University of Sydney*

Editorial Board
Yigal Bronner, *Hebrew University of Jerusalem*
Mario Casari, *Sapienza Università di Roma*
Wiebke Denecke, *Massachusetts Institute of Technology*
Hilde De Weerdt, *Katholieke Universiteit Leuven*
François-Xavier Fauvelle, *Collège de France, Paris*
Mercedes García-Arenal, *Centro de Ciencias Humanas y Sociales, CSIC, Madrid*
Benoît Grévin, *Centre de Recherches Historiques, EHESS-CNRS, Paris*
Racheli Haliva, *Shandong University*
Tomoyasu Iiyama, *Waseda University*
Jun'ichi Isomae, *International Research Center for Japanese Studies, Kyoto*
Alessandra Russo, *Columbia University*
Francesca Trivellato, *Institute for Advanced Study, Princeton*
Ying Zhang, *The Ohio State University*

VOLUME 1

From Confucius to Zhu Xi

The First Treatise on God in François Noël's
Chinese Philosophy (1711)

Edited by
THIERRY MEYNARD, S. J.,
and **DANIEL CANARIS**

BREPOLS

 The GPH series logo of an upside-down Dutch ship draws its inspiration from a similar image found in a seventeenth-century Japanese map of Nagasaki that is now kept in the British Library Asian Collection (Or.75.g.25). Drawn from a particular spatial perspective and in line with local cartographical and pictorial traditions, it represents a historical source that defies a singular reading and works as a constant reminder of the complexity and connectivity of early modern historiographical practices. An upside-down ship inspired by this map was selected as the series logo because it symbolizes the mandate of the series to defamiliarize modes of historical writing and to diversify this field of study.

British Library Cataloguing in Publication Data
A catalogue record for this book is available from the British Library.

© 2023, Brepols Publishers n.v., Turnhout, Belgium.

All rights reserved. No part of this publication may be reproduced, stored in a retrieval system, or transmitted, in any form or by any means, electronic, mechanical, photocopying, recording, or otherwise without the prior permission of the publisher.

ISBN: 978-2-503-60179-3
e-ISBN: 978-2-503-60180-9
DOI: 10.1484/M.GPH-EB.5.130894

Printed in the EU on acid-free paper.

D/2023/0095/3

Table of Contents

List of Illustrations   6

Preface   7

Thierry Meynard and Daniel Canaris
Introduction   9

Yves Vendé
1. Intellectual Biography of François Noël   17

Thierry Meynard
2. Composition and Sources of the First Treatise   33

Thierry Meynard
3. Noël's Interpretation of Neo-Confucianism   79

Wang Ge
4. Evaluation from the Perspective of Chinese Philosophy   109

Pierre Galassi
5. Theological Themes in the First Treatise   129

FRANÇOIS NOËL'S *CHINESE PHILOSOPHY* IN THREE TREATISES

Preface to the Reader   164

First Treatise: On Chinese Knowledge of the First Being, or God
Chapter 1: Did the Ancient Chinese have Knowledge of God,
   the First Being, or were they Atheists?   169
      Question 1: How many Meanings does
         Tian Have in the Ancient Books?   169
      Question 2: What Perfections do the Ancient Classics
         Attribute to *Tian* and *Shangdi*?   171
      Question 3: Whether the Ancient Books and Classics Give
         True Knowledge of the First Being, or God, and whether
         it is False that the Ancient Chinese were Atheists   200
Chapter 2: Do Modern Chinese People Have Knowledge
   of the First Being or God, or Are they Atheists?   205
      Question 1: What Perfections do the Modern Commentators
         Attribute to *Tian* or *Shangdi*?   206
      Question 2: How Do Modern Authors Explain *Tian*,
         and Do they Distinguish *Tian* from *Shangdi*?   248

Question 3: What Do Modern Commentators Recognize as First Origin of the World?	262
Question 4: Definitions, Types, and Properties of the Spirits by Modern Authors	285
Question 5: What does *jiaoshe* or the Sacrifice to Heaven and Earth Mean?	305
Question 6: What does the Two-Character Word *taiji* or First Ultimate of Things Mean among the Chinese?	340
Question 7: Do Modern Works Give True Knowledge of the First Being or God, and Are Modern Chinese Atheists?	351
Chapter 3: True Name of God in China	357
Question 1: Can God be called *Shangdi*, that is the Lord and Ruler of Heaven, or Supreme Lord?	357
Question 2: Can God be Called *Tian* (Heaven)?	378
About the Authors	392
Bibliography	393
Concordance List of Titles and Names	407
Charts	413
Index	419

List of Illustrations

Figure 1. 'Doctrinae Sinicae brevis indagatio', ARSI, Fondo Gesuitico 724/4, fol. 1^r	155
Figure 2. 'Doctrinae Sinicae brevis indagatio', ARSI, Fondo Gesuitico 724/4, fol. 1^v–2^r	156
Figure 3. 'Doctrinae Sinicae brevis indagatio', ARSI, Fondo Gesuitico 724/4, fol. 130^v	158
Figure 4. BnF, collection Bréquigny 15, fol. 1	158
Figure 5. *Summarium NAT*, 1704	159
Figure 6. Cover of the *Libri sex*, 1711; copy given by the author to the Jesuit College of the Holy Trinity, Lyon, 1712	160
Figure 7. Cover of the *Philosophia Sinica*, 1711	161
Figure 8. Manuscript note on the cover of the *Philosophia Sinica*	161

Preface

The Jesuit translations of the Confucian classics that were published in the seventeenth and eighteenth centuries were the primary vehicle through which early modern and Enlightenment Europe was introduced to the intellectual traditions of China. They inaugurated Sinology as a discipline and contributed to the wave of enthusiasm for *chinoiserie* that endured at least until the mid-eighteenth century. Only in the nineteenth century, when academic Sinology was born, were these translations definitively displaced as tools for accessing Chinese thought. These academic Sinologists were often harsh in their judgement of their Jesuit predecessors, whom they criticised as tendentious in their reading of the Chinese classics. As a result, these early Jesuit translations were for a long time side-lined, studied only by missiologists and the Jesuits themselves.

In recent years, there has been a renaissance in the philological study of these texts. Scholars in both China and in the West have uncovered the sources and the translation strategies that were used to convey Confucian concepts to Europe. Nonetheless, the philological study of Jesuit translations remains for the most part separated from studies of their European reception. Moreover, scholars working on China in the Enlightenment have largely tended to cluster around national contexts, while neglecting the diffusion of texts across linguistic boundaries.

In 2019, a group of scholars from across Australia and China met at the University of Sydney to reflect upon future directions for research on Sino-Western intellectual exchange. Their research project, entitled *Transforming the East: Jesuit Readings of the Chinese Classics and their Dissemination in Early Modern Europe (ca. 1590–1773)*, was selected for funding by the Australian Research Council in 2021. The principal aim of this ongoing project is to re-evaluate Europe's first encounter with Chinese thought through the Jesuit translations, and to produce a comprehensive history of the dissemination of these translations in Europe.

This project has brought together scholars from different fields and linguistic backgrounds: Europeanists, sinologists, missiologists, and historians of philosophy and religions are working together to place the history of Sino-European intellectual encounters into dialogue with the philological analysis of Jesuit translations. Another aim of the project is to make primary and secondary sources written in languages other than English accessible to anglophone scholars through the publication of critical editions and an international collaborative digital platform (https://textus-sinici.org/).

The present volume illustrates the interdisciplinary approach taken by this project. This publication was led by two Partner Investigators of the project: Thierry Meynard, a Sinologist and historian of philosophy based at Sun Yat-sen University, and Daniel Canaris, an early modern intellectual historian formerly based in China, who has recently been appointed a DECRA Research Fellow at the University of Sydney. They drew together a team of scholars from China and Europe to analyse, from a systematic and multifocal perspective, the First Treatise of the *Philosophia Sinica* (1711) by the Flemish Jesuit François Noël. Meynard and Canaris also produced the first vernacular translation of the treatise, which they publish here accompanied with rich annotations and punctilious transcriptions of Chinese characters from the corresponding manuscript version of the text. The result is an unprecedented window into Noël's idiosyncratic and innovative marriage of neo-Scholasticism and neo-Confucianism.

Given its focus, it is only fitting that such a book is the first in a series intended to provide a platform for scholarship engaging with the intertwining of philological and hermeneutical methods as the core of research in the humanities, as well as addressing recent debates in the field of comparative historical studies. This study thus clearly represents all that the wider book series *Global Perspectives on Medieval and Early Modern Historiography* advocates for: a return to philological studies as a fertile way to interpret the texts that every civilization has produced, together with their contexts and global connections.

Francesco Borghesi and Yixu Lü

THIERRY MEYNARD AND DANIEL CANARIS

Introduction

From the the late sixteenth century, Jesuit missionaries in China sought to place Christianity in dialogue with Chinese philosophy by translating and interpreting the Chinese classics. Following contemporary Chinese practice, they focussed on the Four Books, that is, the canon of 'Confucian' texts codified in the Song dynasty. At first they were motivated by the view that intimate knowledge of the Confucian classics would facilitate their engagement with Chinese literati and that tracing continuities between the Christian and the Confucian traditions could help Christianity take root in China. But as opposition to the Jesuits' accommodation strategy grew during the Chinese Rites Controversy over whether Chinese Catholics could perform rituals in honour of their ancestors and Confucius the Jesuits began to publish their translations to provide a philological and philosophical justification for their missionary strategy. The most famous and widely read of these translations was the *Confucius Sinarum philosophus*, which was published in 1687. The Jesuits articulated a two-pronged hermeneutic: the ancient Chinese were monotheists who worshipped the true God while the Confucian and ancestor rites were not superstitious but civil and political rites devoid of religious content.

A dimension often forgotten by missiologists focussed on mission history and praxis is that the Jesuits also addressed their published translations to the general European reader. These works influenced, both directly and indirectly, European thinkers such as Pierre Bayle, Nicolas Malebranche, Leibniz, Christian Wolff, and Voltaire. Unprecedented access to Chinese thought contributed at least in part to the deprovincialization of European thought and to the development of globalized and comparative perspectives in the Enlightenment.

The Jesuits' complex interpretation of Confucianism received divergent and perhaps unexpected responses from their European readers: for thinkers with atheist sympathies such as Bayle and Wolff, Confucianism provided evidence that societies can operate without religion whereas for deists such as Voltaire it showed that sophisticated forms of philosophical and theological thinking were possible outside of a Judaeo-Christian framework. While scholars have long appreciated the influence of the Jesuits' translations on the development of Enlightenment thought, the challenge for scholarship today is to reconcile the missionary reading of Chinese philosophy as it was elaborated in China and the Sinological

Thierry Meynard, Sun Yat-sen University, Guangzhou, China

Daniel Canaris, University of Sydney, Australia

production intended for the intellectual scene in Europe. Such an undertaking requires interdisciplinary collaboration between Sinologists and Europeanists, as well as between philologists and philosophers.

The career and intellectual output of the Flemish Jesuit François Noël (1651–1729) are pregnant with implications for this dialogue between missiology and comparative philosophy. Noël was one of the foremost interpreters of Chinese philosophy at the dawn of the Enlightenment, and his translations and commentaries represented the culmination of the Jesuits' Sinological research. In 1711, he published at Prague the *Sinensis imperii libri classici sex* (Six Classics of the Chinese Empire, henceforth *Libri sex*), which contained the first full translation of the Four Books ever published in Europe, as well as the first published translations of the *Xiaojing* (Classic of Filial Piety) and *Xiaoxue* (Elementary Learning) in a Western language.[1] Hence Noël's translations provided the fullest expression of the neo-Confucian canon at the time, and were unrivalled until the birth of academic Sinology in the ninteenth century.

Alongside the *Libri sex*, in the same year and same city Noël also published *Philosophia Sinica* (Chinese Philosophy). The title of the work bespeaks Noël's intent to address not only theologians involved in the Chinese Rites Controversy but also the general European reader. These pretensions are elaborated in the preface: Noël claims that he defines Chinese thought as philosophy not in terms of the modern conception of the discipline taught in university courses, but in terms of the discipline practised by the ancients, who stressed practical concerns and the pursuit of wisdom. This artful preface might have piqued the interest of erudite readers during the early eighteenth century, when many intellectuals, particularly in Italy, were pining for the recovery of ancient philosophy as a counterpoise to arid Scholasticism and the apparently heterodox implications of post-Cartesian philosophy. But Noël quickly reveals that he remains wedded to the Aristotelian-Thomistic frameworks of his predecessors, and that he is focused on the core questions of the Rites and Terms Controversies. Accordingly, Noël reorders Chinese philosophy according to Aristotelian principles over the course of three treatises: the first of Chinese conception of the First Being or God, the second on Chinese rituals, and the third on Chinese ethics.

If we were to judge Noël by his reception, we would probably be compelled to regard him as a failure. Firstly, his works had no effect on the outcome of the Chinese Rites Controversy. The year before their publication, Pope Clement XI publicly confirmed his 1704 decree *Cum Deus optimus* condemning the Chinese Rites and banning any discussion on the topic. By using a secular title like 'Chinese Philosophy' Noël perhaps sought to skirt around the ban, but the *Philosophia Sinica* was suppressed and, to our knowledge, was not consulted again until the end of the eighteenth century, when the wave of European enthusiasm for China had long subsided.[2] Secondly, the effective suppression of the work prevented it from

---

1 François Noël, *Sinensis imperii libri classici sex, nimirum Adultorum schola, Immutabile medium, Liber sententiarum, Memcius, Filialis observantia, Parvulorum schola* (Prague: Kamenicky, 1711).
2 For the suppression of the *Philosophia Sinica*, see Chapter 1 by Yves Vendé.

exerting any influence in Enlightenent perceptions of Chinese philosophy and the development of Western Sinology as a discipline. Arguably, even if the *Philosophia Sinica* had not been suppressed, its obscure scholastic style would have hindered its reception in Enlightenment Europe, which was increasingly favouring discursive texts written in the vernacular.

Noël's translations were more widely distributed than his commentaries but their influence was still rather limited. The *Libri sex* were reviewed in the 1711 and 1712 volumes of the scholarly journal *Acta eruditorum*,[3] and Wolff also referred to them when preparing his notorious lectures on the practical philosophy of the Chinese.[4] Extracts of Noël's text were translated into French by Jean-Baptiste Du Halde in his *Description […] de l'empire de la Chine* (1735), which was widely read by the *philosophes* of the French Enlightenment.[5] Noël's translations would achieve greater diffusion in a French translation published in 1784 by the French philosopher François-André-Adrien Pluquet (1716–1790).[6] However, the Sinologists of the nineteenth century looked poorly on Noël's Sinology. The French Sinologist Jean Pierre Abel-Rémusat (1788–1832) criticized Noël for deviating significantly from his source texts and intermingling neo-Confucian commentaries and his own explanations in his translation.[7] Abel-Rémusat's student, Stanislas Aignan Julien (1797–1873), made ample reference to Noël's translation in his Latin edition of the *Mencius*, but he similarly criticized Noël for obscuring the meaning with 'verbose and tedious paraphrasis'.[8] James Legge echoed this criticism in his introduction to his translation of the *Xiaojing*, noting that Noël's translation was 'decidedly periphrastic'.[9]

While we do not pass judgement on the quality of Noël's translations, Noël's insistence on an open and explicit dialogue between text and commentary in the interpretation of the Confucian classics was a milestone in Jesuit Sinology and paved the way for a richer dialogue between intellectual traditions. Since Matteo Ricci, the Jesuits, in both their Chinese and European writings, consciously opposed neo-Confucianism, that is the Song and Ming dynasty school of commentaries on

---

3 *Acta eruditorum* (Leipzig: Typis Joh. Casp. Mulleri, 1711), pp. 284–86; *Acta eruditorum* (Leipzig: Typis Joh. Casp. Mulleri, 1712), pp. 123–28, 224–29.
4 Mark Larrimore, 'Orientalism and Antivoluntarism in the History of Ethics: On Christian Wolff's "Oratio de Sinarum Philosophia Practica"', *The Journal of Religious Ethics*, 28.2 (2000), 189–219.
5 Jean-Baptiste Du Halde, *Description géographique, historique, chronologique, politique et physique de l'empire de la Chine et de la Tartarie Chinoise*, 4 vols (Paris: P.G. Le Mercier, 1735), 2:389.
6 François Noël, *Les Livres classiques de l'empire de la Chine*, trans. by François-André-Adrien Pluquet, 7 vols (Paris: Chez De Bures, 1784).
7 For discussion, see Wong Ching-him 黃正謙 [Felix Wong], 'Lun Yesuhuishi Wei Fangji de Ladingwen Mengzi fanyi 論耶穌會士衛方濟的拉丁文《孟子》翻譯', *Journal of Chinese Studies*, 57 (2013), 133–72.
8 'Sed illi versioni, perelegantis necnon nervosae dictionis, in Mencio nobis laudatae, ne ulla quidem insunt vestigia; imo saepe saepius sensum, verbosa atque taediosa paraphrasi obrutum, elicere frustra labores'. Stanislaus Julien, *Meng tseu vel Mencium inter sinenses philosophos, ingenio, doctrina, nominisque claritate Confucio proximum* (Paris: Societatis Asiaticae et Comitis de Lasteyrie impensis, 1824), Pars Prior, xvi.
9 James Legge, *The Sacred Books of China: The Texts of Confucianism*, vol. 1 (Oxford: Clarendon Press, 1879), p. 463.

the Confucian classics which they believed corrupted or obscured the monotheism of pre-Qin Confucianism. While their rejection of neo-Confucianism tracked trends in the hermeneutics and philology of the late Ming and early Qing, there was a certain disingenuity in their approach: the Jesuits still relied on neo-Confucian commentators to access and interpret the ancient Confucian classics. This contradiction was pointed out by Ricci's successor as superior to the Jesuit China mission, Niccolò Longobardo (1565–1654), who insisted upon the continuity between the neo-Confucian commentaries and the ancient classics. For Longobardo, however, this continuity entailed that the atheism or pantheism identified by the Jesuits in neo-Confucianism must also be attributed to ancient Confucianism, and thus the entire Confucian tradition had to be rejected as incommensurable with Christianity. After many deliberations, the Jesuits ultimately rejected Longobardo's arguments and persisted with Ricci's hermeneutic strategy, but Longobardo's writings resurfaced in the second half of the seventeenth century, and were paraded by the Jesuits' opponents in the Chinese Rites Controversy as evidence of major philological weakness in the Jesuits' hermeneutic strategy. Noël's interest in neo-Confucianism must be read as an implicit intervention in the dispute between the supporters of Ricci's and Longobardo's hermeneutics. But rather than advocate for either position, Noël forges a new path: he agrees with Longobardo that the neo-Confucian commentaries must be accepted as authentic and reliable witnesses to the Confucian tradition (*daotong*), but he rejects Longobardo's interpretation of the *daotong* through materialist categories as fundamentally mistaken. Noël argues his position by treating neo-Confucian metaphysics with greater sensitivity and subtlety than his predecessors. For example, whereas in previous Jesuit writings *qi* (air) was reduced to a material principle, Noël provides a more sophisticated spiritual understanding of *qi* as a vital principle that encompasses both material and immaterial dimensions.

Noël's intellectual contribution to Sinology has been subject of some piecemeal studies over the past few decades. Notably, his Chinese-language works and translations of the Chinese classics have attracted the attention of Sinologists, including Pan Feng-Chuan and Luo Ying. Missiologists such as Paul Rule and Claudia von Collani have also analysed Noël's writings in depth, particularly in relation to the Chinese Rites Controversy. A promising study on Noël's interpretation of Chinese political philosophy has also been conducted by Carel Wesselius. The originality of Noël's reception of neo-Confucianism has been noted and analysed by Felix Wong and Thierry Meynard.[10]

This book builds upon the philological and intellectual foundation of this incipient scholarship with the first systematic overview and English translation of the First Treatise of Noël's *Philosophia Sinica*. Notably, past work has largely relied on the printed editions of Noël's work, which unfortunately do not reproduce the Chinese characters corresponding to Noël's Latin translations of Chinese texts, thus making the identification of Noël's sources and philological analysis much

---

10 For a list of prior studies on Noël, see the Bibliography, Secondary Sources about Noël.

more difficult. In the translation of the First Treatise by Thierry Meynard, Daniel Canaris, and Wang Ge, the manuscript sources of the First Treatise are used to identify and transcribe almost all Noël's Chinese citations, and Noël's romanizations are updated to modern Pinyin to make the work more accessible to Sinologists. Extensive annotations guide the reader through Noël's Chinese sources, providing an unprecedented window into the textual history of this work.

At the heart of this volume is a transdisciplinary dialogue between the scholastic and neo-Confucian intellectual traditions that was conducted under the auspices of the Jesuit China mission. By providing a philologically accurate translate of Noël's First Treatise with rich annotations exploring and explaining Noël's hermeneutics, this volume will serve as an essential tool for Sinologists, who often lack the linguistic expertise in Latin and other European languages needed to engage with early modern Sinology. Also, historians working on the reception of Chinese philosophy in Europe have long appreciated the role played by the translation and interpretation of the Four Books and Five Classics for the Jesuits' missionary strategy, but we still have a shallow understanding of how the commentaries were used by the missionaries to inform their interpretation of Confucianism. Since the *Philosophia Sinica* places significant emphasis on the commentaries of the Song, Yuan, Ming, and early Qing dynasties, this work can serve as an illuminating case study of cross-cultural hermeneutics in the early Enlightenment.

The intellectual context of the First Treatise is presented with an array of essays analysing Noël's rapprochement between neo-Confucianism and scholastic philosophy. Chapter 1 by Yves Vendé features a copious intellectual biography, detailing Noël's formation, the development of his shift towards neo-Confucianism, and the suppression of the *Philosophia Sinica*. Chapter 2 by Thierry Meynard delves into the composition and sources of the First Treatise. Meynard reveals that the First Treatise was built upon decades of Sinological scholarship by the Jesuits and Chinese Christians, who catalogued relevant citations from the Chinese classics for demonstrating the compatibility between the Confucian and Christian worldviews. In Chapter 3, Meynard examines in minute detail Noël's reading of neo-Confucianism by positioning it in the context of previous Jesuit treatments of neo-Confucianism. Meynard analyses how Noël deploys the two-fold scholastic definition of *natura* to reinterpret the neo-Confucian *taiji* (Great Ultimate) as inhabiting both an active creative dimension (*natura naturans*) and a passive dimension (*natura naturata*). This two-fold definition, which had only marginal currency in Western philosophy before its adoption by Spinoza, allows Noël to identify transcendence in the neo-Confucian tradition. In Chapter 4, Wang Ge reappraises the First Treatise from the perspective of Chinese philosophy, arguing that while Noël's transcendent reading of neo-Confucian metaphysics was flawed, his attempt to bridge Chinese and Western intellectual traditions represented a pioneering achievement that anticipated trends in twentieth century comparative philosophy. In Chapter 5 Pierre Galassi analyses Noël's rapprochement between neo-Confucianism and scholasticism through the lens of sapiential realism, an analogic mode of reasoning that focuses on 'similarity relations' as opposed to analytical correspondences. At the same time, Galassi elucidates Noël's often terse scholastic reasoning by comparing Noël's metaphysical argumentation to that of Aquinas and Suárez.

The *Philosophia Sinica* is a work of great theological relevance. There is an continual need for theologians to contextualize Christianity both in theory and practice. With Ricci's accommodation of Christianity to Confucianism, the Christian faith found a unique expression in China. Noël's contribution to this project of accommodation is historically significant, though little known and underappreciated. Of course, generations of Chinese Christians have continued the work of contextualization, mostly in the areas of liturgy and art, but there is an urgency to delve deeper in the domain of contextualized theology. Noël made a germinal attempt three hundred years ago by stressing the possibility of metaphysical correspondences between Christianity and neo-Confucianism, a school which, like scholasticism, was characterized by a high degree of rationalism. He explored the semantic possibilities of neo-Confucian concepts such as *taiji*, *li*, and *guishen* from a scholastic point of view. Of course, his interpretative choices were not representative of mainstream neo-Confucianism, and there were other schools, such as the School of Mind (*Xinxue*) to which he could have referred. Even so, Noël's philological work was meticulous and detailed, and his readings were supported by a close reading of his source texts. Noël isolated concepts that he could relate to Christian thought, but in the other direction, he was challenged by some concepts and ways of thoughts which were opposed to scholasticism, or occupied a very marginal position. His interpretation of the School of Principle and of the role of neo-Confucianism within Chinese thought may be disputed by modern scholarship (as Wang Ge has argued in his contribution to this volume), but it can still enrich Confucian–Christian dialogue in the twenty-first century. Instead of seeing the plurality of discourses as a threat to orthodoxy, Clooney invites us to embrace positively the 'complexity of the present moment of pluralism' that only allows to construct a way of reading which is viable in the contemporary world.[11]

Since Ruggieri and Ricci, the Western encounter with Chinese philosophy has focused on engaging the dialogue between ancient texts and Western thought, be it Christianity, Greek and Roman ethics, American pragmatism, etc. Despite an entrenched hostility of the missionaries and Chinese Christians towards neo-Confucianism, Noël was the first Christian author to engage in a positive dialogue with neo-Confucianism. His pioneering efforts found a parallel in Leibniz's metaphysical and religious interpretation of neo-Confucian texts and have found a continuation in the work of Julia Ching on the religious thought of Zhu Xi.[12] Noël's efforts to interpret the School of Principle as compatible with Christianity reveals the potential of neo-Confucian ideas to cross linguistic and cultural boundaries and find philosophic relevance in diverse intellectual contexts.

We would like to thank Professor Francesco Borghesi for welcoming this volume in his series *Global Perspectives on Medieval and Early Modern Historiography* and

---

11   Francis Clooney, *Western Jesuit Scholars in India* (Boston: Brill, 2020), p. 81.
12   Julia Ching, *The Religious Thought of Chu Hsi* (Oxford: Oxford University Press, 2000).

Rosie Bonté for her assistance in organizing the publication of this volume, as well as Tang Yulin for his meticulous work in compiling the index. We are also most grateful to the two anonymous peer reviewers for their meticulous and expert feedback. This research received the support of the Australian Research Council Discovery Project 'Transforming the East: Jesuit Translations of the Confucian Classics' (Chief Investigators: Professor Francesco Borghesi and Professor Lu Yixu, University of Sydney).

YVES VENDÉ

1. Intellectual Biography of François Noël

1.1 Noël and his Education in Flanders

On 18 August 1651, François Noël was born at Hestrud in the Hainault, now in France, but then ruled by the Habsburgs until its cession to France as a result of the Treaty of Aix-la-Chapelle in 1668.[1] This may explain why Noël is variously called French, Belgian, German, and Walloon. In the *Philosophia Sinica*, however, he identified himself as a Fleming, and on this basis declared that he would not dare to discuss French grammar.[2] His maternal tongue may have been Flemish, but there are two extant letters to his brother written in French.[3]

On 30 September 1670, at the age of nineteen, Noël entered the novitiate of the French-Belgian province (Provincia Gallo-Belgica) of the Jesuits at Tournai (Doornik).[4] Though his hometown was attached to France in 1668, Tournai remained under the Habsburgs and is now part of Belgium.

After the novitiate, Noël studied philosophy and theology at the Jesuit College d'Anchin while taking additional classes in mathematics and astronomy. From 1573 onwards, this college, which was founded in 1568 and affiliated to the University

---

1 See Joseph Dehergne, *Répertoire des Jésuites de Chine de 1552 à 1800* (Rome: Institutum Historicum Societatis Iesu, 1973), p. 185.
2 See François Noël, 'Tractatus primus', *Philosophia Sinica* (Prague: Kamenicky, 1711), p. 156 (c.3, q.1, §.1); this edition, p. 364. Paul Rule discovered in the Archivum Roman Societatis Iesu [ARSI] a document (Fondo Gesuitico 724/6) in which Noël refers to himself in Italian as 'Fiamingo'. In Italian, the word is 'Fiammingo' (with a double m). Rule records this as 'Fiamingo' (not 'Fiammingo'), but this could just be a spelling variation. Rule also notices that Abel-Rémusat described Noël in his brief bibliographical note in the *Nouveaux mélanges asiatiques* as 'savant jésuite allemand'. See Paul Rule, 'François Noël, SJ, and the Chinese Rites Controversy', in *The History of the Relations between the Low Countries and China in the Qing Era (1644–1911)*, ed. by W. F. Vande Walle and Noël Golvers (Leuven: Leuven University Press, 2003), pp. 137–65 (p. 137 n. 1).
3 The first letter to his elder brother, Nicolas Noël (1648–1703), is dated 22 June 1688 and is in BnF, MS Français, Mélanges sur la Chine, 17239, fols 65^r–83^r. A digital copy is available on *Gallica*. Joseph Dehergne has transcribed the letter based on the text of BnF document. See Vanves, Archives françaises de la Compagnie de Jésus, Noël. The second letter, dated 10 August 1690, is in ARSI, Jap. Sin. 164, fols 283^r–284^v.
4 See Dehergne, *Répertoire des Jésuites de Chine de 1552 à 1800*, p. 186.

Yves Vendé, Catholic University of Lille, France

of Douai,⁵ trained Jesuits of the French-Belgian province in philosophy, and from 1622 also provided instruction in theology.⁶ The college had become renowned after the visit of Louis XIV in 1670.⁷ Around 1673–1675, Noël followed the course of philosophy which was based on Aristotle, including logic, the natural sciences, anthropology, and ethics. Noël was probably familiar with the Aristotelian commentaries produced at the Jesuit College of Coimbra between 1592 and 1603, and in his own *Philosophia Sinica* he mentions the Coimbra commentary on *De physica*.⁸

His four years of theological studies at the College d'Anchin were based on Aquinas, just like in any other Jesuit college. Since the seventeenth century, however, the Spanish Jesuit Francisco Suárez (1548–1617) had become an important reference point in theology with works such as the *De divina substantia ejusque attributis* (1606), which was cited twice by Noël in his First Treatise. We do not have a precise date and place for his ordination to the priesthood, but this most likely occurred around 1680 in Douai.

According to Pfister, Noël taught literature and rhetoric for seven years.⁹ This probably includes two years of a teaching internship, called a Regency, which he conducted around 1676–1677, and also four or five years of teaching prior to his departure for China in 1684. His expertise in the Greco-Roman classics would prove very beneficial for his future career as a translator of the Chinese classics.

While in Douai, Noël would have certainly learnt about Nicolas Trigault (1577–1628) who returned from China to Europe in 1614 as procurator of the Jesuit China mission. During his four-year sojourn in Europe, Trigault promoted the mission, published the Latin translation of Ricci's memoirs, found new recruits and bought thousands of books for the China mission. It is not clear at what time Noël asked to be sent to the missions in the Far East, but he probably obtained permission in 1683, since he departed Europe in January 1684. At that time, all the Jesuits destined for the Far Eastern missions had to sail from Lisbon. Only in 1685 would a group of French Jesuits including Joachim Bouvet (1656–1730) break the Portuguese monopoly by sailing from Brest and not from Lisbon.

Like his fellow Flemish Jesuit and immediate predecessor Antoine Thomas (1644–1709), Noël was under the patronage of Maria de Guadalupe, Duchess of Aveiro (1630–1715), who provided financial help for the cost of the travel.¹⁰

---

5   This university was established in 1559 on the model of Louvain and presented a very international setting with an English College (established in 1662), a Scottish College (established in 1573), and an Irish College (established in 1603).
6   Paul Grendler, 'Jesuit Schools and Universities in Europe 1548–1773', in *Brill Research Perspectives in Jesuit Studies*, 1.1 (2019),. 1–118.
7   In 1667, Louis XIV invaded Douai, and in 1668 through the same Treaty of Aix-la-Chapelle, Douai, like Hestrud, was annexed to France.
8   François Noël, 'Tractatus primus', p. 138 (c.2, q.6); this edition p. 341.
9   Louis Pfister, *Notices biographiques et bibliographiques sur les Jésuites de l'ancienne mission de Chine*, 2 vols (Shanghai: Imprimerie de la Mission Catholique, 1932), I, pp. 414–19.
10 See Rule, 'François Noël, SJ and the Chinese Rites Controversy', p. 138.

1.2 Noël and his Missionary Work in China

Noël stayed in Goa from December 1684 to the beginning of 1685 and arrived in Macao on 9 August 1685.[11] He was destined for the Japanese province of the Society of Jesus and could have worked in Guangdong province or in Vietnam, both of which were under the jurisdiction of the Japanese province. However, his own inclination was to enter Japan, where he would probably have died as a martyr. He obtained permission from his superiors who were generally quite reluctant to send men to certain death. Although he attempted to enter Japan disguised as a layman, in the end he failed to enter the country.[12] On 2 February 1686, he pronounced in Macao his final vows as a Jesuit, which, besides the traditional vows of chastity, poverty, and obedience to the order, included also a fourth vow of obedience to the Pope. Meanwhile, he had started to learn Chinese as part of his preparations for entering mainland China.

On 29 September 1687, Noël stayed a few weeks in Canton where he probably met the Italian Jesuit Francesco Saverio Filippucci (1632–1692), who in the following year would be appointed Visitor of China and Japan (1688–1691). In the last years of his life, Filippucci had been collecting Chinese materials related to the Chinese Rites Controversy and probably encouraged Noël to study the Chinese classics. Still in Canton, on 5 October 1687, Noël and three other Jesuits made their oath of obedience to the apostolic vicar Bernadino della Chiesa (1644–1721), an Italian reformed Franciscan who was sent to China by Propaganda Fide, the Vatican bureau in charge of all missions outside of Europe.[13] As a Jesuit, Noël was bound to obey to the Pope, and now as a missionary in China, he was bound by this oath of obedience to Propaganda Fide. As we shall see, his intellectual work on Chinese philosophy developed later in spite of, or perhaps because of, the great tensions between his obedience to the Jesuit order and his obedience to the Vatican.

His astronomical observations allow us to trace his itinerary: Zhaoqing 肇慶 (28 October 1687), Shaoguan 韶關 (13 November), Nanxiong 南雄 (21 November), Nan'an 南安 (25 November), Ganzhou 贛州 (2 December), Nanchang 南昌 (18 December), Changshu 常熟 (1 February 1688).[14] On 6 February 1688, Noël arrived in Shanghai 上海 where he stayed for one year, studying Chinese language and ministering among the poor on Chongming 崇明 island. In this period, he did not seem to devote much time to the Chinese classics. There is a manuscript letter of 22 June 1688 sent by Noël from Shanghai to his brother Nicolas, who was also a Jesuit and a member of the French-Belgian province.[15] This letter reveals his excitement at

---

11 See François Noël, *Observationes mathematicæ et physicæ in India et China factæ ab anno 1684 usque ad annum 1708* (Prague: Kamenicky, 1710), p. 20.
12 Dehergne, *Répertoire des Jésuites de Chine de 1552 à 1800*, p. 186; Liam Matthew Brockey, *Journey to the East* (Cambridge, MA: Harvard University Press, 2007), p. 228.
13 'Testimonium de iuramento a quattuor iesuitis emisso, Cantone 5 Octobris 1687', in *Sinica Franciscana*, vol. 6.1, ed. by G. Mensaert (Rome: Collegii S. Bonaventurae, 1961), pp. 489–90.
14 See Noël, *Observationes mathematicæ et physicæ*, pp. 31–33.
15 BnF, MS Français, Mélanges sur la Chine, 17239, fols 65ʳ–83ʳ.

the discovery of a new geographical space with the enumeration of many cities and towns where he calculated precisely their latitude and longitude. At the time, his comprehension of written Chinese was limited, but in the following two decades he would fill up this new intellectual space with the words of the Chinese classics. In the year 1689, he stayed in Hangzhou 杭州, Suzhou 蘇州, Yangzhou 揚州, and in the beginning of 1690, he arrived at Huai'an 淮安 in Jiangsu province, where he made precise and frequent astronomical observations which were published much later.[16] From Huai'an, he wrote another letter to his brother, dated 10 August 1690, giving some news about the work of Jean-François Gerbillon (1654–1707) and Joachim Bouvet at the court, mentioning his pastoral visits to Zhenjiang 鎮江, Yangzhou, Xuzhou 徐州, in Jiangsu province, and to Wuhe 五河 in Anhui 安徽 province where he established a new church.[17] According to his astronomical observations, he was still at Zhenjiang in February 1692, and the first observation in Nanchang (Jiangxi 江西 province) is dated 23 May 1693.[18] We can infer from a letter of his from Ganzhou dated 3 October 1692 that he arrived in Jiangxi province sometime between February and October 1692.[19] He stayed in Nanchang for nine years. The relative stability of this long period allowed him to develop his pastoral skills. In 1696, he baptized 1280 people.[20] In his report about the status of China mission written in 1700, he mentions that there were 150,000 Christians in Jiangxi province, and that the number of neophytes had reached more than 4000 in recent years.[21] During his period in Nanchang, he also wrote a short text, dated 30 August 1699, about the Manchu military campaigns between 1674 and 1688 to secure their control of China.[22]

1.3 Noël's Early Rejection of Neo-Confucianism

Apart from his pastoral work, Noël devoted substantial time to the study of the Chinese classics. In 1698, he published his only Chinese work, *Renzui zhizhong* 人罪至重 [Extreme Gravity of Human Sin]. As the Chinese Christian Wu Su 吳宿 wrote in the preface: 'Mr Wei from the Great West loves reading Chinese books, starting from the Four Books to the Classics and Histories, like stars in the sky or chess pieces on the board. With his thorough understanding he cites

---

16 Noël, *Observationes mathematicæ et physicæ*, pp. 6–20.
17 ARSI, Jap. Sin. 164, fols 283ʳ–284ᵛ.
18 Noël, *Observationes mathematicæ et physicæ*, pp. 25, 34.
19 Pfister, *Notices biographiques et bibliographiques*, p. 415.
20 Brockey, *Journey to the East*, p. 171.
21 François Noël and Kaspar Castner, *Relatio de statu Sinicae ecclesiae et progressu S. Fidei in Imperio Sinarum, ab anno 1692 quo data est per edictum Imperatoris Sinarum, praedicandae Legis Divinae libertas ad annum saecularem 1700*, ARSI, Jap. Sin. 125, fols 200ʳ–231ᵛ (fol. 226ᵛ).
22 'Abrégé de l'histoire des guerres civiles de la Chine depuis 1674 jusqu'à 1688', Vanves, Archives françaises de la Compagnie de Jésus, Noël. Two eighteenth-century copies are held in Paris, Archives nationales de France, Section ancienne K. 1375.

methodically to support his assertions, harmonizing the profound and the subtle' (泰西衛先生喜讀中華之書自四子書以及經史，星羅棋布，淹貫條達，有所引證，淵微恰和合).[23] Indeed, Noël continued the tradition started by Michele Ruggieri (1543–1607) and Matteo Ricci (1552–1610) in studying the ancient classics and using them in their own works. Noël's Chinese book has not received much scholarly attention except a paper by Pan Feng-Chuan 潘鳳娟 who calls it 'the most comprehensive and systematic work on the idea of sin in Catholic theology'.[24] For reasons unknown to us, the book was published in Beijing even though Noël never went to the capital. Pan discusses the theological anthropology and moral theology contained in the work, but what concerns us here is Noël's Confucian horizons at the time. Pan notices that in continuity with the Riccian school, Noël quotes the ancient classics (*Mencius*, *Shijing*, *Shujing*, and *Chunqiu*) and distinguishes between the ancient texts cited by early Confucian scholars and those cited by Song Confucian scholars.[25] This passing remark by Pan about the distinction between ancient and Song Confucianism is in fact crucial. In 1940, the Chinese scholar Zhu Qianzhi 朱謙之 (1899–1972) had noticed that the distinction between ancient and Song Confucianism in the *Renzui zhizhong* amounted, in fact, to a complete rejection of what Noël calls 'vulgar Confucianism' (*suru* 俗儒), which was placed on a par with Buddhism and Daoism. Noël shows already a great familiarity with the classics (some thirty citations mentioned) and also with the neo-Confucian interpretation based on *li* 理, the normative principle of reality, which he systematically rejects, writing for example:

> It is clear that *Tian* 天 and *Shangdi* 上帝 cannot be explained with the empty concept of *li* 理 [...] Vulgar Confucianism considers *li*, *dao* 道, and *Tian* as the foundation of the myriad of things, but after investigation, its *li*, *dao* and *Tian* all belong to empty words.[26]

Noël's radical condemnation of neo-Confucianism in 1698 is in complete continuity with the views of Matteo Ricci, Niccolò Longobardo (1559–1654), Prospero Intorcetta (1626–1696), and Philippe Couplet (1623–1693).

---

23 Xu Zongze 徐宗澤, *Ming Qing jian Yesuhuishi yizhu tiyao* 明清間耶穌會士譯著提要 (Shanghai: Shanghai guji chubanshe, 2006), p. 62.
24 Pan Feng-Chuan 潘鳳娟 'God, Sinner, and Saintly Governance: François Noël and *Ren zui zhi zhong*', in *Light a Candle: Encounters and Friendship with China: Festschrift in Honour of Angelo Lazzarotto P.I.M.E.* (Sankt Augustin: Monumenta Serica, 2010), pp. 159–98 (p. 169). For the Chinese version of this article, see Pan Feng-Chuan 潘鳳娟, 'Qingchu Yesuhuishi Wei Fangji de renzuishuo yu shengzhilun 清初耶穌會士衛方濟的人罪說與聖治論', *Xinshixue* 新史學, 23:1 (2012), pp. 9–53.
25 Pan Feng-chuan 'God, Sinner, and Saintly Governance', p. 174.
26 '由是可觀，天與上帝絕不能以理之虛名為解[...]夫俗儒言理，言道，言天，莫不以此為萬物之根本矣。但究其所謂理，所謂道，所言天，皆歸於虛文而已。' Noël, *Renzui zhizhong*, cited in Zhu Qianzhi 朱謙之, *Zhongguo sixiang duiyu Ouzhou wenhua zhi yingxiang* 中國思想對於歐洲文化之影響 (Taiyuan: Shanxi chuban chuanmei jituan, 2014), p. 127.

1.4 Noël's Shift towards Neo-Confucianism

Noël's initial rejection of neo-Confucianism contrasts with his full translation of the *Xiaoxue* 小學 [Elementary Learning] by Zhu Xi (1130–1200) in the *Libri sex*, and of course with the *Philosophia Sinica* which provides many explanations of *Tian* and *Shangdi* based on the neo-Confucian *li* which he had rejected a decade earlier. Felix Wong 黃正謙 even talks about his 'undaunted acceptance of the elucidation of Song authors' in the *Philosophia Sinica*.[27] But what has remained largely unexplained is the reason for this intellectual shift.

In his early engagement with the ancient classics, Noël remained in continuity with the exegesis expressed in the *Confucius Sinarum philosophus* (1687), and his own translation of the *Mencius* was intended to complete what was missing. In 1700, he had already finished his Latin translation of the Four Books.[28] Besides the *Sishu zhijie* 四書直解 [Colloquial Commentary on the Four Books] by Zhang Juzheng 張居正 (1525–1582), Noël also used the *Sishu mengyin* 四書蒙引 [Primer on the Four Books] by Cai Qing 蔡清 (1453–1508). Analysing the printed text of 1711, Felix Wong argues that Noël initially understood the Four Books as mostly concerned with ethics, and consciously refrained from mentioning the more metaphysical interpretation of neo-Confucianism in his translations.[29] Thus on the basis of the printed text it would seem that Noël's interpretation of the Four Books is quite in line with his rejection of neo-Confucianism in the *Renzui zhizhong*.

However, through a careful comparison between Noël's manuscript translation of the *Zhongyong* finished in 1700 and the printed version of 1711, Luo Ying 羅瑩 discovered that Noël had first translated many commentaries of the *Sishu zhijie* and *Sishu mengyin* which expound the neo-Confucian interpretation of the Four Books, but removed some of these commentaries from the printed version. For example, in relation to the incipit of the *Zhongyong* (天命之謂性), Noël gives in the manuscript the neo-Confucian explanation in terms of *li*, the four aspects of Heaven (*yuan heng li zhen* 元亨利貞) according to the *Yijing*, and the four moral principles (*ren yi li zhi* 仁義禮智) according to the *Mencius*, but those comments are absent from the printed version.[30] Could Noël have first accepted those explanations

---

27 Wong Ching Him 黃正謙 [Felix Wong], '*The Unalterable Mean*: Some Observations on the Presentation and Interpretation of *Zhongyong* of François Noël, SJ', *Journal of Chinese Studies*, 60 (2015), 197–224 (p. 220).
28 See Royal Library of Belgium, Brussels KBR 19.930 'Immutabile Medium ex sinico in Latinum idioma traductum a P. Francisco Noël Societatis Jesu, Missionario Sinensi, Nancham in China, 1700'; Royal Library of Belgium, Brussels KBR 19.931 'Mencius ex sinico in latinum idioma traductus a P. Francisco Noël Societatis Jesu, Missionario Sinensi, Nancham in China, 1700'; Saint Petersburg Library, Cordier *Bibl. sin.* p. 1395 'Liber Sententiarum ex sinico in latinum idioma traductus a P. Francisco Noël Societatis Jesu, Missionario Sinensi, Nancham in China, 1700'.
29 Wong, '*The Unalterable Mean*'.
30 Luo Ying 羅瑩, 'Qingchao lai Hua Yesuhuishi Wei Fangji jiqi Ruxue yishu yanjiu 清朝來華耶穌會士衛方濟及其儒學譯述研究', *Beijing xingzheng xueyuan xuebao* 北京行政學院學報 [Journal of Beijing Administrative Institute], 1 (2015), 120–28 (p. 122).

in 1700, but later rejected them? This is unlikely because because the comments which are suppressed in the *Libri sex* are present in the *Philosophia Sinica*.³¹

Luo Ying also notices that, in relation to a citation of the *Shijing* in *Zhongyong* 16 (神之格思, 不可度思), Noël translated a comment by Cai Qing explaining that all things originate from *taiji* 太極 through the two *qi* 氣 of *yin* 陰 and *yang* 陽. Cai's comment does not appear in the printed version.³² However, in the *Philosophia Sinica* there is an entire question dedicated to *taiji* where neo-Confucian cosmology is explained in great detail.³³ Also, Luo Ying notices that in his manuscript Noël sometimes translates *xing* 性 as *natura* (nature), and other times translates it as *natura rationalis* (rational nature), but in the *Libri sex*, Noël consistently translated *xing* as nature.³⁴ In fact, 'rational nature' accords with the neo-Confucian interpretation of *xing* in terms of *li* 理. The elimination of the adjective 'rational' from the *Libri sex* does not mean that Noël rejected the neo-Confucian interpretation because in the First Treatise of the *Philosophia Sinica* there are more than twenty instances of 'natural reason' or 'rational nature'.

All those findings show that in 1700 Noël had already accepted many neo-Confucian concepts, such as *li*, *taiji*, *yin*, and *yang*, but he eliminated them from the *Libri sex* and maintained them in the *Philosophia Sinica* because he considered the books as complementary as shall be explained below.

Noël's shift from rejecting neo-Confucianism to accepting it would have taken place in the years 1698–1700, and he may have been influenced by some literati in Jiangxi. Another important factor came from Bouvet, and here Claudia von Collani provides an important clue:

> The conviction that also the more recent Chinese knew God was shared by Noël and by at least two other missionaries, namely the French Jesuit Joachim Bouvet […] and the Spanish Augustinian Alvaro de Benvavente. It is possible and probable that the three had contact to each other […] In his *Gujin jingtian jian Tianxue benyi*, Bouvet tried to prove the theism of the contemporary Chinese. His manuscripts were sent several times to Rome, and Noël must have known them.³⁵

Collani's hypothesis is correct. We have found evidence directly linking Noël with Bouvet which may partially explain Noël's intellectual shift towards neo-Confucianism. On 6 November 1701, the Vice-Provincial Antoine Thomas (1644–1709) in Beijing sent Noël instructions to depart immediately for Rome to deal with the Chinese Rites Controversy. On 18 November, he sent another letter to Noël:

31　Noël, 'Tractatus primus', p. 31 (c.2, q.1, §.1, B.2), this edition, p. 209.
32　Luo Ying, 'Qingchao lai Hua Yesuhuishi Wei Fangji', p. 122.
33　Noël, 'Tractatus primus', pp. 137–46 (c.2, q.6); this edition, pp. 340–51.
34　Luo Ying, 'Qingchao lai Hua Yesuhuishi Wei Fangji', p. 123.
35　Claudia von Collani, 'François Noël and his Treatise on God in China', in *History of the Catholic Church in China* (Leuven: Ferdinand Verbiest Institute, 2015), pp. 23–64 (p. 36).

> Moreover, I am sending you a remarkable treatise in Chinese about *Tian* drawn from the Classical books through the work and zeal of Father Bouvet. The Chinese literati highly praise it.³⁶

This refers to the *Tianxue benyi* 天學本意 [Basic Meaning of the Study of Heaven]. A letter of Bouvet dated 1704 confirms that Noël received the work and carried it to Europe.³⁷ Bouvet's work probably inspired Noël to take into account new commentaries and to develop a new exegesis based on the School of Principle (*Lixue* 理學).³⁸ In his same letter of 18 November 1701, Thomas also told Noël that he would send from Beijing documents including the *Relatio brevis*, which featured the testimonies of Kangxi, Manchu princes, and high-ranking Han officers:

> Testimonies about [*Tian*] by very important scholars and perhaps by the emperor himself shall soon be sent over if time allows. We shall soon try to have them printed with the approvals. This will convince not only the Europeans but also the Chinese. A distinguished Manchu literatus, Wang Laoye, otherwise known as He-shi-heng [Henkama], who often reports our affairs to the emperor, told me after a few days of careful reading that it is evident and clear from the texts that the ancient sages knew the God that we Christians worship and call *Tianzhu*.³⁹

The Jesuits were confident enough to have found convincing arguments to prove Ricci's identification of *Tian* with God, not only on the basis of the ancient Classics, but also on the basis on recent commentaries following the School of Principle that Bouvet was now using. We contend that Bouvet's work greatly influenced Noël in his shift towards neo-Confucianism. However, Noël would go much further than Bouvet in adopting key neo-Confucian concepts and analysing them through scholastic rationalism. On 6 December, Noël left Nanchang and on 1 January 1702 arrived in Canton.⁴⁰ While staying in Canton for two weeks, he received the books and documents sent from Beijing to be carried to Rome, including Bouvet's

---

36 'Mitto insuper insignem Tractatum Sinicum desumptum ex libris Classicis labore, & studio P. Bouvet de Tien. Valde laudant Literati Sinenses'. Extract of letter of Antoine Thomas to François Noël (18 November 1701), in François Noël and Caspar Kastner, *Summarium novorum autenticorum testimoniorum* [henceforth *Summarium NAT*] (Rome, 1704), p. 87.
37 See David E. Mungello, *The Silencing of Jesuit Figurist Joseph de Prémare in Eighteenth-Century China* (Lanham: Lexington Books, 2019).
38 This does not exclude the possibility that the two may have met before in South China, perhaps in 1696 when Bouvet was sent to France, or in 1698 when Bouvet returned to China.
39 'Testimonia de eo praecipuorum Doctorum brevi mittentur, ac forte ipsius Imperatoris, si opportunum fuerit petere tempori: curabimus brevi imprimi cum approbationibus; neque enim convincit solum Europaeos, sed maxime ipsos Sinenses. Sane *Vam lao ye*, aliter *He Hen* insignis Litteratus, Tartarus, qui res nostras ad Imperatorem deferre solet, postquam his diebus accurate legit, mihi hodie dixit, manifestum, & clarum esse ex textibus, a sapientibus antiquis Deum cognitum fuisse, quem Christiani adoramus, & nominamus *Tien chu*'. Excerpt from the letter of Thomas to Noël and others (18 November 1701), in Noël and Castner, *Summarium NAT*, p. 87.
40 Nicolas Standaert, *Chinese Voices in the Rites Controversy* (Rome: Institutum Historicum Societatis Iesu, 2012), pp. 22–23.

Tianxue benyi and Kangxi's *Brevis relatio*.⁴¹ He also collected documents and books left by Filippucci in Canton.

1.5 Noël's Scholarly Work in Rome

On 14 January 1702, Noël and the Bavarian Jesuit Kaspar Castner (1665–1709) boarded an English vessel in Canton, carrying with them many Chinese documents and books as evidence for the legitimacy of the Chinese Rites. On his first return to Europe in 1702, he and Castner were named procurators of the Jesuit China mission, as well as procurators of the bishop of Macao (João de Cazal,?–1735), of the bishop of Nanjing (Alessandro Ciceri, S. J., 1639–1703), of the Apostolic Vicar of Jiangxi (Álvaro de Benavente, O.S.A, 1647–1709) and of the Apostolic Vicar of Guizhou (Carlo Turcotti, S. J., 1643–1706). The boat of the East India Company passed through Macao on 21 January and sailed for Europe three days later. The boat reached London on 4 October 1702, from where Noël sent a letter to the Superior General in Rome to announce their coming.⁴² Noël and Castner finally reached Rome at the end of December.⁴³

Noël and Castner spent three years in Rome, lobbying cardinals in the attempt to convince them of the compatibility of the Chinese Rites with Christianity. In 1703, Noël wrote a report on the state of the missions in China, which was published one year later in French translation and focused mostly on the pastoral activities among the lower class.⁴⁴ On 27 March 1703, Noël and Castner officially presented to Clement XI the testimonies of Chinese Christians and non-Christians, including the Kangxi emperor, in support of the Chinese Rites. The documents were published in August 1703 at Rome as *Summarium novorum authenticorum testimoniorum* (abridged below as *Summarium NAT*) under the names of Noël and Castner. Most of the content concerns the Chinese Rites, but the eighth and final section (pp. 75–89) is of greater interest for our research since it deals with 'the legitimate meaning of the terms *Tian* and *Shangdi*'.⁴⁵ Some testimonies by Chinese Christians mentioned in this work are found in the *Philosophia Sinica*.⁴⁶ Among non-Christian testimonies is included Kangxi's declaration of 30 November 1700

---

41 Antoine Thomas, *Brevis relatio eorum quae spectant ad declarationem Sinarum Imperatoris Kam Hi circa caeli Confucii et avorum cultum* (Peking, 1701; Augsburg and Dillingen: Johann Kaspar Bencard, 1703).

42 ARSI, Jap. Sin. 167, fols 50ʳ–51ᵛ. Noël also sent two short letters to the Superior General, one from Calais dated 23 October 1702, and one from Paris dated 5 November 1702. See ARSI, Jap. Sin. 167, fols 68ʳ and 77ʳ.

43 Standaert, *Chinese Voices*, p. 23. Dehergne gives different dates which seem incorrect; Dehergne, *Répertoire des Jésuites de Chine de 1552 à 1800*, p. 185.

44 'Mémoire sur l'état des missions de la Chine, présenté en Latin à Rome, au Révérend Père Général de la Compagnie de Jésus, l'an 1703, par le Père François Noël, missionnaire de la même Compagnie, et depuis traduit en Français', in *Lettres édifiantes et curieuses*, vol. 17 (Toulouse: Noël-Étienne Sens, 1810), pp. 128–48.

45 Noël and Castner, *Summarium NAT*, pp. 75–89.

46 Noël, 'Tractatus primus', pp. 151–57 (c.3, q.1); this edition, pp. 357–77.

in favour of the Chinese Rites that the Beijing Jesuits had translated from Manchu into Latin, but Noël made a new Latin translation based on the Chinese version, which is included in the *Philosophia Sinica*.

In early 1704, Noël and Castner received another batch of documents which had been collected by Antoine Thomas in autumn 1702 in favour of the Chinese Rites. This was published at Rome on 26 August 1704 with the title *Memoriale et summarium novissimorum testimoniorum Sinensium*, but since this work has no textual connection with the *Philosophia Sinica*, it is not discussed here.

Already in 1703, Charles-Thomas Maillard de Tournon (1668–1710) had left Europe for China as papal legate, with secret orders to proclaim in China the interdiction of the Chinese Rites. At the end of 1705, Noël sailed once more from Lisbon for Goa, where he made astronomical observations in April and May 1706,[47] and reached Macao on 22 July 1707.[48] Meanwhile, on 17 February 1707, Tournon had promulgated in Nanjing the decree which forbade Chinese Christians from performing the Chinese Rites.

It is quite surprising that after only a six-month sojourn months in Macao, Noël was sent back to Europe. On this occasion he joined the new legation of two Jesuit procurators, Antonio Provana (1622–1720) and José Ramón Arxó (1663–1711). In a letter, Noël mentions that his superiors sent him back to Rome because of the issue (*causa*) of the Rites Controversy.[49] Indeed, the superiors may have thought he could still be of good service in Europe because of his Sinological skills. Claudia von Collani has suggested that the main reason for sending him back was his poor mental health which could not be properly treated in China.[50] A lengthy letter dated 30 December 1707 sent by Noël from Macao to the Superior General narrates the legation of Tournon since his arrival in Macao in 1705, his interaction with the court in Beijing, his travel to Nanjing and his decree against the Chinese Rites and his expulsion to Macao. In this letter, Noël also discusses the negative consequences of Tournon's decree and warns that the Church in China may suffer a harsh persecution, as in Japan, and that all the missionaries may be expelled.[51] Interestingly he does not mention his return to Europe, and this may suggest that the decision of his superiors was not yet made or not yet communicated to him.

On 14 January 1708, Noël, Provana, Arxó, and the Chinese Catholic Fan Shouyi 樊守義 (1682–1753) left Macao.[52] They carried a total of sixty-nine documents, including copies of original documents preserved in the imperial archives that

---

47 Noël, *Observationes mathematicæ et physicæ*, p. 30.
48 Noël, Letter to the Superior General, Macao, 30 December 1707, ARSI, Jap. Sin. 171, fols 200ʳ–211ᵛ (fol. 200ʳ).
49 Noël, Letter to the Superior General, Bahia, 3 July 1708, ARSI, Jap. Sin. 172, fol. 46ʳ.
50 Both a letter by Pieter Van Hamme and the Jesuit catalogue by Kilian Stumpf reported the health problems of Noël. See Collani, 'François Noël and his Treatise on God in China', p. 28.
51 Noël, Letter to the Superior General, Macao, 30 December 1707, ARSI, Jap. Sin. 171, fols 200ʳ–211ᵛ.
52 See Thierry Meynard, 'Fan Shouyi, a Bridge between China and the West under the Rites Controversy', *Annales Missiologici Posnanienses*, 22 (2017), 21–31.

Kangxi himself had examined and approved, as well as the first part of the *Acta Pekinensia* compiled by Kilian Stumpf (1655–1720).[53] In the *Philosophia Sinica*, Noël draws from the *Acta Pekinensia* to relate the catastrophic meeting between Kangxi and the Apostolic Vicar Charles Maigrot (1652–1730) on 2 August 1706.[54] After a stopover at Bahia in Brazil between June and July 1708,[55] the three Jesuits and Fan Shouyi reached Rome in February 1709.

Since 1701, Noël had been working on arranging the classical texts and their commentaries to express their compatibility with Christianity. Already in 1703, he had written a first draft entitled 'Doctrinae Sinicae brevis indagatio', which served as basis for the *Summarium NAT*, and the *Memoriale et summarium novissimorum testimoniorum Sinensium*. It seems that the publication of the *Philosophia Sinica* was put on hold until a suitable time, as we learn from a comment by Kilian Stumpf in February 1706:

> About passages from Classic books, from interpreters, etc. we say nothing in particular here, because without the commentaries in which they are explained and verified, they cannot be understood. And so it is better to keep them until, on either side of the discussion, there are missionaries thoroughly competent in the Chinese language committed to a debate. There are also other references, by no means small in number; but it did not seem opportune to include them in the catalogue. They will be presented at a suitable time, when they are either requested or there is pressing necessity to produce them.[56]

When Noël returned Rome around February 1709, the suitable time had come, and Noël did the final preparations for the publication of his book as a last attempt to save the mission. But the Vatican spoke even before he could publish it. On 25 September 1710, Pope Clement XI publicly promulgated the anti-Rites decree *Cum Deus Optimus*, which had been secretly signed in 1704, and forbade further discussion on the Chinese Rites.

---

53 For a description of these documents, see Antonio Sisto Rosso, *Apostolic Legations to China of the Eighteenth Century* (South Pasadena, California: P. D. and Ione Perkins, 1948), pp. 179–82. These documents were published in Italian translation in the *Atti imperiali autentici di vari trattati, passati nella regia corte di Pekino, tra l'imperatore della Cina, e M. Patriarca Antiocheno al presente Sig. Cardinale di Tournon negli anni 1705, e 1706* (Cologne: 1710). For an English translation of the first part, see Kilian Stumpf, *The Acta Pekinensia or Historical Records of the Maillard de Tournon Legation: Volume I, December 1705 – August 1706*, ed. by Paul Rule and Claudia von Collani (Rome: Institutum Historicum Societatis Iesu, 2015).
54 Noël, 'Tractatus primus', pp. 177–78 (c.3, q.2); this edition, pp. 390–91.
55 Noël, Letter to the Superior General, Bahia, 3 July 1708, ARSI, Jap. Sin. 172, fol. 46ʳ.
56 Stumpf, *The Acta Pekinensia*, p. 170.

1.6 The Publication of the *Philosophia Sinica* and its Censorship

The pope's condemnation of the Chinese Rites was certainly very difficult for Noël to accept. Soon after, he went to Prague, not to teach at the Jesuit Klementinum College in Charles University, but to carry out the publication project which he could not carry out in Italy or in France. In 1710 he published his *Observationes mathematicae et physicae* with Joachim Johannes Kamenicky, the printer of Charles University. In this book of 133 pages, he reported astronomical observations conducted between 1684 and 1708 in India and China. In 1711, he published his voluminous *Sinensis imperii libri classici sex*, or *Libri sex* [Six Classic Books of the Chinese Empire] in 608 pages. This book included a translation of the Four Books, the *Xiaojing* 孝經 [Classic of Filial Piety], and Zhu Xi's *Xiaoxue* 小學 [Elementary Learning]. Noël is often credited for being the first to publish a translation of *Mencius* in a European language, but he should also be recognized for being the first to translate a work by Zhu Xi into a European language. Noël made a conscious decision to keep his translations of the Four Books in the *Libri sex* as close as possible to the original text, without too many neo-Confucian interpretations (a few of them were deleted from the manuscripts of 1700 as shown above) and to leave the neo-Confucian reading of the Confucian classics for the *Philosophia Sinica*. Felix Wong explains the complementarity of the two works this way:

> One may assert that in a sense the publication of *Philosophia Sinica* in conjunction with *Libri Sex* in the same year provided the Catholic author with an opportunity to elucidate the coherent theoretical framework that is manufactured behind his rendition, and to refrain from adulterating the translation with too much argumentation.[57]

For all those reasons, when the *Libri sex* was published in 1711, it may have appeared as an academic and uncontroversial work, but the publication of the *Philosophia Sinica* in the same year appeared as an act of defiance against the papal decision. On the cover, Noël mentions that he had received a special license (*de speciali licentia*) of Clement XI, and indeed, the pope had granted such a license in 1704. Despite the papal prohibition of further discussion on the Chinese Rites in 1710, Noël may have thought that the license of 1704 was still in force, and he chose the neutral phrase 'Chinese philosophy' as the title to make the work seem less controversial. However, the content of the work was in total opposition to the decree *Cum Deus Optimus* since it affirmed that the Chinese concept of heaven (*Tian*) was equivalent to the Christian notion of God and that the Chinese Rites were legitimate cults addressed to the true God. At 678 pages, this work was even longer than the *Libri sex*, and was

---

57 Wong, '*The Unalterable Mean*', p. 222.

followed by a ninety-page historical notice on the Chinese Rites, which was also published in 1711.[58]

Andreas Waibl (1642–1716), the Jesuit Assistant for Germany, may have covered up or even facilitated Noël's act of disobedience. The Jesuits were quickly accused of disobeying the papal decree, and Michelangelo Tamburini (1648–1730), the Superior General of the Jesuits from 1706 to 1730, had to write to the pope a formal declaration of obedience, signed by the procurators of all the provinces gathered in Rome.[59] Tamburini restricted the diffusion of the work within the Jesuit order, as can be gathered from a handwritten note on a copy of the *Philosophia Sinica* now held in the Biblioteca nazionale di Napoli. Carel Wesselius noticed this handwritten note and he translates it as: 'This volume by special license from pope Clement XI, is allowed to be read by members of the Society of Jesus. However, it is not allowed to be made public.'[60]

It seems that Frantz Retz (1673–1750), Superior General from 1730 to 1750, continued the policy of Tamburini because on 10 October 1733 the French Jesuit Antoine Gaubil (1689–1759) had to write to Retz to ask permission for a copy of the *Philosophia Sinica* to be sent to Beijing:

> The Belgian Father François Noël of our Society of Jesus, missionary in China, had three treatises published: the first was about the knowledge of the First Being in China; the second about the ceremonies towards the deceased; the third about ethics. Those three treatises are very useful to us but are missing in the French residence of Beijing and it is said that they cannot be obtained unless permission is first sought and obtained from Your Paternity. I therefore humbly request this permission and ask Your Paternity to have the said book sent from Prague to the Fathers in Paris. The Father Procurator in Paris shall pay the cost of the book and the transportation.[61]

---

58 François Noël, *Historica notitia rituum ac ceremoniarum* (Prague: Kamenicky, 1711). For the textual connection between the two works, see Carel Wesselius, 'The *Ethica Politica*: François Noël's (1651–1729) Description of Confucian Political Thought in his *Philosophia Sinica Tribus Tractatibus*' (unpublished MA thesis, Leiden University, 2020) p. 7.
59 ARSI, Jap. Sin. 197 II, fols 227–30; Printed version (Latin and French): *Solution de la question soy-disant curieuse* (1719), pp. 31–40.
60 See Carel Wesselius, 'The *Ethica Politica*', p. 36.
61 'Pater Franciscus Noel Belga Soc[ietatis] nostrae in Sinâ missionarius Pragae curavit imprimi tractatus tres, scilicet de Cognitione primi Entis apud Sinas, de ceremoniis erga defunctos, de Ethicâ. Tractatus illi nobis omnibus perutiles, in hâc nostrâ gallicâ Pekinensi residentia desunt, neque posse obtineri dicuntur nisi prius petitâ et obtentâ Suae Paternitatis licentiâ. Hanc itaque licentiam suppliciter postulo et V[estr]am Paternitatem rogo ut jubeat Pragâ Parisios mitti praedictos libros. Pater Procurator Parisiensis librorum et vecturae pretium solvet'. ARSI, Jap. Sin. 184, fol. 115; Antoine Gaubil, *Correspondance de Pékin, 1722–1759*, ed. by Renée Simon (Geneva: Librairie Droz, 1970), p. 360.

1.7 Noël's Final Years

Dehergne mentioned that in 1713 Noël returned to Lille, which was in his original French-Belgian province, but on 10 June 1715, he sent from Lille a letter to the Superior General in Rome and in this letter he requested to return to the China mission.[62] He was allowed to go and made two attempts in 1715 and 1716, the second time going as far as Lisbon, but because of his poor health and problems with the vessels, in the end he did not sail.[63]

He continued his literary and scholarly work, but it was seemingly unconnected with China. In 1717, he published his *Opuscula poetica* in four parts, which was approved by Jacob Stessl, the provincial of Bohemia.[64] As we recall, Noël had cultivated literary studies before leaving for China.

It seems that in 1717 he returned for good to his original French-Belgian province, since it is recorded that he lived in the Jesuit College of Lille for twelve years, from 1717 until his death in 1729.[65] There, he turned to theology, writing a manual based on the writings of Suárez, a Jesuit author mentioned in the *Philosophia Sinica*. As he explains in the preface, he had some free time after his return from China and devoted himself to writing this manual for students of theology to help them better understand Suárez's thought. He condensed the twenty-three volumes of the *Summa* into only two volumes. On 18 April 1725, Cornelius Mahy, the provincial of the French-Belgian province, approved the work and gave permission to the publisher Thomas Fritsch at Frankfurt to print the work within six years, but the work was published only posthumously in 1732. The work seemed to have enjoyed modest distribution because it was published simultaneously at Cologne and Madrid, and then was reprinted at Venice in 1733.[66] Noël had died in Lille three years before at the age of seventy-eight on 17 September 1729.

As a result of the restrictions imposed on the distribution of the *Philosophia Sinica*, the work seems to have exerted little influence in the eighteenth century. The earliest reference that we have been able to locate is in the first volume of *Les Livres classiques de l'empire de la Chine* (1784) by the French philosopher François-André-Adrien Pluquet (1716–1790). This work, which was based on Noël's *Libri sex*, includes citations from the Third Treatise, revealing that Pluquet had access to

---

62 Dehergne, *Répertoire des Jésuites de Chine de 1552 à 1800*, p. 186.
63 See Rule, 'François Noël, SJ and the Chinese Rites Controversy', p. 161; Collani, 'François Noël and his Treatise on God in China', p. 30.
64 François Noël, *Opuscula poetica* (Frankfurt: Thomas Fritsch, 1717). This work contains *Life of Jesus Christ under the Name of Divine Love* (*Vita Jesu Christi sub Nomine Divini Amoris*); *Marian Letters* (*Epistolae Marianae*); *Life of St Ignatius of Loyola, Founder of the Jesuits* (*Vita Sancti Ignatii de Loyola Societatis Jesu Fundatoris*); and several tragedies (*Tragoediae*).
65 Pierre Delattre, ed., *Les Établissements des jésuites en France depuis quatre siècles*, vol. 2 (Enghien, Belgium: Institut supérieur de théologie, 1953), col. 1291–1292.
66 François Noël, *Theologiae R.P. doctoris eximii Francisci Suarez, e Societate Jesu, summa* (Madrid: Antonio Sanz, 1732); *Theologiae R.P. doctoris eximii Francisci Suarez, e Societate Jesu, summa* (Cologne: Sumptibus Fratrum de Tournes, 1732); *Theologiae R.P. doctoris eximii Francisci Suarez, e Societate Jesu, summa* (Venice: Apud Nicolaum Pezzana, 1733).

the *Philosophia Sinica*. The *Philosophia Sinica* is mentioned briefly in the writings of the Jesuit philologist Lorenzo Hervás y Panduro (1735–1809), who lived in Rome after the dissolution of the Society of Jesus. Panduro cites the First Treatise in the *Viage estático al mundo planetario* (1793), the Second Treatise in the *Historia de la vida del hombre* (1799), and the Third Treatise in the *Carta del abate don Lorenzo Hervás al excelentísmo señor don Antonio Ponce de Leon* (1805). Only in the first half of the nineteenth century is the *Philosophia Sinica* mentioned outside of a footnote. The French Sinologist Jean-Pierre Abel-Rémusat (1788–1832) devotes a one-page description to the *Philosophia Sinica*, explaining the rarity of the work and the displeasure it gave Noël's superiors. Abel-Rémusat criticizes Noël for two things: firstly, in terms of style, his wordy translation; and secondly, in terms of content, his focus on the Rites Controversy. However, he still considers that 'the work contains a great deal of remarkable principles'.[67] The historian and Sinologist Paul Rule is more appreciative: 'The *Philosophia Sinica* is a quite sophisticated work, and in many ways an advance on its Jesuit predecessors [...] The *Philosophia Sinica* was, of course, conceived in the heat of the Rites Controversy, leading in Rémusat's judgment to distortion, but remains a considerable work of scholarship'.[68]

---

67 Jean-Pierre Abel-Rémusat, 'François Noël, missionnaire à la Chine', *Nouveaux mélanges asiatiques*, 2 vols (Paris: Schubart & Heideloff, 1829), II, pp. 255–56.
68 Rule, 'François Noël, SJ and the Chinese Rites Controversy', pp. 156–57.

THIERRY MEYNARD

2. Composition and Sources of the First Treatise

In a recent paper, Claudia von Collani investigated Noël's sources using the printed text of the *Philosophia Sinica*.[1] However, the ARSI manuscript, which contains the Chinese characters corresponding to Noël's citations of Chinese texts, allows a much more precise and certain identification of Noël's sources. Furthermore, Nicolas Standaert has shown that Noël translated excerpts from the books he and Castner brought to Rome in 1703, preserved until now in ARSI.[2] This chapter investigates the overall structure of the work and demonstrates how the work benefited from previous compilations realized by the missionaries and Chinese Christians. It then discusses the Chinese classics, commentaries, and dictionaries used by Noël, paying special attention to those which were not mentioned by other missionaries before him. Finally, it presents the Chinese works which were contemporary to the Terms and Rites Controversies and mentioned by Noël.

2.1 Overall Structure of the *Philosophia Sinica*

Before dealing with the First Treatise, we need to discuss the overall structure of the *Philosophia Sinica* and its three treatises. The structure is already apparent in the preface in the manuscript 'Doctrinae Sinicae brevis indagatio' (Brief investigation of Chinese Teaching), which is now held in ARSI.[3] This preface was probably written in China since it mentions 'here in China' (*in hac China*), but the entire manuscript was probably completed in Rome between 1703–1704. Only the manuscript of the First Treatise (*Tractatus primus*) is extant today.

In the short preface of seventeen lines that is found in the manuscript, Noël asks three questions. The first question concerns whether the Chinese have any knowledge of *numen* (divinity) and whether they are atheistic. This question reflects the Chinese Terms Controversy about the Chinese names for God that the Jesuit missionaries discussed from 1615 until the late 1620s. In the First Treatise, Noël argues against Longobardo's opposition to indigenous Chinese vocabulary for

---

1 Collani, 'François Noël and his Treatise on God in China'.
2 Standaert, *Chinese Voices*, p. 81.
3 ARSI, *Fondo Gesuitico* 724/4, fols 1ʳ–128ʳ (fol. 1ʳ). As Standaert notices, the handwriting does not belong to Noël. See Standaert, *Chinese Voices*, p. 79 n. 123.

Thierry Meynard, Sun Yat-sen University, Guangzhou, China

expressing the Christian God, and contends that *Shangdi* and *Tian* are legitimate terms for God.[4]

The second question concerns whether the Chinese are superstitious in offering worship to the *manes* (souls of the dead). This second question refers to the Chinese Rites Controversy that raged among the Jesuits, Franciscans, and Dominicans from 1630 until the early eighteenth century. In the Second Treatise Noël argues that the rites to Confucius and the ancestors are not religious but civil, and therefore fully compatible with Christianity.

The third question concerns whether the Chinese have erred in moral philosophy. This refers to the controversy among missionaries about the virtues of the Chinese. This controversy can be traced back to Saint Augustine who had dismissed the virtues of the pagans compared with Christian virtues. In terms of its content, the Third Treatise is more original than the preceding two. Here Noël shows that moral virtues exist in China and, even with the coming of Christianity in China, Confucian ethics is still relevant.

Besides the ARSI manuscript, there is another manuscript in Paris, which lacks the Chinese characters corresponding to Noël's citations of the Chinese classics. The Parisian manuscript follows the Roman manuscript but has a more elaborate title: 'Doctrinae Sinicae brevis indagatio, ex ipsis Sinarum libris eruta in qua dilucidantur pene omnes controversiae Sinenses'.[5] This expanded title makes clear that the work treats the controversies over Jesuit missionary practices in China as distinct: namely, the Rites Controversy, the Terms Controversy, and the controversy over Chinese virtue. We have noticed that on the last folio (fol. 325^r) are mentioned the names of a few towns in Flanders: Tournay, Lisle, Douay, etc. Standaert infers that the Roman manuscript is older than the Parisian manuscript, while the printed text is a revision of the Parisian manuscript.[6]

A manuscript of the *Philosophia Sinica* was also recorded in the catalogue of the Municipal Library of Arras. Unfortunately, the archivist of the library informed us that the entire collection in which this manuscript was found was destroyed by German artillery in July 1915. It is possible that it was an intermediary between the Parisian manuscript and the printed text since it had been observed that the manuscript was heavily corrected.[7]

It is striking that the title shifts from 'Investigation of Chinese Teaching' in the three manuscripts to 'Chinese Philosophy' in the printed version. As explained in

---

4 See Niccolò Longobardo, *A Brief Response on the Controversies over Shangdi, Tianshen and Linghun*, ed. by Thierry Meynard and Daniel Canaris (Singapore: Palgrave Macmillan, 2021).

5 BnF, collection Bréquigny 15–16; 2 vols (I, 394 pages; II, 416 pages; supplement 9 pages). 'Tractatus primus: De cognitione primi entis seu Dei apud Sinas', pp. 1–324; 'Tractatus secundus: De cultu defunctorum apud Sinas', pp. 327–638; plus annex: 'De scopo rituum sinensium controversorum', 26 pages; 'Tractatus tertius: De ethica sinensi', pp. 1–170.

6 Standaert, *Chinese Voices*, p. 79 n. 124.

7 Bibliothèque municipale d'Arras, 1170 (1341–1342), *Doctrinae Sinicae brevis indagatio*, 416 pages with supplement of nine pages. Heavily corrected. See Alcius Ledieu, *Catalogue général des manuscrits des bibliothèques publiques de France: Tome 40, Supplément – tome 1: Abbeville – Brest* (Paris: Plon), Arras, p. 325.

the previous chapter, Noël published his work following the papal condemnation of the Chinese Rites in 1710, and thus had to discard the previous title that made explicit reference to the controversies and adopted instead the more academic and scholarly title of 'Chinese Philosophy'.

With this new concept of philosophy, Noël wrote a new preface running over nine printed pages, and he relabelled the three treatises in terms of three branches of philosophy. The Third Treatise on Chinese ethics (*De ethica sinensi*), is called moral philosophy. The First Treatise on the Chinese knowledge of God (*De cognitione primi entis seu Dei apud Sinas*) is now called rational philosophy. More surprisingly, the Second Treatise on the Chinese Rites for the deceased (*De cultu defunctorum apud Sinas*) is called natural philosophy. As Carel Wesselius remarks, the Second Treatise does not seem to correspond to natural philosophy, a branch of scholastic philosophy related mostly to physics and human body, and 'while the *Philosophia Sinica* indeed discusses parts of Confucian philosophy, such as moral philosophy, it is first and foremost a document defending the policy of accommodation held by the Jesuit order'.[8]

2.2 The Term 'Chinese Philosophy' in the Preface

In the new preface to the printed edition, Noël mentions the conflicts about Chinese philosophy (*de Philosophiae Sinensis rebus contentiones*) and strives to show his impartiality: he chose authors endowed with authority and selected a wide range of works so that readers may make their own judgement. If readers know Chinese, they may even check the correctness of his Latin translation against the Chinese works which are kept in the Jesuit headquarters at Rome. Therefore, the title of the work seeks to convey the idea that Chinese teaching (*doctrina*) is not a superstitious religion, but a philosophy which acknowledges the existence of God without establishing any supernatural and erroneous beliefs.

Behind this tactical decision to describe Chinese thought as philosophy, there was a much deeper intellectual foundation. The *Confucius Sinarum philosophus* had recognized a Chinese learning (*scientia*) and promoted Confucius as the Chinese philosopher par excellence, but did not affirm the existence of a Chinese philosophy as such because of a perceived lack of metaphysics.[9] In contrast, Noël in his preface recognizes a speculative science in China (First Treatise) as in Europe, and he considers Chinese philosophy even more complete than modern European philosophy — a subtle critique of Cartesianism — since it also contains practical and moral philosophy (Second and Third Treatises) as in ancient Greece. Of course, for Noël, Chinese philosophy does not reach

---

[8] Carel Wesselius, 'The *Ethica Politica*', p. 6.
[9] Couplet and others, *Confucius Sinarum philosophus*, p. xxxvii; Thierry Meynard, ed., *Confucius Sinarum Philosophus (1687): The First Translation of Confucian Classics* (Rome: Institutum Historicum Societatis Iesu, 2011), p. 132.

the same degree of precision and correctness as scholasticism, but just like the Greek philosophy, Chinese philosophy is able to find, within the limitations of language and thought, abstract concepts to express the First Being (*primum ens*). The list of the attributes of God enumerated by scholastic philosophers (unicity, eternity, etc.) allows Noël to find equivalents in the ancient classics and their modern commentaries.

Noël's discovery of a true speculative philosophy in ancient China and of its development by the School of Principle from the Song to the Qing dynasties allows him to recognize that China has an authentic and complete philosophy. Noël was not the first to talk about a Chinese philosophy, but he was the first to publish a book under this title. Just like the Jesuits before him, Noël is guilty of reducing the diversity of Chinese culture and thought to Confucianism alone, but we need to recognize that if one school of thought can represent the main intellectual tradition of China it is surely the School of Principle which had dominated the intellectual scene for more than eight centuries from the Song dynasty to the end of the Qing dynasty.

By rejecting Song philosophy, Ricci and Longobardo dismantled the Confucian orthodoxy (*Daotong* 道统). Even the attempts by the authors of the *Confucius Sinarum philosophus* and by Bouvet to disconnect some selected commentaries from the School of Principle (such as the *Sishu zhijie* in the case of the *Confucius Sinarum philosophus*, and the *Sishu rijiang* 四書日講, or Daily Lectures on the Four Books, in Bouvet's case) were unconvincing. Only with Noël do we find a strenuous effort to engage simultaneously with the ancient classics and the modern commentaries, to uphold what he calls 'the ageless and continual tradition',[10] and to reject Ricci's theory of corruption, which held that the ancient Confucian teaching had been corrupted since the coming of Buddhism into China in the Han dynasty. In contrast, Noël believes that the discourses about *Tian* and *Shangdi* in the commentaries 'explain more explicitly, efficiently and clearly what the ancients had said in a general way'.[11]

2.3 The Hermeneutical Principles in the Preface

In his preface, Noël fully admits the difficulty of interpreting obscure passages in the Chinese classics, but he makes a daring parallel with the Bible, quoting a few passages from Genesis, Exodus, Kings, Tobias, Esther, Job, Psalms, Ecclesiasticus (Sirach), Ecclesiastes, and Luke, which suggest polytheistic faith or idolatrous practices. Noël seems to be aware of the new trend in the critical exegesis of the Bible, which had been developed by Richard Simon (1638–1712) in his *Histoire critique du Vieux Testament* (1685). Similarly, Noël develops hermeneutical principles in reading Chinese classics. He shows that it is not always possible to maintain a

---

10 'perpetua successivae doctrinae traditio'. Noël, 'Tractatus primus', p. 24 (c.1, q.3); this edition, p. 201.
11 'imò videntur subinde expressiùs, efficaciùs & clariùs explicare quod generaliter illi dixerant'. Noël, 'Tractatus primus', p. 62 (c.2, q.1, §.9); this edition, p. 247.

literal meaning, but a metaphorical meaning (*simile*) should be sometimes preferred, taking into consideration the context (*limites*), the rhetorical effects (*auxesis*), and the intention of the writer.

Other expressions should not be understood literally but as a particular way of speaking (*modus loquendi*). For example, Noël gives an excerpt from the chapter 'Duofang' 多方 in the *Shujing*: 'Only the princes of our Zhou dynasty, due to their particular skill in gathering all souls and due to the splendor of their virtue, were found worthy and became the masters of the spiritual Heaven' (惟我周王, 靈承于旅, 克堪用德, 惟典神天). The character *dian* 典 here means 'to master', but this seems to attribute to Wen Wang a divine power. In a note, Noël explains:

> Here and elsewhere the Chinese emperor is called the master of spiritual Heaven and of all the spirits (that is, pontifex or priest). This is both because he is the master of the sacrifices which are made to the spirits, and also because those spirits depend upon his rule for worship […] It is clear that this way of speech does not mean that the emperor is superior to or controls the Master of Heaven, but this way of speaking is similar to how we say that this man is the commander or the tribune of such and such a king, or that he is the governor of such and such a king, that is to say, he is a tribune or governor established by the king or in his name.[12]

For Noël, it is only possible to understand this passage of the *Shujing* as a particular way of speaking that should be understood in terms of how when we are entrusted authority by a leader, we assume a particular office 'of that leader'.

But could *Shangdi* or *Tian* be understood also as metaphors or ways of speaking? Very early on, some missionaries like Longobardo raised doubts about the intention of the Chinese writers in the classical texts. In his *Brief Response on the Controversies*, Longobardo affirms that both ancient and modern writers mention *Shangdi*, *Tian*, *taiji*, and *li*, as if referring to God or to an absolute principle, but their language is purely metaphorical and intentionally deceptive. These atheistic writers use symbolic language about God, but they themselves do not believe in God or in any reality beyond the present world.[13]

If Longobardo's interpretative frame is accepted, the words of Confucius and of the wise men of antiquity would lose their persuasive power; the Chinese Rites would lose also their reverence; and the classical texts would not be credible. Against Longobardo's hermeneutic of suspicion, Noël holds a more generous and trusting interpretation, asserting that the Chinese believe in what they say, especially when the God-language found in many texts is internally coherent and expressed with proper actions, like the ritual worship of the ancient rulers Yao and Shun. In Question 3 of Chapter 1, Noël invokes the authority of Saint Augustine who advocated in his *De doctrina Christiana* (III.10) that the literal meaning should be followed as much as possible, unless something absurd or false would ensue from

---

12 Noël, 'Tractatus primus', p. 19 (c.1, q.2, §.6); this edition, p. 195.
13 See Longobardo, *A Brief Response on the Controversies*, pp. 111–17 (prelude 5).

a literal interpretation. Therefore, while many things are said metaphorically in the Chinese classics, *Tian* and *Shangdi* are not be taken metaphorically but as literally.

In the preface, Noël quotes *Mencius* in support of an exegesis which aims at expressing the general intention of the writer: 'A prudent commentator of the *Book of Odes* should not misuse individual words to harm the meaning of the sentences, nor abuse individual sentences to harm the general meaning'.[14] For Noël, his own method of selecting passages of the classics and their commentaries respects the hermeneutical principles given in the *Mencius*:

> I have carefully selected not only those things which accord with philosophic truth, but also many other things which appear to go against it. I have presented to myself many objections just as any adversary would have done, but I took care also to resolve these difficulties with evidence drawn from the source of the Chinese books so that they cannot be attributed to the free invention of my own intelligence or to my own personal judgement. Even though the particular solutions taken separately do not always convince the intellect, which can hardly be demanded or expected in every matter, when considered collectively, the solutions do not seem to leave any place for hesitation, or for holding the contrary position. Moreover, the Chinese books that I quote frequently cannot be suspected of favouring one opinion over the other, because almost all the things I am quoting were written before the controversy about Chinese philosophy arose, and those books written after the start of the controversy freed of any suspicion by the situation of the earlier time and the reputation of their authors. A prudent man will never convince himself, I suppose, that either Christian or pagan authors would have wanted to expose their name to the shame of ignorance and the mockery of the literati.[15]

For sure, Noël is not neutral in the Terms and Rites Controversies, yet his method is to select many excerpts about *Shangdi* and *Tian* from representative texts, to classify the textual material and to translate as accurately as possible. It is especially important to distinguish literal and metaphorical meanings to attribute divine power to God and not to Confucius or the wise kings.

In the first chapter, Noël warns that denying the theistic reading of the Chinese classics may undermine the theistic reading of the Bible as well, and thus facilitate atheism in Europe.[16] In other words, the enemies of the true religion are not the Jesuits who are able to recognize theism in the scriptures of China, but those who are led by fear and suspicion to interpolate atheism into the Chinese texts. Those people indirectly promote a hermeneutic of suspicion which becomes a weapon in the hands of the atheists in Europe to attack Christianity itself.

---

14 Noël, 'Praefatio', in *Philosophia Sinica*, p. b; this edition, p. 167. Cf. *Mencius* 3A:「故說《詩》者，不以文害辭，不以辭害志」.
15 Noël, 'Praefatio', p. b; this edition, pp. 167–68.
16 Noël, 'Tractatus primus', p. 26 (c.1, q.3); this edition, p. 203.

2.4 Structure of the First Treatise

This volume focuses on the First Treatise for both practical and theoretical reasons. First, the *Philosophia Sinica* is a bulky work which requires a precise analysis of the sources. A comprehensive analysis of the entire work is beyond the scope of a single volume. Our analysis of Noël's Chinese sources was aided by the fact that the manuscript of the First Treatise in ARSI includes the Chinese characters corresponding to Noël's citations. We do not have this luxury for the Second and Third Treatises, making the textual analysis of these works more difficult. Second, the question of God in China was of great philosophical and theological importance both for the mission and for comparative philosophy, and Noël's treatment of this topic allows us to understand his pioneering contribution to this topic.

The First Treatise comprises three chapters. The first two chapters present in chronological order the knowledge of God, first in ancient China (first chapter) and second in modern China (second chapter). The ancient period described in the first chapter is not clearly defined but loosely corresponds to Spring and Autumn period, as well as the Qin and Han dynasties, a long period when the Five Classics, the *Lunyu*, and the *Mencius* were formed and finally edited. The second chapter deals with the knowledge of God among modern commentators, and this corresponds to the Song, Yuan, Ming, and Qing dynasties. The third chapter is historically situated in the late Ming and the early Qing, but the sources are no longer the classical texts and their commentaries, but the written testimonies of missionaries, Chinese Christians, Jews and Muslims, and even pagan Chinese, including above all Kangxi.

Each chapter is divided into questions, and most questions are divided into paragraphs. In each paragraph, there is a summary explanation of the question and a general answer (*succintus sensus* or *compendium*) which is cross-referenced to excerpts or summaries of textual testimonies arranged alphabetically. These textual references are usually placed in a separate section (*textus librorum*) at the end of a question.

The method used in the first two chapters consists mainly in an accumulation of authoritative references related to some key concepts whereas the third chapter features scholastic argumentation with question, affirmation, objections, and resolution.

The *Philosophia Sinica* functions as a reference book since the reader can search for Chinese texts in translation according to the period (ancient/modern/contemporary) and according to the attribute for God (dominion, power, knowledge, etc.). However, it is more than a reference book since there is argumentation running through each question, and the three parts of the *Philosophia Sinica* are called treatises.

Before we proceed to a deeper analysis of the content of the *Philosophia Sinica*, it is important to situate it in relation with different works produced before or around that time.

2.5 *Summarium NAT*

While most of the content of the *Summarium NAT* deals with the Chinese Rites, its eighth and last section deals with 'the legitimate meaning of the terms *Tian* and *Shangdi*, and of the *jing Tian* tablet', that is to say, the Terms Controversy which is the object of the First Treatise. This section of the *Summarium NAT* contains excerpts from the Chinese classics and their commentaries, as well as declarations of missionaries and Chinese Christians, pagans, and Jews in favour of the Chinese Rites. Much of this discussion can be found already in the 'Doctrinae Sinicae brevis indagatio', the manuscript of the First Treatise.[17]

As for Chinese texts written by missionaries, the *Summarium NAT* quotes only two Franciscan works, the *Tian Ru yin* 天儒印 [Imprints of the Heavenly Teaching and the Literati Teaching, 1664] by Antonio de Santa María Caballero (1602–1669) and the *Chuhui wenda* 初會問答 [Questions and Answers at the Initial Meeting, 1680] by Pedro de la Piñuela (1650–1704). In the context of the Terms Controversy, the mention of two Franciscan works in support of the monotheism of ancient China and of Confucius is strategically important since these works show that the Franciscans had previously been very close to the Jesuit position.

As for the Chinese who were either Christian or sympathized with Christianity, the testimonies of Feng Yingjing 馮應京 (1555–1606), Yang Tingyun 楊廷筠 (1562–1627), Zhu Zongyuan 朱宗元 (c. 1615–1660), Han Lin 韓霖 (1601–1644) and Zhang Geng 張賡 (c. 1570–1647) almost exactly match the text in the 'Doctrinae Sinicae brevis indagatio', and almost in the same order. However, the testimonies of Xu Guangqi 徐光啓 (1562–1633) and Chen Yi 陳儀 (1575–1634, *jinshi* 1610) in the 'Doctrinae Sinicae brevis indagatio' are more elaborate than in the *Summarium NAT*, and this suggests that the 'Doctrinae Sinicae brevis indagatio' served as one source for the *Summarium NAT*, unless there was also a proto-source from which both the 'Doctrinae Sinicae brevis indagatio' and the *Summarium NAT* were derived. Nonetheless, the 'Doctrinae Sinicae brevis indagatio' could hardly be the sole source, since the *Summarium NAT* quotes other Chinese Christians, such as Yan Mo 嚴謨 (1640–?) and Qiu Sheng 丘晟 (*jinshi* 1706),[18] as well as documents which were not originally written in Chinese.

Among non-Christian testimonies, Noël includes a new translation of Kangxi's testimony of 30 November 1700 in favour of the Chinese Rites. While the Beijing Jesuits had already published a Latin translation of Kangxi's testimony based on the Manchu text in the *Brevis relatio* of 1703, Noël based his translation on the Chinese version, which is included in the 'Doctrinae Sinicae brevis indagatio'. The *Brevis relatio* deals mostly with the Rites Controversy, but there is a statement

---

17 Noël and Castner, *Summarium NAT*, pp. 75–89 (Number 8); Noël, 'Tractatus primus', pp. 151–56 (c.3, q.1); this edition, pp. 357–77.
18 Qiu Sheng is not mentioned among the testimonies of the Chinese Christians in Chapter 3, but in Chapter 2 about the *jiaoshe* ritual (Question 5); Noël, 'Tractatus primus', p. 130 (c.2, q.5); this edition, p. 325.

in favour of the use of *Shangdi* and *Tian*: 'As for the ritual of sacrifice performed on the suburban earthen mound, we consider that it is not done to the blue or material heaven, but offered to the Principle, Lord and Ruler of Heaven, Earth and all things, like Confucius says: "The ritual of sacrifice to Heaven and Earth is to serve the Master and Guide of Heaven, or *Shangdi*". Sometimes He is called Master of Heaven (*Shangdi*) and sometimes, Heaven (*Tian*)'. Because of this statement, Noël decided to give the full text of the *Brevis relatio* at the end of the First Treatise. The eighth section of *Summarium NAT* also mentions the above passage of the *Brevis relatio*.[19]

On the issue of *Shangdi*, *Tian*, and *jing Tian*, there is also a strong textual connection between the eighth section of the *Summarium NAT* and the First Paragraph of Question 2 in Chapter 3 in the First Treatise of the *Philosophia Sinica*.[20] However, the quotes in the *Philosophia Sinica* are longer. This suggests that the 'Doctrinae Sinicae brevis indagatio' indeed served as a source for the *Summarium NAT* and that the 'Doctrinae Sinicae brevis indagatio' was very likely completed before 1704, perhaps in 1703.

2.6 Bouvet's *Gujin*

In the context of the Rites and Terms Controversies, Bouvet wrote a Chinese work which was given the Latin title 'Observata de vocibus sinicis Tien et Chang-ti' (Observations on the characters *Tian* and *Shangdi*) and was probably finished by November 1701. Indeed, the Vice-Provincial Antoine Thomas in Beijing sent a letter, dated 18 November 1701 to Noël, which mentions the work:

> Moreover, I am sending to you a remarkable Chinese treatise about *Tian* drawn from the [Chinese] classics through the work and zeal of Father Bouvet. The Chinese literati praise it highly.[21]

This refers to the *Tianxue benyi* 天學本意 [Basic Meaning of the Study of Heaven]. A letter of Bouvet dated 1704 confirms that Noël received the work and carried it to Europe.[22] While Noël was in Rome, Bouvet continued to correct and expand his work. Han Tan 韓菼 (1636–1704), then president of the Ministry of Rites (*Libu shangshu* 禮部尚書), wrote a preface dated the first month of the forty-second year of Kangxi (around February–March 1703), expressing his support for the

---

19 Noël, 'Tractatus primus', pp. 175–76 (c.3, q.2); this edition, p. 387. Noël and Castner, *Summarium NAT*, p. 82.
20 Noël and Castner, *Summarium NAT*, pp. 75–81; Noël, 'Tractatus primus', pp. 166–72 (c.3, q.2, p. 1); this edition, pp. 378–83.
21 'Ex epistola P. Antonii Thomas S. I. Vice-Provincialis Sinarum data Pekini 18. Novembris 1701. P. Francisco Noel S. I.: "Mitto insuper insignem Tractatum Sinicum desumptum ex libris Classicis labore, & studio P. Bouvet de Tien. Valde laudant Literati Sinenses"'. Noël and Castner, *Summarium NAT*, p. 87.
22 See Mungello, *The Silencing of Jesuit Figurist Joseph de Prémare in Eighteenth-Century China*.

publication. Around the same time, Bishop Álvaro de Benavente also gave ecclesiastical approval for the publication.[23]

However, when Maillard de Tournon arrived China in 1705, he asked two missionaries to review Bouvet's work and in the end decided to forbid the publication. He also ordered the confiscation of the many manuscripts in circulation. But on 18 December 1705, Kangxi, who had already read an initial draft, ordered the revised version to be translated into a European language for Tournon since he could not read Chinese.[24] Joseph de Prémare (1666–1736) and Julien-Placide Hervieu (1671–1746) finished their translation in 1706, which they titled 'De cultu coelesti Sinarum veterum et modernorum'.[25] However, Tournon did not change his stance. In 1707, Bouvet wrote a preface to his work, mentioning that the draft examined by Han Tan in 1703 did not include the excepts from the *Sishu rijiang*.

Mungello has examined seven Chinese manuscripts and proposed a chronological sequence for Bouvet's work. The first draft of twenty sheets was written in 1701 (BnF, MS Chinois 7160), and a new version expanded to fifteen folio pages was written in 1703 (BAV, Borgia Cinese 317), but those two early drafts did not include excerpts from the *Sishu rijiang*. In 1705, there was a new version that was greatly expanded, reaching seventy-two folio pages (Shanghai, Biblioteca Zi-ka-wei, 250.1), followed by a version with a total of ninety-nine folio pages and with a preface of May 1707 (BAV, Borgia Cinese 316), and followed by another version with a total of eighty-five folio pages (BnF, MS Chinois 7162). Finally, there is a version of sixty-nine folio pages, with a preface dated 1707 by Bouvet (BnF, MS Chinois 7161).[26]

Initially the work was titled *Tianxue benyi* but later Bouvet expanded the title as *Gujin jing Tian jian tianxue benyi* 古今敬天鑑天學本意 [Examination of 'Revere Heaven' in Past and Present; Essentials of the Heaven Learning]. However, the final versions of 1707 have only *Gujin jing Tian jian* 古今敬天鑑 [Examination of 'Revere Heaven' in Past and Present]. Strangely enough, ARSI does not hold a copy of the *Gujin*, but the Vatican has two copies which probably came from ARSI. Bouvet's work were printed for the first time in 2009 when the two late versions (BnF MS Chinois 7161 and 7162) were reproduced in facsimile.[27] A punctuated edition of the text (based on a comparison between BnF MS Chinois 7161 and BnF MS Chinois 7162) was published in 2013.[28]

---

23 Claudia von Collani, *P. Joachim Bouvet S. J., Sein Leben und sein Werk* (Nettetal: Steyler, 1985), p. 53.
24 Stumpf, *The Acta Pekinensia*, p. 48.
25 'Cu kin kim tien kien, Liber novus e sinico idiomate in latinum versus a patribus Placido Hervieu et Jos. Hen. de Premare, auct. P. Joach. Bouvet, anno 1706', BnF, MS NAL 155, fols 1ʳ–80ᵛ, <https://gallica.bnf.fr/ark:/12148/btv1b10035396v#>.
26 David E. Mungello, 'Unearthing the Manuscripts of Bouvet's *Gujin* after Nearly Three Centuries', *China Mission Studies*, 10 (1988), 34–61 (pp. 37–38).
27 Nicolas Standaert and Ad Dudink, eds, *Chinese Christian Texts from the National Library of France*, XXVI (Taipei: Ricci Institute, 2009), pp. 25–160 (MS Chinois 7161); pp. 161–330 (MS Chinois 7162).
28 Zhou Zhenhe 周振鶴, *Ming Qing zhiji xifang chuanjiaoshi Hanji congkan* 明清之際西方傳教士漢籍叢刊, 6 vols (Nanjing: Fenghuang chubanshe, 2013), III, pp. 113–319. The description of the text was written by Xiao Qinghe 肖清和 and Guo Jianbin 郭建斌. This volume also includes the punctuated text of a similar work by Bouvet, called *Zaowuzhu zhenlun* 造物主真論 (BnF MS Chinois 7163). The *Zaowuzhu*

In the *Gujin*, Bouvet collected many quotes to show that the Chinese terms *Tian* and *Shangdi* expressed a true understanding of God. We have discovered that some sixty citations used by Bouvet in the *Gujin* are also found in the 'Doctrinae Sinicae brevis indagatio', the first draft *Philosophia Sinica*. This includes ten citations from the 132 citations of the *Sishu rijiang* in the *Gujin*. We may infer that Noël had in his hands not only the first draft of 1701 but also an expanded version including the citations of the *Sishu rijiang*. The printed version of the *Philosophia Sinica* also has a rather long quote from the dictionary *Xiesheng pinzijian* 諧聲品字箋 about the meaning of *Tian*, which likely came from Bouvet's preface of 1707 (see below for further details about the *Xiesheng pinzijian*).[29] All this indicates that Noël paid a close attention to the different versions of Bouvet's work, constantly updating new contents.

Noël not only found new important materials like the *Sishu rijiang* in Bouvet's *Gujin*, but he also found a methodology. As Mungello has shown, Bouvet's work is divided in two parts, each of which differs not in argument but in style of argumentation: 'While the second part uses people's proverbs, scholars' maxims and quotations from the classical texts in a manner alien to traditional Chinese literary forms, the first part in the later versions follows a more traditional Chinese form in which each proposition is supported with several passages from the classical texts'.[30] Bouvet arranges the Chinese classics and commentaries according to forty-two topics dealing with *Tian* or *Shangzhu* 上主 (first *juan* of 1707 manuscript), while Noël concentrates the discussion on eight perfections of *Tian* or *Shangdi*. Also, while Bouvet quotes a commentary such as the *Sishu rijiang* immediately after a classical text, Noël arranges the classical texts in the first chapter of the First Treatise, and the corresponding commentaries in the second chapter of the First Treatise.

Despite the strong influence of Bouvet's work, there are some crucial differences. First, Bouvet's work is written in Chinese to convince a Chinese audience that Chinese thought is compatible with Christianity, while Noël intends to convince Europeans that Confucianism is compatible with Christianity.

Second, Bouvet inserts many biblical and Christological explanations to induce the Chinese to adopt Christianity while Noël in his First Treatise stays within the bounds of philosophy and natural theology.

Third, when quoting from the *Sishu rijiang*, Bouvet made references to key concepts of the School of Principle, such as *li* and *qi*, for interpreting the classics. However, like Ricci, Longobardo, and Couplet, Bouvet was staunchly opposed to Song Confucianism, and he specifically criticized in his preface to the *Gujin* the literati of his time for reducing Heaven to the workings of *li* and *qi*.[31] In the

---

zhenlun is very eclectic in its sources: besides the Confucian classics and the orthodox commentaries (*Daquan*, *Rijiang*, etc.), the work also cites the *Daodejing* 道德經, *Zhuangzi* 莊子, *Huainanzi* 淮南子, *Liezi* 列子, etc. Compared to the *Gujin*, the *Zaowuzhu zhenlun* contains fewer elaborations and comments by Bouvet.

29 Noël, 'Tractatus primus', pp. 74–75 (c.2, q.2, E.6); this edition, p. 263.
30 Mungello, 'Unearthing the Manuscripts of Bouvet's *Gujin* after Nearly Three Centuries', p. 43.
31 Mungello, 'Unearthing the Manuscripts of Bouvet's *Gujin* after Nearly Three Centuries', p. 56.

same preface, he writes: 'Among the Song Confucians there are those who did not understand the doctrine that the True Lord is one, and they indulged in their own theories with the result that the classics became obscure' (宋儒有不明真主唯一之旨者，各逞其臆說，而經乃晦矣。).³² Bouvet also criticizes Zhu Xi for having deleted *wuji* 無極; in contrast, Noël follows Zhu Xi in having *wuji* 'the being without ultimate' as a redundant term for *taiji*, the 'first ultimate'.³³ In relation to Zhu Xi's comment on Gaozong's 高宗 dream-vision of Fuyue 傅說 in the *Shujing*, Bouvet admits that Zhu Xi had recognized there was *Tiandi* 天帝 (Heavenly Emperor), but for Bouvet this recognition of Zhu Xi was only momentary (*yishi* 一時). In fact, when Bouvet titles his work 'Examination of "Revere Heaven" in Past and Present', 'present' does not refer to the mainstream ideas of the School of Principle at the beginning of the Qing dynasty but mostly to the fact that Kangxi seemingly supported the idea of 'revering Heaven' (*jing Tian* 敬天), an idea that the Song Confucians had lost and made them unable to understand the classics. On the contrary, Noël does not criticize Zhu Xi and quotes him very positively.

A fourth difference between Noël and Bouvet is that Noël takes seriously the continuity of Confucian orthodoxy (*daotong* 道統), adopting the mainstream interpretations of the School of Principle running through the commentaries of the Song, Yuan and Ming dynasties until the Qing dynasty, such as the *Sishu mengyin* 四書蒙引, *Zhouyi zhengjie* 周易正解, and *Shijing shuoyue jijie* 詩經說約集解 (see next chapter for further discussion of those works). Therefore, Noël deals much more broadly with the commentaries than Bouvet, who only cites in the *Gujin* the above-mentioned *Sishu zhijie* and *Sishu rijiang*, as well as the *Sishu daquan* 四書大全 [Compendium of the Four Books] which was published at the beginning of the Ming dynasty.

2.7 Yan Mo's *Ditian kao*

Noël quotes only once the *Shishu biancuojie* 詩書辨錯解 [Explaining how to Distinguish Errors in the *Shijing* and the *Shangshu*] by the Chinese Christian Paul Yan Mo 嚴謨 (1640–?) about the meaning of the expression of *Huangtian houtu* 皇天后土, which Noël translates as Highest Heaven and Thick Earth.³⁴ The work is lost but a section of it was published in the early 1680s with the title *Ditian kao* 帝天考 [Study on *Tian* and *Di*], which systematically examines the question of *Shangdi* and *Tian*, concluding that they are equivalent with *Tianzhu*: 'This examination reveals that what is called *Shangdi* in the ancient classics is the same as what is called *Tianzhu* by the West' (以今考之，古中之稱［上帝］，即

---

32 Joachim Bouvet, 'Gujin jingtian jian zixu' 古今敬天鑒自序, in *Ming Qing zhiji Xifang chuanjiaoshi hanji congkan*, III, p. 122.
33 Bouvet, *Gujin*, pp. 132–33. Concerning *wuji* and *taiji*, see our analysis below in section 3.7, p. 97.
34 Noël, 'Tractatus primus', pp. 128–29 (c.2, q.5, CC.31); this edition, p. 321.

太西之稱「天主」). The *Ditian kao* itself is a very rare work with only two extant manuscript copies.³⁵

In light of the similarity between the *Ditian kao* and the First Treatise of the *Philosophia Sinica*, it is worth investigating further a possible connection between the works. Yan Mo gave a list of quotes, with short explanations, of the Five Classics and Four Books: Among his thirty-three quotes from the *Shujing*, twenty are found in the *Philosophia Sinica*; among his twenty-six quotes from the *Shijing*, sixteen are in the *Philosophia Sinica*. Overall, among the sixty-five quotes in the *Ditian kao*, thirty-nine are found in Chapter 1 of the First Treatise of the *Philosophia Sinica*, a chapter which deals precisely with the ancient classics. Some translations of those passages by Noël are very close to the explanations given by Yan Mo. Also, after the list of the sixty-five quotes of the Five Classics and Four Books, Yan Mo classifies the same quotes according to theological themes corresponding to the scholastic classification of the divine attributes: power, immensity-eternity, knowledge, simplicity (that is, God being indivisible, and thus purely spiritual without any material dimension), etc. Bouvet's own classification schema of forty-themes themes goes much beyond the divine attributes, whereas Noël's classification of seven attributes for *Tian* and *Shangdi* bears many similarities with Yan Mo's work.

Yet it is quite unlikely that Noël directly used the *Ditian kao*, since he mentions Yan Mo only once. It seems more likely that the influence of the *Ditian kao* was mediated through Bouvet's *Guijin*, for we have discovered that, among the thirty-nine quotes of the *Ditian kao* which are also quoted by Noël, twenty-seven are found in the *Gujin*.

This suggests a cumulative work realized by the Jesuit missionaries and the Chinese Christians over time. In his *True Meaning of the Lord of Heaven*, Ricci had established with the help of Chinese sympathizers a short list of eleven quotes mentioning *Shangdi* in the *Shujing* and the *Shijing*. In the 1680s, Yan Mo produced sixty-five quotes (fifty-nine from the *Shujing* and the *Shijing*, and six from the Four Books). Later, Bouvet added more quotes from the Five Classics and Four Books, reaching a total of 205 passages; to this amount, many commentaries, especially the *Sishu rijiang*, should be added.³⁶ Compared to Bouvet, Noël has fewer quotes from the classics, only 110, but he expanded considerably the number of quotes of the commentaries to reach 269 and also added more commentaries.

Noël agrees with Yan Mo on the monotheistic interpretation of the ancient texts. As Standaert has shown, Yan Mo in the *Ditian kao* adopted a few explanations by Zhu Xi and by his disciple Cai Chen 蔡沈 (1167–1230). However, Yan Mo continued to follow Ricci in rejecting Song Confucianism. In particular, he deliberately omitted and deleted Zhu Xi's interpretation of *Tian* or *Shangdi* according to the concept

---

35 The two extant copies are in BAV: R.G Oriente III 248 and Borgia Cinese 316.9. We are using this punctuated version: Nicolas Standaert [Zhong Mingdan 鐘鳴旦], *Keqin de Tianzhu: Qing chu jidujiaotu lun 'di' tan 'tian'* 可親的天主：清初基督教徒論「帝」談「天」 (Taipei: Guangqi chubanshe, 1998), pp. 27–56.
36 See Mungello, 'Unearthing the Manuscripts of Bouvet's *Gujin* after Nearly Three Centuries', p. 46.

of *li*, claiming to revert to the ancient authentic meaning before the corruption of the texts in the Han and Song dynasties.³⁷ On the contrary, Noël adopted the concepts and interpretations of the Song and Ming philosophers, as we shall see. His specific and unique contribution was to develop a Christian interpretation of the Song, Yuan, Ming and Qing commentaries.

2.8 *Tianjiao he Ru*

Although the Chinese Christian Zhang Xingyao 張星曜 (1633–c. 1715) is not mentioned by Noël, there are some similarities between the *Philosophia Sinica* and the first *juan* of Zhang's *Tian Ru tong yi kao* 天儒同異考 [Examination of Similarities and Differences between the Heavenly and Confucian Teachings]. Research by Xiao Qinghe reveals that this *juan*, which is titled *Tianjiao he Ru* 天教合儒 (Union of the Teaching of Heaven with Confucianism), was in fact written by Bouvet in 1702.³⁸ Unlike the *Gujin*, the *Tianjiao he Ru* generally does not include commentaries, and classifies the classical texts into twenty sections. There are only a very few exceptions like two explicit references to two commentators: Zhang Juzheng 張居正 (n. 2, p. 16) and Chen Dayou 陳大猷 (n. 8, p. 30). There is also a quote by Chengzi about the connection between material (*xingti* 形體) heaven and *Shangdi*, pointing out that the connection does not constitute a formal identity, but only a metaphoric relation (n. 1, p. 15).³⁹

Strikingly, most of the quotes in Chapter 1 of the First Treatise of the *Philosophia Sinica* are common to the *Ditian kao*, the *Gujin* and the *Tianjiao he Ru*. This suggests that there was a database of quotes which provided most of the content of the four texts in question. In the First Treatise and the *Tianjiao he Ru*, the quotes are also arranged in a similar way. In the first section of the *Tianjiao he Ru*, the different meanings of *Tian* and *Di* are listed; similarly, six different meanings of *Tian* are listed in the *Philosophia Sinica*. The second and third sections of the *Tianjiao he Ru* provide information similar to the attributes of dominion and power of *Tian* discussed by Noël. The fourth section of the *Tianjiao he Ru* matches with Noël's discussion of the attribute of knowledge (c.1, q.2, §.3). Sections 5 to 10 correspond to Noël's discussion of the attribute of the will (§.4), while sections 11 to 20 of the *Tianjiao he Ru* correspond to the attribute of justice (§.5). Only the two last attributes given by Noël (immensity and eternity; simplicity) do not have clear

---

37 See Standaert, *Keqin de Tianzhu*, pp. 65–73.
38 Xiao Qinghe 肖清和, *Tian Ru tong yi kao: Qingchu Rujia jidutu Zhang Xingyao wenji* 天儒同異考：清初儒家基督徒張星曜文集 (Taipei: Ganlan chubanshe, 2015), p. xli. Note that citations from *Tianjiao he Ru* are taken from this edition. Xiao Qinghe overturns Mungello's view that Bouvet had borrowed from Zhang. Cf. David E. Mungello, *The Forgotten Christians of Hangzhou* (Honolulu: University of Hawaii Press, 1994), p. 174. The same error was already mentioned in his 1988 article; Mungello, 'Unearthing the Manuscripts of Bouvet's *Gujin* after Nearly Three Centuries', pp. 44–47.
39 This quote by Chengzi is mentioned three times in the First Treatise: Noël, 'Tractatus primus', p. 59 (c.2, q.1, §.8, D.3); p. 66 (c.2, q.2, B.5); p. 67 (c.2, q.2, B.7); this edition, pp. 243, 250, 251.

correspondence in the *Tianjiao he Ru*. Although Noël may have been inspired by the classification proposed by the *Tianjiao he Ru*, the specific quotes within each section are quite different, showing the freedom of the compilers in assigning the quotes to a specific category. Occasionally, the *Tianjiao he Ru* assigns a quote to two or three different categories.

It cannot be discounted that Noël used other materials compiled by the Jesuits and Chinese Christians. For example, Filippucci collected for his library in Canton the Chinese classics and their commentaries, as well as works by Chinese Christians,[40] and also wrote a treatise on the Chinese Rites.[41]

2.9 Other Materials Added to the Printed Text of 1711

A comparison of the ARSI manuscript with the printed text reveals which materials were subsequently added. In addition to the the new preface of the printed version, Noël added some proofs based on the testimony of Muslims, Jews, and Chinese pagans.[42]

There are also some twenty quotes coming from commentaries and dictionaries which were not mentioned in the ARSI manuscript: *Shujing daquan* 書經大全, *Zhengzitong* 正字通, *Xiesheng pinzi jian* 諧聲品字箋, *Da Ming huidian* 大明會典 and *Wenxian tongkao* 文獻通考.

In Chapter 2, most of the content of the question titled 'Whether the modern commentators are moving away from the original meaning of *Tian* or *Shangdi* in the ancient classics?' is new.[43]

In Chapter 3, even more substantial content was added, such as the fourth objection of Question 1, which includes a quote from *De divina substantia ejusque attributis* by Francisco Suárez,[44] and the refutation to the first objection of Question 2.[45] Also are added the names of five persons at the court who testified in favour of the Chinese Rites in 1702.[46] Finally, Noël adds two testimonies given by Kangxi himself on two separate occasions, one on 22 July 1706 through Henkama and Zhao Chang, the second on 1 August 1706 while interviewing Maigrot.[47] Those testimonies are said to be recorded in a document kept in Rome. This corresponds to the first part of the *Acta Pekinensia* which was brought to Europe in the luggage of Antonio Provana (1662–1720) who departed together with Noël from Macao on 14 January 1708. Noël probably directly consulted the *Acta Pekinensia* and copied

---

40 Standaert, *Chinese Voices*, p. 220.
41 'Tractatus P. is Francisci Xaverij Philippucci de Ritibus Sinicis', Rome, Biblioteca nazionale centrale Vittorio Emmanuele [BNCVE], Ges., 1248/3, fol. 169ʳ. See Standaert, *Chinese Voices*, p. 64.
42 Noël, 'Tractatus primus', pp. 166–79 (c.3, q.2); this edition, pp. 378–91.
43 Noël, 'Tractatus primus', pp. 61–63 (c.2, q.1, §.9); this edition, p. 246.
44 Noël, 'Tractatus primus', p. 160 (c.3, q.1, §.2); this edition, p. 376.
45 Noël, 'Tractatus primus', p. 167 (c.3, q.2, §.1); this edition, pp. 382–83.
46 Noël, 'Tractatus primus', p. 176 (c.3, q.2, §.3); this edition, p. 389.
47 Noël, 'Tractatus primus', p. 177 (c.3, q.2, §.3); this edition, pp. 390–91.

related excerpts. All the additions were probably carried out during Noël's second stay in Rome, in the year 1709.

At the very end of the Treatise, Noël expresses his hope of a decision of Rome in favour of the Chinese Rites and Terms, and he must therefore have written this before the promulgation of *Cum Deus Optimus* on 25 September 1710.

2.10 Five Classics and Four Books

The first chapter asks: 'Whether ancient Chinese had knowledge of God, or the First Being, or were they atheists?' (*An Sinae antiquae habuerint aliquam Dei, seu primi Entis cognitionem, nec fuerint Athei?*) Above it has been shown how Noël used, either directly or indirectly, material drawn from the Five Classics and the Four Books which had been compiled by his predecessors. Out of the 110 quotes of the classical texts in Chapter 1 of the First Treatise (see Chart 1 at the end of this volume), seventy-three can be found either in the *Ditian kao*, *Gujin*, or *Tianjiao he Ru*. Some thirty-seven quotes are specific to the *Philosophia Sinica*. For example, in Question 1 of Chapter 1 of the First Treatise, Noël introduces meanings for *Tian* based on two quotes of the *Shijing* (A.1, B.2) and one quote of the *Mencius* (E.5) not found in his predecessors.[48] Similarly, in relation to the first attribute of the dominion of *Tian*, there are five quotes from *Zhoushu* 周書 (Book of Zhou) in the *Shujing* (C.3, D, G, L.11, O.14, T.23) and one quote from the 'Biaoji' 表記 in the *Liji* (O.15).[49] Besides the Five Classics and the Four Books, on one occasion Noël also quotes from the *Kongzi jiayu* 孔子家語 in Chapter 1.[50]

Also in Chapter 1, Noël has four quotes coming from a source apparently not used by his predecessors: the *Quanshi xiangyao* 全史詳要 [Detailed Summary of the Complete History, 30 *juan*, 1630] by the Shanghai scholar Wang Changhui 王昌會.[51]

---

48 Noël, 'Tractatus primus', p. 2 (c.1, q.1); this edition, pp. 170–71.
49 Noël, 'Tractatus primus', pp. 4–6 (c.1, q.2, §.1); this edition, pp. 173–77.
50 Noël, 'Tractatus primus', p. 17 (c.1, q.2, §.5, L.10); this edition, p. 192. From a very early stage, the Jesuits noticed and quoted the *Kongzi jiayu*. Copies of this work are held in ARSI, Jap. Sin. I, 2 (Ming edition, 1554); Jap. Sin. I, 4 (late Ming or early Qing edition), Jap. Sin. I, 5 (late Ming edition). See Albert Chan, *Chinese Books and Documents in the Jesuit Archives in Rome: A Descriptive Catalogue* (Armonk: M.E. Sharpe, 2002), pp. 3–5. Noël also quotes the *Kongzi jiayu*, or *Liber sermonorum familiarium seu domesticorum*, on two occasions in Chapter 2; Noël, 'Tractatus primus', pp. 83, 103 (c.2, q.3, M.14 & q.4, DD.34); this edition, pp. 268, 299.
51 Noël, 'Tractatus primus', p. 6 (c. 1, q.1, §.1, V.24, X.25, X.26 & §.8, H.8); this edition, pp. 178, 200. There are also two other quotes of the *Quanshi xiangyao*, or *Liber annalium universalium*, in Chapter 2 (p. 137) and two other quotes in Chapter 3 (p. 165). The work is present in ARSI, Jap. Sin. III, 11–14. According to the preface by Chen Renxi 陳仁錫 (1579–1634) dated 1629, Wang Changhui had consulted Sima Guang's 司馬光 (1019–1086) *Zizhi tongjian* 資治通鑑, Zhu Xi's *Tongjian gangmu* 通鑑綱目, Liu Shu's 劉恕 (1032–1078) *Tongjian waiji* 通鑑外籍 among others. Chan remarks that the *Quanshi xiangyao* starts with the earliest traditional legends. Chan, *Chinese Books and Documents in the Jesuit Archives in Rome*, p. 488. Indeed, from the *Quanshi xiangyao*, Noël sources quotes about Fu Xi 伏羲, Zhuanxu 顓頊 and

For the eighth attribute of simplicity, only two quotes of this section can be found in the *Ditian kao*, *Gujin*, and *Tianjiao he Ru* whereas the other five quotes are specific to Noël: two drawn from the *Liji* (C.3, D.4), one from the *Shujing* (E.5, I.9), one from the *Yijing* (F.6), and one from the *Quanshi xiangyao* (H.8).[52]

There is a preponderance of the quotes from the *Shujing* and the *Shijing* (see Chart 2 at the end of this volume), which express a vision of *Tian* or *Shangdi* that is closer to the Christian idea of God as person, while *Tian* in the *Lunyu* and the *Mencius* appears more distant. From the beginning of the Jesuit China mission, the Jesuits had focused on the Four Books rather than on the Five Classics for several reasons. First, the Four Books and its commentary by Zhu Xi were prevalent in the philosophical landscape and the examination system of the late Ming. Furthermore, the Four Books provided a comparatively condensed corpus of texts compared to the Five Classics. Finally, the missionaries considered the Four Books easier to understand than the Five Classics.[53]

The gradual shift of the Jesuits from the Four Books to the Five Classics during Kangxi's reign can be explained in the context of the Rites and Terms Controversies. Compared to the Four Books, in the *Shujing* and in the *Shijing* the Jesuits and the Chinese Christians could find more hints of the ancient Chinese belief in *Tian* or *Shangdi* as a personal God who establishes rulers and sends rewards and punishments.

Moreover, this strategic shift towards the *Shujing* and the *Shijing* corresponded to the broader shift of Chinese intellectuals under Kangxi who increasingly distanced themselves from the Four Books and Zhu Xi's commentaries and promoted a new movement called evidential learning (*kaozheng* 考證), which gave greater attention to the Five Classics.[54]

In Chapter 1, Noël intends to present the meaning based on the classical texts alone. The Song commentators all claimed the same. Starting with Ricci, the Jesuits distinguished the ancient meaning of the classics from their interpretation by the Song commentators, and in some way, the Jesuits were preparing the way for the evidential learning. But Noël is atypical among the Jesuits since he distinguishes the classics from their Song interpretation only to show a continuum of meaning. Therefore, when we are reading his translation of the classical texts in Chapter 1, we should be aware that it is already informed by the gloss of the Song commentators. Consider *Zhongyong* 30: 'Small virtue flows like a stream; great virtue is genuinely transforming' (小德川流, 大德敦化). Noël translates this passage as follows: 'There is a particular underlying power that diffuses itself into all individual things in various ways, and there is a universal virtue extending itself broadly to produce all things'.[55] This supposed translation of the ancient classic is, in fact, heavily influenced by Zhu Xi's gloss in *Zhongyong zhangju* 中庸章句: 'Small virtue is part

---

Huangdi 黃帝. Though the *Quanshi xiangyao* is a Ming text, Noël inserts those quotes in the first chapter because he considers them as historical documents which prove the early ritual worship of God.

52 Noël, 'Tractatus primus', pp. 21–23 (c.1, q.2, §.8); this edition, pp. 199–200.
53 See Meynard, ed., *Confucius Sinarum Philosophus (1687)*, pp. 97–105.
54 Xiao Qinghe, *Tian Ru tong yi kao: Qingchu Rujia jidutu Zhang Xingyao wenji*, p. xlvii.
55 Noël, 'Tractatus primus', p. 9 (c.1, q.2, §.2, S.18); this edition, p. 182.

of the complete whole. Large virtue is the basis of the ten thousand differences'
(小德者，全體之分；大德者，萬殊之本).[56] Clearly, the Jesuits at that time
did not have the proper tools to engage with evidential learning, and only in the
nineteenth century scolars like James Legge (1815) built on the methods and results
of the evidential learning to propose translations closer to the original meaning.

2.11 Commentaries on the Five Classics

Chapter 2 asks the same question as Chapter 1, but this time applied to the 'the more recent Chinese' (*Sinae recentiores*). We have observed that Bouvet started to compile quotes from the *Sishu rijiang* to explain the ancient classics while following the traditional Chinese method of placing a commentary immediately after a short passage from a classical text. The translations of the Four Books in the *Sapientia Sinica* (1662) and the *Confucius Sinarum philosophus* (1687) also adopted this method. However, Noël's method differs in that he placed the the quotes from the commentaries that he compiled in Chapter 2. He cross-referenced the commentaries with the corresponding classical passages in Chapter 1 through a system of letters and numbers. Noël's new method is quite innovative because it presented for the first time a large number of quotes (more than 250) from the commentaries, which run over 123 printed pages. The fact that Chapter 1 contains only 110 quotes of the ancient classics over only twenty-seven pages already signals an important shift of focus. Also, compared to the *Confucius Sinarum philosophus* and Bouvet's writings, the *Philosophia Sinica* features an expanded range of commentaries, especially with the inclusion of Cai Qing's *Sishu mengyin* 四書蒙引 and the *Zhouyi zhengjie* 周易正解, as discussed below. In Question 1 of Chapter 2, Noël classifies the quotes related to *Tian* and *Shangdi* according to the same eight attributes as in Chapter 1, showing that the more recent Chinese, the same as the ancient, believe that *Tian* or *Shangdi* is endowed with the same eight attributes. Though Noël applies this scholastic frame to read neo-Confucian texts, an attentive reader can easily notice that Noël's discourse on *Tian* or *Shangdi* is deeply shaped by the neo-Confucian categories of *li*, *qi* and *taiji*.

Most of the quotes in Chapter 1 come from the Five Classics, and hence it is no surprise that the majority of the quotes from the commentaries in Chapter 2 come from the commentaries of the Four Books (143 out of 268). It seems that Noël purposefully chose one commentary for each of the Five Classics, except for the *Chunqiu* which is not mentioned at all.

---

56 *Daxue & Zhongyong*, Translated and annotated by Ian Johnston and Wang Ping (Hong Kong: Chinese University of Hong Kong Press, 2012), p. 483.

1. Zhouyi zhengjie

The *Shujing* and the *Shijing* are the most cited classics in the *Philosophia Sinica*, but we can see the growing importance attached to the *Yijing* in the early Qing. While there are only ten quotes from the *Yijing* in Chapter 1, in Chapter 2 there are some forty-seven quotes from the *Zhouyi zhengjie* 周易正解, which in Latin is called *Vera libri mutationum ac productionum explicatio*. This is the most quoted work after Cai Qing's *Sishu mengyin* (fifty-six quotes). According to Albert Chan, the book was intended for students preparing for civil examinations.[57]

Strangely, there are only three citations from Cai Qing's *Yijing mengyin* 易經蒙引 [Primer on the *Yijing*].[58] Noël may have preferred to cite the *Zhouyi zhengjie* because it was a more recent work, published only in 1693.[59] As Noël mentions, this work was written by three persons: Wu Sunyou 吳蓀右, Ding Keting 丁柯亭 and Wu Nanzou 吳南騶.[60] Noël could not but notice the influence of Cai Qing in the *Zhouyi zhengjie* since he gives eight excerpts with explicit quotes from Cai Qing's *Yijing mengyin*. This may have been an important reason for Noël to choose the *Zhouyi zhengjie*.

Both the *Yijing mengyin* and the *Zhouyi zhengjie* are based on Zhu Xi's *Zhouyi benyi* 周易本義.[61] For example, *Yijing mengyin* quotes Zhu Xi more than 500 times.[62] Also, Cai Qing inherits from Zhu Xi the idea that the teaching of the *Yijing* is devoid of soul, mind, and intention (無思無為) because it is only through human virtue and intelligence that the teaching acquires soul, mind, and intention.[63]

Besides Zhu Xi's ideas, many ideas which are mentioned by Noël as coming from Cai Qing through the *Zhouyi zhengjie* can ultimately be traced back to Zhang Zai 張載 (1020–1078), a philosopher who exerted some influence in the understanding of the *Xici* 繫辭 [Appendix to the *Yijing*] through his work *Yishuo* 易說. In the *Philosophia Sinica*, we can notice Zhang Zai's ideas, such as the importance of the *Yijing* for the *shengren* 聖人 (Sage) for understanding the Way of Heaven and the concrete changes happening in the mundane reality.[64] Also, Cai Qing inherits from Zhang Zai the idea that the spiritual *shen* 神 is one and undifferentiated since the *Xici* states that *shen* has no determinate place or object (*fangti* 方體). Also, like

---

57   Chan, *Chinese Books and Documents in the Jesuit Archives in Rome*, p. 19. This work has no connection with another work of the same title by Hao Jing 郝敬 (1558–1639).
58   See Noël, 'Tractatus primus', p. 32 and p. 60; this edition, pp. 217, 245. ARSI does not have this work.
59   This book is preserved in ARSI, Jap. Sin. I, 19. The original edition of 1693 comprises twenty-two *juan*, twenty-four *ce*, printed by Cishu tang 賜書堂 in Danyang 丹阳, Jiangsu province.
60   Noël, 'Tractatus primus', pp. 32–33; this edition, p. 211.
61   Interestingly, Cai Qing's *Yijing mengyin* has an edition with a title making the connection with Zhu Xi even more explicit: *Zhouyi benyi zhengjie* 周易本義正解, which is kept today in the library of Fujian Normal University.
62   Song Yecao 宋野草, *Cai Qing Yixue sixiang yanjiu* 蔡清易學思想研究 (Beijing: Zhongguo shehui kexue chubanshe, 2015), p. 18.
63   Song Yecao, *Cai Qing Yixue sixiang yanjiu*, pp. 18–19, pp. 68–74.
64   Noël, 'Tractatus primus', p. 102 (c.2, q.4, AA.29–31); this edition, p. 258.

Zhang Zai, Cai Qing insists on the role of *yuan* 元 among the four powers (*side* 四德) embracing Heaven (*tongtian* 統天).⁶⁵

Chapter 2 of the First Treatise also features four quotes from the *Yijing rijiang* 易經日講.⁶⁶ This work was compiled by the Grand Secretary (*daxueshi* 大學士) Kulena 庫勒納 (or Kurene in Manchu, ?–1708) and approved for publication by Kangxi on 3 February 1684.⁶⁷ There is also one single quote from the *Zhouyi daquan* 周易大全 (*Liber magnus commentarius libri Ye kim*).⁶⁸

2. Liji jishuo

The Yuan scholar Chen Hao 陳澔 (1261–1341) wrote the authoritative *Liji jishuo* 禮記集說 [Collected Commentaries on the *Book of Rites*] which is extensively quoted in the *Philosophia Sinica*.⁶⁹ According to Albert Chan, this book was widely used during the Ming and Qing dynasties because it was concise and easy to understand.⁷⁰ In fact, an important reason for the influence of the *Liji jishuo* is its inclusion in the *Wujing daquan* 五經大全 [Compendium of the *Five Classics*], edited by Hu Guang 胡廣 (1369–1418) under the Yongle 永樂 Emperor (r. 1403–1424) of the Ming dynasty. Longobardo had quoted the Five Classics from the *Wujing daquan* and made reference to the *Liji jishuo*.⁷¹ To refute the interpretation of the Dominican Domingo Navarrete (1610–1689), Francesco Brancati (1607–1671) wrote in 1668 seventeen Sinological notes on Chinese rituals drawn mostly from the *Liji jishuo*.⁷² The *Liji jishuo* was also quoted by Filippucci.⁷³ Also, in his *Jili paozhi* 祭禮泡製 (1698), the Chinese catechist Matthias Xia Dachang 夏大常 derived most of his explanations of the rituals from Chen Hao.⁷⁴ Since Matthias Xia was based at Ganzhou in Jiangxi province, he certainly would have had contact with Noël who was based at Nanchang. ARSI has a 1633 edition of the *Liji jishuo*, which was edited by Min Qiji 閔齊

---

65 For the connection between the ideas of Cai Qing and Zhang Zai about the *Yijing*, see Song Yecao, *Cai Qing Yixue sixiang yanjiu*, pp. 12–13.
66 Noël, 'Tractatus primus', p. 86 (c.2, q.3, X.29), this edition, p. 276; pp. 102–03 (c.2, q.4, BB.32), this edition, p. 299; pp. 135–36 (c.2, q.5, GGG.68), this edition, p. 338; p. 145 (c.2, q.6, R.17), this edition, p. 349. Two of the four quotes are found in Noël and Castner, *Summarium NAT*, pp. 72–73.
67 A copy of this work is held in ARSI, Jap. Sin. I, 18.
68 Noël, 'Tractatus primus', p. 86 (c.2, q.3, X.28); this edition, p. 276. This citation is also mentioned in Noël and Castner, *Summarium NAT*, p. 74. A copy of the *Zhouyi daquan* is held in ARSI, Jap. Sin. I, 20.
69 Collani mistakenly identifies Chen Hao as Cheng Hao 程顥. See Collani, 'François Noël and his Treatise on God in China', p. 39.
70 See Chan, *Chinese Books and Documents in the Jesuit Archives in Rome*, p. 415.
71 Thierry Meynard, 'Longobardo's Reading of Song Confucianism,' in Meynard and Canaris ed., *A Brief Response on the Controversies over Shangdi, Tianshen and Linghun* (Singapore: Palgrave, 2021),p. 65. See Meynard, 'Longobardo's Reading of Song Confucianism', p. 65.
72 Prospero Intorcetta, *Testimonium de cultu sinensi, 1668* (Paris: Nicolas Pepié, 1700), pp. 65–138.
73 Saverio Filippucci, 'Tractatus', BNCVE, Ges., 1248/3, fol. 159ʳ. See Standaert, *Chinese Voices*, p. 62.
74 See Chan, *Chinese Books and Documents in the Jesuit Archives in Rome*, p. 42.

伋 (1580–?) in ten *juan*.[75] There are also two quotes from the *Liji jishuo* in the *Summarium NAT*.[76]

In the First Treatise of the *Philosophia Sinica*, the great majority of quotes (twenty-eight out of a total thirty-eight) from the *Liji jishuo* are found in Question 5 of Chapter 2 in connection with the *jiaoshe* 郊社 rituals. Those rituals are performed on the Altar of Heaven (*tiantan* 天壇) and on the Altar of Earth (*ditan* 地壇). There is a great debate within the Chinese tradition over how to understand the status of those two rituals performed on two different altars. From a Christian perspective, these two rituals are polytheistic if they have the same standing and are addressed to two different divinities. The Jesuits, however, favoured a monotheistic interpretation whereby two different rituals are performed on two different altars but are ultimately addressed to the same divinity. Another sensitive issue is the relationship between the rituals performed on the outdoor altars and the rituals performed inside the ancestor hall nearby. On this point, Chen Hao in his commentary closely follows Zhu Xi who asserts that the ritual offered inside ancestor hall is also addressed to the same *di* 帝.[77] Zhu Xi is also the point of reference for the discussion about the timing of the *jiao* ritual and the form of the altar.[78]

3. *Shijing shuoyue jijie*

In 1688, Fan Zhiheng 范之恆 (dates unknown) and Wan Jing 萬經 (1659–1741) published the *Bianzhitang dingzheng shijing shuoyue jijie* 辨志堂訂正詩經說約集解 in eight *juan*. Filippucci, who died in 1692, had already made use of his book just after its publication.[79] This book is quoted in the seventh section of *Summarium NAT* in relation to the Rites Controversy.[80] A copy can be found in ARSI and the BnF.[81]

The work, whose title is translated by Noël as as 'Extensive Compilation of Commentators on the *Book of Odes*' (*Compendiosa libri Carminum interpretum compilatio*), is quoted thirty-six times in the First Treatise of the *Philosophia Sinica*.[82] Noël mentions that the work also includes the commentary of Zhu Xi, and indeed, among the thirty-six quotes, eight of them are drawn from Zhu Xi's *Shijing jizhuan* 詩經集傳 (Collected Commentaries on the *Book of Odes*).[83] Yan Mo quotes also from Zhu Xi's *Shijing jizhuan*.

---

75 ARSI, Jap. Sin. II, 103–04, 111–12.
76 Noël and Castner, *Summarium NAT*, pp. 73–74.
77 Noël, 'Tractatus primus', pp. 122–23 (c.2, q.5, G.9); this edition, p. 311.
78 Noël, 'Tractatus primus', p. 123 (c.2, q.5, H); this edition, p. 312.
79 Filippucci, 'Tractatus', BNCVE, Ges., 1248/3, fol. 159r. See Standaert, *Chinese Voices*, p. 62.
80 Noël and Castner, *Summarium NAT*, p. 73.
81 ARSI, Jap. Sin. II, 92; see Chan, *Chinese Books and Documents in the Jesuit Archives in Rome*, pp. 405–06. BnF, MS Chinois 2750. The BnF copy is available on Gallica: <https://gallica.bnf.fr/ark:/12148/bpt6k9818196r> (accessed on 16 September 2022).
82 Collani misidentifies the Latin title as referring to the *Shijing daquan* 詩經大全. See Collani, 'François Noël and his Treatise on God in China', p. 40.
83 Noël, 'Tractatus primus', p. 41 (c.2, q.1, P.8); this edition, p. 221. The upper section gives the comments of various scholars, while the lower section gives the comments by Zhu Xi.

Obviously, the Jesuits needed a commentary for the *Shijing* since this classic contains a few passages mentioning *Shangdi*. Filippucci and Noël chose this newly published commentary probably because it included Zhu Xi's authoritative commentary and also other alternative interpretations from which they could find support for their monotheistic reading of the *Shijing*, such as this quote by Zhu Xi: 'Although Heaven is so high and remote and does not seem to think about those things, His intelligent spirit which cannot be comprehended is the Author of things and can stop, prevent and control any dangerous turmoil' (惟天高遠，雖若無意於物，然其功用神明不測，雖危亂之極，亦無不能鞏固之者).[84]

4. Shujing jizhuan

The *Shujing jizhuan* 書經集傳 [Collected Commentaries on the *Shujing*] was written by the scholar Cai Chen 蔡沈 (1167–1230). In his *Ditian kao*, Yan Mo had used this work.[85] There are twenty-two quotes in the First Treatise, including ten in the section dealing with the *jiaoshe* ritual.[86] ARSI has one copy of a Qing edition of the work.[87]

5. Shujing daquan

The *Wujing daquan* 五經大全 [Compendium of the *Five Classics*] was edited under the Yongle Emperor by Hu Guang, and as mentioned above, Longobardo in his *A Brief Response on the Controversies* quotes the Five Classics from the *Wujing daquan*.[88] In the *Philosophia Sinica*, there is only of quote from the *Wujing daquan*, more precisely from *Shujing daquan* 書經大全 (*Xukim taciuen, Magnus libri annalium imperalium commentarius*).[89] This single insertion requires close inspection because it concerns Gaozong's dream-vision of Fuyue, as mentioned in the chapter 'Yueming' 説命. The *Confucius Sinarum philosophus* criticizes the explanation of Zhu Xi, which was reproduced in the *Shujing daquan*, and considers Zhu Xi an atheist or 'atheo-politician' (*atheo-politicus*):

> It is quite amusing to see how Zhu Xi, as an interpreter of the first authority and whom we call a late atheo-politician, struggles with this passage; he was very unhappy in not being able to surmount the difficulty. Because of the authority of ancient texts, which are sacred among the Chinese, it is forbidden to undermine the veracity of past events. From there, in whatever direction

---

84 Noël, 'Tractatus primus', p. 41 (c.2, q.2, §.2, Q.9); this edition, p. 222.
85 See Standaert, *Keqin de Tianzhu*, p. 73.
86 Noël, 'Tractatus primus', pp. 107–37 (c.2, q.5); this edition, pp. 305–40.
87 ARSI, Jap. Sin. I, 1b, but incomplete (the two first *juan* missing), with only the *juan* 3 to 6. See Chan, *Chinese Books and Documents in the Jesuit Archives in Rome*, p. 3.
88 See Meynard, 'Longobardo's Reading of Song Confucianism', p. 65.
89 Noël, 'Tractatus primus', p. 52 (c.2, q.1, §.6, A.1); this edition, p. 235.

he moved, he could not escape the presence and power of the divine Being. [...] Evidently Zhu Xi could not grasp how it is possible that, not having a body, he could assume a visible shape, [...] and Zhu Xi says: 'It is impossible to say that nothing happened, but it is also impossible to say that it is nothing but the heavenly reason, or *li*'. By this, the interpreter Zhu Xi shows himself to be ignorant; or because of his ignorance of so many things and because of his own confusion, he was unwilling to support the idea of Truth and Divine Providence. In fact, the *li* is a fiction of the atheo-politicians, invented by the new interpreters some four thousand years later. They understand *li* as a kind of power or natural influence, devoid of mind and will. And yet, they make it the principle of all things, to which all things should return, distorting all the wisdom and records of the whole antiquity with their opinion.[90]

As mentioned above, Bouvet completely overturns the condemnation of Zhu Xi in the *Confucius Sinarum philosophus*, saying: 'Evidently, Zhu Xi truly recognized there was a *Tiandi*, and that the *Di* whom he recognized was not *tianli* (heavenly principle); and we also know that for Zhu Xi, the *Tiandi* whom he recognized at one point of time was a Master without form'.[91] Noël follows Bouvet's interpretation and seems to rebuke the *Confucius Sinarum philosophus*: 'Please note here how incorrectly some are calling Doctor Zhu Xi the chief of the atheists, or atheist'.[92] Since this single quote of the *Shujing daquan* is not present in the ARSI manuscript, we can infer that Noël added it at a later stage to rebuke the judgement of the *Confucius Sinarum philosophus* of Zhu Xi as an atheist. Noël also quotes once from the *Shujing rijiang* 書經日講.[93] This book, published in 1680, is still preserved in the ARSI.[94] It is also quoted five times in the *Summarium NAT*.[95]

2.12 Commentaries on the Four Books

Although the Four Books are not frequently quoted in the section on the classics (only fourteen of the 110 quotes in Chapter 1), there are four commentaries on the Four Books which play a central role in the argumentation about neo-Confucianism in Chapter 2. Indeed, the quotes from the four commentaries used on the Four Books (*Sishu jizhu*, *Sishu zhijie*, *Sishu mengyin* and *Sishu rijiang*) represent 107 quotes out of 269.

---

90 Thierry Meynard, ed., *The Jesuit Reading of Confucius: The First Complete Translation of the* Lunyu *(1687) Published in the West* (Leiden: Brill, 2015), pp. 456–59. Cf. Couplet and others, *Confucius Sinarum Philosophus, Liber tertius*, p. 109.
91 '據上可見朱子真認有個天帝，而其所認之帝，非為天理；又知朱子一時之人，所認之天地，真為無形容之主宰'. Bouvet, *Gujin*, p. 134.
92 Noël, 'Tractatus primus', p. 53 (c.2, q.1, §.6, A.1); this edition, p. 235.
93 Noël, 'Tractatus primus', p. 171 (c.3, q.2, §.1); this edition, pp. 382–83.
94 ARSI, Jap. Sin. I, 28. See Chan, *Chinese Books and Documents in the Jesuit Archives in Rome*, p. 24.
95 Noël and Castner, *Summarium NAT*, p. 82.

1. Sishu jizhu

Many of the early Jesuits studied the Four Books by reading Zhu Xi's *Sishu jizhu* 四書集註 [Collected Commentaries on the Four Books]. The earliest partial translation of the Four Books in a Western language can be traced back to the Italian Jesuit Michele Ruggieri who offered in 1590 to Philip II (1527–1598), king of Spain (1556–1598), the Spanish translation of the *Daxue, Zhongyong*, and the first two chapters of the *Lunyu*. Ruggieri read the classical text as arranged and segmented by Zhu Xi, and also translated many explanations from 'the commentator' (*el comentador*), often placed in the margin of the main text. Ruggieri translated also Zhu Xi's preface (*xushuo* 序說) to the *Lunyu*.[96]

The Jesuits in China usually became familiar with the *Sishu jizhu* during their Chinese-language studies. Albert Chan found a copy of the *Sishu jizhu* in ARSI with Brancati's handwritten annotations, which were probably written in Hangzhou in 1637 and 1638 while Brancati was studying the Chinese language. Brancati indicated the dates marking the progress of his studies, including the five months he spent reading the *Lunyu*.[97] Around 1660, Inácio Da Costa (1603–1666) worked with his Jesuit students in translating the Four Books, and he naturally chose the Zhu Xi edition as basis for the classical text of the Four Books, as clearly mentioned in the preface ('Ad lectorem') of the *Sapientia Sinica* (1662).[98]

From 1662 to 1687, the manuscript and printed Jesuit translations of the Four Books use the same symbols (fol., p., §) to refer to the Zhu Xi edition. Those references can be matched to a Ming edition of the *Sishu jizhu* preserved today in the Yenching Library at Harvard University. The Ming editions of the *Sishu jizhu* adopt the same pagination, with the same book size and the same arrangement in nine columns for each half folio and in seventeen characters for each column. There is an obvious reason why the Jesuits used the Zhu Xi edition for the classical text: it was the standard version of the Four Books during the Ming and Qing dynasties. The Jesuits were often moving residences and sometimes worked separately, so they had to use the standard Nanjing edition, readily available all over the country.

The use of the Zhu Xi edition has important consequences. The Jesuits follow Zhu Xi in adopting the standard division of the Four Books, and they follow exactly the same segmentation of a given passage of the Four Books. Zhu Xi tends to fragment the text of the Four Books into small units or segments, and the Jesuits systematically follow Zhu Xi's edition in presenting the text in this way.[99]

---

96 Thierry Meynard and Roberto Villasante, *La filosofía moral de Confucio por Michele Ruggieri SJ: La primera traducción de las obras de Confucio al español en 1590* (Madrid: Mensajero – Sal Terrae, 2018).
97 See Chan, *Chinese Books and Documents in the Jesuit Archives in Rome*, pp. 9–11.
98 'Notae appositae in margine sunt: f, p, §. Prima denotat folium textus iuxta ordinem impressionis 南京 nân kim editae Authore 朱熹 chū hì, qui liber vulgò dictur 四書集注 sū xū siĕ chú. Secunda indicat paginam. Tertia signat periodum illam, quae aliquali spatio distat ab alia periodo in ipsomet textu sinico'. Prospero Intorcetta, *Sapientia Sinica* (Jianchang, 1662), fol. 2ʳ.
99 Examples can be found in the comments on *Lunyu* 1.8, 2.4, 2.10, 7.6, 10.6, 10.8, 12.5, 12.8, and 12.22.

However, the use of the *Sishu jizhu* became more and more problematic. In his *True Meaning of the Lord of Heaven*, Ricci explicitly rejected Song Confucianism and its key concepts, even criticizing some explanations of the *Sishu jizhu* as incorrect. In the context of the Terms and Rites Controversies, most of the Jesuits were trying to salvage ancient Confucianism, and the differentiation of ancient Confucianism from Song Confucianism became more radical. The authors of the *Confucius Sinarum philosophus* feared the contamination of Zhu Xi's 'materialistic' and 'atheistic' philosophy in their interpretation of the Four Books. Thus, the *Confucius Sinarum philosophus* rarely mentions the name of Zhu Xi, and where it does, it is to criticize him.

The *Philosophia Sinica* is a turning point because it has more than fifty quotes which are explicitly attributed to Zhu Xi and can be traced back to the *Sizhu jizhu* or to the *Yulei*.[100] Noël never criticizes Zhu Xi but calls him a 'famous commentator'. As we shall see, Noël did not consider Zhu Xi's philosophy to be materialistic and atheistic, and therefore he could freely quote him. Perhaps because the Jesuits had for so long kept distance from Zhu Xi, at least formally, Noël only once quoted directly from the *Sishu jizhu*.[101] Also, the *Sishu jizhu* is a very condensed text, and therefore it was more convenient for the Jesuits to search for authoritative commentaries based on the *Sishu jizhu* with more elaborate explanations. Such was the main advantage of the *Sishu zhijie*, *Sishu mengyin* and *Sishu rijiang*.

2. Sishu zhijie

The *Sishu zhijie* 四書直解 [Colloquial Commentary on the Four Books] corresponds to the Daily Lectures on the Four Books that were given orally to the Wanli Emperor for a period of more than twenty years, from 1572 to the 1590s. Library catalogues often state that the *Sishu zhijie* was published in 1573. However, this date simply corresponds to the preface written by Zhang Juzheng and to the publication of the commentary of the *Daxue*. The first edition of a complete *Sishu zhijie* only appeared in the 1590s after Zhang Juzheng's death. Though the *Sishu zhijie* is often attributed to Zhang alone, he cannot be the sole author since he died at the beginning of the instructions on the *Mencius*. The *Sishu zhijie* should be seen as a collective work, involving the initial work of six lecturers, the input of Zhang, and the final work of the revisers. The commentaries necessarily reflected the official reading and could not deviate too much from the standard interpretations.[102]

---

100 According to Felix Wong, there are ninety quotes by Zhu Xi in the Third Treatise. See Wong, 'Lun Yesuhuishi Wei Fangji de Ladingwen Mengzi fanyi', p. 144.
101 Noël, 'Tractatus primus', p. 132 (c.2, q.5, VV.51); this edition, p. 334. ARSI (Jap. Sin. I, 10) holds a copy of the *Sishu jizhu* printed in Nanjing. See Chan, *Chinese Books and Documents in the Jesuit Archives in Rome*, pp. 9–11; Meynard, *The Jesuit Reading of Confucius*, p. 19.
102 See Meynard, ed., *Confucius Sinarum Philosophus (1687)*, pp. 22–34.

The Jesuits used the *Sishu zhijie* from very early on. In the 1610s, the Jesuits already had a copy of Zhang's commentaries in their library in Nanjing,[103] and the plan of studies of 1624 explicitly mentions the use of Zhang's commentaries for the training of the Jesuit missionaries coming to China.[104] According to the preface of the *Sapientia Sinica* of 1662, the Jesuit translations of the *Lunyu* and the *Daxue* are based on twenty different commentaries, but 'mostly' (*praecipue*) on the commentary by the Grand Secretary Zhang (*Colao Cham*),[105] and the translation part also contains a few references to the 'Chinese commentator and Grand Secretary Zhang' (*Commentator sinensis Cham Colao*). An exemplar of the *Sapientia Sinica* held in the Jesuit Archives in Rome has on the cover the inscription: *Xiwen sishu zhijie* 西文四書直解 (Colloquial Commentary of the Four Books in Western Language), which is a clear reference to Zhang's commentary.[106] Later, when the Jesuits were preparing in Guangzhou what would become the *Confucius Sinarum philosophus*, they naturally continued to use Zhang's commentaries as their primary point of reference.

The Jesuits turned to Zhang Juzheng for different reasons. Clearly the political authority of Zhang Juzheng and his imperial student may have played a certain role, as well as the simplicity of the language being used since the Wanli Emperor was only eight years old when he started his lessons on the Confucian classics. Compared to the *Sishu jizhu* and the *Sishu daquan* which collects different interpretations, the *Sishu zhijie* has the great advantage of presenting a unified interpretation. But the more decisive reason is that Zhang Juzheng is closer to ancient Confucianism on two crucial points: the reverence for *Tian* and the worship of the *guishen*. Indeed, Zhang was instructing the young emperor Wanli and since there is no higher human power over the emperor, Zhang wanted to convey that Wanli was still under the power of *Tian* and *guishen*.

As for reverence for *Tian*, Confucius is recorded in *Lunyu* 3.13 as having said: 'Whoever sins against heaven does not have any higher spirit to pray' (獲罪於天，無所禱也). In a note, the *Confucius Sinarum philosophus* alludes to the conflicting interpretations of *Tian* by Zhu Xi and Zhang Juzheng. For Zhu Xi, 'Heaven means

---

103 See Ad Dudink, 'The Inventories of the Jesuit House at Nanking, Made Up during the Persecution of 1616–1617 (Shen Que, *Nangong shudu*, 1620)', in *Western Humanistic Culture Presented to China by Jesuit Missionaries (XVII–XVIII Centuries)*, ed. by Federico Massini (Rome: Institutum Historicum Societatis Iesu, 1996), pp. 119–57 (p. 147). Jensen mentions that Ricci used the *Sishu zhijie* in translating the Four Books into Chinese; however, he provides no evidence in support of this. See Jensen, *Manufacturing Confucianism* (Durham, NC: Duke University Press), p. 85.

104 See Brockey, *Journey to the East*, 266. According to Mungello, the translation of the first sentence of the *Daxue* by the Portuguese Jesuit missionary Gabriel de Magalhães (1610–1677) in his *Nouvelle relation de la Chine* (1668), 'appears to be a very-loose translation-paraphrase' of Zhang's commentary. David E. Mungello, *Curious Land: Jesuit Accommodation and the Origins of Sinology* (Honolulu: University of Hawaii Press, 1985), p. 102.

105 Intorcetta, *Sapientia Sinica*, fol. 1ᵛ.

106 ARSI, Jap. Sin. III, 3a.

principle' (天即理). However, the *Confucius Sinarum philosophus* is not satisfied with the mere identification of heaven with a kind of anonymous principle (*li*) and considers this interpretation as 'twisted'.¹⁰⁷ In reference to this same passage of *Lunyu* 3.13, Noël quotes the same passage of Zhu Xi but instead affirms that 'Heaven as Reason is not something material'.¹⁰⁸ For Noël there is no contradiction between Zhu Xi's *tianli* and Zhang Juzheng's *Tian* because both express the same idea of a spiritual Heaven.

As for the worship of the *guishen*, Zhang Juzheng emphasizes this more strongly than Zhu Xi and other Song philosophers, and Zhang alludes to a personal relationship with heaven and spiritual beings. For the Jesuits, the references to the worship of the spirits in the Four Books were important evidence proving that the ancient Chinese believed in the immortality of the soul in the afterlife, and about the efficacy of worship and prayer, as in Christianity. They wanted to reinforce the idea that, when the ancient Chinese prayed to heaven or the *guishen*, they believed that heaven or the *guishen* could understand and answer their prayers, and also bring rewards or punishments. Clearly, Zhang's understanding of heaven and spirits is quite different from the Western conceptions of God and angels. However, the *Confucius Sinarum philosophus* approved of Zhang for having retrieved from the ancient texts the original faith in God and angels. In continuity with the *Confucius Sinarum philosophus*, Noël quotes a few passages from the *Sishu zhijie* which demonstrate the actions of *guishen* in rewarding the good and punishing the evil.¹⁰⁹

In the *Libri sex*, Noël based his translations of the Four Books mostly on the *Sishu zhijie*, but in the *Philosophia Sinica*, the *Sishu zhijie* does not hold the same importance, being quoted only twenty times. ARSI holds a late Ming edition, which is entitled *Zhang Gelao zhengzi sishu zhijie* 張閣老正字四書直解 in 26 *juan* and 24 *ce*.¹¹⁰ Felix Wong noticed that this edition has the *Mencius* divided in three parts (上孟, 中孟, 下孟), while the *Libri sex* divides the *Mencius* into two parts.¹¹¹ In the *Philosophica Sinica*, Noël also divides the *Mencius* into two parts. Therefore, it seems that Noël did not use the edition of the *Sishu zhijie* kept in ARSI, but another edition.

---

107 In relation to this passage of the *Lunyu*, Zhang still uses the neo-Confucian concept of 'principle' (*li*) or 'heavenly principle' (*tianli*), with its automatic and anonymous moral law of retribution, but he also states that 'there is only one heaven which should be honoured to the highest degree and that nothing else is equal to it'. Couplet and others, *Confucius Sinarum philosophus*, Pars secunda, liber tertius, p. 7. The *Confucius Sinarum philosophus* reads this to mean that heaven (*Tian*) is above the 'heavenly principle' (*tianli*), and it used this as definitive proof that the ancient Chinese were not deist but believed in a personal God.
108 Noël, 'Tractatus primus', p. 68 (c.2, q.2, G.16); this edition, p. 253.
109 Noël, 'Tractatus primus', pp. 91–106 (c.2, q.4); this edition, pp. 303–05.
110 ARSI, Jap. Sin. I, 14. See Chan, *Chinese Books and Documents in the Jesuit Archives in Rome*, pp. 13–14.
111 Wong, 'Lun Yesuhuishi Wei Fangji de Ladingwen Mengzi fanyi', p. 148.

3. *Sishu mengyin*

Cai Qing 蔡清 (1453–1508) is also known by his literary name, Cai Xuzhai 蔡虛斎齋. Cai Qing is considered as an orthodox representative of the School of Principle (*Lixue* 理學), and the most important follower of Zhu Xi's thought during the Ming dynasty.[112] His influence grew even stronger during the early Qing dynasty, and in 1724 his commemorative tablet entered the Temple of Confucius, making him an authoritative reference.[113]

The *Sishu mengyin* 四書蒙引 [Primer on the Four Books] was published posthumously in 1520, and was republished three times in the late Ming (1527, 1587, 1635). It appeared in several editions during the Qing dynasty, both in China and in Japan, and in 1773, it entered into the imperial collection, *Siku quanshu* 四庫全書 [Complete Book of the Four Storehouses]. The work aims first to help students prepare for the imperial examination, but also to reveal the moral meaning of the classics to foster the personal cultivation of the students.

The *Sishu mengyin* is based on the *Sishu jizhu* and *Sishu quanshu*, but unlike the latter two editions and similar to the *Sishu zhijie*, the *Sishu mengyin* presents a unified interpretation and develops the explanations of the Four Books according to the School of Principle, such as its neo-Confucian interpretation of *guishen*, which greatly influenced Noël.[114] Unfortunately, there has been little research on Cai Qing's thought since he is usually considered as an historically important but unoriginal author. However, two recent studies by Song Yecao 宋野草 in 2015 and Wang Suqin 王素琴 in 2019 have deepened our appreciation of Cai Qing's thought.[115]

Cai Qing follows and develops the ideas of Zhu Xi, but his thought is also greatly influenced by Zhang Zai, an author who lived before Zhu Xi but who did not play a great role in the Song and Yuan dynasties after the synthesis of Zhu Xi. Only during the Ming and Qing dynasties did Zhang Zai's works exert significant influence on scholars such as Cai Qing.[116]

Cai Qing attempts at reconciling Zhang Zai with Zhu Xi. For Zhang Zai, first there is *qi* and then the forms (*xiang* 象), but for Zhu Xi, although *li* cannot concretely exist apart from *qi*, *li* is ontologically prior to *qi*. For Cai Qing, *qi* can be understood on two levels: the material and visible *qi*, and the invisible and essential *qi*. Similarly, for Cai Qing *taixu* 太虛 can be understood as material and

---

112 About his relationship with the Fujian branch of the School of Principle, see Liu Yong 劉勇, 'Zhong wan Ming Lixue xueshuo de hudong yu diyuxing Lixue chuantong de xipuhua jincheng: yi Minxue wei zhongxin' 中晚明理學學說的互動與地域性理學傳統的系譜化進程——以「閩學」為中心, *Xinshixue* 新史學, 21.2 (2010), 1–60.
113 Huang Zongxi 黃宗羲 (1610–1695) mentions briefly his life and work; see Huang Zongxi 黃宗羲, 'Zhuru xue'an shang 4' 諸儒學案上四, *Ming Ru xue'an* 明儒學案, *juan* 46.
114 See Wong, 'The Unalterable Mean', p. 221.
115 Song Yecao 宋野草, *Cai Qing Yixue sixiang yanjiu* 蔡清易學思想研究 (Beijing: Zhongguo shehui kexue chubanshe, 2015); Wang Suqin 王素琴, 'Cai Qing jiqi Sishu mengyin yanjiu' 蔡清及其《四書蒙引》研究 (unpublished doctoral thesis, National Taichung University of Education, 2019).
116 See Anne Cheng, *Histoire de la pensée chinoise* (Paris: Seuil, 1997), p. 425.

as an invisible principle (*li*) without the visible *qi*. This allows Cai Qing to reconcile Zhu Xi's concept of *taiji* with Zhang Zai's concept of *taixu*.

As Felix Wong shows, the *Libri sex* relies not only on Zhang Juzheng, but also on Cai Qing.[117] Luo Ying 羅瑩 inspected Noël's manuscript of 1700 held in the Library of Brussels, and discovered references to the *Sishu mengyin*.[118] Similarly, Chapter 2 of the First Treatise of the *Philosophia Sinica* contains fifty-six quotes from the *Sishu mengyin*. ARSI holds one late Ming edition of the *Sishu mengyin* in fifteen *juan*, which was revised by Song Zhaoyue 宋兆檜 (1600–1642): *Daxue* (*juan* 1 and 2), *Zhongyong* (*juan* 3 and 4), *Lunyu* (*juan* 5 to 8), *Mencius* (*juan* 9 to 15).[119]

While the *Sishu zhijie* occupies a relatively minor position in the School of Principle, by selecting the *Sishu mengyin* as primary commentary of the Four Books, Noël was able to enter into a deeper dialogue with mainstream Confucian thought at the beginning of the Qing. Very daringly he adopts the expression of *taiji* as *taixu*, which he renders as *primum vacuum* (First Emptiness), despite the common association of *taixu* with Buddhism or Daoism. He faithfully reports Cai Qing's ideas about the interpenetration of *li* and *qi*, though those ideas clearly challenged the Western division between the spiritual and the material. He explains *taiji* and *taixu* in terms of an ontology of being and, following neo-Confucianism, understands this First Being as a Rational Being which truly exists, despite the fact that scholasticism tended to see a Rational Being as mere possibility, without necessarily having real existence. Noël's explanation of *taiji* and *taixu* as a Rational Being with real existence makes it an equivalent of God.[120]

4. Sishu rijiang

The *Sishu rijiang* 四書日講 [Daily Lectures on the Four Books, or *Quotidania quatuor librorum explicatio* according to Noël's Latin rendering of the title] consists of a series of daily lectures given to Kangxi by his ministers at the Imperial Study Hall. It was edited by the Grand Secretary Kulena and approved by Kangxi on 11 January 1677. The First Treatise of the *Philosophia Sinica* has thirty-three quotes from the work. Hence there are more citations from the *Sishu rijiang* than the *Sishu zhijie* but less than the *Sishu mengyin*.

As explained above, after 1701 Noël had received a few versions of Bouvet's *Gujin*. While Bouvet's initial draft of 1701 did not contain any quote from the *Sishu rijiang*, Bouvet expanded his work in 1702 by adding new materials from the *Sishu rijiang*, such that the revised version of 1707 contains in total 159 quotes. Ten citations from the *Sishu rijiang* in the *Philosophia Sinica* can also be found in

---

117 Noël, *Libri sex, Immutabile medium*, p. 41; see Wong, 'The Unalterable Mean', p. 199.
118 Luo Ying, 'Qingchao lai Hua Yesuhuishi Wei Fangji', p. 122.
119 ARSI, Jap. Sin. I, 15. See Chan, *Chinese Books and Documents in the Jesuit Archives in Rome*, pp. 14–16. The text of the Qing edition of *Sishu mengyin* in the *Siku quanshu* is quite different from the Ming editions.
120 Noël, 'Tractatus primus', pp. 137–46 (c.2, q.6); this edition, pp. 340–51.

the *Gujin*. In his *Libri sex* Noël did not make use of the *Sishu rijiang*, and before 1701, he was mostly using the *Sishu zhijie* and *Sishu mengyin*. Only after Noël had received the revised version of the *Gujin* with the citations from the *Sishu rijiang* did Noël start to pay attention to the *Sishu rijiang*.

Both the *Sishu zhijie* and the *Sishu rijiang* enjoyed very high political authority because they featured lectures given to Wanli and Kangxi respectively. Indeed, the *Sishu rijiang* was even prefaced and promulgated by Kangxi. While the *Sishu rijiang* reinforced the orthodoxy of the School of Principle even more forcefully than the *Sishu zhijie*, it similarly emphasized the religious dimension of *Tian* as a judge over the emperor. As Noël says:

> The books and commentaries that we examined in the second chapter [...] recognize one supreme divinity which produces, controls and plans everything, and remunerates virtue and punishes vices. The commentaries published by the emperor Kangxi, just like the others, lead to the same interpretation. There is not a single text or passage teaching atheism; rather, in various passages it is often taught with clear words that there is one true and supreme Master of all things, especially the entire course of the commentary *Shujing rijiang*.[121]

In fact, the idea of a providential *Tian* is already present in the classics, but was greatly downplayed by the Song commentators. Before the arrival of the Jesuits, late Ming intellectuals like Zhang Juzheng were faced with political and moral decay, and they wanted to convey to the emperor the idea of *Tian* as a judge watching him. The missionaries also promoted the idea of God as rewarding good and punishing evil. In this way, Christianity strengthened a religious tendency which had already been present for some time. The Chinese and Christian influences are clearly seen in the person of Kangxi, under whom the *Sishu rijiang* was written. ARSI holds a copy of the *Sishu rijiang* in twenty-four *juan*, with the first *juan* corresponding to the lectures on the *Daxue*, the *juan* 2 and 3 to the *Zhongyong*, and the *juan* 4 to 26 to the *Mencius*.[122] The *Sishu rijiang* is also quoted twice in the *Summarium NAT*.[123]

2.13 Compendia of Philosophy

1. Xingli daquan

The Jesuits were quite familiar with the *Xingli daquan* 性理大全 [Compendium on Nature and Principle], a work edited by Hu Guang, who also edited the *Wujing daquan* and the *Sishu daquan*. In *A Brief Response on the Controversies*, Longobardo made great use of this work, especially *juan* 1 (on the *Taiji tu* 太極圖), *juan* 4 (on Zhang Zai), *juan* 11 and 12 (on Shao Yong), *juan* 26 (on *li* and *qi*), *juan* 28 (on

---

121 Noël, 'Tractatus primus', p. 171 (c.3, q.2); this edition, p. 382.
122 ARSI, Jap. Sin. I, 13. See Chan, *Chinese Books and Documents in the Jesuit Archives in Rome*, pp. 12–13.
123 Noël and Castner, *Summarium NAT*, p. 73; p. 83.

guishen), and *juan* 34 (on *dao* 道 and *li*).¹²⁴ While the *Confucius Sinarum philosophus* defends Ricci's interpretation of the ancient classics, it still adopts Longobardo's interpretation of neo-Confucianism, criticizing the *Xingli daquan* as a fraudulent interpretation grounded in a single mention of *taiji* in the *Xici*.¹²⁵ Noël has only one explicit reference to the *Xingli daquan* (*juan* 28), and he may have deliberately avoided this work because it had been largely rejected by the Jesuits before him. The only mention in the printed text is not present in the ARSI manuscript and was added later. It consists of two short quotes by Cheng Yi 程頤 (1033–1107), translated by Noël as: 'the producing and destroying Spirit is the Author of things, in Chinese *zaohua*' (鬼神便是造化也) and 'Air is spirit' (只氣便是神).¹²⁶ Noël comments that the reader should not understand *qi* as purely material since it has a spiritual dimension.¹²⁷ There is one copy of a Ming edition of the *Xingli daquan* in 70 *juan* in ARSI.¹²⁸

2. Xingli biaoti

Instead of the *Xingli daquan*, Noël prefers using the *Xingli biaoti* 性理標題 (*Liber dictus naturae & rationis brevis expositio*) which is mentioned eighteen times in the First Treatise. This work is, in fact, a six-*juan* summary of the seventy-*juan Xingli daquan* according to the Ming edition mentioned above. ARSI has one copy under the title of *Xingli biaoti jielan* 性理標題捷覽, which was edited by Huang Hongxian 黃洪憲 (1541–1600).¹²⁹

2.14 Chinese Dictionaries

During the Chinese Rites and Terms controversies, the missionaries drew not only on the ancient classics and authoritative commentaries but also on Chinese dictionaries to clarify the meaning of specific words. Among the different meanings provided by the Chinese dictionaries, they tended to choose the meaning which favoured their own position. The most frequently used dictionary is the *Zihui*, but three other dictionaries are also mentioned: *Zhengzitong*, *Xiesheng pinzijian*, *Wenxian tongkao* and *Baihu tong*.

---

124 See Meynard, 'Longobardo's Reading of Song Confucianism', p. 65.
125 Meynard, ed., *Confucius Sinarum Philosophus (1687)*, pp. 107, 158.
126 Noël, 'Tractatus primus', p. 75 (c.2, q.3); this edition, pp. 263–64.
127 Noël, 'Tractatus primus', p. 75; this edition, p. 264.
128 ARSI, Jap. Sin. II, 89. See Chan, *Chinese Books and Documents in the Jesuit Archives in Rome*, pp. 400–01.
129 ARSI, Jap. Sin. II, 89. See Chan, *Chinese Books and Documents in the Jesuit Archives in Rome*, pp. 398–99. ARSI has another abridged version of the *Xingli daquan*: *Xingli daquan huiyao* 性理大全彙要 in 22 *juan* by Zhan Huai 詹淮. ARSI, Jap. Sin. II, 88. See Chan, *Chinese Books and Documents in the Jesuit Archives in Rome*, pp. 399–400.

1. Zihui

The *Zihui* 字彙 or *Dazihui* 大字彙 [Collection of Characters] was compiled by Mei Yingzuo 梅膺祚 in the late Ming. The work was first published with a preface dated 1615 and then republished with a second preface dated 1686. It contains 33,179 characters. For each character is indicated first the pronunciation and then the meanings, with the most important meaning first. Apart from quotations from literature, the *Zihui* also gives examples from colloquial language to highlight lexical usage. The content is mainly based on the earlier dictionary *Hongwu zhengyun* 洪武正韻 (1375) in which entries are typically arranged according to rhyme groups. The real merit of the *Zihui* is that it condensed the 540 radicals (*bushou* 部首) of the *Shuowen jiezi* 說文解字 to 214 radicals only. The *Zihui* served as a model for later dictionaries, like the *Zhengzitong* 正字通 and the famous *Kangxi zidian* 康熙字典.[130]

This dictionary was systematically used by the missionaries in Canton in 1668 during their debates on the Chinese Rites. Navarrete made use of the *Zihui* to explain the meaning of some fifty Chinese characters, such as *miao* 廟.[131] Caballero also discusses the meaning of *miao* according to the *Zihui*.[132] But Brancati criticizes the friars' mistaken understanding of the *Zihui* and instead provides detailed explanations from the *Zihui* for technical terms connected to the Chinese Rites such as *ji* 祭, *si* 祀, *zhuwen* 祝文, *gao* 告, *jian* 荐, *shecaili* 释菜礼, *muzhu* 木主, etc.[133] Noël quotes the *Zihui* (*Dictionarium Tsu guey*) seven times to explain the characters *li* 吏, *hua* 化, *qi* 氣, *she* 社, *bi* 璧, *zhi* 時 and *Di* 帝. ARSI holds the 1686 edition of the *Zihui* in fourteen *juan*.[134]

2. Zhengzitong

Zhang Zilie 张自烈 (1597–1673) compiled the *Zhengzitong* 正字通 [Comprehensive Dictionary of Orthodox Characters] in 12 *juan*. This dictionary follows the *Zihui* in arranging the characters according to 214 radicals. According to the dates of the five prefaces included in the work, we can infer that it was first published in 1670. The work was reprinted a few times until the publication of the Kangxi Dictionary in 1716.

---

130 See ChinaKnowldege.de: <http://www.chinaknowledge.de/Literature/Science/zihui.html> (accessed 29 October 2021).
131 'El Diccionario que yo tenia, y se me perdiò en el viaje, que es el ordinario, contenia 33375 letras. Otro ay mas numeroso, y mas antiguo, el qual tiene setenta mil'. Domingo Navarrete, *Tratados históricos, ethicos y religiosos de la monarchia de China* (Madrid, 1676), *Tratado* 3, cap. XI, fol. 169. See Ana Busquets Alemany, 'Más allá de la *Querella de los Ritos*: el testimonio sobre China de Fernández de Navarrete', *Anuario Historia de la Iglesia*, 24 (2015), 229–50 (p. 245).
132 Antonio de Santa María Caballero [Antoine de Sainte-Marie], *Traité sur quelques points importants de la mission de la Chine* (Paris: Guérin 1701), pp. 5–6.
133 Francesco Brancati, 'Explicatio litterarum seu vocum quorumdam Sinicarum', in Intorcetta, *Testimonium*, pp. 65–143.
134 ARSI, Jap. Sin. II, 121–22. See Chan, *Chinese Books and Documents in the Jesuit Archives in Rome*, pp. 425–26.

2. COMPOSITION AND SOURCES OF THE FIRST TREATISE   65

The copy held in ARSI was printed in 1678 in Hunan and bears the seal: *Lingnan Guangjutang cangban* 嶺南廣居堂藏板 [Engraved Woodblocks Kept at the Guangju House of Guangdong], suggesting that the Jesuits acquired the copy in Guangdong.[135] Filippucci who spent the final years of his life in Canton before dying in Macao makes reference to the *Zhengzitong*.[136] Noël quotes from the *Zhengzitong* (*Dictionarium Chim tsu tum*) five times: once for each of the characters *qi* 氣, *zhu* 主, *hou* 后 and twice for *di* 帝. Those quotes are absent from the ARSI manuscript, indicating that Noël added those references later.

3. Xiesheng pinzijian

Another dictionary is the *Xiesheng pinzijian* 諧聲品字箋, compiled by Yu Xianxi 虞咸熙 and his son Yu Desheng 虞德升, and published in 1673 in fifty-seven *juan*, with reprints in 1677 and 1684. While the two previous dictionaries were produced in the Ming dynasty, Noël mentions this work as a recent dictionary (*recens sinicum dictionarium*).[137]

In 1701 in Nanjing, the apostolic vicar Artus de Lionne MEP (1655–1713) proposed to the two other apostolic vicars, Álvaro de Benavente and Basilio Brollo da Gemona OFM (1648–1704), some ninety-two propositions against the Chinese Rites. The thirty-fourth proposition argued that the three important dictionaries, the *Zihui*, *Zhengzitong* and *Pinzijian*, all attest that the spirit of the deceased reside in the tablet.[138] This shows that the *Pinzijian* was already a reference in the discussions among missionaries as early as 1701.

Bouvet quotes from the *Pinzijian* only once in the 1707 preface of his *Gujin jingtian jian* 古今敬天鑒. Noël cites exactly the same passage, which is the sole quote from the *Pinzijian* in the First Treatise, though it is absent in the ARSI manuscript. The fact that the *Pinzijian* is one of the very few works quoted by Noël but not physically present today in the ARSI collection suggests that Noël did not have the *Pinzijian* at hand and that he may have quoted directly from Bouvet's preface. Noël gives also the quote with the same translation in the *Summarium NAT*.[139] Even before Bouvet wrote his preface to the *Gujin* in 1707, he may have mentioned this quote to Noël who later inserted it in the *Summarium NAT* (1704) and in the final version of the *Philosophia Sinica*.[140] Noël had good reason to add this single

---

135   ARSI, Jap. Sin. II, 115–20. See Chan, *Chinese Books and Documents in the Jesuit Archives in Rome*, pp. 421–24.
136   'Tractatus', BNCVE, Ges. 1248/3. See Standaert, *Chinese Voices*, p. 76, note 112.
137   Noël, 'Tractatus primus', pp. 74, 82 (c.2, q.3, E.6); this edition, p. 263.
138   Noël and Castner, *Summarium NAT*, p. 17.
139   Noël and Castner, *Summarium NAT*, p. 88.
140   There is also an early reference to the *Pinzijian* in a 1705 work by Álvaro de Benavente OSA (1647–1707): 'An Chinenses Deum vivum, et verum sub litteris, seu characteribus 天, cujus vox est Tien, et 上帝 quorum voces Xam Ti aliquando coluerint?', BNCVE, Fondo Gesuitico 1251/5. Also, in 1706, Stumpf made a reference to the *Pinzijian*: see Stumpf, *The Acta Pekinensia*, p. 170 n. 379. Later, Foucquet also referred to the *Pinzijian*. See John Witeck, *Controversial Ideas in China and in Europe: A Biography of Jean-François Foucquet* (Rome: Institutum Historicum Societatis Iesu, 1982), p. 211 n. 142.

quote of the *Pinzijian* because it explains *Tian* not only in terms of *li* and *qi*, but also in terms of 'an extremely spiritual true Master' (至靈之真宰) and 'Supreme *Shangdi*' (皇皇之上帝), responsible for rewarding the good and punishing the evil.

4. Wenxian tongkao

The *Wenxian tongkao* 文獻通考 [Comprehensive Investigations Based on Ancient Books and Ancient Sages] is an administrative history written during the Yuan dynasty by Ma Duanlin 馬端臨 (1254–1325). Noël translates the title as 'Universalis inquisitio priscorum tum librorum tum Sapientum' [Universal Investigation into both Ancient Books and Ancient Sages]. During the Ming dynasty, Wang Qi 王圻 (*jinshi* degree 1565) wrote a sequel (*xu* 續) to the *Wenxian tongkao*. All the quotes from the *Wenxian tongkao* are absent from the ARSI manuscript and were therefore added later. ARSI has one copy of a Qing edition in twenty-one *juan*.[141] In total, there are twelve quotes from this work, including eight related to the question of the *jiaoshe* ritual.[142]

5. Baihu tong

The literal meaning of *Baihu tong* 白虎通 [The Discussions of the White Tiger], is a reference to the White Tiger Pavilion in Luoyang where the discussions on the true meaning of the classics took place in 79. Ban Gu 班固 (32–92) is considered as the editor of the work, following the orders of emperor Zhang of Han 漢章帝 (57–88; r. 75–88). Noël translates the title as 'Communis regiorum professorum sensus' [Ordinary Meaning of the Royal Scholars], which reflects the official dimension of this work. The First Treatise quotes directly from the *Baihu tong* three times, and there is also an indirect quote of *Baihu tong* drawn from the *Zihui*. The four occurrences are all related to the rituals (c.2, q.4 and q.5). Carel Wesselius has noticed the presence of three quotes from the *Baihu tong* in the Third Treatise on ethics, which also contains some discussion on rituals.[143] ARSI does not hold this work.

2.15 Other Chinese Works

1. Da Ming huidian

The editorial project of the *Da Ming huidian* 大明會典 [Collected Statutes of the Ming Dynasty], also shortened to *Ming huidian* 明會典, started in 1497 under the supervision of Xu Pu 徐溥 (1428–1499), and was continued after his death by Li Dongyang 李東陽 (1447–1516), who completed it in 1502. It was officially

---

141 ARSI, Jap. Sin. II, 128–48. See Chan, *Chinese Books and Documents in the Jesuit Archives in Rome*, pp. 433–34.
142 Noël, 'Tractatus primus', pp. 86, 124, 127, 131–32 (c.2, q.5); this edition, pp. 276, 313, 317–19, 332, 343, 371.
143 Carel Wesselius, 'The *Ethica Politica*', p. 28.

published in the sixth year of the Zhengde 正德 Emperor (1511). This first edition, called the Zhengde edition, includes 180 *juan*.[144] There was a first supplement of fifty-three *juan* under the the Jiajing 嘉靖 Emperor (1507–1567; r. 1521–1567), which was completed in 1529, but unpublished. The *Da Ming huidian* was fully revised and expanded from 1576 to 1585, and published in the fifteenth year of the Wanli Emperor (1587). With this second edition, called the Wanli edition, the collection reached its definitive size of 228 *juan*. It was not printed in many copies, and already under the Qianlong 乾隆 Emperor, the Wanli edition was so hard to find that the *Siku quanshu* included the Zhengde edition instead. The statutes are arranged according to the Six Ministries (*liubu* 六部), and the rituals to Confucius are under the Ministry of Rites (*libu* 禮部), in the section called Bureau of Sacrifices (*sijiqinglisi* 祠祭清吏司).

In 1668, missionaries in Guangzhou extensively discussed the ritual to Confucius based on *juan* 84 of the *Da Ming huidian*. On 8 March 1668, Navarrete presented a *declamatio* to the Jesuits where he adduced the authority of *juan* 84 of the *Da Ming huidian* to show that the *jiding* 祭丁 rituals in honour of Confucius, so called because they were performed the first day, *ding* 丁, of the second and eighth month, were religious and thus incompatible with Christianity. Navarrete translated the prescriptions of the ritual according to the Ming emperor Hongwu 洪武 (r. 1368–1398).[145] However, in Chapter 12 of the first part of *De sinensium ritibus*, Brancati rebuked Navarrete's translation and interpretation.[146]

Noël has eight references to the *Da Ming huidian* (Wanli edition of 1587), with seven of them dealing with the *jiaoshe* ritual.[147] The eight references are not present in the ARSI manuscript, and hence were added at a later stage. When discussing the ritual to Earth, Noël is scathing of *juan* 94 of the *Da Ming huidian* for having introduced superstitions, such as the rituals towards Chenghuang 城隍, the spirit protecting a city, which were not based on any classical text. Noël criticizes the Jiajing Emperor, a follower of Daoism, for being responsible for this.[148] As mentioned above, under the Jiajing Emperor, the *Da Ming huidian* was expanded by fifty-three *juan*. ARSI has a full set of the Wanli edition (1587) of the *Da Ming huidian*.[149]

---

144 The general editors (*zongcaiguan* 總裁官) are listed as: Li Dongyang 李東陽, Jiao Fang 焦芳, and Yang Tinghe 楊廷和. See *Jingyin Wenyuange Siku quanshu* 景印文淵閣四庫全書 (Taipei: Taiwan shangwu yinshuguan, 1986), *ce* 617, p. 5a. In the Wanli edition, the names of Li Dongyang and the two others do not appear.

145 Domingo Navarrete, *Controversias antiguas y modernas entre missionarios de la gran China* (Madrid, 1679), pp. 296–324.

146 Francesco Brancati, *De sinensium ritibus politicis acta. seu R. P. Francisci Brancati, Societatis Jesu, apud Sinas per annos 34. missionarii, responsio apologetica ad R. P. Dominicum Navarette Ordinis Praedicatorum* (Paris: Nicolas Pepié, 1700), pp. 136–44. See Thierry Meynard, 'Conflicting Interpretations on the *Collected Statutes of the Ming Dynasty*: The debate between Navarrete and Brancati on the Ritual to Confucius in Canton in 1668' (to be published).

147 Noël, 'Tractatus primus', pp. 107–36 (c.3, q.5); this edition, p. 268, 306, 318–23, 329.

148 Noël, 'Tractatus primus', p. 111 (c.2, q.5); this edition, p. 322.

149 ARSI, Jap. Sin. IV, 13–24. See Chan, *Chinese Books and Documents in the Jesuit Archives in Rome*, pp. 547–49.

2. Gu Zhouli and its Commentary by Chen Renxi

According to Albert Chan, the *Gu Zhouli* 古周禮 has little connection with ritual but describes the different offices under the Zhou dynasty, like the Office of Heaven (*tianguan* 天官) and the Office of Earth (*diguan* 地官). Chen Renxi 陳仁錫 (1579–1634) wrote a commentary titled *Chongding Gu Zhouli* 重訂古周禮. Noël selected three quotes from the *Gu Zhouli* and twice mentioned the name of the commentator as Chen Renxi.[150] ARSI holds two copies of the *Gu Zhouli* with the commentary by Chen Renxi.[151] The work is mentioned twice in the *Summarium NAT*.[152]

3. Mingxin baojian

The *Mingxin baojian* 明心寶鑒 [Precious Examination which Enlightens the Mind] was probably written at the end of the Yuan dynasty or the beginning of the Ming dynasty. Sometimes attributed to Fan Liben 范立本, it was one of the first Chinese works ever translated into a European language. Around 1592, Ruggieri translated the work into Latin,[153] and in the same year in Philippines, the Dominican Juan Cobo (1546–1592) translated it into Spanish.[154] Later, Navarrete also included a Spanish translation in his *Tratados*.[155] Noël describes it as a common book (*libellus trivialis*).[156] Indeed, it mixes Confucianism with Daoism and Buddhism. Noël surprisingly cites this work on one occasion to express an idea dear to the missionaries, namely the retribution of good and evil (為善者，天報之以福；為不善者，天報之以禍).[157] ARSI has one copy of the Ming edition of the work.[158]

2.16 Chinese Works by Missionaries and Chinese Christians

Chapters 1 and 2 of the First Treatise present the case that the Chinese had knowledge of the Christian concept of God prior to their encounter with Christianity in the late Ming by citing the ancient classics and their commentaries from the Song to the Qing dynasties. The approach of these two chapters was mostly based on philology and comparative philosophy. Nevertheless, five works from the early

---

150 Noël, 'Tractatus primus', p. 135 (c.2, q.5, FFF.66); p. 156 (c.3, q.1, C3 & D4); this edition, pp. 337, 369–70.
151 ARSI, Jap. Sin. I, 8; ARSI, Jap. Sin. II, 96. See Chan, *Chinese Books and Documents in the Jesuit Archives in Rome*, pp. 6–7; p. 410.
152 Noël and Castner, *Summarium NAT*, pp. 74–75.
153 BNCVE, Fondo Gesuitico, MS [3314] 1185, fols 78ʳ–93ᵛ.
154 Juan Cobo, *Beng Sim Po Cam o Espejo rico del claro corazón*, Biblioteca Nacional de Madrid, MS 6040; Madrid: Librería General, 1959.
155 Domingo Navarrete, *Tratados históricos*, pp. 173–245.
156 Noël, 'Tractatus primus', p. 52 (c.2, q.1, §.5, D.4); this edition, p. 234.
157 Noël, 'Tractatus primus', p. 52 (c.2, q.1, §.5, D.4); this edition, p. 234.
158 ARSI, Jap. Sin. I, 137. See Chan, *Chinese Books and Documents in the Jesuit Archives in Rome*, pp. 180–83.

Qing were used: the *Zhouyi zhengjie*, *Shijing shuoyue jijie*, *Xiesheng pinzi jian*, *Sishu rijiang*, and the *Zhengzitong*. With the exception of the *Sishu rijiang*, none of these works were influenced by Christianity.[159]

The third chapter is very different in nature because it provides explicit evidence drawn directly from the encounter between Christianity and Chinese culture and from people who have participated in and fashioned this encounter. This chapter presents the prevalent view since Ricci, according to which the ancient Chinese had a true, though incomplete, knowledge of God. At the beginning of the chapter, Noël has a very lengthy section to show that two Franciscan missionaries and a dozen of Chinese Christians wrote texts showing that *Shangdi* is a legitimate name for God.[160] Then follows another section on *Tian* as legitimate name for God, but this is based not on the testimonies of the Chinese Christians, but on the testimonies of Muslims, Jews, and other non-Christians.[161] The chapter ends with the famous declaration of Kangxi on *Shangdi* and *Tian*.

The debate about the legitimacy of *Tian* and *Shangdi* should be understood in the context of the Terms Controversy. The discussions held among missionaries at Jiading 嘉定 in 1628 and the subsequent decision to forbid the use of *Tian* and *Shangdi* did not alter the prevalent view. However, facing the opposition of the Dominicans and Franciscans about the Chinese Rites since the 1630s, the Jesuits had to present to Rome more arguments to prove the legitimacy of the Chinese Rites and also the legitimacy of Chinese Terms like *Shangdi* and *Tian*. In Question 1 of Chapter 3, Noël adopts a scholastic framework with an affirmative part consisting of three arguments from reason (*a ratione*), from tradition (*ab usu*), and from authority (*ab authoritate*), followed by objections and their resolution. The first point of the argument from reason is presented as follows:

> Words are arbitrary signs which obtain their power of signifying meaning from a decision made at the time of their institution. The word *Shangdi*, as it results from the discussion in Chapter 1, was instituted very early to express the true God, and its institution has been maintained until now, as shown in Question 1 of Chapter 2. Therefore, the true God can be called *Shangdi*.[162]

Noël follows here an Ockhamist conception of language by which the universals are natural signs which the mind cannot help forming, like the notion of God, whereas the words themselves are arbitrary, *signa ad placitum*, or conventional terms, like *Deus* for the Romans, or *Shangdi* for Chinese.[163] Accordingly, there is nothing sacred in the terms *Deus* or *Shangdi* as such. By reducing the question of

---

159 The *Xingmipian* and the *Shuwenpian* are the only two Christian writings in Chapters 1 and 2 of the First Treatise. Noël, 'Tractatus primus', pp. 129–30 (c.2, q.5, EE.32–FF.33); this edition, pp. 324–25.
160 Noël, 'Tractatus primus', pp. 150–66 (c.3, q.1); this edition, pp. 359–60.
161 Noël, 'Tractatus primus', pp. 166–74 (c.3, q.2); this edition, pp. 379–81.
162 Noël, 'Tractatus primus', p. 151 (c.3, q.1, §.1); this edition, p. 358.
163 'signa ad placitum instituta, tantum dum sunt signa, sive non [...] Ex quibus omnibus colligi potest, quod quaedam nomina significant praecise *signa ad placitum instituta*, & non nisi dum sunt *signa*'. Ockham, *Summa totius logicæ*, Cap. 11.

God to an issue of terminology, Noël succeeds in desacralizing the issue itself. The authority of the term of 'God' lies only on human convention, and Noël needs thus to show that *Shangdi* was indeed commonly accepted as equivalent for God.

Noël proceeds in two steps to show the equivalence of *Shangdi* to God, first through the tradition (*ab usu*) of the missionaries in China, and second through the authorities (*ab authoritate*) of the Chinese Catholics. Strategically, he shows that two Franciscans had drawn an equivalence between *Shangdi* and God. He first quotes an excerpt from the *Tian Ru yin* 天儒印 (1664) by Caballero (in Chinese Li Andang 利安當): '*Shangdi* is the same as the one Lord of Heaven and should be venerated with the highest majesty since He controls and governs all things' (上帝者, 即主宰萬有, 至尊無二之天主也).[164] The mention of Caballero is especially significant since it shows that, before the Canton Conference (18 December 1667–26 January 1668), the Franciscan had supported the idea of *Shangdi* as an equivalent of God. Later, Caballero changed his stance, and in 1668 in Canton, was strongly opposed to the term *Shangdi*.[165] Noël was very much aware of Caballero's final rejection of *Shangdi*, but he purposefully selected a passage from an early work of his to show that he had once supported the term. ARSI has two copies of the *Tian Ru yin*.[166]

The second Franciscan author is Pedro de la Piñuela (1650–1704), who was born in Mexico to Spanish parents and was known in Chinese as Shi Duolu 石鐸祿. Noël cites from La Piñuela's *Chuhui wenda* 初會問答 (1680). The quote is quite long but the main point is: 'The words of Confucius clearly mean that there is a single Lord and Ruler who watches us and reaches us, so that we do not dare to offend Him even slightly. How could this be called the blue sky?' (孔子此言, 正謂明明上天之中有一主宰, 鑒我臨我, 朝夕不敢稍有獲罪也。豈謂此蒼蒼之天乎)[167] The lengthy quote is also found in the *Summarium NAT*.[168] La Piñuela arrived China in 1677 and, unlike Cabellero, did not participate in the disputes between the missionaries during the Canton exile of 1666–1671. This might explain why he held a very tolerant view on the Confucian notion of *Tian*. His work is held in ARSI.[169]

After the two quotes revealing the use of *Tian* and *Shangdi* among the friars in China, Noël turns his attention to nine Chinese Christians who Noël believes are more qualified to express the Christian faith into Chinese language because of their

---

164 Noël, 'Tractatus primus', p. 152 (c.3, q.1, A.1); this edition, p. 359.
165 Caballero, *Traité sur quelques points importants de la mission*, p. 79: 'Ce qu'ils conçoivent par le nom de XANGTI n'est pas notre vrai Dieu'. For the original document, see 'Tratado que se remitio al muy R. P. Luis de Gama de la Compania de Jesus, Visitator de la Provincias de Japon y China de la misma Compania sobre alguns puntos a este mision de la gran China', Rome, Archive of Propaganda Fide, *Scritture, Indie Orientali e Cina 1623–1674*, Tomo 1, 272ʳ–312ᵛ.
166 ARSI, Jap. Sin. I, 122 and 151. See Chan, *Chinese Books and Documents in the Jesuit Archives in Rome*, pp. 169–70, 203.
167 Noël, 'Tractatus primus', p. 152 (c.3, q.1, B.2); this edition, p. 359. The ARSI manuscript has instead a quote from another work of La Piñuela, his *Moxiang shengong* 默想神功 (1694), *juan* 1: 「想已罪, 『获罪』之心, 是全无畏惧佁然自纵不复知, 有上帝右临汝」.
168 Noël and Castner, *Summarium NAT*, p. 78.
169 ARSI, Jap. Sin. I, 119. See Chan, *Chinese Books and Documents in the Jesuit Archives in Rome*, p. 167.

knowledge of both the Chinese classics and Christian doctrine.[170] As explained above, many quotes of the Chinese Christians inserted in Chapter 3 are also found in the same order in the eighth section of the *Summarium NAT* in relation to the terms *Shangdi*, *Tian* and *jing Tian* 敬天 (reverence towards Heaven), but the content may have slight differences. Noël and Castner have drawn excerpts from books of the late Ming already present in Rome, such as those by Xu Guangqi, Yang Tingyun, Li Zhizao 李之藻 (1571–1630). Those books were written during the Terms Controversy and before the Rites Controversy. Noël and Castner also quoted texts which were specifically written during the Rites Controversy. Many texts had been previously collected by Filippucci in Canton before his death in 1692. In 1702, Noël and Castner brought these documents to Rome, as well as more recent texts and documents.

Xu Guangqi is named first, with supporting evidence from four writings. The *Piwang* 闢妄, an apology of Christianity against Buddhism, says that '*Shangdi* is the Lord of the living and the dead' (無分人鬼，皆上帝為主).[171] The quote is also found in the *Summarium NAT*.[172] ARSI has four copies of the *Piwang*.[173] Other words of Xu come from the memorial he presented to the court in 1616, called the *Bianxue zhangshu* 辨學章疏: The missionaries 'want all people to follow virtue to respond to the will of God on high who loves them, and to serve openly *Shangdi* as their first origin' (欲使人人为善，以称上天爱人之意，以昭事上帝为宗本).[174] Quite surprisingly, ARSI does not hold this important work, but the Vatican Library has two copies.[175] Noël also mentioned two postfaces written by Xu Guangqi, the first for Ricci's *Ershiwu yan* 二十五言 (1604) and second for Aleni's *Tianzhu jiangsheng yanxing jilüe* 天主降生言行記略 (1635), where the term *Shangdi* can be found. ARSI has two copies of the *Ershiwu yan*,[176] as well as two editions of the *Tianzhu jiangsheng yanxing jilüe*.[177]

Noël wants to show that Xu Guangqi, like Ricci, believed that ancient China had a monotheistic faith, and the terms of *Shangdi* and *Tian* are equivalent to the Christian God. It seems that Noël here criticizes the words that Longobardo attributed to Xu Guangqi:

---

170 Noël, 'Tractatus primus', p. 153 (c.3, q.1); this edition, p. 360.
171 Noël, 'Tractatus primus', p. 153 (c.3, q.1, C); this edition, p. 360. The *Piwang* 闢妄 is an anti-Buddhist work by a Chinese Christian. It has been attributed for a long time to Xu Guangqi, as attested here by Noël. However, scholars have recently raised doubts about this attribution. See Ad Dudink, 'The Image of Xu Guangqi as Author of Christian Texts', in *Statecraft and Intellectual Renewal in Late Ming China*, ed. by Catherine Jami, Peter Engelfriet, and Gregory Blue (Leiden: Brill, 2001), pp. 99–223 (pp. 115–24).
172 Noël and Castner, *Summarium NAT*, p. 83.
173 ARSI, Jap. Sin. I, 132, 139, 139a, and 159. See Chan, *Chinese Books and Documents in the Jesuit Archives in Rome*, pp. 175, 184, 209.
174 Noël, 'Tractatus primus', p. 153 (c.3, q.1, D); this edition, p. 360.
175 BAV, Borgia Cinese, 324.13; BAV, Raccolta Generale Oriente, III, 213.10.
176 ARSI, Jap. Sin. I, 53.1 and 53.B. See Chan, *Chinese Books and Documents in the Jesuit Archives in Rome*, pp. 84–86 and 90.
177 ARSI, Jap. Sin. I, 58 and 76. See Chan, *Chinese Books and Documents in the Jesuit Archives in Rome*, pp. 107–10. Xu Guangqi's postface can only be found in ARSI, Jap. Sin. I, 76.

Shangdi in no way can be our true God with the attributes which we ordinarily attribute to God, such as the fact that God is one uncreated substance distinct and different from all creation, has neither beginning nor end, and is the Creator of all things visible and invisible, which he made from nothing, and is the end and beginning of all things, arranging and ruling all things by His nod alone, and so on.[178]

In fact, the words of Xu Guangqi which were reported to Longobardo through an intermediary are most probably incorrect as proven here by Noël with the quotes of Xu Guangqi mentioning the term *Shangdi*. The second Chinese person mentioned by Noël is Feng Yingjing, though Noël wrongly assumes that he was baptized. Feng wrote a preface to *The True Meaning of the Lord of Heaven* with the following words:

天主何?上帝也。「實」云者，不空也。吾國六經四子，聖聖賢賢，曰「畏上帝」，曰「助上帝」，曰「事上帝」，曰「格上帝」。

> What does *Tianzhu* mean? This means *Shangdi*, not to be understood as something which is lifeless, but true and real. Our six classical books and our four doctors, Confucius, Mencius, Zisi and Zengzi, and all those famous in the past for their virtue, knowledge and wisdom say: 'fear *Shangdi*, assist *Shangdi*, serve *Shangdi*, to approach *Shangdi*, to unite with *Shangdi*'.[179]

This same quote is mentioned in the *Summarium NAT*.[180] ARSI has two copies of the 1607 edition of *The True Meaning of the Lord of Heaven*,[181] as well as two later editions.[182] Yang Tingyun collaborated with Diego de Pantoja in writing the *Qike* 七克 [Seven Victories, *c*. 1612] and wrote in the preface:

大指不越兩端，曰：欽崇天主万物之上，曰：愛人如己。夫「欽崇天主」，即吾儒「昭事上帝也」。

> The two commandments of Christianity are: first, to worship one God, *Tianzhu*, above all things; second, to love your neighbour as yourself. To worship one God is what our doctors have called 'serving openly *Shangdi*'.[183]

---

178 Longobardo, *A Brief Response on the Controversies*, pp. 194–95 (prelude 17, part 2, n. 14). Recently, Liu Yu 劉豫 has taken the words of Xu Guangqi as reported by Longobardo at face value and wrongly argues that Xu Guangqi did not accept the monotheistic interpretation of the ancient classics by Ricci. See Liu Yu, *Harmonious Disagreement: Matteo Ricci and his Closest Chinese Friends* (New York: Peter Lang, 2015), p. 142. For my review of the book by Liu Yu, see Thierry Meynard, *Archivum Historicum Societatis Iesu*, 85.169 (2016), pp. 245–48.
179 Noël, 'Tractatus primus', p. 153 (c.3, q.1, §.1, F); this edition, p. 360.
180 Noël and Castner, *Summarium NAT*, p. 83.
181 ARSI, Jap. Sin. I, 44 and 45. See Chan, *Chinese Books and Documents in the Jesuit Archives in Rome*, pp. 72–75.
182 ARSI, Jap. Sin. I, 46 and 47. See Chan, *Chinese Books and Documents in the Jesuit Archives in Rome*, pp. 75–76.
183 Noël, 'Tractatus primus', pp. 153–54 (c.3, q.1, G); this edition, p. 361.

This quote is mentioned the *Summarium NAT*.[184] ARSI holds two late Ming editions of *Qike*, as well as one Qing edition (1694).[185] Noël also mentions a preface of Yang Tingyun to Aleni's *Zhifang waiji* 職方外紀 (1623),[186] as well as two works by Yang Tingyun himself, the *Daiyipian* 代疑篇 (1621)[187] and the *Tianshi mingbian* 天釋明辨 (1645).[188] Noël also mentions the third pillar of the Catholic Church, Li Zhizao, and his preface to two works of Ricci, the second edition of *True Meaning of the Lord of Heaven* (1607) and the *Jiren shipian* 畸人十篇 (1608). ARSI only has a 1695 edition of the *Jiren shipian*.[189] Noël also cites from Li Zhizao's preface to the *Shengshui jiyan* 聖水紀言 (c. 1616) by Sun Xueshi 孫學詩:

> 其教專事天主，即吾儒知天、事天、事上帝之說。不曰「帝」，曰「主」者，譯語，質朱子曰：「帝者，天之主宰」。以其為生天、生地、生萬物之主也，故名之主則更切，而極其義，則吾六合萬國人之一大父母也。

> The Christian religion consists only in serving *Tianzhu*; and this corresponds to what our doctors say: to know Heaven, to serve Heaven, to serve *Shangdi*. He is not called *di*, but *zhu*, and this can be explained by quoting doctor Zhu Xi: 'This word *di* means *zhuzai*, or lord and ruler'. Since God is the lord who produced heaven, earth and all things, this single word *zhu* or lord better expresses what [God] is. Finally, if we want to penetrate more deeply what [God] is, [we can say that] He is our only great Father and Mother of all people on earth.[190]

The quote above is also mentioned in the *Summarium NAT*.[191] ARSI has copies of two late Ming editions of the *Shengshui jiyan*.[192] Next, Noël mentions Chen Yi who specifically mentions that *Tianzhu* and *Shangdi* are the same in his preface to Aleni's *Xingxue cushu* 性學觕述 (1646).[193] The quote is also given in the *Summarium NAT*.[194] ARSI holds two copies of the 1646 edition, as well as another edition.[195]

---

184 Noël and Castner, *Summarium NAT*, p. 83.
185 ARSI, Jap. Sin. I, 84, 85 and 86. See Chan, *Chinese Books and Documents in the Jesuit Archives in Rome*, pp. 136–38.
186 ARSI, Jap. Sin. II, 19 and 20. See Chan, *Chinese Books and Documents in the Jesuit Archives in Rome*, pp. 299–301.
187 ARSI, Jap. Sin. I, 165b–165c; Chan, *Chinese Books and Documents in the Jesuit Archives in Rome*, pp. 217–18.
188 ARSI, Jap. Sin. I, 165a; Chan, *Chinese Books and Documents in the Jesuit Archives in Rome*, p. 216.
189 ARSI, Jap. Sin. I, 52; Chan, *Chinese Books and Documents in the Jesuit Archives in Rome*, pp. 83–84.
190 Noël, 'Tractatus primus', pp. 153–54 (c.3, q.1, I.9); this edition, p. 361.
191 Noël and Castner, *Summarium NAT*, p. 84.
192 ARSI, Jap. Sin. I, 53.3 and 131. See Chan, *Chinese Books and Documents in the Jesuit Archives in Rome*, pp. 86–87.
193 Noël, 'Tractatus primus', p. 155 (c.3, q.1, L.11); this edition, p. 362. For an English translation of the full preface, See Giulio Aleni, *A Brief Introduction to the Study of Human Nature*, trans. by Thierry Meynard and Dawei Pan (Boston: Brill, 2020), pp. 64–69.
194 Noël and Castner, *Summarium NAT*, p. 84.
195 ARSI, Jap. Sin. II, 16–16a and 21. See Chan, *Chinese Books and Documents in the Jesuit Archives in Rome*, pp. 295–97 and 301.

Noël mentions also Chen Yi's preface to the *Qike*, but seems to confuse Chen Yi with Chen Liangcai 陳亮采 (*jinshi*, or advanced scholar, in 1595).[196]

There is also a lengthy quote from the *Duoshu* 鐸書 (*c*. 1641) by Han Lin. This quote is not present in the ARSI manuscript and hence was added later. Interestingly, Han Lin mentions the metaphoric use of language: 'When we use the word heaven to refer to the visible heaven, this is like using the word imperial court to refer to the emperor since the supreme power resides there' (今指蒼蒼而言天，猶以朝廷稱天子也).[197] The quote is given in the *Summarium NAT*.[198] ARSI has one copy of the *Duoshu*.[199] There is also a quote from the *Tianxue zhengfu* 天學證符 (1628–1636) by Zhang Geng, which repeats the metaphorical interpretation of the word *Tian*, and interestingly enough mentions that there is no contradiction with Zhu Xi.[200] Zhang Geng's citation is also found in the *Summarium NAT*.[201] Albert Chan remarks that this work, which is held in ARSI, is very rare.[202]

In his *Zhengshi lüeshuo* 拯世略說 (1644), Zhu Zongyuan, like Ricci, draws an equivalence between *Shangdi* and *Tianzhu*,[203] and the same quote is found in the *Summarium NAT*.[204] ARSI has three copies of the works.[205] There is also a mention of Zhu's *Dakewen* 答客問 (1643), but without any text. Li Jiugong 李九功 (1605–1681) in his *Shensilu* 慎思錄 (1682) makes the same identification: 'The name *Shangdi* which is always mentioned in the books of our doctors refers clearly and without any doubt to *Tianzhu*' (儒書上帝之稱，固明指天主).[206] The quote is also mentioned in the *Summarium NAT*.[207] ARSI has two copies of the first edition of this work.[208] Finally, Noël mentions that the term *Shangdi* appears in three other prefaces, but without mentioning their author: prefaces to the *Qike*,[209] to the *Shengjiao sigui* 聖教四規 (*c*. 1662)[210] and to the

---

196 Noël, 'Tractatus primus', p. 154 (c.3, q.1); this edition, p. 362.
197 Noël, 'Tractatus primus', pp. 154–55 (c.3, q.1, M.12); this edition, p. 362.
198 Noël and Castner, *Summarium NAT*, pp. 84–85.
199 ARSI, Jap. Sin. I, 144. See Chan, *Chinese Books and Documents in the Jesuit Archives in Rome*, pp. 190–91.
200 Noël, 'Tractatus primus', p. 155 (c.3, q.1, N.13); this edition, p. 363.
201 Noël and Castner, *Summarium NAT*, p. 85.
202 ARSI, Jap. Sin. I, 141. See Chan, *Chinese Books and Documents in the Jesuit Archives in Rome*, p. 186.
203 Noël, 'Tractatus primus', p. 155 (c.3, q.1, O.14); this edition, p. 363.
204 Noël and Castner, *Summarium NAT*, p. 84.
205 ARSI, Jap. Sin. I, 145–145a and 166a. See Chan, *Chinese Books and Documents in the Jesuit Archives in Rome*, pp. 192–94, 220–21.
206 Noël, 'Tractatus primus', p. 156 (c.3, q.1, P.15); this edition, pp. 363–64.
207 Noël and Castner, *Summarium NAT*, p. 86.
208 ARSI, Jap. Sin. I, 34/37, 136. See Chan, *Chinese Books and Documents in the Jesuit Archives in Rome*, pp. 30–32, 179.
209 Besides Yang Tingyun mentioned above, there are quite a number of people who wrote prefaces to the *Qike*: Cao Yubian 曹于汴 (1558–1634), Zheng Yiwei 鄭以偉 (?–1633), Xiong Mingyu 熊明遇 (1579–1649), Peng Duanwu 彭端吾 (*jinshi* 1601), Fan Dingyu 樊鼎遇, Cui Chang 崔淐 (*jinshi* 1601), Wang Ruchun 汪汝淳, and Chen Liangcai 陳亮采 (*jinshi* 1595), also mentioned above.
210 As for Brancati's *Shengjiao sigui*, two Chinese Christians wrote a preface: Xu Erjue 徐爾覺, who was the grandson of Xu Guangqi, and Qiu Yuezhi (baptismal name Augustine 奧定).

Piwang tiaobo he 闢妄條駁合 (1689), a work which is perhaps mentioned last in Noël's list because it was the most recent of all the Chinese Christian works.

In conclusion, Noël shows that from the beginning of the China mission Chinese Christians identified *Shangdi* with *Tianzhu* and that in spite of the Jiading conference which forbade the use of *Shangdi* they continued to make this identification up until his time of writing. Noël suggests that the best judges for evaluating which Chinese terms should be used for designating God are the Chinese Christians themselves, and that the missionaries and the Vatican should hear their views. The fifteen quotes reflect the attempt of the Chinese Christians to ground their Christian faith on the monotheism of the ancient classics, but we may notice that they consciously stay away from neo-Confucianism and refrain from discussing *Tian* or *Shangdi* in terms of *li* and *taiji*. As mentioned above, many Chinese Christians like Zhang Xingyao were eager to express the distinctiveness of their faith by accepting ancient Confucianism while rejecting neo-Confucianism. However, as shall be argued below, Noël's hermeneutic of combining Christianity with neo-Confucianism in Chapter 2 of the First Treatise allows for a deeper cross-fertilization of the two traditions.

After having presented the affirmative side of the issue of *Shangdi* through reason, ecclesiastical use and Chinese authorities, Noël deals with five objections and their resolution. But let us move further to the issue of *Tian*.

2.17 Contemporary Documents by Non-Christians

As seen above, Noël has argued for the legitimate use of *Shangdi* by invoking the testimonies of the Chinese Christians. Now, in relation to the legitimate use of *Tian* for God, he provides only one extra piece of evidence, the tombstone of the first Chinese bishop, Luo Wenzhao 羅文炤 (1617–1691), upon which was written the word *Tianxue* 天學 (Heavenly teaching). In addition, Noël gives the testimonies of Muslims, Jews, and other non-Christians. First, he mentions three Islamic works: the *Zhengjiao zhenquan* 正教真詮 [The True Explanation to the Correct Teaching] (1642) by Wang Daiyu 王岱輿 (c. 1570–1660), the *Qingzhen jiaokao* 清真教考 [Investigation of the Pure and True Teaching] (Kangxi era) by Zhan Yingpeng 詹應鵬 (*jinshi* in 1616) and Sun Ke'an 孫可庵, and the *Sipian yaodao buzhu bianmeng qianshuo* 四篇要道補注便蒙淺說 [Basic Introduction to the Key Teachings of the Four Chapters] (1653–1660) by Zhang Zhong 張中 (c. 1598–1698).[211] Those three works are not found in ARSI, and Noël probably did not have the texts at hand, but found in a letter of a fellow Jesuit the mention of those three titles with the number of occurrences of *Tian*, *Tianming*, *Tianli*, *Tianjing* 天經, *Tianzhi* 天志, *shitian* 侍天, *baitian* 拜天, and even *Shangdi*.

In relation to the Jewish use of *Tian* and *jing Tian*, Noël gives a more precise source, that is, a letter of Gianpaolo Gozani (1659–1732) from Kaifeng dated 30

---

211 Noël, 'Tractatus primus', p. 168 (c.3, q.2); this edition, pp. 379–80.

June 1705. Noël presents three stone tablets of the Kaifeng synagogue: the first erected in 1487 (明弘治二年), the second in 1511 (明正德七年), and the third in 1663 (康熙二年).²¹² From 1698 to 1724, Gozani intermittently resided in Kaifeng and sent a few reports and letters about the Jewish community there. Noël also mentions a book called *Mingjiao* 明教 which was offered by a Jew to the Jesuits in Beijing, but no information about this book could be found.

Noël also mentions an anti-Christian book called *Pi Xiyang xiejiao lun* 闢西洋邪教論 which accepts the idea that *Tian* and *Shangdi* is a supreme lord, but refutes the idea of incarnation. There is also a reference to the proclamation called *Jiangzhou Zhengtang Lei wei zun Tian qu xie* 絳州正堂雷为尊天祛邪 [Proclamation Issued by Prefect Lei of Jiangzhou Regarding the Worship of Heaven and the Elimination of Heterodoxy] by Lei Chong 雷翀, the *zhifu* 知府 of Jiangzhou in Shanxi province. Noël does not provide a translation for the text and he might not have had the document at hand. Also, Noël mistakenly ascribes the date of 1633 to the text: it should be 1635.

Finally, Noël cites from a document which carries the highest political authority, the so-called *Brevis relatio* which contains the testimonial of Kangxi in favour of the Chinese Rites. On 30 November 1700, four Jesuits had sent a memorial to Kangxi asking if their interpretation of *jitian*, *jisi*, *jikong* was correct. On the same day, Kangxi gave a written answer in Manchu, which was later translated into Chinese and Latin:

> 康熙三十九年十月二十日奏是日奉旨：這所寫甚好，有合大道。敬天及事君親、敬師長者，係天下通義。這就是無可改處。

> The things you have written are well said, and greatly cohere with the Great Way (the True Teaching common to all mankind). To worship Heaven, to serve rulers and parents, to respect teachers and superiors, this is the law and opinion common to the whole world. All the things contained in this writing are completely true and there is nothing that should be changed or corrected.²¹³

In 1701, the Jesuits in Beijing had published a version in Manchu, Chinese, and Latin of their memorial and the answer by Kangxi, and added other testimonies by court officers. Noël finishes the First Treatise with the text of Kangxi's testimonial, showing that Chinese monotheism is not only found in the ancient classics and their commentaries, but also in the person of Kangxi. For Noël, this proves that there is no conflict between the Confucian reverence towards *Tian* and the Christian worship of God alone.

Interestingly Noël does not promote the proposition suggested in the second chapter of the First Treatise that *taiji* or *li* could also be equivalents for God. Following his argumentative frame in three points, he may have shown in the first point that

---

212 Noël, 'Tractatus primus', p. 169 (c.3, q.2); this edition, pp. 380–81.
213 Noël, 'Tractatus primus', pp. 175–79 (c.3, q.2); this edition, p. 388.

this identification agrees with reason. But he would have encountered difficulties with the second point since only a few Jesuits before him had supported *taiji* as a possible equivalent for God. In relation to the third point, Noël would have had even more difficulties in finding Chinese Christians who accepted the idea of *taiji* as God, not only because Ricci had shaped Chinese Christianity in the refutation of *taiji*, but also because Chinese Christians like Zhang Xingyao would have strongly opposed such a move which may have been perceived as threatening the distinctiveness of Christianity.

THIERRY MEYNARD

3. Noël's Interpretation of Neo-Confucianism

Since Ricci, all missionaries in China had rejected neo-Confucianism, including the neo-Confucian interpretation of *Tian* and *Shangdi*, as well as key concepts developed by neo-Confucianism, such as *li*, *qi*, and *taiji*. Bouvet may have quoted many passages of the *Sishu rijiang*, but he did not make great effort to understand Song philosophy. His adoption of the *Sishu rijiang* is mostly strategic, and his interest is in recovering the meaning of the ancient classics. Therefore, Bouvet explicitly rejected Zhu Xi's notion of *taiji* and developed his own Figurist reading of the *Yijing*.

Chinese Christians like Zhang Xingyao were also strongly opposed to Song Confucianism. For Zhang, it was essential to express the radical difference between Christianity and Song Confucianism to prevent Christianity from being completely absorbed by Confucianism. He accepted Bouvet's main idea in the *Tianjiao he Ru* that Christianity and Confucianism share many similarities, and as mentioned above, he copied the quotes compiled by Bouvet which express similarities, but he was even more eager to express in what way Christianity completed what was missing in Confucianism (*buru* 補儒) and even went beyond Confucianism (*chaoru* 超儒).[1]

In Chapter 2 of the First Treatise, Noël deals with neo-Confucianism but, unlike other missionaries and the Chinese Christians, he develops a positive interpretation of it. He investigates the concepts of *Tian* and *Shangdi* (questions 1 and 2), *li* and *qi* (question 3), *guishen* (question 4), the *jiaoshe* ritual (question 5), *taiji* (question 6). He concludes with a discussion of whether the neo-Confucians are atheist or not (question 7). As we shall see below, after a careful study of neo-Confucian texts, Noël interprets neo-Confucianism as theistic and, therefore, compatible with Christianity. His adoption of neo-Confucianism is an attempt to overthrow the deep misunderstanding among missionaries and Chinese Christians about the incompatibility of neo-Confucianism with Christianity.

---

[1] On Zhang Xingyao, see Xiao Qinghe 肖清和, *Tian Ru yitong: Qingchu Rujia jidutu yanjiu* 天儒異同：清初儒家基督徒研究 (Shanghai: Shanghai daxue chubanshe), 2019.

Thierry Meynard, Sun Yat-sen University, Guangzhou, China

3.1 Jesuit Interpretation of the Neo-Confucian *Tian* and *Shangdi*

In his Christian-Confucian synthesis, Ricci makes use of scholastic categories to interpret the meaning of *Tian* and *Shangdi* in the ancient Chinese classics, arguing for their similarity with Christian monotheism. Noël applies a similar method but differs in that he extends the method to the commentaries written since the Song dynasty, arguing that the commentaries have basically kept the same monotheistic meanings as found in the classics.

Just like his predecessors, Noël applies the traditional attributes of God to *Tian* and *Shangdi*. While these attributes represent the intrinsic properties of God, for Noël the Chinese never developed a theological discourse that describes these properties in and of themselves, but always consider these properties in relation to the human world. Therefore, Noël's list of attributes mostly reflects the relationship of *Tian* or *Shangdi* with human beings. The eight attributes are: dominion, power, knowledge, will, justice, life, immensity-eternity, simplicity. For each attribute, Noël provides a series of quotes from the ancient classics in Chapter 1 and from their commentaries in Chapter 2 (see Charts 3 and 4 at the end of this volume).

The human orientation of *Tian* is already apparent in the first attribute (*perfectio*) discussed by Noël, the dominion of *Tian* or *Shangdi*: 'His power of jurisdiction, that is to say his power of governing all people as His subjects, of appointing and changing kings, of enacting laws, and punishing those who disobey'.[2] Among the twenty-seven quotes from the ancient classics, twelve come from the *Shujing*, and Noël concludes: 'I am asking you, what could be more complete and more straightforward in declaring the supreme dominion of the Ruler of Heaven, or in expressing the complete subjection of humanity towards Him'.[3] Among the eight quotes from the commentaries, the first one comes from the *Sishu rijiang* commenting on the chapter 'Liang Hui Wang' (2) in *Mencius*:

上天降生下民，立之君，以主治；立之師，以主教。其意但欲為君師者，代天宣化，輔助上帝之所不及。

> When the Supreme Heaven establishes kings to rule over the people whom He produces and doctors to teach them, He wants one single thing, that the kings and doctors transmit and teach the correct way of living, in His name as His assistants (*vicarii*), helping *Shangdi* in what He cannot reach.[4]

Accordingly, rulers and doctors are like assistants (*vicarii*) of Heaven and their herald. It is also stated here the idea that *Shangdi* needs help. This shows that there is a mutual interaction between *Tian* and mankind. *Tian* does not act in human history from the outside, but though the rulers and teachers. Noël did not further

---

2 Noël, 'Tractatus primus', p. 3 (c.1, q.2, §.1); this edition, p. 171.
3 Noël, 'Tractatus primus', p. 3 (c.1, q.2, §.1); this edition, p. 172.
4 Noël, 'Tractatus primus', p. 29 (c.2, q.1, §.1, A.1); this edition, p. 206.

comment, but this seems similar to the idea in Christianity that God cannot save people without their cooperation.⁵

The interaction between *Tian* and mankind is only possible according to the neo-Confucians because *Tian* endowed human beings with *li*, as the *Sishu rijiang* states in commenting *Zhongyong* 1: 'When producing man, Heaven first endowed him with sensible matter (*materia sensibilis*) to form his body and then infused into him right reason to establish his rational nature' (天之生人，既與之氣以成形，即賦之理以成性).⁶ According to the ancient classics, Heaven entrusted its dominion to the rulers. Through the concept of *li*, neo-Confucianism recognizes that each human being in virtue of his own nature potentially participates in the dominion of Heaven. For Noël, the neo-Confucian idea of a rational nature infused into human beings is similar to the natural law (*lex naturalis*) existing in us as 'participation in the eternal law'. Noël corroborates his point by making reference to Aquinas' *Summa theologiae*.⁷

The second attribute is the power (*potentia*) of *Tian* to create and sustain all things. Among the nineteen quotes from the ancient classics, Noël has six citations from the *Yijing*, including a citation frequently quoted by the missionaries since Ricci which Noël renders as: 'While issuing commands, the Lord or Ruler of Heaven came out or started to come out into act from the enigmatic symbol *Zhen* which represents the equinoctial region [equator] of the world' (帝出乎震).⁸ Elsewhere, Noël suggests that for the Chinese the creation of the world started around the spring equinox (March 20–21) and refers to the *Annales ecclesiastici* (1619) by the Avignonese Jesuit Jacques Salian (1557–1640).⁹ While the association between the biblical creation at spring and *Di* starting motion at spring might seem fortuitous, it reflects a common archetype that relates the beginning of life with spring. It also suggests that Noël at least in part shared Bouvet's Figurism, a hermeneutic that sought historical correspondences between the Bible and the classics. However, there are only two Figurist arguments in the First Treatise.¹⁰ Moreover, Noël refrains from applying to *Tian* the theological notion of creator, and prefers using the Platonic notion of 'first maker of things' (*primus rerum effector*).¹¹ From the commentaries, Noël provides twenty-six quotes, including ten from the *Zhouyi*

---

5   'The one who created you without you, He cannot save you without you' (*Qui ergo fecit te sine te, non te justificat sine te*). Augustine, *Sermo* 169, 13.
6   Noël, 'Tractatus primus', p. 29 (c.2, q.1, §.1, B.2); this edition, pp. 206–07.
7   Noël, 'Tractatus primus', p. 30 (c.2, q.1, §.1); this edition, p. 207. Noël refers to Aquinas, *Summa theologiae*, I^a–II^ae, q.90, a.4.
8   Noël, 'Tractatus primus', p. 8 (c.1, q.2, §.2, D.4); this edition, p. 180. See also Matteo Ricci, *The True Meaning of the Lord of Heaven*, ed. by Thierry Meynard (Boston: Jesuit Sources, 2016), p. 99 (§ 106).
9   Noël, 'Tractatus primus', p. 24 (c.1, q.3); this edition, p. 201. See also Jacobus Salianus, *Annales ecclesiastici*, vol. 1 (Paris, 1625), p. 12: 'Probatio petitur ex scriptura. Germinet, inquit, terra herbem virentem et lignum pomiferum faciens fructum, id enim verno tempori maxime convenire nemo negare potest'.
10 Collani identified another Figurist argument in the Third Treatise identifying Fu Xi as a son of Noah: François Noël, 'Tractatus tertius', *Philosophia Sinica*, p. 245. See Collani, 'François Noël and his Treatise on God in China', p. 45.
11 In Greek: protourgos.

zhengjie, such as: 'Therefore, the force of movement (*vis motrix*) immediately breaks into motion or into act, and soon the production of things, both in terms of reason [*li*] or form, and in terms of air [*qi*] or matter begins to emerge' (故化機一動、而物之生理、生氣皆此發端).[12] *Tian* is endowed with a power of creation, and creation is explained in terms of *li* and *qi*. Commenting the hexagram *qian* 乾, the *Zhouyi zhengjie* describes the production of things as a complete process with four powers (*side* 四德) representing four stages: the first and great power (*yuan* 元), the participative power (*heng* 亨); the directive power (*li* 利), and the perfective power (*zhen* 贞), but while the four powers are usually juxtaposed as four parallel powers, the *Zhouyi zhengjie* singles out *yuan* as an equivalent of Heaven and as the basis for the three other powers (*heng, li, zhen*). This leads Noël to understand the relation of things to *Tian* in terms of the Platonic and Thomistic 'participation' (*participatio*).[13] An important concept mentioned by the *Zhouyi zhengjie*, but which comes from Cai Qing, is *qiji* 氣機, which Noël translates as the force of movement of vital breath (*vitalis aurae vis motrix*) which comes from *Shangdi* and starts the process of generation of things.[14] To illustrate this, Noël gives the following metaphor from the *Zhouyi zhengjie*: 'Take the example of a few grains of millet. Each grain contains in itself the meaning of life; the power of Heaven resides in it and the force of movement hides in it' (今只以一粒粟言之，各有一點生意，即便是天德之所在，機之所伏也).[15]

As for the third attribute of the knowledge (*scientia*) of *Tian* or *Shangdi*, Noël provides only six quotes from the classics, including four from the *Shijing*, such as 'The Great Lord and Guide of heaven [*Shangdi*] inspected the four regions' (監觀四方) or 'The Lord and Guide of heaven [*Di*] paid attention to Wang Ji and directed his mind' (維此王季，帝度其心).[16] There is also the famous exclamation of Confucius in *Lunyu* 14.37: 'I am not angry at Heaven and I don't blame people, but through the study of lower things I penetrate to the intelligence of higher things; how could Heaven not know me?' (不怨天，不尤人。下學而上達。知我者，其天乎).[17] Noël also cites from Zhu Xi's commentary on the *Shijing*: 'Approaching the lowest things, Heaven understands all and seeks the peace and tranquillity of the people' (天之临下甚明，但求民之安定而已).[18] In relation to the exclamation of Confucius, there is a comment from Zhang Juzheng mentioning Confucius's 'close union with Heaven' (與天合一).[19]

As for the fourth attribute of will (*voluntas*), Noël provides some fourteen quotes from the classics showing that Heaven has not eyes or ears, but still sees and hears what the eyes and ears of all the people see or hear. He shows

---

12 Noël, 'Tractatus primus', p. 36 (c.2, q.1, §.2, A.1); this edition, p. 215.
13 Noël, 'Tractatus primus', p. 34 (c.2, q.1); this edition, p. 248.
14 Noël, 'Tractatus primus', p. 39 (c.2, q.1, §.2, I); this edition, p. 213.
15 Noël, 'Tractatus primus', p. 37 (c.2, q.1, §.2, B); this edition, p. 218.
16 Noël, 'Tractatus primus', p. 10 (c.1, q.2, §.3, A & C); this edition, pp. 183–84.
17 Noël, 'Tractatus primus', pp. 10–11 (c.1, q.2, §.3, E.3); this edition, p. 184.
18 Noël, 'Tractatus primus', p. 43 (c.2, q.1, §.3, A.1); this edition, p. 183.
19 Noël, 'Tractatus primus', pp. 43–44 (c.2, q.1, §.3, D.3); this edition, pp. 224–25.

that the commentators hold the view that Heaven is endowed with will, and he has four quotes from Zhang Juzheng's *Sishu zhijie* to this effect, including: 'It is clear that the command of the Master of Heaven should mostly look at the hearts of the people, and the will of Heaven should incline to what the people are inclined to' (可見帝天之命主于民心, 而民心所歸, 莫非天意).[20] According to Zhu Xi, 'a man perfect in wisdom and science is one with Heaven and Earth', and Cai Qing specifies that this union is permanent both in essence and in its effects (*ti yong* 體用); however, Noël misreads Zhu Xi and Cai Qing when he asserts that the union between the sage and Heaven is only about effects (*yong*), but not in nature (*ti*). His misunderstanding is determined by the Christian idea of an union with God where human beings keep their own substance distinct from God.[21] Also, Noël translates a comment from the *Shijing shuoyue jijie* about Wen Wang in the ode 'Weitian zhiming' 維天之命 (The Mandate of Heaven) as: 'Although it is often said that a man of perfect virtue and knowledge is like Heaven, Heaven and the perfect man are still two things'. (凡言聖人如天者, 天與聖人猶為二).[22]

According to scholastic theology, God does not follow a strict egalitarian retribution towards people but follows a distributive justice which allows for differences in retribution according to merits (fifth attribute).[23] Hence Noël identifies eighteen quotes in the classics, of which most come from the *Shujing*. Generally speaking, Heaven does not interfere directly but through the wise rulers. Nonetheless, Noël cites the *Kongzi jiayu* 孔子家語 about the retribution of Heaven (*tianbao* 天報) in rewarding good and punishing evil.[24] The idea of divine retribution mostly reflects the theory of the 'mutual interaction between Heaven and man' (*tianren ganying* 天人感應) in the Han dynasty. This theory has a strong religious dimension with Heaven sending rewards and punishments. However, Zhu Xi and most Song Confucians understood this mutual interaction as an anonymous moral law. Ricci devoted a large part of Chapter 6 of *The True Meaning of the Lord of Heaven* to demonstrate the existence of paradise and hell. When Longobardo asked the Christian literatus Yang Tingyun whether the literati believed in afterlife, Yang Tingyun replied that they do not discuss this.[25] However, Intorcetta and Couplet discovered that Zhang Juzheng frequently discussed divine retributions in his lectures to emperor Wanli. From the late Ming, there was indeed a revival of the notion of 'reverence towards Heaven' (*jing Tian* 敬天) and of the theory of the

---

20 Noël, 'Tractatus primus', p. 44 (c.2, q.1, §.4, C.3); this edition, p. 225.
21 Noël, 'Tractatus primus', p. 71 (c.2, q.2, R.30); this edition, p. 258.
22 Noël, 'Tractatus primus', p. 72 (c.2, q.2, X.37); this edition, p. 260.
23 Aquinas, *Summa theologiae* II^a II^{ae}, q.61.
24 Noël, 'Tractatus primus', p. 7 (c.1, q.2, §.5, L.10); Noël, 'Tractatus primus', pp. 50–51 (c.2, q.1, §.5, D.3); this edition, pp, 192, 234.
25 Longobardo, *A Brief Response on the Controversies*, p. 187 (prelude 17, part 2, n. 3): 'In relation to invisible things, such as the angels, the rational soul, the afterlife, and the like, they spoke with great uncertainty, and indeed were greatly mistaken. Therefore, on these matters one must not wish to adhere to their judgment'.

mutual interaction between Heaven and man. Also, in relation to *Lunyu* 3.13 (獲罪於天, 無所禱也), the *Confucius Sinarum philosophus* harshly criticizes Zhu Xi for identifying *Tian* with *li* (天即理也) but praises Zhang Juzheng for his reverence towards Heaven.[26] On the contrary for Noël, there is no opposition between Zhu Xi's anonymous *li* and Zhang Juzheng's purposeful Heaven. In connection with this same passage of *Lunyu* 3.13, Noël quotes Cai Qing:

蓋孔子出一天字, 特地是以壓竈與奧, 而其所主則在道理上。

> Confucius used the word Heaven to lower down the power of the spirits of hearth and of the South-West corner of the room; what matters the most is the guiding and teaching Reason, and thus, the interpretation [of Zhu Xi] proposed the word Reason.[27]

As we can see, Noël draws upon Zhang Juzheng's theory of mutual interaction, but unlike Longobardo, Intorcetta, and Couplet, he understands this mutual interaction at a metaphysical level, with the insistence on a common *li* connecting Heaven and human beings.

Since God is omniscient, He is also said to be living (sixth attribute), and endowed with the powers to offer (*oblatio*), to give (*datio*), to command (*jussio*), to speak (*locutio*), to listen (*auditio*), to see (*visio*), etc.[28] Noël has thirteen quotes from the *Shujing* and the *Shijing* showing that *Tian* sees and hears, speaks with Wen Wang, etc. The first commentary provided by Noël is Zhu Xi's interpretation of Gaozong dreaming about Fuyue in the *Shujing*. We have discussed above how the *Confucius Sinarum philosophus* had condemned Zhu Xi as an atheo-politician, and how Bouvet overturned this condemnation while affirming that Zhu Xi truly recognized *Tiandi*. Noël mentions Zhu Xi's explanation of the dream as a mutual motion (*motus reciprocus* or *ganying* 感應) and criticizes those who consider Zhu Xi as an atheist.[29] We should note that it is very rare for Zhu Xi to adopt explicitly the Han theory of the mutual interaction between Heaven and people, but he does not provide further explanation. Without affirming the objective reality of this divine dream (only Gaozong could know this), the knowledge obtained by Gaozong in the dream could be well explained by the common *li* that he shares with *Tian*.

While the six attributes mentioned above mostly deal with the external operations of *Tian*, the seventh attribute deals with an inner propriety: immensity-eternity. On this topic, Noël presents only six quotes from the classics and eight from the commentaries, including Zhu Xi's citation of Zhang Zai: 'Heaven penetrates so closely into things that [things] cannot be separated from [Heaven]' (天體物而不遺, 猶仁體事而無不在也).[30] Also, Heaven and Reason are the same (天者,

---

26 Couplet and others, *Confucius Sinarum philosophus*, Liber Tertius, p. 7; Meynard, *The Jesuit Reading of Confucius*, p. 167.
27 Noël, 'Tractatus primus', p. 68 (c.2, q.3, G.16); this edition, p. 253.
28 Noël, 'Tractatus primus', pp. 17–20 (c.1, q.2, §.6); this edition, p. 193.
29 Noël, 'Tractatus primus', p. 54 (c.2, q.1, §.6, A.1); this edition, p. 235.
30 Noël, 'Tractatus primus', p. 54 (c.2, q.1, §.7, A.1); this edition, p. 237.

理也) and omnipresent.³¹ There are also four quotes from the *Zhouyi zhengjie* to explain that Heaven and Earth are constantly active through the transformations of *yin* into *yang*, and vice-versa, and Heaven like the teaching of the *Yijing* has no fixed object (無體)'.³² As for the eternity of Heaven, there is a single reference to *Lunyu* 16.8 (君子之三畏) that the *Sishu rijiang* explains as: 'The wise knows well that the Law of Heaven, which turns and acts with constant course, does not exist in any place; thus, he keeps reverence and caution at all times with great diligence'.³³

God does not include any matter which is always a combination of the four natural elements, and therefore scholastic theology gives to God the attribute of simplicity (*simplicitas*). Longobardo had determined that the Chinese had no idea of a spiritual substance separated from matter.³⁴ On the contrary, Noël renders a quote from the *Yijing* (觀天之神道) as: 'Look at Heaven's spiritual mode of action',³⁵ and then cites from the *Zhouyi zhengjie* to clarify that this expression is empty because human eyes cannot see the spiritual mode of action of Heaven but only its effects in the world.³⁶ Therefore, the word *guan* 觀 should not be understood literally, but 'in a spiritual way through the intellect, either in abstraction or about something which cannot be perceived'.³⁷ In relation to this same citation from the *Yijing*, the *Zhouyi zhengjie* states: 'The vital breath in Heaven acts always secretly and without interruption. What mode of action could be even more spiritual?' (氣化流行於穆不已，其道何神也).³⁸

Noël draws support for a spiritual reading of the Chinese classics from Aquinas himself who considers that there are only three ways to know God: the *via negationis* by which the essence of God is known; the *via causalitatis* by which the virtue or power of God is known; the *via excellentiae* by which the ultimate end is known.³⁹ Noël recognizes that the Chinese used the *via causalitatis* and *via excellentiae* to know *Tian* as purely spiritual, quoting a passage from the *Zhuzi yulei* stating that 'the teaching of the *Yijing* was born out of suspended emptiness' (《易》之爲書，是懸空做出來) and that 'As for this teaching, before the shaping of the enigmatic symbols and their numerical lines, a unique and pure Reason pre-existed' (未有爻畫先，在《易》則渾然一理).⁴⁰ Noël comments that emptiness should be understood as abstract from matter, that is, as spiritual, so that the object of the teaching is a Real Being (*Ens reale*) with a foundation in the things itself. Here Noël adopts Suárez's concept of Being of reason (*Ens rationis*), a Being considered real

---

31 Noël, 'Tractatus primus', p. 54 (c.2, q.1, §.7, B.2); this edition, p. 238.
32 Noël, 'Tractatus primus', pp. 55–56 (c.2, q.1, §.7, D.4, E.5, F, G); this edition, pp. 238–39.
33 Noël, 'Tractatus primus', pp. 55–56 (c.2, q.1, §.7, H.6); this edition, p. 240.
34 Longobardo, *A Brief Response on the Controversies*, p. 138 (prelude 10, n. 1).
35 Noël, 'Tractatus primus', pp. 22–23 (c.2, q.1, §.8.C); this edition, p. 243.
36 Noël, 'Tractatus primus', p. 59 (c.2, q.1, §.8.C); this edition, p. 243.
37 Noël, 'Tractatus primus', p. 57 (c.2, q.1, §.8); this edition, p. 243.
38 Noël, 'Tractatus primus', p. 59 (c.2, q.1, §.8, B.2); this edition, p. 242.
39 Noël, 'Tractatus primus', p. 57 (c.2, q.1, §.8); this edition, p. 240.
40 Noël, 'Tractatus primus', p. 60 (c.2, q.1, §.8, M.9); this edition, p. 245.

in our mind.⁴¹ Noël explains further Reason as reasoned reason (*ratio ratiocinata*), that is a reason in abstraction but with a foundation in the thing itself (*cum fundamento in re*). This would mean that the Being of Reason is not only real in our mind but has also a reality in the concrete world. Here Noël seems indebted not so much to Suárez who criticized the multiple meanings of the term 'reasoned reason', but perhaps to the English Jesuit Thomas Compton Carleton (1591–1666) based at Liège.⁴²

In conclusion, through the analysis of *Tian* according to eight attributes of God, Noël shows that the *Tian* explained by the neo-Confucians as *li* is also an equivalent to the philosophical notion of God. Because *Tian* is a transcendental Reason, this explains how the Chinese commentators could know through human reason alone God and His attributes. According to this philosophical understanding, God should not be construed as an external transcendence (*waizai chaoyue* 外在超越), a notion recently developed by Chinese scholars to characterize Christianity who contrasts it with the Chinese *Tian* as internal transcendence (*neizai chaoyue* 內在超越).⁴³ Perhaps more fitting is the term proposed by Yu Yingshi 余英時 of inward transcendence (*neixiang chaoyue* 內向超越) which maintains the tension between the objective reality of *Tian* and the human mode of inward knowledge.⁴⁴ Through the two favoured methods of scholasticism, the *via causalitatis* and the *via excellentiae*, Noël shows that the neo-Confucians have true knowledge of God, but he also invokes the *via negationis* by referring to seven citations which describe *Tian* as being known in 'a deep and mysterious mist' (*in arcana ac mysteriosa caligine*; *mingming zhizhong* 冥冥之中). Furthermore, Noël accepts the neo-Confucian idea of a union between *Tian* and the sage but he (mis)understands this union as limited to the functional level only.

3.2 Jesuit Interpretation of *li* and *qi* before Noël

In the first two chapters of the First Treatise, Noël's method was to start from the traditional attributes of the Christian God and find corresponding passages in the Chinese texts. This method required a painstaking work of finding in the classics and commentaries relevant passages mentioning *Tian* and *Shangdi*, and then sort them out according to their attributes or properties. Fortunately, Noël did not start from scratch and could build upon the works of Ricci, Yan Mo, and Bouvet as mentioned above. In the third chapter, Noël uses a reverse method, starting from

---

41 Noël, 'Tractatus primus', p. 58 (c.2, q.1, §.8); this edition, p. 241.
42 For the position of Suárez and Compton Carleton on *ratio ratiocinata*, see Sven K. Knebel, 'Entre logique mentaliste et métaphysique conceptualiste: la distinctio rationis ratiocinantis', *Les Études philosophiques*, 61.2 (2002), 145–68.
43 See Tang Yijie 湯一介, *Rudaoshi yu neizaichaoyue wenti* 儒道釋與內在超越問題 (Nanchang: Jiangxi renmin chubanshe, 1991).
44 Yu Yingshi 余英時, *Lun Tianren zhi ji: Zhongguo gudai sixiang qiyuan shitan* 論天人之際：中國古代思想起源試探 (Beijing: Zhonghua shuju chubanshe, 2014).

the key notions of Chinese philosophy, *li* and *taiji*, to show that they express a true transcendence. This method presents the great advantage that many compilations and detailed discussions were easily available. For example, *Zhuzi yulei* had individual chapters discussing *taiji*, *li* and *qi*, *guishen*, etc. Similar discussions are found in the *Xingli daquan*, and many other *compendia*. Noël probably knew those discussions and consulted them, but he rarely mentions them: there is only one citation from the *Zhuzi yulei*, one citation from the *Xingli daquan* and eighteen citations from the *Xingli biaoti*. Besides these relatively rare instances, Noël prefers quoting from the commentaries of the ancient classics.

The dual method used by Noël in Chapters 1–2 and Chapter 3 seems circular and tends to reinforce the idea of a compatibility between the Christian God and the neo-Confucian notions of *Tian*, *Shangdi*, *li*, and *taiji*. Noël could easily be accused of isolating quotes from their context and drawing undue conclusions. In defense of Noël's dual method, it can still be argued that the sheer number of quotes he presents through this dual method already demonstrates strong internal coherence, as he himself suggested in the Preface.

Since Ruggieri, the Jesuits translated *li* as reason (*ratio*), and this could have provided a common ground for the philosophical dialogue. However, in the *True Meaning of Lord of Heaven*, Ricci examines the neo-Confucian *li* and criticizes the many defects of this concept. From the point of view of Christian creationism, *li* is 'unable to produce things' (不得生物).[45] From the point of view of Christian theism, *li* lacks intelligence (*ling* 靈) and righteousness (*yi* 義).[46] From the point of view of Aristotelian philosophy, *li* is only an 'accident' (依賴之品) and therefore lacks true substance.[47] From the point of Western moral philosophy, *li* cannot be equated to human nature or *xing* 性.[48] As for *qi*, Ricci identifies it as the air, one of the four natural elements according to Empedocles and Aristotle, and therefore he considers it as only material,[49] and unable to be the basis for life (生活之本).[50]

As we can see, Ricci's understanding of *li* and *qi* is quite superficial, but was very influential among the missionaries. For Longobardo, the Chinese teaching is similar to the Platonic theory of the world-soul: 'The ancient Chinese held that all things come from infinite chaos, which they imagined to be the first material principle and prime matter. They were persuaded themselves that this [the First Principle] is one and the same with the parts of the world and that there is nothing beyond it or outside it'.[51] In the preface to the *Confucius Sinarum philosophus* understands *li* and *qi* as two immanent causes, *li* being a formal cause, and *qi* being a material cause, and therefore lacking true transcendence.[52]

---

45 Ricci, *The True Meaning of the Lord of Heaven*, p. 87 (c.2, n. 87).
46 Ricci, *The True Meaning of the Lord of Heaven*, p. 89 (c.2, n. 91).
47 Ricci, *The True Meaning of the Lord of Heaven*, p. 285 (c.7, n. 426).
48 Ricci, *The True Meaning of the Lord of Heaven*, p. 287 (c.7, n. 426).
49 Ricci, *The True Meaning of the Lord of Heaven*, p. 55 (c.1, n. 55).
50 Ricci, *The True Meaning of the Lord of Heaven*, p. 165 (c.1, n. 204).
51 Longobardo, *A Brief Response on the Controversies*, p. 155 (prelude 13, n. 1).
52 Meynard, ed., *Confucius Sinarum Philosophus (1687)*, pp. 157–64.

3.3 Noël's Interpretation of *li* and *qi*, and the First Being

In Question 3 of Chapter 2, Noël asks what the literati understand as first origin of the world and replies by explaining the concepts of *li* and *qi*, as well as their relationship. Just like his Jesuit predecessors, he translates *li* as Reason (*ratio*), but unlike them, he understands it as an intellectual principle which is an active Reason (*ratio activa*) and therefore endowed with the power of generation.[53]

As for *qi*, Noël maintains the notion of air, which was used by his predecessors, to render it, but he explicitly rejects the materialist interpretation of *qi*: 'In order to make the Chinese speak consistently and without contradiction, *qi* should not be understood only as material air (*sensibilis aër*)'.[54] He bestows upon *qi* a much deeper meaning than inert matter, which he translates as 'vital breath' (*vitalis aura*) and which he understands as vital principle (*principium vitale*). In support of this, he refers to the notion of *qi* as something spiritual (只氣便是神) which was espoused by Cheng Yi 程頤. For Noël, there is a process by which *shen* comes to spiritualize (*spiritualizare*) *qi*.

For Noël, all reality cannot be reduced to the two principles of *li* and *qi*, and he understands that 'an infinite *suppositum* acting with life and intelligence is included in the universal reason and breath'.[55] The scholastic concept of *suppositum* is the equivalent of an individual substance underlying all the accidents of a thing, and Noël suggests that within *li* and *qi* there is such an underlying infinite substance. To support his view, Noël provides a quote from the Chinese dictionary *Xiesheng pinzijian* 諧聲品字箋 (1677) which he probably copied from Bouvet's preface (1707) to the *Gujin*:

使其中止此渾然渾行之理若氣，而絕無至靈之真宰焉，則所云「無親惟親」者誰所云?「難諶靡常」，而「降祥降殃」者又誰?倘所謂皇皇之上帝非乎?乃吾人日在鑒茲之下，不知時加警惕以畏天威，且敢以小智私心與帝天角，弗思甚矣。

> If only the active reason *li* and the breath *qi* are found in the midst of it and if there is not at all a true guide, unique and very intelligent, then when the *Book [of Imperial Annals]* says that he does not love some, but loves others, I am asking you who else he could be? Who else he could be when it is said 'Do not trust rashly since his command and providence changes easily'? Could he not be indeed the one called *Shangdi*, the King of kings? We who are living under his constant gaze not only do not know how to revere the terrible majesty of Heaven but with fear and tremor, and we do not dare to oppose ourselves to the Lord of Heaven with our opinion and perverse heart. What greater stupidity could it be?[56]

---

53 Noël, 'Tractatus primus', p. 75 (c.2, q.3); this edition, p. 264.
54 Noël, 'Tractatus primus', p. 34 (c.2, q.1, §.2); this edition, p. 213.
55 Noël, 'Tractatus primus', p. 37 (c.2, q.3, §.1); this edition, p. 263.
56 Noël, 'Tractatus primus', p. 75 (c.2, q.3); this edition, p. 263.

Accordingly, besides *li* and *qi*, there is the need for *Tian* or *Shangdi*, endowed with a supreme intelligence or spirit (*zhiling* 至靈) to direct the people. It is difficult to tell if the *Pinzijian* intends to express the ancient meaning of Heaven according to the *Shangshu*, or whether it adopts positively this understanding. For Noël, this quote expresses that within *li* and *qi* there is the equivalent of a personal God acting. Besides *Shangdi* and *Tian*, Noël holds that *taiji*, *taixu*, and *yuan* 元 refer similarly to a First Being (*primum ens*) who is active within *li* and *qi*, so that the activity of this First Being is communicated to *li* and *qi*. As for the relationship between *li* and *qi*, there is a debate in Song philosophy as to whether priority should be granted to *li* or *qi*. Cai Qing attempts here to harmonize the position of Zhu Xi (priority of *li*) and the one of Zhang Zai (priority of *qi*), holding that both positions are correct.[57]

In Question 3 of Chapter 2, Noël briefly investigates the Chinese cosmogenesis, a topic which is for him more related to physics than to metaphysics. He rejects Longobardo's analysis according to the world-soul theory, and instead argues that the Chinese make a distinction between something that is spiritual and uncreated and something material and created, that is, the primordial air or ether. However, since Noël is still committed to the scholastic strict separation between the spiritual and the material, he expresses some regret about the lack of clarity:

> The Chinese do not make clearly enough the distinction, and apparently mix spirit with matter, and reason with body. In my opinion, because of the ambiguity of the word 'air' –*qi* in Chinese, which originally means material air — it comes also to mean anything material and corporeal, as well as human life, human spirit, time, action and motion, etc.[58]

In short, while Noël accepts the neo-Confucian concepts of *li* and *qi*, he also attempts to show that they receive their being and activity from a first being, which is not detached from them, but within them.

3.4 Jesuit Interpretation of *guishen* before Noël

When the first Jesuits came to China, the worship of *guishen* was very widespread in the popular religions. The initial reaction of Michele Ruggieri was to condemn their worship as a sin (*zui* 罪), as can be seen from his catechism of 1584.[59] Later he discovered also positive meanings of the *guishen* in the Four Books. Ruggieri's ambivalence about the *guishen* can be seen in his Spanish translation of 1590. Influenced by his knowledge of popular religion, he translates *guishen* in *Lunyu* 2.23

---

57 Noël, 'Tractatus primus', p. 74 (c.2, q.3); this edition, p. 262.
58 Noël, 'Tractatus primus', p. 76 (c.2, q.3); this edition, p. 266.
59 See *Michele Ruggieri's* Tianzhu shilu *(The True Record of the Lord of Heaven, 1584)*, ed. and trans. by Daniel Canaris (Leiden: Brill, 2022), p. 164 (n. 13.6).

as demons not to be worshipped.⁶⁰ However, he considers the *guishen* in *Zhongyong* 29 to be good spirits and angels.⁶¹

Following the steps of Ruggieri, Ricci in Chapter 4 of his *True Meaning of the Lord of Heaven* developed from the Chinese classics a positive meaning of *guishen* as good angels, sent by God while rejecting the neo-Confucian interpretation of *guishen* in terms of contractions and extensions of *qi* and in terms of *yin* and *yang*.⁶² Ricci did not intend to explicitly endorse the ancient worship of the *guishen*, and only quoted the *Shujing* and the *Shijing* to prove that ancient Chinese believed in the immortality of the soul and the possibility of communication between the living and the dead.⁶³ Ricci was correct in considering the ancient belief in the *guishen* as religious, but it was impossible for him explain on the basis of the classics how the *guishen* receive commands from God, have their own independent substance, and even enjoy free will in accordance with the Catholic discourse on angels.

In Chapter 11 of *Brief Response on the Controversies*, Longobardo refutes Ricci's affirmation that *guishen* are independent substances obeying God, but like *Shangdi* are of the same substance as *li*, *qi*, and *taiji* and, therefore, are inseparable from matter. In that same chapter, Longobardo makes reference to *Zhongyong* 16 — the most important classical text for understanding the *guishen* — which cites Confucius as saying that the *guishen* 'constitute the being and substance of things, and cannot be divided or separated from things without things being immediately destroyed' (體物而不可遺).⁶⁴ Of course, all of Longobardo's analysis is founded on the erroneous premise that *qi* corresponds to air, one of the four material elements in Ancient Greek thought. This assumption was first made by Ricci and was followed by generations of Jesuits during the seventeenth century.

In 1687, the *Confucius Sinarum philosophus* argues for the interpretation of *guishen* in the classics as spiritual substances and angels, but adopts Longobardo's argument that the neo-Confucian philosophers are materialist, atheistic, and even use religion for political control. For example, in translating *Lunyu* 3.13 and 14.43, the *Confucius Sinarum philosophus* criticizes the interpretation of the *guishen* by Zhu Xi who is labelled an atheo-politician.⁶⁵

---

60 'No conveniendo sacrificar, sacrificas al demonio, es de hombres baxos y hechizeros'. Michele Ruggieri, *Disciplina de los varones*, San Lorenzo de El Escorial, MS c.III-27, fol. 30a. See Thierry Meynard and Roberto Villasante, *La filosofía moral de Confucio por Michele Ruggieri*, p. 142.

61 'Presentados delante de los ángeles, no les pase por el pensamiento que son malos. Y, aun aquel Santo que vendrá después de cien siglos, no dudará de aprobarlos'. Michele Ruggieri, *Disciplina de los varones*, San Lorenzo de El Escorial, MS c.III-27, fol. 22a. See Thierry Meynard and Roberto Villasante, *La filosofía moral de Confucio por Michele Ruggieri*, p. 126.

62 Ricci, *The True Meaning of the Lord of Heaven*, pp. 153–55 (nn. 189–92).

63 Ricci, *The True Meaning of the Lord of Heaven*, pp. 143–45 (nn. 171–76).

64 Longobardo, *A Brief Response on the Controversies*, p. 142 (prelude 11, n. 7).

65 Meynard, ed., *Confucius Sinarum Philosophus (1687)*, pp. 165, 457.

3.5 Noël's Interpretation of *guishen* as Active Producing-Destroying Causes

In contrast to his predecessors, Noël discusses the neo-Confucian interpretation of the *guishen* and reconciles it with Western philosophy and Christianity. Question 4 of Chapter 2 of the First Treatise is titled 'Definitions, types and properties of the Spirits by modern authors'.[66] Felix Wong has considered Noël's translation of *guishen* as 'producing and destroying spirit' (*spiritus producens & destruens*) as influenced by the *Sishu mengyin*:

> We can see the impact of *Sishu mengyin* again on Noël in his rendering of *guishen* as 'producing and destroying Spirit' (*Spiritus destruens & producens*). *Gui* does not play an active part of 'destroying' in the context of *Zhongyong*, for Confucius overtly says that 'in their being virtuous, how great are ghosts and spirits' (鬼神之為德, 其盛矣乎, in article 16). Zhu Xi merely said that '*gui* is the spirit of *yin*' (鬼者陰之靈也) and that 'those who go back are called *gui*' (反而歸者為鬼); he did not ascribe any negative elements to the word *gui*. To think of *gui* as necessarily a destroying spirit may have been partly influenced by its general usage in Chinese. But what decisively assured Noël of the legitimacy of *destruens* is the explanation given in *Sishu mengyin*. The author Cai stressed that 'although this Spirit is void of corpus, it makes and destroys all corporeal substances of the universe' (惟鬼神也, 雖無其形、無其聲, 而實有其理也, 故陰陽之合, 實有是合也, 陰陽之散, 實有是散也。惟其實有是合, 故合則為物之始；惟其實有是散, 故散則為物之終).[67]

Felix Wong insists above on the passive dimension of the *guishen* according to Zhu Xi and contrasts this with Cai Qing's stress on the active dimension of the *guishen*. However, the sentence of Cai Qing mentioned by Wong is not found in the *Philosophica Sinica*, and in fact, Noël bases his understanding of the *guishen* on Zhu Xi's commentary of *Zhongyong* 16 from the *Zhongyong zhangju* (物之終始, 莫非陰陽合散之所為也), which Noël translates as: 'The producing and destroying Spirit makes and destroys all the corporeal substances of the world.'[68] Since Zhu Xi talks about the actions (*suowei* 所為) of the *yin* and *yang*, merging (*he* 合) and dispersing (*san* 散), Noël quite logically attributes those actions to *guishen*. Furthermore, Cai Qing follows Cheng Hao 程顥 and Zhu Xi in holding that '*guishen* are the effective agents of Heaven and Earth' (鬼神, 天地之功用). Therefore, *guishen* is not purely passive as Felix Wong understood, and Noël's interpretation of an active part 'destroying' and an active part 'producing' could be traced back to Zhu Xi, through the mediation of Cai Qing. However, for Zhu Xi and the Song Confucians, the *guishen* are not understood as persons, deliberately and purposefully acting in the world, but as anonymous forces.

---

66 Noël, 'Tractatus primus', p. 91 (c.2, q.4); this edition, p. 285.
67 Wong, '*The Unalterable Mean*', p. 221.
68 Noël, 'Tractatus primus', p. 85 (c.2, q.3); this edition, p. 273.

Another likely influence on Noël is Longobardo's interpretation which was mentioned above: the *guishen* 'constitute the being and substance of things, and cannot be divided or separated from things, otherwise things would be immediately destroyed' (體物而不可遺). This idea of an immediate destruction in case of separation of the *guishen* from the concrete object is neither in the Chinese text nor in the commentaries, but Longobardo's interpretation was probably influenced by his understanding of Shao Yong's cosmology which posited a cycle of production and extinction of the cosmos every 129,600 years.[69] Longobardo draws a parallel between the production and destruction of things with Aristotle's notions of generation and corruption, considering *yin* and *yang* as 'natural causes of generation and corruption'.[70] In brief, for Noël as it is for Longobardo, the *guishen* is an operative cause, the difference being that Longobardo reduces the operative cause to a material principle, while Noël recognizes that the *guishen* are endowed with a spiritual substance.

In Question 4 of Chapter 2 of the First Treatise, Noël gives four descriptions of the spirit (*guishen* or *shen*). First, while drawing upon the *Xici* and the explanation given by Zhou Dunyi 周敦頤 in chapter 'Dongjing' 動靜章 of the *Tongshu* 通書, Noël explains *shen* in terms of an alternation of motion (*yang*) and stillness (*yin*), and yet '*shen* is incomprehensible' (陰陽不測之謂神). Instead of comparing *yin* and *yang* with form and matter, Noël rightly sees that *yin* and *yang* are not static entities, but dynamic and interrelated:

> To bring this back to our European manner of speaking, this expression 'union and separation of rest (*yin*) and motion (*yang*)' could be understood as union and separation of matter and form. However, in a more general and universal way of speaking, it seems that it should be understood as the passage from non-action or rest to action or motion. The passage from non-action to action whereby something which was not existing is made to exist can be called union because matter is united with form, nature with substance, or subject with accidents. The passage from action to non-action results in something existent becoming non-existent, and this could be called a separation because things are obviously disjoined. Thus, the words *yin* and *yang* in their most general meaning, as it can be gathered from here, and as it will appear below, signify nothing else than rest and motion. *Yin* means rest, either positive as conservation, or negative as cessation. *Yang* means motion, or a continuing action. More precisely, the words *yin* and *yang* mean the mode resulting from rest and motion, that is, a transcendental relationship. Surely, according to the Philosophers, every continuous action allows for a brief delay or rest, so that after the first action there is a little delay, and after this, another action follows; then, another little delay, etc. Thus, the Chinese mutual alternation or production of rest (*yin*) and motion (*yang*) has some resemblance, and is perhaps even identical, to this way of action.[71]

---

69 See Longobardo, *A Brief Response on the Controversies*, p. 121 (prelude 5, n. 1).
70 See Longobardo, *A Brief Response on the Controversies*, p. 122 (prelude 5, n. 3).
71 Noël, 'Tractatus primus', p. 98 (c.2, q.4, K.10); this edition, p. 292.

On the basis of the Aristotelian concepts of relation and movement, Noël explains here that *yin* and *yang* constitute a transcendental relation, not only in the sense that *yin* and *yang* cannot exist without each other, but also in the sense that *yang* tends to become *yin*, and vice-versa.

The second description of *shen* is based on Zhu Xi's commentary of the *Tongshu* 通書註, in which *shen* is explained in terms of substance and function (*tiyong* 體用): 'a substance transcending by far all things' (妙萬物之體) and 'a cause perfecting wonderfully all things' (妙萬物之用).[72] This means that *shen* never leaves the alternation of motion and rest, nor does it leave the concrete things, and yet it transcends all things, causing them to exist.

The last two descriptions refer to the *guishen*. Referring to the writings of Zhang Zai and Zhu Xi, Noël explains *guishen* as 'the natural principle of a double vital operation' (二氣之良能), with the producing spirit *shen* being 'the intelligence of motion (*yang*)' (*yangzhiling* 陽之靈) and the destroying Spirit *gui* being 'the intelligence of rest (*yin*)' (*yinzhiling* 陰之靈). Considering Noël's translation of *liangneng* as natural principle (*naturale principium*), Felix Wong concludes that Noël adopts a materialistic reading.[73] However, there is a metaphysical dimension to the concept of nature in Noël's thought. Indeed, the *guishen* are endowed with intelligence (*intelligentia* or *ling* 靈), and also Noël points out that 'the word natural should not be taken here as being opposed to voluntary, but as being opposed to violent; indeed, what is voluntary and free can be natural'.[74] This deterministic view of nature may have received some Stoic or even Spinozist influences.

The fourth and last description, which refers to Cheng Hao and Zhu Xi, discusses *guishen* as 'traces of the Author of things' (造化之迹). However, following Cai Qing, Noël understands traces *ji* 迹 as metonymic causes. In this way, the *guishen* are not the visible effects but the transcendental causes of an 'Author' (*Effector*). The term 'Author' suggests *guishen* as person, but this is not explicit in the commentaries. Also, Noël does not follow Ricci, Longobardo, and Couplet in understanding *qi* simply as a material principle, but also considers *qi* as life. Therefore, when he accepts *guishen* as defined in terms of a double *qi*, he describes them as 'the natural principle of the double vital breath, or of the double second life, that is, the intelligence of rest (*yin*) and motion (*yang*)'.[75] With the term 'second life' (*vita secunda*), Noël suggests two levels of life: a spiritual life at the level of the vital spirits or *guishen*, and a 'second life' at the level of *yin* and *yang*. At the level of the spiritual life, there is a single and potential cause (*yigushen* 一故神); at the level of the operation, there is a double efficient cause (*duplex causa effectiva* or *liangguhua* 兩故化) consisting of *yin* and *yang*. The different dimensions of *guishen* have been schematized in Chart 5 at the end of this volume.

---

72 Noël, 'Tractatus primus', p. 92 (c.2, q.4); this edition, p. 286.
73 Wong, '*The Unalterable Mean*', p. 220.
74 Noël, 'Tractatus primus', p. 92 (c.2, q.4); this edition, p. 286.
75 Noël, 'Tractatus primus', p. 97 (c.2, q.4, K.10); this edition, p. 290.

In brief, Noël understands the *guishen* or *shen* as being within the sensible world and yet as 'a certain invisible and immaterial cause, removed from the sensible world, and incomprehensible to the human mind', or 'the transcendental being' (*Ens longè transcendens*).[76] Also, within the invisible realm, *shen* is the efficient cause for *guishen*, so that there are not two but three different levels to understand *shen* and *guishen*. As we can see Noël developed a sophisticated understanding of the neo-Confucian concept of *guishen*, while his Jesuit predecessors had simply reduced the neo-Confucian concept of *guishen* to some materialist monism. It seems that Noël was intellectually challenged to think about substances which could be at the same time both immanent and transcendent, something that scholasticism does not usually allow.

After the metaphysical descriptions of the *guishen*, Noël lists five kinds of spirits: the Spirit of Heaven (*tianshen* 天神), the spirits of mountain and rivers (*shanchuan shenqi* 山川神祇), the domestic spirits (*wusizhe* 五祀者), the spirits of the living (*renzhi shenming* 人之神明) and the spirits of the dead (*shengshen* 聖神). In relation to the spirits of the dead, Noël affirms that for the literati the human soul perishes after death. Like Pietro Pomponazzi (1462–1525), Noël may have thought that the immortality of the soul cannot be proven by philosophy, unlike the existence of God, or that the Chinese literati had not found a philosophical argumentation to support the belief in the immortality of the soul, and therefore, despite Ricci, one should not criticize the neo-Confucian philosophers for having eventually abandoned the ancient belief in the immortality of the soul.

As for the spirits of the living, Noël pays particular attention to the method of spiritual life. According to the Song philosophers, spiritual life is based on the meditation of the Four Books and of the *Shujing*, but Noël considers the new method of spirituality developed in the early Qing that was based on the *Yijing*. Noël provides a series of citations from the *Zhouyi zhengjie* 周易正解 about the *Xici* which emphasizes the importance of its teaching to understand the way of Heaven and Earth, to transform the mundane reality into something spiritual, and 'to spiritualize the work of virtue' (此便是《易》有以神其德行也).[77] Noël compares this spiritual method to the art of algebra, suggesting that it has nothing mystical but proceeds through abstract intelligence.

Finally, Noël lists eight properties of the spirits. The first four can be said to reflect the understanding of the Song Confucians: incorporeal (*wuxing wusheng* 無形無聲), imperceptible (*shizhi er fujian* 視之而弗見), intelligent (*congming* 聰明) and righteous (*zhengzhi* 正直). However, Noël continues with four other properties: rewarding good and and punishing evil (*siqifumei, huoyinzhibing* 司其福美、禍淫之柄), knowing secret things (*zhide* 知得), being offended by sins (*manguishen* 慢鬼神), and producing effects and returning sensible things (*guishen zhi wei* 鬼神之為). Those four last properties of the *guishen* are not emphasized by the Song Confucians, and in fact, they are hard to reconcile with

---

76   Noël, 'Tractatus primus', p. 99 (c.2, q.4); this edition, p. 293.
77   Noël, 'Tractatus primus', p. 101 (c.2, q.4, Y.27); this edition, p. 297.

the Song conception of the *guishen* based on *yin* and *yang* as discussed above. Here Noël draws from late Ming and early Qing authors who emphasize the personal dimensions of the *guishen* and their purposeful actions in the world. Noël mentions some quotes from Zhang Juzheng linked to the theory of the 'mutual interaction between Heaven and men' by Dong Zhongshu 董仲舒, with Heaven personally sending rewards and punishments. However, Zhang Juzheng considers that it is not morally proper to worship the *guishen* or investigate in depth their nature, and it is enough 'to show reverence at a distance to fulfil one's obligation' (*jingeryuan zhikeye* 敬而遠之可也). While Noël acknowledges that the Chinese writers hardly make mention of paradise, just as in the case of the immortality of the soul, Noël might have refrained from criticizing the neo-Confucians because the existence of paradise and hell are not demonstrable by philosophical reason, but accepted through faith and revelation.[78]

After the question on the *guishen*, Noël turns to the question of the *jiaoshe* ritual. While this question may appear out of place in a metaphysical treatise, Noël does not dissociate the intellectual knowledge of Heaven and the practical rituals to Heaven and the Spirits. He addresses here the issue of the hierarchy between the sacrifice given to Heaven and the one given to the Earth, and wants to show that ultimately the different rituals are addressed to the same *Shangdi*. This is the longest section of the First Treatise which discusses a large number of historical records concerning the evolution of the rituals. Since this question would make a digression in our philosophical discussion, we do not analyse it here, and the reader may refer to our English translation with the annotations. We move therefore to Question 6, concerning *taiji*.

3.6 Jesuit Interpretation of *taiji* and Noël's Interpretations

The concept of *taiji* was consistently dismissed by the Jesuits as intellectually flawed. In 1603, in his *True Meaning of the Lord of Heaven*, Ricci considered it a late invention by neo-Confucianism and determined that it could not be a substance.[79] In a Latin manuscript summary added to the printed Chinese book sent to Rome, Ricci stated explicitly that *taiji* is an equivalent for the Western notion of 'prime matter' (*prima materia*), but 'if they would accept *taiji* to be the First Principle, substantial, intelligent, infinite, then we could assure it is in nothing different from God'.[80] However, Ricci did not follow up on this possible interpretation which could have provided the basis of an agreement. Consulting the *Xingli daquan*, Longobardo offered a detailed description of *taiji*, listing seventeen attributes: perfection, origin of the world, first cause of movement, eternity, etc. He recognized that those attributes of *taiji* seem divine, but he surprisingly concluded that *taiji*

---

78 Noël, 'Tractatus primus', p. 95 (c.2, q.4); this edition, pp. 303–04.
79 Ricci, *The True Meaning of the Lord of Heaven*, p. 81.
80 Ricci, *The True Meaning of the Lord of Heaven*, p. 377.

is nothing but prime matter.[81] In 1687, the *Confucius Sinarum philosophus* mostly follows Longobardo's analysis in rejecting *taiji*.[82]

In many parts of the First Treatise Noël mentions *taiji*, and he investigates 'whether the double-character word *taiji* is used by the Chinese for the supreme Master of Heaven, or God, in the sense that God is the first cause of all things'.[83] In particular, Question 5 of Chapter 2 is dedicated to this topic. In opposition to his predecessors' interpretations of *taiji*, Noël creatively proposes that *taiji* should be understood through the concept of nature or *physis* with which the ancient Greek philosophers, such as Democritus and Epicurus, had expressed the idea of God.[84] Based on Chinese texts, he systematically presents four different meanings, as origin of the world, totality of the world, essence of a particular thing and origin of movement.

3.7 First Meaning of *taiji* as 'Producing the World'

For the first meaning of *taiji*, Noël makes recourse to the medieval idea of a unitary concept of *natura*, as expressing the totality of the being in its double and complementary dimensions: in its creative dimension, nature is divine, called 'creating nature' (*natura naturans*), and thus meaning God the creator; in its passive dimension, nature is produced, called 'created nature' (*natura naturata*), thus meaning the created world. According to Mittelstrass, this two-fold concept of *natura* was used by Averroes and Duns Scotus.[85] Aquinas mentioned *natura naturans* only once, and without adopting it.[86] The Coimbra commentary on Aristotle's *Physics* mentions that this term was used by 'good philosophers' (*boni philosophi*), albeit with poor classical Latin style, and considers it equivalent to Augustine's description of God's creative nature (*natura creatrix*) in *De Trinitate* 15.1.[87] This double concept of nature allows going beyond the traditional dualism of Christian theology with its strong division between God and its creature, uniting them under the single category of nature, and yet it preserves the transcendence of God over the world and avoids the problem of pantheism.

Noël first shows the transcendental dimension of the concept of *taiji* by quoting from Shao Yong's *Wuming gong zhuan* 無名公傳 (Biography of Mr No One):

---

81 Longobardo, *A Brief Response on the Controversies*, p. 168 (prelude 14, n. 20).
82 Meynard, ed., *Confucius Sinarum Philosophus (1687)*, pp. 157–62.
83 Noël, 'Tractatus primus', p. 29 (c.2); this edition, p. 206.
84 Noël, 'Tractatus primus', p. 142 (c.2, q.6); this edition, p. 350.
85 Jürgen Mittelstrass 'Nature and Science in the Renaissance', in *Metaphysics and Philosophy of Science in the 17th and 18th Centuries: Essays in Honour of Gerd Buchdahl*, ed. by R. S. Woolhouse (Dordrecht: Kluwer Academic Publishers, 1988), pp. 17–43 (p. 19).
86 Aquinas, *Summa theologica*, Ia IIae q.85, a.6.
87 Noël, 'Tractatus primus', p. 138 (c.2, q.6); this edition, p. 341; *Commentarii Collegii Conimbricensis Societatis Iesu, in octo libros Physicorum Aristotelis Stagiritae* (Coimbra: Antonius à Mariz, 1592), p. 217 (II, c.2, q.1, a.1).

3. NOËL'S INTERPRETATION OF NEO-CONFUCIANISM   97

能造萬物者，天地也；能造天地者，太極也。太極其可得而名乎？
可得而知乎？故強名之曰太極。太極者，其無名之謂乎？

> It is heaven and earth which produces all things; and it is *taiji* which produces heaven and earth; therefore, how could *taiji* be expressed with a true name? How could it be fully understood? *Taiji* is a conventional name, and what is called *taiji* is in fact without any name.[88]

For Shao Yong, the ultimate reality is beyond human language, because, if there is a word to name the ultimate reality, this would mean that this ultimate reality is still part of the world. The mere impossibility of naming it shows that it transcends the world itself. Noël comments on the passage by referring to the *via negationis* mentioned above, quoting from Francisco Suárez similar opinions held by Plato, Hermes Trismegistus, who was the purported author of the Hermetic Corpus, and the Church Father John of Damascus.[89] Being without name, *taiji* is also beyond the sensible world, and thus Noël quotes from the first few lines of Zhu Xi's *Taiji tushuo jie* 太極圖說解 (Commentary on the explanation of the *taiji* diagram):

「上天之載，無聲無臭，而實造化之樞紐，品彙之根底也。」故曰：
「無極而太極。」非太極之外複有無極也。

> 'The operation, or nature, of heaven above is without voice, smell or sensation', yet it is truly the efficient cause, the hinge and the root of all the things being produced. Thus, it is said: '*Wuji*, the being without ultimate, and at the same time, *taiji*, the first ultimate'. Besides the first ultimate, there is no such thing as the being without ultimate.[90]

Here, Zhu Xi begins with a quote of the *Shijing* found in the *Zhongyong*, expressing the idea that *taiji* is beyond the sensible world, before any differentiation, and yet it is the basis of the concrete and visible world. Zhou Dunyi's *Taiji tushuo* 太極圖說 (Explanation of the *taiji* diagram) may suggest that *wuji* is prior to *taiji*, but Zhu Xi clearly states that *taiji* and *wuji* are in fact the same, and as Robin Wang mentions, Zhu Xi has little say about *wuji*.[91] Noël follows here Zhu Xi's orthodox commentary, and not Zhou Dunyi's original text. In interpreting *shuniu* 樞紐 and *gendi* 根底, he uses the Aristotelian notion of efficient cause (*causa effectiva*) which had been interpreted by the Scholastics as transcendental (unlike the material and formal causes considered as immanent). In this way, Noël builds his argument for *taiji* as being the transcendental cause of the world, or as he says, creating nature (*natura naturans*).

---

88 Noël, 'Tractatus primus', p. 138 (c.2, q.6); this edition, p. 341.
89 See Noël, 'Tractatus primus', pp. 138–39 (c.2, q.6); this edition, p. 342.
90 Noël, 'Tractatus primus', p. 139 (c.2, q.6); this edition, p. 342.
91 Robin Wang, 'Zhou Dunyi's Diagram of the Supreme Ultimate Explained (*Taijitu shuo*): A Construction of the Confucian Metaphysics', *Journal of the History of Ideas*, 66.3 (2005), 307–23 (p. 316).

Even though *taiji* is a transcendental cause of the world, it is active within the world. In this vein, Noël quotes from Cai Qing's commentary on *Zhongyong* 26 in the *Sishu mengyin*:

> 天道之至誠無息,如何?[...] 此正是「上天之載無聲無臭」處,以主宰者言也。至於「覆載生成」處,乃其功用也。

> The true Way of Heaven never ceases. 'How secret and mysterious the Law of Heaven running its course without interruption!' refers to what is said elsewhere: 'the nature of Heaven above without sound and smell', that is, the Master and Guide. Concerning 'protecting and sustaining, producing and accomplishing', this refers to His effects.[92]

The *Zhongyong* does not mention the word *taiji*, but for Cai Qing, the words 'nature of heaven above, without voice and smell' in Chapter 33 of the *Zhongyong* refer to *taiji*, which Cai Qing interprets further in terms of mastery (*zhuzai* 主宰). The phrase 'protecting, sustaining, producing and accomplishing' in Chapter 26 of the *Zhongyong* are interpreted by Cai Qing as meaning the efficiency of *taiji*. Thus, for Cai Qing, *taiji* has two complementary dimensions: one metaphysical or transcendental, and the other operative, or immanent. In other words, *taiji* is both the cause of the world and its active operating principle, or in Scholastic terms, *natura naturans*. In Noël's translation, we can see already a subtle semantic transformation since the term *zhuzaizhe* 主宰者 means 'what masters and directs', and can be understood as a non-personal entity, while the Latin words *dominus* and *rector* suggest a personification, similar to the idea of a personal God.

Noël also wants to show that this meaning of *taiji* in China is not completely new and finds its roots in ancient texts. His argument unfolds as a logical deduction. First, according to the *Wenxian tongkao*, the word *taiyi* 泰一, or the Greatest Unity (*maxima unitas*), was used during the Han dynasty as an equivalent for *Shangdi*, the Lord on High. Secondly, Chen Hao in his *Liji jishuo* quoted a certain scholar referring to *taiji* in the *Xici* as meaning *taiyi*, and that all the scholars later accepted this interpretation. The logical conclusion is that *Shangdi*, *taiyi*, and *taiji* are all identical to the 'highest and first maker of the universe' (*summus ac primus rerum effector*) with only different names that were given at different periods of Chinese history. Noël's logical deduction is valid only if the premise of the argument is true, but the Ricci's idea of *Shangdi* as an equivalent for God was precisely object of debate among missionaries.

In his search for terms for expressing the transcendental dimension of *taiji*, Noël cites two important passages from Cai Qing. In the first passage, Cai Qing adopts Zhang Zai's concept of *taixu* 太虛 (*primum vacuum*) and, in an attempt to 'harmonize the positions of Zhu Xi and Zhang Zai' (合張朱之意), Cai Qing makes *taixu* an equivalent for *taiji* (太虛即太極之謂), interpreting *taixu* in terms of principle and without the dimension of visible energy (是太虛以理

---

92 Noël, 'Tractatus primus', p. 139 (c.2, q.6); this edition, p. 342.

言, 不以形氣言也).⁹³ Thus, *taixu* does not mean something empty, as it may be conceived in Buddhism or Taoism, but something invisible, incorporeal, and yet real. Because Noël understands principle in terms of reason, he interprets further *taixu* as a 'being consisting in reason' (*ens ratione constans*) and elsewhere 'a living intellectual being' (*ens vitale intellectuale*).⁹⁴ Noël mentions a second passage by Cai Qing, giving another equivalent for *taiji* as *shen* 神, or spirit (單言神, 則當得太極).⁹⁵ This is another attempt by Noël to express the transcendental nature of *taiji*.

Noël concludes in this way: 'It is clear now that *taiji*, or first ultimate, often means spirit, reason, the unique and spiritual cause, the Lord of Heaven, God as seen objectively [independently from the subjective mind], the first creator of all things, and *natura naturans*'.⁹⁶ By identifying *taiji* with God as *natura naturans*, Noël expresses its two-fold transcendence, as producer of the world and as the active principle within the world. This would mean that *taiji* or God is both transcendent and immanent to the world.

Against the tradition of dualism between spirit and matter in Western philosophy and Christianity, Noël's interpretation of *taiji* affirms that the immanent world is not utterly separated from transcendence, and it can be seen as its extension and domain of activity. Despite the boldness of his analysis, Noël shows a kind of reserve about its radical consequences since this would mean that God as *natura naturans* can never be conceived as distinct from the concrete world, thus countering the traditional view that God created the world at some point in history. As I mentioned above, the concept of *natura naturans* is quite marginal in Western thought. Most probably Noël considers this concept because Baruch Spinoza (1632–1677) used it in his *Ethica*, which was published just after his death in his *Opera posthuma* in 1677:

> [B]y *Natura naturans* we must understand what is in itself and is conceived through itself, *or* such attributes of substance as express an eternal and infinite essence, that is [...] God, insofar as he is considered as a free cause. But by *Natura naturata* I understand whatever follows from the necessity of God's nature, or from God's attributes, that is, all the modes of God's attributes insofar as they are considered as things which are in God, and can neither be nor be conceived without God.⁹⁷

If this is truly the case, Noël would not have been the first to make an association between Spinoza and Asian thought. The French intellectual Pierre Bayle (1647–1706), having learnt about Buddhism by reading the *Confucius Sinarum philosophus*, wrote the entry 'Spinoza' for his *Dictionnaire critique* (1697), which associates Spinoza's thought with Buddhism, and considers them both as atheistic.⁹⁸ Similarly, Nicolas

---

93   *Sishu mengyin*, *Mencius*, Jinxin 盡心 (1); Noël, 'Tractatus primus', p. 69 (c.2, q.2, L.19); this edition, p. 254.
94   Noël, 'Tractatus primus', p. 69 (c.2, q.2, L.19); this edition, p. 254; p. 73 (c.2, q.3); this edition, p. 262.
95   *Zhongyong* 16 in *Sishu mengyin*; Noël, 'Tractatus primus', p. 99 (c. 2, q.4, M.13); this edition, p. 293.
96   Noël, 'Tractatus primus', p. 139 (c.2, q.6); this edition, p. 342.
97   Spinoza, *Ethics*, trans. by Edwin Curley (London: Penguin, 1996), p. 20 (pars I, prop. 29).
98   Meynard, ed., *Confucius Sinarum Philosophus (1687)*, p. 15.

Malebranche (1638–1715) portrayed his fictive Chinese philosopher in *Dialogue between a Christian Philosopher and a Chinese Philosopher on the Existence and Nature of God* as holding ideas similar to the 'impious Spinoza'.⁹⁹ Even though the *Ethica* was condemned by the Church and forbidden by many countries, it circulated across Europe, and Noël would have surely known about it. However, unlike Bayle and Malebranche's complete rejection of Spinozism, Noël may have been positively influenced by the Spinozist idea of God as *natura naturans*, mentioned in the passage above from the *Ethica*, and used it to describe *taiji*. With Noël, Spinoza's words of *Deus sive natura* had become *taiji sive natura sive Deus*.

Noël's own training did not prepare him to understand *taiji* in terms of *natura naturans*, since this concept was marginal in Western philosophy and theology. On the contrary, his discovery of the concept of *taiji* in Chinese philosophy may have led him to rethink his own idea about God and to go beyond a strict dualism between the creator and the created world. Most probably, when he came back to Europe in 1703–1705, he may have observed the similarity between the neo-Confucian's *taiji* and the Spinozist idea of God as *natura naturans*. There is some debate whether Spinoza also identified God with *natura naturata*, but whatever Spinoza's idea on the question, Noël may not have accepted this, and wanted only to underline *taiji* as *natura naturans*. Even though Noël may have received Spinozist influence, he was not a Spinozist for whom the divine cause (*natura naturans*) would be immanent to its effects (*natura naturata*). By identifying *taiji* with the concept of God as *natura naturans*, Noël makes a significant contribution to comparative philosophy, a contribution which has been ignored until today.¹⁰⁰

Noël's understanding of *taiji* in terms of *natura naturans* and *natura naturata* would be followed by a similar attempt much later by Samuel Taylor Coleridge (1772–1834). Coleridge read an English translation based on the Spanish translation of Longobardo's *Brief Response on the Controversies*, which quoted Chengzi 程子: 'Taken as to its shape, and Celestial Body, it is call'd Heaven; in respect to its Government it is called Governor' (以形體謂之天, 以主宰謂之帝).¹⁰¹ Recently, Chris Murray has shown that this view is reflected in Coleridge's dualistic conception of Nature as *natura naturans* and *natura naturata*,¹⁰² though Coleridge does not make any explicit reference to Chinese thought. Unlike Noël who primarily stresses the active and transcendent power of *natura naturans*, Coleridge's interpretation is committed to a metaphysical monism. The Chinese philosopher Zhang Dongsun

---

99 Nicolas Malebranche, *Œuvres complètes* (Paris: Vrin, 1958), vol. 15. P. 42.
100 More recently, comparative philosophers like Franklin Perkins have explored other similarities between neo-Confucianism and Spinozism; see Franklin Perkins, *Leibniz and China: A Commerce of Light* (Cambridge: Cambridge University Press 2014), p. 22.
101 Awnsham Churchill and John Churchill, eds, *A Collection of Voyages and Travels*, 6 vols (London: John Walthoe, 1732), I, p. 209.
102 Chris Murray, 'Coleridge's Daoism? Joseph Needham, Dominican Sinology, and Romantic Pantheism', *The Wordsworth Circle*, 51.2 (2020), 205–20. Murray attributes ideas to the Dominican Domingo Navarrete (1610–1689) while ignoring the fact that Navarrete was translating from Longobardo's *A Brief Response on the Controversies*.

張東蓀 (1886–1973) also affirms that 'there two meanings of *Tian*: one is equivalent to nature and the other equivalent to God. In combining the two, this is quite similar to the medieval concept of *natura naturans*'.[103]

3.8 Second Meaning of *taiji* as 'Essence of a Thing'

For Noël, *taiji* is also understood as 'essence of a thing, either created or uncreated' (*essentia rei tam increatae quam creatae*) and provides this excerpt from Zhu Xi's *Taiji tushuo jie*: 'If we consider all things, each one has its own specific nature, and at the same time all things have the same *taiji* in common' (自萬物而觀之, 則萬物各一其性, 而萬物一太極也).[104] Noël misreads the passage and gives it an Aristotelian meaning: *taiji* represents the essence of a thing, and therefore there would be as many *taiji* as there are different species or genus of things. However, Zhu Xi claims that each individual thing has *taiji*, that is, the fullness of *taiji* in itself, saying for example: 'Everything has its *li*, but all *li* are one and the same' (物物各有理, 總只是一箇理).

Indeed, the idea that *taiji* as ultimate reality could be fully present, even potentially, in each individual thing runs against most of Western philosophy. In Aristotelian thought, there is a clear distinction between the essence of each individual thing and the essence of the whole cosmos. For Christianity, to say God is present in each individual thing is also a heresy.

In order to make the Chinese text intelligible from the point of view of Western mentality, Noël was forced to afford *taiji* a second meaning which seems completely disconnected from the first meaning. He uses thus a reduction of the concept of *taiji*, from the ultimate essence, which is fully present in each individual thing, to the essence of a specific thing. Of course, with this second definition of *taiji*, Zhu Xi's words have been completely transformed. This is enough to indicate that the different meanings of *taiji* given by Noël are not complementary aspects or dimensions of *taiji*, but different meanings which may contradict each other. Yet, for Zhu Xi, the two meanings should not be disconnected since he claims that the *taiji* at the level of universe is also the *taiji* at the level of each individual thing.

Furthermore, Noël indirectly quoted Zhen Dexiu 真德秀 (1178–1235), a disciple of Zhu Xi, who had expressed the relationship between the universal and the singular with the category of *li*:

萬物各具一理。萬理同出一原[...]太極者, 乃萬理統會之名。

---

103 '天有二個意義: 一是等於西方的nature, 一是等於西方的God。會合起來卻頗似中世紀學者的natura naturans'. Zhang Dongsun 張東蓀, *Lixing yu Liangzhi: Zhang Dongsun wenxuan*, 理性與良知: 張東蓀文選 (Shanghai: Yuandong chubanshe, 1995), p. 290.
104 Noël, 'Tractatus primus', p. 139 (c.2, q.6); this edition, p. 344.

Each thing contains in itself one substantial principle, and all the principles come from one source [...] The first ultimate is the word which includes all the substantial principle of things.¹⁰⁵

Noël did not attempt to explain further the axiom that 'the principle is one but its manifestations many' (*liyi fenshu* 理一分殊) that Zhu Xi had borrowed from Cheng Yi. The idea that the first ultimate is immanent in the individual examples of each category of things was qualified by the twentieth-century Chinese scholar Feng Youlan as 'mystical'.¹⁰⁶ Noël did not offer any further comment or explanation articulating the particular with the universal since he may have felt a great difficulty in explaining neo-Confucian ideas so foreign to Western thought.

3.9 Third Meaning of *taiji* as 'Total Aggregate of the Natural Agents'

After having discussed *taiji* as transcendental origin of the world and as essence of a particular thing, Noël introduces a third meaning as being 'total aggregate of the natural agents' (*tota aggregatio agentium naturalium*). He provides only two passages, both drawn from the *Zhouyi zhengjie*. The first quote is, in fact, drawn from the *Zhouyi benyi tongshi* 周易本義通釋 [General Explanation of the Original Meaning of the *Yijing*] by Hu Yunfeng 胡雲峰 (1250–1333), providing a commentary on the *Xici*:

> 一卦六爻之間，莫不有三才太極之理，此曰「三極」，是卦爻已動之後，各具一太極。後曰「易有太極」，是卦爻未生之先，統體一太極也。
>
> Each enigmatic symbol [hexagram] and each of its six numerical lines [line statements] always contain the principle of *taiji* of the first three beginnings (heaven, earth and human being, that is, the total aggregate of the natural agents), thus called 'the Three Ultimates'; this means that, after each symbol and its numerical parts have been applied to a particular thing through motion or change and put into practice, each symbol contains its own *taiji*. When it is further said that 'the doctrine of the *Book of Changes and Productions* contains in itself *taiji*', this means that, before each symbol and its numerical parts have been attached to and practically inserted in a particular thing through motion or change, their universal substance (or more exactly their universal aggregate) is this unique *taiji*, this common and unique nature.¹⁰⁷

---

105 Noël, 'Tractatus primus', p. 140 (c.2, q.6); this edition, p. 344.
106 Fung Yu-lan, *A Short History of Chinese Philosophy*, ed. by Derk Bodde (New York: Free Press, 1976), p. 298.
107 Noël, 'Tractatus primus', p. 140 (c.2, q.6); this edition, p. 345.

In this passage, Hu Yunfeng considers two aspects of *taiji*. The first aspect concerns *taiji* as present in individual things, that is, after the differentiation into the myriad of things, but Noël has just explained this in the second meaning of *taiji*. Noël's concern lies with the second aspect by which heaven, earth, and humanity constitute all together an aggregate of the natural world, also called *taiji*, that is, before the differentiation into the myriad of things.

The second quote is from the *Zhouyi zhengjie* and describes the relationship between *taiji* and *yin-yang* by quoting the Song scholar Cai Jiezhai 蔡節齋:

主太極而言，則太極在陰陽之先。主陰陽而言，則太極在陰陽之內。蓋自陰陽未生之時而言，則所謂太極者，其理已具。自陰陽既生之時而言，則所謂太極者，即在乎陰陽之中也。

> If you consider *taiji*, it is prior to rest *yin* and motion *yang*; and if you consider rest *yin* and motion *yang*, then *taiji* is contained in them. Indeed, before rest *yin* and motion *yang* happen, what we call *taiji* is their cause, mentally represented. After they are produced, what we call *taiji* is the same thing contained inside rest *yin* and motion *yang*, that is, inside this substantial composite of rest and motion, which has nature or *taiji* as substantial element.[108]

For Zhu Xi, *yin* and *yang* belong to the realm of the physical world and thus cannot mix with *taiji*; only their energy (*yinyang zhi qi* 陰陽之氣) can be found in *taiji* but not *yin* and *yang* themselves. Cai Jiezhai here seems to have been influenced by Zhu Xi's rival Lu Jiuyuan 陸九淵 (1139–1193), who considers *yin* and *yang* as belonging to the realm of what is without shape, and thus holds, unlike Zhu Xi, that *taiji* contains *yin* and *yang* even before the differentiation into concrete things. By following the interpretation of Cai Jiezhai, and not that of Zhu Xi, Noël can show more clearly the third meaning of *taiji* as representing the totality of the cosmos including all its rational principles and physical elements.

It should be observed that this third meaning of *taiji* is completely different from the first meaning as transcendental cause. Here *taiji* is considered as the totality of all things brought into a single whole, and thus quite similar to the idea of a world-soul as expressed by Pythagoras or Plato, an idea which was harshly criticized by Aristotle and rejected by Christian thinkers as pantheistic. It was beyond Noël that *taiji* could have been both the totality of beings and also their transcendental cause. Julia Ching precisely holds that such is the opinion of the neo-Confucians.[109]

---

108 Noël, 'Tractatus primus', p. 144 (c.2, q.6); this edition, p. 346.
109 Julia Ching, *The Religious Thought of Chu I* (Oxford: Oxford University Press, 2000), p. 46.

3.10 Fourth Meaning of *taiji* as 'Internal Principle of Motion and Rest'

Noël also provides a detailed account of the Aristotelian idea of nature or *physis* as principle of movement. Noël recalls the Aristotelian definition of nature as 'an essential part of a complete substance' (*pars essentialis substantiae completae*). Owing to the metaphysical autonomy of concrete things with their own specific nature or essence, 'it is evident in this meaning that neither God nor an angel can be properly called nature'.[110] In other words, neither God nor an angel can enter into the substance of a thing which has its own specific essence, distinct from God. Furthermore, for Aristotle, nature concerns the natural world, which is the realm of movement. As Bodnar argues, when an entity moves or is at rest according to its nature, reference to its nature may serve as an explanation of the event.[111] As a good Aristotelian, Noël holds that, at the level of an individual thing, its own essence is the true nature which makes it move, or as he says, nature is 'the principle and cause of motion and rest, in itself and not by accident'.[112] All those arguments above exclude having God as principle of movement of things.

Yet Noël holds that it is still possible to talk 'loosely' (*impropriè*) about God as nature because God is indirectly and ultimately 'the principle of all the movements of the whole' (*principium operationum totius*). Similar to the Aristotelian definition of nature as movement, *taiji* has been also defined as a principle of motion and rest by Zhou Dunyi. Noël cites the following from the *Zhouyi zhengjie*:

太極者，乃所以動而陽、靜而陰之本體也。動而陽者，陰之根也。太極之用，所以行也。靜而陰者，陽之根也。太極之體，所以立也。

> The first ultimate is this same substance by which there is a motion from the *yang*, and rest from *yin*. The motion producing *yang* is the source of *yin*, and the first ultimate through this acts as a cause. The rest which produces *yin* is the source of *yang*, and the essence of the first ultimate subsists through this.[113]

Following Zhu Xi, *taiji* is explained here in terms of an ontology (*ti*, or *substantia*) of movement and rest, making *taiji* fulfil the Aristotelian definition of nature.[114] Noël understands quite well that *yin* and *yang* are not static entities, but always in the state of becoming something else, and so he talks in terms of two 'transcendental

---

110 Noël, 'Tractatus primus', p. 138 (c.2, q.6); this edition, p. 341.
111 See Istvan Bodnar and Pierre Pellegrin, 'Aristotle's Physics and Cosmology', in *A Companion to Ancient Philosophy*, ed. by Mary Louise Gill and Pierre Pellegrin (Malden, MA: Blackwell, 2006), pp. 270–91 (p. 276).
112 Noël, 'Tractatus primus', p. 138 (c.2 q.6); this edition, p. 341.
113 Noël, 'Tractatus primus', p. 140 (c.2, q.6); this edition, p. 347.
114 Noël, 'Tractatus primus', p. 141 (c.2, q.6); this edition, p. 348.

relationships', in the sense that the relationship tends towards an object which is not in oneself: *yang* tends to become *yin*, and vice-versa, as we said above.[115]

3.11 Evaluation of Noël's Interpretation of *taiji*

Just as the concept of nature in the West has different meanings, for Noël *taiji* has not one but four meanings. This already shows that *taiji* should not be understood, and often dismissed on the account of one single meaning, but four meanings need to be taken into account. The first meaning of *taiji* as *natura naturans* is clearly theistic, and the fourth meaning of *taiji* as the principle of movement of all things is also a loose way of describing God. Noël briefly mentions *taiji* as essence of individual thing and as aggregation of the cosmos, but there was no need for him to deal in greater detail with those two meanings which he considers as immanent.

What is striking is that Noël fails to articulate the relationship of the four meanings to each other. As noted, he remains silent on the key axiom 'the principle is one but its manifestations many'. This silence is understandable because human language can hardly express this axiom in philosophical terms, and indeed the neo-Confucians themselves use metaphors.

In Chapter 3 of the First Treatise, Noël asks what name the Chinese Christians should call God, and he states that the term *taiji* is 'vague, uncertain, and applied indiscriminately to different objects, indicating the whole, the part, the substance, the accident, the creature or the creator', and thus the Fathers of the China mission have always rejected the term for expressing God.[116] Some writings by Chinese Catholics around that time show the same rejection. For example, Wang Ge 王格 has recently analysed the writing of a catechist near Beijing in the 1720s, which dismisses *taiji* as being 'inside things and not outside' (皆在物之內, 不在物之外).[117] Though Noël attempts to rehabilitate *taiji*, he does not push for using the term inside the Church and considers *Tian* as the best term for God.

Since the many neo-Confucian texts consulted by Noël sometimes contradict each other, or are even internally inconsistent, Noël is unable to schematize coherently the different meanings of *taiji*, which is at the same transcendent, individual, immanent, and source of movement. Hence thus he retains the impression of *taiji* as 'applied indiscriminately to different objects'. Despite this limitation, he was probably the first European to go this far in understanding *taiji* directly from Chinese sources.

In conclusion, Noël's understanding of neo-Confucianism was shaped by the School of Principle. Though he rarely cites directly Zhu Xi, there are many quotes

---

115 Noël, 'Tractatus primus', p. 141 (c.2, q.6); this edition, p. 347.
116 Noël, 'Tractatus primus', p. 150 (c.3); this edition, p. 357.
117 Wang Ge 王格, *Cong Tian dao Tianzhu de Ruye huitong quanshi: Fandigang suocang Lun Rujia zhi Tian, Taiji yu Tianzhu* 從「天」到「天主」的儒耶會通詮釋——梵蒂岡所藏《論儒家之天、太極與天主》析論 [Confucian-Christian Comprehensive Hermeneutic from Heaven to the Lord of Heaven; Analysis of the Discourse on the Confucian Notions of Heaven, *taiji* and on the Lord of Heaven], *Guoji hanxue* 國際漢學, 19.2 (2019), 78–85.

making references to the *Sishu zhangju, Zhouyi benyi, Zhuzi yulei,* and *Zhuzi quanshu*. Noël often quotes from the works of Zhu Xi's disciples, like Cai Chen's *Shujing jizhuan*. Also, the *Liji jishuo* is representative of the School of Principle during the Yuan dynasty, the *Sishu mengyin* by Cai Qing during the Ming dynasty, and the *Zhouyi zhengjie* during the Qing. Therefore, the quotes mentioned by the First Treatise of the *Philosophia Sinica* provide a detailed reflection into the School of Principle under the Song, Yuan, Ming, and Qing dynasties. Noël discusses in the First Treatise the neo-Confucian understanding of *Tian, Shangdi, jiaoshe* in view of the Chinese Terms and Rites Controversies, but he also discusses in detail the key concepts of the School of Principle, such as *li, qi, taiji* and *guishen*.

The *Philosophia Sinica* is an important but overlooked work. On the basis of his predecessors, he selects many commentaries from the Song to the Qing dynasty and organizes the material in a very logical way. In the First Treatise, he focuses on the core question of the Western tradition, that is, the possibility of a human knowledge of God, and this was precisely the key issue of the Chinese Terms Controversy. Because Noël investigates neo-Confucianism from this rather Eurocentric framework, he does not reach the point of thinking within the Chinese tradition. But what remains meaningful is that he is challenged by neo-Confucianism to find ways to go beyond the traditional divide in Western thought between the creator and the created world, between spirt and matter, beyond the idea of an anthropomorphic God, and creativey applies the concept of nature to explain *taiji* as God.

Furthermore, Noël moves away from Ricci's radical break between ancient Confucianism and neo-Confucianism, and he re-establishes the tradition or *daotong*. He successfully shows the continuity of the Chinese tradition, overturning the judgement of his predecessors about the pantheism and atheism of neo-Confucianism. Though he may have projected his understanding of ancient Chinese monotheism onto neo-Confucianism, he nonetheless appreciates the neo-Confucian shift towards the inner moral law.

The classics and their commentaries had a double function: first, to prepare students for the imperial examination; secondly, to foster practical personal cultivation. The Jesuits' reading is somewhat more theoretical because it focusses on the possibility of extracting from the classics and their commentaries definitions and attributes of *Tian, Shangdi, guishen, linghun,* etc., which could align with the philosophical definitions of God, angels, souls in the Christian scholasticism. This is the reason why Noël is able to find in the commentaries of the School of Principle many resources which allow his First Treatise to conduct a metaphysical engagement between the two traditions. But Noël does not ignore the practical and moral dimensions of the classics and their commentaries, and deals with those in the Second and Third Treatises.

Despite the limitations of his method, Noël was the first Westerner to go so far in the understanding of the School of Principle. However, the *Philosophia Sinica* remained the work of a single person, and since the Vatican had condemned ancient Confucianism, Noël's effort to reconcile neo-Confucianism with Christianity may appear very futile and did not gain traction.

Around the same time, and apparently without knowing the *Philosophia Sinica*, Leibniz (1646–1716) read Longobardo's treatise that was highly critical of Confucianism, and through his own genius was able to discover the value of neo-Confucianism as corresponding to his own metaphysical system. In the final year of his life, he wrote the *Discours sur la théologie naturelle des Chinois*, which was published only in 1735, nineteen years after his death.[118] In China, French Jesuits like Joseph de Prémare, Jean-Joseph-Marie Amiot (1718–1793), and Pierre-Martial Cibot (1727–1780) studied and translated some pieces related to neo-Confucianism, but their publication in Europe failed to attract much attention. Only in the nineteenth century, did the study of neo-Confucianism resume with Jean-Pierre Abel-Rémusat and Guillaume Pauthier (1801–1873) in France, Charles de Harlez (1832–1899) in Belgium,[119] Georg von der Gabelentz (1840–1893) and Wilhelm Grube (1855–1908) in Germany. There were also the Protestant missionary W. H. Medhurst (1796–1857) and the Jesuit Stanislas Le Gall (1858–1916), both based in China.[120] The encounter with China has truly enriched and deepened the modern understanding of the perennial question of God and His presence in the world.

---

118 See Thierry Meynard, 'Leibniz as Proponent of neo-Confucianism in Europe', *Studia Leibnitiana Sonderhefte*, 52 (2017), 179–95.

119 See Yves Vendé, 'Hermeneutical Conflicts on ZHU Xi — Some Remarks about Late 19th Century Debate De Harlez and Le Gall', *Lumen: A Journal of Catholic Studies*, 5.2 (2017), 23–54.

120 Knud Lundbaek, 'Notes sur l'image du Néo-Confucianisme dans la littérature européenne du XVIIe siècle à la fin du XIXe siècle', in *Actes du 3e Colloque International de Sinologie* (Paris: Les Belles Lettres, 1983), pp. 131–76.

WANG GE

4. Evaluation from the Perspective of Chinese Philosophy[1]

4.1 Introduction

The *Philosophia Sinica* (*Chinese Philosophy*, 1711) by François Noël (1651–1729) is currently the earliest known work to be published under the title 'Chinese philosophy'. In this work, Noël seeks to probe Chinese philosophy from the perspective of 'ancient philosophy', which he called 'the pursuit of correcting virtue and thought, as well as the operation of a correct reason and a way of life', and the probing of 'the knowledge of divine and human matters'.[2] The First Treatise of Noël's work focuses on the Chinese understanding of the First Being (*primus Ens*), and is thus primarily metaphysical in its content. The Second Treatise concerns Chinese rituals while the Third concerns ethics in Chinese thought in relation to individual moral cultivation (*xiushen* 脩身), familial management (*qijia* 齊家), and political governance (*zhiguo ping tianxia* 治國平天下).[3] Strictly speaking, however, Noël's methodology diverges from modern academic approaches to Chinese philosophy because Noël explicitly aims to prove that orthodox neo-Confucianism fully agrees with Judaeo-Christian doctrine on a philosophical level despite the lexical and cultural differences between Chinese and European traditions. For this reason, Noël believes that orthodox Confucian thought can constitute a Christian Confucian philosophy.[4] For Noël, Confucian philosophers were not

---

[1] The research contained in this chapter was supported by the National Social Science Fund of China under the grant 18CZX037. It also received significant support from the Zhejiang University Institute for Advanced Study in Humanities and Social Sciences. The author would like to thank Thierry Meynard and Daniel Canaris for their valuable insights in the revision of the manuscript. This chapter was translated into English by Daniel Canaris.

[2] Noël, 'Praefatio', p.(a)2; this edition, p. 164.

[3] Noël, 'Praefatio', p.(a)2; this edition, p. 165. Noël's description of Chinese philosophy as an intellectual and moral pursuit parallels the description of the superior man (*junzi* 君子) in *Zhongzhong* 28, which also mentions intellectual inquiry (*daowenxue* 道問學) and the honouring of the virtuous nature (*zundexing* 尊德性). This passage was discussed extensively by neo-Confucians, especially in the controversy between School of Principle and School of Mind.

[4] See Thierry Meynard [Mei Qianli 梅謙立] and Wang Ge 王格, 'Chaoyue eryuan, maixiang tongyi: Yesuhuishi Wei Fangji *Zhongguo zhexue* (1711 *nian*) ji qi Rujia quanshixue de chutan' 超越二元、邁向

Wang Ge, Department of Philosophy, Shanghai University of Finance and Economics

further away from knowledge of God or the First Being than the philosophers of Greco-Roman antiquity. In fact, in certain respects, Confucian philosophers were superior in their knowledge of God.[5] However, unlike his forebears in the Jesuit China mission, Noël did not believe that neo-Confucianism had been corrupted into atheism or idolatry by Buddhism. Rather, he endeavours to demonstrate that neo-Confucianism was even better than that which had been expounded by the Confucian sages of antiquity.[6]

The *Philosophia Sinica* sought to articulate Noël's staunch defense of Confucian thought and its value within the context of the Chinese Rites Controversy, which spanned the Ming and Qing dynasties. Noël almost unreservedly believes that the entire Confucian tradition possesses a correct understanding and knowledge of God, and that contemporary Chinese only lack a sensory knowledge of God, thereby making them 'impious' (*impii*).[7] In other words, he believes that the problem of Chinese religious teaching does not consist in their knowledge (*cognitio*) of God but in their desire (*volitio*) for God.[8] In undertaking a defense of Confucianism from the perspective of knowledge, Noël's exposition resembles debates in Chinese philosophy over the relationship between knowledge (*zhi* 知) and praxis (*xing* 行). The neo-Confucian philosopher Wang Yangming 王陽明 (1472–1529) believes that the equivalence between *zhi* and *xing* consists in *xincong* 信從, that is, true knowledge is knowledge which is sincerely put into practice. True knowledge is a present commitment that requires complete dedication.[9] However, Noël does not emphasize the differences in praxis,[10] devoting his energy to expounding the uniformity in Chinese and Western knowledge. Obviously, the uniformity of knowledge was the foundation of the Jesuits' missionary enterprise and at the heart of their missionary strategy of accommodating Confucianism. Nevertheless, in their view these differences in praxis justified their efforts to change the status quo in China.

Be that as it may, the *Philosophia Sinica* still has some relevance for contemporary research on Chinese philosophy. If we consider from the perspective of cross-cultural dialogue that our modern discipline of 'Chinese philosophy' essentially originated from the universalization of 'philosophy' in China during the age of globalization, Noël ought to be considered a pioneering figure because he paved the way for a cross-cultural approach to philosophic inquiry and values.[11] Regardless of whether

---

統一——耶穌會士衛方濟《中國哲學》（1711年）及其儒家詮釋學的初探, *Zhexue yu wenhua* 哲學與文化, 11 (2017), 45–61.
5   Noël, 'Tractatus primus', pp. 77–78 (c.2, q.3, §.2); this edition, pp. 270–71.
6   Noël, 'Tractatus primus', p. 62 (c.2, q.1, §.9); this edition, p. 247.
7   Noël, 'Tractatus primus', p. 149 (c.2, q.7, 8); this edition, p. 365.
8   Noël, 'Tractatus primus', p. 28 (c.2); this edition, p. 205.
9   See Wang Ge 王格, 'Wang Yangming "Zhixing heyi" yili zaitan' 王陽明「知行合一」義理再探, *Daode yu wenming* 道德與文明, 5 (2015), pp. 137–42.
10 Except for the ritual sacrifice, which was the core topic in the Chinese Rites Controversy.
11 See Wang Ge 王格, '"Zhongguo zhexue" heyi zhengdang de zui zao lunshuo––Ming Qing zhi ji Xiren zhi zhengyan' 「中國哲學」何以正當的最早論說——明清之際西人之證言, *Zhexue yanjiu* 哲學研究, 7 (2019), pp. 57–66.

his approach was appropriate, in his pursuit of universal values, Noël must be recognised for his attempt to embrace non-European thought and civilizations with a tolerant and open-minded perspective.

In this chapter, I attempt to re-appraise Noël's *Philosophia Sinica* from the perspective of Chinese philosophy, focussing on the First Treatise concerning metaphysics. In particular, this chapter will consider the debates in Chinese philosophy over classical studies (*jingxue* 經學) and the School of Principle (*lixue* 理學), the relationship between *li* 理 (principle) and *qi* 氣 (air) in the School of Principle, as well as contemporary neo-Confucian understandings of religion and transcendence. By uncovering Noël's approach for investigating Chinese philosophy and the orientation of his values, we can better appreciate how intercultural understanding and misunderstanding can occur.

4.2 Antiquity and Modernity: *jingxue* and *lixue* in Western Eyes

It is well known that under the Jesuits' policy of cultural accommodation in East Asia, Matteo Ricci (1552–1610) implemented the missionary strategy of extolling ancient Confucianism. However, his successor Niccolò Longobardo (1559–1654) radically opposed the entire Confucian tradition. While Longobardo's writings are full of misunderstandings, his understanding of neo-Confucianism was much deeper than that of his predecessor. His view that the School of Principle was a development in continuity with the Confucian tradition is not a distortion.[12]

While in the *Philosophia Sinica* Noël stresses the continuity between ancient and modern Confucianism, he still points out two differences: compared to ancient Confucianism, the vocabulary employed in the commentaries and expositions of the School of Principle are more universal and abstract in character, while also being more difficult to understand.[13] Overall, pre-Qin Confucianism was formulated in more everyday language, while its exposition was much more directly based on our lived experience and common knowledge.[14] In contrast, neo-Confucianism used numerous concepts which were more abstract, rational, and metaphysical. From these concepts was developed a unique and highly systematic discursive system. The finalization of this discursive system is ordinarily attributed to Zhu Xi 朱熹 (1130–1200),[15] but Noël relied primarily upon the Cheng-Zhu School of Principle (Cheng-Zhu *lixue* 程朱理學) that had been officially established as the state orthodoxy in the Ming and Qing dynasties.

---

12 See Daniel Canaris, 'Mediating Humanism and Scholasticism in Longobardo's "Resposta Breve" and Ricci's Reading of Confucianism', *Renaissance Quarterly*, 74.2 (2021), pp. 498–527.
13 Noël, 'Tractatus primus', p. 66 (c.2, q.2, 3); this edition, p. 258.
14 See Chen Shaoming 陳少明, 'Jingdian shijie zhong de ren, shi, wu––dui Zhongguo zhexue shuxie fangshi de yi zhong sikao' 經典世界中的人、事、物——對中國哲學書寫方式的一種思考, *Zhongguo shehui kexue* 中國社會科學, 5 (2005), pp. 57–67.
15 See Chen Lai 陳來,'Songdai lixue huayu de xingcheng' 宋代理學話語的形成, *Hebei xuekan* 河北學刊, 1 (2008), pp. 32–35.

For this reason, I will first address the question of the relationship between ancient and modern Confucianism. In the Confucian tradition of philosophic inquiry, the study of ancient Confucianism was conducted primarily through classical studies (*jingxue* 經學). However, the neo-Confucianism of the Song and Ming dynasties — which in Chinese writings of the period is mostly termed 'later Confucianism' (*hou Ru* 後儒) — has been called the School of Principle (*lixue* 理學), or, as it is better known today, the Song-Ming School of Principle (Song-Ming *lixue* 宋明理學) or neo-Confucianism.[16]

The Song and Ming scholars of the School of Principle professed to follow the Confucian orthodoxy (*daotong* 道統): that is to say, they believed they inherited the spirit of orthodox Confucianism dating to Confucius and Mencius and stressed their unbroken continuity with this tradition. However, there are undeniably significant differences between early Confucianism and the Song-Ming School of Principle in terms of intellectual context, methodology, and lexicon. But how then can there be continuity between the classics of pre-Qin Confucianism and the argumentation of the time? This is a difficulty that the School of Principle faced from the beginning, and it became even more serious in the School of Mind developed by Lu Jiuyuan 陸九淵 (1139–1193) and Wang Yangming. In asserting that 'the Six Classics are all records of our mind-heart' (六經皆吾心之記籍), Wang Yangming did not seek to deny the supreme status of the ancient Confucian classics, and indeed he continually emphasized his 'respect for the classics' (*zun jing* 尊經).[17] For this reason, he argued that 'the learning of the sage is School of Mind' (聖人之學，心學也).[18] However, as far as ethical action was concerned, Wang Yangming extolled the innate deductive powers of the mind at the moment of action. As the School of Mind became prominent in the late Ming, the chasm between the classics and argumentation became even more pronounced. Wang's School of Mind presented a crisis for orthodox Confucian thought.[19] Among later

---

16   The seventeenth century neo-Confucian scholar Huang Zongxi understood *lixue* in broad terms as referring to the Confucian intellectuals of the entire Song-Ming period. This usage corresponds to the term neo-Confucian, which is commonly used in Anglophone scholarship today. In the narrow sense, however, *lixue* refers to the Cheng-Zhu School of Principle. The neo-Confucianism described by the Jesuit missionaries in the Ming and Qing dynasties was the orthodox Cheng-Zhu School of Principle. For example, Philippe Couplet (1623–1693) in the *Confucius Sinarum philosophus* used the Greek term *neoterici*, which literally means 'modern' but carries negative connotations. Due to prejudice, the Ming dynasty School of Mind did not figure prominently in their discussion. For discussion, see Chen Lai 陳來, *Song Ming lixue* 宋明理學 (Shanghai: Huadong shifan daxue chubanshe, 2004), pp. 1–2; Hoyt Cleveland Tillman, 'A New Direction in Confucian Scholarship: Approaches to Examining the Differences between Neo-Confucianism and Tao-Hsüeh', *Philosophy East and West*, 43.3 (1993), pp. 455–74; William Theodore de Bary, 'The Uses of Neo-Confucianism: A Response to Professor Tillman', *Philosophy East and West*, 43.3 (1993), pp. 541–55.
17   See Wang Shouren 王守仁, 'Jishan shuyuan zunjingge ji' (*yiyou*, 1525) 稽山書院尊經閣記（乙酉）, in *Wang Yangming quanji* 王陽明全集 (Hangzhou: Zhejiang guji chubanshe, 2010), *juan* 7, *wenlu* 4, book 1, pp. 271–72.
18   See Wang Shouren 王守仁, 'Xiangshan wen ji xu' 象山文集序, in *Wang Yangming quanji* 王陽明全集, *juan* 7, *wenlu* 4, book 1, p. 260.
19   See Wang Ge 王格, 'Zhou Rudeng de jingdian quanshi: yi qi sishuxue yu shixue wei zhu de tantao' 周汝

proponents of the School of Mind there were some who were 'no longer restrained by Confucian ethics' (非名教所能羈絡),[20] causing great anxiety in Chinese scholarly circles. For example, the early Qing Confucian scholar Gu Yanwu 顧炎武 (1613–1682) proposed that 'classical studies is the School of Principle indeed' (經學即理學):

> [愚獨以為「理學」之名，自宋人始有之。古之所謂理學，經學也，非數十年不能通也。故曰：「君子之于《春秋》，沒身而已矣。」今之所謂理學，禪學也，不取之五經而但資之語錄，校諸帖括之文而尤易也。又曰：「《論語》，聖人之語錄也。」舍聖人之語錄而從事於後儒，此之謂不知本也。][21]

> I believe the term *lixue* has been in use since the Song dynasty. In antiquity what was called the School of Principle was in fact classical studies, and many decades of study are needed to understand properly [these disorderly Confucian classics]. Therefore it was said, 'For a gentleman scholar to study the *Spring and Autumn Annals* requires a lifetime of study'. Today's School of Principle is in fact Chan Buddhism. They do not study the Five Classics but rather are immersed in records of conversations. When compared to undertaking the compositions for the civil examinations, [this sort of learning] is much easier. It is also said, '*The Analects* are the sayings of a sage'. To neglect the sayings of the sage while devoting oneself to later Confucianism, this is tantamount to not knowing the source.

For Gu Yanwu, the greatest problem in the School of Principle was its neglect of the Five Classics for records of conversations (*yulu* 語錄) and its neglect of sages and classical texts for the writings of later Confucians.[22] It was as if the School of Principle was a frivolous movement that had abandoned its roots. Gu believed that the true School of Principle should be completely based on classical studies. In other words, classical studies was the true School of Principle. This was the question over the relationship between ancient Confucianism and neo-Confucianism within Chinese philosophy of the Ming and Qing periods. The critique of neo-Confucianism and the exhortation to return to ancient classics was already taking shape and by the eighteenth century had become the dominant mode of scholarship in Chinese thought.

Putting aside Gu Yanwu's judgements over which form of scholarship was superior, what was the difference between these two modes of learning? Generally speaking, what classical studies sought to address were ancient texts written two

---

登的經典詮釋——以其四書學與詩學為主的探討, *Kongzi yanjiu* 孔子研究, 4 (2015), pp. 103–10.
20 Huang Zongxi 黃宗羲, *Ming Ru xue'an* 明儒學案 (Beijing: Zhonghua shuju, 2008), *juan* 32, 'Taizhou xue'an I', p. 703.
21 Gu Yanwu 顧炎武, 'Yu Shi Yushan shu' 與施愚山書, in *Gu Tinglin Shiwen ji* 顧亭林詩文集 (Beijing: Zhonghua shuju, 1983), p. 58.
22 Concerning the *yulu* of neo-Confucians, see Chen Lisheng 陳立勝, 'Lixuejia yu yulu ti' 理學家與語錄體, *Shehui kexue* 社會科學, 1 (2015), pp. 129–42.

thousand years before, and to resolve the lacunas, fragmentations, inconsistencies, and incomprehensible passages within classical texts that resulted from historical changes in language and textual transmission. Moreover, the classical texts examined in classical studies had both perennial and sacred value that was far greater than that of historical documents. For this reason, commenting on the classics must involve a thorough understanding of many different types of classical texts. In other words, 'understanding the classics' (*tongjing* 通經) is the perennial pursuit of a classical scholar. However, in the end, our understanding of the classics will always fall short of fully grasping their contents. Hence the task of the classical scholar is interminable.

The missionaries addressing the Confucian tradition would also encounter the same dilemma: on the one hand ancient Confucian texts were difficult to decipher, archaic, and fragmentary, but these ambiguities also gave them greater interpretative space; on the other hand, neo-Confucianism possessed a highly systematic discursive language, which was expansive in scope but stable in meaning. If outsiders completely accept and engage with this system, then it is very easy to be drowned in it. Hence, out of strategic and intellectual considerations, when introducing Western learning into China, the Jesuits from Ricci onwards borrowed heavily from the discursive system of the School of Principle or coined new terms that were derived from it. At the same time, however, they bestowed new meanings on these terms which were incompatible with neo-Confucianism and entered into discursive competition with the School of Principle.[23] Likewise, when introducing the Chinese classics into Europe, they inevitably adopted the exegesis of the School of Principle.[24] This was not only because the discursive system of neo-Confucianism was dominant in Chinese thought at the time but also because the School of Principle provided a rather clear and orderly commentary on the classics. A rash rejection of the School of Principle would have led the missionaries into greater exegetic difficulty. In the history of Chinese philosophy, the discursive system of the School of Principle was only truly challenged in the mid eighteenth century, when the philological study movement (*puxue* 樸學) came into prominence. Chinese scholars in the seventeenth century made attempts at textual criticism, but they had yet to reach the stage in which they could realize it fully. The missionaries were even less in a position to do so.

As a product of the early eighteenth century, the *Philosophia Sinica* was by no means an exception. Noël primarily based his work on the Cheng-Zhu School of Principle as articulated in the Ming and Qing periods, citing the orthodox and officially sanctioned expositions of scholars such as Cai Qing 蔡清 (1403–1508). While Noël actively accepted the School of Principle tradition, he also attempted

---

23 See Wang Ge 王格, '"Gewu qiongli": wan Ming Xiyang zhexue yu Song Ming lixue zhi jian de huayu jingzheng' 「格物窮理」：晚明西洋哲學與宋明理學之間的話語競爭, *Shijie zhexue* 世界哲學, 4 (2021), pp. 123–31.

24 See Thierry Meynard: 'La première traduction des Entretiens de Confucius en Europe: entre le li néoconfucéen et la ratio classique', *Études chinoises*, 30 (2011), pp. 173–92.

to fashion Confucianism into a Christian Confucian philosophy or a Confucian Christian philosophy. In terms of exegesis, Noël sought to connect ancient and modern Confucianism with medieval Scholasticism. He can be considered a Western exponent of 'classical studies, or the School of Principle indeed' (經學即理學).[25]

4.3 Understanding the Classics: Tensions between the Classics and Exegesis

In Confucianism, the aim of understanding the classics (*tong jing* 通經) was to apply ancient knowledge to practice (*zhiyong* 致用). In the Ming and Qing periods this constituted an intellectual trend known as *jingshi zhiyong* 經世致用, which stressed the political benefit of learning. Unlike the Confucian scholars of the time, the Jesuit missionaries who arrived in China during the seventeenth century did not have particular political ambitions. However, they still used politics to push their religious agenda, not only in the Chinese court but also in the Roman Curia. Like the Confucian intellectuals, they sought to curry favour with political leaders, even if their ideals were very different. As for their religious agenda, the Jesuits' role in internal Catholic debates even imperilled the future of the order, leading to its suppression in 1773. In other words, the Chinese learning of the missionaries at the time more closely resembled the 'antiquity studies' (*guxue* 古學) in vogue in East Asian countries such as Japan and Korea. They also had to confront the imposing discursive system of the Song-Ming neo-Confucianism and attempt to pursue the 'ancient meaning' (*guyi* 古義) from it.[26] Of course, due to their very different cultural and intellectual backgrounds, the Jesuits' philological skills in interpreting the Chinese classics were no match for the those of these East Asian scholars.

Like his predecessor Matteo Ricci, Noël considered the Five Classics and Four Books as early Confucian classics, and used them to probe and evaluate whether the intellectual concepts of ancient Confucianism were compatible with Christianity. In this investigation, they were confronted with the vexed question of how to interpret the ancient classics.

First, in terms of methodology, Noël reviewed and reflected on the exegetic methods used to interpret the texts of Sacred Scriptures. He advocated that the interpretation of the Chinese classics should follow similar principles, that is not rigidly literal yet restrained in judgement, while calmly and prudently addressing the complexities and ambiguities in the text.[27] Noël probably was influenced by the emergence of biblical textual criticism in seventeenth-century Europe; however, similar positions and discussions could also be found in the interpretative traditions

---

25 Gu Yanwu 顧炎武, 'Yu Shi Yushan shu', p. 58.
26 See Wang Ge 王格, 'Yesuhuishi *Lunyu* fanyi (1687 nian) zhong de "guxue" qingxiang' 耶穌會士《論語》翻譯（1687年）中的「古學」傾向, *Xixue dongjian yanjiu* 西學東漸研究, vol. 6 (Beijing: The Commercial Press, 2017), pp. 109–23.
27 Noël, 'Praefatio', p.(a)3; this edition, pp. 166–67.

of the School of Principle, such as Zhu Xi's famous 'method of reading', which stressed the importance of not interpolating or superimposing interpretations and taking a step back.²⁸

In confronting the ancient Confucian classics, Noël took full advantage of the Jesuits' earlier studies, which provided a ready catalogue of references to *Shangdi* 上帝 and *Tian* 天 in the ancient classics. On this foundation, Noël used a scholastic framework to classify these references according to the attributes of God. In this way, he sought to verify whether the ancient Confucians had a correct knowledge of God or 'the First Being' and to prove that they were not atheists.

Noël's exegesis was selective and tendentious. For example, he especially stressed the literal meaning of the words *tianli* 天吏 and *tianzi* 天子 to show the transcendence of *Tian* 天.²⁹ Another example is his explanation of the passage from the chapter 'Taishi' 泰誓 of the *Shujing* 尚書經: 'Heaven sees as my people see; Heaven hears as my people hear' (天聽自我民聽，天視自我民視). According to the Confucian tradition, this passage is understood in people-oriented (*minben*, 民本) terms as a moral restraint on a ruler's political activity.³⁰ However, Noël deviates from this theme, stressing that Heaven can see and hear as well as people.³¹

A further example can be found in Noël's interpretative linking of two passages from the 'Shuogua' (Explanation of the *gua*): '*Di* comes forth in *Zhen*' (帝出乎震) and 'All things come forth from *Zhen*' (萬物出乎震). He understands these two passages as indicating a 'first mover' akin to that found in Christian creationism. Noël translates *chuhu* 出乎 in two different ways: in the former passage it is rendered as 'to begin to come out into act' (*coepit exire in actum*) whereas in the latter passage it is rendered as 'to emanate' (*emanant*).³² In reality, there are many divergent interpretations of the 'Shuogua'. The original text can be divided into two parts:

[帝出乎震，齊乎巽，相見乎離，致役乎坤，說言乎兌，戰乎乾，勞乎坎，成言乎艮。]

> (A) *Di* comes forth in *Zhen* [to His producing work]; He brings [His processes] into full and equal action in *Xun*; they are manifested to one another in *Li*; the greatest service is done for Him in *Kun*; He rejoices in *Dui*; He struggles in *Qian*; He is comforted and enters into rest in *Kan*; and He completes [the work of the year] in *Zhen*.

---

28 See Chen Lisheng 陳立勝, 'Zhuzi dushufa: quanshi yu quanshi zhi wai' 朱子讀書法：詮釋與詮釋之外, in *Song Ming ruxue zhong de 'shenti' yu 'quanshi' zhi wei* 宋明儒學中的「身體」與「詮釋」之維 (Beijing: The Commercial Press, 2019), pp. 193–96.
29 Noël, 'Tractatus primus', pp. 18–19 (c.1, q.1, §.6, E.5); this edition, pp. 195–96.
30 Chen Yun 陳贇, 'Zifa de zhixu yu wuwei de zhengzhi: Zhongguo gudian sixiang zhong de zhengzhi zhengdangxing wenti' 自發的秩序與無為的政治——中國古典思想中的政治正當性問題, *Shehui kexue* 社會科學, 1 (2003): 79–86.
31 Noël, 'Tractatus primus', p. 18 (c.1, q.1, §.6, K.10); this edition, p. 196.
32 Noël, 'Tractatus primus', p. 8 (c.1, q.2, §.2, D.4), and pp. 23–24 (c.1, q.3, I); this edition, pp. 180, 201.

[萬物出乎震，震，東方也。「齊乎巽」，巽，東南也，齊也者，言萬物之絜齊也。離也者，明也，萬物皆相見，南方之卦也，聖人南面而聽天下，向明而治，蓋取諸此也。坤也者，地也，萬物皆致養焉，故曰「致役乎坤」。兌正秋也，萬物之所說也，故曰「說言乎兌」。戰乎乾，乾，西北之卦也，言陰陽相薄也。坎者水也，正北方之卦也，勞卦也，萬物之所歸也，故曰「勞乎坎」。艮，東北之卦也，萬物之所成終而所成始也，故曰「成言乎艮」。]

(B) All things are made to issue forth in *Zhen*, which is placed at the east. [The processes of production] are brought into full and equal action in *Xun*, which is placed at the south-east. The being brought into full and equal action refers to the purity and equal arrangement of all things. *Li* gives the idea of brightness. All things are now made manifest to one another. It is the trigram of the south. The sages turn their faces to the south when they give audience to all under the sky, administering government towards the region of brightness: the idea in this procedure was taken from this. *Kun* denotes the earth [and is placed at the south-west]. All things receive from it their fullest nourishment, and hence it is said, 'The greatest service is done for Him in Kun'. *Dui* corresponds [to the west] and to the autumn, the season in which all things rejoice. Hence it is said, 'He rejoices in *Dui*'. He struggles in *Qian*, which is the trigram of the north-west. The idea is that there the inactive and active conditions beat against each other. *Kan* denotes water. It is the trigram of the exact north, the trigram of comfort and rest, what all things are tending to. Hence it is said, 'He is comforted and enters into rest in *Kan*. *Zhen* is the trigram of the north-east. In it all things bring to a full end the issues of the past [year], and prepare the commencement of the next'. Hence it is said, 'He completes [the work of the year] in *Zhen*'.

It can be seen from the structure of these two passages that B is a sort of commentary (*zhuan* 傳) on a classical text (*jing* 經). Such commentaries were extremely common in pre-Qin sources. Each of the sentences in B essentially correspond to the order in which the *gua* are presented in A. Thus, 'All things come forth from *Zhen*' (萬物出乎震) is a reasonable interpretation for '*Di* comes forth in *Zhen*' (帝出乎震). In this way, the production of text B would have occurred after A, and B interpreted A with the expression *wanwu* 萬物 (all things) in order to dispel the religious meaning of *Di* 帝 in the original text.[33] This perhaps reflected a trend in early Confucian thought to secularize primitive beliefs. However the Tang dynasty scholar Kong Yingda 孔穎達 (574–648) combined these two passages in his interpretation, understanding them as 'If *Di* created all things, then it happened in *Zhen*' (帝若出萬物，則在乎震). He based this on the commentary by Wang Bi 王弼 (226–49): '*Di* is the master that produces all things and the author of flourishing' (帝者，生物之主，興益之宗). Kong Yingda understood Wang

---

[33] See Xin Yamin 辛亞民, '"Shuogua zhuan" "Di chu hu zhen" zhang xilun' 〈說卦傳〉「帝出乎震」章析論, *Zhongguo zhexue shi* 中國哲學史, 4 (2015), 66–70.

Bi's commentary to mean 'This *Di* is used to mean *Tiandi*' (以此帝為天帝也).³⁴ In this way, Noël's interpretation broadly agrees with Kong Yingda's commentary. Where they differ is in the fact that Kong Yingda used a conditional structure ('If 若 …, therefore 則'), which reflected an undeveloped Confucian religious attitude towards *Tiandi*.

In the preface to his entire work, Noël cited the following passage from Mencius: 'Those who explain the odes may not insist on one term so as to do violence to a sentence, nor on a sentence so as to do violence to the general scope' (說詩者不以文害辭, 不以辭害志). With this passage, Noël advocated a comprehensive and precise understanding of Chinese philosophical works that avoids one-sided and decontextualized interpretations. In this way, Noël sought to deal with those expressions that seemed to contradict the literal meaning.³⁵ However, decontextualization (*duanzhang quyi* 斷章取義) played a significant role in pre-Qin interpretations of the *Shijing*. In particular, during the late Zhou dynasty, when the *Shijing* was used for political and diplomatic occasions, most of the commentaries would break away from the context of the *Shijing* and interpret the poems as commentaries, satire, and political exhortations in relation to their contemporary context while gradually infusing Confucian moral values into the poems.³⁶ Mencius' commentary on the *Shijing* was also based on this decontextualist approach, and thus says, 'They must try with their thoughts to meet that intention, and then we shall apprehend it' (以意逆志, 是為得之). In fact, Noël is precisely 'using his thoughts to meet that intention' because he is applying medieval scholasticism to appraise Confucianism. In particular, when citing and explaining the *Shijing*, he is overly eager to prove the equivalence of *Shangdi* and *Tian* with the Christian God, and thus often departs from the context of the passages. One notable example is his reading of the ode 'Yunhan' 雲漢:

[祈年孔夙，方社不莫。
昊天上帝，則不我虞。
敬恭明神，宜無悔怒。]

> In praying for a good year I was abundantly early; I was not late [in sacrificing] to [the Spirits] of the four quarters and of the land.
>
> *Shangdi* in the great heaven does not consider me.
>
> Reverent to the intelligent Spirits, I ought not to be thus the object of their anger.

---

34 Wang Bi 王弼 *zhu*, Kong Yingda 孔穎達 *shu*, *Zhouyi zhengyi* 周易正義 (Beijing: Beijing daxue chubanshe, 2000), *juan* 9, p. 385.
35 Noël, 'Praefatio', p.(b); this edition, p. 167.
36 See Meng Qingnan 孟慶楠, 'Deyi zhi fu: *Shi* de jingdianhua ji qi yiyi' 德義之府：《詩》的經典化及其意義, *Zhongguo ruxue* 中國儒學, 13 (Beijing: Zhongguo shehui kexue chubanshe, 2019), pp. 185–99.

Noël's citation of this passage excludes the verse 'In praying for a good year I was abundantly early; I was not late [in sacrificing] to [the Spirits] of the four quarters and of the land' (祈年孔夙，方社不莫), thus the 'intelligent Spirits' (*mingshen*) are understood as 'the intelligent Spirit of *Shangdi*'.[37] In fact, on this verse, Zheng Xuan (127–200) comments as follows:

> [我祈豐年甚早，祭四方與社又不晚。天曾不度知我心，肅事明神如是，明神宜不恨怒於我，我何由當遭此旱也？][38]
>
> I prayed for a rich harvest extremely early, and was not late in sacrificing to the [spirits] of the four quarters (*sifang*) and of the land (*she*). Heaven does not consider or know my heart. I solemnly worshipped the intelligent spirits (*mingshen*) like this; the intelligent spirits should not nurse hatred toward me. Why must I suffer this drought?

Evidently, the *mingshen* must be the spirits of the four quarters and of the land. Noël's method is to decontextualize the passage, although he perhaps is not doing this deliberately.

Thus, Noël's methodology for interpreting the classics faces a dilemma. On the one hand he stresses that some expressions in the ancient classics should not be understood metaphorically (*metaphoricum*) and in this way he proves that the ancient Confucians were not materialists because it can be seen from the literal meaning of the passage that *Tian* possesses personal characteristics.[39] On the other hand, however, when some passages can be easily understood as materialist, Noël stresses that their metaphoric or metonymic connotations (*metonymiam*), thereby suggesting that they should not be understood as materialist.[40] In this respect, Noël could substantiate his argument by referring to the interpretative tradition of the School of Principle. For example, Cai Qing understood the character *ji* 迹 (traces) in 'traces of the spirit' (鬼神之迹) as something that 'cannot be seen or heard' (說「迹」字略涉於見聞). Noël astutely points out this metaphoric reading.[41]

In this way, Noël has fallen into the trap of self-contradiction because the criterion by which he determines whether a passage should be interpreted rhetorically or literally is his pre-determined conclusion, that is to say, he uses his predisposed understanding about the orientation of Confucian values to determine the method by which he probes the meaning of classical texts. In this way, he leads the Confucian texts towards Christian doctrine. Of course, Noël is not oblivious to this contradiction. He cites the exegetic principles of Saint Augustine (354–430): if the literal meaning of a scriptural method seems erroneous, then it must be

---

37 Noël, 'Tractatus primus', pp. 22 (c.1, q.2, §.8, A.1); this edition, p. 199.
38 Mao Heng 毛亨 *zhuan*, Zheng Xuan 鄭玄 *jian*, Kong Yingda 孔穎達 *shu*, *Mao shi zhengyi* 毛詩正義 (Beijing: Beijing daxue chubanshe, 2000), *juan* 18, p. 1412.
39 Noël, 'Tractatus primus', pp. 24–25 (c.1, q.3, III); this edition, pp. 201–02.
40 Noël, 'Tractatus primus', p. 79 (c.2, q.3, §.4, W.34); this edition, p. 275.
41 Noël, 'Tractatus primus', p. 92 (c.2, q.4, K.10); this edition, p. 289.

interpreted metaphorically.⁴² However, Augustine did not truly solve the problem, or rather he proposed an 'exegetic circle' in that literal and overall meaning of the text serve as basis for each other. Noël is somewhat conscious of this, because he uses some supplementary evidence to promote his reading of the text. For example, he points out that *Tian* 天 is used metaphorically for God, that this expression can be found in the traditions of all countries of both the New World and the Old Continent, and that if this metaphoric reading were to be rejected, then problems would emerge in the interpretation of Sacred Scripture itself.⁴³

There is a very famous paragraph in the introduction to the *Shumu dawen* 書目答問 [Answers to Questions on Bibliography] by the late Qing scholar Zhang Zhidong 張之洞 (1837–1909):

[由小學入經學者，其經學可信；由經學入史學者，其史學可信；由經學、史學入理學者，其理學可信。]⁴⁴

> Trustworthy are the classical studies of someone entering into classical studies from elementary studies; Trustworthy are the historical studies of someone entering historical studies from classical studies; Trustworthy are the neo-Confucian studies of someone entering neo-Confucian studies from classical studies and historical studies.

Evidently, the first 'trustworthy' (*kexin* 可信) is based on the historical and linguistic investigation of classical texts whereas the second and third 'trustworthy' are based on their sacred value and canonical status. Therefore, as for as methodology is concerned, the Figurism of the Jesuit Joachim Bouvet (1656–1730) to a certain extent could be seen as 'entering classical studies from elementary studies' and 'entering historical studies from classical studies'. Although Noël placed great stress on ancient dictionaries, he hardly never applied Figurist interpretations to texts. An exception would be his citation of the entry on the character *zhu* 丶（主）in the *Zhengzitong* 正字通: 'By combining the character 丶 with the character 王, Heaven, earth and all things are ruled by One' (从丶配以王，天地萬物統於一也). This reading seems to have traces of Figurism.⁴⁵ In this case, Noël rationalist exegesis of Confucian texts could be seen as 'entering into the School of Principle from classical studies and historical studies'.

As for the interpretation of classics in the School of Principle tradition, Noël believes that there is continuity between the School of Principle and ancient Confucianism. In terms of investigative methodology, Noël claims to focus on those passages in the School of Principle which seem to diverge from ancient Confucianism while passing over those which are identical.⁴⁶ However, the School of Principle

---

42 Noël, 'Tractatus primus', p. 25 (c.1, q.3, III); this edition, p. 202.
43 Noël, 'Tractatus primus', pp. 25–26 (c.1, q.3, III); this edition, pp. 202–03.
44 Zhang Zhidong 張之洞, *Shumu dawen buzheng* 書目答問補正, ed. Fan Xizeng 范希曾 (Shanghai: Shanghai guji chubanshe, 2001), p. 257.
45 Noël, 'Tractatus primus', p. 87 (c.2, q.3, §.3, Y.35); this edition, p. 277.
46 Noël, 'Tractatus primus', p. 28 (c.2); this edition, p. 205.

contained references not only to the extremely common *Tian* and *Shangdi*, but also to *li*, *Taiji*, *guishen*, *qi*, *xing*, *ming* and other abstract metaphysical concepts. Furthermore, they constituted the tightly knit discursive system of the School of Principle. Hence Noël had to penetrate the discursive system of the School of Principle, and to grasp and explain the conceptual terms from within this system.

4.4 Probing the Reason of Things: Systematic Philosophic Exposition

Above it was mentioned that unlike classical studies, the School of Principle employed an abstract and meticulous metaphysical framework that resembled in certain respects Christian theology. Therefore, when interpreting the metaphysical concepts of the School of Principle, Noël made extensive reference to mediaeval Scholasticism, especially the theology of Thomas Aquinas (1225–1274).

According to the contemporary neo-Confucian scholar Mou Zongsan 牟宗三 (1909–1995), the incipit of the *Zhongyong* 'What heaven has conferred is called Nature' (天命之謂性) reflected a sort of 'inner transcendence' (內在的超越) in the Confucian tradition, bridging ethics and religion.[47] For the scholars of the Song-Ming School of Principle, *tianming* 天命 (mandate of Heaven) was the same as *tianli* 天理 (reason of heaven). Noël understood this reason as akin the *lex* (law) in the Western tradition,[48] thereby introducing the scholastic concept of natural law. In this way, *tianfa* 天法 (the law of heaven) is the natural law. For Aquinas, law is rational, while the eternal law is the rational embodiment of God.[49] Hence Noël borrows this concept corresponding to *tianli* 天理, which is a core concept in the School of Principle, and applies Aquinas' theology of natural law to understand basic notions in the School of Principle, such as 'Heaven is the basic substance of Reason' (天者，理之本體也) and 'the great origin of morality comes from Heaven' (道之大原出於天).[50] For this reason, the core discursive system of the entire School of Principle is interpreted within the rationalist framework of natural law: 'In Heaven this Reason (*li* 理) is the mandate (*ming* 命); in human beings and other things, it is called nature (*xing* 性); in actions, it is called the way (*dao* 道); they are all Reason (*li* 理)' (此理在天則為命，在人物則為性，在事物則為道，皆理也)[51] In Noël's translation, this sentence is transformed into an

---

47 See Mou Zongsan 牟宗三, *Zhongguo zhexue de tezhi* 中國哲學的特質, in *Mou Zongsan xiansheng quan ji* 牟宗三先生全集 (Taipei: Lianjing chuban shiye youxian gongsi, 2003), vol. 28, pp. 21–22.
48 It must be noted that when Noël's predecessors translated the term *siwen* 斯文 in the *Lunyu*, they also used the term 'law'. Perhaps they were influenced by the traditional Confucian emphasis on 'decrees and systems' (*dianzhang zhidu* 典章制度). See Wang Ge 王格, 'Yesuhuishi *Lunyu* fanyi (1687 nian) zhong de "guxue" qingxiang' 耶穌會士《論語》翻譯 (1687 年) 中的「古學」傾向, *Xixue dongjian yanjiu* 西學東漸研究, vol. 6 (Beijing: The Commercial Press, 2017), p. 111.
49 John Finnis, *Natural Law and Natural Rights* (Oxford: Clarendon Press, 1980), pp. 35–36.
50 Noël, 'Tractatus primus', p. 63 (c.2, q.2, E.12); this edition, pp. 248, 251–52.
51 Noël, 'Tractatus primus', p. 63 (c.2, q.2, E.14); this edition, p. 248.

expression of Aquinas' natural law theory. This strained comparison, however, is not entirely mistaken. In fact, unlike the meaning of 'nature' during the birth of natural science in the early modern period, the concept of 'nature' in scholastic philosophy was metaphysical and its origin was God.[52] Precisely for this reason, when Western learning was translated into Chinese in the late Qing dynasty, *xingfa* 性法 and *tianfa* 天法 were used to translate the concept of natural law. The translation *ziranfa* 自然法 for natural law only came into common usage through Japanese-language translations.[53]

In the Song-Ming School of Principle, the term *ming* 命 had two levels of meaning: *li* 理 and *qi* 氣.[54] For this reason, Noël has another way for translating *ming*, namely, *providentia* (providence). Corresponding to *ming* discussed at the level of *qi* 氣 in neo-Confucianism — that is to say, what is usually called fate, luck, or fortune — Noël translates as 'the cycle of time' (*temporis revolutio*).[55] However, in the Christian tradition, providence is divine and arranges everything.[56] Hence like Mou Zongsan, Noël especially likes to cite the verse 'How profound and unceasing are the mandates of Heaven!'(維天之命, 於穆不已) from the ode 'The Ordinances of Heaven' (維天之命) in the *Shijing*, as well as the neo-Confucian explanations of it. Nevertheless, what Noël stresses in his reading of this passage is the obscurity and mysteriousness (*arcane et mysteriose*) of the operation of the heavenly law operates.[57] In contrast, Mou Zongsan believes that this passage is about the profundity and penetration of the Mandate of Heaven:

> [我們試觀這個宇宙，山河大地變化無窮，似乎確有一種深邃的力量，永遠起著推動變化的作用，這便是《易經》所謂「生生不息」的語意。正因為「於穆不已」的天命，天道轉化為本體論的實在 (ontological reality)，或者說本體論的實體(ontological substance)。此思想的型態一旦確定了，宗教的型態立即化掉，所以中國古代沒有宗教。]

When we observe this universe, we can see endless changes of the mountains, rivers, and lands. It might seem like there is indeed a profound force which eternally drives these changes. This is the meaning of what the *Yijing* calls 'unceasing generation' (生生不息). Precisely because of the 'profound and unceasing' (於穆不已) Mandate of Heaven, the way of Heaven is transformed into an ontological reality, or rather an ontological substance. Once the form

---

52 For the concept of nature in the Western tradition, see Pierre Hadot, *Le voile d'I sis: Essai sur l'histoire de l'idée de Nature* (Paris: Gallimard, 2008).

53 Cheng Liaoyuan 程燎原, 'Xingfa, Tianfa, Zira nfa: Qing mo de yilun lüeshu'「性法」、「天法」、「自然法」：清末的譯論略述, *Jindai fa yanjiu* 近代法研究 (Beijing: Beijing daxue chubanshe, 2007), vol. 1, pp. 95–106.

54 Chen chun 陳淳, Beixi ziyi 北溪字義 (Beijing: Zhonghua shuju, 1983), pp. 1–2.

55 Noël, 'Tractatus primus', p. 64 (c.2, q.2, K.18); this edition, p. 248.

56 Noël, 'Tractatus primus', p. 80 (c.2, q.3, §.5); this edition, p. 282.

57 Noël, 'Tractatus primus', pp. 79–80, 87–88 (c.2, q.3, AA.36 & CC.40); this edition, pp. 278, 282–83.

of this thought has been determined, the form of religion is immediately cast off. Thus Chinese antiquity did not have religion.[58]

Mou Zongsan believes that the notion of a personal divinity is negated by this 'profound and unceasing' Mandate of Heaven, which he reconfigures in a philosophical sense as a body of unceasing generation and flow. This obviously is closer to the systematic explanations of Song-Ming neo-Confucianism. For example, as Xiong Shili 熊十力 (1885–1698) wrote:

[天非具有人格之神，無形體，無方相。故言天者，亦只合於發用或流行處置詞，其流行不已，發用無窮者，即天也。離發用流行而言天，天果何物乎？]

> *Tian* is not a divinity with personhood. It is without shape and appearance. Therefore, when we speak of *Tian*, this term should only be discussed on the level of functioning (*fayong* 發用) or operation (*liuxing* 流行). *Tian* is something with endless operation and limitless functioning. If we were to speak about *Tian* without functioning or operation, what would *Tian* be?[59]

In contrast, Noël's understanding was perhaps closer to the concept of a personal divinity that could be found in early primitive belief systems. In fact, however, Noël's understanding of *yi* 易 (change) was very close to that of the Song-Ming neo-Confucianism. Noël views the neo-Confucian concept of *xuyan* 虛言 (function word), which contrasts to *shiyan* 實言 (notional word) as an abstract and metaphysical discourse. In neo-Confucianism, *yi* 易 often does not indicate the actual *Yijing* or the sixty-four hexagrams, but rather is an abstract formulation that indicates the overall basic order of the entire universe in its unceasing generation and change. Its special characteristics include non-change (*buyi* 不易), changing into something else (*bianyi* 變易), and simple change (*jianyi* 簡易). With this meaning, *yi* is equivalent to *dao* 道 or *li* 理.[60]

In the School of Principle, *li* is opposed to *qi*. Noël understands *qi* as a sort of 'vital principle' and *li* as an 'intellectual principle' in opposition to it.[61] In particular, he cites a passage from the *Xingli daquan* 性理大全: '*qi* is *shen* (spirit)';[62] however, when Cheng Yi 程頤 (1033–1107) made this claim, he was not suggesting that *qi* was *shen* but rather that *shen* was in *qi*, and that there could be no *shen* without *qi*. To use a neo-Confucian mode of expression, the operation (*liuxing* 流行) of *qi* is

---

58 Mou Zongsan 牟宗三, *Zhongguo zhexue de tezhi* 中國哲學的特質, in *Mou Zongsan xiansheng quanji* 牟宗三先生全集, vol. 28, pp. 22–23.
59 Xiong Shili 熊十力, *Dujing shiyao* 讀經示要, in *Xiong Shili quanji* 熊十力全集, vol. 3 (Wuhan: Hubei jiaoyu chubanshe, 2001), p. 574.
60 Noël, 'Tractatus primus', p. 58 (c.2, q.1, §.8); this edition, p. 241.
61 See Thierry Meynard [Mei Qianli 梅謙立] and Wang Ge 王格, 'Chaoyue eryuan, mai xiang tongyi: Yesuhuishi Wei Fangji *Zhongguo zhexue* (1711 nian) ji qi Rujia quanshixue de chutan' 超越二元、邁向統一——耶穌會士衛方濟《中國哲學》（1711年）及其儒家詮釋學的初探, *Zhexue yu wenhua* 哲學與文化, 11 (2017), 45–61.
62 Noël, 'Tractatus primus', p. 75 (c.2, q.3, §.1); this edition, pp. 263–64.

shen. Indeed, this notion is based on the common idea of the relation between *li* and *qi* in Cheng-Zhu School of Principle: '*li* and *qi* are neither separate nor identical' (理、氣不離不雜). It is also internally consistent with the neo-Confucian theory concerning the operations of the Mandate of Heaven (天命流行). When citing this passage, Noël stresses its literal meaning,[63] but does not undertake any detailed study of its meaning in the neo-Confucian context. Hence he was unable to fully understand the meaning of 'the principle is one but its manifestations many' (理一分殊).[64]

As a matter of fact, in the Chinese Daoist tradition, *qi* or *xi* 息 (breath) is closely related to life, as illustrated in the chapter 'Xiaoyaoyou' 逍遙遊 (Carefree Wandering) of the *Zhuangzi* 莊子: 'living creatures are blown about with breath' (生物之以息相吹). The Daoist pranayama (*tiaoxi* 調息) significantly influenced neo-Confucianism, especially Zhu Xi's *Exhortation for Regulating Breath* (*Tiaoxi zhen* 調息箴).[65] Although the content of this work principally concerns breathing practices, it was based on Zhu Xi's theory of *qi*.

When citing Zhu Xi's claims that '*sheng* 生 (life) is called *qi*, and the *li* 理 (principle) of *sheng* is called *xing* 性 (nature)' (生之謂氣，生之理之謂性) and '*sheng* is the *qi* that people receive from *Tian*' (生者，人之所得於天之氣也), Noël could not avoid being perplexed and thinking that Chinese philosophy confuses these terms in many passages.[66] Since Zhu Xi's use of the term *sheng* here likely originates from the critique of Gaozi's claim that '*sheng* (life) is what we call *xing* (nature)' (生之謂性) in *Mencius* 11.3, here *sheng* is a vital energy or temperament, that is to say, the psychological characteristic of a person or even the material characteristic of a thing. Hence, *qi* is related with matter. However, the understanding of human life in Chinese philosophy included both the material or psychological dimension as well as a spiritual, intellectual and even moral dimensions. Chinese philosophy also viewed these elements as inseparable, fusing them into the harmonious unity of a substance. Human life participates in the totality of the universe and 'assists in the transforming and nourishing process of Heaven and Earth' (贊天地之化育, in *Zhongyong* 中庸 23). Only according to this meaning can we understand 'the operations of *qi*' (氣之流行), and then the 'Learning of Life' (*Shengming de xuewen* 生命的學問).[67] Nevertheless, Noël notes that *qi* has spiritual and vital elements, and thus does not consider *qi* in Chinese philosophy as mere materialism. This represents a greater deepening of Western understanding about Chinese philosophy. However, metaphysical theory in Chinese philosophy is never completely detached from material things, and *dao* 道 (way) or *li* is in material things. Therefore, Noël would discover with some puzzlement

---

63 Noël, 'Tractatus primus', p. 78 (c.2, q.3, §.2, T.26); this edition, p. 270.
64 Noël, 'Tractatus primus', pp. 139–40 (c.2, q.6, G.7 & L.11); this edition, pp. 344–46.
65 See Wu Zhen 吳震, 'Shen xin jifa "jingzuo":Shi xi zhuzixue de xiuyang lun' 身心技法：靜坐——試析朱子學的修養論, in *Zhuzi xuekan* 朱子學刊 (Hefei: Huangshan shushe, 2000), pp. 206–24.
66 Noël, 'Tractatus primus', p. 108 (c.2, q.5, §.1, K.11, L.12 & L.13); this edition, pp. 306–07.
67 See Mou Zongsan 牟宗三, *Shengming de xuewen* 生命的學問 (Guilin: Guangxi shifan daxue chubanshe, 2005), pp. 30–35, 61–68.

that for Chinese people the *guishen* seemingly cannot be detached from form.⁶⁸ In the same way, in seeing the ideal, natural and moral dimensions as equivalents to the neo-Confucian *Tian*, *xing* and *xin*,⁶⁹ Noël fundamentally misinterprets Cheng Yi's neo-Confucianism:

[心也，性也，天也，一理也。自理而言，謂之天；自稟受而言，謂之性；自存諸人而言，謂之心。]⁷⁰

> *Xin*, *xing*, and *Tian* are all the same *li*. When speaking about principle, it is called *Tian*; when speaking about temperament, it is called *xing*; when speaking about what is harboured inside people, it is called *xin*.

For Cheng Yi, *xin*, *xing*, and *Tian* are about the operation of the heavenly principle in uniting heaven and people. Only this is the true meaning of the *xing*: the heavenly decree and individuals below are interlinked and that which is possessed by individuals is *xing*. It is very different from Aquinas' theological system of natural law.

The Confucian tradition almost has no equivalent to Christianity's theory of Creation by God; however, *Tian* or *Di* (Emperor) still has priority. In neo-Confucianism, this priority is explained philosophically as a sort of 'logical priority', while the philosophical substance of the logical priority is 'ontological priority'.⁷¹ For this reason, when in neo-Confucianism *Tian* or *Di* is described as prior to all things, this should not be considered something which took place in space or time, but rather a sort of ontological exposition or metaphysical discourse. Creation in Christianity took place in time, and God's Creation really took place.⁷² Creationism is one of the central beliefs of Christianity. Above Noël mentions that he found vestiges of Creationism in his reading of the *Yijing* passage '*Di* comes forth in *Zhen*'. While it would have been very difficult for Noël to find any suitable correspondence to Creationism in neo-Confucian thought and texts, Noël realizes that *Tian* in neo-Confucianism is the reason for the generation of all things. He drew inspiration from this and even attempts to compare *taixu* 太虛, *yuanqi* 元氣, *tiandi* 天地, and *wanwu* 萬物 to the Creation process.⁷³ But when he addresses the term *zaohua* 造化, he understands it as *author*, which implies personhood and subjectivity.⁷⁴ In fact, *zaohua* in neo-Confucian discourse corresponds to a philosophy of 'observing things' (*guanwu* 觀物). Neo-Confucian philosophers engaged in the observation of 'the operating substance of Heavenly Mandate' (天命流行之體), such as Cheng Hao 程顥 (1032–1085) in the poem 'Autumn Day' (*Qiuri*

---

68 Noël, 'Tractatus primus', p. 133 (c.2, q.5, YY.55); this edition, p. 335.
69 Noël, 'Tractatus primus', p. 63 (c.2, q.2); this edition, p. 248.
70 Zhu Xi 朱熹, *Sishu zhangju jizhu* 四書章句集注 (Beijing: Zhonghua shuju, 1983), p. 349. For Noël's translation, see Noël, 'Tractatus primus', pp. 67–68 (c.2, q.2, E.13); this edition, p. 252.
71 See Su Dechao 蘇德超, 'Zai lun "luoji zaixian"' 再論「邏輯在先」, *Jiangsu shehui kexue* 江蘇社會科學, 4 (2011), pp. 8–13.
72 Noël, 'Tractatus primus', p. 7 (c.1, q.2, §.2); this edition, pp. 178–79.
73 Noël, 'Tractatus primus', pp. 75–76 (c.2, q.3, §.1, I.10); this edition, pp. 265–66.
74 Noël, 'Tractatus primus', pp. 92–93, 96, 101 (c.2, q.4, K.10 & Y.27); this edition, p. 286, 289–90, 294, 297.

秋日) wrote, 'When left alone, nature suffices in itself, resembling human life in that each of its four seasons has an enjoyable part'. (萬物靜觀皆自得，四時佳興與人同).[75] *Tian* in the School of Principle is *tianli* 天理 (heavenly principle), and the ruling master without a ruling master. However, this is precisely where neo-Confucianism differs from Christianity in the understanding of transcendence.

4.5 Conclusion

Longobardo and Noël considered the same texts, but their understanding and evaluation were diametrically opposed. This awkward situation would not have been unfamiliar to neo-Confucian scholars from the late Ming onwards. One way of resolving this difficulty would be to conduct textual research. When addressing the text, Noël simultaneously stresses the need to consider both the literal meaning of a text and the implications beyond this literal meaning. Gu Yanwu's assertion 'classical studies is the the School of Principle indeed', the emergence of textual studies in the mid Qing dynasty, and pan-Asian antiquity studies movement of the eighteenth century can all be considered as different approaches for solving this problem.[76] Another approach would be through pure philosophical argumentation. Noël borrows concepts from the scholastic tradition, especially Aquinas' theological system, to syncretic exposition of neo-Confucianism, especially the Cheng-Zhu School of Principle. He pays particular attention to Cai Qing, who was Zhu Xi's most influential follower in the Ming dynasty, because in his exposition of many neo-Confucian categories Cai Qing employs an inclusive hierarchy to syncretize the many points of divergence in the Confucian tradition, such as those relating to *taixu*, *taiji* and *guishen*.[77]

Noël's *Philosophia Sinica* was born in the age of the early Enlightenment when globalization had already begun. Noël's exposure to various cultures of the world, especially the ancient civilization of East and West, gave him a broad perspective and understanding.[78] For example, he used a poem from Mexico as an example to illustrate the metaphorical use of the world 'heaven' in various cultural traditions throughout the world.[79] He firmly believed that both Eastern and Western sages, as

---

75 English translated by Lü Danian 呂大年.
76 See Wang Ge 王格, 'Yesuhuishi *Lunyu* fanyi (1687 nian) zhong de "guxue" qingxiang' 耶穌會士《論語》翻譯（1687年）中的「古學」傾向, *Xixue dongjian yanjiu* 西學東漸研究, vol. 6 (Beijing: The Commercial Press, 2017), pp. 109–23.
77 For discussion, see Thierry Meynard [Mei Qianli 梅謙立] and Wang Ge 王格, 'Chaoyue eryuan, mai xiang tongyi: Yesuhuishi Wei Fangji Zhongguo zhexue (1711 nian) ji qi Rujia quanshixue de chutan'; Thierry Meynard [Mei Qianli 梅謙立], 'Yesuhuishi Wei Fangji dui guishen de lijie' 耶穌會士衛方濟對鬼神的理解, *Beijing xingzheng xueyuan xuebao* 北京行政學院學報, 5 (2018), pp. 110–15; Thierry Meynard, 'François Noël's Contribution to the Western Understanding of Chinese Thought: *Taiji sive natura* in the *Philosophia Sinica* (1711)', *DAO: A Journal of Comparative Philosophy*, 17 (2018), 219–30.
78 Noël, 'Praefatio', p. (a)3; this edition, pp. 165–66.
79 Noël, 'Tractatus primus', pp. 25–26 (c.1, q.3, III); this edition, pp. 202–03.

well as people of past and present, all share the same mind and rational faculties.[80] This is the open-minded attitude of a cosmopolite in the age of globalization. Because of circumstances outside of Noël's control, when the *Philosophia Sinica* was published in 1711, it did not achieve the success that it should have achieved. However, as Europe entered deeper into the age of the Enlightenment, other translations of Chinese translations filled the void.

---

80 Noël, 'Tractatus primus', p. 87 (c.2, q.3, §.3, Z.33); this edition, pp. 276–77.

PIERRE GALASSI

5. Theological Themes in the First Treatise

5.1 A Broader Perspective: Sapiential Realism

> That which is last with respect to all human knowledge is that which is knowable first and chiefly in its nature. And concerning these there is 'wisdom, which considers the highest causes', as stated in the *Metaphysics* [I. I, 2, 981b28; 982b9]. Therefore it rightly judges all things and sets them in order, because there can be no perfect and universal judgment that is not resolved into first causes. But in regard to that which is last in this or that genus of knowable things, it is science that perfects the intellect. Therefore according to the different genera of knowable things, there are different habits of sciences; although there is but one wisdom.[1]

In recent years much has been written on Second Scholasticism: that is, the revival and reform of scholastic thought. In this scholarship, however, there is a relative lack of reflection on how Second Scholasticism informed the development of evangelic methods in the Jesuit China mission. The abundance of specialist studies on the Jesuit China mission have privileged historical approaches over theological reflection. This chapter proposes that a closer analysis of the Thomistic-realist background of this mission can shed light on inculturation, interculturality, and evangelization. Since this multidisciplinary field of study oscillates between theology and philosophy, as well as history and Sinology, a critical evaluation that goes beyond historical or comparativist approaches is needed to obtain a broader perspective, which can be called, according to the definition given by the Dominican theologian Antonio Olmi, 'sapiential realism'.[2]

This perspective allows us to catch a glimpse of that thread connecting the theology of Aquinas, the mysticism of Ignatius of Loyola, the missionary method of Matteo Ricci and his followers in the East, and the intellectual output of François

---

[1] Aquinas, *Summa theologiae*, I^a–II^{ae}, q.57, a.2, resp. The English translations of the *Summa* have been drawn from *The Summa Theologica of Saint Thomas Aquinas*, trans. by the Fathers of the English Dominican Province, rev. by Daniel J. Sullivan, 2 vols (Chicago: Encyclopaedia Britannica, 1952), II, p. 36.
[2] For a complete exposition and application of this vision both to Aquinas and Matteo Ricci, see Antonio Olmi, *P. Matteo Ricci e san Tommaso d'Aquino* (Bologna: Edizioni Studio Domenicano, 2020).

Pierre Galassi, Theological Faculty of Emilia Romagna, Bologna, Italy

Noël. Of course, we need not seek only explicit connections, because this perspective permeates Catholic thought as a *Weltanschauung*:

> Adopting this approach, in thought and in life, means accepting all the original certainties and the first principles of implicit philosophy (the most important of which is the 'primacy of reality'), and being willing to know reality itself not simply with the help of 'natural' reason (concrete but limited), or 'scientific' reason (rigorous but also limited), or 'philosophical' reason (rigorous but abstract), but by means of 'sapiential' reason. Aimed only at the search for the truth that is good and the good that is true, this mode of reason is more analogue than analytical, synthetic or dialectical; it signals instead of demonstrating; it 'tastes' the truth instead of 'seeing it'; and in order to express this ineffable sentiment, use thought to force words to go beyond thought and words directly to the heart of the created reality and mystery of the Creator.[3]

Sapiential realism underlies the mission of many Jesuits in China, especially that of Matteo Ricci, and can also be identified at the origin of the Society itself and, above all, of the personality of Ignatius of Loyola. This chapter synthesizes this Ignatian-Thomistic contribution to the Jesuit mission in China through the lens of two fundamental dimensions: the logic of Incarnation and the method of accommodation.

According to Aquinas, the logic of the Incarnation can be likened to a principle of universal order that starts from the frank consideration of the 'condition of human nature to which it is proper to be led by things corporeal and sensible to things spiritual and intelligible'.[4] This relation between the Eternal Mystery and the created reality has meant that this cornerstone of the Christian faith also became, in a certain sense, a worldview or a thought and an attitude:[5] 'Not to be restrained by the greater, but to be contained by the smaller, this is divine' (*Non coerceri a maximo, contineri tamen a minimo, divinum est*).[6]

The method of accommodation was famously applied by Alessandro Valignano (1539–1606), and above all Matteo Ricci (1552–1610), who affirmed: 'I accommodated myself to them [the Chinese] in everything, when necessary, I have adapted the sayings and sentences of our philosophers and some things taken from our own'.[7] However, the Ignatian source of this method is much less well known.[8] This rhetorical strategy finds expression in many of the twenty Introductory Explanations to

---

3 Olmi, P. *Matteo Ricci e san Tommaso d'Aquino*, pp. 147–48. The translation is mine.
4 Aquinas, *Summa theologiae*, III^a, q.61, a. 1, resp.
5 For a broader perspective Ignatius of Loyola, *Spiritual Exercises and Selected Works*, ed. by George E. Ganns (New York: Paulist Press, 1991).
6 *Elogium sepulcrale S. Ignatii*, in *Imago primi saeculi Societatis Iesu* (Antwerp: Officina Plantiniana, 1640), p. 280.
7 Matteo Ricci, 'Letter to Fr. Girolamo Costa S. J., 14 August 1599', in *Lettere (1580–1609)*, ed. by Francesco D'Arelli (Macerata: Quodlibet, 2001), p. 363.
8 For further study on this topic, see Stephen Schloesser, 'Accommodation as a Rhetorical Principle: Twenty Years after John O'Malley's The First Jesuits (1993)', *Journal of Jesuit Studies*, 1 (2014), 347–72.

the Spiritual Exercises.⁹ For example, Ignatius insists that 'the Spiritual Exercises should be adapted to the disposition of the persons who desire to make them, that is, to their age, education, and ability'.¹⁰ In particular, the realistic enhancement of human nature and its relation with Grace has led the history of the Society of Jesus, and above all of its missionary component, to elaborate positions and methods of evangelization which also found application in the East:

> The basic assumption of the compatibility between 'nature and grace', between 'reason and revelation' that underlay the Thomistic synthesis coincided with the Jesuits' conviction that in their pastoral activities they should not only rely upon God's grace but also use all the 'human means' at their disposal, as the Constitutions prescribed. [...] Intimately related to the Thomistic assumption that 'grace perfects nature' was an understanding of the relationship between grace and 'free will' that allowed for human activity under the influence of grace. In this view, the will was wounded and enfeebled by Original Sin, but not vitiated or destroyed. Grace, always the primary factor, allowed the will to 'cooperate' with it, so that in some mysterious way human responsibility played its part in the process of salvation.¹¹

This basic sapiential realism in the Society found correspondence in Aquinas' thought, which the Jesuits assumed without hesitation from the Society's foundation despite their reservations about restricting themselves to a particular school of theology.¹²

The various versions of the Jesuit curriculum or *Ratio studiorum* followed the same line, although they also included a broader range of Renaissance authors.¹³ In fact, the theological formation described in the *Ratio studiorum* was structured around the scheme of the *Summa theologiae*,¹⁴ which contributed to the replacement of Peter Lombardo's *Liber sententiarum*. For instance, the *Ratio studiorum* of 1599 requests that professors 'follow [...] entirely the doctrine of St Thomas [Aquinas] in scholastic theology, consider him as their own teacher and do everything possible so that the disciples are fond of him'.¹⁵

By Noël's time more than a century had passed since the writing of this *Ratio Studiorum*, and in the meantime the thought of Francisco Suárez had become dominant in the Jesuit order. In highlighting the differences and continuities

---

9   Ignatius of Loyola, *Spiritual Exercises*, pp. 121–28 (§ § 1–20).
10 Ignatius of Loyola, *Spiritual Exercises*, p. 126 (§ 18).
11 John W. O'Malley, *The First Jesuits* (Cambridge, MA: Harvard University Press, 1993), p. 249.
12 O'Malley, *The First Jesuits*, p. 247. See also *The Constitutions of the Society of Jesus and Their Complementary Norms*, ed. by John W. Padberg (Saint Louis: Institute of Jesuit Source, 1996), p. 156.
13 These texts can be found in *Ratio atque institutio studiorum Societatis Iesu (1586, 1591, 1599)*, ed. by Ladislaus Lukàcs, vol. 5 of *Monumenta paedagogica Societatis Iesu*, 7 vols (Rome: Institutum Historicum Societatis Iesu, 1986).
14 *Ratio atque institutio studiorum Societatis Iesu (1586, 1591, 1599)*, pp. 7–13.
15 *Ratio atque institutio studiorum Societatis Iesu (1586, 1591, 1599)*, p. 386.

between Aquinas' thought and Suárez's elaboration of it,[16] the most important point is to maintain the perspective of sapiential realism.

5.2. *Materia Sinica – Forma Scholastica*

Although less read than his other works, the *Philosophia Sinica* is arguably Noël's most important work. The title of the work reveals how Noël confronts and exhibits Chinese thought through typical scholastic categories and discourse. The Flemish Jesuit also employs a scholastic structure to develop his argumentation: the work is divided into treatises (*tractatus*), consisting of chapters (*capita*), which are further divided into issues (*quaestiones*). Each issue sometimes further subdivided into paragraphs (*paragraphi*) and occasionally in detailed points (*puncta*). The Third Treatise (*De ethica sinensi*) is also divided into three parts (*partes*), the chapters of which are further subdivided into sections (*sectiones*), followed by the same divisions used in the two previous Treaties.

The systematic discussion of each topic borders on rigidity. Each topic is structured around a supporting thesis, which include letters serving as cross references to the citations from Chinese-language works inserted at the end of each section (*textus librorum*).

Despite being titled *Philosophia Sinica*, the long and detailed index of the work reveals that Noël does not restrict himself to philosophical discussion, but considers also the questions that often arise in the interstices between philosophy and theology. This was not unusual, since contemporary treatises often did not make rigid disciplinary distinctions. However, the title was probably prudential political choice made in light of the fact that discussion of the Chinese Rites had been prohibited by the decree *Cum Deus optimus* of 1704. A more outspoken theological title addressing taboo issues, such as Chinese monotheism or the civil nature of Chinese rituals, would have raised the ire of the authorities and prevented the publication of Noël's work.

The index also helps us to identify Noël's method and his key points. The first treatise, *De cognitione primi Entis, seu Dei apud Sinas*, elaborates a natural theology from ancient and modern Chinese sources. The first chapter, which is divided into three *quaestiones*, discusses whether the ancient Chinese possessed an idea of God (First Being), or whether they were atheist. Noël first considers the multiple meanings of the term *Tian* 天 in ancient books; then he reviews the

---

16 For the Spanish Jesuit's thought on religion and preaching, see Robert Fastiggi, 'Francisco Suárez and the Non-Believers', *Pensamiento: Revista de Investigación e Información Filosófica*, 74.279 (2018), 263–70; Aaron Pidel, 'Francisco Suárez on Religion and Religious Pluralism', in *Francisco Suárez (1548–1617): Jesuits and the Complexities of Modernity*, ed. by Robert Alexander Maryks and Juan Antonio Senent de Frutos (Leiden: Brill, 2019), pp. 128–53. For the relevance of Suárez's thought to the Jesuit mission in China, Iralia Morali, '*Religioni ac bonis artibus*: l' "apostolato scientifico" dei Gesuiti in Cina', in *Pianeta Galileo 2009*, ed. by Alberto Peruzzi (Florence: Regione Toscana – Consiglio Regionale, 2009), pp. 399–415.

perfectiones or attributes of *Tian* and the classic term *Shangdi* 上帝 in the footsteps of the scholastic tradition; finally he offers a synthetic assessment in response to the question of ancient Chinese theism. The same pattern is repeated for the treatment of modern Chinese theism (*recentiores*). The catalogue of divine attributes according to these authors is followed by six other important questions concerning the different meanings of *Tian* and *Shangdi*, the recognition of a First Principle as the basis of reality, the notion and division of spirits in Chinese cosmology, the role of *jiaoshe* 郊社 (an important sacrificial ceremony offered once a year by the emperor to Heaven and Earth), and the correct interpretation of *taiji* 太極 (Supreme Ultimate). It concludes, like the first chapter, with a synthetic response to the question of whether the contemporary Chinese know God. The third chapter discusses the question of the divine names of *Tian* and *Shangdi*, and concludes with the famous declaration of the Kangxi 康熙 Emperor on the correct meaning of these divine names.

5.3. Divine Names – Divine Attributes

As for the link between the divine name and the knowability of the divine essence, Noël refers to the etymological, patristic, and Thomistic-Suárezian understanding of the divine name as indicating the divine substance starting from the divine operation. Interestingly, however, when comparing the Western and Chinese names for God, the Flemish Jesuit makes the classical distinction between the proper and common name for God, the latter of which is more suitable for transposing the name of the Christian God to the Chinese context. Noël's thesis insists on the licitness of converging the terms *Deus* (Θεός) and *Shangdi* 上帝, as *nomina appellativa et communia*. The risk lies in the possibility that both terms may be juxtaposed with proper names of deities, and thus be misunderstood as idolatrous:

> *Shangdi* is the name of an idol. Therefore, God cannot be called by this name, just as God cannot be called Jupiter, since this is the name of an idol. I answer that *Shangdi* is not the proper name of the idol but rather the epithet of an idol. The proper name of the idol Yuhuang or rather the person living at the end of the Han dynasty was Zhang Yi. He lacked an honorific because he was a common man (I). However, Jupiter is a proper name which is not shared by anybody else. Surely, the true divinity can be called with the name an idol because in the Church's earliest period the same word *deus* was used to express Jupiter, Saturn, Apollo and other idols, as well as the true divinity of the Christians.[17]

A lengthy selection of biblical, patristic, and theological sources follows to confirm this thesis.[18] The procedural basis of these passages is deeply Thomistic.[19] According

---

17   Noël, 'Tractatus primus', p. 159 (c.3, q.1, §.2); this edition, p. 373.
18   Noël, 'Tractatus primus', p. 159 (c.3, q.1, §.2); this edition, p. 373.
19   Aquinas, *Summa theologiae*, Iª, q.13, a.9, ad 2.

to Aquinas, *Deus* is not the proper name of God, because a proper name is something exclusive, while a common name is inclusive. Now, since *deus* can be used in relation to false gods, *deus* is an analogous name. *Deus* only signifies the Christian God by convention. The proper, exclusive name of God is 'Being itself subsisting by itself' (*Ipsum esse per se subsistens*), because there can only be one proper name, and this corresponds to the expression used in Exodus 3:14 (*Ego sum qui sum*).[20]

Following this logic we can understand why Noël does not consider here terms like *Caelum* even though the Chinese call God *Tian* 天. The operation is precisely the opposite: Noël does not claim that what Christians call in Latin *Deus* is the same as what the Chinese call *Tian* 天, but that what the Chinese call *Tian* corresponds to what the Christians call *Deus*. The logic of appropriation is reversed because Noël does not stick a Christian label on Chinese terms, but tries to elicit the implicit Christian connotations of some Chinese divine names. Moreover, this also emerges from the titles of the *quaestiones* of the First Treatise: 'What perfections do the ancient (*antiqui*) and modern (*recentiores*) attribute to *Tian* (Heaven) and *Shangdi* (Lord and Ruler of Heaven)?'[21]

The partition of attributes indicates that we are not faced with a criterion for assessing what the Chinese refer to but a correspondence of terms (*correspondentia terminorum*) for the divine names. Moreover, the sequence of attributes is almost entirely drawn from the Chinese texts themselves, thus implying that the God presented here is the God as known by the Chinese themselves, and not merely a scholastic interpretation of Chinese theism.[22] It is precisely in this respect that Noël differs from the procedure of Aquinas and Suárez. Hence the common ground between Aquinas, Suárez, and Noël must be sought in their common background in metaphysical realism rather than a common language or methodology.

The sequence of divine perfections that Noël elaborates follows neither the schema of Aquinas nor that of Suárez. Divine perfections, in Christian theology, are innumerable, and it would be a vain undertaking to attempt a complete enumeration. However, some perfections, which are called 'attributes', are recognized as being of fundamental importance, although there is no strict agreement on their number or classification. Aquinas' classification, which has become conventional, is based on the analogy of entitative and operative perfections in creatures: the former qualifies God's very nature or essence as abstracted from activity, whereas the latter refers specifically to the activity of His nature.

Now, Aquinas' first proof of God's existence comes to show that 'it is necessary to arrive at a first mover which is moved by no other. And this everyone understands to be God'.[23] This unmoved mover is pure actuality or act, because it moves (and

---

20 Aquinas, *Summa theologiae*, I^a, q.13.
21 Noël, 'Tractatus primus', p. 2 (c.1, q.2); this edition, p. 171; Noël, 'Tractatus primus', p. 29 (c.2, q.1); this edition, p. 204.
22 Noël Probably draws on the work *Ditian kao* 帝天考 (*c.* 1680s) [Study on *Di* and *Tian*] by Christian Paul Yan Mo 嚴謨, especially for the order and typology of sources mentioned, as well as for their classification according to theological themes corresponding to the Western classification of divine attributes.
23 Aquinas, *Summa theologiae*, I^a, q.2, a.3, resp.

therefore is act) but is not moved (so there is no transition from potency to act). Starting from the idea of pure act, Aquinas deduces that God is absolutely simple. However, in the paragraph on the attribute of simplicity, Noël seems to deduce simplicity from divine spirituality, quoting in this passage Aquinas himself:

> In order to prove the simplicity of God, Saint Thomas says that God is Spirit: 'God is spirit' (Job 6). Indeed, a spirit is not made of quantitative parts, and therefore it is simple and much more noble than a body, because the spirit is the means with which a body lives.[24]

On closer examination, Noël's reasoning turns out to be exactly the opposite: he does not prove God's simplicity from spirituality — which at best implies incorporeality, that is, a form of simplicity — but he derives spirituality from simplicity.[25] Only after stating that God, as pure act, cannot contain any potency, and that without potency there can be no matter, does Noël come to immateriality, incorporeality and finally spirituality. Hence it is from the absolute simplicity of God that additional attributes are derived.

Simplicity excludes potency and composition; since the first level of potency is the hylomorphic compound, whereby matter lies in form just as potency is in act, if there is no potency in God, then God is pure form, and therefore immaterial and incorporeal.[26] Also excluded is the composition of subject and essence, which are related to each other as potency to act. Therefore, for the divinity, form is an essence that identifies with the subject. Moreover, there can be no composition between essence and act of being, since the essence that exists inheres in the act of being like potency in the act. Excluding this composition, it is concluded that God is 'Being itself subsisting by itself', that is His metaphysical proper name.

This metaphysical identification between God and Being lyrically echoed in the Latin translation of the Nestorian Stele cited by Noël:[27]

> An ancient stone recording the entry of Christianity in China[28] begins as follows: 'I attentively contemplate the true and perpetual Tranquility [*ji*], the Being which precedes all beginnings, itself without beginning, spiritual and empty [*lingxu*] like something very profound, the most universal, perfect, mysterious Ultimate of all things [*xuanshu*] and the efficient Cause [*zaohua*] which adorns and perfects all the Saints through its exemplary and grand

---

24 Noël, 'Tractatus primus', p. 21 (c.1, q.2, §.8); this edition, p. 198. The biblical reference is wrongly attributed to Job, whereas it's a quote from John 4:24.
25 Aquinas, *Summa theologiae*, Iª, q.3.
26 Aquinas, *Summa theologiae*, Iª, aa.1–2.
27 For Noël this source served as 'a proof that God had and has different names and circumscriptions in China'. See Collani, 'François Noël and his treatise on God in China', p. 58.
28 This section L.20 is not present in the Roman manuscript and was later added by Noël. The Chinese text of the Nestorian stele was published by Li Zhizao in 1625. Nicolas Trigault, Michael Boym, and Antonio de Gouvea made Latin translations. The Chinese and Syrian texts with the Latin translation was first published in Europe by Athanasius Kircher in his *Monumenta Sinica* (Amsterdam, 1667). In translating those few excerpts here, Noël does not copy other translations but proposes his own translation.

Majesty [*yuanzun*]. Can this be that I (I am who I am),[29] Three and One, the most perfect substance [*miaoshen*] without beginning, the true Lord [*zhenzhu*], Eloho [*Aluoheyu*]?'[30]

In God being and essence coincide, and consequently so do will, intelligence, science, knowledge, etc. This Thomistic awareness is implicit in the exposition of divine attributes, when Noël states, for example, that 'since the knowledge and power of God are interrelated attributes and knowledge extends itself to everything that power does',[31] or elsewhere, 'God's understanding is His living'.[32]

The operative attributes are found among the attributes derived from immateriality. Immateriality is a condition of knowability and knowledge, because Aquinas' Treatise on Man in the *Summa* considers becoming the other as the condition of knowledge.[33] This point, which is important for the metaphysical substratum of the *Philosophia Sinica*, needs clarification. Aristotle states the following about divine knowledge:

> *Itself*, therefore, is what it thinks, seeing that it is the greatest thing, and its thinking is a thinking of thinking [νόησις νοήσεως] […]. Since what is thought and the intellect are not, then, different, in respect of things which have no matter, they will be the same thing; and its thinking will be one with what is thought. A yet further difficulty remains, if what is thought is composite: for it would change in the parts of the whole. Or is everything which has no matter indivisible? — as human intellect, or at least the intellect of composites, is in this condition in some period of time (for it does not have the good in this or in that, but has the best in some whole, being something other than itself), so its thinking is in this condition, being itself of itself, throughout all time.[34]

Knowledge is possible only in the immaterial order, because in materiality, when one thing becomes another, it ceases to be itself, just as burning wood becomes ash; on the contrary, man does not become red when he knows what 'red' is, but remains substantially unchanged in the cognitive act: only his intellect is changed by the other. If God is absolutely immaterial, He is absolute knowledge and absolutely knowable, because immateriality is the condition of knowledge and knowability; God knows absolutely himself and is, as Aristotle says, 'Thought of Thought' (νόησις νοήσεως or *intelligentia intelligentiae*). This Aristotelian elaboration should not be understood in a conceptualist or rationalist sense, and can provide an evocative point of comparison with Chinese thought. In fact, to properly understand scholastic

---

29 Exodus 3:4: 'Sum qui sum'. This is the Latin version of YHWH, the name God.
30 Noël, 'Tractatus primus', p. 69 (c.2, q.2, L.20); this edition, pp. 254–55.
31 Noël, 'Tractatus primus', p. 9 (c.1, q.3, §.8); this edition, p. 183.
32 Noël, 'Tractatus primus', p. 17 (c.1, q.2, §.6); this edition, p. 193.
33 Aquinas, *Summa theologiae*, I^a, q.79, a.3.
34 Aristotle, *Metaphysics: Book Λ*, trans. and ed. by Lindsay Judson (Oxford: Clarendon Press, 2019), pp. 38–39 (1074b31–1075a10).

terms such as *intelligere*, *ratio*, and the like you have to understand their realist implications. In this lies Aquinas' great metaphysical achievement, as Bernard Lonergan explains:

> 'In his quae sunt sine materia, idem est intelligens et intellectum'.³⁵ [...] If you object that modern interpreters translate *noesis noeseos* as 'thinking thought', I readily grant what this implies, namely, that modern interpreters suppose Aristotle to have been a conceptualist. But also I retort that medieval translators did not write 'cogitatio cogitationis' but 'intelligentia intelligentiae'. It seems to follow that medieval translators did not regard Aristotle as a conceptualist. Aquinas accepted and developed Aristotle. [...] Aquinas transposed this appeal into his own 'participatio creata lucis increatae' to secure for the Aristotelian theory of knowing by identity the possibility of self-transcendence in finite intellect. On his own, Aquinas identified intelligible species with intellectual habit to relate species to *intelligere* as form to *esse*, a parallel that supposes a grasp of the real distinction between finite essence and existence. [...] Sense differs from the sensible, intellect differs from the intelligible, only inasmuch as they are in potency. But in God there is no potency. Hence in God substance, essence, esse, intellect, species, *intelligere* are all one and the same.³⁶

Returning to the entitative attributes, Aquinas, after stating that God is the 'Being itself subsisting by itself' that exists, claims that it possible to establish that God is also the Supreme Good, because 'being and good (and true) are convertibile' (*ens et bonum et verum convertuntur*), and therefore God is also Goodness itself.³⁷ God is also infinite,³⁸ not in the sense of something indeterminate, but in the sense of perfection, since if God is the absolute being, you cannot subtract anything from Him or add add anything to Him.

Turning more specifically to the operative attributes, it can be noted that, with regard to the attribute of divine justice, Noël agrees with Aquinas that distributive justice is the only kind of justice attributable to God independently. In fact, God can certainly not be assigned retributive justice, since all creation comes from God and only creatures can return to God and not the other way round. The fact that Noël mentions *superjustitia* — a term absent in Aquinas — probably implies that all the divine attributes are understood eminently (*super* or ὑπέρ), as in Neoplatonic philosophy:

---

35 Aristotle, *De Anima*, trans. and ed. by Mark Shiffman (Newburyport: Focus Publishing R Pullins Co, 2011), p. 86 (III.4, 430a3–5).
36 Bernard Lonergan, *Word and Idea in Aquinas*, ed. by Frederick E. Crowe and Robert M. Doran (Toronto: Lonergan Research Institute – University of Toronto Press, 2005), pp. 196–97.
37 Aquinas, *Summa theologiae*, Iª, qq.5–6.
38 Aquinas, *Summa theologiae*, Iª, q.7.

> According to Saint Thomas, the distributive justice of God, or rather His super-justice, is that which gives to all according to their merit: namely, reward to the good, and punishment to the bad.[39]

A final reflection on the operative attribute of divine dominion deserves our attention:

> As they say, when the Supreme Heaven appoints kings to rule and doctors to teach the people whom It produces, Its only intention is that that the kings and doctors transmit and spread the correct way of living, in Its name as Its assistants, helping the Lord of Heaven [*Shangdi*] in what He cannot reach (A). When producing man, Heaven first endowed him with sensible matter (*materia sensibilis*) to form his body and then infused into him right reason to establish his rational nature. The correct reason, insofar as it is in Heaven, is the first, participative, directive and perfective power of Heaven. Insofar as it is in human beings, [the correct reason] is a human being's innate duty, justice, honesty and intelligence, or rather, the natural seeds of duty, justice, honesty and intelligence. The infusion and reception of reason is like a commandment imposed by Heaven, and can be called the Law of Heaven (B).[40]

Then he makes the following analogy of proportionality: Heaven stands for eternal law (*lex aeterna*), just as right reason (*recta ratio*) stands for natural law (*lex naturalis*), and the Emperor, in turn, who is a member of the world's government as vicar of Heaven, bears the seeds of eternal law. This structure is perfectly Thomist: human nature, which is infused with virtues, participates in a right reason of Heaven (*lex coelestis*), just as natural law is a reflection of the eternal law in human nature:

> Generally speaking, the Law of Heaven or infused reason of nature encompasses all created things, but understood specifically, it is the lucid and intelligent faculty which encompasses only human beings (C). Saint Thomas affirms in questions 90 and 91 of the *Prima Secundae* that the law is something rational and that the eternal law is the idea of governing things, in God as a Ruler, or a reason of divine wisdom directing all actions and motions. [He adds that] the natural law within us is a participation in the eternal law by which all things are regulated towards their own end, but the rational creature [is regulated] in a more excellent way insofar as it provides both for itself and for others, as well as that this natural human law is 'a dictate of practical reason', namely that it is impressed by God, instructing under obligation to perform or avoid actions. These principles of Saint Thomas appear to match closely the principles given by the Chinese commentators in relation to the Law of Heaven.[41]

In the final passage, the Emperor is also subject to natural law. It is no coincidence that Noël links this lengthy comparison, which is enriched by different sources, to the parable of the Prodigal Son (Luke 15:18). This parable contains a double

---

39 Noël, 'Tractatus primus', p. 14 (c.1, q.2, §.5); this edition, p. 189.
40 Noël, 'Tractatus primus', pp. 29–30 (c.2, q.1, §.1); this edition, p. 207.
41 Noël, 'Tractatus primus', p. 30 (c.2, q.1, §.1); this edition, p. 207.

confession: the son first converts inwardly and then manifests his repentance to his father. In this same way, Noël suggests that in Chinese thought there are two closely united dimensions: consciousness (the inner law of man's heart) and the cosmos (outer or celestial law). This passage also echoes the Chinese awareness that the breakdown of human relations and fidelity to right reason also implies a rupture with Heaven:

> From this you see that the kings and doctors of the people are appointed by Heaven or the supreme Lord, that Heaven produces the human body and infuses the rational nature, that on a general level the Law of Heaven is understood to be reason infused with nature and on a specific level is understood to be a reason endowed with lucid and intelligent nature. Thus, whoever transgresses reason sins against Heaven. Offerings are made to Heaven as the Lord, the intelligent Spirit, the Author of things. Heaven is above and obeyed by emperors. The emperors of the first three dynasties served Heaven. I ask you, can there be a clearer affirmation about God as Lord? Did not the prodigal son in the Gospel of Luke 15[:21] say, 'Father, I sinned against Heaven and against you?'[42]

The fundamental consequence emerges that the Emperor acts honestly only when he applies heavenly law. This means that in its own way Chinese thought, just as Western thought, distinguishes between political power and celestial power; moreover, it entails that the actions of the emperor are conditioned and bound by respect for the Mandate of Heaven (*Tianming* 天命), which reveals a surprising correspondence with the 'universal medieval belief that commands of princes contrary to natural law were not binding on their subjects, and could therefore lawfully be resisted'.[43]

Even among the Chinese, Noël says, the law of Heaven is the eternal law; secondly, natural law would be nothing more than a reflection of the eternal-heavenly law in human natural reason; finally there is the emperor who is vicar of Heaven with his Law. This is true not because the emperor is the perfect realization of the heavenly law, but because the first realization of eternal law in the world is what is infused as proportion/order (*ut ratio*) in the nature of things and above all as right reason (*ut recta ratio*) in men. Such a consideration accurately reflects the same operation as Aquinas in treating natural law in its relation with the eternal law.

---

42 Noël, 'Tractatus primus', p. 31 (c.2, q.1, §.1); this edition, p. 208.
43 Joseph Needham, *Science and Civilization in China. Volume 2: History of Scientific Thought* (Cambridge: Cambridge University Press, 1959), pp. 537–38.

5.4. Taiji 太極 as ἀρχή – yin 陰 and yang 陽 as Transcendental Relations

Fundamental to understanding the theology of the *Philosophia Sinica* is Noël's discussion of the translatability of the term *taiji* 太極 (Supreme Ultimate) and its possible Western equivalences in question 6 of chapter 2 of the First Treatise. Noël renders this in Latin as *primus rerum terminus*, which literally translates as 'First Term of Things'. For Noël, this term encompasses the same polysemia implied by the Western term nature (φύσις), which requires a preliminary clarification:

> 'Nature' comes from the Latin root **gna*, which means 'generation', hence *nasci*, 'come to be by generation'; similarly the corresponding Greek word, φύσις, belongs to the root φύω, 'to generate'. The way and time in which the thing is generated, and above all what it derives determine what the thing itself is, its essence (which as such is what it consists of) is nature as a principle of action, of behaviour (*naturum* = what is about to be born, which is destined to be born, to bloom, and also what it is going to generate, from which *natura naturans* = generating nature, which is expressed by generating, producing). The meaning of nature is first and foremost specified in two general semantic classes, depending on whether the emphasis is placed on all the things that have come to light, or on the intrinsic principle that each thing blooms, comes to light. We talk about nature in the first sense whenever by nature we mean natural things [...]. We talk about nature in the second sense when [...] we do not identify nature with the things themselves, but from them we go back to the immanent principle that each is what it is and acts in the way it acts. The contrast between nature in the first sense and nature in the latter sense can be likened to the contrast between nature considered in material terms (*natura materialiter spectata*) and nature considered in formal terms (*natura formaliter spectata*) — in other words, the contrast between *natura naturata* and *natura naturans*.[44]

Even with this common definition of nature, it must be noted that even in Aquinas this term can cause confusion between the first cause (*causa prima*) and secondary causes.[45] In fact, the blurring of this distinction was diffused in Noël's intellectual context, particularly in the work of Baruch Spinoza.[46] It is no coincidence that in the late seventeenth century and eighteenth century there was extensive philosophical and theological discussion on parallels between Chinese thought and Spinozism.[47] In this historical perspective can be understood Noël's lexical

---

[44] Augusto Guzzo, Vittorio Mathieu, and Virgilio Melchiorre, 'NATURA (*nature; Natur; nature; naturaleza*)', in *Enciclopedia filosofica*, ed. by Centro di Studi Filosofici di Gallarate, 12 vols (Milan: Bompiani, 2008), VIII, p. 7729.

[45] Aquinas, *Summa theologiae*, I[a]– II[ae], q.85, a.6, resp.

[46] Guzzo, Mathieu, and Melchiorre, 'NATURA (*nature; Natur; nature; naturaleza*)', pp. 7739–40.

[47] For an overview of the topic, see Thijs Weststeijn, 'Spinoza sinicus: An Asian Paragraph in the History of the Radical Enlightenment', *Journal of the History of Ideas*, 68.4 (2007), 537–61.

choices for translating the notion of a first constitutive principle of reality that is present in Chinese thought.

Having supposed the overlap between *natura* and *taiji*, Noël then lists the possible meanings:

> Please note that [Western] philosophers understand the concept of nature in many ways. First, nature may be God, or the Creator of all things, called *natura naturans*, in contrast with Creation called *natura naturata*. Second, nature may be the essence of a thing. Third, it may be the total aggregate of the natural agents. Fourth, it may be the birth or generation of life, arising from an internal principle of a thing. Fifth, it is an internal principle by which something is first moved. According to the Coimbra commentaries, this principle resides in living and non-living things. Aristotle adopts the fifth meaning, defining nature as the principle and cause of motion and rest, by itself and not by accident. You should understand motion as any change, successive or instantaneous, insofar as motion can be called *actio* or *passio*. You should understand rest as something positive, like the preservation of the end acquired through motion. […] Since Aristotle defined nature as an essential part of a complete substance, it is clear that, in this meaning, neither God nor angels can be properly called nature. However, due to a similarity with true nature, inasmuch as God and angels are the principle of operations of the whole, they can be loosely called nature. Hence we often speak of 'divine nature' or 'angelic nature', even though they lack the conditions required for nature. Now that I have finished discussing these preliminary points, I can respond to the question above. I argue that *taiji*, or the First Ultimate, can be best understood as nature explained here in various ways.[48]

The first meaning postulates the equivalence of *taiji* to *natura naturans*, that is, to God as the creator. Interestingly, this equivalence is discussed through the lens of negative theology, insofar as the First Principle manifests itself, *de facto*, as without a term (*sine termino* or *wuji* 無極):

> *Taiji*, or the First Ultimate, can be understood as *natura naturans*, or God as author of all things. This is proven by what the Chinese say: 'It is Heaven and Earth which produce all things; and it is *taiji* which produces Heaven and Earth; therefore, how could *taiji* be expressed with a true name? How could it be fully understood? *Taiji* is only a conventional name, and that which is called *taiji* is in fact without any name'. (A). Suárez says something similar about the ineffability of God in his work (Volume 1, Book 2, Chapter 3[1]): 'The Fathers of the Church praised Plato and Trismegistus for saying that God is difficult to understand, but impossible to name'. Further below Suárez says: 'According to John of Damascus in Chapter 4 of Part 1 of his book, it is impossible to say what God's essence or nature is'. The Chinese also say: 'The operation, or nature, of

---

48 Noël, 'Tractatus primus', p. 138 (c.2, q.6); this edition, p. 341.

highest Heaven is without voice, smell or sensation, yet it is truly the efficient cause, or the hinge and root of all the things that have been produced. Thus, it is said, "*Wuji*, or the Being without Ultimate, and at the same time, *taiji*, or the First Ultimate". Beyond the First Ultimate, there is no such thing as the Being without Ultimate'. (B) This is because the Being without Ultimate is the First Ultimate.[49]

Even in recent times the philosopher Feng Youlan 馮友蘭 observed that 'the Supreme Ultimate is very much like what Plato called the Idea of the Good, or what Aristotle called God'.[50] Other than the Western sources listed in the citation above, even starker similarities can be seen between the *wuji* and the thought of Pseudo-Dionysius the Areopagite: 'The theologians celebrate it [the Thearchy] as nameless [ανώνυμον] and in accordance with all names. Thus, they call it nameless'.[51] Precisely for this reason, however, this being-without does not indicate *strictu sensu* an absence, but *transcendence*:

> By identifying *taiji* with God as *natura naturans*, Noël expressed its two-fold transcendence, as producer of the world and as the active principle within the world. This would mean that *taiji* or God is both transcendent and immanent to the world.[52]

If *taiji* 太極 is considered as a causal origin of movement and rest, as Noël suggests in the fifth (which includes the fourth) sense of the term, a very particular reflection can be noted. In fact, at the level of created nature (*natura naturata*), all things are *yin* 陰 and *yang* 陽, that is, they participate in the principle of rest and motion. Noël renders this famous polarity of Chinese thought with the pairing of *quies* (rest) and *motus* (motion):

> In their general and proper sense, as evidenced here, *yin* and *yang* mean nothing else but the two modes or transcendental relations of motion and rest: *yang* is a transcendental relation, or the essential order of motion towards rest; and *yin* is the essential order of rest towards motion. To avoid confusion, I have always translated *yin* and *yang* as rest and motion respectively, though in reality one exists only in relation to the other, and vice-versa.[53]

From a Thomistic point of view, transcendental relations are essential relations, just like the relation between matter and form, which are not separate or separable entities, but co-principles. For example, if matter is considered from a metaphysical

---

49 Noël, 'Tractatus primus', pp. 138–39 (c.2, q.6); this edition, p. 342.
50 Fung Yu-lan 馮友蘭, *A History of Chinese Philosophy*, 2 vols (Princeton: Princeton University Press, 1983), II, p. 537.
51 Pseudo-Dionysius the Areopagite, *The Divine Names and the Mystical Theology*, trans. and ed. by John D. Jones (Milwaukee: Marquette University Press, 1999), p. 114 (1.§ 6.25, 596a).
52 Thierry Meynard, 'François Noël's Contribution to the Western Understanding of Chinese Thought: *taiji sive natura* in the *Philosophia sinica* (1711)', *DAO: A Journal of Comparative Philosophy*, 17.2 (2018), 219–30 (p. 224).
53 Noël, 'Tractatus primus', p. 141 (c.2, q.6, §.5); this edition, p. 347.

point of view, its totality is inextricably linked to its form; likewise, if form is considered from a metaphysical point of view, its totality is inextricably linked to its matter. Thus matter is not form, and form is not matter, but there is no matter without form and there is no form without matter, because the *res* is composed of matter and form, which are two elements that cannot exist separately:

> There are, however, says Suárez, some real relations which are inseparable from the essences of their subjects [...] These relations, called by Suarez *relationes transcendentales*, are not mental relations; they are real; but they cannot disappear while the subject remains, as predicamental relations (that is, relations belonging to the category of relation) can disappear. A predicamental relation is an accident acquired by a thing which is already constituted in its essential being; but a transcendental relation is, as it were (*quasi*), a *differentia* constituting and completing the essence of that thing of which it is affirmed to be a relation.[54]

According to Aquinas, there are two complementary aspects of a relationship: 'being to' (*esse ad*) and 'being in' (*esse in*). A relation termed as *esse ad* expresses the essence of the relation *qua* relation. In contrast, *esse in* indicates the transcendental aspect of the relation. 'Being to something else' can be interpreted in two ways: it can be considered a rational relation or a real relation, whereby the former relation is established by the knowing subject, such that it is not in the *res*, and the latter relation is in the subject (*esse in subiecto*) and is therefore real.

Now, in and of itself the real relation lies in reality at the predicamental level, and is thus accidental. For example, being a father adds to being a subject of human nature, in the form of an entitative relation (*secundum esse*). However, being a father is not constitutive of human nature, but rather can be described in terms of a real relation that is not inherent but essential. This is also called *secundum dici*, which can be understood in the sense of a relation that is established by virtue of the definition given of the subject. For example, in the act of knowing the knowing subject is related to the known, and vice-versa. It is precisely this last gnoseological analogy that offers an eloquent example: if you consider the relation of knowledge on the side of the knowing subject, then it is a transcendental and real relation, while on the part of the known as knowable it is a relation of reason. Thus, to return to the discourse on *yin* and *yang*, if one considers the relationship between motion (*yang*) and rest (*yin*), one stands to the other by transcendental relation:

> Following Zhu Xi, *taiji* is explained here in terms of an ontology (ti 體, or *substantia*) of movement and rest, and thus Noël considered that *taiji* fulfills the Aristotelian definition of nature. Noël understood quite well that Yin and Yang are not static entities, but always in the state of becoming something else, and so he talked in terms of two 'transcendental relationships'.[55]

---

54 Frederick Copleston, *A History of Philosophy. Volume 3: Late Medieval and Renaissance Philosophy* (New York: Doubleday, 1993), p. 371.
55 Meynard, 'François Noël's Contribution to the Western Understanding of Chinese Thought', p. 228.

If *taiji* corresponds polysemically to nature, it is necessary to investigate whether *yin* and *yang* are two emanations or two modes of the same nature, conceived in a general sense. If they are two modes of the same nature, the first two determinations of nature would be understood as *natura naturans* and *natura naturata*: there would therefore be nature in the general sense and then its first determinations, with the corollary that nature as such is contained within *natura naturans* and *natura naturata*. By considering this non-emanationist but constitutive perspective, we can better understand nature as a fundamental constitutive principle (ἀρχή), especially in the second definition ascribed by Noël to the term *taiji*: we no longer have a generic nature from which the *natura naturans* would proceed (such a generic nature would be paradoxical, because if nature as such made nature proceed, it would itself be *naturans*), but nature as a fundamental constitutive principle. Therefore, *taiji* is not a principle from which things proceed, but a fundamental principle of which things are constituted.[56]

As a fundamental principle, nature inevitably is actuality and the operative principle. While essence and nature are the same per se, it must be pointed out that nature is its structuring principle, or more specifically the principle of its operations, while the essence is more precisely the determination of a subject.

Returning to the discourse of polarity, we have seen how the principle of rest (*yin*) and motion (*yang*) are in all the things created (*natura naturata*). From an Aristotelian-Thomistic point of view, they can be read both as matter and form and as essence (*essentia*) and act of being (*actus essendi*). If this second equivalence could be demonstrated, it would be not only a remarkable achievement from the point of view of a Sino-Western philosophical-theological encounter, but also evidence of Noël's return to Aquinas which, as is known, unlike Suárez, noted a *distinctio realis* between essence and the act of being. To be precise, in fact, if the two Chinese elements were matter and form, this would contradict the fact that not all realities other than God are composed of matter and form, such as angels or the soul, something which a theologian like Noël could not ignore. So, in what sense can all the things that proceed from God, and therefore are not God, have a composition of *yin* and *yang*, with the result that some things are negative or passive and other things positive or active? The only appropriate correspondence would seem to be that with *essence* and *act of being*: everything that is different from God is composed of essence and act of being, but not necessarily of matter and form. All that comes from *taiji*, or *natura naturans* as the productive principle of all things, is *yin* and *yang*:

> 'Since *yin* and *yang* are always found in the production of everything, the First Ultimate and the Two Formalities are always present' (P). From the perspective of the First Ultimate, it is prior to rest (*yin*) and motion (*yang*) since it is their efficient cause (*ratio productiva*); but from the point of view of *yin* and *yang*,

---

56 Noël, 'Tractatus primus', pp. 139–40 (c.2, q.6); this edition, p. 344.

the First Ultimate is contained in them insofar as it is the essential principle of the whole (Q).⁵⁷

As an essential principle, *taiji* could therefore be defined as the ἀρχή: indeed, here you can find a correspondence between Chinese thought and the thought of Greek Presocratic philosophers. For the latter, the ἀρχή is together the essential constitutive principle, the matrix of all things and the generative principle of all things. However, this generative principle is not separate from things; otherwise, it would not be the constitutive principle. For this reason, it is both an immanent and dominant principle. Noël's equivalence between *taiji* and *natura* can be understood as follows: as a constitutive principle, it is the essence; however, as that from which activity proceeds, it is called nature. This could also serve as further confirmation of Zhu Xi's well-known passage:

> *Question*: The Great Ultimate is not a thing existing in a chaotic state before the formation of heaven and earth, but a general name for the principles of heaven and earth and the myriad things. Is that correct? *Answer*: The Great Ultimate is merely the principle of heaven and earth and the myriad things. With respect to heaven and earth, there is the Great Ultimate in them. With respect to the myriad things, there is the Great Ultimate in each and every one of them. Before heaven and earth existed, there was assuredly this principle. It is the principle that 'through movement generates the that'. It is also this principle that 'through tranquillity generates the yin'. (49: 8b–9a)⁵⁸

If you consider this principle as prior to *yin* and *yang*, then it is the producer; if you consider the aforementioned polarity with respect to this principle, you can see how it permeates them, and is essential and constitutive. This is, after all, also the logic of Creation, according to which God does not create a reality that is totally different from Himself. Although the presence of God's immensity in Creation is not the essence of things, this presence is more deeply ingrained in everything than the essence of the thing itself. In this sense, similarities can also be found with the λόγος of Heraclitus, which in Latin Stoicism is translated as *ratio*.⁵⁹

It is therefore necessary to understand *taiji* as the principle that operates in things and not only as the principle that is within things: one can therefore speak of the nature of things in the essential sense, provided that it is not considered in a strictly immanent sense; otherwise, it would coincide with human nature, which in fact is the intrinsic principle of its actions. As Aquinas states in his first proof for God, 'Everything which is moved is moved by something else' (*Omne quod movetur ab alio movetur*): a finite nature acts by virtue of its own abilities and therefore is a second cause, but precisely for this reason a first cause is required for the second cause to act as second cause. That first cause is always present in

---

57 Noël, 'Tractatus primus', p. 141 (c.2, q.6, §.5); this edition, p. 348.
58 Wing-Tsit Chan 陳榮捷, ed., *A Sourcebook in Chinese Philosophy* (Princeton: Princeton University Press, 1963), p. 638.
59 Noël, 'Tractatus primus', pp. 141–42 (c.2, q.6); this edition, p. 348.

the action of the second cause, but not as a nature in the strict sense of principle that is intrinsic to the action of a subject; the second cause has its own nature and acts in virtue of it, and in this sense it is said to be *causa sui*. But a second cause depends on the first cause, which in virtue of its nature as an operating principle also acts where there is the second cause, because it makes it act as a second cause, although it is not intrinsic to it as the nature from which the second cause makes its operations emanate.

The polysemia of *taiji* therefore leads Noël to a decisive inference: since it is 'the principle and cause of motion and rest' (*principium et causa motus et quietis*), if its last and strictest meaning is true, that is, of a principle operating 'by itself and not accidently' (*per se et non per accidens*), we can say in a broader sense that God, as *natura naturans* acting in *natura naturata*, is present in it. It is true that *natura naturata* has its own way of operating; however, it is and remains *naturata*. Therefore, *natura naturata* needs the presence of *naturans*, just as the second cause acts by virtue of its operations, but it is and remains a second cause, and thus depends on the first cause. Everything leads us to think of a notion of participation, as suggested by Zhu Xi's well-known analogy of the moon:

> *Question*: [You said], 'Principle is a single, concrete entity, and the myriad things partake it as their substance. Hence each of the myriad things possesses in it a Great Ultimate.' According to this theory, does the Great Ultimate not split up into parts? *Answer*: Fundamentally there is only one Great Ultimate, yet each of the myriad things has been endowed with it and each in itself possesses the Great Ultimate in its entirety. This is similar to the fact that there is only one moon in the sky but when its light is scattered upon rivers and lakes, it can be seen everywhere. It cannot be said that the moon has been split.' (49: 10b–11a)[60]

Although it would be rash to define Zhu Xi's thought as panentheistic, in essence I agree with Julia Ching's observations:

> By analogy, we might say the Great Ultimate is like God or necessary being in Thomas Aquinas's system, that which *subsists*, in and of itself, without depending on others, while all others *exist*, in and of the Great Ultimate. But the analogy is imperfect, as the Great Ultimate is, on another level, immanent as well as transcendent. It is above all things and yet present in all things. It is above motion and rest and yet involved in a cyclical cosmic process.[61]

Considering this structure, Noël associates the terms nature and *taiji* drawing inspiration from certain patristic authors who interpreted pagan philosophers in these terms.[62] This better validates the thesis of an ontological correspondence between *taiji* and the ἀρχή (even if it is not explicitly present in Noël's reflection), since only the latter concept is at once both the dominant and constitutive operating principle of things.

---

60 Chan, *A Sourcebook in Chinese Philosophy*, p. 638.
61 Ching, *The Religious Thought of Chu Hsi*, p. 52.
62 Noël, 'Tractatus primus', p. 142 (c.2, q.6); this edition, pp. 350–51.

5.5 *Vacuum sive abstractum*

When asked whether Chinese voices agree on the identity of the designated divine reality, in many passages Noël responds positively. When writing about divine names, Noël elaborates his thesis by gradually introducing all the subsequent theoretical fundamental questions, including that concerning *taiji*:

> In the stone tablet recording the entrance of Christianity into China in AD 700, God is expressed with the word *lingxu*, or spiritual and empty, with the word *xuanshu*, or mysterious ultimate of things, with the word *zaohua*, or efficient Cause, and with the word *shentian*, or Spiritual Heaven (L). First Emptiness is the same as *taiji*, the First Ultimate of things (M). *Taiji* can even be understood as Heaven […]. Also, Emptiness is understood as something alive and not as something dead (N). Finally, Heaven or the Master of Heaven as being the Author, Founder, Creator, is called the producing and destroying Spirit [*guishen*] (O). As vital principle, it is called air, or vital breath […]. From all this, you can see that all the different names with which Heaven is called can be very well applied to the true Lord of Heaven and Earth.[63]

The underlying question of this text seems to be what the Chinese mean when they use the word 'spirit'. In first place, the spirit can be what presides over the voice, or the breath of the voice (*flatus vocis*) and aether; both of these are material realities. Finally it can mean void/emptiness (*vacuum*), which can be understood as *ratio* and is therefore immaterial. Thus the first void (*Primum Vacuum*) must be understood as devoid of matter, and indicates God (or the angel, when it is not qualified as *Primum*).

Noël not only proposes the term *taiji* as a possible divine name, but also *vacuum*. This term, which corresponds to *xu* 虛 (or *taixu* 太虛), is of Daoist and Buddhist derivation and penetrated into Chinese thought with the advent of neo-Confucianism. Unlike Matteo Ricci, Noël on this point interacts with the latter current as a legitimate continuation and interpretation of orthodox Confucianism; yet, unlike the Figurists,[64] he avoids excessive superimpositions of Christian revelation on Chinese terminology, adopting instead a realist interpretation:

> You see from this that the object of the teaching is the one pure Reason, namely Real Being (elsewhere they say that the word Reason should be understood as something true and real, and not false), and abstracted from perceptible and extended matter, and this is what philosophers call generally the object of metaphysics. It is abstract for philosophers, either in reality, like God and the Angels, or in reason like the predicates of Being and substance. Therefore, 'empty way' should neither be taken as fictitious and chimerical, nor as a Being

---

63 Noël, 'Tractatus primus', p. 64 (c.2, q.2, §.1); this edition, p. 249.
64 For the Figurists, see Claudia von Collani, *Die Figuristen in der Chinamission* (Frankfurt: Lang, 1981).

of Reason reasoning without a foundation in reality, but it should be taken either as abstract reality, or abstractly reasoned reason with a foundation in reality.[65]

As far as the distinction between real being (*ens reale*) and being of reason (*ens rationis*) is concerned, further clarification is needed. A being can be considered a being of reason reasoning (*ratio ratiocinans*) or a being of reasoned reason (*ratio ratiocinata*), depending on whether it is based on a distinction or an abstraction.[66] Now, the body of *ratio ratiocinata* can be 'without foundation in reality' (*sine fundamento in re*), that is to say a mere fantasy as in the case of a chimera (*chymaerice*), or 'with foundation in reality' (*cum fundamento in re*), that is to say terms such as substance, man, animal, species, or gender. This can be illustrated with the following example: simply speaking, man does not exist in reality, because only individuals exist; rather, man is an entity elaborated by reason, but with foundation in reality, insofar as man indicates human nature as abstracted from individuality and exists either in an individual or in the mind of God. There are three kinds of universals: a universal prior to reality (*ante rem*), that is, the very essence of God; a universal in reality (*in re*), corresponding to the individual, and finally a universal after reality (*post rem*), that is, the aforementioned abstraction, which would then be the direct universal.

Emptiness/void is therefore nothing more than an abstraction, which in turn is conceived as an equivalent to immateriality. Such an abstraction can be positively immaterial, such as God and the angels, which exclude matter themselves, or negatively immaterial, such as entity and substances, which can be conceived without matter, without being *tout court* immaterial, and are the result of the simple abstraction of the mind. For this reason, Noël elsewhere states:

> Emptiness here is understood neither as a perceptible and material Being, such as an immense and empty space of aether [*taikong*], nor as something fictitious or non-existent, but as a truly existing Being and as Reason, with its double meaning: something immaterial and something existing before things.[67]

In this same context, after listing the divine perfections among the modern Chinese, Noël explains the link between *Tian* and *Shangdi* in terms of the link between *abstractum* and *suppositum*:

> The Spirit of Heaven is neither the Soul of Heaven nor the substantial form of the physical heaven. The Chinese neither follow and nor know anything about the error of the ancient philosophers who affirmed that Heaven is animated and made up of a body and soul or spirit. This is evident because they say

---

65 Noël, 'Tractatus primus', p. 58 (c.2, q.1, §.8); this edition, pp. 241–42.
66 Being of Reason (*ens rationis*) is a medieval concept referring to beings which exist truly in the mind but have no reality in the concrete world. This concept was developed by Suárez. See Daniel Novotný, 'Suárez on Beings of Reason', *Conimbricenses.org Encyclopedia*, Mário Santiago de Carvalho, Simone Guidi (eds) < www.conimbricenses.org/encyclopedia/suarez-on-beings-of-reason/> (accessed on 1/16/2021).
67 Noël, 'Tractatus primus', p. 64 (c.2, q.2, §.1); this edition, p. 249.

that *Tian* is exactly the same as the Lord of Heaven, and the Lord of Heaven is the same as Heaven, or that Heaven is the Lord of Heaven and the Lord of Heaven is Heaven (R). It is impossible to hold that body and soul are the same. […] They always accept the Lord of Heaven as a *suppositum*, and not as a part of the *suppositum*. They never oppose Heaven to the Lord of Heaven, as if one partakes in the other, but they always use Heaven when referring to one aspect, and the Lord of Heaven when referring to another aspect, while affirming that they are both the same. Clearly, the Chinese do not make out of Heaven and the Lord of Heaven a composite which would be partly material, partly spiritual.[68]

For Chinese authors, saying *Shangdi* and *Tian* is basically the same thing. Noël goes further, collecting and reapplying to the terms *Shangdi* and *Tian* the theoretical elaboration carried out just before about the combination emptiness-spirit: they are not the same thing *sic et simpliciter*; however, they do not even indicate two different realities or two parts of the same reality, but only one same reality. In fact, when we say *Shangdi* we mean the *suppositum*, which also does not come into opposition to what is called *Tian*. Consequently, one could say analogically in reference to the debate on *vacuum*, that the expression *Shangdi* is the concrete entity, while *Tian* is the abstract entity, just like saying God and divine. According to this process, just as in the Aristotelian principle that being is said in multiple meanings, but always in reference to a unity and a determined reality,[69] even some Chinese terms are said in many ways, without falling into misunderstanding. We now better understand why the identification of *vacuum* with the *Primus rerum terminus* seemed almost obvious to father Noël.[70]

5.6. A Theoretical Conclusion

By way of conclusion, let us recapitulate the theme of faith and grace as a theological *Weltanschauung* for re-reading the *Philosophia Sinica*.

Aquinas interrogates the explicit and implicit faith in the context of the inner act of faith, where faith is an act of the intellect.[71] The triple classification of the act of faith according to the Angelic Doctor is well known:[72]

> It is one thing to say: 'I believe God' (*credere Deum*), for this indicates the object. It is another thing to say: 'I believe God' (*credere Deo*), for this indicates the one who testifies. And it is still another thing to say: 'I believe in God' (*in Deum*), for this indicates the end.[73]

---

68 Noël, 'Tractatus primus', p. 65 (c.2, q.2, §.2); this edition, pp. 256–57.
69 Aristotle, *Metaphysics: Book Λ*, pp. 32–33 (1003a).
70 Noël, 'Tractatus primus', p. 69 (c.2, q.1, L.19); this edition, p. 254.
71 See Aquinas, *Summa theologiae*, II^a–II^{ae}, q.2, and also *Quaestiones disputatae de veritate*, q.14, aa.11–12 (English translation *Truth: Questions I–XXIX*, trans. by Robert W. Mulligan, 3 vols (Eugene: Wipf and Stock Publishers, 2008)).
72 'The Angelic Doctor' refers to Aquinas.
73 Aquinas, *Super Evangelium S. Ioannis lectura*, c. 6, lectio 3, § VII; *Commentary on the Gospel of John*, trans.

With regard to the statement of the act of faith, Aquinas makes it immediately clear that the act of the believer does not end in the statement, but in reality.[74] Secondly, it is always Christ through Whom man is saved, in every time and in every place. As for the way in which this object of faith is accepted, it can be implicit or explicit, without altering the foundation of faith in Christ the only Mediator; hence even if not all the saved witnessed revelation, they were not saved without faith in the Mediator.[75]

These clarifications allow us to understand why Aquinas affirms the need for an explicit preaching for engendering faith, a need which would be echoed throughout the debates of early modern scholasticism over the salvation of infidels in newly discovered lands. In fact, the distinction between explicit and implicit faith allows the act of faith to be extended from a mere statement of faith to a deeper statement of the heart's intention. These different levels of faith trace a gradation in the relationship with the divine. Finally, the need for both faith and explicit preaching sheds more light on the relation between divine action (first cause of salvation) and ecclesial proclamation (second cause):

> Granted that everyone is bound to believe something explicitly, no untenable conclusion follows even if someone is brought up in the forest or among wild beasts. For it pertains to divine providence to furnish everyone with what is necessary for salvation, provided that on his part there is no hindrance. Thus, if someone so brought up followed the direction of natural reason in seeking good and avoiding evil, we must most certainly hold that God would either reveal to him through internal inspiration what had to be believed, or would send some preacher of the faith to him as he sent Peter to Cornelius (Acts 10:20).[76]

With regard to the concept of faith and religion in Suárez,[77] we can identify a thread connecting Suárez's elaboration back to the thought of Aquinas and the earliest patristic sources within the logic of sapiential realism. This can be illustrated with the following passage in which Suárez seems to agree with Aquinas:

> Even to those infidels to whom people have not preached the Gospel or faith, God provides sufficient means for them to be enlightened and be enticed to faith, provided that they have not opposed themselves, either by extraordinarily sending preachers sent to them, or by instructing them through the ministry of angels, or by enlightening them and calling them inwardly by Himself. This

---

by Fabian Larcher and James A. Wiesheipl, 3 vols (Washington: The Catholic University of America Press, 2010), II, p. 21.
74 Aquinas, *Summa theologiae*, II^a-II^{ae}, q.1, a.2, ad 2.
75 Aquinas, *Summa theologiae*, II^a-II^{ae}, q.2, a.7, ad 3.
76 Aquinas, *Quaestiones disputatae de veritate*, q.14, a.11, ad 1; *Truth: Questions I–XXIX*, trans. by Robert W. Mulligan, 3 vols (Eugene: Wipf and Stock Publishers, 2008), I, p. 262.
77 Francisco Suárez, 'De natura et essentia virtutis religionis', book 1, c. 1, § 6, in *Opera omnia*, 28 vols (Paris: Vivès, 1856–1878), XIII, p. 5.

is done so that [what is proclaimed in that] passage of Revelations 3[:20] may take place among all people: 'Behold, I am standing at the door and knocking'.[78]

Despite the different nuances of each school and historical period, we can observe among them continuities ripe for further application in the mission field. By reflecting on these continuities, we can better understand the remote and implicit background of the *Philosophia Sinica*.

Returning to the concept of *religio* in Aquinas and Suárez, the theologian Ilaria Morali points out:

> [Suárez] emphasized the multifaceted meanings and interpretations of the word *religio* in the Christian tradition. He openly stated that he preferred and considered more comprehensive the classical definition: religion is what unites us to God [...]. Suárez adds nothing new, but appropriates a doctrine that penetrates from Augustine in the patristic age into the Middle Ages and is further articulated by Aquinas, on whom Suárez is among the most famous commentators of the modern era. *Religio*, therefore, comes from *religare*: Aquinas had stated that *religatio* meant tying again, reconstituting a bond that has begun to loosen or that was lost. Every creature, including man, coming into existence also begins to distance itself from its creator, a detachment that evidently presents two facets: a positive facet of creaturely autonomy and the negative facet of sin as a detachment from God. Aquinas's interpretation therefore expresses the richness of the patristic element: religion is in fact the movement of man's return to God, a new reunification: it constitutes the first bond (*ligatio*) with which man is bound to God through faith. Religion is therefore a vital relation with God.[79]

For Suárez, the religious experience is located both at the level of 'true or false knowledge of God and worship' (*cognitio vera aut falsa Dei et cultus*), as an expression of the intellect, and at the level of virtue (*virtus*), as an expression of the will in relation to the divine.[80]

Having assumed the original gratuitousness of salvation and faith, and assumed the truth of the Christian religion, Suárez addresses the implications of this for the infidels. Suárez notes that in some cases ignorance could render the rejection of faith involuntary and, therefore, guilt-free. This notion is based on the common axiom 'God will not deny his grace to anyone who does what lies within him' (*facienti quod in se est Deus non denegat gratiam*),[81] that is, if a man through natural

---

78 Suárez, 'De gratia', book 4, c. 11, in *Opera omnia*, VIII, p. 318.
79 Morali, '*Religioni ac boni artibus*', p. 406.
80 Suárez, 'De natura and Essentia virtutis property religionis property', book 1, c. 2, *Opera omnia*, XIII, pp. 6–8.
81 Jean Rivière, 'Quelques antécédents patristiques de la formule "Facienti quod in se est"', *Revue des Sciences Religieuses*, 7.1 (1927), 93–97.

light and the good use of freedom does what can and should be done, he will be illuminated, and vice versa in the negative case.[82]

This preliminary assumption leads Suárez to distinguish three orders of infidels (*tres ordines infidelium*):[83] first there are those to whom the faith has been sufficiently announced and proposed, but who have refused to believe, and consequently cannot be excused. At the opposite extreme, the second group of infidels is made up of those who have heard nothing about the Christian faith; their degree of awareness and consequent responsibility, however, was a subject of discussion already in the patristic age. The third group of infidels is composed of those who have heard some element of the Christian faith, but in a form not sufficient for a right conversion and awareness of faith.[84] He finds support for this conclusion in John 15:22 and Romans 10:14, as well as drawing on the earlier elaborations of two distinguished Dominicans, Francisco de Vitoria OP (1486–1546) and Tommaso de Vio, the Caietan OP (1469–1534).[85]

However, while there is some agreement on the invincible ignorance of those who act unknowingly against a faith that they have never heard, there is a consensus that these people can still be blamed if they act against the natural law, at least in its universal principles.[86]

On the cause and manner of the unfaithful's salvation, Suárez reaffirms the universal divine will that every man be saved, as well as the prevenience of Grace in our ability to access salvation. On the part of man, however, faith is required, which can exist in reality (*in re*) or at least by desire (*in voto*), which are both signs of the prevenient action of supernatural Grace. Furthermore, the one who is to be saved must have ecclesial membership *in re* or at least *in voto*.[87] Even if salvation were to take place through the fulfilment of the latter condition, salvation is always the work of Christ.

In concluding the *quaestio* of *taiji* 太極, Noël curiously opens up one last problem, which remains only adumbrated and not solved:

> Someone may ask now whether the Chinese books mention not only the unity of God, but also the Trinity of Persons. I answer that this mystery [of the Trinity] cannot be known by natural reason, but only through faith according to Suárez, and thus it would be vain to seek this. We can only ask whether the Chinese know through natural (not supernatural) reason the supreme and infinite Divinity in every type of essential perfection, leaving aside notional attributes. They seem to hint obscurely very few things about this mystery [of

---

82 Suárez, 'De fide theologica', tractatus 1, disputatio 17, sectio 1, § 3.
83 Suárez, 'De fide theologica', tractatus 1, disputatio 17, sectio 1, § 3, p. 425.
84 Suárez, 'De fide theologica', tractatus 1, disputatio 17, sectio 1, § 3, p. 425.
85 Suárez, 'De fide theologica', tractatus 1, disputatio 17, sectio 1, § 9.
86 Suárez, 'De fide theologica', tractatus 1, disputatio 17, sectio 1, § 11. For Suárez's treatise on eternal and natural law see Suárez, 'De legibus', book 2, in *Opera omnia*, V, pp. 84–172.
87 Suárez, 'De fide theologica', tractatus 1, disputatio 12, sectio 4, § 22.

Divine Perfection] under the cloak of general vocabulary, but it is better to omit those things because this is irrelevant to the question.[88]

Noël suspends judgement on whether the Chinese have come to implicitly guess some Trinitarian aspects of the divine with the natural light of reason. The underlying reasoning is as follows: to know the Mystery of the Trinity you need the supernatural light of faith; however, Noël wonders if, with natural reason, regardless of all notional attributes,[89] the Chinese may have glimpsed some aspect of the Trinity even in general terms. The point of concern, however, is the suspension of judgement on this issue. The remote cause of Noël's suspension of judgement could be the heated political and diplomatic controversies between the Holy See and the Chinese Empire, and the proximate cause could be the deviations of some Figurist interpretations which had caused many problems for the Society of Jesus and were well known to Noël.

However, one fundamental point remains that Noël performs two cultural operations: an act of *inculturation* because he wants to show how Christianity can present itself in comprehensible terms to the Chinese, and an act of *acculturation*, because he seeks, and sometimes identifies, Western terms with fundamental elements in Chinese thought. Indeed, just as the Fathers of the Church sought to see under the veil of the pagan philosophy a *representation* of God the Creator, so the Flemish Jesuit tries to see in the Chinese thought such a representation. It is as if Noël says that behind this veil of Chinese philosophy is hidden that Christian Creator God, who is at the same time a dominant yet immanent principle in reality.

Yet Noël does not construct overlapping identities, but analogies. To construct analogies means to say that something similar is also found in Chinese thought, even if it is not the same thing. Only the analogy, in fact, allows us to say that *Shangdi* does not coincide with the explicit recognition of the Christian Creator God, although that term can be used to present the concept of Creator. The analogous reality is deeper: He whom the Chinese call *Shangdi* is really He whom a Christian calls *Deus*, and this is the similarity (*similitudo*); however a Christian, calling him *Deus*, articulates greater depth than what the Chinese articulate by *Shangdi*, and this is the difference (*dissimilitudo*).

Noël, an apologist *in* China, *for* China, and *from* China, shows, as it were, that Christ already works in Chinese thought in some way. However, a clarification is needed: Noël does not want to show that Chinese philosophy is equal to Christianity, because in this sense there is no philosophy equal to Revelation; even Aristotelianism in this sense is not fully suitable, as Thomist and scholastic philosophers were fully aware.

'We have the mind of Christ':[90] this is the philosophical and theological criterion of judgement. Theologically speaking, the relation between reason and

---

88   Noël, 'Tractatus primus', p. 143 (c.2, q.6, §.5); this edition, p. 351.
89   They are, according to Aquinas, innascibility, fatherhood, filiation, active and passive spiration. See *Summa theologiae*, 1ᵃ, q.32.
90   1 Corinthians 2:16.

Revelation can be configured in two ways: if reason establishes what Revelation can propose, we would end up in rationalism; alternatively, reason can be limited to saying what are *the conditions of possibility* of Revelation, provided that one is not faced with the evidently absurd. With such theological reason, we can deepen both our understanding of how God acts through Revelation, which takes place in contexts and terms that are accessible to man, and the means with which Revelation is proclaimed, namely, preaching. Noël made an excellent attempt in all these directions.

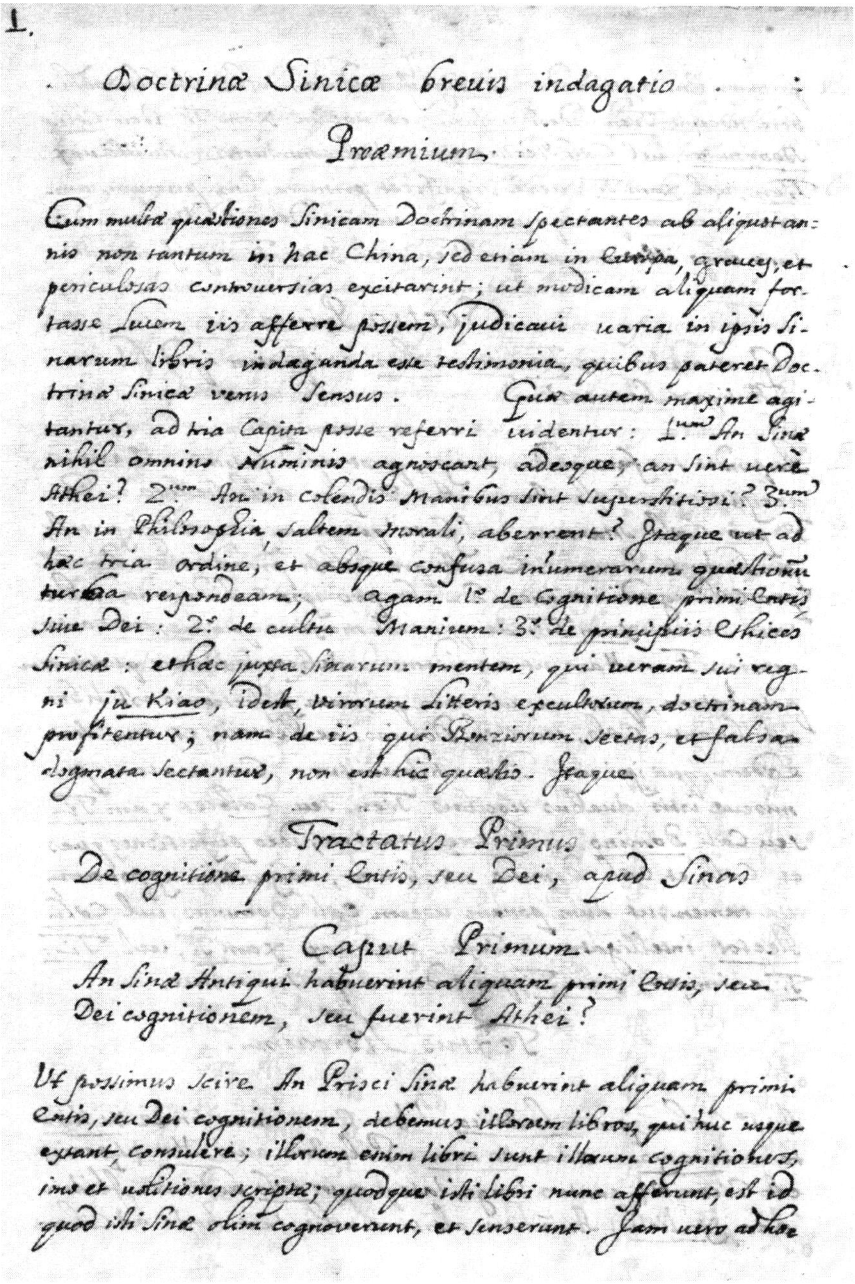

1.

Doctrinæ Sinicæ brevis indagatio.

Proœmium

Cum multæ quæstiones Sinicam Doctrinam spectantes ab aliquot annis non tantum in hac China, sed etiam in Europa, graves, et periculosas controversias excitarint; ut modicam aliquam fortasse lucem iis afferre possem, judicavi varia in ipsis Sinarum libris indaganda esse testimonia, quibus pateret Doctrinæ Sinicæ verus Sensus. Quæ autem maxime agitantur, ad tria Capita posse referri videntur: 1.um An Sinæ nihil omnino Numinis agnoscant, adeoque, an sint vere Athei? 2.um An in colendis Manibus sint superstitiosi? 3.um An in Philosophia, saltem morali, aberrent? Itaque ut ad hæc tria ordine, et absque confusa innumerarum quæstionum turba respondeam; agam 1.o de Cognitione primi Entis sive Dei: 2.o de cultu Manium: 3.o de principiis Ethices Sinicæ: et hæc juxta Sinarum mentem, qui veram sui regni Ju Kiao, idest, virorum litteris excultorum, doctrinam profitentur; nam de iis qui Bonziorum sectas, et falsa dogmata sectantur, non est hic quæstio. Itaque

Tractatus Primus

De cognitione primi Entis, seu Dei, apud Sinas

Caput Primum.

An Sinæ Antiqui habuerint aliquam primi Entis, seu Dei cognitionem, seu fuerint Athei?

Ut possimus scire An Prisci Sinæ habuerint aliquam primi Entis, seu Dei cognitionem, debemus illorum libros, qui huc usque extant, consulere; illorum enim libri sunt illorum cognitionis, imo et volitionis scripta; quodque isti libri nunc afferunt, est id quod isti Sinæ olim cognoverunt, et senserunt. Jam vero ad hæc

Figure 1. 'Doctrinae Sinicae brevis indagatio', ARSI, Fondo Gesuitico 724/4, fol. 1r (with permission).

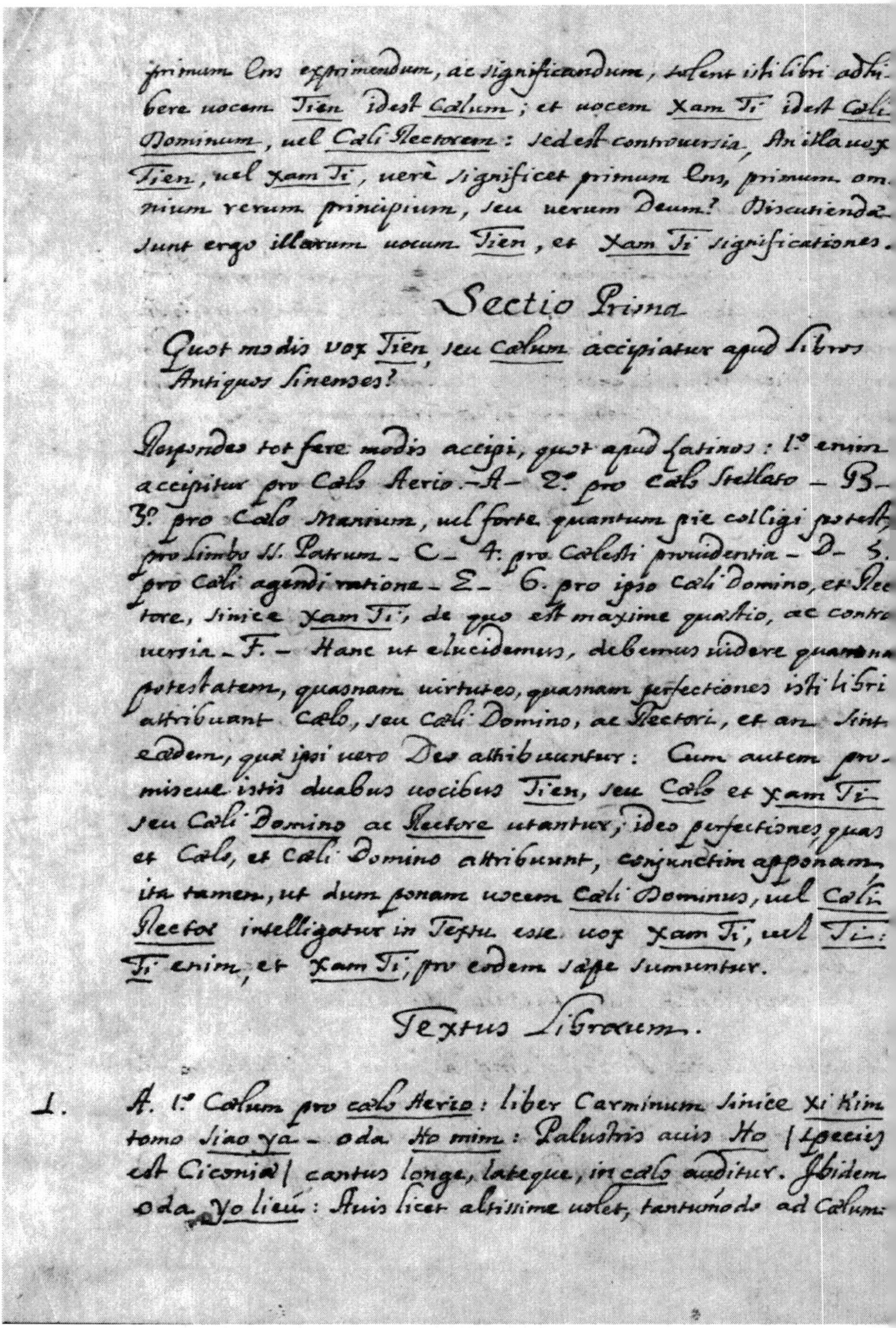

primum Ens exprimendum, ac significandum, solent isti libri adhibere vocem Tien idest Cælum; et vocem Xam Ti idest Cæli Dominum, vel Cæli Rectorem: sed est controversia, An illa vox Tien, vel Xam Ti, verè significet primum Ens, primum omnium rerum principium, seu verum Deum? Discutiendæ sunt ergo illarum vocum Tien, et Xam Ti significationes.

Sectio Prima

Quot modis vox Tien, seu Cælum accipiatur apud libros Antiquos Sinenses?

Respondeo tot fere modis accipi, quot apud Latinos: 1.º enim accipitur pro Cælo Aerio - A - 2.º pro Cælo Stellato - B - 3.º pro Cælo Manium, vel forte quantum pie colligi potest, pro Limbo SS. Patrum - C - 4. pro Cælesti providentia - D - 5. pro Cæli agendi ratione - E - 6. pro ipso Cæli Domino, et Rectore, Sinice Xam Ti, de quo est maxime quæstio, ac controversia - F. - Hanc ut elucidemus, debemus videre quamnam potestatem, quasnam virtutes, quasnam perfectiones isti libri attribuant Cælo, seu Cæli Domino, ac Rectori, et an sint eædem, quæ ipsi vero Deo attribuuntur: Cum autem promiscue istis duabus vocibus Tien, seu Cælo et Xam Ti seu Cæli Domino ac Rectore utantur; ideo perfectiones quas et Cælo, et Cæli Domino attribuunt, conjunctim apponam, ita tamen, ut dum ponam vocem Cæli Dominus, vel Cæli Rector intelligatur in Textu esse vox Xam Ti, vel Ti: Ti enim, et Xam Ti, pro eodem sæpe sumuntur.

Textus Librorum.

1. A. 1.º Cælum pro cælo Aerio: liber Carminum Sinice Xi Kim tomo Siao ya - oda Ho mim: Palustris avis Ho (species est Ciconiæ) cantus longe, lateque, in cælo auditur. Ibidem oda Yo lieu: Avis licet altissime volet, tantummodo ad Cælum

Figure 2. 'Doctrinae Sinicae brevis indagatio', ARSI, Fondo Gesuitico 724/4, fol. 1v–2r (with permission).

…que pertingit : Ibidem, Oda Cai Ki: Celerrima illa auis Sin bi ad cælum peruenit quiescit. — B. 2. Pro cælo stellato. B. 2.
…b. Carminum, tom. quadrum, Oda Cheu Leao: Constellatio An…res (nempe Sinica) seu cor Scorpij in Cælo apparet. — C. 3. pro Cælo C. 3.
…anicum, uel limbo. L. 6. Carm. to. tn ya: Oda Hia uu: Tres …ti defuncti Principes, scilicet Tay iam, Vam Ki, Ven uam in… …elo existunt. — Et lib. Annalium Jmperialium, Sinicè Xu Kim… …m. 5. cap. Chao Kao: Hujus imperij in plures defuncti Jmperato…o intelligentia, ac prudentia inclyti in Cælo existunt. — D. 4. pro D. 4.
…lesti prouidentia. Lib. Sententiarum, Sinicè Lun yu, art. 12. Pro …ita, et morte datur ~~med~~ lex: diuitiæ, et paupertas à cælo pendent.
…5. 2 pro cæli agendi ratione. Mencius lib. 2. cap. 5. Vnicum At… E. 5
…tium, quod potest uere dici magnum, et unicus est princeps Yao ipsi …uit q illud perfectè imitari. — F. 6. — pro ipso Cæli Domino, et F. 6
…ctore, seu Xam Ti. Lib. Annal. Jmpir. cap. Tay xi: maximum …tud cælum tremenda ira concitatum justi defunctorum Patrem me… …m Ven uam Sumâ cum reuerentia adiuri cæli maiestatem asta… …iere ad expellendam tyrannidem.

1. 詩經小雅鶴鳴鶴鳴于九皐聲聞于天。
2. 詩經小雅菀柳有鳥高飛亦傅于天。
3. 詩經小雅采芑駭彼飛隼其飛戾天亦集爰止。
4. 詩經國風綿蠻三星在天。
5. 詩經大雅下武三后在天。
6. 書經誥誓殷多先哲王在天。

4. 論語下第十二死生有命富貴在天。
5. 孟子上滕文公惟天為大惟堯則之。
6. 書經泰誓皇天震怒命我文考肅將天威。

Figure 3. 'Doctrinae Sinicae brevis indagatio', ARSI, Fondo Gesuitico 724/4, fol. 130ᵛ (with permission).

Doctrinæ Sinicæ breuis Indagatio
ex ipsis Sinarum libris eruta,
in qua dilucidantur penè
omnes Controuersiæ
Sinenses.

Authore
P. Francisco Noël Belga
Societatis IESV
Missionario Sinensi.

Tractatus primus
De Cognitione primi Entis
Seu Dei apud Sinas.

Figure 4. BnF, collection Bréquigny 15, fol. 1.

SVMMARIVM

Nouorum Autenticorum Teftimoniorum tam Europæorum, quam Sinenfium nouiffimè è China allatorum

CIRCA VERITATEM, ET SVBSISTENTIAM FACTI,

C V I

Innitur Decretum fa: me: ALEXANDRI VII.

Editum die 23. Martij 1656.

ET PERMISSIVVM RITVVM SINENSIVM;

ITEMQVE

Circa vfum vocum Tien, & Xam tj, ac tabellæ Kim Tien

SANCTISSIMO DOMINO NOSTRO

CLEMENTI PAPÆ XI.

O B L A T V M

A PP. FRANCISCO NOEL, & CASPARO CASTNER S.I.

Procuratoribus Illmorum, & Rmorum Epifcoporum

Macaenfis, Nankinenfis, Afcalonenfis, & Electi Andreuillenfis, & pro Miffionibus Societatis IESV in Imperio Chinæ, & adiacentibus Regnis.

Figure 5. *Summarium NAT*, 1704.

SINENSIS IMPERII LIBRI CLASSICI SEX,

NIMIRUM

ADULTORUM SCHOLA,
IMMUTABILE MEDIUM,
LIBER SENTENTIARUM,
MEMCIUS,
FILIALIS OBSERVANTIA,
PARVULORUM SCHOLA.

E Sinico idiomate in latinum traducti

A

P. FRANCISCO NOËL Societatis JESU MISSIONARIO.

SUPERIORUM PERMISSU.

PRAGÆ, Typis Univerſitatis Carolo-Ferdinandeæ, in Collegio Soc. Jesu ad S. Clementem, per Joachimum Joannem Kamenický p.t. Factorem, Anno 1711.

Figure 6. Cover of the *Libri sex*, 1711; copy given by the author to the Jesuit College of the Holy Trinity, Lyon, 1712.

PHILOSOPHIA
SINICA
TRIBUS
TRACTATIBUS,

Primo Cognitionem Primi Entis,
Secundo Ceremonias erga
Defunctos,
Tertio Ethicam,

Juxta Sinarum mentem

complectens,

AUTHORE

P. Francisco Noël Societ. JESU Missionario.
De speciali licentia
SS. D. N. D. CLEMENTIS PAPÆ XI.
ET
SUPERIORUM PERMISSU.

PRAGÆ,

Typis Universit: Carolo-Ferdinandeæ, in Collegio Soc.
Jesu ad S. Clementem, per Joachimum Joannem Kamenicky
Factorem, Anno 1711.

Figure 7. Cover of the *Philosophia Sinica*, 1711.

PRAGÆ,

Typis Universit: Carolo-Ferdinandeæ, in Collegio Soc.
Jesu ad S. Clementem, per Joachimum Joannem Kamenicky
Factorem, Anno 1711.

Tomus hic ex speciali Licentia Clem. XI Papæ privatim legi potest à Religiosis Societ. Jesu, non autem publicari.

Figure 8. Manuscript note on the cover of the *Philosophia Sinica*.

Chinese Philosophy in Three Treatises

1 - Knowledge of the First Being;
2 - Ceremonies towards the dead;
3 - Ethics,
According to Chinese thought

By
Father François Noël, missionary of the Society of Jesus

With special permission of
Pope Clement XI
and of his superiors.[1]

Published at Prague
with the Press of Charles-Ferdinand University
in the College of the Society of Jesus at the Klementinum,
Charles-Ferdinand University,
by Joachim Joannes Kamenicky in 1711.

Translated from Latin into English by
Thierry Meynard and Daniel Canaris, with
Chinese transcribed by Thierry Meynard
and revised by Wang Ge 王格

---

1 In 1703, Noël received permission from Pope Clement XI to publish on the Chinese Rites. Hence, he published with Kaspar Castner in Rome *Summarium novorum autenticorum testimoniorum* (1703) and *Summarium novissimorum testimoniorum sinensium* (1704). However, on 25 September 1707, Clement XI published a decree confirming the decisions of 1704 against the Chinese Rites and also forbade the future publication of any book on the Chinese Rites without special papal authorization. Noël may have thought that his permission of 1703 was still valid, though it may be argued that he and the Jesuit superiors in Prague disobeyed the pope in publishing the work. In November 1711, the Jesuit Superior General Michelangelo Tamburini (r. 1706–1730) had to write a formal declaration of obedience to the pope, signed by the procurators of all the provinces gathered in Rome. Subsequently, the diffusion of the *Philosophia Sinica* was restricted within the Jesuit order, and even Jesuits needed a special authorization from their Superior General. See Collani, 'François Noël and his Treatise on God in China', pp. 31–33.

Preface to the Reader[1]

Dear Reader, when you observe the term 'Chinese Philosophy' on the cover of this book, do not think that I mean a philosophical course like those taught by modern philosophers. I am speaking about concepts (*res*), not a system (*ars*); I am indicating content and knowledge and not form or methodological order.[2] I am referring to philosophy as it was conducted by the ancients. For them, philosophy was called the pursuit of correcting virtue and thought, as well as the operation of correct reason and a way of life; it was called the knowledge of divine and human matters, and also a habit of the intellect,[3] which consists in wisdom and prudence and governs human actions. From this, a two-fold philosophy emerges: a speculative philosophy which diligently scrutinizes the truth of things, as well as a practical philosophy which prescribes certain laws for guiding the order of human action. With the help of the former, we reach truth; with the help of the latter, we attain morality.[4] I follow this mode of philosophy in this work, which I have divided into three parts or treatises. In the First Treatise, I examine mostly the truth of speculation, whereas in the second and third, I focus on the morality of action.[5]

The First Treatise discusses the most sublime inquiry of ancient [Chinese] philosophers, that is, the true knowledge of the First Being, to which almost the entire philosophy of Aristotle can be reduced. I investigate both whether the Chinese in the past had true knowledge of the First Being, the first Origin, the first Producer of things and whether the Chinese of today still have this knowledge. I not only discuss the intrinsic perfections of the First Being and its external operations according to Chinese thought, but also investigate what they mean by intelligent beings or spirits [*guishen*].

The Second Treatise reviews and evaluates the different Chinese ceremonies used towards deceased parents and benefactors, and discusses their moral integrity. It also investigates whether these funeral rites for parents, which are both unique and many, include anything that contradicts the light of natural reason imprinted on

---

[1] This printed preface replaces a much shorter preface found in the ARSI manuscript. See ARSI, Fondo Gesuitico 724/4, fol. 1ʳ.

[2] In the *Proemium* to the Third Treatise, Noël reiterates that Chinese thought does not follow the rules of Western logic: 'Sinae ut antiqui sapientes, absque praeceptorum methodo Philosophantur; rem non artem dicunt'. For Noël, the Chinese do not use modern formal logic, but through the natural logic common to everyone they have reached the substance of the topic matter. Noël, 'Tractatus tertius', p. 1.

[3] The habit of the intellect, which was developed by Aristotle and later adopted by the scholastics, concerns the practical process by which the intellect is shaped.

[4] This account of Chinese philosophy resembles Stoicism, which associates the pursuit of knowledge through logic with the pursuit of the good life through morality.

[5] In the original preface to the manuscript (ARSI, Fondo Gesuitico 724/4, fol. 1ʳ), Noël sets his work against the background of the Chinese Terms and Rites Controversies by raising three questions. See Chapter 2.1. In the published version, Noël reshapes the framework in two parts, theoretical and practical, with the second part further divided into rituals and ethics.

us by God, or whether they possess the innate and special justice of due gratitude [for the ancestors and the deceased parents].⁶

In the Third Treatise, I have organized examples and precepts, which are scattered in Chinese books without any order, in relation to the correct standard of human actions, both in the private or domestic realm, and the political realm. From these I have composed a short treatise on ethics for the individual, family, and politics.⁷

Finally, in order to make the discussions on Chinese matters clearer, as well as more meaningful and pleasant for you, dear reader, I have added at the end of this book a historical notice, drawn from their books, on the Chinese rites and the spirits known to the Chinese.⁸

Just as the ancient philosophers, especially the Platonists, divided philosophy into the rational, natural, and moral spheres, so you will find expressed — or at least outlined — rational philosophy in the First Treatise, natural philosophy in the Second Treatise, and moral philosophy in the Third Treatise.⁹

Concerning the true knowledge of the First Being, you may not be surprised that the more recent Chinese veil it with somewhat more abstract or obscure terms, often expressing the First Principle with the general terms Heaven [*Tian*], Nature [*xing*], Reason [*li*], etc. Since those terms and expressions were often used by ancient Greek philosophers while discussing the first cause of all things, they should be very familiar. What was more frequent among them than that term λόγος, or Reason? What more common than Nature? Abstract words are certainly not enough to indicate the true essence of God, but should we condemn the Chinese, as well as all ancient philosophers, with the black stain of atheism, and affirm that, in so many centuries preceding the birth of Christ, the entire world, except the

---

6   Without a knowledge of the controversies, it may be difficult for a European reader to understand the connection between the Second Treatise on the Chinese Rites with the First Treatise on metaphysics and the Third Treatise on ethics.
7   Noël composed an independent treatise on Chinese ethics, following the structure of *Commentarius in Aristotelis Moralem* by Pierre Barbay (died 1664). This work was first published in Paris in 1675 and reprinted a few times afterwards (Paris, 1676, 1680, 1684, 1690; Lyon 1692). Barbay, who was born in Abbeville, was a student of Antoine Arnauld (1560–1619), and became professor of philosophy at the Beauvais College of Paris University. He wrote commentaries on Aristotle's logic, physics, metaphysics, and ethics, which were published posthumously by his students. He is sometimes said to be a Jesuit, but this is doubtful since he is not mentioned by the *Bibliothèque des Écrivains de la Compagnie de Jésus* (1853).
8   Noël, *Historica notitia rituum ac ceremoniarum Sinicarum in colendis parentibus ac benefactoribus defunctis*. This work has a preface and eight chapters, with a total of ninety-one pages.
9   As Carel Wesselius notes, 'This division of philosophy, ascribed to the philosopher Xenocrates, the second successor of Plato in the Academy, was widespread in Western philosophy'. Carel Wesselius, 'The *Ethica Politica*: François Noël's (1651–1729) Description of Confucian Political Thought in his *Philosophia Sinica Tribus Tractatibus*' (unpublished master's thesis, Leiden University, 2020, p. 6. The First Treatise can be matched with rational philosophy and the Third Treatise with ethics, but it is difficult to match the Second Treatise on the Chinese Rites with natural philosophy which deals with the physical world and the human body. According to Catholic teaching, the souls of the dead are detached from the body; therefore, the honours paid to the dead have more to do with rational philosophy than with natural philosophy.

minuscule region of Judaea, had laboured in the ignorance of its true Founder and Rewarder? This certainly could not be admitted by sober Reason, nor does it seem to conform to Divine Providence.

Indeed, those ambiguous, obscure, and somehow contradictory words, which are sometimes found in the Chinese books, are not in opposition to the innate knowledge of the true divinity because those words are explained or refuted elsewhere very clearly. Could you please tell me what books in the world, especially those relating the foundations of learning, lack obscurity and ambiguity? Even in the Bible, you can find many difficulties and apparent contradictions if you adhere only to the literal meaning of words! I provide here only a few examples to illustrate my point: faith teaches that God is one, yet God said to Moses, 'I have made you like God to Pharaoh' (Exodus 7:1); 'The strong gods of the earth are exceedingly exalted' (Psalm 46:10); 'God stood in the congregation of gods, and in their midst judges them' (Psalm 81:1); 'I saw the gods ascending from the earth' (1 Kings 28:13). From these passages you do not infer that there are many gods. Likewise, the spirit of God is good, but it is said, 'The next day, the evil spirit of God entered Saul' (1 Kings 18:10). Furthermore, there is no void or nothingness in the world, and yet it is said, 'He stretched out the north over the empty space, and he hung the earth upon nothing' (Job 26:7). Also, the celestial harmonies are the dreams of Pythagoras, but it is said, 'Who can declare the order of heavens, or can make the celestial harmony sleep?' (Job 38:37). You do not infer from this that all these claims contradict God's infinite goodness, truth and wisdom. Moreover, angels in the Book of Job are called the sons of God: 'Now on a certain day when the sons of God came to stand before the Lord' (Job 1:6). But in Genesis 6:2 it is said, 'The sons of God seeing that the daughters of men were beautiful selected a few of them and took them as wives'. You don't infer from this that angels marry, nor you attribute those things to them. Indeed, those passages of the Bible do not contradict the true notion of God or angels. Without placing the Bible and Chinese books on the same level, those obscure and complex passages found in the Chinese texts should not be understood as contradicting knowledge of the true divinity and secondary intelligences or spirits, when they are clearly explained elsewhere.

Similarly, during the funeral rites for deceased parents, it might seem that the norm of moral behaviour is transgressed by the unusual pomp of the external actions, and the occasional words expressing extreme pain or love. But you should not rashly conclude that there is any unlawful or superstitious worship hidden in those rites. You should pay attention not to untrustworthy appearances, but to the purpose of those rituals and to the intention of the one speaking. Very often, when interpreting the Bible, you cannot make judgement from only the exterior appearance or the literal meaning of words, otherwise you may fall into error. For example, the Bible says, 'Lay out your offerings of bread and wine over the tomb of a just man' (Tobias 4:18),[10] and 'Good things that are hidden in a mouth that is

---

10 In the printed version this verse is misattributed to Job. We have corrected this mistake in our translation.

shut, are like food set above a grave' (Ecclesiasticus 30:18). Would you say that the food is brought to the tomb for the deceased to eat it? And when it is said, 'After the liver of the fish is burnt, the demon will be driven away' (Tobias 6:19), would you consider this as superstition? When it is said, 'The death of human beings and of animals is one, and both of them have the same condition […]; human beings have nothing more than beasts' (Ecclesiastes 3:19), and 'The dead know nothing at all, neither they have any reward' (Ecclesiastes 9:5), would you infer from this that the human souls perish? When it is said, 'Lord, you will preserve human beings and animals' (Psalm 35:7), and 'I myself arrange for you […] to eat and drink at my table in my kingdom' (Luke 22:30), would you think that the animals shall be blessed with human beings in Heaven, and that human beings eat and drink there? I mention those passages so that you do not demand from the Chinese books a level of clarity which makes explanation or interpretation redundant, since you do not find nor expect such clarity in the Bible.

Also, when the Bible affirms that King Solomon was wiser than all those before and after him, should he be compared with Adam, the Prophets, the Apostles, the Blessed Virgin, and Christ? Does this claim need explanation? When the Chinese extol their teacher Confucius with much — and perhaps excessive — praise, you should understand that that praise must be bound within some limits. Thus the biblical commentators circumscribe the following statement about King Assuerus within the bounds of truth, 'King Assuerus made every land and all the islands of the ocean give him tribute' (Esther 10:1). In the same way, the Chinese also know how to stretch hyperbole to the limits of fair moderation.

To understand correctly the foundational books of Chinese philosophy, the entire scope and the true meaning of their ideas need to be considered. Words should not be isolated and torn from their contexts, as the Chinese doctor Mencius says in Chapter 3 of the second part [of his book]: 'A prudent commentator of the *Book of Odes* should not abuse individual words to harm the meaning of the sentences, nor abuse individual sentences to harm the general meaning'.[11] Therefore, I have cited not only those passages which conform to philosophical truth, but also many other passages which seem to contradict it. I have presented to myself more objections than any adversary could have presented, but I have also taken care to resolve those difficulties. I have sourced evidence from Chinese books so that my reasonings cannot be attributed to the free invention of my own intelligence or to my own personal judgement. Even though the particular solutions taken separately do not always convince the intellect — which can be hardly be required or expected — when taken together, the solutions do not seem to leave any room for doubt, or the contrary position. Nor can the Chinese books that I

---

11 *Mencius* 5.1: '故說 《詩》 者, 不以文害辭, 不以辭害志'. Noël provides the same translation in *Libri sex*, p. 369. Notice that Noël divides the *Mencius* in two parts, with the first part including 'Lianghui wang' (chapters 1 and 2), 'Gongsun Chou' (chapters 3 and 4) and 'Teng Wen Gong' (chapters 5 and 6), and the second part including 'Lilou' (chapters 1 and 2), 'Wan Zhang' (chapters 3 and 4), 'Gaozi' (chapters 5 and 6) and 'Jinxin' (chapters 7 and 8). In this volume, see Chapter 2 by Meynard and Chapter 4 by Wang Ge for further discussion on Noël's use of this citation.

quote frequently be suspected of favouring one opinion over the other, because almost all the things I am quoting were written before the controversy about Chinese philosophy had emerged, and if the books were written after the start of the controversy, the social status and the reputation of their authors absolve those books from any suspicion. I believe a prudent man will never be persuaded that these authors, be they Christian or non-Christian, would want their name to be exposed to the reproach of ignorance and the mockery of the literati. Finally, I would like to warn you about a few points.

First, bear in mind that throughout this work I always speak according to the thinking of the Chinese literati who profess the true teaching of their country, called *Rujiao*. Thus, there is no discussion here about those who follow the perverse sects of the idolaters Lao[zi] and Fo [Buddha] and their false teaching and fables.

Second, almost all the Chinese books, which I will cite in the ensuing discussion, have been brought from China to Europe and are kept in Rome. If needed, the original quotes can be easily checked.[12]

Third, to signify the funeral ceremonies for deceased parents, which in Chinese are called *ji* [祭], I have deliberately refrained from using the Latin word *oblationes* (offerings), but have used the neutral and common word *ceremonia* (*ji*), because *oblationes*, according to Calepillo and other writers,[13] are strictly speaking offerings to gods, whereas in China the deceased are not considered as gods. In order to avoid any appearance of superstition, I have refrained from using this word. However, the word *oblatio* in and of itself can be used to signify either a sacred or a secular offering.

Fourth, to lessen the burden of reading so many quotes drawn from the foundational books of Chinese philosophy, I have inserted a brief summary at the beginning of each Question, Section, and Paragraph, and I have placed abundant quotes at the end, just as they appear in the Chinese books. In both parts I have maintained the same alphabetical order. Thus, the reader can decide to read the summary alone, the quotes alone, or both.

Fifth, although the Chinese do not have grape wine, I consistently use the word *vinum* (wine) to signify the drinks made from rice and other things which they use in their rituals and daily life because their alcohol has some kind of resemblance with grape wine.

Those are the things that I judged should be mentioned beforehand so that the reader may understand better the things to be discussed. If you find a mistake in my thinking, please correct it. If you are expert in Chinese language and literature, you may improve the translation. Enjoy the fruit of my long labours. Farewell.

---

12 See the charts in the Appendix of this volume.
13 Ambrogio Calepino (*c.* 1440–1510) was the author of a famous Latin dictionary that was published in 1502 and reprinted many times until the eighteenth century.

FIRST TREATISE
ON CHINESE KNOWLEDGE OF THE FIRST BEING, OR GOD

Chapter 1: Did the Ancient Chinese have Knowledge of God, the First Being, or were they Atheists?

To know whether the ancient Chinese had knowledge of the First Being, or God, we need to examine the extant books in which they wrote down their knowledge and intentions, and which tell us today what they knew and thought.[1] Those books use generally the words *Tian*, or Heaven, and *Shangdi*, that is the Lord or Ruler of Heaven, to express and signify the First Being.[2] But there is a controversy as to whether the words *Tian* or *Shangdi* mean the First Being and the First Principle of everything, namely the true God. We need thus to discuss the meanings of *Tian* and *Shangdi*.[3]

Question 1: How many Meanings does *Tian* Have in the Ancient Books?

I answer there are as many meanings as found among the Latin authors, such as aerial heaven (A.1); starry heaven (B.2); the Heaven [where] souls [reside] after death (C.3); heavenly Providence (D.4); Heaven's method of action (E.5); and the Lord and Ruler of Heaven (*Shangdi*), about which there is greatest controversy (F.6). To resolve the controversy, we must examine what power, virtues, and perfections are attributed to *Tian* and *Shangdi* by the Chinese books, and whether they are the same attributes as those of the true God. Since they use the two words *Tian* and *Shangdi* indiscriminately,[4] I shall mention together the perfections attributed to

---

1 Ricci had affirmed that the ancient Chinese had some knowledge of God, but not long after his death, this affirmation was fiercely debated, leading to the question of the suitability of using Chinese terms to express God. This resulted in the Jiading conference in 1628 where Longobardo played an important role, but he was eventually silenced. See Brockey, *Journey to the East*, p. 87.
2 *Tian* is translated as Heaven with a capital letter when referring to God, and with a lower case when it refers to material sky. A more literal translation of *Shangdi* would be the Master/Ruler-on-High. Many Chinese commentators associate *Tian* and *Shangdi*, but Jesuits like Noël strove to strengthen further the association between *Tian* and *Shangdi*, making *Shangdi* an equivalent to *Tian*.
3 Noël refers here to the Terms Controversy that embroiled the Jesuits from 1612 onwards.
4 This claim is repeated several times by Noël, but in fact, in the history of Chinese thought, the status of *Shangdi* is not as elevated as that of *Tian*.

both, but for clarity, I shall mention *Tian* as Heaven, and *Shangdi* or *Di* as Lord and Ruler of Heaven.

NOTES

A.1 Aerial heaven:

《詩經・小雅・鶴鳴》：「鶴鳴于九皋,聲聞于天。」

Ode 'Heming' in the volume 'Xiaoya' of the *Book of Odes* (*Shijing*): 'The song of the marsh bird *he* (a type of stork) is heard far and wide in heaven'.

《詩經・小雅・菀柳》：「有鳥高飛,亦傅于天。」

Ode 'Yuliu' in the same volume: 'Although the bird flies so high, it only reaches heaven'.

《詩經・小雅・采芑》：「鴥彼飛隼,其飛戾天,亦集爰止。」

The ode 'Caiqi' in the same volume: 'The bird called *sun*, which is extremely swift, rests when it reaches heaven'.

B.2 As starry heaven:

《詩經・國風・綢繆》：「三星在天。」

Ode 'Choumou' in the volume 'Guofeng' of the *Book of Odes*: 'The Chinese constellation Antares, or heart of the Scorpius, appears in heaven'.[5]

C.3 As the Heaven [where] souls [reside] after death:

《詩經・大雅・下武》：「三后在天。」

Ode 'Xiawu' in the volume 'Daya' of the *Book of Odes*: 'The three deceased rulers (Tai Wang, Wang Ji, Wen Wang) are in Heaven'.[6]

《書經・周書・召誥》：「茲殷多先哲王在天。」

Chapter 'Zhaogao' in volume 5 of the *Book of Imperial Annals* (*Shujing*): 'Many deceased rulers of the Yin dynasty, renowned for their intelligence and prudence, are in Heaven'.[7]

---

5 Literally, 'the three stars appear in heaven'. According to the *Maoshizhuan* 毛詩傳 (Mao commentary on the *Book of Odes*, Han dynasty), the three stars designate the three stars of the constellation of Orion (參宿三星), but according to the *Maoshizhuan jian* 毛詩傳箋 (Annotations to the Mao commentary on the *Book of Odes*, Han dynasty) by Zheng Xuan 鄭玄 (127–200), they refer to the three stars of the constellation of Scorpius (心宿三星), with Antares being the brightest of the three. Noël follows this explanation which was probably taken from the *Bianzhitang dingzheng shijing shuoyue jijie* 辨志堂訂正詩經說約集解 by Fan Zhiheng 范之恆 and Wan Jing 萬經, mentioned many times in Noël's work. More recently, in his *Tianwen kaogu lu* 天文考古錄, the scholar Zhu Wenxin 朱文鑫 (1883–1939) demonstrated that the three stars refer in fact to the three constellations of Orion (參宿三星), Scorpio (心宿三星) and Hegu (河鼓三星).

6 Quoted in the *Tianjiao he Ru*, p. 50 (n. 19).

7 This statement suggests the possibility of the salvation for non-Christians. This possibility was affirmed by some Fathers of the Church but became more controversial since the sixteenth century. Quoted in Bouvet's *Gujin*, p. 210 (n. 40) and in the *Tianjiao he Ru*, p. 50 (n. 19).

D.4 As heavenly Providence:

《論語・顏淵》：「死生有命, 富貴在天。」

Chapter 12[.5] in the *Book of Sentences* (*Lunyu*): 'Death and life are fixed by law; wealth and poverty depend upon Heaven'.[8]

E.5 As Heaven's method of action:

《孟子・滕文公上》：「惟天為大, 惟堯則之。」

Chapter 5 in the second part of the *Mencius*: 'Only Heaven can be said great, and only the ruler Yao was able to imitate it perfectly'.[9]

F.6 As Lord and Ruler of Heaven, or *Shangdi*:

《書經・周書・泰誓》：「皇天震怒, 命我文考, 肅將天威。」

Chapter 'Taishi' in volume 4 of the *Book of Imperial Annals*: 'Great Heaven was moved with a terrible anger and ordered my deceased father Wen Wang to assume with the highest respect His authority which had been damaged and to expel the tyrant'.[10]

Question 2: What Perfections do the Ancient Classics Attribute to *Tian* and *Shangdi*?

I answer that their books attribute to *Tian* and *Shangdi* the same perfections that we attribute to the true God. To prove it, I shall go briefly through each of the main attributes of God, which the books ascribe to *Tian* and *Shangdi*. From this, it will be clear that the ancient Chinese understood *Tian* and *Shangdi* as signifying the true God.

§.1. Dominion of *Tian* and *Shangdi* according to Ancient Authors

I do not deal here with the supreme dominion of God as a property of God in Himself, but as His power of jurisdiction, that is to say his power of governing all people as His subjects, of appointing and changing kings, of enacting laws, and punishing those who disobey. From this, human beings have the obligation to serve, obey, and worship Him as the Supreme Lord, and if they do not comply, they sin.[11] Chinese books seem to attribute to *Tian* and *Shangdi* such a supreme dominion.

---

8   Quoted in *Gujin*, p. 195 (n. 33) and in the *Tianjiao he Ru*, p. 44 (n. 15). See Noël's translation in *Libri sex*, p. 149; Meynard, *The Jesuit Reading of Confucius*, p. 367.
9   See Noël's translation in *Libri sex*, p. 302.
10 Quoted in the *Gujin*, p. 177 (n. 27) and in the *Ditian kao* 帝天考 by the early Qing Chinese Christian Yan Mo 嚴謨, p. 33 (n. 21). Quoted partially in the *Tianjiao he Ru*, p. 37 (n. 11).
11 Noël does not discuss the divine attributes of God in Himself (such as His unity) because in the classical texts or in their commentaries, nothing similar can be found, but Noël expounds the relationship between *Tian* and humanity by using the external attributes of God over the world, especially over humanity. Scholastic authors mention first the creative power of God, and then His power, knowledge, will, etc. To accommodate Chinese intellectual traditions, Ricci's *Tianzhu shiyi* first expressed the

They say that *Tian* or *Shangdi* appoints kings and doctors as its vicars (A);[12] changes dynasties (B); commands them (C); entrusts them with duties (D); declares law (E); is angered by sins and orders that sins be punished (F); and generously grants prayers (G); that the emperor assumes power in the hall [of *Shangdi*] (H); officers receive power from the emperor, but the emperor receives authority from Heaven (I); [*Shangdi*] is served, like a son serves his parents (K); kings obey Him (L); and that it will be criminal not to obey, serve, and worship Him (M); that, if one sins against Heaven, there will be no one to whom one can turn to beseech the pardon of his crime (N); that the king does not dare to belittle the service due to Him, to neglect the order received from Him or disregard His will (O); that all the people and the officers direct all their efforts to managing the rites necessary for His worship (P); that even the emperor himself tills the ground to prepare the rice and wine used for His worship (Q); sacrifices or offerings are made to Him (R); that the rulers roast the sheep that are to be offered to Him (S); that the ruler Wen Wang served Him very diligently and promoted the ritual worship due to Him (T); Wu Wang made a burnt offering as a sacrifice to Him (V); Huangdi made a palace for Him (X); Zhuanxu composed music to present Him offerings (Z).[13] I am asking you, can there be a more complete and more explicit declaration of the supreme dominion of the Lord of Heaven, or statement of the complete subjection of humanity towards Him and of the necessity of serving Him? Is it not the case that their books attribute to *Tian* or *Shangdi* the same dominion that we attribute to the true God? Since the power or omnipotence of God is related to His dominion, I add this to the discussion.

NOTES

A.1 《書經·周書·泰誓上》：「天佑下民，作之君，作之師。惟其克相上帝，寵綏四方。」

Chapter 'Taishi' in volume 4 of the *Book of Imperial Annals* (in Chinese *Shujing*): 'Heaven appointed kings and teachers to help the people. But these kings and teachers, or doctors, can only cooperate and associate with the Lord of Heaven to cherish and pacify the people of the whole empire'.[14]

Dominion of God over the world and humanity and then expressed the idea of creation, which is marginal in China. See Ricci, *The True Meaning of the Lord of Heaven*, p. 50 (n. 33).

12 Noël calls kings and teachers vicars, which in Christianity refer to persons who have an authority in the absence of Christ; thus, the pope is said to be the vicar of Christ on earth.

13 Noël first explains how *Tian* or *Shangdi* appointed kings (A–I), and next how the kings obeyed Him (K–X). Based on the classical texts, Noël understand the relationship between *Tian* and the rulers as genuine, but João Rodrigues and Longobardo had argued on the contrary that the rulers were in fact atheistic and were only manipulating the people.

14 Quoted in the *Gujin*, p. 180 (n. 28) and in the *Ditian kao*, p. 34 (n. 23) where Yan Mo understands *you* 佑 not as helping but as listening (*ting* 聽), suggesting a reciprocal relationship between *Tian* and people: *Tian* listens to the people because the people are talking to Him. This passage is also quoted in its entirety in the *Tianjiao he Ru*, p. 24 (n. 7) and partially on p. 36 (n. 11).

B.2 《書經・周書・召誥》：「皇天上帝,改厥元子。」

Chapter 'Zhaogao', in volume 5 of the *Book of Imperial Annals*: 'The Supreme Lord of Great Heaven, or Great-Heaven-Supreme-Lord (in Chinese *Huangtian Shangdi*), removes the heirs from the throne'.[15]

C.3 《書經・周書・大誥》：「予造天役。」

Chapter 'Zhaogao' in volume 4 of the *Book of Imperial Annals*: 'I am doing what Heaven orders, says the ruler Cheng Wang'.

D. 《書經・周書・大誥》：「遺大投艱于朕身。」

[Chapter 'Zhaogao' in volume 4 of the *Book of Imperial Annals*] 'He imposed upon me this great and difficult task, entrusting it to me'. See below E.5 and M.12.

E.4 《書經・商書・太甲上》：「先王顧諟天之明命。」

Chapter 'Taijia' in volume 3 of the *Book of Imperial Annals*: 'The emperor before you had always this clear Law of Heaven before his eyes'.[16]

E.5 《中庸・第一》：「天命之謂性。」

Chapter 1 of the *Book of the Unalterable Mean* (in Chinese *Zhongyong*):[17] 'The Law of Heaven[18] is the infused reason of nature'.[19]

E.6 《詩經・大雅・大明》：「明明在下,赫赫在上。天難忱斯。」

Ode 'Daming' in the volume 'Daya' of the *Book of Odes*: 'Though bright virtue lies low, the power on high is terrible; thus, it is difficult to trust in Heaven'.[20]

---

15 Quoted in the *Gujin*, p. 194 (n. 32), in the *Ditian kao*, p. 36 (n. 33), and in the *Tianjiao he Ru*, p. 25 (n. 7).
16 Quoted in the *Gujin*, p. 161 (n. 19) and p. 217 (n. 42), and in the *Ditian kao*, p. 32 (n. 15) where Yan Mo, like Noël, understands *yuanzi* 元子 as meaning 'heirs to the throne'. It is also quoted in the *Tianjiao he Ru*, p. 32 (n. 9).
17 Ruggieri translates the title *Zhongyong* as 'estar siempre en el medio'. See Thierry Meynard and Roberto Villasante, *La filosofía moral de Confucio* (Madrid: Mensajero, 2018), p. 100. Just as in *Libri sex*, Noël translates here the title *Zhongyong* as 'Book of the unalterable mean', and Felix Wong has argued that Noël's translation of *yong* was influenced by the interpretation of Cheng Yi (不易之謂庸). See Wong, 'The Unalterable Mean', p. 202.
18 Wong criticizes Noël's translation of *tianming* as 'Law of Heaven' (*Coeli lex*) since it fails to see that *ming* is here a verb. See Wong, 'The Unalterable Mean', p. 206.
19 Ruggieri follows Zhu Xi and understands *xing* 性 as an equivalent of *li* 理, translating *xing* as reason (*razón*). The *Confucius Sinarum philosophus* translates *xing* as rational nature (*natura rationalis*) and Noël follows here the same line of interpretation with 'infused reason of nature'. Yet Noël had some doubt about translating *xing* as 'rational nature', because he deleted the adjective 'rational' in his manuscript of the *Zhongyong* in the *Libri sex*. See *Libri sex*, p. 41, and Wong, 'The Unalterable Mean', p. 209. Quoted also in the *Tianjiao he Ru*, p. 17 (n. 3) and p. 23 (n. 6).
20 Quoted in the *Gujin*, p. 155 (n. 14) and the *Tianjiao he Ru*, p. 17 (n. 2).

F.7 《書經・周書・泰誓》:「商罪貫盈, 天命誅之。予弗順天, 厥罪惟鈞。予小子夙夜祗懼, 受命文考, 類于上帝, 宜于冢土, 以爾有眾, 底天之罰。天矜于民, 民之所欲, 天必從之。」

> In the chapter 'Taishi' in volume 4 of the *Book of Imperial Annals*, Wu Wang addresses his courtiers: 'The crimes accumulated by the Shang dynasty have become outrageous. Heaven commands that the dynasty be punished. If I do not obey Heaven, my sin would be the same as theirs. I am filled everyday with fear and reverence and I have received the command of my deceased father Wen. Then, I have offered a sacrifice to *Shangdi* and to the Spirit of Earth so that I could exact the punishment of Heaven for all you companions and accomplices. Heaven is generous and compassionate towards people. If people seek anything from him, He shall give it to them'.[21]

G. 《書經・周書・泰誓》:「爾尚弼予一人, 永清四海, 時哉弗可失!」

> [Chapter 'Taishi' in volume 4 of the *Book of Imperial Annals*]: 'Help me alone to purify the whole empire for all eternity. Time should not be wasted'.

H.8 《書經・周書・金縢》:「乃命于帝庭, 敷佑四方。」

> Chapter 'Jinteng' in volume 4 of the *Book of Imperial Annals*: 'Wu Wang received the power in the hall of the Ruler of Heaven and spread far and wide the radiance of his virtue to help all the people of the empire'.[22]

I.9 《禮記・表記》:「子曰: 唯天子受命于天, 士受命于君。故君命順則臣有順命; 君命逆則臣有逆命。」

> Chapter 32 'Biaoji' in volume 9 of the *Book of Rites* (in Chinese *Liji*): 'Confucius says, the emperor receives his command from Heaven, and the literati from the emperor. If the emperor obeys the command of Heaven, a literatus obeys the order of the emperor; but if the emperor does not obey the order of Heaven, the literatus does not obey either'.[23]

K.10 《禮記・哀公問》:「仁人之事親也如事天, 事天如事親。」

> Chapter 27 'Aigong wen' in volume 9 of the *Book of Rites*: 'A pious son serves his parents as if he serves Heaven, and he serves Heaven as if he serves his parents'.[24]

---

21 Quoted in the *Gujin*, p. 193 (n. 32) and in the *Ditian kao*, p. 34 (n. 24–25). It is also partially quoted in the *Tianjiao he Ru*, p. 30 (n. 8) and in Noël's *Renzui zhizhong*. See Zhu Qianzhi, *Zhongguo sixiang duiyu Ouzhou wenhua yingxiang*, p. 127.
22 Ricci mentions this passage among eleven testimonies for the worship of *Shangdi*. See Ricci, *The True Meaning of the Lord of Heaven*, p. 101 (n. 108). This passage is also cited in the *Ditian kao*, p. 36 (n. 30) where Yan Mo, like Noël, understands *fuyou sifang* 敷佑四方 as meaning 'to propagate virtue to help in the four directions'. It is further mentioned in the *Tianjiao he Ru*, p. 26 (n. 7) and in Noël's *Renzui zhizhong*. See Zhu Qianzhi, *Zhongguo sixiang duiyu Ouzhou wenhua yingxiang*, p. 127.
23 The beginning is quoted in the *Tianjiao he Ru*, p. 24 (n. 7).
24 This passage is mentioned in the *Tianjiao he Ru*, p. 23 (n. 6) and p. 30 (n. 8).

L.11 《書經‧周書‧泰誓》：「惟天惠民,惟辟奉天。」

Chapter 'Taishi' in volume 4 of the *Book of Imperial Annals*: 'Heaven loves the people, and the rulers should obey Heaven'.

M.12 《書經‧周書‧泰誓》：「今商王受, 弗敬上天, 降災下民。沈湎冒色, 敢行暴虐, 罪人以族, 官人以世, 惟宮室、臺榭、陂池、侈服, 以殘害于爾萬姓。焚炙忠良, 刳剔孕婦。皇天震怒, 命我文考, 肅將天威, 大勳未集。肆予小子發, 以爾友邦冢君, 觀政于商。惟受罔有悛心, 乃夷居, 弗事上帝神祇, 遺厥先宗廟弗祀。」

In chapter 'Taishi' in volume 4 of the *Book of Imperial Annals*, Wu Wang addressed his court before attacking Emperor Zhou: 'But now, this emperor Shou (also called Zhou) does not reverence Supreme Heaven, and he inflicts many calamities on the people. He is a drunkard, lustful, and cruel. He extends the punishment of offenders to all their relatives. He awards dignities to children because of their parents. He exhausts all your strength and wealth to build for himself palaces, pavilions, and pools. He burns the good and loyal people with terrible torments and tears the wombs of pregnant women. Hence Great Heaven was moved with an extreme anger, and ordered my late father Wen to assume, with the highest respect, His authority which had been damaged, and expel the tyrant. But he could not complete the task before his death. On this account, I, Fa, a little child, see how at the hands of all of you, the nobles and assistants of the empire, the government of the Shang dynasty completely fell into ruin; but Shou has not come to senses. He spends his days at home in laziness and extravagence. He does not serve the Lord of Heaven or the spirits of heaven and earth, neglecting also the usual offerings to his deceased parents in the ancestor hall, etc.'[25] See above F.7.

N.13 《論語‧八佾》：「獲罪於天, 無所禱也。」

Chapter 3 of the *Book of the Sentences* [*Lunyu* 3.13]: 'If you sin against Heaven, there is no one to whom you can pray to escape punishment'.[26]

O.14 《書經‧周書‧泰誓上》：「有罪無罪, 予曷敢有越厥志?」

Chapter 'Taishi' in volume 4 of the *Book of Imperial Annals*: Wu Wang says, 'If someone is found guilty or innocent, how could I transgress the will (of Heaven)?'

---

25 The last sentence is quoted in the *Gujin*, p. 177 (n. 27) and in the *Ditian kao*, p. 34 (n. 22). The first sentence is quoted in the *Tianjiao he Ru*, p. 30 (n. 8) with a comment by the Song scholar Chen Dayou 陳大猷 (1188–1275), father of Chen Hao and proponent of the School of Principle. Fa 發 stands for the name of the child.

26 A literal translation of *Lunyu* 3.13 would be: 'If you sin against Heaven, there is no need to pray'. Ricci had quoted this in relation to the idea of keeping the *guishen* at distance. See Ricci, *The True Meaning of the Lord of Heaven*, p. 167 (n. 206). This passage is also quoted in the *Gujin*, p. 146 (n. 9) and in the *Ditian kao*, p. 44 (n. 60) where Yan Mo like Noël understands *wusuodao* 無所禱 as meaning 'unable to escape punishment'. In his *Renzui zhizhong*, Noël explicitly rejected Zhu Xi's interpretation based on *li*: '故孔云: "獲罪於天"者, 非獲罪於理, 乃獲罪於賦理之天主也。夫天之不可謂理者, 由諸書所言, 無不著明矣'. Cited in Zhu Qianzhi, *Zhongguo sixiang duiyu Ouzhou wenhua yingxiang*, p. 126. See Noël's translation in *Libri sex*, p. 95; Meynard, ed., *Confucius Sinarum Philosophus*, p. 166.

O.15 《禮記‧表記》：「子言之：『昔三代明王皆事天地之神明，無非卜筮之用，不敢以其私，褻事上帝。』」

Chapter 32 'Biaoji' in volume 9 of the *Book of Rites*: 'Confucius says, "In the past, the three earliest dynasties (Xia, Shang and Zhou) always used oracles in serving *Tian Di zhi shenming* (the intelligent spirit of Heaven and Earth), and they did not dare to despise the service and worship of *Shangdi* by their individual will and decision"'.[27] See here the contradictory opinions about the oracles.

P.16 《禮記‧月令》：「是月也，命四監，大合百縣之秩芻，以養犧牲。令民無不咸出其力，以共皇天上帝。」

Chapter 6 'Yueling' in volume 3 of the *Book of Rites*: 'In this month, the emperor orders that the officers in charge of mountains, lakes, forests, and rivers, together with all the other officers of his empire, quickly gather the forage to feed the animals used for sacrifices, and that all the people unite all their forces to worship the Supreme Lord of Great Heaven (*Huangtian Shangdi*)'.[28] See the Second Treatise.

Q.17 《禮記‧表記》：「天子親耕，粢盛秬鬯，以事上帝。」

Chapter 32 'Biaoji' in volume 9 of the *Book of Rites*: 'The emperor with his own hands tills the earth and prepares rice and wine to serve the Lord of Heaven'.[29]

R.18 《中庸‧第十九》：「郊社之禮，所以事上帝也。」

Chapter 19 of the *Book of the Unalterable Mean*: 'This ritual with which sacrifices are made to Heaven and Earth was instituted to serve the Lord and Ruler of Heaven'. This is to say: this sacrifice which was made to Heaven and Earth is that by which the Lord and Ruler of Heaven is served.[30]

---

27 The words *bu* 卜 and *shi* 筮 are translated with the vague terms of oracles (*sortes*). *Shenming* is translated as intelligent spirit in the singular form. The same quote is given in c.1, q.2, §.8, B2.
28 This passage is quoted in the *Tianjiao he Ru*, p. 15 (n. 1) and p. 33 (n. 10).
29 Ricci mentions this passage among his eleven testimonies for the worship of *Shangdi*. See Ricci, *The True Meaning of the Lord of Heaven*, p. 99 (n. 107). This passage is also quoted in the *Gujin*, p. 152 (n. 13) and in the *Tianjiao he Ru*, p. 35 (n. 10).
30 In his *Zhongyong zhangju* 中庸章句, Zhu Xi follows Zheng Xuan 鄭玄 (127–200) and sees an elision in the text, with the meaning that there was a double sacrifice, offered separately to *Shangdi* and to *Houtu* (不言后土者, 省文也). This passage was often discussed by the missionaries and Chinese Christians. Among his eleven testimonies for the worship of *Shangdi*, Ricci places this quote in the first position and criticizes Zhu Xi's interpretation of a double sacrifice as polytheistic. See Ricci, *True Meaning of the Lord of Heaven*, p. 97 (n. 104). Later, the *Confucius Sinarum philosophus* accepts the duality of the sacrifices, offered separately to Heaven and Earth, but holds that their finality is to worship *Shangdi*, accusing Zhu Xi of being a political-atheist in acknowledging two sacrifices given to Heaven and Earth but failing to recognize their ultimate finality in *Shangdi*. See 'Liber secundus', Couplet and others, *Confucius Sinarum philosophus*, p. 59. Bouvet quotes this passage of the *Zhongyong* and admits there were two rituals (*erli* 二禮) but dedicated to the unique *Shangdi*. See Bouvet, *Gujin*, p. 147. As can be seen from his translation, Noël accepts Zhu Xi's explanation of a double sacrifice, but he uses the singular form to express that it was one single ritual sacrifice to *Shangdi*. See also Noël's translation in Noël, *Libri sex*, p. 55. Noël was perhaps influenced by Zhang Juzheng's comment on this passage of the *Zhongyong*; see below (c.2, q.5, VV.51). This passage is also quoted in the *Gujin*, p. 147 (n. 9) and in *Ditian kao*, p. 45 (n. 62) where Yan

R.19 《孟子・離婁上》：「雖有惡人, 齋戒沐浴, 則可以祀上帝。」

Chapter 1 in the second part of the *Mencius*: 'Even someone completely defiled by disgrace can still make offerings to the Lord and Ruler of Heaven if he puts himself in order and washes himself'.[31]

R.20 《易經・渙卦》：「先王以享于帝, 立廟。」

Symbol 'Huan' in the *Books of Changes and Productions* (in Chinese *Yijing*): 'The ancient wise emperors used to make offerings to the Lord of Heaven and to erect buildings to commemorate deceased parents'.[32]

S.21 《易經・鼎卦》：「聖人亨, 以享上帝。」

Symbol 'Ding' in the *Yijing*: 'A ruler with perfect virtue and knowledge cooks and seasons himself the animal, a tender calf, to make an offering to the Lord of Heaven'.[33]

T.22 《詩經・大雅・大明》：「維此文王, 小心翼翼, 昭事上帝。」

Ode 'Daming' in the volume 'Daya' of the *Book of Odes*: 'Wen Wang, with great care, diligence and reverence, openly served the Lord of Heaven'.[34]

T.23 《書經・周書・立政》：「亦越文王、武王, 克知(三有宅心, 灼見)三有俊心, 以敬事上帝。」

Chapter 'Lizheng' in volume 5 of the *Book of Imperial Annals*: 'Wen Wang and Wu Wang knew very well that their three most important ministers intended to worship and serve the Lord of Heaven both before and after their appointment'.

Mo like Noël affirms that the rituals were to worship *Shangdi*. This passage is cited in the *Tianjiao he Ru*, p. 16 (n. 2) with a comment about the unicity of *Shangdi*. For the citation of this passage in Noël's *Renzui zhizhong*, see Zhu Qianzhi, *Zhongguo sixiang duiyu Ouzhou wenhua yingxiang*, p. 126.

31 This passage is quoted in the *Gujin*, p. 149 (n. 11) but Bouvet misinterprets *eren* 惡人 in the moral sense. This passage is also quoted in the *Ditian kao*, p. 45 (n. 65) and in the *Tianjiao he Ru*, p. 41 (n. 13). See also Noël's translation in Noël, *Libri sex*, p. 353.

32 Noël adopts the neutral translation of *miao* (temple) as buildings (*aedificia*). This passage is quoted in the *Gujin*, p. 145 (n. 9). For the citation of this passage in Noël's *Renzui zhizhong*, see Zhu Qianzhi, *Zhongguo sixiang duiyu Ouzhou wenhua yingxiang*, p. 127.

33 Noël adopts the neutral translation of the term *shengren* as ruler of absolute virtue and knowledge. The text does not specify the nature of the offering, but Noël understands it is a calf (*du* 犢), as is explained in the commentary in c.2, q.1, §.1, H.7. This small example shows that Noël's explanation of the classical text is influenced by later interpretations. This passage is quoted in the *Gujin*, p. 146 (n. 9) and in the *Tianjiao he Ru*, p. 34 (n. 10).

34 Ricci mentions this passage among his eleven testimonies for the worship of *Shangdi*. See Ricci, *True Meaning of the Lord of Heaven*, p. 99 (n. 105). Ricci mentions it a second time in the same work, commenting: 'How can anyone who refuses to believe in the existence of the Sovereign on High be called a superior man?' Ricci, *The True Meaning of the Lord of Heaven*, p. 275 (n. 406). This passage is also quoted in the *Ditian kao*, p. 40 (n. 45) and in the *Tianjiao he Ru*, p. 49 (n. 19).

V.24 王昌會《全史詳要·卷二》：「諸侯受命于周，尊武王為天子。柴于上帝，望于山川，大告武成。」

> Volume 2 of the *Book of Universal Annals*:[35] 'After being greeted as emperor by the small kings, Wu Wang made a sacrifice to the Lord of Heaven by burning victims and offerings. He made an offering to the spirits of mountains and rivers, and he announced the complete end to the war everywhere'.[36]

X.25 王昌會《全史詳要·卷一》：「帝廣宮室之制，遂作合宮，祀上帝，接萬靈，布政教焉。」

> Volume 1 of the *Book of Universal Annals*: 'After having handed down the regulations for buildings everywhere, Emperor Huangdi built the Palace of Union in which he sacrificed to the Lord of Heaven, received the nobles and the people, and taught the precepts for a good life and a good government'.

X.26 王昌會《全史詳要·卷一》：(顓頊)「於是鑄為之鐘，作五基六英之樂，以調陰陽，享上帝，朝群侯。」

> Volume 1 of the same *Book of Universal Annals*: 'Emperor Zhuanxu, grandson of Emperor Huangdi, casted a bronze bell and composed music out of five fundamental notes and with six modes for harmonizing strong and gentle passions, for making sacrifices to the Lord of Heaven, and for receiving petty kings'.

§.2. Power of *Tian* or *Shangdi* according to Ancient Authors

The immense power (*potentia*) of God is revealed especially in the fact that all things of world depend on it not only in terms of their beginning but also in terms of their preservation and operation. [The power of God is also shown] by the fact that nothing can be made without it, and all things could be stopped or destroyed by it.[37] The Chinese books attribute to *Tian* or *Shangdi* similar things, saying: everything draws its origin from Heaven (A); all things depend on a great and primaeval force to come into being (B); the active force of Heaven knows and rules the great beginnings of things (C); the Lord and Ruler of Heaven started to come out into act from the enigmatic symbol representing the equatorial region of

---

35 The *Book of Universal Annals* refers to the *Quanshi xiangyao* 全史詳要 (Detailed summary of the complete history; 30 *juan*, 1630) by the Shanghai scholar Wang Changhui 王昌會. The full set of thirty *juan* is found in ARSI, Jap. Sin. III, 11–14. The work is quoted only five times in the First Treatise: c.1, q.2, §.6, A.1, V.24, X.25 and X.26; c.1, q.2, §.8, H.8; and c.2, q.5, OOO. Though the *Quanshi xiangyao* was written during the Ming dynasty, Noël inserts those quotes in the first chapter because he considers them as historical documents which prove early ritual worship of God.

36 Noël is not shy to mention rituals offered to mountains and spirits because he understands them not as polytheistic but addressed ultimately to Heaven or *Shangdi*, as he argues below.

37 In scholastic treatises dealing with the external attributes of God, the creative power usually comes first. The Chinese texts express *Tian* as being the origin and source of everything, but do not stress the idea of *Tian* as Creator. If there is an idea of Creation in the Chinese texts, it is mostly philosophical, and not historical as in the Bible. Here Noël understands the power of God not only as origin of the physical world, but also as origin of human desires, politics, and culture.

the world [i.e. the equator] according to the charts of the *Yijing*, and all the things and productions of the world flow from this (D);³⁸ matter and form are found in all human beings produced by Heaven (E); the Lord of Heaven infused in human beings the inner correctness of a rational nature (F); Heaven placed people in China and circumscribed [their land] with boundaries (G); He produces people full of passions, yet made some men wise so that they can rule over them (H); without His command and providence, nothing can happen (I); He helps the people who are obedient and remarkable for their virtue (K); He does not allow any remnant of the family of [the tyrant] Zhou, nor does He allow them to escape (L); He can stop everything (M); He confers power (N); People pray to Him to confer the blessing of a long life and peaceful life (O); People pray to Him for a good harvest (P); with a hidden virtue He settles people down so that they can live together (Q); Heaven is the author and cause of what no human forces can achieve (R); finally, the universal and particular force of Heaven makes that all things, without conflicting with each other, are produced on earth and revolve in heaven (S).

Thus, the Chinese books attribute to Heaven or the Lord of Heaven the same power that we attribute to God. However, while they do not distinguish the Divine Power from [the attributes of] knowledge and will, except in reason of a beginning, we add knowledge and will below Divine Power, examining first knowledge [before will].³⁹

NOTES

A.1 《禮記‧郊特牲》：「萬物本乎天，人本乎祖，此所以配上帝也。郊之祭也，大報本反始也。」

> Chapter 11 in volume 5 of the *Book of Rites*: 'All things draw their origin from Heaven; human beings, from their ancestors. Thus, human beings are compared with the Lord of Heaven. By this sacrifice to Heaven, the highest thanksgivings were paid to the Principle of all things, and this sacrifice was cherished in the heart'.⁴⁰

B.2 《易經‧乾卦》「彖曰：大哉乾元，萬物資始，乃統天。」

> Symbol 'Qian' in the *Book of Changes and Productions*: 'How great is the power of Heaven as agent. All things in order to come to existence depend upon it. Its virtue encompasses all of Heaven and includes in itself all the other powers of Heaven'.

---

38 This is the closest idea of Creation as an historical event that the Jesuits could find.
39 Noël makes an interesting remark which reveals his method: the ancient Chinese texts do not distinguish between divine power, knowledge, and will, but he uses those scholastic distinctions to exhibit the scholastic attributes of God. In other words, scholasticism supplies a framework for reading the ancient Chinese texts.
40 The mention of the mind seems to be an addition by Noël. The same instance on the mind is found below in translating the same expression. See c.2, q.5, B.3 and KKK.72. The term *pei* 配 is translated as 'to be associated with' (*conferri*). This passage is quoted in the *Tianjiao he Ru*, p. 18 (n. 3) and p. 34 (n. 10).

C.3 《易經・繫辭傳上・第一章》：「乾知大始，坤作成物。」

Chapter 1 of 'Zhuan shang' in the *Book of Changes and Productions*: 'The active power of Heaven knows and rules the great beginning of things, and the compliant power of Earth gives them completion'.

D.4 《易經・說卦・第五章》：「帝出乎震…萬物出乎震。」

Chapter 5 of 'Shuogua' in the *Book of Changes and Productions*: 'While issuing commands, the Lord or Ruler of Heaven came out or started to come out into act from the enigmatic symbol *Zhen* representing the equinoctial region of the world'.[41] Further down is added: 'All the things of the world emanate from the symbol *Zhen*'. This Chinese character means a violent and great motion.

E.5 《詩經・大雅・烝民》：「天生烝民，有物有則。民之秉彝，好是懿德。」

Chapter 'Zhengmin' in the volume 'Daya' of the *Book of Odes*: 'Matter and form are found in all men produced by Heaven, and since all human beings are endowed with a common nature, everyone chooses naturally the beauty of virtue'.[42]

F.6 《書經・湯誥》：「惟皇上帝，降衷于下民。」

Chapter 'Tang gao' in volume 3 of the *Book of Imperial Annals*: 'The supreme Lord of Heaven infused man with the inner rectitude of rational nature'.[43]

G.7 《書經・梓材》：「皇天既付中國民，越厥疆土于先王。」

Chapter 'Zicai' in volume 4 of the *Book of Imperial Annals*: 'After the Supreme Lord of Heaven had established people in China, he immediately fixed territorial boundaries under the rule of the first emperors'.

---

41 Ricci mentions this passage among his eleven testimonies for the worship of Shangdi, commenting: 'This word Sovereign or emperor does not connote the material heavens. Since the blue sky embraces the eight directions, how can it emerge from one direction only?' Ricci, *The True Meaning of the Lord of Heaven*, p. 99 (n. 106). This passage is quoted in the *Tianjiao he Ru*, p. 15 (n. 1). *Zhen* 震 is associated with the east, but Noël renders it as 'equinoctial region of the world', which would suggest the equatorial region, where the length of day and night is roughly equal. Noël is attempting to link *zhen* to the equinox. See below (c.1, q.3, I). with the mention of the biblical scholar Jacques Salian. See Wang Ge's chapter in this volume.

42 Noël expresses the notions of human bodies (*wu*) and human rules (*ze*) with the Aristotelian categories of matter and form, which are used to describe the relationship between the human soul and the body. This passage is quoted in the *Gujin*, p. 136 (n. 4) and in the *Ditian kao*, p. 43 (n. 57) where Yan Mo like Noël explains *yi* 彝 as *changxing* 常性, as well as in the *Tianjiao he Ru*, p. 17 (n. 3).

43 Ricci mentions also this among his eleven testimonies. See Ricci, *The True Meaning of the Lord of Heaven*, p. 99 (n. 108). The term *zhong* in the Classical text means inner moral feelings. Noël's interpretation of the term as rational nature is consistent with his rationalistic reading of the texts based on neo-Confucianism. Though he claims to interpret the classical text independently from the neo-Confucian interpretations, he sometimes fails to do so. In fact, this passage is quoted in the *Gujin*, p. 138 (n. 5) and in the *Ditian kao*, p. 30 (n. 11) where Yan Mo like Noël understands *zhong* 衷 as meaning 'unbiased principles' (*zhongzheng zhi li* 中正之理). It is also quoted in the *Tianjiao he Ru*, p. 22 (n. 6) which similarly understands *zhong* as 'principle of great centrality and perfect correctness' (*dazhong zhizheng zhi daoli* 大中至正之道理).

H.8 《書經·仲虺之誥》：「惟天生民有欲，無主乃亂；惟天生聰明時乂。」

Chapter 'Zhonghui zhi gao' in volume 3 of the *Book of Imperial Annals*: 'Since Heaven produces people filled with desires and passions, if they are without a leader, ruler, and master, they are immediately confused; Heaven produces intelligent men to rule over the people'.⁴⁴

I.9 《易經·無妄》：「天命不佑，行矣哉？」

Symbol 'Wuwang' in the *Book of Changes and Productions*: 'Without the help of the Providence of Heaven, how could anything be done?'

K.10 《易經·繫辭傳上·第十二章》：「子曰：『祐者，助也。天之所助者，順也；人之所助者，信也。』」

Chapter 12 of 'Zhuan shang' in the [*Appendix to the*] *Book of Changes and Productions*: 'Confucius says, "If someone wants Heaven's help, he needs to be obedient; and if he wants people's help, he needs to be sincere and upright"'.

K.11 《易經·大有》：「上九自天祐之，吉，無不利。」

Symbol 'Dayou' in the *Book of Changes and Productions*: 'The supreme virtue, or the ruler of supreme virtue, is helped by Heaven, and thus, nothing bad or unpropitious will fall upon him'.⁴⁵

L.12 《詩經·大雅·雲漢》：「昊天上帝，則不我遺。昊天上帝，寧俾我遯。」

Ode 'Yunhan' in the volume 'Daya' of the *Book of Odes*: 'The Lord and Ruler of the most immense Heaven [*Haotian Shangdi*] does not allow any of us to be left over'. A little further down is added: 'O Lord and Ruler of the most immense Heaven, why do you not allow us to flee far away?'⁴⁶

M.13 《詩經·大雅·瞻卬》：「藐藐昊天，無不克鞏。無忝皇祖，式救爾後。」

Ode 'Zhanyang', in the volume 'Daya' of the *Book of Odes*: 'There is nothing at all that the most immense and excellent Heaven cannot stop. Do not bring any more disgrace to your ancestors, so that you can save your posterity'.⁴⁷

N.14 《詩經·魯頌·閟宮》：「致天之屆，于牧之野。無貳無虞，上帝臨女。」

Ode 'Bi gong' in the volume 'Lusong' in the *Book of Odes*: 'It happened that Heaven abandoned Emperor Zhou in the plain of Muye. Then, to dispel doubt, all people said: "Discard all your worries; the Lord and Ruler of Heaven approaches you", that is to say, He wants you to rule'.

---

44 This passage is quoted in the *Gujin*, p. 179 (n. 28), in the *Ditian kao*, p. 30 (n. 9) and in the *Tianjiao he Ru*, p. 25 (n. 7).
45 This passage is quoted in the *Tianjiao he Ru*, p. 36 (n. 11).
46 This passage is quoted in the *Ditian kao*, p. 43 (n. 56) and in the *Tianjiao he Ru*, p. 15 (n. 1). This passage is partially mentioned in Noël's *Renzui zhizhong*. See Zhu Qianzhi, *Zhongguo sixiang duiyu Ouzhou wenhua yingxiang*, p. 127.
47 This passage is quoted in the *Ditian kao*, p. 44 (n. 59).

O. 《詩經·魯頌·閟宮》：「天錫公純嘏,眉壽保魯。居常與許,復周公之宇。」

[Ode 'Bi gong' in the volume 'Lusong' in the *Book of Odes*]: 'May Heaven grant our ruler the great blessing of a long life to preserve the kingdom of Lu, and after the lands of our royal clan Zhou are recovered, may He allow [our ruler] to live happily in the cities of Chang and Xu'.

P.15 《禮記·月令》：「是月也,天子乃以元日,祈穀于上帝。」

Chapter 6 'Yueling' in volume 3 of the *Book of Rites*: 'On the first day of this spring, called *xin*, the emperor prays to the Lord and Ruler of Heaven for harvest'.[48]

Q.16 《書經·洪範》：「惟天陰騭下民,相協厥居。」

Chapter 'Hongfan' in volume 4 of the *Book of Imperial Annals [Shujing]*: 'Through Its hidden power, Heaven settles the people and helps and brings them to live together'.[49]

R.17 《孟子·萬章上》：「莫之為而為者,天也；莫之致而至者,命也。」

Chapter 3 'Wan Zhang shang' in the second part of the *Mencius*: 'When something happens which no human strength can achieve, Heaven is the author and cause of this'.[50]

S.18 《中庸·第三十》：「辟如四時之錯行,如日月之代明。萬物并育而不相害,道并行而不相悖,小德川流,大德敦化。」

Chapter 30 of the *Book of the Unalterable Mean*: 'We see every day countless things of different types produced together on Earth and yet they do not conflict with each other; we see the four seasons, the Sun and the Moon revolving in the sky, and yet they are not in opposition to each other. This happens certainly because of a particular underlying power that diffuses itself into all individual things in various ways, and because of a universal power that extends itself broadly to produce all things'.[51]

---

48 The classical text does not mention the name of the first day as *xin* (*sin*). Noël is reading in fact the *Liji jishuo* by Chen Hao. This quote and the commentary are found below (c.2, q.5, QQQ.78). This passage is also quoted in the *Tianjiao he Ru*, p. 43 (n. 14).

49 Quoted in the *Gujin*, p. 134 (n. 2) and in the *Ditian kao*, p. 35 (n. 28) where Yan Mo, like Noël, understands *yin* 陰 as meaning 'in darkness' (*mingmingzhizhong* 冥冥之中).

50 Noël in his translation conflates *Tian* and *ming* into a single idea of Heaven. See also his translation in Noël, *Libri sex*, p. 374. This passage is also quoted in the *Gujin*, p. 95 (n. 33) and in the *Tianjiao he Ru*, p. 44 (n. 15).

51 Noël's translation of *xiaode* and *dade* is clearly influenced by Zhu Xi's comment: 'Small virtue is part of the whole; great virtue is the root of the myriad of things' (小德者, 全體之分；大德者, 萬殊之本). See also Noël's translation in Noël, *Libri sex*, p. 70. This shows the difficulties faced by the Jesuits in expressing the original meaning of the classical texts without the neo-Confucian meaning.

§.3. Knowledge of *Tian* or *Shangdi* among Ancient Authors

Since the knowledge and power of God are interrelated attributes and knowledge extends itself to everything that power does, if the power of *Tian* or *Shangdi* is the same as the power of God, as we have shown in the preceding paragraph, we can deduce and infer what sort and how great the knowledge of [*Tian* or *Shangdi*] is. Let us see what the Chinese authors say in particular about it. They say that the Lord of Heaven has regard for the lowest things and holds awe-inspiring authority, and while looking at the four regions of the world or empire, He searches for a peaceful home for the people (A); He inspected all the kingdoms of the empire (B); He examined and directed the mind of Wang Ji (C); Heaven surveys everything with utmost clarity, and despite being so high up, He ascends and descends, approaching our affairs and doings, and every day has regard for us (D); Confucius says, how could Heaven not know me? (E); does He want me to cheat Heaven and to deceive It? (F).

If those few quotes about vision, simple intelligence, and approval are compared with the knowledge of God, surely you would conclude that they are all the same thing?[52] Since God's knowledge directs His will in its workings, let us now examine the will of Heaven or the Ruler and Lord of Heaven.

NOTES

A.1 《詩經・大雅・皇矣》:「皇矣上帝, 臨下有赫。監觀四方, 求民之莫。維此二國, 其政不獲。維彼四國, 爰究爰度。上帝耆之[憎其式廓]乃眷西顧, 止維與宅…帝遷明德…天立厥配。」

> Ode 'Huangyi' in the volume 'Daya' of the *Book of Odes*: 'That Most Excellent Lord and Ruler of Heaven, while looking at the lowest things, holds awe-inspiring authority; while inspecting the four regions of the empire, He searches for a peaceful home for the people. Since both the Xia and Shang dynasties had lost the correct way of government, during his search He inspected all the kingdoms of the empire. Once He has found someone suitable, the Ruler of Heaven immediately confers upon him power and government. Inspecting carefully the Western region, He gave this region to our ruler Tai Wang for the purpose of inhabitation'. A little further down is added: 'The Lord and Ruler of Heaven moved into this place our ruler Tai Wang, who was renowned for his virtue, and He gave him a wife as partner'.[53]

---

52 Noël makes reference to three types of knowledge of God according to scholasticism: the knowledge of the vision of God which allows Him to know existing objects; the knowledge of simple intelligence of God which allows Him to know possible objects; and the knowledge of approbation which allows Him to approve the good. Among the excerpts chosen here, (A), (B), (C), and (D) belong to the knowledge of vision; (E) and (F) belong to the knowledge of simple intelligence.

53 This passage is quoted in the *Gujin*, p. 155 (n. 14) and partially in the *Ditian kao*, p. 37 (n. 35–36). It is also partially quoted in the *Tianjiao he Ru*, p. 20 (n. 5). The expression *Tian li jue pei* 天立厥配 means that Heaven established Tai Wang as partner. Yan Mo omits this, and Noël understands it as meaning that Heaven gave Taiwang a wife as a partner. The same mistake is present in the ARSI manuscript, unless Noël wants to suggest that *Shangdi* had established human marriage, as in Genesis. For the citation of this

B. 《詩經・大雅・皇矣》：「帝作邦作對。」

[Ode 'Huangyi' in the volume 'Daya' of the *Book of Odes*]: 'The Lord and Ruler of Heaven [*Di*] inspected the mountain Qi and from there made a kingdom, and appointed someone to govern it properly'.[54]

C. 《詩經・大雅・皇矣》：「維此王季, 帝度其心。」

[Ode 'Huangyi' in the volume 'Daya' of the *Book of Odes*]: 'The Lord and Ruler of Heaven [*Di*] examined and directed the mind of Wang Ji'.[55]

D.2 《詩經・周頌・敬之》：「敬之敬之, 天維顯思, 命不易哉。無曰高高在上, 陟降厥士, 日監在茲。」

Ode 'Jingzhi' in the volume 'Zhousong' of the *Book of Odes*: 'Pay attention to reverence! Heaven watches carefully everything, and so it is not easy to keep the empire and the favour of Providence. Make sure you do not say that Heaven is high and placed on high. In fact, while ascending and descending, It constantly approaches our affairs and doings, and inspects this place'.[56]

E.3 《論語・憲問》：「子曰：不怨天, 不尤人。下學而上達。知我者, 其天乎！」

Chapter 14 of the *Book of Sentences* [*Lunyu* 14.37]: 'Confucius says: I am not angry at Heaven and I don't blame people, but through the study of lower things I arrive at the understanding of higher things; how could Heaven not know me?'[57]

F.4 《論語・子罕》：「吾誰欺？欺天乎？」

Chapter 9 of the *Book of Sentences* [*Lunyu* 9.11]: 'Confucius says: who does he want me to deceive? Does he want me to deceive Heaven?'[58]

---

passage in Noël's *Renzui zhizhong*, see Zhu Qianzhi, *Zhongguo sixiang duiyu Ouzhou wenhua yingxiang*, p. 127.

54 The classical text, does not mention the name of the mountain but the commentaries talk about Mount Qi 岐山. This passage is quoted in the *Ditian kao*, p. 38 (n. 37) where Yan Mo, like Noël, understands *zuodui* 作對 as meaning 'to choose someone to govern a place'.

55 This passage is quoted in the *Ditian kao*, p. 38 (n. 38) where Yan Mo, like Noël, understands *du* 度 as meaning 'to direct'. This passage is also quoted in the *Tianjiao he Ru*, p. 23 (n. 6) and in Noël's *Renzui zhizhong*. See Zhu Qianzhi, *Zhongguo sixiang duiyu Ouzhou wenhua yingxiang*, p. 127.

56 This passage is quoted in the *Gujin*, p. 147 (n. 10), the *Ditian kao*, p. 41 (n. 50) and in the *Tianjiao he Ru*, both partially on p. 17 (n. 2) and p. 27 (n. 8), and in its entirety on p. 19 (n. 4).

57 This passage is quoted in the *Gujin*, p. 155 (n. 14) and p. 197 (n. 33), and in the *Tianjiao he Ru*, p. 29 (n. 8) and p. 39 (n. 12). See also Noël, *Libri sex*, p. 167; Meynard, *The Jesuit Reading of Confucius*, p. 449. For the citation of this passage in Noël's *Renzui zhizhong*, see Zhu Qianzhi, *Zhongguo sixiang duiyu Ouzhou wenhua yingxiang*, p. 126.

58 This passage is quoted in the *Gujin*, p. 165 (n. 20) and in the *Tianjiao he Ru*, p. 30 (n. 8). See also Noël, *Libri sex*, p. 132; Meynard, *The Jesuit Reading of Confucius*, p. 300. For Noël's citation of this passage in Noël's *Renzui zhizhong*, see Zhu Qianzhi, *Zhongguo sixiang duiyu Ouzhou wenhua yingxiang*, p. 126.

§.4. Will of *Tian* or *Shangdi* according to Ancient Authors

I am discussing not the necessary will of God, by which God loves Himself and finds pleasure in His Infinite Goodness, but His free will, which is both effective and executive, as well as His love towards both the moral and physical good of all creatures, and His hate towards their moral evil.

In regard to Heaven [*Tian*] or the Lord of Heaven [*Shangdi*], [the ancient authors'] books say: it is not Emperor Yao but Heaven who gave the empire to Shun (A); anyone can be proposed for Heaven to give him the mandate, but Heaven cannot be forced to give it to him, just as an emperor cannot be forced by a petty king to give him a kingdom (B);[59] since Emperor Jie scorned virtue, offended the spirits, and harassed the people, Heaven removed him from the throne, and replaced him with Tang, a ruler endowed with the truest virtue (C); he ordered Tang to establish the borders of all the countries (D); Tang as minister of Emperor Yin could by his virtue win over the heart of Heaven (E); in the past, Emperor Jie did not obey Heaven and filled the whole empire with his crimes; thus, Heaven helped Tang and ordered him to remove Jie from the throne (F); [Heaven] does not reject a prince from succeeding his father's throne, unless he is similar to Jie or Zhou (G); they were all intoxicated with wine, and the foul smell of their vices reached heavenly heights; hence Heaven destroyed the power of the Yin dynasty and because of their excesses He did not show any love for them; it is not that Heaven is cruel, but that those people brought bad things upon themselves because of their crime (H); Heaven does not always love everyone, but loves those who pay respect to It (I); Tang started to make so much progress every day in the pursuit of perfection that his virtue reached Heaven with an immense splendour and could continue for some time without interruption; the Lord and Ruler of Heaven [*Shangdi*] was his only object of reverence, and hence the Lord of Heaven [*Di*] commanded him to rule over China (K); Heaven loves the people (L); [Heaven] commands those who come first in knowledge and moral behaviour to instill intelligence and moral sense into those who come later in this respect (M); the virtue of this princess was most upright, and thus the Lord of Heaven [*Shangdi*] protected her (N); all those peoples crushed by hardship look toward Heaven as someone dreaming who sees nothing, but then the Great Lord of Heaven [*Huang Shangdi*] exists; who can say that He holds anyone in contempt?[60] (O); Alas, secret Heaven poured out Its terrible anger on this lowly land, and the public policy of the government was corrupted (P); Confucius said, 'If I have done anything in this matter which violates fairness, may Heaven reject me; may Heaven reject me!' (Q).

What could be said more clearly about this multiform will of God? Could it be that all those passages agree with the will of God? But now let us discuss justice, which is His constant and eternal will of distributing His law to everyone.

---

59 Here Noël stresses the free will of *Tian*/God.
60 These passages emphasize God's fairness in punishing evil not out of hatred but out of justice.

NOTES

A.1 《孟子・萬章上》：「萬章曰：『堯以天下與舜，有諸？』孟子曰：『否。天子不能以天下與人。』『然則舜有天下也，孰與之？』曰：『天與之。』『天與之者，諄諄然命之乎？』曰：『否。天不言，以行與事示之而已矣。』」

> Chapter 3 'Wan Zhang shang' in the second part of the *Mencius*: 'The disciple Wan Zhang asks his master Mencius, "I have often heard that Emperor Yao had agreed to give his empire to his minister Shun; isn't it the case?" But Mencius answered that an emperor cannot give his empire to someone else. Wan Zhang continued asking, "When Shun obtained the empire, who gave it to him?" Mencius replied, "Heaven". Wan Zhang objected: "Did Heaven confer the empire upon Shun through precise words?" Mencius says, "Not at all; Heaven does not speak, but made it known through the excellent virtues and admirable deeds for which Shun was illustrious"'.[61]

B. 《孟子・萬章上》：「曰：『以行與事示之者，如之何？』曰：『天子能薦人於天，不能使天與之天下；諸侯能薦人於天子，不能使天子與之諸侯；大夫能薦人於諸侯，不能使諸侯與之大夫。昔者，堯薦舜於天而天受之，暴之於民而民受之。』」

> [Chapter 3 'Wan Zhang shang' in the second part of the *Mencius*]: 'When Wan Zhang asked further how, Mencius replied, "When the emperor discovers someone fit for the empire, he can propose to Heaven that he be made emperor, but he cannot force Heaven to confer the empire upon him. Similarly, when a petty king discovers someone suitable for a kingdom, he can propose to the emperor that this person be made a petty king, but he cannot force the emperor to give him a kingdom. In the past, the emperor Yao proposed to Heaven Shun for the office of emperor. Heaven accepted the proposal and made this acceptance well known far and wide among the people. The people of the empire accepted this clear action"'.[62]

C.2 《書經・咸有一德》：「夏王弗克庸德，慢神虐民。皇天弗保，監于萬方，啟迪有命，眷求一德，俾作神主。惟尹躬暨湯，咸有一德，克享天心。」

> Chapter 'Xianyou yide' in volume 3 of the *Book of Imperial Annals*: 'Emperor Jie was ruining virtue, scorning the spirits, and harassing the people. The Greatest Heaven (namely the King of Heaven) did not keep him on the throne, and looking in all directions, summoned someone to receive the empire. It looked for a man endowed with the truest virtue to appoint him as the lord of the spirits [*Shenzhu* 神主] (that is, the presider over the rituals).[63] There was only the minister Yin and the ruler Tang who were endowed with the truest virtue and could win over the heart of Heaven'.[64]

---

61 See Noël's translation in *Libri sex*, p. 370.
62 See Noël's translation in *Libri sex*, p. 371.
63 Being a human being, the emperor cannot be the master of spirits, but he presides over the ceremonies due to them.
64 The expression 'able to win over the heart of Heaven' (克享天心) does not suggest a unidirectional relationship, but a mutual and interactive relationship between Heaven and human beings. This passage

D.3 《詩經·商頌·玄鳥》：「古帝命武湯, 正域彼四方。」

Ode 'Xuanniao' in the volume 'Shangsong' of the *Book of Odes*: 'Long ago, the Lord of Heaven [*Di*] appointed the bellicose prince Tang to demarcate the borders of all the kingdoms'.[65]

E.4 See C.2.

F.5 《書經·周書·泰誓中》：「惟天惠民, 惟辟奉天。有夏桀, 弗克若天, 流毒下國。天乃佑命成湯, 降黜夏命。」

Chapter 'Taishi' in volume 4 of the *Book of Imperial Annals*: 'Heaven loves the people; kings should obey and assist Heaven. In the past, Emperor Jie disobeyed Heaven and polluted all the kingdoms subject to him with his crimes. Then, Heaven helped Prince Cheng Tang and ordered him to overthrow Jie's mandate'.[66]

G.6 《孟子·萬章上》：「繼世以有天下, 天之所廢, 必若桀紂者也。」

Chapter 3 'Wan Zhang shang' in the second part of the *Mencius*: 'For Heaven to reject a prince from succeeding his father's throne, he needs to be like Jie or Zhou'.[67]

H.7 《書經·周書·酒誥》：「庶群自酒, 腥聞在上。故天降喪于殷, 罔愛于殷, 惟逸。天非虐, 惟民自速辜。」

Chapter 'Jiugao' in volume 4 of the *Book of Imperial Annals*: 'All of them were intoxicated with wine; the stench of their vices …'. See above.[68]

I.8 《書經·商書·太甲下》：「惟天無親, 克敬惟親。」

Chapter 'Taijia' in volume 3 of the *Book of Imperial Annals*: 'Heaven does not always love all, but loves those who pay respect to It'.[69]

K.9 《詩經·商頌·長發》：「帝命不違, 至于湯齊；湯降不遲, 聖敬日躋；昭假遲遲, 上帝是祗。帝命式于九圍。」

Ode 'Changfa' in the volume 'Shangsong' of the *Book of Odes*: 'The emperors of the Xia dynasty had not yet abandoned the mandate of the Lord of Heaven [*Di*]. When the time was ripe, Tang was born in a propitious moment and started to make so much progress every day in the pursuit of perfection that his virtue reached Heaven with an immense splendour and continued for some time without

---

is quoted in the *Gujin*, p. 163 (n. 19) and p. 194 (n. 32), as well as in the *Ditian kao*, p. 32 (n. 17) which omits the mention of *shenzhu* 神主. This passage is also quoted in the *Tianjiao he Ru*, p. 32 (n. 9) and p. 47 (n. 17).

65 The first half of this passage is quoted in the *Tianjiao he Ru*, p. 14 (n. 1) and the entire passage is quoted in *Tianjiao he Ru*, p. 23 (n. 6).

66 An abbreviated form of this passage is quoted in the *Gujin*, p. 180 (n. 28), and in the *Tianjiao he Ru*, p. 25 (n. 7).

67 See Noël's translation in *Libri sex*, p. 374.

68 This passage is quoted in the *Gujin*, p. 170 (n. 24) and the *Tianjiao he Ru*, p. 37 (n. 11) and p. 47 (n. 17).

69 This passage is quoted in the *Gujin*, p. 167 (n. 22) and in the *Ditian kao*, p. 32 (n. 16) where Yan Mo like Noël understands *ke* 克 as meaning 'to be able', as well as in the *Tianjiao he Ru*, p. 39 (n. 12).

interruption. The Lord and Ruler of Heaven [*Shangdi*] was his only object of reverence. Thus, the Lord of Heaven [*Di*] commanded him to rule over all the nine provinces (or the the whole China, which had been then divided in this way)'.[70]

L.10 See F.5.

M.11 《孟子・萬章上》：「天之生此民也，使先知覺後知，使先覺覺後覺也。」

Chapter 3 'Wan Zhang shang' in the second part of the *Mencius*: 'Of all those people whom [Heaven] produces, Heaven commands those who come before others in their knowledge of things to instill understanding into those who come later in knowledge of things; and He commands those who come before others in their understanding of moral norms to impart a sense of mind to those who come later in their understanding of right conduct'.[71]

N.12 《詩經・魯頌・閟宮》：「其德不回，上帝是依。」

Ode 'Bigong' in the volume 'Lusong' of the *Book of Odes*: 'The virtue of this princess was very upright, and hence the Lord of Heaven [*Shangdi*] protected her'.[72]

O.13 《詩經・小雅・正月》：「民今方殆，視天夢夢。既克有定，靡人弗勝。有皇上帝，伊誰云憎。」

Ode 'Zhengyue' in the volume 'Xiaoya' of the *Book of Odes*: 'All those peoples when crushed by hardships and confronted with all sorts of dangers look toward Heaven as if it were a dreamer who sees nothing. But then, when the time comes for [Heaven] to accomplish what It has destined, there is no one whom Heaven does not overcome. The Greatest Ruler of Heaven exists (in Chinese *you Huang Shangdi*)! Who then can say that He hates anyone?'[73]

P.14 《詩經・小雅・小旻》：「旻天疾威，敷于下土。」

Ode 'Xiaomin' in the volume 'Xiaoya' of the *Book of Odes*: 'Alas, Heaven is hidden, etc.' See above.[74]

Q.15 《論語・雍也》：「夫子矢之曰：『予所否者，天厭之！天厭之！』」

Chapter 6 of the *Book of Sentences* [*Lunyu* 6.26]: 'After making an oath, Confucius said, "If I have done anything in this matter (concerning Nanzi, a petty king's wife, whom he had visited) that violates honesty, fairness, and reason, may Heaven reject me; may Heaven reject me!"'[75]

---

70 Ricci mentions the second part of this quote among his eleven testimonies for the worship of *Shangdi*. See Ricci, *The True Meaning of the Lord of Heaven*, p. 99 (n. 105). This passage is also quoted in the *Gujin*, p. 182 (n. 28), the *Ditian kao*, p. 37 (n. 34) and the *Tianjiao he Ru*, p. 31 (n. 9).
71 This passage is quoted in the *Tianjiao he Ru*, p. 17 (n. 3). See also Noël's translation in *Libri sex*, p. 377.
72 This passage is quoted in the *Tianjiao he Ru*, p. 37 (n. 11).
73 This passage is quoted in the *Gujin*, p. 206 (n. 38), the *Ditian kao*, p. 43 (n. 58) and *Tianjiao he Ru*, p. 37 (n. 11).
74 This passage is quoted in the *Tianjiao he Ru*, p. 46 (n. 16).
75 According to the classical text of *Lunyu* 6.26 and to the commentaries by Zhu Xi and Zhang Juzheng,

§.5. Justice of *Tian* or *Shangdi* according to Ancient Authors

According to Saint Thomas, the distributive justice of God, or rather His super-justice, is that which gives to all according to their merit: namely, reward to the good, and punishment to the bad.[76] Since the fullness of God's justice is His mercy, we shall also touch upon it here. Now let us see what the ancient books say about justice and mercy.

When the later emperors of the Xia dynasty discarded the splendid examples and virtues of their ancestors, Heaven cast down various calamities and used the hand of Prince Tang to transfer the empire to him (A); [Heaven] did not transfer this empire to him unjustly since Heaven, as the facilitator of virtue, considers only the truth or falsity of virtue in order to send good or evil things (B). Emperor Jie, who was the last of the Xia dynasty, is very guilty, and Heaven decrees that he should be punished. Prince Tang says, 'I fear the Lord of Heaven and I do not dare to punish Emperor Jie' (C). Emperor Jie, brimming with crimes, fraudulently abused the highest Heaven to rule over the people, but the Lord of Heaven made use of his crimes and chose the Shang dynasty and Prince Tang to receive the empire (D). The correct way for Heaven to act is to bless the good and curse the wicked. It sent forth several evils upon the Xia dynasty to reveal its crimes; thus, Prince Tang says, 'I obey the commands of the greatly angered majesty of Heaven, and I do not dare to spare him' (E). He continues, 'Some of you have a lot of virtue and wisdom, and I dare not to disregard you. If I myself sin, I do not dare to forgive myself. Indeed, I only consider what the heart of the Lord of Heaven considers and has ratified' (F). Finally, about the following dynasty, known as the Yin or Shang: 'They were drinking wine, and the stench of their vices reached up high; therefore, Heaven destroyed the rule of the Yin dynasty and did not love the people of that family because of their unrestrained passions. Heaven is not cruel, but because of their sin, those people brought this evil upon themselves'. (G). 'The Lord of Heaven punished cruelly the reigning emperor Zhou, the last of the Yin dynasty' (H). 'The people of the Miao region corrupted justice either through money or through power, and oppressed the innocent; hence the Lord of Heaven correctly punished them,

---

Confucius was calling upon Heaven to make an oath. This passage presented a difficulty for the authors of the *Confucius Sinarum philosophus* since it is a violation of the Second Commandment for Christians to invoke God as a witness (Exodus 20:7, Deuteronomy 5:21). Therefore, the *Confucius Sinarum philosophus* makes the point that Confucius did make the oath to Heaven but was not bound by the religious obligation of Judaism. See Meynard, *The Jesuit Reading of Confucius*, p. 238. Obviously, Chinese Catholics were not allowed to make an oath to Heaven, as Confucius had done. *Lunyu* 6.26 is also quoted in the *Gujin*, p. 199 (n. 34) and in the *Tianjiao he Ru*, p. 37 (n. 11). See Noël's translation in *Libri sex*, p. 117.

76 Distributive justice is done between unequals, like a ruler or God distributing in a fair way rewards and punishments towards men. Commutative justice is done between equals, like men exchanging goods, money, or duties. See Aquinas, *Summa theologica*, IIa IIae q.58, a.2. In certain circumstances justice needs to go beyond positive law due to the inherent imperfections of positive law; see Aquinas, *Summa theologica*, IIa IIae 120.1 ad 2. The concept of *superjustitia* is not used by Aquinas but by Suárez. See the chapter by Galassi in this volume, p. 137.

and those who could not escape the punishment were completely destroyed' (I). 'The Lord of Heaven does not always keep the same mode of action: He sends forth countless good things to those who act well and countless bad things to those who act badly' (K). Confucius said, 'Heaven rewards those who act well, and punishes those who act badly' (L). May punishment always instill fear in you; Heaven does not bring unjust punishment, but people bring punishment upon themselves (M). Alas, am I alone in misery? What reason did I give to Heaven? What is my crime? (N) O Heaven, you are called the Father and Mother or parent of people and yet I am still buried under dreadful calamities despite being innocent (O). Heaven is merciful towards people and loves them (P).

I refrain from citing more because these passages are enough to show clearly on a general level God's true justice and mercy. I am not sure whether even Christian books could express this more explicitly.⁷⁷ But let us now see if life is an attribute of *Tian* or *Shangdi*, thus implying there is nothing dead in Him.

NOTES

A.1 《書經‧商書‧伊訓》：「于其子孫弗率, 皇天降災, 假手于我有命。」

Chapter 'Yi Xun' in volume 3 of the *Book of Imperial Annals*: 'When the emperors of the later Yin dynasty ...' See above.

B.2 《書經‧商書‧咸有一德》：「非天私我有商, 惟天祐于一德[...]惟天降災祥在德。」

Chapter 'Xianyou yide' in volume 3 of the *Book of Imperial Annals*: 'It was not unjust for Heaven to confer power on Prince Tang. Indeed, Heaven supports him who shines with the purest virtue'. And a little further down: 'In order to send good or evil Heaven only considers whether the virtue is pure, mixed, or false'.⁷⁸

C.3 《書經‧商書‧湯誓》：「有夏多罪, 天命殛之[...]予惟聞汝眾言, 夏氏有罪, 予畏上帝, 不敢不正。'

Chapter 'Tang Shi' in volume 3 of the *Book of Imperial Annals*: 'That emperor Jie, who was the the last of Xia dynasty, is very guilty, and Heaven decrees that he should be punished'. A little further down: 'I have heard', Prince Tang says, 'all your complaints; Emperor Jie is greatly guilty; I fear the Lord of Heaven [*Shangdi*], and I do not dare to leave [Jie] unpunished'.⁷⁹

---

77 Noël suggests that Christians can learn something about God's justice in Chinese classics.
78 The classical text expresses only the idea that Heaven's justice depends on virtue. Here three different states of virtue are given — being pure, mixed or false. This passage is quoted in the *Gujin*, p. 167 (n. 22) and in the *Ditian kao*, p. 32 (n. 17).
79 Ricci mentions this among his eleven testimonies for the worship of *Shangdi*. See Ricci, *The True Meaning of the Lord of Heaven*, p. 99 (n. 108). This passage is quoted in the *Gujin*, p. 193 (n. 32) and in *Ditian kao*, p. 29 (n. 8).

D.4 《書經・商書・仲虺之誥》:「夏王有罪,矯誣上天,以布命于下。帝用不臧,式商受命。」

Chapter 'Zhonghui zhi gao' in volume 3 of the *Book of Imperial Annals*: 'Emperor Jie, brimming with crimes …' See above.[80]

E.5 《書經・商書・湯誥》:「天道福善禍淫,降災于夏,以彰厥罪。肆台小子,將天命明威,不敢赦。敢用玄牡,敢昭告于上天神后,請罪有夏。」

Chapter 'Tang gao' in volume 3 of the *Book of Imperial Annals*: 'The correct way for Heaven to act is to bless the good and to curse the wicked. It sent forth several evils upon the Xia dynasty to reveal its crimes. I am a little child', says Prince Tang, 'I obey the commands of the greatly angered majesty of Heaven, and I have dared not to spare It, but to use a tender little black calf to sacrifice to It,[81] and to openly inform the Spirit of the highest Heaven and of the dense Earth, which in Chinese is called *Shangtian shenhou* (just as a Christian bachelor [scholar] in his book addresses the spiritual king of the highest Heaven),[82] requesting permission to punish the crimes of the Xia dynasty'.[83]

F. 《書經・商書・湯誥》:「爾有善,朕弗敢蔽;罪當朕躬,弗敢自赦,惟簡在上帝之心。」

Shortly after [in chapter 'Tang gao' in volume 3 of the *Book of Imperial Annals*], Prince Tang continues before a large assembly: 'I do not dare not to examine those among you who excell virtue and wisdom. If I myself sin, I do not dare to forgive myself. Indeed, I only consider what the heart [*xin*] of the ruling Heaven considers and has approved'.[84] Chapter 20 of the *Book of Sentences* [*Lunyu*] quotes this passage with a few changes: 'I, Li (the name of Prince Tang), am a little child, and yet have dared to use a tender black calf for sacrificing to [Heaven], and to inform openly the Spirit of the Great Heaven and of the Thick Earth, which in Chinese is *Huanghuang houdi*'.[85] As Zhang Juzheng, prime minister of the empire, states in his famous commentaries: 'Emperor Jie is guilty of many crimes, and I do not dare to forgive him and to turn a blind eye. All those wise men are your ministers, Ruler of Heaven. I won't allow that they live in obscurity, without honour and official position. Indeed, I only consider what your heart [*xin*], Lord of Heaven, considers and has approved'.[86]

---

80 This passage is quoted in the *Gujin*, p. 193 (n. 32) and in the *Ditian kao*, p. 30 (n. 10).
81 As mentioned in the *Confucius Sinarum philosophus*, black was the colour used by the Xia dynasty. See Meynard, *The Jesuit Reading of Confucius*, p. 582.
82 Noël is possibly alluding here to the spiritual writings of Li Jiugong 李九功 (c. 1605–1681).
83 The *Confucius Sinarum philosophus* commenting on *Lunyu* 20.1 also translates this passage of the *Shujing*. See Meynard, *The Jesuit Reading of Confucius*, p. 583. This passage is quoted in the *Ditian kao*, p. 31 (n. 12) and partially in the *Tianjiao he Ru*, p. 38 (n. 12) and p. 47 (n. 17).
84 Quoted in the *Gujin*, p. 154 (n. 14) and in the *Ditian kao*, p. 31 (n. 13).
85 *Lunyu* 20:「予小子履,敢用玄牡,敢昭告于皇皇后帝:有罪不敢赦。帝臣不蔽,簡在帝心」. The *Shujing* mentions the two divinities, *Shangtian shenhou* 上天神后, given in the *Lunyu* as *Huanghuang houdi*. In translating this passage of the *Lunyu*, the *Confucius Sinarum philosophus* conflated the two divinities into one: the Thrice-Great and Most August King and Emperor of Heavens, with the expression of thrice-great alluding to Hermes Trimegistus. Here Noël refrains from any Figurism. This passage of the *Lunyu* is also quoted in the *Tianjiao he Ru*, p. 15 (n. 1) and p. 39 (n. 12). See Noël's translation in *Libri sex*, p. 196.
86 Zhang Juzheng's commentary is misplaced and should be inserted in Chapter 2. For the Chinese text of

NOTE: In the *Book of Imperial Annals* is written '*Shangtian shenhou*', that is, 'the spiritual king' or 'princely Spirit of highest Heaven', as I have written above. However, in the *Book of Sentences* is written *Huanghuang houdi*, which literally translates to 'king of kings', 'ruler', or 'lord'. Indeed, those four characters in the word *Huanghuang houdi* each signify 'king', 'prince', 'ruler', 'sovereign', or 'lord', although the Chinese take the first three characters differently, as we will see below.

G.6 《書經·周書·酒誥》：「庶群自酒, 腥聞在上。故天降喪于殷, 罔愛于殷, 惟逸。天非虐, 惟民自速辜。」

Chapter 'Jiugao' in volume 4 of the *Book of Imperial Annals*: 'They were drinking wine, etc.'

H.7 《書經·周書·立政》：「帝欽罰之。」

Chapter 'Lizheng' in volume 5 of the *Book of Imperial Annals*: 'The Lord of Heaven severely punished that emperor [the emperor Zhou]'.

I.8 《書經·周書·呂刑》：「惟時庶威奪貨, 斷制五刑, 以亂無辜, 上帝不蠲, 降咎于苗。苗民無辭于罰, 乃絕厥世。」

Chapter 'Lüxing' in volume 6 of the *Book of Imperial Annals*: 'Those peoples of the Miao region, etc.'[87]

K.9 《書經·商書·伊訓》：「惟上帝不常, 作善降之百祥, 作不善降之百殃。」

Chapter 'Yixun' in volume 3 of the *Book of Imperial Annals*: 'The Lord of Heaven does not always, etc.'[88] See above.

L.10 《孔子家語·在厄》：「由也, 昔者聞諸夫子：『為善者, 天報之以福；為不善者, 天報之以禍。』」

Chapter 20 of the *Book of the Domestic Sayings of Confucius* [*Kongzi jiayu*]: 'Teacher', he says addressing Confucius, 'I, your disciple You, remember that you once said, "Heaven rewards those who act well, and punishes those who act badly"'.

M.11 《書經·周書·呂刑》：「永畏惟罰。非天不中, 惟人在命。天罰不極, 庶民罔有令政在于天下。」

Chapter 'Lüxing' in volume 6 of the *Book of Imperial Annals*: 'Punishment in you, etc.'[89] See above.

Zhang's commentary, which is not found in the ARSI manuscript, see Zhang Juzheng 張居正, *Zhang Juzheng jiangping Lunyu* 張居正講評論語, ed. by Chen Shengxi 陳生璽 (Shanghai: Shanghai cishu chubanshe, 2007), p. 311: 「今夏王無道, 得罪于天, 乃天討必加, 我當明正其罪而不敢赦。其賢人君子為上天所眷命者, 這都是帝臣, 我當顯揚于朝而不敢隱。蓋凡此有罪有德的人, 都一一簡在上帝之心」. In the second chapter, Noël quotes the *Sishu rijiang* with a similar interpretation.

87 This passage is quoted partially in the *Tianjiao he Ru*, p. 48 (n. 18).
88 This passage is quoted in the *Ditian kao*, p. 31 (n. 14) and in the *Tianjiao he Ru*, p. 15 (n. 1) and p. 38 (n. 12).
89 This passage is quoted in the *Tianjiao he Ru*, p. 40 (n. 12), p. 46 (n. 16), p. 48 (n. 17) and p. 49 (n. 18); an abbreviated form of this passage is also quoted in the *Gujin*, p. 170 (n. 24).

N.12 《詩經‧小雅‧小弁》：「我獨于罹。何辜于天?我罪伊何?」

Ode 'Xiaobian' in the volume 'Xiaoya' of the *Book of Odes*: 'Alas, I am alone, etc.' See above.

O.13 《詩經‧小雅‧巧言》：「悠悠昊天, 曰父母且。無罪無辜, 亂如此憮。昊天已威, 予慎無罪。」《詩經‧小雅‧何人斯》：「不愧于人, 不畏于天。」

Ode 'Qiaoyan' in the volume 'Xiaoya' of the *Book of Odes*: 'O most distant, hidden and immense Heaven! You are called the Father and Mother of mankind, and though myself I am without a crime, I am buried under dreadful calamities for no reason. O strict majesty of the immense Heaven, I consider myself innocent in this affair'.[90] In the following ode 'He ren si': 'Are you not ashamed in front of people? Do you not fear Heaven?'[91]

P.14 《書經‧周書‧泰誓上》：「天矜于民」;《書經‧周書‧泰誓中》：「惟天惠民。」

Chapter 'Taishi' in volume 4 of the *Book of Imperial Annals*: 'Heaven is merciful towards people'; and shortly after: 'Heaven loves people'.[92]

§.6. Life of *Tian* or *Shangdi* according to Ancient Authors

Since God's understanding is His living,[93] and since we have seen in paragraph 3 that knowledge or understanding is an attribute of *Tian* or *Shangdi*, we can thus deduce that He is also endowed with life. But I do not investigate here the essence of what it means to live, that is, to move oneself mostly through action or an immanent operation, but I shall discuss only the internal and external operations, with which the principle from which they proceed or the subject (*suppositum*) towards which they are oriented is indicated to be living.[94] These operations include offering, giving, command, speech, hearing, vision, adoption, and prayer.

Therefore, their books say: the Lord of Heaven presented the best minister in dreams to Emperor Gaozong (A); Wu Wang dreamt that the Lord of Heaven offered him nine teeth, i.e., nine years (B); the Lord of Heaven was angered at the depravity of Prince Gun and He did not confer on him the nine laws of good government (C); while the Ruler of Heaven had torn down the power of the Yin dynasty, He stimulated the virtue of Wu Wang and amassed all power in him (D);

---

90 With the quotes in N.12 and O.13, Noël suggests a crisis of faith in Heaven, who fails to protect the just person. Those passages are quite limited in comparison to the many quotes that Noël provides in support of the Jesuit thesis of a monotheistic China. Those two quotes are not intended to support atheism, and Noël could probably feel safe to introduce them here because the Bible itself contains passages suggesting a crisis of faith in God's justice, such as the recriminations of Job. The first sentence is quoted in the *Tianjiao he Ru*, p. 22 (n. 6).
91 This passage is quoted in the *Tianjiao he Ru*, p. 30 (n. 8).
92 This passage is quoted in the *Tianjiao he Ru*, p. 37 (n. 11).
93 Aquinas, *Summa contra gentiles*, I.99: 'Intelligere autem et vivere Dei ipse est Deus'.
94 The scholastic concept of *suppositum* corresponds to an individual substance underlying all the accidents of a thing.

when Heaven was looking for a prince who was suited to rule, only the princes of the Zhou dynasty were found worthy to become emperors, and He instructed them in a remarkable way (E); since Wu Wang has visited the kingdoms of the petty kings, Heaven adopted him as a son, choosing him as emperor (F); the Lord of Heaven has made the famous emperors Cheng and Kang rule (G); the Lord of Heaven speaks with Wen Wang (H); the emperor must pray to Heaven for the preservation of his rule (I); Heaven sees and hears according to what the people see and hear (K).

Do not all those figures of speech indicate clearly enough that there is life in that which we are discussing? From what has been said, there is clearly a kind of life, and this will be shown further below. But let us now turn to Immensity and Eternity.

NOTES

A.1　《書經・說命上》：「夢帝賚予良弼。」

In chapter 'Yueming' in volume 3 of the *Book of Imperial Annals*, Emperor Gaozong says: 'The Lord of Heaven offered to me in dreams the best minister and servant of the empire'. The same is said in the volume 2 of the *Book of Universal Annals*.[95]

B.2　《禮記・文王世子》：「文王謂武王曰：『女何夢矣？』武王對曰：『夢帝與我九齡。』」

Chapter 8 'Wenwang shizi' in the *Book of Rites*: 'Wen Wang said when talking to his son Wu Wang, "Please tell me what your dream was". Wu Wang answered back: "I dreamt that the Ruler of Heaven gave me nine teeth". Wen Wang explained then how to understand the nine teeth'.

C.3　《書經・洪範》：「鯀陻洪水，汩陳其五行。帝乃震怒，不畀洪範九疇。」

Chapter 'Hongfan' in volume 4 of the *Book of Imperial Annals*: 'In order to hold back the waters of the raging deluge, Prince Gun had disturbed the five universal primary principles of natural things. The Lord and Ruler of Heaven was moved by a terrible anger, and He did not confer on him the common nine laws or rules for correct government'.[96]

D.4　《書經・君奭》：「在昔上帝，割申勸寧王之德，其集大命于厥躬。」

Chapter 'Junshi' in volume 5 of the *Book of Imperial Annals*: 'In the past the Lord of Heaven had torn down the rule of the Yin dynasty, and strenuously promoted the virtue of Wu Wang and amassed the full power of the whole empire in him'.

95　This passage is quoted in the *Gujin*, p. 158 (n. 16).
96　This passage is quoted in the *Gujin*, p. 177 (n. 27) and in the *Ditian kao*, p. 35 (n. 29). It is also partially quoted in the *Tianjiao he Ru*, p. 37 (n. 11). For the citation of this passage in Noël's *Renzui zhizhong*, see Zhu Qianzhi, *Zhongguo sixiang duiyu Ouzhou wenhua yingxiang*, p. 127.

E.5 《書經・多方》:「天惟求爾多方, 大動以威, 開厥顧天。惟爾多方, 罔堪顧之。惟我周王, 靈承于旅, 克堪用德, 惟典神天。天惟式教我用休, 簡畀殷命, 尹爾多方。」

> Chapter 'Duofang' in volume 5 of the *Book of Imperial Annals*: 'Heaven was searching all those regions for someone who could hold the power. It used weighty signs to impress a strong motion so that someone's soul would be induced to receive the decree of a favourable Heaven. There was no one anywhere who could match the order of a favourable Heaven. Only the princes of our Zhou dynasty, because of their particular skill in gathering all souls and the splendour of their virtue, were found worthy of becoming the masters of the spiritual Heaven,[97] that is to say, they received office and power. Therefore, Heaven instructed and chose them in a remarkable way, and transferred the power of the Yin dynasty to them, to manage and organize all your provinces'.

《詩經・大雅・卷阿》:「俾爾彌爾性, 百神爾主矣。」[非徒為祭主, 乃神之精靈依為主也。]

> NOTE: Here and elsewhere the Chinese emperor is called the master of spiritual Heaven and of all the spirits (that is, pontifex or priest). This is both because he is the master of the sacrifices made to the spirits, and also because those spirits depend upon his rule for worship.[98] Fan [Zhiheng] & Wan [Jing], who collated [the commentaries of] various interpreters, comment on these words in the ode 'Juan A' [卷阿] in the volume 'Daya' of the *Book of Odes*: 'May you become the master of all spirits for your entire life!'[99] According to them, the word 'master' means not only that he becomes the master of the sacrifices, but also that the perfect intelligence of the spirits depends on his control.

《書經・夏書・胤征》:「天吏逸德, 烈于猛火。」

> This way of speaking clearly does not mean that the emperor is superior to or controls the Lord of Heaven, but it is similar to how we say that this man is the commander, governor, or the tribune of such and such a king, that is to say, he was appointed tribune or governor by the king, or in the king's name. For this reason, the Chinese emperor is called the legate of Heaven. In the chapter 'Yinzheng' of volume 2 of the *Book of Imperial Annals* is written: 'If the legate of Heaven (the emperor) punishes indiscriminately good and evil people, then he will become crueller than a burning fire'.

---

97 Noël reads *shentian* together as spiritual Heaven, but it should be *shen Tian* (the spirits and Heaven). Legge translates *dian shen tian* as 'to preside over (all services to) spirits and to Heaven'. In the note just below, Noël expresses the correct meaning. In commenting 'Duofang', Bouvet states that God has planned from all eternity to send His own son to rule all humanity. See *Gujin*, p. 183 (n. 28).

98 Noël is correct in referring to the role of the emperor in the sacrifices made to Heaven and the spirits. In ancient Rome, the *pontifex* exercised religious functions within the college of pontiffs. The leader of this college was the *pontifex maximus*, the functions of which were subsumed by the emperor during the imperial period. In ancient China, the ruler exercised individually the religious function of communicating with his ancestors.

99 Fan Zhiheng 范之恆 (dates unknown) and Wan Jing 萬經 (1659–1741) published the *Bianzhitang dingzheng shijing shuoyue jijie* 辨志堂訂正詩經說約集解 in eight *juan*. See Chapter 2.11.

《字彙·吏字》：「交所使者曰吏。受命於天謂之天吏。受命於君謂之官吏。」

There are similar metaphors elsewhere. Under the entry for the character *Li* [吏] the dictionary *Zihui* explains the double-character word 'legate of Heaven' [天吏] as 'the one who receives order from Heaven', while the one receiving orders from the prince is called 'the legate or officer of the prince'.[100] Similarly, the Chinese emperor is appointed emperor by Heaven or the Lord of Heaven and is called the son of Heaven. The Lord of Heaven is said to be the emperor's superior, as can be seen here above and below, as well in the following chapter, especially in §.6.n. 1 [c.2, q.1, §.6, A.1].

F.6 《詩經·周頌·時邁》：「時邁其邦，昊天其子之。」

Ode 'Shimai' in the volume 'Zhousong' of the *Book of Odes*: 'When I', says Wu Wang 'visited at the appointed times the kingdoms of petty kings, Heaven adopted me as son (i.e., emperor)'.[101]

G.7 《詩經·周頌·執競》：「不顯成康，上帝是皇。」

Ode 'Zhijing' in the volume 'Zhousong' of the *Book of Odes*: 'Did not the emperors Cheng and Kang shine most brightly? The Lord of Heaven appointed them to rule'.[102]

H.8 《詩經·大雅·皇矣》：「帝謂文王：『予懷明德，不大聲以色。』」

Ode 'Huangyi' in the volume 'Daya' of the *Book of Odes*: The Lord of Heaven spoke to Wen Wang: 'I favour your secret and remarkable virtue, which springs forth in your heart without many words or external appearance'.[103]

I.9 《書經·召誥》：「王其德之用，祈天永命。」

Chapter 'Zhaogao' in volume 5 of the *Book of Imperial Annals*: 'The emperor should use his own virtue to pray to Heaven for the permanence of his empire'. A little further down Prince Zhao Gong continues as follows: 'I, the emperor, offer to you this reel of silk to be used for the sacrifices in the future and to pray to Heaven for the permanence of the empire'.

K.10 《書經·周書·泰誓中》：「天視自我民視，聽自我民聽。」

Chapter 'Taishi' in volume 4 of the *Book of Imperial Annals*: 'Heaven sees and hears according to what our people see and hear'.[104]

---

100 The dictionary *Zihui* 字彙 was compiled by Mei Yingzuo 梅膺祚, published in 1615. It is arranged according to 214 radicals. ARSI has an edition in fourteen *juan* printed in Zhejiang in 1687. For a discussion of Noël's translation of *tianli* and *tianzi* to show the transcendence of *tian*, see Wang Ge's chapter in this volume, p. 116.
101 This passage is quoted in the *Ditian kao*, p. 41 (n. 48).
102 Ricci mentions this among the eleven testimonies for the worship of *Shangdi*. See Ricci, *The True Meaning of the Lord of Heaven*, p. 46 (n. 105). This passage is also quoted in the *Ditian kao*, p. 41 (n. 49).
103 This passage is quoted in the *Ditian kao*, p. 38 (n. 40) and in the *Tianjiao he Ru*, p. 21 (n. 5). For reference to the passage in Noël's *Renzui zhizhong*, see Zhu Qianzhi, *Zhongguo sixiang duiyu Ouzhou wenhua yingxiang*, p. 127.
104 This passage is quoted in the *Gujin*, p. 155 (n. 14) and in the *Tianjiao he Ru*, p. 21 (n. 5). This passage is discussed by Wang Ge in Chapter 4 of this volume, p. 116.

§.7. Immensity and Eternity of *Tian* or *Shangdi* according to Ancient Authors

I discuss here the double perfection of God, that is, his Immensity and Eternity. Understand what the books hint about both these things with these few words: as they say, the Law of Heaven runs its own course in a silent and mysterious way without interruption and end (A); whoever reveres the anger and changes of Heaven does not dare to trifle and enjoy oneself; wherever you go and wander, Heaven sees very clearly and reaches (B); behold, I offer the sacrificial offering to Heaven, and I beseech Heaven to stay on the right side of the offering (C); the immense Lord of Heaven is the king of the people living in this world below (D); the spirit does not have a specific place (E); O very vast and immense Heaven, do you not think or do you not devise plans? (F).

These few things suffice to express the immense existence of the Lord of Heaven in time and place.[105]

NOTES

A.1 《詩經·周頌·維天之命》：「維天之命,於穆不已。於乎不顯,文王之德之純。」

Ode 'Weitian' in the volume 'Zhousong' in the *Book of Odes*: 'How secretly and mysteriously does the Law of Heaven continuously run its own course without interruption or end! How could it be more apparent? The virtue of Wen Wang, perfect before all, has never ceased'.[106]

B.2 《詩經·大雅·板》：「敬天之怒,無敢戲豫；敬天之渝,無敢馳驅。昊天曰明,及爾出王。昊天曰旦,及爾游衍。」

Ode 'Ban' in the volume 'Daya' in the *Book of Odes*: 'Whoever fears the anger of Heaven does not dare to trifle and laugh; whoever reveres the changes of Heaven, does not dare to enjoy and indulge himself. The term "very vast and hidden Heaven" means that [Heaven] sees very clearly and reaches wherever you go. Indeed, "very vast and hidden Heaven" means that [Heaven] illuminates everything and reaches wherever you wander'.[107]

C.3 《詩經·周頌·我將》：「我將我享,維羊維牛,維天其右之。」

Ode 'Wojiang' in the volume 'Zhousong' of the *Book of Odes*: 'I offer in person here a lamb, there a calf. May Heaven stand (or Heaven stands) at its right side'.[108]

---

105 Noël stresses that *Tian, Shangdi,* or *shen* transcends time and space, not being bound to a particular time or place.
106 This passage is quoted in the *Gujin*, p. 132 (n. 1).
107 This passage is quoted in the *Gujin*, p. 155 (n. 14), in the *Ditian kao*, p. 42 (n. 54), and in the *Tianjiao he Ru*, p. 19 (n. 4) and p. 46 (n. 16).
108 This passage is quoted in the *Gujin*, p. 152 (n. 13), in the *Ditian kao*, p. 40 (n. 47), and in the *Tianjiao he Ru*, p. 35 (n. 10).

D.4 《詩經・大雅・蕩之》：「蕩蕩上帝,下民之辟。」

Ode 'Dangzhi' in the volume 'Daya' in the *Book of Odes*: 'The immense Lord of Heaven is the king of the people living in this lowest sphere'.[109]

E.5 《易經・繫辭傳上・第四章》：「神無方而《易》無體。」

Chapter 4 of 'Zhuan shang' in the *Book of Changes and Productions*: 'The spirit lacks a specific place; the teaching of the *Book of Changes and Productions* or *Yijing* lacks a specific object'.

F.6 《詩經・小雅・雨無正》：「浩浩昊天, 不駿其德。降喪飢饉, 斬伐四國。旻天疾威, 弗慮弗圖。舍彼有罪, 既伏其辜。若此無罪, 淪胥以鋪。」

Ode 'Yuwuzheng' in the volume 'Xiaoya' in the *Book of Odes*: 'Alas, the extremely vast, immense, and secret Heaven does not spread the benefits of His virtue, but sends forth the deadly disasters of barrenness, and destroys all the kingdoms. O strict majesty of merciful Heaven, do not you think or make plans? If you abandon and destroy the guilty and wicked, when they are found guilty, they receive willingly the punishment for their crimes. But how could it seen that those who are innocent are indiscriminately cast down to their death?'[110]

§.8. Simplicity of *Tian* or *Shangdi* according to Ancient Authors

In order to prove the simplicity of God, Saint Thomas says that God is Spirit: 'God is spirit' (Job 6).[111] Indeed, a spirit is not made of quantitative parts, and therefore it is simple and much more noble than a body, because the spirit is the means with which a body lives. Let us see now whether *Tian* or *Shangdi* is a spirit according to those books. They say, 'O very vast Ruler of Heaven, or very vast Heaven, Supreme Lord and Ruler, do you not consider us? While we so reverently worship you, intelligent spirit, surely you should not be angry at us?' (A). The first three Chinese dynasties served the Spirit of Heaven and Earth, who was called the Lord and Ruler of Heaven (B). 'Without the rites', Confucius says, 'there are no rules for managing the service and worship of the Spirit of Heaven and Earth' (C). All the rites established for nourishing the living, burying the dead, and serving the spirits and the Lord of Heaven, came from that first origin (D). Spiritual Heaven gave the sceptre to the princes of the Zhou dynasty (E). Spiritual Heaven's way of action directs the four seasons of the year without error (F). The thing of the highest Heaven is free from sound and smell, or sense perception (G). Prince Fuxi offered sacrificial victims to the Spirit (H). Prince Cheng Tang warned the spiritual

---

109 This passage is quoted in the *Gujin*, p. 135 (n. 2), the *Ditian kao*, p. 42 (n. 55), and the *Tianjiao he Ru*, p. 22 (n. 6). The first half of the passage is also quoted in the *Tianjiao he Ru*, p. 19 (n. 4).
110 The first four characters of this passage are quoted in the *Tianjiao he Ru*, p. 19 (n. 4).
111 Following Saint Augustine, Aquinas defines the simplicity of God as being beyond every form of composition used by the intellect to apprehend an object, and this means that God is unlike corporeal objects with parts and quantity. See Aquinas, *Summa theologiae*, Iª pars, q.3. Aquinas cites John 4:24, not Job 6 as Noël indicates.

king or spirit of the highest Heaven; this means that he inquired about His will or sought from Him permission (I).

Since they affirm that spiritual Heaven, Heaven's spiritual way of action, and the spiritual Lord or King of Heaven, are free from sense perception, the Spirit certainly resides in Heaven. Indeed, they call the Lord of Heaven Spirit. Therefore, the simplicity of the Spirit is suggested, but this unity of the Spirit will be discussed later.

I am omitting here the other attributes of God, insofar as they have been included in what has already been discussed or will be sufficiently included later on. For the sake of brevity, I have decided to not discuss in particular how each text can be applied to a corresponding attribute of God, or to the formality of an attribute. The reader can easily do it by himself.

NOTES

A.1 《詩經·大雅·雲漢》:「昊天上帝,則不我虞。敬恭明神,宜無悔怒。」

Ode 'Yunhan' in the volume 'Daya' of the *Book of Odes*: 'O Ruler of the very vast Heaven, or very vast Heaven, Supreme Lord and Ruler (in Chinese *Haotian Shangdi*), do you not consider us while we worship you, intelligent spirit, with internal and external reverence? Certainly, you should not hate us or get angry at us'.[112]

B.2 《禮記·表記》:「子言之:『昔三代明王皆事天地之神明,無非卜筮之用,不敢以其私,褻事上帝。』」

Chapter 32 'Biaoji' in volume 9 of the *Book of Rites*: 'Confucius says, "In the past, the three dynasties always used oracles in serving the intelligent spirit of Heaven and Earth, and they did not dare to despise the service and worship of *Shangdi* with their private will and decision"'.[113]

C.3 《禮記·哀公問》:「孔子曰:『非禮無以節事天地之神也。』」

Chapter 27 'Aigong wen' in volume 9 of the *Book of Rites*: 'Confucius says, "Without the rites, etc." See above.

D.4 《禮記·禮運》:「以養生送死,以事鬼神上帝,皆從其朔。」

Chapter 9 'Liyun' in volume 4 of the *Book of Rites*: 'All the rites, etc.'

---

[12] The characters *jing* 敬 and *gong* 恭 are understood as internal and external reverence. *Mingshen* 明神 is understood as intelligent spirit in the singular form. This interpretation strengthens the monotheistic nature of Chinese ancient religion. However, according to Couvreur, *mingshen* refer to the four spirits of the four directions: *Cheu king*, trans. by Séraphin Couvreur (Taipei: Éditions Kuangchi Press, 1966), pp. 411, 429. Couvreur like Legge understands *ming* in *mingshen* as meaning intelligent. This passage is quoted in the *Tianjiao he Ru*, p. 15 (n. 1). For analysis of Noël's translation of this passage, see Wang Ge's chapter in this volume.

[13] Noël has already translated this passage above (q.2, §.1, O.15).

E.5 《書經·多方》：「惟我周王，靈承于旅，克堪用德，惟典神天。」

Chapter 'Duofang' in volume 5 of the *Book of Imperial Annals*: 'Only the princes of our Zhou dynasty, because of their particular skill in gathering all souls and due to the splendour of their virtue, were found worthy of becoming the masters of the spiritual Heaven', that is to say, they received office and power.[114]

F.6 《易經·觀卦》：「觀天之神道而四時不忒，聖人以神道設教而天下服矣。」

Symbol 'Guan' in the *Book of Changes and Productions*: 'Look at Heaven's spiritual mode of action, or the way in which the four seasons of the year revolve without error'.

G.7 《詩經·大雅·文王》：「上天之載，無聲無臭。」

Ode 'Wenwang' in the volume 'Daya' of the *Book of Odes*: 'The thing of the highest Heaven, etc.' See above.[115]

H.8 王昌會《全史詳要·卷一》：「伏羲氏養六畜以充庖厨，且以為犧牲，享神祇，又曰『庖犧氏』。」

Volume 1 of the *Book of Universal Annals* [*Quanshi xiangyao*]: 'Prince Fuxi was feeding all sorts of animals, so that they could be used in the kitchen and be available to be offered as sacrificial victims to the Spirit or the spirits; and thus, he was called the slaughterer'.

I.9 《書經·湯誥》：「敢昭告于上天神后。」

Chapter 'Tanggao' in volume 3 of the *Book of Imperial Annals*: Prince Cheng Tang says, 'I have dared to warn publicly the spiritual King of the Highest Heaven, or the Spirit of the Highest Heaven and of Dense Earth'.

Question 3: Whether the Ancient Books and Classics Give True Knowledge of the First Being, or God, and whether it is False that the Ancient Chinese were Atheists

It seems almost useless to ask this question because the clear testimonies of those books convince the intellect to conclude that the Chinese truly knew the supreme divinity. However, in order to set out these [testimonies] more clearly, I briefly recapitulate what they say, and from many texts I draw together these few points.

    I. According to their books, all things draw their first origin from Heaven, or the Lord and Ruler of Heaven, and they depend on His virtue for the beginning of their existence. This means that Heaven or the Lord of Heaven is the first cause of all things, and then produces human beings, infusing into them right reason and a rational nature. Nothing can happen without His command and Providence;

---

114 This passage is translated above (q.2, §.6, E.5).
115 This passage is quoted in the *Ditian kao*, p. 40 (n. 44) and in the *Tianjiao he Ru*, p. 20 (n. 5).

He presides over the principles of things, etc. Would not this indicate the First Being, unlimited and infinite in every perfection? Indeed, there is nothing prior by which it or its perfections are limited, since their books acknowledge there is nothing before Heaven or the Lord of Heaven. Also, you will not find it mentioned anywhere that the Lord of Heaven began at some time, had a starting point or parents, or that He was a human, but everywhere they call Him Spirit. Furthermore, the *Yijing* says through the enigmatic symbol *Zhen* representing the equinoctial region of the world, that Heaven came into act and then diffused itself in all the processes of the world. Are they not tacitly hinting that [the Lord of Heaven] began the Creation of the world at the spring equinox, just as Salian and others have said?[116] As the interpreters say, Prince Wen Wang through this arrangement of enigmatic symbols hinted at the processes and changes which take place in the course of a year, though this may refer to the processes of the first year of the world and their beginnings. Deeply entrenched in the minds of all Chinese is the ageless and continual tradition that the origin of all things and the beginning of all processes are found in this progressive arrangement of enigmatic symbols, or rather, that they are represented and outlined in it.

II. Their books attribute to Heaven (*Tian*) or the Lord of Heaven (*Shangdi*) the perfections proper to God, as listed above. According to them, He appoints kings for the people, delegates or ministers of justice as His helpers. They say that people worship, fear, pray to, serve, sacrifice to, and obey Him. He is angered by sins and is bound by virtue. He confers rewards on the good, and He punishes the wicked. He observes all things, scrutinizes all souls, guides hearts, reaches everywhere, and cannot be deceived. He is the greatest, the highest, immense, intelligent, loving, merciful, helping and protecting. Are not all those things very similar to how the Bible refers to God? For example, 'all the power comes from above' [Romans 13:1]; 'The kings rule through me and the lawgivers determine justice' [Proverb 8:15]; 'Every knee shall bend to me' [Philippians 2:10]; 'the Lord is exceedingly angry' [Psalm 106:40]; 'God is the lord of retributions' [Psalm 93:1]; 'He scrutinizes hearts and minds' [Psalm 7:10]; 'The Lord is on high and looks down on low things' [Psalm 112:6]; 'The highest gave His own voice' [Psalm 17:14], etc.

III. Do not tell me that those expressions should be understood allegorically in relation to the material heaven, to its material force, or to some empty and chimeric heaven. How could such forceful wording and expressions be used in such important affairs to signify the material heaven, its material force, or a chimeric heaven? Indeed, the emperor uses such expressions to exhort his princes, dukes, fellow soldiers when fighting against the unjust oppressor of the people, when approving laws and public rituals, when offering sacrifices and petitions; and the royal minister uses them when giving his sovereign testimonies about correct

---

116 This refers to the Avignonese Jesuit Jacques Salian (1557–1640) and his *Annales ecclesiastici* (1619). Noël here is influenced by Figurism, a school of hermeneutics pioneered by Bouvet that sought to apply symbolic interpretation of divine revelation in the Chinese classics. In the First Treatise, there is another Figurist element below; see c.2, q.3.

living and just rule; the court historian uses them when refering to the illustrious deeds of the ancients. This can be seen in volumes 2 to 5 of the *Book of Imperial Annals* [*Shujing*], in volume 8 of the *Book of Odes* [*Shijing*], in volumes 1 and 2 of the *Book of Universal Annals* [*Quanshi*], and in the *Mencius*, etc.

If indeed those expressions refer to a chimeric heaven (the same can be said about the material heaven or its material force), what are they there for? What kind of incitement can they bring in the exhortations, threats, and advice? What kind of respect in the sacrifices, rituals, and prayers? What kind of credibility could they lend to the histories? Indeed, if they refer to the material heaven or its material force, what is the purpose of so many unusual metaphors?

Why are there so expressions which can hardly agree with this material heaven or its material force? Indeed, and here I omit many other things, the material heaven cannot be a spirit or intelligence. The same could be said about its material virtue. Indeed, if you make it either purely spiritual, a composite of matter and spirit, or a spirit coexisting with material heaven, you would certainly say something contradictory. Indeed, to say that something is both material and immaterial, or spiritual is the same as as saying that it is both body and spirit, which is contradictory. Even if you take here spiritual as accident and not as substance, you cannot deny that it belongs to the spirit, because the spiritual quality according to the philosophers cannot be received or dwell in material subject, but can only inhabit a spiritual subject.

Do not mention again the metaphorical meaning![117] Where do you find something material said to be metaphorically spiritual, unless there is something spiritual in it, or out of consideration of something spiritual by which the material could be said spiritual by derivation? Finally, in order to cover all things, I ask you, where do you find so many similar metaphors in the histories, public rituals, laws, and such important things? Saint Augustine in chapters 10 and 11 of *De doctrina Christiana* establishes this rule for assessing the true meaning of the Bible: whenever the words of the Bible can be taken literally, they should not be reconstrued with a metaphoric meaning or any other less literal reading, unless something absurd or false follows from the literal meaning.[118] Can this rule be used here? Nothing absurd or false follows from a literal reading; but on the contrary, something absurd or false follows from another interpretation. Another thing is to use the word Heaven as a figure for the Lord of Heaven or the Spirit of Heaven because this metaphor is used by all peoples, especially Europeans. The other day, I was reading in a recently published French book some verses about the newly discovered territories of Mexico. The poem consistently uses the word Heaven for the Lord of Heaven. Finally, if someone wishes without reason to distort all those attributes of God,

---

117 Noël seems here to reply to Longobardo's treatise. See Longobardo, *A Brief Response on the Controversies*, pp. 111–12.
118 Augustine, *De doctrina Christiana*, 3.10: 'Demonstrandus est igitur prius modus inveniendae locutionis, propriane an figurata sit. Et iste omnino modus est, ut quidquid in sermone divino neque ad morum honestatem neque ad fidei veritatem proprie referri potest, figuratum esse cognoscas'.

which are expressed with such clarity and energy, with a metaphorical reading, an impious atheist could similarly employ a metaphoric reading of almost everything said about God in the Bible, and thus could shamelessly deny being convinced by them that God exists.

IV. From all this we can conclude whether the ancient Chinese were atheist. An atheist can be understood in two ways: in negative terms it indicates someone who has no knowledge at all of a supreme and invisible divinity, whereas in positive terms it indicates someone who may have some obscure knowledge, but rejects it, and denies the existence of God. Atheism of the first type involves only the intellect, or rather, in the negation of the act of the intellect, but I do not discuss here whether this is possible. Indeed, the theologians Francesco Amico [SJ, 1578–1651], Bartolomé de Medina [OP 1527–1580], Luis Molina [SJ, 1535–1600], Francisco Zumel [OP, 1540–1607], and Luis de Granada [OP, 1504–1588] generally say that it is possible for a child or a wild man to be negatively ignorant of God, that is to say, to lack awareness about God's existence of God, at least for a short time with the result that no thought about God occurs to him, but it is impossible for the whole community to have such ignorance.[119]

Atheism of the second type involves not only the intellect, but also an act of the will. Since the proposition 'God exists' is not self-evident to us, an act of the will is needed for the intellect to decide upon giving assent to it. Hence positive atheists are indeed guilty when the idea of God's existence occurs to them, but they do not want to examine the reasons needed for the intellect to give assent to a judgement about God's existence, or having examined those reasons, they do not let the intellect give assent to them; or when their intellect is brought to assent by the force of the incontrovertible reasons, they reject this conclusion in their heart. In those latter two cases, they should be called semi-atheists, or impious, more than atheists. 'What is known about God is clear to them; they keep the truth of God in injustice because while they acknowledged God, they did not honour Him as God' (Romans 1:19–21); 'The unwise said in his heart that there is no God' (Psalm 13:1).

Regarding the ancient Chinese, generally speaking, they do not seem to be atheist in terms of intellect or will. The ancient Chinese books contain their thoughts which attribute to Heaven, or the Lord and Ruler of Heaven the perfections proper to God, as we saw. Their opinions are expressed in their books chronicling that the first three empires Xia, Shang, and Zhou, which lasted around 1976 years,[120] honoured the Lord of Heaven or the Spirit of Heaven and Earth; that Fuxi, the founder of the Chinese race, sacrificed to the Spirit or spirits, while the emperors Zhuanxu, Huangdi, and Wu Wang sacrificed to the Lord of Heaven; that Wen Wang honoured Him with great care and diligence; that Cheng Tang feared and obeyed Him; that all the magistrates and the people prepared everything necessary

---

119 This expresses the classical idea of the *homo religiosus*, which was found in Cicero and in the Church Fathers, and became also very influential in Renaissance with the discovery of ancient civilizations.
120 This is an almost exact match with Couplet's *Tabula chronologica monarchiae Sinicae* (Paris: Horthemels, 1686) which has 458 years for Xia, 644 years for Shang and 873 years for Zhou, with a total of 1975 years.

for His worship. Thus, we can conclude that the ancient Chinese were not atheist. From this, you may not immediately infer that they were holy, immune from sins and already saved. It seems that no other nation before the coming of Christ was so diligent and careful in establishing rituals for worshipping the spirits of heaven, earth, mountains, rivers, and other worldly things, with the exception of the Jews.[121] Thus, how could the Chinese be considered atheist? Someone may say, 'I confess, the ancient Chinese seem to have some knowledge about the First Being or God, and were not atheists, but after the Buddhist idolatry came into China, more recent Chinese slowly moved toward atheism so that they would seemingly not share any beliefs with these [idolaters]. They have lost the knowledge of the First Being or God and think differently now than in the past'. Let us analyse and discuss this since this is the crux of the controversy.[122]

---

121 Noël gives here a special status to the Jewish people. In the preface to the *Confucius Sinarum philosophus*, Couplet was much bolder, affirming that, even before the Jews, the Chinese people were the first nation ever to build a temple to the true God. See Meynard, ed., *Confucius Sinarum philosophus*, p. 189.
122 In fact, the controversy was essentially a dispute between the Jesuits and the Franciscans, Dominicans, and Propaganda Fide about ancient Confucianism. The missionaries generally agreed that neo-Confucianism should be rejected. Noël attempts to move beyond the controversy over ancient Confucianism and to develop a new controversy with neo-Confucianism.

Chapter 2: Do Modern Chinese People Have Knowledge of the First Being or God, or Are they Atheists?

In order to solve the question correctly, we need to consult not one or two but many Chinese books, including books written by modern Chinese, books in common usage, books that have been commended for the erudition and fame of their authors, as well as well-worn books from which Chinese scholars today draw their knowledge (*cognitiones*). In this way, we may know what knowledge Chinese people have today and what understanding they have of the First Being. For example, if the Chinese would like to know what understanding we have in Europe of the Most Holy Trinity, wouldn't it be prudent and safe to consult the most important books taught now in the European universities? Similarly, if we wanted to know whether the Greek Orthodox are not only schismatic but also heretical, we should read the books they are now using. If after investigating their books we are still unsure about their true meaning, we should rely on the opinion of learned Greeks who can explain their own books orally. Let us now return to the question.[1]

I mentioned ideas (*cognitiones*) and not desires (*volitiones*). Indeed, one thing is to know God; another, to desire Him. Even though the intellect may know some truth, the will very often refuses to be subjected to it and is much less inclined to put that truth into practice.

Let us now discuss all these matters. First, to know whether the more recent Chinese have not lost or disfigured the knowledge of the First Being of the ancients, in the First Question [of this chapter] we will consider how they explain the original text of the ancient books we have discussed in the First Chapter. If their explanations and interpretations match the meaning of the original text, then it should be acknowledged that their ideas are the same as those of the ancient Chinese who wrote the original texts. You already have the meaning of the original texts in the preceding chapter. Let us examine their interpretations, following the same order as before. But for sake of brevity, when the interpretation coincides with the original meaning already explained, or does not express much more, I shall omit it. This needs to be noted to understand this whole chapter. I shall refer here only to interpretations which seem to express something more fully or offer a contradictory view.[2]

To solve all the objections which could be raised, we shall see in Question 2 how these more recent authors explain the word *Tian*, or Heaven, and *Shangdi*, or

---

1 This method was first used by Longobardo with his research on the *Xingli daquan* and then with his interviews with Chinese literati. Noël uses the same method but ends up with opposite conclusions.
2 Noël is a bit misleading here since he rarely if ever presents opposing arguments.

Lord of Heaven, and whether this explanation stands in the way of or contradicts the true knowledge of God. Then, in Question 3, we shall show what they recognize as first source of things in the world and how it is named. We shall then explain in Question 4 the views of both the modern and ancient authors on the definition, classification, and properties of the Spirits [*guishen*]. We shall examine in Question 5 whether the *jiao* sacrifice to Heaven is directed towards the material heaven or the immaterial Heaven, namely the Spirit of Heaven (God). Similarly, we will investigate whether the *she* sacrifice to the Earth is directed towards the material earth, or to that same Spirit of Heaven and Earth, or something else. In Question 6, we shall discuss that two-character word *taiji*, i.e., the first ultimate or nature of things. Since more recent Chinese often use *taiji* interchangeably with *li*, that is Reason (*Ratio*), and associate *li* with *Tian* or Heaven [*Tianli*], we shall investigate whether the Chinese use the two-character word *taiji* for the supreme Lord of Heaven, or God, in the sense that God is the first cause of all things. Finally, in Question 7, we shall summarize all the things drawn from the books of the more recent Chinese and investigate whether they hold any true knowledge of the First Being, that is God, or rather whether the Chinese today can be called atheist.

Now, let us begin with the perfections, which the modern Chinese commentaries on the ancient classics attribute to Heaven (*Tian*) and to the Lord of Heaven (*Shangdi*). In this way, we may know whether the modern Chinese understanding of God is different from that of the ancient Chinese.

Question 1: What Perfections do the Modern Commentators Attribute to *Tian* or *Shangdi*?

They appear to attribute the same things as the ancient books, although often veiled under different terms. In the previous chapter, we went through each of the main attributes of God and saw that they were ascribed to *Tian* and *Shangdi* by the ancient books and classics. We shall use here the same method and examine whether the modern commentators ascribe all the same attributes of God to *Tian* and *Shangdi*.

§.1. Dominion of *Tian* or *Shangdi* according to the Modern Commentators

I refer here to the meaning of certain commentators on this matter. As they say, when the Supreme Heaven appoints kings to rule and doctors to teach the people whom It produces, Its only intention is that that the kings and doctors transmit and spread the correct way of living, in Its name as Its assistants, helping the Lord of Heaven [*Shangdi*] in what He cannot reach (A).[3] When producing man, Heaven first endowed him with sensible matter (*materia sensibilis*) to form his body and

---

3 Accordingly, the ruler is like an assistant (*vicarius*) of Heaven and its herald. It is also stated here the idea that *Shangdi* needs help, like God in Christianity cannot save people without themselves. As Augustine says, 'The one who created you without you, He cannot save you without you' (*Qui ergo fecit te sine te, non te justificat sine te*). Augustine, *Sermo* 169, 11.

then infused into him right reason to establish his rational nature.[4] The correct reason, insofar as it is in Heaven, is the first, participative, directive and perfective power of Heaven. Insofar as it is in human beings, [the correct reason] is a human being's innate duty, justice, honesty, and intelligence, or rather, the natural seeds of duty, justice, honesty, and intelligence.[5] The infusion and reception of reason is like a commandment imposed by Heaven, and can be called the Law of Heaven (B). Generally speaking, the Law of Heaven or infused reason of nature encompasses all created things, but understood specifically, it is the lucid and intelligent faculty which encompasses only human beings (C). Saint Thomas affirms in questions 90 and 91 of the *Prima Secundae* that the law is something rational and that the eternal law is the idea of governing things, in God as a Ruler, or a reason of divine wisdom directing all actions and motions. [He adds that] the natural law within us is a participation in the eternal law by which all things are regulated towards their own end, but the rational creature [is regulated] in a more excellent way insofar as it provides both for itself and for others, as well as that this natural human law is 'a dictate of practical reason', namely that it is impressed by God, instructing under obligation to perform or avoid actions.[6] These principles of Saint Thomas appear to match closely the principles given by the Chinese commentators in relation to the Law of Heaven about which they say, 'The way of Heaven, or Heaven's way of action, is devoid of any iniquity; it always holds fast to morality and justice; the ruler, as the assistant of Heaven, governs in the name of Heaven, and this is why he puts forward the morality and justice of Heaven to rule the people' (D).[7]

Confucius says, 'I do not think it is appropriate to flatter the spirit of the South-West corner of the room, or the spirit of fire; above the spirits, there is no power higher than Heaven, and being the highest, it cannot be compared with anything else. Heaven grants good things to whoever acts according to right reason but sends bad things to whoever acts against right reason. Anyone who transgresses duty and does not follow right reason sins against Heaven. To whom can he turn to seek forgiveness of this sin against heaven (E)?[8] A disfigured man after fasting

---

4   Noël understands this as a process of creation in two steps that resembles Genesis 2:7. Noël translates *qi* with the scholastic concept of sensible matter (*materia sensibilis*). Concerning this concept, see Kurt Smith, *Matter Matters: Metaphysics and Methodology in the Early Modern Period* (Oxford: Oxford University Press, 2010), pp. 55, 60.
5   The concept of seeds (*semina*) translate the concept of *duan* 端 in the *Mencius*. Noël probably chose the term *semina* from Stoicism because the *semina* or seeds are rational entities.
6   These citations are drawn from Summa theologiae I^a–II^{ae}, qq.90–91. The concepts of natural law and participation in Aquinas enable Noël to stress the continuity between the rationality of Heaven or God and its rational decrees, known by human beings through reason.
7   Noël had shown that the ancient texts conceived the dominion of Heaven not as purely external and immediate but as mediated by the virtuous kings, and he shows here that neo-Confucian texts conceives the way of Heaven as morality and justice (*liyi* 理義). In other words, there is a moral continuity between Heaven and human beings. Noël establishes further an interesting parallel with the Scholastic notion of natural law: the way of Heaven and the natural law have a transcendental foundation (respectively in Heaven and in God) and both are immanent in human actions.
8   The *Confucius Sinarum philosophus* rebuked Zhu Xi and the neo-Confucians for identifying Heaven as

and ablutions can approach the intelligent spirit and present offering to the Lord of Heaven (F).⁹ The ancient emperors made offerings to the Lord of Heaven and erected ancestor halls to show that there are masters in the empire (G). The reason why the emperor makes a sacrifice to the Lord of Heaven is that there is nothing in the world which the Lord of Heaven does not produce, and there is nothing which the emperor does not rule (H).¹⁰ When worshipping the Lord of Heaven, the emperor is adorned with the dignity received from Heaven and thus has someone above himself to obey. In appointing the inspectors of the peoples and kingdoms, he strengthens the whole body of the monarchy and has below himself those to whom he entrusts the management of affairs. Watching above or below, he is not ashamed of anything. The dignity of the emperor is found between the two extremities of Heaven and human being.¹¹ The Xia dynasty is said to have respected the Lord of Heaven; the Shang dynasty to have glorified [Him]; and the Zhou dynasty to have worshipped Him through a reverential liturgy. These all mean the same thing (I).'

From this you see that the kings and doctors of the people are appointed by Heaven or the supreme Lord,¹² that Heaven produces the human body and infuses the rational nature, that on a general level the Law of Heaven is understood to be reason infused with nature and on a specific level is understood to be a reason endowed with lucid and intelligent nature. Thus, whoever transgresses reason sins against Heaven. Offerings are made to Heaven as the Lord, the intelligent Spirit, the Author of things. Heaven is above and obeyed by emperors. The emperors of the first three dynasties served Heaven. I ask you, can there be a clearer affirmation about God as Lord? Did not the prodigal son in the Gospel of Luke 15[:21] say, 'Father, I sinned against Heaven and against you?'¹³

---

    li 理 and opposed the neo-Confucian reading to that of Zhang Juzheng, who they believed was more theist in his interpretation. See Meynard, *The Jesuit Reading of Confucius*, p. 167. Here Noël adopts the neo-Confucian point of view: to follow heaven means to follow *li* 理.

9 The Five Classics make mention of *shenming* 神明 or an even more archaic expression, *mingshen* 明神. Noël translates both these expressions as intelligent spirit, always in the singular form, insisting again on the rational and monotheistic nature of Heaven or God.

10 The universal domination and ownership of all things by the ruler appears very shocking for modern democratic thought, but it was practically mitigated by the moral imperative for the ruler to master his desire.

11 Cai Chen means here that the emperor is not only responsible towards Heaven but also towards the people.

12 The Chinese concept of *tianming* suggests that the emperor is directly selected by Heaven, but as the texts show, this was mediated through the wise and the people. Similarly, in the Western tradition, the kings were often anointed by the Church, but yet they were not considered as rulers by divine right in the sense that God directly appointed them.

13 With this quote from Saint Luke, Noël suggests an interesting connection between Christianity and neo-Confucianism. Just as the son was able to recognize within him an inner law, explained as natural law in scholasticism, the kings and ancient wise men in China were following an inner law, explained in terms of reason and nature in neo-Confucianism.

NOTES

A.1 大學士庫勒納等編《日講四書解義‧卷十四‧孟子‧梁惠王下》:「上天降生下民,立之君,以主治;立之師,以主教。其意但欲為君師者,代天宣化,輔助上帝之所不及。」

> Corresponding to quote A.2 in the paragraph on dominion (c.1, §.1), there is the following interpretation in the *Daily Commentary on the Four Books* (in Chinese *Sishu rijiang*), which was recently published by the Kangxi Emperor. In volume 14, the second part of the chapter 'Lianghui wang' of the *Mencius* is reproduced with few changes and is explained as follows: 'When the Supreme Heaven appoints the people …' See above.[14]

B.2 《日講四書解義‧卷二‧中庸‧第一》:「天之生人,既與之氣以成形,即賦之理以成性。故在天則為『元亨利貞』,而四時、五行、庶類、萬化莫不由是而出。在人則為『仁義禮智』,而四端、五典、萬事、萬物之理無不統於其間。其稟受賦畀,即如天之命令,所謂性也。」

> Corresponding to quote C.3 in the paragraph on dominion (c.1, §.1), volume 2 of the *Daily Commentary [on the Four Books]* has the following interpretation of *Zhongyong* 1: 'Heaven produces man, and after It has given him a matter endowed with sensations to form his body, It then infused into him right reason to establish his rational nature.[15] Therefore, insofar as this reason is in Heaven, it is the great or first power; it is participative or extensive, directive and perfective. Out of it flow the four seasons of the year, the Five Primary Universal Principles of things, all the species of things, and all the changes and productions of things. In human beings, this corresponds to inborn duty, justice, honesty, and intelligence. The four natural affections of mercy, shame, reverence, and knowledge, the five-fold order of human condition (the love between father and son, the justice between king and subject, the correct distinction between husband and wife, the correct obedience between elder and youth, the correct sincerity between friends), all those things are regulated by this. The infusion and reception of reason is like the law or commandment imposed by Heaven, and this is why it is called the infused reason of nature'.[16]

---

14 This passage is quoted in the *Gujin*, p. 180 (n. 28).
15 The *Rijiang* here follows closely Zhu Xi's *Zhongyong zhangju* and does not imply an historical process in two steps, although Noël understands it this way (before …, then …). In this respect, Noël was probably influenced by the narration of Genesis 2:7: 'Then the Lord God formed man from the dust of the ground, and breathed into his nostrils the breath of life; and the man became a living being'. Furthermore, according to the theory of human nature in the *De anima*, Aristotle does not describe a historical unfolding, but holds the theory of hylomorphism in which matter (body) and form (soul) form a unity. Noël's equation of *qi* and *li* with matter and reason respectively, and of *xing* with rational nature, is problematic.
16 A slightly abbreviated form of this passage is quoted in the *Gujin*, p. 139 (n. 5). Neo-Confucianism expresses the unity between Heaven and human beings through the concept of *xing* 性. Similarly, in Christianity, the commandments of Heaven are not external but inscribed in human nature.

C. 蔡虛齋《四書蒙引・卷一・大學》：「《大學》之『明德』，即《中庸》天命之性也。但《中庸》性字兼人、物，而『明德』則專指人非物，所得而同矣。」

> Concerning the beginning of the *Teaching of Adults* (in Chinese *Daxue*), the interpreter Cai Xuzhai in volume 1 of his commentary *Sishu mengyin* writes as follows: 'That which the *Daxue* calls a "faculty" or "lucid and intelligent nature" [*mingde*] is the same as what the *Zhongyong* or *Unalterable Mean* relates: "the Law of Heaven is the infused reason of nature" [*Tianming zhi xing*]. But the words "infused reason of nature" in the *Zhongyong* include human beings and all other things, while the characters for "faculty" or "lucid and intelligent nature" in the *Daxue* refer to human beings alone because other things do not have this faculty and they do not share the same nature as human beings'.[17]

C. 《日講四書解義・卷一・大學》：「人之明德，乃天所昭然付予之理，所謂『天之明命』也。」

> Volume 1 of the *Daily Commentary [on the Four Books]* states in the section on the *Daxue*: 'The lucid faculty of human beings is right reason which Heaven infuses into them like light. This is what is called the lucid Law of Heaven'. Does not this resemble Psalm 4[.7]: 'Let the light of your face shine on us, O Lord'?[18]

D.3 陳澔《禮記集說・表記・第三十二》：「呂氏曰：天道無私，莫非理義；君所以代天而治者，推天之理義以治斯人而已，天敘、天秩、天叙、天命、天討，莫非天也。」

> Corresponding to quote I.9 (c.1, §.1) from chapter 32 'Biaoji' of the *Book of Rites*, Chen Hao in volume 9 [of the *Liji jishuo*] cites the author Lü as follows: 'The way of Heaven …' See above. He also adds: 'Heaven's order, disposition, law, and retribution are all Heaven'.[19]

E.4 《日講四書解義・卷四・論語上・八佾》：「媚奧、媚灶，吾皆以為不然。奧、灶之上，至尊無對，莫過於天。順理而行，則天降之祥；逆理而行，則天降之災。倘所行不能安分，不能循理，即為得罪於天。天之所罪，將何所禱以求免哉？」

> Corresponding to quote N.13 from chapter 3 of the *Lunyu* [3.13], volume 4 of the *Daily Commentary* states, 'I myself', says Confucius … See above.[20]

F.5 張居正《四書直解・孟子・離婁下》：「至於醜惡之人，本人情之所憎厭者，使能齋戒沐浴以致其潔，則雖對越神明而奉上帝之祀，亦無不可。」

> Concerning quote R.19 from chapter 2 'Lilou xia' in the second part of the *Mencius*, the interpreter Zhang Juzheng, commonly called Zhang Gelao, once the Chief Minister of the empire wrote in volume 20 [of his commentary *Sishu zhijie*]:

---

17 Compared with Zhu Xi's *Sishu zhangju*, Cai Qing added the parallel between the *mingde* of the *Daxue* and the *tianming zhi xing* of the *Zhongyong*.
18 This passage is quoted in the *Gujin*, p. 144 (n. 8). Noël draws a parallel with Psalm 4:7 since this passage may be read as a theory of enlightenment: God's rational imprint in human mind.
19 The Yuan scholar Chen Hao 陳澔 (1261–1341) wrote the authoritative *Liji jishuo* 禮記集說 [Collected commentaries on the *Liji*], which is frequently cited in this work.
20 Quoted in the *Gujin*, p. 146 (n. 9).

'Some people usually despise a worthless man with a disfigured face; but if this person practices abstinence, cleans himself carefully and removes uncleanness, then he can approach the intelligent spirit and present offerings to the Lord of Heaven [Shangdi]'.[21]

G.6 《周易正解·卷十五·渙卦》：「享帝立廟, 以示天下之有主, 正是收拾人心之大機括處。」

Corresponding to quote R.20, volume 15 of the *True Explanation of the Book of Changes and Productions* (in Chinese *Zhouyi zhengjie*), written and published recently by three literati from the town of Danyang in the province of Nanjing, which was the most important center for Chinese learning in the whole empire,[22] states the following about the symbol 'Huan': 'Offerings are presented to the Lord of Heaven and ancestor halls are erected to show that there are masters in the empire. It is truly in this way that people are stirred up to recollect their mind'.

H.7 《周易正解·卷十三·鼎卦》：「聖人所以享上帝者, 以天下無一物非上帝之所生, 亦無一物非聖人之所統。禮記小注有云：『天下之物皆天之所生, 無物足以稱其德, 故牲則以特；天下之物皆天子之所有, 故諸侯膳之以犢。』」

Corresponding to quote S.21, volume 13 of the *True Explanation of the Book of Changes and Productions* states the following about the symbol 'Ding': 'The reason why the emperor makes a sacrifice to the Lord of Heaven is that nothing in the world or the empire exists without being produced by the Lord of Heaven, and there is nothing which is not ruled by the emperor'. Afterwards, this work cites the commentary of Doctor Zhu Xi, which further states: 'Heaven produces all things in the world, and there is nothing which can explain enough Its power; therefore, only an animal is offered to Heaven. However, the emperor possesses all things and has dominion over them. Therefore, a petty king offers to Heaven only a little calf as offering'.[23]

I.8 蔡沈《書經集傳·卷五·周書·立政》：「以是敬事上帝, 則天職修, 而上有所承；以是立民長伯, 則體統立而下有所寄。人君位天人之兩間, 而俯仰無作者, 以是也。夏之尊帝、商之不鼇、周之敬事, 其義一也。」

Corresponding to quote T.23, the commentator Cai Chen writes the following about the chapter 'Lizheng' in volume 5 of the *Book of Imperial Annals* [*Shujing*]: 'In worshipping, the emperor …, etc.' See above.[24]

---

21 Here *duiyue* 對越 means 'to join with' but Noël translates as 'to approach' (*accedere*), strengthening the difference between man and the divine.
22 For the *Zhouyi zhengjie*, see Chapter 2.11.
23 The attribution of the quote to Zhu Xi is erroneous; in fact, it comes from the scholar Ma Rong 馬融 (79–166) who is quoted by Wei Shi 衛湜 (Song dynasty) in the *Liji jishuo*.
24 For Cai Chen and his *Shujing jizhuan*, see Chapter 2.11.

§. 2. Power of *Tian* or *Shangdi* according to Modern Commentators

As they say, the great and first power of Heaven is the mind (*animus*) that always and constantly produces things. When the force of movement (*vis motrix*) breaks into act, the production of things, both in terms of matter and form, starts to emerge.[25] The power of Heaven is operative not only at the beginning [*yuan*] but also at the completion of a thing. In general terms, it encompasses the whole power of the Ruler of Heaven, including three other powers of Heaven, namely the participative, directive, and perfective [*heng li zhen*] (A). Amid secret and mysterious darkness, the four-fold power of Heaven revolves silently and produces all things by its motion. Insofar as this power of Heaven is great and primary, it governs the beginning of things. As participative, the power of Heaven makes things grow; as directive, it makes each thing tend towards its own end; as perfective, it makes things reach their completion and end (B). From this, each thing has a four-fold participation in the power of Heaven according to its own nature. The participation received from Heaven is something extremely sublime, pure, and simple, for the thing of Heaven insofar as it lacks anything perceptible through senses cannot be comprehended by thought or expressed through any sense or figure (C). When it is said that the active power of Heaven knows the beginnings of things, the word 'to know' means that the Lord acts, rules, and directs, just as the expression 'he knows the city' refers to the governor of the city who acts in the whole city as a master, rules over all things and manages the city (D). What controls the production of all things is the active power of Heaven which, when actualized with the passive power of Earth, perfects all things (E).

The production and perfection of all things originate in Heaven. Since Heaven controls the production and perfection of things, Heaven is called the Lord and Ruler of Heaven. The Lord of Heaven's force of movement (*vis motrix* or *virtus movens*), which comes into act and stops acting, diffuses itself into all the directions of the eight symbols [trigrams] representing the productions and mutations of things in the *Yijing*. All the eight symbols are governed by and depend upon the Lord of Heaven (F). Who produces all things of the world? Who makes them reach perfection? There must be a Lord and Ruler, and thus he is called *Shangdi*, or the supreme Lord (G). In order that all things are produced and perfected, there must be something by which they are produced and perfected. Hence, there is *Di*, or *Shangdi*. It can be further investigated what the beginning of all things is. As the author [Cai Qing] says below, there is nothing else but the force of movement of air [*qi*] or the vital breath, that is to say the force of movement of the vital

---

25 The notion of force of movement (*vix motrix*), or intrinsic and active force, was put forward by Francis of Marchia (*c.* 1290–*c.* 1344) in his commentary on Peter Lombard's *Sentences* (*c.* 1320). The notion was discussed further in the sixteenth century by Giacomo Zabarella (1533–1589) in his *De rebus naturalibus* (1599), by Pierre Gassendi in his *De motu impresso a motore translato* (1642), and by Leibniz in his *Specimen dynamicum* (1695). Johannes Kepler (1571–1630) also uses the notion as a power acting at a distance. For Gassendi, the force of movement was endowed into matter by God, and Noël seems to embrace here this theological foundation of the physical world.

principle. Where the force of movement of this air or vital breath acts, all things immediately follow (H).²⁶

In order to make Chinese thought coherent and not self-contradictory, this word air [*qi*] can be understood as vital breath (*vitalis aura*) or rather should be understood as something like vital principle (*principium vitale*), and not material air (*sensibilis aër*). Please see Question 3 below for more information. The same commentator [Wu Sunyou], who quoted the author mentioned above [Cai Qing], wrote at the beginning of the passage: 'When it is called the force of movement (*vis motrix*) of air, or vital breath, things are not yet existing (not even the material air), but because the Lord of Heaven cannot be seen coming into act or ceasing His act, thus, it is said that all things follow the Lord of Heaven in acting or stopping. Therefore, that which or he who cannot be seen [i.e. the Lord of Heaven] can still be known through what can be seen. After this, he [Wu Sunyou] says, "The Lord of Heaven coming into act and ceasing act cannot be seen. If you wish to know Him coming into act and ceasing act, why do you not consider Him in all things that have been produced? How could things make themselves? Since the Lord of Heaven governs them, their action and cessation, or motion and rest, can be seen. From this can be known the Lord of Heaven's action and cessation (I)". Again: the active force of Heaven [*qian*] is placed first in the series of the eight symbols [trigrams], and it plays the role of King [*jun*] and Lord [*zhu*]; indeed, the Lord is the maker of things, and there is nothing that He does not encompass and rule. All the other agents depend on [this force], as well as being ruled and encompassed by it, and they perform their functions at its command (K). All this shows that the writers recognize an invisible principle before the material existence of things, and they call it the Lord of Heaven, in Chinese *Di* or *Shangdi*. Hence by this word air or vital breath [*qi*], air or vital breath, should be understood as a vital principle, which is invisible and the prime mover (*primum movens*), and they do not recognize anything prior to it. As I shall state in Question 3, they always understand *qi* as life, inner motion, vital breath, and, according to the ancient meaning, exhalations of vital breath.²⁷

Now let us briefly pursue other matters.²⁸ As they say, all human beings produced by Heaven have a sensitive body for their matter and right reason for their form. With this right reason they naturally love virtue (L). Whoever does

---

26 Cai Qing developed this important concept of *qiji* 氣機 (cause of *qi*), picked up by Wu Sunyou in his commentary on the *Yijing*. The term *qiji* appears once in *Zhuangzi* and once in *Zhuzi yulei*. The term is also used in Chinese medicine.
27 While Ricci, Longobardo, Intorcetta, and Couplet have all argued for a materialist interpretation of *qi*, Noël makes a breakthrough here in understanding *qi* as a vital principle which is immaterial. He goes also beyond the traditional idea of an active force being imposed from the outside to a passive matter, and he adopts the idea of an intrinsic force. See our note just above about *vis motrix*. In Question 3, Noël identifies *qi* with life itself.
28 After having discussed the power of *Tian* from the point of view of cosmology, Noël deals with anthropology, showing that the power of *Tian* supports human efforts without replacing them, and instigates human freedom.

not follow the correctness of the mind violates the Law of Heaven, and is not given any special assistance by Heaven. Without Heaven's help, he encounters many difficulties in his affairs, and even if he wishes to do anything, how could he achieve it (M)? Heaven always has a reason for helping human beings: whoever follows the correct reason faithfully can win over Heaven's heart, and the obedient man receives Heaven's help (N). The sentence 'the highest virtue, or the prince of the highest virtue, is helped by Heaven; nothing ill or unlucky will befall him' is said on the basis of emptiness [*kong*] (that is, a thing or foundation which is imperceptible, invisible and divorced from matter, as I will say below). However, Confucius' explanation of these words is neither false nor rash (O). O Ruler of immense Heaven, or immense Heaven, the Supreme Lord and Ruler, you who have the power to allow us to escape evil and seek goodness, why do you not allow us to flee afar (P)? Although the highest Heaven seems not to think at all about these things, Its intelligent spirit, being the maker of things, cannot be comprehended and wards off all dangers (Q). In Its secret and mysterious darkness, Heaven has something by which It stabilizes silently the people, assists them, and joins them to live together (R). When something which no human effort can accomplish is done naturally, it is said to be Heaven which governs and rules in that deep and immense darkness. It can never be comprehended nor conceived (S). Each person is given according to individual needs something called natural reason, which cannot be comprehended. It is given without any apparent traces of the Maker, who in that deep and mysterious darkness has full freedom to give and take away, as well as to come and depart (T). The universal and particular power of Heaven is nothing other than Its fourfold power, which is first or great, participative, directive and perfective, and can be understood in a particular and universal sense (V). What is understood through all the things of the world is something external and perceptible, but what is understood through this universal and particular power is something internal and free (X). Finally, this universal power is the first root of all things and the first principle of all productions (Z).

More time would be needed to link each of these things to God, as the first and universal cause, to His omnipotence, providence, assistance, simultaneous workings, and wisdom.[29] However, all those things seem clear enough and I shall move forward.

---

29 *Concursus simultaneus*, or simultaneous workings, refers to divine workings which parallel human activity. It is contrasted with *concursus previus*, which explores divine activity as a cause or precondition of human activity. Jesuits (Molina, Suárez) tended to de-emphasize *concursus previus*.

NOTES

A.1 《周易正解·卷一·乾卦》：「物之所資以始者元也。」「大矣哉乾之元乎,何也?天以生物為心,而元即其生生之心也。故化機一動,而物之生理、生氣皆此發端,是萬物資元以始也。然此元氣流行,初無間斷,物之由始而終,皆其貫徹。亨者,元之通；利者,元之遂；貞者,元之成。是元非止為萬物資始,乃統貫于天德者也。此乾元所為大也。」

> Corresponding to quote B.2 in the paragraph on the power of Heaven [c.1, q.2, §.2, B.2], volume 1 of the *True Explanation of the Book of Changes and Productions* states the following about the symbol 'Qian': 'The power upon which things rely to commence their existence is called first or great [*yuan*]'.[30] A little further down is written: 'What is the great and first power of Heaven? Heaven attentively considers the production of things; this first and great power is the mind that constantly produces things. Therefore, the force of movement (*vis motrix*) immediately breaks into motion or into act, and soon the production of things, both in terms of reason [*li*] or form and in terms of air [*qi*] or matter, begins to emerge.[31] All things depend on that great and first power to commence their existence. The regular motion of this power pertains not only to the beginnings of things but also to their completion. The participative power [*heng*] of Heaven is the communication of the first and great power; the directive power [*li*], its direction; and the perfective power [*zhen*], its perfection. All things not only rely upon this first power to commence their existence, but also on a general level the first power encompasses in itself all the powers of Heaven, and this is why it is called great'.[32]

A.2 《周易正解·卷一·乾卦》：「是元非止為萬物資始,乃統攝帝天之柄,如天王之大一統者然,故曰統天。」

> Not far below [in volume 1 of the *True Explanation of the Book of Changes and Productions*]: 'This first and great power of Heaven operates not only at the beginning of all things, but also on a general level embraces the whole rulership of Heaven, called in Chinese *ditian* [帝天]. Its power can be said to embrace the whole heaven, just as the great and immense power of the emperor rules over the whole monarchy'.[33]

---

30 This quote appears in Cai Qing's *Yijing mengyin*, juan 1, and what follows next is an explanation of Cai Qing's idea about *yuan* as equivalent of the power of Heaven (*tiande* 天德).
31 The production of things is explained here not as a combination of *yin* and *yang*, but as something more fundamental, the combination of *li* and *qi*.
32 The four powers (*side* 四德: *yuan, heng, li, zhen*) are usually juxtaposed as four parallel powers, but here *yuan* is singled out as an equivalent of Heaven and becomes the basis for the three other powers (*heng, li, zhen*), stressing the continuity between the first great power of Heaven and the three other powers. To single out the role of *yuan* among the four powers is, in fact, an idea of Zhang Zai. See Song Yecao, *Cai Qing Yixue sixiang yanjiu*, p. 12.
33 Here again the *Zhouyi zhengjie* adopts the commentary (*tuanzhuan*) of the hexagram 'qian' in the *Zhouyi* (大哉乾元萬物資始乃統天, juan 1).

B. 《周易正解・卷一・乾卦》：「問：天德之元在何處?而萬物則何從而資之以為始耶?曰：此問甚善,此理甚妙。蓋天之四德默運於冥漠之間,而萬物之所以為'元亨利貞'者,惟其機之所動耳。」「今只以一粒粟言之,各有一點生意,即便是天德之所在,機之所伏也。故機發動之時,一段滋溫之氣,是得於乾之元；至其露生之時,則得於乾之亨；既而得利而向於實；得其貞而實之成：無他也。」

> A little further below [In volume 1 of the *True Explanation of the Book of Changes and Productions*]: 'You ask where the first and great power of Heaven is located? From where does it operate at beginning of all things? I answer that your question is excellent and the answer is most sublime. The fourfold power of Heaven dwells silently amid a secret and mysterious darkness. All things commence their existence, grow, are directed, and are perfected by participating in this fourfold power. But the break-through is done by the force of movement'.[34] And the text continues a little further down: 'Take the example of a few grains of millet. Each grain contains in itself a sense of life; the power of Heaven resides in it and the force of movement hides in it. When a little bit of air causes fermentation and the force of movement breaks into act or motion, the first and great power of Heaven is operative in the grain; then humidity is increased, the participative or expansive power of Heaven is operative in the grain; when the grain tends to produce fruit, the directive power of Heaven is operative; and when the grain finally produces fruit, the perfective power of Heaven is operative'.[35]

C. 《周易正解・卷一・乾卦》：「『大哉乾乎,剛健中正,純粹精也。』精者元始、亨通、利遂、貞成,皆維天之命,至微至妙。上天之載,無聲無臭,有不可思議形容者。」

> Finally, [in the *Yijing* the following is stated about the symbol 'Qian']: 'How great is the active power of Heaven! Its strength, constancy, equity and rectitude are most pure, whole and perfect'. [The *True Explanation of the Book of Changes and Productions*] comments on this passage as follows: 'The fourfold active power of Heaven is the most sublime and excellent Law of Heaven. The thing of the Supreme Heaven is without sound and smell, and cannot be perceived through the senses, comprehended by any thought or expressed by any concrete meaning or figure'.[36]

---

34 This unfolding of the First Principle into three different stages may have suggested to Noël something similar to the idea of a continuous creation (theory of a unique act of creation unfolding in time), already present in Saint Augustine's *De genesi ad litteram* and Aquinas' *Summa theologiae* and *Disputatae questiones de potentia Dei*. The idea of a continuous creation was developed further by Francisco Suárez in his *On Creation, Conservation, & Concurrence* (1597), and adopted by Descartes in his *Discourse on the Method* (1637). Francisco Furtado and Li Zhizao 李之藻 presented a philosophical of creation in *Huan you quan 寰有詮* (1628). Still, in c.1, q.3, Noël expresses the conventional idea of a historical creation at spring and mentions Jacques Salian.

35 The idea of *yuan* as a force of movement and the metaphor of the millet come from Cai Qing's *Sishu mengyin*, *juan* 1. This vitalist explanation in four steps explains the production of things.

36 Same as the quotes above, this quote is a paraphrase of Cai Qing's explanation about the hexagram *Qian* in the *Yijing mengyin*, *juan* 1.

D.2 《周易正解・卷十七・繫辭傳上・第一》：「知猶主, 即主宰也, 如知州、知縣之知, 謂主一州、一縣之事。」

> Corresponding to quote number 3 [C.3], volume 17 of the *True Explanation of the Book of Changes and Productions* states the following about chapter 1 of 'Zhuan shang': 'The character "to know" [*zhi*] refers here to a master who acts, rules and directs things. This is similar to the meaning of the character "to know" [*zhi*] in reference to the governor of the city; the expression "he knows the city" or "he knows the small city" means that he acts as master of the whole city or of the small city, ruling and directing everything'.37

E. 《周易正解・卷十七・繫辭傳上・第一》：「故萬物之生, 形質未成而胚胎先露者, 皆乾之所主。蓋乾道一倡而陰陽交合, 則氣以始其形, 理以始其性。盡物而資始之, 知大始者也。及夫機緘已露, 而形質斯成者, 皆坤之所為。蓋坤道順承, 而資生品物, 則承天之氣以成其形, 承天之理以成其性。盡物而成就之, 作成物者也。」

> A little further down [the *True Explanation of the Book of Changes and Productions*] adds: 'The active power of Heaven controls the productions of all things before they become perceptible and before the formation of offspring. When the active power of Heaven breaks into act, reveals itself as leader, and stillness (*yin*) and motion (*yang*) are joined together, then the air [*qi*] gives rise to a perceptible figure [*xing* 形], and reason [*li*] gives rise to an imperceptible nature [*xing* 性]. That which the beginning of this whole situation depends is that power which knows the great beginnings. Then, the passive power of Earth [*kun*], unfastened by Heaven's force of movement, perfects the perceptible figure. Indeed, only when Earth's way of action obeys Heaven in aiding the production of all things, it receives the air of Heaven to perfect their perceptible figure and the reason of Heaven to perfect their imperceptible nature. This way the Author of things makes everything complete'.38

F.3 《周易正解・卷二十二・說卦・第五》：「『帝出乎震。』朱熹：『帝者, 天之主宰』。昔者文王以先天卦位有其體而未有其用, 於是取而更置之始, 於東方之震, 而終於東北之艮, 以明造化一歲流行之用。蓋萬物之生成, 皆本於天, 而天之所以主宰乎生成者, 謂之帝。是帝也, 其出入之機, 即流行於後天之卦位焉。卦位起於震, 是其出於此也。蔡虛齋《易經蒙引》曰：『此乾坤乃偏言之, 乾坤與六子同例者也, 統之於帝矣。』」

> Corresponding to quote number 4 [D.4], volume 22 of the *True Explanation of the Book of Changes and Productions* states the following about chapter 5 of the 'Shuogua': 'Doctor Zhu Xi says, "The word *Di* means the Lord and Ruler of

---

37 The explanation of 'to know' as 'to govern' is given by Zhu Xi in his *Zhouyi benyi* 周易本義 (*zhang* 1, *juan* 3): '知, 猶主也'. However, the etymology for prefect (*zhizhou* 知州) comes from 'Xici shang' 繫辭上 in *Zhuzi yulei, juan* 74: '知, 主之意也, 如知縣、知州'.

38 In his translation, Noël tends to adopt a chronological frame, talking about the active power of Heaven (*qian*) before things become perceptible, and talking about the passive power of Heaven (*kun*) as being chronologically after the active power of Heaven. In fact, the text does not suggest temporal progression, and the active power of Heaven and the passive power of Earth are never separated. It is only possible to talk about a priority of *qian* over *kun* in terms of logical priority.

Heaven".³⁹ In the past, Wen Wang saw that the symbols [trigrams] invented by Fuxi were arranged according to their substance, but lacked purpose and use, and so he had them arranged in a different circular order, placing first the symbol [trigram] for motion (*Zhen*) in view of the equinoctial region of the world [i.e. the east]. He placed last the symbol for cessation (*Gen*) in the north-eastern region of the world in order to display the successive works of the Author of things within a full year. All the productions of things have Heaven as their first beginning. Since Heaven controls the production and perfection of things, Heaven can be called Lord and Ruler of Heaven. The Lord of Heaven's force of movement, which comes into act and ceases act, diffuses itself into all the directions of the eight symbols as arranged by Wen Wang. Since the order of these eight symbols starts from the symbol for motion, Heaven comes into act from there'.⁴⁰ Then, [the *True Explanation of the Book of Changes and Productions*] quotes Cai Xuzhai: 'All those eight symbols depend upon the Lord of Heaven who rules and controls them'.⁴¹ With the eight symbols, Cai Xuzhai shows the order of the productions and changes of things during a full year, progressing from spring to summer, from summer to autumn, and from autumn to winter, where the annual cycle finishes. He shows also the diverse mutations of the air and the temporal cycles according to the seasons of the year, temperature changes, and the diverse conditions of the air.

G. 《周易正解・卷二十二・說卦・第五》：「雲峰胡氏曰：『自出震, 以至成言乎艮, 萬物生成之序也。然孰生孰成之, 必有為之主宰者, 故謂之帝。』」

Next, the *True Explanation of the Book of Changes and Productions* quotes Hu Yunfeng:⁴² 'The order of all created and perfected things runs from the first symbol for motion (in Chinese *Zhen*), until the last symbol for cessation (in Chinese *Gen*), but who produces them and who perfects them? There must be a Lord and Ruler, who is thus is called *Di*'.

---

39 See Zhu Xi, *Zhouyi benyi*, juan 4. Interestingly, Noël quotes Zhu Xi for the identification of *Di* with 'Lord and Ruler' of Heaven (*Tian zhi zhuzai* 天之主宰), but he does not quote Zhang Juzheng who identifies *Di* with the ruler of *Shangdi* (*Shangdi zhi zhuzai* 上帝之主宰). Zhang's explanation is adopted in the preface of the *Confucius Sinarum philosophus* because of the explicit mention of *Shangdi*. See Meynard, ed., *Confucius Sinarum Philosophus*, pp. 141–42.
40 The order of the eight trigrams is explained by Couplet in the preface of the *Confucius Sinarum philosophus*. See Meynard, ed., *Confucius Sinarum Philosophus*, p. 141. The arrangement attributed to Wen Wang (Posterior Heaven) is probably more ancient than the arrangement attributed to Fu Xi (Anterior Heaven).
41 While Cai Qing stresses from a metaphysical point of view that all the eight trigrams are on the same level (*tongli* 同例), Noël adds below his own commentary stressing the temporal priority of Zhen. We can notice here and in six other quotes from the *Zhouyi zhengjie* the mention of Cai Qing. Noël quotes abundantly from Cai Qing's *Sishu mengyin*, but he does not seem to have the *Yijing mengyin*, which indeed is not present today in ARSI.
42 Hu Bingwen 胡炳文 (1250–1333), *hao* Yunfeng 雲峰 was a Yuan 元 dynasty scholar and a follower of Zhu Xi. Hu Yunfeng wrote a commentary on the *Yijing* in his *Zhouyi benyi tongshi* 周易本義通釋 (General explanation of the original meaning of the *Yijing*), in 12 *juan*. Bouvet gives exactly the same quote but draws upon the *Yijing daquan*. See Bouvet, *Gujin*, n. 1 (p. 131).

H. 《周易正解・卷二十二・說卦・第五》：「蔡虛齋曰：『此節主帝言，下節主萬物之隨帝言。蓋萬物之生成，必有所以生成之者。故帝為天之主宰。究竟亦無他，只是氣機耳。氣機之所在，萬物即隨之。』」

> A little further below, the *True Explanation of the Book of Changes and Productions* quotes Doctor Cai Xuzhai: 'This passage deals mostly with the Lord of Heaven, while the next passage deals with all the things insofar as they ensue from the Lord of Heaven. For all things to be produced and made perfect there must be something by which they are produced and perfected. Hence *Di* (that is *Shangdi*) is the Lord and Ruler of Heaven. If the question is further investigated, there is nothing other than the force of movement of the vital breath or air. When the force of movement of the vital breath acts, all things immediately follow'.[43]

I. 《周易正解・卷二十二・說卦・第五》：「首節言帝乘卦位以出入，就氣機說猶未著物，然帝之出入不可見。故次節言物之隨帝以出入。蓋因其可見以明其不可見也。」「鄭氏圖注云：『帝字宜自為句，八者皆帝所為，故以帝冠之。』」

> However, take note of what [Wu Sunyou] quoting [Cai Qing] says about the force of movement of air or vital breath at the beginning of the passage [chapter 5 of 'Shuogua']: 'The first passage deals with the Lord of Heaven coming into act and ceasing act according to the order of the eight symbols; when the force of movement of air or vital breath is mentioned this means that things do not yet exist, and nothing has emerged into being. Since the Lord of Heaven cannot be seen coming into act or ceasing act, the next passage says that all things ensue from the Lord of Heaven in acting or ceasing. In this way, that which or he who cannot be seen [the Lord of Heaven] can still be known through that which can be seen'. After this, [Wu Sunyou] quotes the writer Zheng [Xuan] explaining the eight symbols as follows: 'With the single character *Di* (that is the Lord of Heaven) means one thing by itself. It is this *Di* who makes the eight symbols and has been put in charge of them'.[44]

《周易正解・卷二十二・說卦・第五》：「夫帝之出入不可見，而欲知帝之出入者，盍自萬物觀之乎？」「此萬物一歲之出入也，然豈萬物能自為之哉？惟帝主之也，則觀萬物之出入，而帝之出入可知矣。」

> The same writer [Wu Sunyou] begins his explanation of chapter 5 [of 'Shuogua'] as follows: 'It is impossible to see the Lord of Heaven coming into act and ceasing act, and if you wish to know him coming into act and ceasing to act, why do you not consider everything that has been produced?' He then enumerates the productions of the whole year that take place in succession according to seasonal

---

43 Cai Qing distinguishes *Di* (or *Shangdi*) from *qiji* 氣機 (cause of *qi*) which comes from *Di* and starts the process of generation of things.
44 Noël is correct in referring the number eight to the number of hexagrams or *gua*, but a more accurate translation of Zheng's commentary should be: 'Starting from the character *Di*, there is one sentence, and since the eight items constitute the actions of *Di*, they are all under *Di*'. The eight actions of *Di* are: to emerge from Zhen; to bring order in Xun; to display beauty in Li; to do great work in Kun; to rejoice in Dui; to struggle in Qian; to rest in Kan; to complete in Gen (出乎震，齊乎巽，相見乎離，致役乎坤，說言乎兌，戰乎乾，勞乎坎，成言乎艮).

variations, starting from winter and going through the eight symbols. Afterwards, he concludes: 'This is the action and cessation of all things in the course of a full year. How can things make themselves? Since the Lord of Heaven controls them, their action and cessation, that is their motion and rest, can be seen, and thus the action and the cessation, or rest, of the Lord of Heaven can be known'.[45]

K. 《周易正解・卷二十二・說卦・第四》：「乾次兌而居圖之始，有君之之道焉，為造物之主，而於萬物無所不統。凡夫雷動風散之屬，皆統攝於乾，而分職以德者也。」「君猶主也。」

The same author [Wu Sunyou] says on chapter 4 of the same section ['Shuogua' in volume 22 of the *True Explanation of the Book of Changes and Productions*]: 'The active force of Heaven (or Heaven itself) is placed first in the series of the eight symbols [trigrams] and exercises the function of a ruler. It is indeed the Lord Author of things, and there is nothing that it does not embrace or rule. For example, thunder, which is the symbol for motion, and wind, which is the symbol for diffusion, and all the others rely on it, are encompassed and ruled by it, and exercise their own function according to its command'. Little further below it is said: 'The word ruler [*jun*] means lord [*zhu*]'.

L.4 《日講四書解義・卷二十三・孟子・告子上》：「天生眾民，有形氣者為物，有天理者為則。此民所秉執之常性，無不好是懿美之德者。夫物與則有精粗之分。」

Corresponding to quote 5 [R.17], volume 23 of the *Daily Commentary on the Four Books* states the following about chapter 6 'Gaozi shang' in the second part of the *Mencius*: 'All human beings produced by Heaven have a perceptible body for matter and right reason for form. All human beings receive this common nature, and there is no one who does not like the beauty of virtue. Matter and form differ in terms of greater and lesser perfection'. The Gelao Zhang Juzheng explains this in detail.[46]

M.5 《周易正解・卷十七・无妄卦》：「故不正則逆天之命，而天下不祐之。天既不祐，則動多窒礙。雖欲有所行也，其能行矣哉？」

Corresponding to quote 9 [K.10], volume 7 of the *True Explanation of the Book of Changes and Productions* states the following about the symbol 'Wuwang': 'Whoever does not follow the correctness of the mind ...' See above.

---

45 *Di*, its action and cessation (*Di zhi churu* 帝之出入) as well as the cause of *qi* (*qiji* 氣機) are all metaphysical realities which cannot be perceived by senses but can be known through their effects. On the contrary, Longobardo understands *Di* and *Dizhu* 帝主 as a physical dominance. See Longobardo, *A Brief Response on the Controversies*, pp. 130–31 (prelude 6, n. 2).

46 This passage is quoted in the *Gujin*, p. 138 (n. 5). The mention of Zhang Juzheng seems here a mistake, with Noël confusing the *Sishu rijiang* with the *Sishu zhijie*.

N.6 《周易正解・卷二十一・上傳・第十二》：「夫祐之為言助之義也。然助之有得之天者,有得之人者,而要皆非漫然而助我也。理之自然而無矯拂者,為順處有者。能順乎天理而不違,則克當乎天心矣；是天之所助者,順也。理之誠實而無偽妄者,為信處有者,能以信而感乎乎人,則克合乎人心矣；是人之所助者,信也。」

> Corresponding to quote number 10, volume 21 of the *True Explanation of the Book of Changes and Productions* states the following about chapter 12 of 'Shang zhuan': 'To be helped, or to receive assistance, can be understood in two ways: to obtain assistance from Heaven, and to obtain it from human beings, but in both cases, neither Heaven nor human beings help someone without a reason. Someone who follows the natural command of correct reason and does not resist it wickedly can be called obedient. The person who obeys the correct reason of Heaven by following it and not resisting to it can win over the heart of Heaven. Such an obedient man receives the help of Heaven. Someone who embraces the true morality of reason and does not do anything false and deceitful can be called sincere. By embracing the truth of morality and arousing other people through his own purity, the sincere man can win over the minds of others; such a sincere and truthful man receives the help of others'.

O.7 《周易正解・卷五・大有卦》：「『上九:自天祐之,吉无不利。』憑空說出此兩句。若无孔子繫辭之說,恐朱子亦未知所解,方知聖人之言不苟也。」

> Corresponding to quote number 11 [K.11], volume 5 of the *True Explanation of the Book of Changes and Productions* states the following about the symbol 'Dayou': 'The sentence "The highest virtue, or the prince of the highest virtue, is helped by Heaven; nothing bad or unlucky will befall him" is said insofar as it depends on emptiness, namely something of anything material or perceptible.[47] If Confucius had not explained in his appendix [the *Xici*] the words of Wen Wang and Zhou Gong (see c.1, §.2, F.6 and K.10), I am afraid that Doctor Zhu Xi would have been unable to explain them since he acknowledges that the explanation of Confucius is well conceived'.[48]

P.8 《詩經說約集解・大雅・雲漢》：「昊天上帝,乃司禍福趨避之權者也,寧不使我得逃遁而去乎?」

> Corresponding to quote number 12 [L.12], the *Exhaustive Compilation of the Book of Odes*, which was recently published by Fan [Zhiheng] and Wang [Jing] and includes Zhu Xi's commentary in the appendix, states the following about the ode 'Yunhan' in the volume 'Daya': 'O Ruler of immense Heaven …' See above.[49]

---

47 This explanation about the word *kong* here is not found in the ARSI manuscript.
48 This quotation is found in Cai Qing's *Sishu mengyin* and *Yijing mengyin*, and was copied into the *Zhouyi zhengjie*.
49 On the *Bianzhitang dingzheng shijing shuoyue jijie* 辨志堂訂正詩經說約集解, see Chapter 2.11.

Q.9 　《詩經說約集解・大雅・瞻卬》：朱熹：「惟天高遠,雖若無意於物,然其功用神明不測,雖危亂之極,亦無不能鞏固之者。幽王苟能改過自新而不忝其祖,則天意可回,來者猶必可救,而子孫亦蒙其福矣。」

> Corresponding to quote number 12 [M.13], the famous commentator Zhu Xi says the following about the ode 'Zhanyang' in the tome 'Daya': 'Although Heaven is so high and remote and does not seem to think about these things, His intelligent spirit which cannot be comprehended is the Author of things and can stop, prevent, and control any dangerous turmoil. If Youwang wishes to return to his senses, to pursue a new way of life, and not to inflict dishonour to his ancestors with his despisable conduct, then the will of Heaven can return and take care of his posterity so that his descendants may receive his paternal prosperity.'[50]

R.10 　蔡沈《書經集傳・卷四・周書・洪範》：「天於冥冥之中,默有以安定其民,輔相保合其居止。」

> Corresponding to quote number 16 [Q.16], Cai Chen in volume 4 of his commentary on the *Imperial Annals* [*Shujing jizhuan*] writes the following about the chapter 'Hongfan': 'Heaven in its hidden ...' See above.

S.11 　《日講四書解義・卷二十一・孟子・萬章上》：「天下事,凡人力莫之作為而自然為者,是之謂天。主宰於沖漠之中,不可得而測也。」

> Corresponding to quote number 17 [R.17], volume 21 of the *Daily Commentary on the Four Books* writes the following about the chapter 'Wan Zhang shang' of the *Mencius*: 'When something is done naturally ...' See above.[51]

T. 　張居正《四書直解・孟子・萬章上》》：「堯舜禹之時,相不皆久,子不皆賢,固皆有天命存乎其間,而所謂天命,又非可以強為而力致也。蓋凡事有待於經營而成者,皆屬人為,未可以言天。惟是因物,不見其作為之迹。而予奪去就,冥冥之中,自有主張,此則理之自然而不可測者。」

> In volume 21 [of the *Sishu zhijie*], the Gelao Zhang Juzheng explains in greater detail: 'Under the emperors Yao, Shun [and Yu], their ministers did not all last the same amount of time, nor were their children equally wise, and thus the law and disposition of Heaven [*tianming*] is present in all things. That which is called the law and disposition of Heaven cannot be taken by force. Everything that needs to be perfected through well-thought plans and stratagems is considered human and cannot be called Heaven. Each person is given to each according to his needs ...' See above.

V.12 　蔡虛齋《四書蒙引・卷四・中庸・第十三》：「究其實,則只是元亨利貞之分合言也。」

> Corresponding to quote number 18 [S.18], Cai Xuzhai says in volume 4 of the *Sishu mengyin* about the *Zhongyong*: 'If the universal and particular power of Heaven is correctly understood', See above.

50　The original quote comes from Zhu Xi's *Shijing jizhuan, juan* 7.
51　This passage is quoted in the *Gujin*, p. 155 (n. 33).

X. 蔡虛齋《四書蒙引・卷四・中庸・第十三》：「蓋萬物、日月、四時, 皆在外者；小德、大德, 是在內主張之者。」

> Also, as it is said just below [in the *Sishu mengyin*]: 'All the countless things of different species, the sun, the moon, the four seasons, are all external, but the particular and universal virtue [*xiaode dade*] is something internal, exercising its freedom among external things'.

Z. 張居正《四書直解・中庸・哀公問・政第十三》：「天地有揪會的大德, 為萬物之根抵, 為萬物之本原。但見其敦厚盛大, 自然生化出來, 無有窮盡。」

> The Gelao Zhang [Juzheng] says in volume 3 [of his *Sishu zhijie*]: 'Heaven and Earth embrace the one great and universal virtue which is the first root of all things and the first beginning and origin of all productions; you observe the extremely abundant and immense natural productions and changes which unfold outside endlessly'.

§.3. Knowledge of *Tian* or *Shangdi* according to Modern Commentators

The great Lord of Heaven, though residing in the highest realm, approaches the smallest things, inspires awe and understands everything. He watches over all the kingdoms because He wishes a stable peace and tranquility for people (A). Tai Wang wanted to give people peace and tranquility and he did not disappoint the Lord of Heaven [*Di*] or make Him angry (B). Make sure not to say that Heaven is the Most High and placed above, and thus has nothing to do with us. You should know that He is intelligent, attentive, and awe-inspiring, since He is constantly coming up and down as if to approach our affairs and to watch over us each day. If someone lacks respect, surely Heaven rejects him and the favour of Providence leaves him. Surely you should revere [Heaven] (C)? When I am alone, could it possibly happen that Heaven in Its deep and mysterious darkness is unable to know me? The perfect man cannot be known by people, but only Heaven knows him. (D) There is no greater crime than people cheating or deceiving Heaven. Heaven cannot be cheated, but people deceive only themselves (E). Those few words are clear enough, and I proceed to discuss the will.

NOTES

A.1 《詩經說約集解・大雅・皇矣》：「凡天命之君, 皆以安民而已。彼皇矣上帝, 雖高高在上, 而其臨下, 則赫然威明, 所以監觀乎西方。惟欲求民之安定也。」朱熹：「天之臨下甚明, 但求民之安定而已。」「苟上帝之所欲致者, 則增大其疆境之規模。」

> Corresponding to the first quote of the section on knowledge in the previous chapter [c.2, q.2, §.3, A.1], the *Exhaustive Compilation of the Book of Odes* states the following about the ode 'Huangyi' in the volume 'Daya': 'The king appointed by the command of Heaven has to insure the tranquility and peace of the people. The great Lord of Heaven (in Chinese *Huangyi Shangdi*), though residing in the highest, approaches the these things below, inspires awe and understands everything. He watches over all the kingdoms because He wishes a stable

peace and tranquility for the people'. Zhu Xi comments on this passage saying: 'Approaching these things below, Heaven understands all and seeks peace and tranquility for people'.[52] A little further below he adds: 'When the Lord and Ruler of Heaven [*Shangdi*] chooses someone, He makes him a ruler and promotes his rule and his power far and wide'.

B 《詩經說約集解・大雅・皇矣》：「曰『帝遷明德』者，推本輿宅之意，見太王之真能莫民不負帝心也。」

The same compilation [*Exhaustive Compilation of the Book of Odes*] states: 'Through His bright virtue, *Di* is said to have transferred Tai Wang to this place. If you carefully assess the first and true intention for this, you shall see that Tai Wang honestly gave people peace and tranquility, and he did not exasperate the mind and intention of the Lord of Heaven [*Di*]'.

C.2 《詩經說約集解・周頌・敬之》：「无曰天高高在天，而于吾无輿。當知其聰明明畏，常若陟降于吾所為之事，而日日監視于此。使一有不敬，天必棄之而命去矣，其可不敬哉？」朱熹：「天道甚明，其命不易保也，無謂其高而不吾察。當知其聰明明畏，常若陟降於吾所為，而無日不臨監於此者，不可以不敬也。」

Corresponding to quote 2 [c.2, q.2, §.3, D.2], the *Exhaustive Compilation of the Book of Odes* states the following about the ode 'Jingzhi' in the volume 'Zhousong': 'Make sure not to say ...' See above. As Zhu Xi says in reference to this quote: 'The way of Heaven or Heaven's mode of action is very clever; the favour of Providence is not easy to maintain. You should not say that Heaven is so high up that it does not examine or observe us. You should know that Heaven is intelligent and clever, and therefore, you should fear It as if It were always either coming up or down to approach our affairs. There is not a single day in which It does not approach and observe. Thus, you cannot but revere It'.[53]

D.3 《日講四書解義・卷九・論語・憲問》：「惟是心存焉為己，仰不愧天，或者上天於冥冥之中能知我耳。人之所以莫我知者，正在此也。」 張居正《論語直解》：「惟是心存為己，仰不愧天，或者上天于冥冥之中能知我耳，所以說『知我者其天乎』。」「大聖人盡性至命，與天合一，其獨德之妙，真有人不能知而天獨知之者。」

Concerning quote 3 [c.2, q.2, §.3, E.3] from the *Lunyu* [14.37], volume 9 of the *Daily Commentary on the Four Books* states: 'By recollecting the soul and by spending time alone, if I raise the eyes to Heaven and experience no shame, could it possibly happen that the highest Heaven, in Its deep and mysterious darkness, does not know me?' Concerning the same quote, Zhang Juzheng in the ninth volume [of the *Sishu zhijie*] adds: 'The perfect man who adheres to and follows the Law of Heaven in accomplishing all parts of his rational nature reaches the singular excellence

---

52 Zhu Xi, *Shijing jizhuan*, juan 6.
53 The *Shijing shuoyue jijie* quotes here Zhu Xi, and transforms the ancient religious meaning of *Tian* going up and down (*zhijiang* 陟降) into a moral law 'as if Heaven was going up and down' (*ruo zhijiang* 若陟降). The relation is no more a religious relation with a personal *Tian*, but expressed as reverence (*jing* 敬) towards *Tian*.

of a close union with Heaven. The people cannot know and notice him, but only Heaven knows him'.⁵⁴

E.4 張居正《四書直解 · 卷七 · 論語 · 子罕》:「我將誰欺, 無乃欲欺天乎?人而欺天, 莫大之罪, 況天不可欺, 徒自為虛詐而已。」

Concerning quote 4 [c.2, q.2, §.3, F.4] of the *Lunyu* [9.11], Zhang Juzheng states in volume 7 [of the *Sishu zhijie*]: 'Whom does he want me to cheat or deceive? Does he want me to deceive Heaven? There is no greater crime than for man to cheat or to deceive Heaven. Furthermore, Heaven cannot be cheated or deceived. But out of his evilness, man deceives only himself'.⁵⁵

§.4. Will of *Tian* or *Shangdi* according to Modern Commentators

Modern authors indicate clearly enough that there is intention and will in Heaven. The ascension to the imperial throne results from an order of Heaven, and the office of the Emperor is called the office of Heaven. The wealth of the emperor is called the wealth of Heaven, and it cannot be made or given through human forces. However, it is difficult to know the will of Heaven since the reality of Heaven lacks sound and cannot be perceived by senses. Therefore, [Heaven] shows Its will and intention not through distinct and clear words, but silently. The ascension of Prince Shun to the empire, in whom the heart of Heaven was delighted, was not fixed when emperor Yao transferred the power to him, but was predetermined in that obscure and mysterious darkness (A).⁵⁶ The mysterious and secret substance of Heaven does not speak. When the emperor proposes someone as successor, he cannot know whether the will of Heaven will agree, let alone force Heaven to confer the empire on the one that he is proposing (B). Although Heaven has neither eyes to see nor ears to hear, there is nothing related to human virtues and vices that It does not see or hear. Indeed, Heaven is thought to see and hear what the eyes and ears of all the people see or hear. Thus, it is clear that the Lord of Heaven's command considers especially people's hearts, and Heaven's will is inclined to what the people are inclined (C). The Lord and Ruler, namely Heaven, performs all these various things amid a deep and mysterious mist. How could human strength accomplish such things? Human strength cannot make someone stay in an office for a long time or make someone wise or stupid. Therefore, both long and short durations, as well as wisdom and stupidity, come from the will of Heaven which must be obeyed (D). We are not allowed to prevent the intention or will of Heaven from achieving its end (E).

---

54 In translating *Lunyu* 14.37, the *Confucius Sinarum philosophus* translated in a similar way Zhang Juzheng's comment about not feeling ashamed. See Meynard, ed., *Confucius Sinarum Philosophus*, p. 449. However, the *Confucius Sinarum philosophus* did not translate the comment about the union with Heaven (*Tian ren heyi* 天人合一).
55 An abbreviated form of this passage is quoted in the *Gujin*, p. 165 (n. 20).
56 Noël mentions nineteen excerpts, most of which connect the key notions of *yi* 意 to Heaven. On four occasions, the term *tianyi* 天意 is used.

Once the Lord of Heaven ordered the fierce prince [Cheng] Tang to act as emperor in order to settle the boundaries of all the surrounding kingdoms (F). The Lord of Heaven commanded prince [Cheng] Tang to be the ruler and doctor of the people. Each day, this prince made such progress in the pursuit of perfection that his virtue could reach up to Heaven with great splendour. He bound and joined the heart of Heaven to himself, and became one with it (G). The people groan after being exposed to every sort of danger and evil. They look at Heaven as if It were asleep and not discerning anything. Neither certain happiness blesses the good, nor certain unhappiness oppresses the wicked. It is as if [Heaven] had no intention to distinguish between the two. In fact, Heaven does not behave like this towards people. If Heaven wishes to afflict them at the appointed time, It will do so. How great is the Lord of Heaven! Who could say that Heaven hates anyone? (H). Out of Its holiness and mercy, the hidden and mysterious Heaven now pours out the rigour of Its fearsome anger onto Earth (I). If what I have done does not agree with right reason, I have surely sinned against Heaven, and Heaven needs to reject me (K). But since you, Prince, are the obedient son of Heaven, Heaven loves, preserves and protects you (L). While Prince Yu was kneeling, he questioned the mind of Heaven, and he complied very respectfully and faithfully (M). Anyone who always strives to adhere to right Reason with constant thought will be certainly helped by the heart of Heaven (N). Confucius said, 'If Heaven had no intention or will towards me, It surely would not have endowed my intellectual faculty with life; indeed, Heaven controls my life and shall help me amid a deep and mysterious darkness' (O). There is a will in Heaven, which constantly turns. Hence Confucius said, 'If Heaven had wished to destroy the knowledge of the ancient wise men, He would not have given it to a mortal like me. Therefore, if Heaven does not want to destroy it, how is it that the inhabitants of that place Kuang could harm me?' (P) Evidently Heaven in Its deep and mysterious darkness silently helps Confucius, not on Confucius' account alone, but because of the knowledge of the ancient wise men in which he excelled (Q). Mencius says, 'Heaven does not yet wish the peace of the empire' (R). Some obtain what they desire, others do not, while some obtain it but only in a limited way and not in accordance with their desires. All these things depend on the judgement of the Maker of things and cannot be attributed to efforts of human intelligence and prudence (S).⁵⁷ The law and providence of Heaven is truly found in those things which He directs and governs secretly (T).

While you listen to the modern Chinese writers speaking in this way, would not you believe that the ancients whom we now admire are followers of true wisdom?⁵⁸ And would not you believe that all these affirmations could be truly applied to the multiform will of God, namely the will of good pleasure (*voluntas beneplaciti*) and the signified will (*voluntas signi*), the antecedent will of goodness

---

57 Zhang Juzheng has in Chinese *zaowu* 造物, which is translated in Latin as *effector* (maker or author).
58 Noël seems to be saying here that if our understanding of the ancient texts is purely filtered through the modern commentators, we would still conclude that the ancients were theists. This passage is a refutation of both Ricci and Longobardo.

or the consecutive will of justice, the absolute, conditional, effective, and ineffective will of His most wise providence, etc.⁵⁹ But as my readers are learned men, I do not need to dwell on these points. Let us move to other things.

NOTES

A.1   張居正《四書直解・孟子・萬章上》：「萬章問說：『帝王之統, 必有所與, 而後有所承。舜有天下, 既非堯之所與, 果誰與之乎?』孟子答說：『帝王之興皆由天命, 故其位曰天位, 祿曰天祿。見其為天之所授, 非人力可得而與也。』『天意難知, 人事易見, 舜之受命於天, 天固非諄諄然命之也, 天載無聲。何嘗有言, 惟就舜之行事, 默示其意而已。』『意之所在, 即命之所在, 豈待諄諄然以言命之乎?知舜為天心所眷, 則其奄有天下不在于禪授之時, 而於穆之中固已預為之地矣, 堯安得而與之哉?』」

> Corresponding to quote 1 [A.1] in the fourth paragraph of the previous chapter about will [c.2, q.2, §.4, A.1], Zhang Juzheng in volume 21 [of the *Sishu zhijie*] writes the following about Chapter 5 'Wan Zhang shang' in the second part of the *Mencius*: 'As for the monarchy of the emperor, the disciple Wan Zhang says that there must first be someone to give before it can be conceived that there is someone to receive it. Since the emperor Yao did not give the monarchy to Prince Shun, who, I ask, actually gave it to him? Mencius answers that the ascension to the imperial throne results from an order of Heaven. Since the office of the emperor is called the office of Heaven, and the wealth of the emperor is called the wealth of Heaven, it is therefore proven that dignity and wealth is bestowed by Heaven, not by human efforts'. Shortly after, Mencius answers again: 'It is difficult to know the will and intention of Heaven while it is easy to see human affairs. Since Prince Shun received the empire from Heaven, it was certainly not through distinctly expressed words that Heaven ordered Shun to be emperor. Indeed, the reality of Heaven lacks voice as said in the *Zhongyong*. How could Heaven speak? Heaven showed silently Its will and intention through the excellent virtues and remarkable deeds by which Prince Shun was resplendent'. Then, a few more words are added: 'The will of Heaven is precisely where the empire is. What need was there for distinctly expressed words to bestow the empire on him? If you know that Prince Shun was such that the heart of Heaven delighted in him, surely his ascension to obtain the empire was not fixed only when Emperor Yao transmitted it to him, but it was predetermined long ago in the secret and mysterious darkness'.⁶⁰

---

59   Concerning the multiform will of God (*multiplex Dei voluntas*), see Noël, *Theologiae R.P. doctoris eximii Francisci Suarez e Societate Jesu, Summa*, Tract. 3, Disput. 11, p. 325.
60   Zhang Juzheng interprets here the words of Mencius. Noël translates *wumuzhizhong* 於穆之中 as 'amid this secret and mysterious darkness' (*in arcana ac mysteriosa caligine*). It seems that Noël thinks in terms of the pillar of cloud in Exodus 13, with the double aspects of things being concealed and being revealed. Quoted in the *Gujin*, n. 16 (p. 158).

B.2 《日講四書解義·卷二十一·孟子·萬章上》:「天之體於穆無言,其與舜也,固非諄諄然教命之也。」「但就舜之行與事默示其與之之意而已矣。」「天子能舉而薦之於天,然天意之從違尚未可知,不能使天必與之天下。」「舜之行事當乎天心而天受之。」「此豈人力能為也哉,吾故曰實天使之。」

> Concerning the same passage, volume 21 of the *Daily Commentary on the Four Books* states: 'The mysterious and secret substance of Heaven does not speak, etc.' Shortly after it adds: 'The emperor can choose anyone and propose him to Heaven, but he cannot know whether the will of Heaven will agree, and he cannot force Heaven to confer the empire on him'. It is also said: 'The deeds and virtues of Prince Shun have subdued the heart of Heaven, which has accepted him'. Then a little further down: 'How could human effort alone could accomplish all those things? Therefore, I argued that he was truly ordered by Heaven to become emperor'.

C.3 張居正《四書直解·孟子·萬章上》:「《書經·泰誓》篇有云:『天未嘗有目以視,而于人之善惡無所不見,但從我民眾目所視以為視耳;未嘗有耳以聽,而于人之淑慝無所不聞,但從我民眾耳所聽以為聽耳。』《書》之所言如此,可見帝天之命主于民心,而民心所歸,莫非天意。」

> Concerning the passage of the *Book of Imperial Annals* that we mentioned in quote 10 of paragraph six about life in the previous chapter [c.2, q.2, §.6, K.10], Zhang Juzheng states the following in volume 21 [of the *Sishu zhijie*]: 'Although Heaven has no eyes, etc.' See above.

D. 張居正《四書直解·孟子·萬章上》:「以氣數言,若似乎不齊;以機會言,則適相湊合。是皆冥冥之中有為之主宰者,一天之所為而已,豈人力之所能與哉?蓋人力可以薦賢于天,而不能使為相之皆久;人力可以傳位于子,而不能使其子之必賢。其有久、近、賢、不肖者,皆天意之所為。聖人一惟聽天之命而順受之耳。」

> Later, Zhang Juzheng discusses why certain people were not made emperors: 'If you observe the unfolding of time, there are things which are not sufficiently consistent, but if you observe the occasion and the circumstances of time, then all things are consistent between each other. At least regarding the unfolding of time and the circumstances and occasion of time,[61] in the deep and mysterious darkness there is a certain Lord and Ruler, that is, one Heaven alone, which makes all things. Indeed, how could human strength accomplish these things? Human forces may propose a wise man to Heaven, but they cannot cause anyone to remain in the supreme office of the first minister for a long time. They may transmit the sceptre to a son, but they cannot make a son wise or stupid. Indeed, both the length or shortness of time and wisdom or stupidity come from the will of Heaven. Thus, a man with perfect virtue and knowledge desires to obey the command of Heaven'.

---

61 The concept of *qishu* 氣數 appears in the Han-dynasty *Huangdi neijing* 黃帝內經 (Inner canon of the Yellow Emperor) and refers to temporal cycles.

E.4 《日講四書解義・卷二十一・孟子・萬章上》:「予於天所生民之中幸為先覺者也,其可負天意哉?」

Around the end of the chapter containing the passage of the Mencius, the *Daily Commentary on the Four Books* states as follows: 'Mencius says, "Since Heaven has made me excell in terms of right living among the people that It has produced, could I prevent the intention of Heaven from achieving Its end?"'[62]

E.5 《詩經說約集解・商頌・玄鳥》:「迨至于湯,備武德以為號,故上帝命之為君,以正彼四方之疆域。」

Corresponding to quote 3 [c.2, q.2, §.6, D.3], the *Exhaustive Compilation of the Book of Odes* states in relation to the ode 'Xuanniao' in the volume 'Shangsong': 'Prince Cheng Tang was called fierce because of his fierce courage. When he rose up, the Lord of Heaven ordered him to act as emperor to settle the boundaries of all the surrounding kingdoms'.

G.6 《詩經說約集解・商頌・長發》:「天命未嘗有違,延至于湯,遂以會合。湯之降生,適應其期而不遲。天意已有所屬矣。湯之聖敬,又曰積而升。以至昭明感格于天,遲遲不息,一惟上帝之是敬。無間間斷,是以上帝之命為君師,以式法于九圍,而作之極焉。」「昭假,有與天心合一之意。」

Corresponding to quote 8 [c.2, q.2, §.6, I.9], the *Exhaustive Compilation of the Book of Odes* states the following about the ode 'Changfa' in the volume 'Shangsong': 'The emperors of the Xia dynasty had not yet rejected the Law of Heaven up until the time of Prince [Cheng] Tang, who was born in a suitable time and was growing so well each day in the pursuit of perfection with the result that his virtue reached up to Heaven with immense splendour. He persisted in this pursuit with great constancy for a long time. The Lord of Heaven was the only object of his reverence without any interruption whatsoever. Therefore, the Lord of Heaven commanded him to act as the ruler and teacher of the people so as to arrange duly all the nine provinces, that is all of China, and to produce the perfect model of teaching'. Below is added: 'To reach up to Heaven with immense splendour means to bind the heart of Heaven to oneself, to unite it with oneself, and to become one with it'.[63]

H.7 《詩經說約集解・小雅・正月》:「瞻彼中林,大者維薪,小者維蒸,甚為分明。人之視物則有然矣。乃民今方危殆,痛訴於天,而視天夢夢然,善者未必福,惡者未必禍,若無意分別者,豈天之於人反如是乎?然此亦特其未定之時耳。及天道復其常然,而既克有定,雖淫惡橫肆之人,天欲禍既禍之,靡有弗勝之者。大哉上帝!伊於誰而云有所私憎之乎?淫與之禍,理之自然,而惜乎今未定也。」

Corresponding to quote 11 [c.2, q.2, §.6, O.13], the *Exhaustive Compilation of the Book of Odes* states the following about the ode 'Zhengyue' in the volume 'Xiaoya': 'See that trees in that forest are very clearly distinguished from thickets and other

---

62 These are not the words of Mencius, but an interpretation.
63 This comment expresses the strong conviction held by Song and Ming Confucianism of a union between Heaven and the human mind (*Tianren heyi* 天人合一). Noël accepts the possibility of this union which he understands not at the substantial but at functional level.

things. Indeed, people groan when exposed to all sorts of dangers and evils and bring their complaints to Heaven, but they see that Heaven distinguishes nothing as if It were asleep: real happiness does not bless the good, and real unhappiness does not punish the wicked just as if there were no mind to distinguish between the two. In fact, Heaven does not behave like this towards people, but it only happens like this because the appointed time has not yet come. Although Heaven's way or mode of action shall return to its ordinary course and the determined time shall come, perverse men can thrust upon themselves the license to sin without restraint. If Heaven wishes to afflict and punish them, It could immediately do so. There is no one whom It cannot overcome. How great is the Lord of Heaven! Who could say that Heaven hates someone? Right reason demands that the evil are punished, but the appointed time has not yet arrived'.

I.8 《詩經說約集解·小雅·小旻》：「彼幽遠之旻天, 本仁覆憫下者也, 乃疾怒之威, 敷布于下土, 使王之謀猶邪僻, 不知何日斯止乎?」

Corresponding to quote 12 [c.2, q.2, §.6, P.14], the *Exhaustive Compilation of the Book of Odes* states the following about the ode 'Xiaomin' in the volume 'Xiaoya': 'That hidden, remote, and mysterious Heaven, which is holy and merciful in Itself, protects and takes pity on the lowest things, now pours the rigour of Its tremendous anger down onto earth, and makes the emperor's plan perverse and ill-conceived. I do not know when this shall end'.

K.9 《日講四書解義·卷五·論語·雍也》：「若使我之所為不合於理, 不由其道, 是獲罪於天也。天必棄絕之, 天必棄絕之。」

Corresponding to quote 13 [c.2, q.2, §.6, Q.15], the *Daily Commentary on the Four Books* states the following about chapter 6 of the *Book of Sentences* [Lunyu 6.26]: 'Confucius says, "If what I have done does not agree with right reason and if I have not kept the right path, surely I would have sinned towards Heaven, and Heaven may reject me, and even must reject me"'. Zhang Juzheng has the same.[64]

L.10 《詩經說約集解·小雅·天保》：「吾君奉天為子, 天之仁愛吾君也, 保爾受命有常, 定爾而厥位無危。」[65]

The *Exhaustive Compilation of the Book of Odes* states the following about the ode 'Tianbao' in the volume 'Xiaoya': 'But since you, our Prince, are the obedient and compliant son of Heaven, Heaven loves you, Prince. Indeed, may Heaven preserve you and may you reign forever. May Heaven secure your throne so that it may never be endangered'.

---

64 This comment refers to *Lunyu* 6.26. Bouvet also cites this passage of the *Rijiang* in his *Gujin*, p. 199 (n. 34). In his *Renzui zhizhong*, Noël had in fact rejected the neo-Confucian interpretation based on *li*: '孔子曰：「予所否是」者, 天厭之天厭之[...] 此類語者, 若直以理之名自解, 其謬易見'. Cited in Zhu Qianzhi, *Zhongguo sixiang duiyu Ouzhou wenhua yingxiang*, p. 126. Clearly, Noël had changed his mind on the neo-Confucian *li*.

65 Starting from here, the eight remaining excerpts from the modern commentators are not directly linked to any passage mentioned by Noël in the first chapter.

M.11 蔡沈 《書經集傳・卷五・周書・召誥》：「禹亦面考天心, 敬順無違。」

About chapter 'Zhaogao', Cai Chen in volume 5 of the *Book of Imperial Annals* states the following: 'Prince Yu, etc.' See above.

N.12 《日講四書解義・卷一・孟子・離婁上》：「大雅文王之詩曰：『永言配命, 自求多福, 』言人能常作思維, 務合天理, 於是天心佑助。」

About Chapter 1 'Lilou' in the second part of the *Mencius*, volume 1 of the *Daily Commentary on the Four Books* states the following: 'This passage of the *Book of Odes* means: "If someone with constant, etc."'[66]

O.13 張居正《四書直解・卷五・論語・第七》：「若天無意于我, 必不生我以如是之德。既生我以如是之德, 則我之命, 天實主之, 必將佑我于冥冥之中矣。」蔡虛齋《四書蒙引・卷六・論語》：「天字以主宰言。」

About the chapter 7 of the *Book of Sentences* [*Lunyu* 7.22], the commentator Zhang Juzheng in volume 5 [of the *Sishu zhijie*] states the following: 'If Heaven, etc.' Cai Xuzhai in volume 6 of the *Sishu mengyin* states: 'Here the word Heaven should be understood as Lord and Ruler'.[67]

P.14 蔡虛齋《四書蒙引・卷一・大學》：「言天運亦自有意。」蔡虛齋《四書蒙引・卷一・大學》：「雖孔子亦曰『天之將喪斯文也』,『天之未喪斯文也』。孟子亦曰：『吾之不遇魯侯者, 天也』。」

Also, about the preface of the *Daxue*, Cai Xuzhai in volume 1 of the *Sishu mengyin* states the following: 'When it is said that Heaven constantly turns and changes, this means that Heaven has some intention and will'. A few words later is added: 'Confucius himself said in chapter 9[.2] of the *Book of Sentences*, "If Heaven had wished the knowledge of the ancient wise men, etc."' The same commentator continues: 'Mencius even said in chapter 2 of the first part of the *Mencius*: "I could not meet or speak with the petty king of Lu, nor could I get his favour; this came from Heaven"'.

Q.15 蔡虛齋《四書蒙引・論語上・第九》：「故知匡人之不能加害, 是則天之默相夫子於冥冥之中者, 非為夫子一身計, 為斯文計也。」

About the chapter 9[.5] of the *Book of Sentences*, the same Cai Xuzhai in his *Sishu mengyin* states the following: 'From this you can see that the inhabitants of the place Kuang cannot harm the life of Confucius. In a deep and mysterious darkness, Heaven silently helps him, not only because of him alone, but also because of the knowledge of the ancient wise men'.

---

66 Quoted in the *Gujin*, p. 211 (n. 40).
67 The *Confucius Sinarum philosophus* translated this comment of *Lunyu* 7.22 by Zhang Juzheng. See Meynard, *The Jesuit Reading of Confucius*, p. 260.

R. 蔡虛齋《四書蒙引・孟子・公孫丑下》：「『夫天，未欲平治天下也』，以此見天之一說自不可廢。故聖賢往往有屈於氣數者。」

> [Cai Xuzhai in *Sishu mengyin* states the following about the chapter 'Gong Sun Chou xia' of the *Mencius*]: 'Mencius says elsewhere: "Heaven still does not want peace and tranquility of the empire". From this you can therefore see that the explanation and interpretation of the word Heaven cannot be omitted nor rejected. Men famous for their wisdom and virtue have debased the meaning of this word and applied it to the succession of times'.[68]

S.16 張居正《四書直解・卷二十六・孟子・盡心下》：「然其間有得，有不得，亦有得之，而品節限制不能如意者，其權都是造物主張，不可以智力而取。」「性也而命，存乎間矣。」

> About chapter 8 'Jinxin xia' in the second part of the *Mencius*, Zhang Juzheng states the following in volume 26 [of the *Sishu zhijie*]: 'Some, etc.' See above. [The commentator] concludes as follows: 'This indeed is nature, but the law and providence of Heaven remains inside this'.

T.17 張居正《日講四書解義・卷二十六・孟子・盡心下》：「然有遂其欲者，有不得遂其欲者，實『有命焉』，以默為限制。君子惟安命而已矣。」「是以命衡性，而命為重矣。」

> About the same passage of chapter 8 in the second part of the *Mencius*, volume 26 of the *Daily Commentary on the Four Books* states as follows: 'Some can obtain what they desire, but others not. Surely, the law and providence of Heaven which secretly directs and regulates things is truly found there. The wise man tries only to submit to the Law of Heaven'. A little further down is added: 'Since the law or providence of Heaven directs and regulates nature, therefore it is highly esteemed'.[69]

§.5. Justice of *Tian* or *Shangdi* according to Modern Commentators

From what we have already discussed it is clear that the modern authors attribute justice to *Tian* (Heaven) and *Shangdi* (Lord of Heaven), but here are a few extra things. They say that Heaven's correct way of action, or the way of Heaven in blessing good people and punishing evil people, should be feared (A). In punishments and rewards, a fair ruler observes only what the heart of Heaven observes and sanctions (B). Heaven observes and investigates very clearly all things, and there is nothing obscure that It does not scrutinize. Therefore, do you not fear Heaven? (C). Confucius said, 'Heaven rewards good people with happiness, and evil people with infelicity' (D). I omit many [other] similar things. Let us now briefly discuss life.

---

68 Cai Qing stresses the importance of *Tian* and makes the connection with the Song cosmology based on numbers and on *qi*. However, Noël misreads this passage to indicate that Cai Qing criticized the Song cosmologists for having debased the real meaning of *Tian*. Here Noël shows himself still attached to a critical view on Song philosophy, which was accused by Ricci and his followers of having diluted the transcendental nature of *Tian*.

69 The translation of *ming wei zhong yi* 命為重矣 as 'made for several things' departs rather significantly from the original text.

NOTES

A.1 蔡沈《書經集傳·卷三·商書·湯誓》：「按《仲虺之誥》，其大意有三：先言天立君之意，桀逆天命，而天之命湯者不可辭；次言湯德足以得民，而民之歸湯者非一日；末言為君艱難之道，人心合離之機，天道福善禍淫之可畏。」

> Corresponding to quote 4 of paragraph 5 concerning justice in the preceding chapter [c.1, q.2, §.5, D.4], Cai Chen states the following about the chapter 'Zhonghui zhi gao' in volume 3 of the *Book of Imperial Annals*: 'This chapter principally contains three things. First, it refers to the intention of Heaven in appointing kings; since Emperor Jie had not obeyed the command of Heaven, Prince Tang could not exempt himself from obeying the command of Heaven. Second, the virtue of Prince Tang could subdue the hearts of the people, although the people did not immediately submit themselves to him. Finally, ruling the country correctly is a difficult art, and the occasion of alienating or reconciling people, as well as Heaven's correct way of action, or the way of Heaven, which blesses good people and afflicts evil people, should be feared'.

B.2 《日講四書解義·卷十二·論語·堯曰》：「湯既伐桀，而作誥以告諸侯，先述其初請命於帝，而伐桀之詞曰：『予小子履，敢用黑色之牡牲，敢昭告於皇天后土之神。今夏桀有罪，己必討之，而不敢赦。天下賢人皆上帝之臣，己必用之而不蔽。蓋其罪其賢皆簡閱在上帝之心；己安敢違之而自任其私意乎？予之初請命者如此。』」

> Concerning quote 5 [c.1, q.2, §.5, E.5] about chapter 20 of the *Book of Sentences* [*Lunyu* 20.1], volume 12 of the *Daily Commentary on the Four Books* states the following: 'After Prince Tang had defeated Emperor Jie, he gave a speech to the petty kings and nobles. He refers first to the words with which he had asked the Lord of Heaven for permission to attack Emperor Jie: "I am Lü, a little child, and I dare to use a little black calf for sacrificing to Him (this colour was in use under the Xia dynasty, whose last emperor was Jie) and to openly alert the spirit of the Great Heaven and of the Dense Earth that Emperor Jie has committed many crimes, and therefore he should be punished. I myself do not dare to forgive and turn a blind eye. All the wise people of the whole empire are your princes, Ruler of Heaven, and thus should be promoted to offices. I myself do not dare to allow them spend their life in obscurity without honour and office. Concerning [Jie's] crimes and the wisdom [of the wise people], I consider only a single thing, O Lord of Heaven: what your heart observes and sanctions. How would I dare to go against Heaven and claim this for myself according to my own mind? Indeed, I first asked for permission"'. Please see the explanation with clearer words in volume 12 of Zhang Juzheng's [*Sishu zhijie*].[70]

---

[70] Noël gave the translation of Zhang Juzheng's comment in c.1, q.2, §.5, F.

C.3 《詩經說約集解・小雅・何人斯》：「彼以人為可欺，飾其巧智，固不愧于人矣。然天之明察，無隱不彰也。汝獨不畏于天乎？而何以若此也？」

> Corresponding to quote 13 [c.1, q.2, §.5, O.13], the *Exhaustive Compilation of the Book of Odes* states the following about the ode 'Herensi' in the volume 'Xiaoya': 'Having thought that people could be deceived, he embellishes his shrewd skills and clever plans, being not at all ashamed in front of people. But Heaven observes and investigates very clearly all things, and there is nothing obscure which It does not scrutinize. Do you alone not fear Heaven? Why do you act in such a way?'

D.4 《明心寶鑒・第一》：「子曰：為善者，天報之以福；為不善者，天報之以禍。」

> Chapter 1 of the small common book called *Mingxin baojian* states as follows: 'Confucius said: "Good people, etc."'[71] See above.

§.6. Life of *Tian* or *Shangdi* according to Modern Commentators

Regarding the vital operations that modern commentators attribute to *Tian* and *Shangdi*, I say only a few things. As they say, the Lord of Heaven talked to Emperor Gaozong in dreams: 'I offer to you the best minister and servant' (A). Prince Wu Wang says: 'Without me realizing it, Heaven appointed me as the master of people and spirits (i.e., pontifex and king) and adopted me as son, or ordered me to be emperor' (B). The Lord of Heaven appointed the emperors Cheng Wang and Kang Wang, and he ordered them to follow the flourishing government of the predecessor Wu Wang; the Lord of Heaven controlled and directed their virtues (C). The Lord of Heaven kindly considered Prince Wen Wang (D). The Lord of Heaven says: 'I myself love and cherish the shining virtue or capacity of Prince Wen Wang, which is growing significantly without great noise or external appearance' (E). What Heaven sees and hears comes from the people. Since I judge the will and intention of Heaven in the souls of the people. I myself should go to punish Emperor Zhou (F).

All these operations (to say, to offer, to consider kindly, to cherish, to love, to appoint an emperor, to adopt as son, to see, to hear, to order, to intend) sufficiently indicate that there is a vital principle from which they proceed. Now let us discuss immensity and eternity.

---

71 For the *Mingxin baojian* see Chapter 2.15. The quote here is drawn from *Kongzi jiayu*, and it is mentioned above. See c.1, q.2, §.5, L.10.

CHAPTER 2   235

NOTES

A.1 《書經大全·説命》：「高宗夢傅說,據此,則是真有箇天帝與高宗對答,曰：『吾賚汝以良弼。』今人但以主宰說帝,謂無形象,恐也不得。若如世間所謂『玉皇大帝』,恐亦不可。[畢竟此理如何？學者皆莫能答。] 偁夢之事,只說到感應處。高宗夢帝賚良弼之事,必是夢中有帝賚之說之類。只是夢中事,說是帝真賚,不得；說無此事,只是天理,亦不得。」

> Corresponding to quote 1 of paragraph 6 about life in the previous chapter [c.1, q.2, §.6, A.1], volume 5 of the *Shujing daquan*, or *Great Commentary on the Book of Imperial Annals* states the following about the chapter 'Yueming': As Doctor Zhu Xi says, 'Emperor Gaozong had a dream that the minister Fu Yue was offered to him. Therefore, it was truly the Lord of Heaven (*Tiandi*) who said to Emperor Gaozong: "I myself offer to you the best minister and servant". Now the doctors explain very often the character *Di* with the words *zhu zai* (Lord and Ruler), and they interpret very often *Di* as Lord and Ruler. They say that *Di* does not have any appearance and cannot be perceived by the senses. I myself think that this is impossible. I also think that it cannot be that idol of the Daoist sect which the common people call *Yuhuang Dadi* (the Precious Ruler and Great Lord of Heaven). If the dream can only be explained through mutual motion [*ganying*], there was necessarily a Lord of Heaven, *Di*, who offered Fuyue to Gaozong when Emperor Gaozong dreamt about being offered the best minister and servant by the Lord of Heaven. It cannot be said that this did not take place or that it was only the principle of heaven, or *tianli*'.[72] Please note here how some people incorrectly call Doctor Zhu Xi the chief of the atheists, or atheist.[73]

B.2 《詩經說約集解·周頌·時邁》：「我周當商命交革之初,正人心望治之始。我也以時往,於諸侯之邦而巡之。不知昊天其以我為神人之主而子之乎！是固非偶然者矣。」

> Corresponding to quote 6 in paragraph 6 of the previous chapter [c.1, q.2, §.6, F.6], the *Exhaustive Compilation of the Book of Odes* states the following about the ode 'Shimai' in the volume 'Zhousong': Prince Wuwang says, 'Our Zhou dynasty started to disturb the power of the Yin dynasty through warfare. Then everybody's souls started to pant with ardent desire for a good and new government. I myself proceeded to visit the kingdoms of the petty kings at the appointed time. Without me realizing it, the very vast heaven appointed me as master of the spirits and human beings, and adopted me as son. This certainly did not happen by chance'.

---

72 This commentary from the *Shujing daquan* is not present in the ARSI manuscript, and we have therefore retrieved the passage of Zhu Xi directly from *Zhuzi yulei*, *juan* 79. Bouvet gives the same quote, but abbreviated. See Bouvet, *Gujin*, pp. 133–34. Quote mentioned in Noël's *Renzui zhizhong* with a complete rejection of *li*: '夫理也奚能賚弼?' See Zhu Qianzhi, *Zhongguo sixiang duiyu Ouzhou wenhua yingxiang*, p. 127.

73 Noël does not consider Zhu Xi as an atheist or atheo-politician. Concerning this passage of the *Shujing daquan*, see Chapter 2.11.

C.3 《詩經・周頌・執競》:「不顯成康,上帝是皇」; 《詩經說約集解・周頌・執競》:「豈不顯哉,成王、康王之德乎?著當時,昭來世,而大業不墜。上帝于是亦以之為君,而使之繼武王之盛焉。」;朱熹《集傳》:「成王康王之德,亦上帝之所君也。」

> Corresponding to quote 7 [c.1, q.2, §.6, G.7], the same [*Exhaustive*] *Compilation* [*of the Book of Odes*] states the following about ode 'Zhijing' in the volume 'Zhousong': 'Was not the virtue of the emperors Cheng Wang and Kang Wang shining very bright? Their virtue at that time was emitting rays and illuminating the centuries to come, not allowing the great undertakings of their predecessors to fall in vain. Thus, the Lord and Ruler of Heaven appointed them as emperors and ordered them to follow the prosperous reign of the emperor Wu Wang'. Zhu Xi says: 'It was indeed the Lord of Heaven who ruled and controlled their virtues'.[74]

D.4 《詩經・大雅・皇矣》:「帝謂文王:予懷明德,不大聲以色,不長夏以革。」朱熹《集傳》:「言上帝眷念文王,而言其德之深微不暴著其形迹。」

> Corresponding to quote 8 [c.1, q.2, §.6, H.8], Zhu Xi says the following about the ode 'Huangyi' in the chapter 'Daya' of the *Book of Odes*: 'The Lord of Heaven kindly and favourably considered the prince Wen Wang'. Zhu Xi also says: 'His virtue was essentially internal, deep and hidden so that it could not be shown externally with any visible appearance'.

E.5 《日講四書解義・卷三・中庸・第三十三》:「上帝自言,予眷懷文王之明德,不張大其聲音與顏色,似可形容不顯之德矣。」

> Corresponding to the same quote [c.1, q.2, §.6, H.8], volume 3 of the *Daily Commentary on the Four Books* states the following about *Zhongyong* 33: 'The Lord of Heaven Himself thus says, "I myself love and cherish, etc."'[75] See above.

F.6 蔡沈《書經集傳・卷四・商書・泰誓中》:「武王言,天之視聽皆自乎民。今民皆有責於我。」

> Concerning quote 10 [c.1, q.2, §.6, K.10], Cai Chen states the following in volume 4 of the *Book of Imperial Annals* about the chapter 'Taishi': 'Wuwang says, "What Heaven sees and hears comes from the people, etc."' See above.

---

74 Noël brings here a quote of Zhu Xi from his *Shijing jizhuan* 詩經集傳, which suggests that Zhu Xi was not an atheist, but had recognized the power of God.

75 In fact, the quote was taken directly from the *Shijing*, while the comment here refers to *Zhongyong* 33 which quotes the same passage of the *Shijing*.

§.7. Immensity and Eternity of *Tian* or *Shangdi* according to Modern Commentators

Let us see whether those writers hint at the immensity and eternity of God. Indeed, they say the following things about *Tian* or *Shangdi*. There is nothing that the intelligence and vision of Heaven does not reach, and hence [Heaven's intelligence] should indeed be honoured. As Doctor Zhang [Zai] says, just as the soul's piety or rectitude penetrates actions so deeply that it is always found in them, so Heaven penetrates things so closely that they cannot be separated from [Heaven] (A).[76] Heaven and Reason are the same; Reason extends itself to all things and exists everywhere, and thus Heaven extends to all things and can see everywhere (B). The immense Lord of Heaven is the king of people living in this lowest sphere (C). He who controls and rules in the midst of all things, Heaven, Earth, days, and nights, could be here or there, or could be and not be at the same time, since no one can conceive or comprehend His place. Could His incomprehensibility be the same as the highest spirituality of the Law of Heaven, or could He be the same as the incomprehensible spirit?' (D). Reason is what controls stillness (*yin*) and motion (*yang*), or the production of things; this Reason is a Spirit, because it exists here and does not exist here, and therefore it is said to be an incomprehensible Spirit. When stillness (*yin*) changes into motion (*yang*), Reason exists in motion (*yang*); when motion (*yang*) changes into stillness (*yin*), Reason exists in stillness (*yin*). Since Reason exists in both, it is said to exist here and not to exist here. Moreover, since it exists here and does not exist here, it is said to be incomprehensible. Since it is imcomprehensible, it is a Spirit (E). Obviously, this means that the Spirit is found in all actions and cessations or conservations, in all vicissitudes and changes. Indeed, the Spirit does not exist in any place and does not have a fixed place (F). Next, Reason is called Spirit because it is Lord and Ruler, or because it controls and rules all things (G). The Law of Heaven is constantly revolving and acting without stopping at any place; therefore, the wise man keeps reverence at all times (H).

If someone pays attention to how God sees, penetrates, and rules all things everywhere, how all things are in God, and encompassed by God, how God resides in things, not as a part but as agent and cause, or Reason, how He is in one place as well as beyond that place, how He acts in an unchangeable way, then all the things said here could apply to His incomprehensible immensity and eternity.[77]

---

[76] Concerning the relation between *ti* and *wu* as expressed in *Zhongyong* 16 (體物而不可遺), Noël understands it as a metaphysical relationship. In contrast, Longobardo understands it as a physical relationship: 'All the spirits constitute the being and substance of things, and cannot be divided or separated from things, otherwise things would be immediately destroyed'. Longobardo, *A Brief Response on the Controversies*, pp. 142–43 (prelude 11, n. 7).

[77] Noël adopts here the metaphysics of Zhang Zai and identifies it with the Christian metaphysics postulating the existence of a transcendental God who is present in the world and all things, yet distinct from the world. Noël draws certainly from the metaphysics of Saint Aquinas, but also of mystics like Saint Ignatius of Loyola.

NOTES

A.1 朱熹《詩經集傳・大雅・板》：「天之聰明，無所不及，不可以不敬也。張子曰：『天體物而不遺，猶仁體事而無不在也。』」

Corresponding to quote 2 of paragraph 7 on immensity and eternity in the previous chapter [c.2, q.2, §.7, B.2], Zhu Xi writes the following about the ode 'Ban' in the volume 'Daya' of the *Book of Odes*: 'There is nothing, etc.'[78] See above.

B.2 《詩經說約集解・大雅・板》：「天者，理也；理無往而不在，故天無往而不鑒；敬天，此一詩之要旨也。」

Corresponding to the same quote, the *Exhaustive Compilation of the Book of Odes* states the following: 'Heaven, etc.' See above.

C.3 《詩經說約集解・大雅・蕩》：「曰：天下之大亂必有所由致者。彼蕩蕩然廣大之上帝，乃下民之君，而主之以善者也。」

Corresponding to quote 4 [c.2, §.7, D.4], the *Exhaustive Compilation of the Book of Odes* states the following about the ode 'Dang' in the volume 'Daya': 'The great disorders and commotion of the empire necessarily arise from some cause. The immense and very vast Lord of Heaven is in reality the king of people living in the lowest sphere, and He controls them through true goodness'.

D.4 《周易正解・卷十七・傳上・第四》：「主宰于天地萬物晝夜之中，或在此，或在彼，無在而無不在，莫得而測其方所焉，不與命之至神者，同其不測乎？」

Corresponding to quote 5, volume 17 of the *True Explanation of the Book of Changes and Productions* states the following about chapter 4 of the 'Zhuan shang': 'The one controlling in the midst, etc.' See above.

E.5 《周易正解・卷十七・傳上・第四》：「天地之化、萬物之生、晝夜之循環，不外一陰陽而已。陰變陽，陽變陰，是之謂易。陰陽，氣也。所以主宰是氣者，理也。陰陽之變易皆是理主宰之。故夫子于下章指，陰陽之迭運者，而謂之道；神只是這箇道。因其無在、無不在，故謂之神。張子曰：『兩在，故不測。』蓋當其陰變為陽也，而此理則在陽。當其陽變為陰也，而此理則在陰。陰陽只管變易，而理皆無不在焉，是謂『兩在』也。『兩在，故不測』，『不測』即神也。」

Corresponding to the same passage, the [*True*] *Explanation* [*of the Book of Changes and Productions*] states the following: 'The constant activity of Heaven and Earth, the productions of all things, and the course of days and nights do not go beyond the limits of stillness (*yin*) and motion (*yang*). Stillness (*yin*) is changed into motion (*yang*), and motion (*yang*) in its turn is changed or transitions into stillness (*yin*), that is, into a state of conservation. Thus, stillness (*yin*) and movement (*yang*) are both air, or something which can be perceived by the senses, or the activity and passivity of the vital principle. Reason is what controls and rules the air, since indeed Reason controls and rules the alternating productions and changes of stillness (*yin*) and motion (*yang*). In the following chapter, Confucius

---

78 Quoted in Bouvet, *Gujin*, p. 155 (n. 14), but without Zhang Zai's words.

shows that this alternating production and change of stillness (*yin*) and motion (*yang*) is Reason, and this Reason, which exists here and does not exist here, is truly a Spirit. Zhang [Zai] says: "It cannot be comprehended because it exists here and does not exist here".[79] When stillness (*yin*) changes or transforms into motion (*yang*), Reason exists in motion (*yang*); and when motion (*yang*) transforms into stillness (*yin*), Reason exists in stillness (*yin*). Stillness (*yin*) and motion (*yang*) only revolve around productions and changes while Reason exists in both and exists nowhere. Thus, it is said to exist here and not to exist here, or to exist in two different places. Since it cannot be comprehended, it is a Spirit'.

F. [《周易正解・卷十七・傳上・第四》]:「曰『神无方』,言神之無所不在,無有一定方所也。曰『《易》无體』,言陰陽只管變易,無箇一定形體也。」「天地之化、萬物之生、晝夜之循環,皆有箇神易。《易》則模寫乎此理者也。故在《易》亦有神易。」「此无方體,亦是言聖人之神易,與天命之神易合一,而見其能至命也。」

[the *True Explanation of the Book of Changes and Productions*]: 'Hence in the *Book of Changes and Productions* it is said, "The Spirit lacks any fixed place", that is, it does not exist in any place nor does it have any fixed place. Thus, "the teaching of the *Book of Changes and Productions* has no fixed object" means that stillness (*yin*) and motion (*yang*) which revolve around changes and productions do not have any determinate matter which can be perceived by the senses'. Shortly after is added: 'The constant action of Heaven and Earth, the productions of all things, the course of days and nights, all these things contain in themselves the changing and producing Spirit. Change and production are shaped by Reason. Therefore, the changing and producing Spirit resides in the teaching of the *Book of Changes and Productions*'.[80]

G. [《周易正解・卷十七・傳上・第四》]:「神易,一也。自其主宰而言謂之神,自其運用而言謂之易。神易二字已盡了。」

Still further below [the *True Explanation of the Book of Changes and Productions*]: 'The changing and producing Spirit is unique. As Lord and Ruler, it controls and guides, and it is called Spirit. As constantly revolving and moving, it revolves and moves, and it is called changing and producing. This is adequately expressed by the words "changing and producing Spirit"'.

---

79 Zhang Zai's words are found in his *Hengqu Yi shuo* 橫渠易說 [Explanation of the *Yijing* by Master Hengqu]. Zhu Xi praised the words of Zhang Zai as very insightful. See *Zhuzi yulei, juan* 98.

80 For Zhang Zai, the impossibility of a determinate place or object (*fang* 方 or *ti* 定體) for the spirit and the mutations (*shenyin* 神易) means that the spiritual (*shen* 神) is one and undifferentiated. In the *Yijing mengyin*, Cai Qing quotes and develops similar ideas. See Song Yecao 宋野草, *Cai Qing Yixue sixiang yanjiu* 蔡清易學思想研究 (Beijing: Zhongguo shehui kexue chubanshe, 2015), p. 13.

H.6 《日講四書解義・卷十・論語・季氏》：「孔子曰：『君子有三畏：畏天命, 畏大人, 畏聖人之言。』君子之三畏, 具切於脩身行己如此者, 皆由識得天命流行, 無在不有。故小心敬慎, 無時不然耳。」

> Corresponding to chapter 16 of the Book of Sentences [Lunyu 16.8] ('There are three things that the wise man fears: the Law of Heaven, the illustrious men, the words of the wise'), volume 10 of the Daily Commentary on the Four Books states: 'The three fears of the wise man concern most of all moral behaviour, the guarding and vigilance of oneself and they come from the fact that the wise man knows well that the Law of Heaven, which turns and acts with constant course, does not exist in any place. Thus, he maintains reverence and caution at all times with great diligence'.

§.8. Simplicity of *Tian* or *Shangdi* according to the Modern Commentators

We have already said many things about the Spirit or Simplicity of Heaven and still more things will be discussed further below, but here I cite only a few things. Some authors say that Wen Wang and Wu Wang could truly become the spiritual Master of Heaven (obviously like pontifex), or as mentioned above, could be appointed by spiritual Heaven as Master (A). The Spirit is something excellent and incomprehensible. The four seasons of the year do not stray and are controlled by the Spirit of the way of Heaven, or by the Spirit of Heaven's way of action, and nothing more spiritual can exist or be conceived than the way of Heaven (B). The Spirit of Heaven cannot be observed and seen, but Its spiritual way of action can be seen in the four seasons of the year which are constantly revolving without error (C). Surely, Heaven is that supreme excellence which is called Spirit; as the creator of operations it is called the Author that produces and destroys (D).[81] Finally, Heaven is not like something corporeal like the earth and cannot be perceived by the senses (E). The Lord of Heaven does not use any external sound or perceptible voice in directing people towards peace (F). That woman with her splendid ornament seems to refer to Spirit of Heaven, or the Ruler of Heaven (G).

From this you see that spirituality as well as simplicity can be attributed to Heaven, that Heaven itself is called Spirit, and they explain it everywhere either as an incomprehensible excellence, or as the Creator and Author of things.[82]

Also, Saint Thomas in [his commentary on] the first chapter of the Letter to the Romans explains God by way of excellence, negation, and causality, saying that the invisible things of God constitute the invisible divine essence which is known by way of negation; the virtue of God constitutes the divine power which is known by way of causality; the divinity is the ultimate end and the supreme good to which all things tend, and is known by way of excellence.[83]

---

81 Noël's translation of *guishen* as producing and destroying spirit appears more than eighty times in the First Treatise. For further explanations, see Chapter 3.4–3.5.
82 Simplicity should be understood in a scholastic way. Something is simple because it is not mixed with another element, here matter. Thus, simplicity means being spiritual, that is, unmixed with matter.
83 Aquinas, *Commentary on Romans*, n. 115, trans. by Fr. Fabian R. Larcher, OP: 'But man is capable of knowing God from such creatures in three ways, as Denis says in *The Divine Names*. He knows him, first

In relation to the words 'Consider Heaven's spiritual way of action', take note of what the Chinese commentator [Cai Qing] says: 'Those words are said in an empty way'. This does not mean that the words are false and hollow, but they are said in a spiritual way through the intellect, either in abstraction or about something which cannot be perceived. A spiritual way cannot be observed, inasmuch as it cannot be perceived and is invisible, but is an abstraction perceived through the intellect (H).

At a later point, he explains another text as follows: 'The word *shen* when taken to mean "to make spiritual" or "to spiritualize" (*spiritualizare*) is said in an empty way (obviously abstractly and intentionally or spiritually), but when taken to mean "to help the Spirit" it is said in physical and in real terms' (I). 'To make spiritual' means here that the Reason which spiritualizes its operation or makes it spiritual is found in the teaching of the *Book of Changes and Productions* (K).[84] Next, the word *yi*, that is the teaching of the *Book of Changes and Productions*, is said in an empty way, or in abstract terms, like a separation from perceptible matter (L). On the contrary, for Zhu Xi, this teaching comes from a suspended emptiness because before the formation of the enigmatic symbols [*gua* 卦] and their numerical lines or constitutive parts [*yao* 爻] pre-existed a single and pure Reason in terms of this teaching and a single and tranquil soul or mind existing in terms of man (M).

You see from this that the object of the teaching is the one pure Reason, namely Real Being (elsewhere they say that the word Reason should be understood as something true and real, and not false), and abstracted from perceptible and extended matter, and this is what philosophers call generally the object of metaphysics.[85] It is abstract for philosophers, either in reality, like God and the Angels, or in reason like the predicates of Being and substance. Therefore, 'empty way' should neither be taken as fictitious and chimerical, nor as a Being of reason reasoning without a foundation in reality,[86] but it should be taken either as abstract reality,

---

of all, through causality. For since these creatures are subject to change and decay, it is necessary to trace them back to some unchangeable and unfailing principle. In this way, it can be known that God exists. Second, he can be known by the way of excellence. For all things are not traced back to the First Principle as to a proper and univocal cause, as when man produces man, but to a common and exceeding cause. From this it is known that God is above all things. Third, he can be known by the way of negation. For if God is a cause exceeding his effects, nothing in creatures can belong to him, just as a heavenly body is not properly called heavy or light or hot or cold. And in this way, we say that God is unchangeable and infinite; and we use other negative expressions to describe him'. <https://aquinas.cc/la/en/~Rom> (accessed 1 October 2020). It seems that Noël cites this passage of Aquinas through Cornelius à Lapide, *Commentaria in Epistulam ad Romanos* (Lyon, 1664), p. 35.

84 The term *spiritualizare* is used in late Scholasticism, for example: Thomas Albert Tranquillus, OP, 'De generatione et anima', *Theses ex Universa Philosophia* (Prague, 1682), p. 17: 'The agent intellect spiritualizes and illuminates the phantasma'. It is used also by Jean Gabriel Boyvin, OFM (died 1680) in *Theologia Scoti* (Paris, 1677), p. 358: 'To spiritualize the species which are perceived'. It was also used by John Ponce. See Leen Spruit, *Species intelligibilis*, 2 vols (Leiden: Brill, 1995), II, pp. 341–45.

85 Noël reads neo-Confucian metaphysics through the prism of Aristotelian and scholastic metaphysics, in which the object of metaphysics or the spiritual is defined as being remote from matter.

86 'Being of reason' is a medieval concept which was later developed by Francisco Suárez (1548–1617) who argued that such being really exists in our mind though it has no reality in the concrete world. See Daniel Novotný, 'Suárez on Beings of Reason', *Conimbricenses.org Encyclopedia*, Mário Santiago de Carvalho,

or abstractly reasoned reason[87] with a foundation in reality, as I have said, but this is enough for now.[88]

NOTES

A.1 蔡沈《書經集傳・卷五・周書・多方》：「文武善承其眾, 克堪用德, 是誠可以為神天之主矣。」

> Corresponding to quote 5 of paragraph 8 on simplicity in the previous chapter [c.1, q.2, §.8, E.5], Cai Chen in volume 5 [of the *Shujing jizhuan*] writes the following about the chapter 'Duofang' in the *Book of Imperial Annals*: 'Since the Wen Wang and Wu Wang knew very well how to reconcile and gather the souls of all, and to fulfill every part of virtue, they could thus truly become the masters or or pontifices of the spiritual Heaven'.

B.2 《周易正解・卷六・觀卦》：「神者, 妙不可測之謂；『四時不忒』, 即是天道之神。」「極而言之, 觀之于天, 氣化流行於穆不已, 其道何神也!」「至若聖人之所以為觀, 則誠在此, 動于彼, 不假形聲, 不著事迹。其設教之道何神也, 而不顯篤恭之妙!直與帝載之無聲臭者同, 亦非人所得而測。」

> Concerning quote 6 [c.1, q.2, §.8, F.6], volume 6 of the *True Explanation of the Book of Changes and Productions* states the following about the symbol 'Guan': 'The character Spirit means an excellence which cannot be well conceived or expressed. The phrase "the four seasons of the year revolve without error" means that the Spirit of the way of Heaven, or of Heaven's mode of action'. Shortly after is written: 'For a thorough explanation, consider that the vital breath in Heaven acts always secretly and without interruption. What mode of action could be even more spiritual?' A few words later: 'A man with perfect knowledge and virtue can indeed be observed. Since he is dedicated to the pursuit of truth, he stirs up the courage

---

Simone Guidi (eds) <www.conimbricenses.org/encyclopedia/suarez-on-beings-of-reason/> (accessed on 1/16/2021).

87 See Sven K. Knebel, 'Entre logique mentaliste et métaphysique conceptualiste: la distinctio rationis ratiocinantis', *Les Études philosophiques*, 61.2 (2002), 145–68.

88 There is a paragraph in the ARSI manuscript (fol. 45ʳ–45ᵛ) which was removed in the published text: 'From all the things which we have said in this section made of 8 paragraphs, you can notice how the more recent Chinese seem to attribute the same perfections to Heaven or the Lord of Heaven that the Europeans attribute to the true God, and therefore it is correct to assume that they express the true God with the words of *Tian* and *Shangdi*. If you object that they more frequently express it as Reason, law, air or vital breath, time or course of time, First Emptiness, and perceptible body, and that they confuse the Lord of Heaven with Heaven, so that the meaning of their words seem to disagree with the true meaning of the supreme divinity, then we shall answer all these things in the following sections' (*Jam vero ex iis, quae tota hac sectione per octo paragraphos deducta diximus, potes conspicere quommodo Recentiores Siniae videantur etiam easdem Caelo, Coelive Domino, quasi Europaei vero Deo, attribuere perfectiones, adeoque jure possit prosumi per ipsas voices Coelum, Coeli Dominus ac Rector, ab iis verum Deum utcumque exprimi. Si autem opponas quod istam vocem Coelum saepius explicent per vocem Ratio, per vocem Lex, per vocem aer seu vitalis aura, per vocem tempus seu temporis revolutio, per vocem primum vacuum, per vocem corpus sensibile, et similes; coelique Dominum confundant cum Coelo, atque adeo videatur harum vocum significatio discrepare a vera Suprimi Numinis significatione, nunc ad haec omnia in sequentibus sectionibus respondebimus. Itaque*).

of the people and acts without using his voice or body and without leaving any trace of his operations. What mode of promoting the teaching could be even more spiritual? Certainly, man is unable to comprehend or express the unique excellence of that inner virtue that is scarcely visible from the outside and resembles the the Lord of Heaven's reality or operation, which lacks sound, odour and anything perceptible by the senses'.

C.   [《周易正解·卷六·觀卦》]：「『觀天之神道』，此數字虛說。『四時不忒』，正是天之神道處。須看一『觀』字：天之神, 安可得而觀？於四時之不忒觀之，可以見天之神道矣。」

A little further down [in the *True Explanation of the Book of Changes and Productions*]: 'The words "Observe Heaven's spiritual mode of action" are in fact empty, and the words "The four seasons revolve without error" are indeed that in which the mode of action of Heaven consists. The word "Observe" should be considered. For how could the Spirit of Heaven be seen? Heaven's spiritual way or Its mode of action can only be observed in the four seasons revolving without error'.[89]

D.3   《性理標題·卷三·天文》：「[或問：『天帝之異？』] 程子曰：『以形體謂之天, 以主宰謂之帝, 以至妙謂之神, 以功用謂之鬼神, 以性情謂之乾；其實一而已, 所自而名之者異也。』」

In the chapter 'Tianwen' in volume 3 of the *Summary of the Book of Nature and Reason* (in Chinese *Xingli biaoti*), the author Cheng asks about the difference between *Tian* (Heaven) and *Shangdi* (Lord of Heaven),[90] and says as follows: 'From the point of view of perceptible matter, it is called Heaven; from the point of view of its mastery and rule, it is called *Di*, the Lord and Ruler or Emperor of Heaven; from the point of view of its excellence, it is called *shen* or Spirit; from the point of view of operations and effects, it is called *guishen*, the producing and destroying Spirit, or an invisible Author;[91] from the point of view of nature and efficiency, it is called *qian*, Power or active Force; *Tian* and *Shangdi* are the same thing in reality, but the things out of which their names are taken are different'.[92]

---

89   This quote from the *Zhouyi zhengjie* comes in fact from Cai Qing in his *Yijing mengyin*: '「觀天之神道」，此數字虛說，下言「四時不忒」，正是天之神道處。故曰：天之所以為觀也，須看觀之一字。天之神, 安可得而觀？於四時之不忒焉觀之，可以見天之神道矣'. In several occurrences, we can detect the influence of Cai Qing on the *Zhouyi zhengjie*, sometimes even explicit through the use of quotes. Cai Qing's concept of *xu* 虛 or emptiness should not be understood in the Buddhist sense of something lacking reality because its existence is conditional, but in the sense of something lacking any positive characterization beside what exists.
90   The Chinese text has instead: 'someone asked, and Cheng answered'.
91   Noël adds here the meaning of invisible Author since he understands the *guishen* as an invisible Author between *Tian* and the concrete world.
92   For the *Xingli biaoti*, see Chapter 2.13. Ricci mentioned this quote of Master Cheng 程子 and criticized the identification of a material heaven with *Di* as transcendental being. See Ricci, *The True Meaning of the Lord of Heaven*, pp. 101–02 (nn. 109–10). Longobardo also mentioned this Chinese quote of Master Cheng, drawn from *juan* 26 of the *Xingli daquan*, which he summarized as: '*Shangdi* (spirit of heaven) is the same thing as heaven, and by extension, or at least by analogy, the same ought to be said about the spirits of other things'. Longobardo concludes that 'all spirits adored by the Chinese are the same

E. 《性理標題・卷三》：「致堂胡氏曰：夫天，非若地之有形也。」

Hu Zhitang says a little further down [in the *Summary of the Book of Nature and Reason*]: 'This Heaven is unlike earth because it is not something corporeal and cannot be perceived by the senses'.[93]

F.4 蔡沈《書經集傳・卷五・周書・多士》：「呂氏曰：『上帝引逸者，非有形聲音之接也。人心得其安，則亹亹而不能已，斯則上帝引之也。』是理坦然，亦何閒于桀，第桀喪其良心，自不適於安耳。帝實引之，桀實避之，帝猶未遽絕也，乃降格災異以示意嚮於桀，桀猶不知警懼，不能敬用帝命，乃大肆淫逸，雖有矯誣之辭，而天罔念聞之。」

The commentator Cai Chen writes the following in volume 5 of the [*Shujing jizhuan*] about the chapter 'Duoshi' in the *Book of Imperial Annals*: 'According to the writer Lü: "The Lord of Heaven does not use anything external or any perceptible voice when guiding people to peace. When a man's soul pursues peace, it does not know where to rest and always aspires to greater perfection. It is clear that the Lord of Heaven guides it". Emperor Jie overturned the guidance of right reason and thus could not pursue peace. The Lord of Heaven guided him but Jie refused. However, the Lord of Heaven did not abandon him and sent him several evils and disasters to show His intention and goodwill. But Jie did not understand that he should fear, revere and obey the Lord of Heaven's order. He indulged himself in all kinds of pleasures without any restraint. Even though he decorated his crimes with nice words, Heaven did not look at him and or hear him'.[94]

G.5 《詩經說約集解・鄘風・君子偕老》：「胡然而有此天之神也，胡然而有此帝之神也。」

The *Exhaustive Compilation of the Book of Odes* states the following about the ode 'Junzi xielao' in the volume 'Yongfeng': 'Why is there the Spirit of Heaven? Why, I say, is there the Spirit of the Lord of Heaven?'

H.6 See above C.2.

---

substance as the things in which they subsist and exist'. For Longobardo this is proof that Chinese monism does not allow for true transcendence. See Longobardo, *A Brief Response on the Controversies*, pp. 142–43 (prelude 11, n. 7). Yan Mo had also difficulties with this passage which he omitted on purpose. See Nicolas Standaert [Zhong Mingdan], *Keqin de Tianzhu*, p. 67. However, *Tianjiao he Ru*, p. 15 (n. 1) quotes Master Cheng and comments: 'By *Tian*, the classical texts refer to *Shangdi*, and [Chengzi] does not dare to use directly the character *Di*. This is because when *Tian* is mentioned it is like a minister who speaks about the emperor to refer to the court' (經書之言天，即指上帝也。不敢斥言帝，故言天，猶臣子稱皇帝朝廷). For the argument of metaphoric language, see below the quote from the *Duoshu* by Han Lin (c.3, q.1, M.12). Like Bouvet and Zhang Xingyao, Noël has no difficulties with this statement of Master Cheng, repeated in an abbreviated form twice below (c.2, q.2, B.5 and B.7).

93 Hu Yin 胡寅 (1098–1156), *hao* Zhitang 致堂.
94 Cai Chen's expression 'to send several evils and disasters' (*jiangge zaiyi* 降格災異) has a strong religious meaning in the sense of *Tian* as divine judge.

I.7 《易經‧繫辭傳上‧第九》：「顯道神德行,是故可與酬酢,可與祐神矣。」《周易正解‧卷十八》：「二神字不同,上是虛字,下是實字。」

Chapter 9 of 'Zhuan shang' states: 'By revealing itself, the correct way of action spiritualizes or makes spiritual the work of virtue. In this way, it can respond to the Spirit and help It or co-operate with It'. Volume 18 of the *True Explanation of the Book of Changes and Productions* comments as follows: 'The character *shen* (to spiritualize, or to make spiritual) is understood in two ways: first in an empty way, and second in a real way'.

K. 蔡虛齋《易經蒙引》：「神是《易》中有理以神之。」

A little further down [in the *True Explanation of the Book of Changes and Productions*], Cai Xuzhai states: 'To make spiritual means that the Reason which spiritualizes or makes spiritual is contained in the teaching of the *Book of Changes and Productions*'.

L.8 《易經‧繫辭傳下‧第三》：「是故易者,象也。象也者,像也。」《周易正解‧卷二十》：「蔡虛齋曰：易字虛說。」

Chapter 3 of 'Zhuan xia' in the *Book of Changes and Productions* states as follows: '*Yi*, or the *Book of Changes and Productions*, is the figure of things, that is, symbolic; however, the figure is the representation or image of things'. Commenting on this passage, volume 20 of the *True Explanation of the Book of Changes and Productions* cites Cai Xuzhai: 'The character *Yi*, or the *Book of Changes and Productions*, is said in an empty way'.

M.9 《周易正解‧易說綱領》：「朱子曰：《易》之爲書,是懸空做出來；如《書》便眞個有這政事謀謨,方做出《書》來；《詩》便眞個有這人情風俗,方做出《詩》來。《易》却都无這已往的事,只是懸空做的。未有爻書⁹⁵之先,在《易》則渾然一理,在人則湛然一心。」

The preliminary volume of the *True Explanation of the Book of Changes and Productions* cites Zhu Xi as follows: 'The teaching of the *Book of Changes and Productions* arose out of suspended emptiness. The teaching of the *Book of Imperial Annals* arose out of the preexisting norm of a good government; the teaching of the *Book of Odes* came from people's preexisting affections and mores; but nothing similar existed before the teaching of the *Book of Changes and Productions*, insofar as it arose out a suspended emptiness (obviously a Being abstracted from matter).⁹⁶ Before the shaping of the enigmatic symbols and their numerical lines pre-existed a unique and pure Reason in terms of this teaching and a unique and tranquil soul in terms of man'.⁹⁷

---

95 Mistake in the ARSI manuscript for 畫.
96 Cf. *Zhuzi yulei, juan* 67. Here *xuankong* 懸空 means literally to be suspended in the air. Zhu Xi stresses here the historical background of the composition of the *Yijing* which did not rely on presupposed magical practices of divination. From the standpoint of the metaphysical thought of Zhu Xi, *xuankong* could be interpreted as a logical priority of the abstract figures of the *Yijing* before any manifestation with concrete forms, but this is not necessarily identical to an abstraction from matter, as Noël says here.
97 This sentence in *Zhuzi yulei* is in fact attributed to Zhu Xi's disciple Shen Xian 沈僴.

§.9. Whether the Modern Commentators are Moving Away from the Original Meaning of *Tian* or *Shangdi* in the Ancient Classics?

We have seen in the first chapter that the original books and classics attribute to Heaven and Lord of Heaven the perfections that we attribute to the true God, and we concluded that *Tian* and *Shangdi* meant God for the ancient Chinese. We have now been investigating in the eight paragraphs above whether the modern commentators had corrupted the meaning of the ancients, and for sake of brevity, I summarize below what those paragraphs say about each attribute.[98]

1. As for dominion, they say that *Tian* or *Shangdi* appoints kings and doctors as their vicars and assistants to rule and educate the people; He sends good things to those who follow correct reason, but evil things to those who transgress; He produces the human body and infuses in the body an intelligent nature; He makes sacrifices to be offered to Him as the Lord and Ruler of Heaven, and also as Intelligent Spirit; and He makes the Chinese emperors and the people serve Him.

2. As for power, they say that His virtue is the first root and beginning of all things; it is something internal and free; acting amid a mysterious darkness, it gives beginning, increase, direction, and the perfection of its being to everything; it cannot be comprehended by thought or expressed by figure; it directs all things; it produces and perfects all things of the world; it cannot be seen except in its effects; it helps those who obey it; it wards off dangers; make the people firm and unites them so they can live together.

3. As for knowledge, they say that He is very clever and intelligent, and observes all the kingdoms of China and everyday looks at what we are doing; He knows people in His mysterious darkness; and people cannot deceive Him.

4. As for will, they say that it is difficult to know the will of Heaven; Heaven shows Its intention in a silent way; people cannot prevent the will of Heaven from achieving its end; the ruler by his virtue subdues the heart of Heaven and Heaven commands him to pacify the kingdoms; Heaven does not hate anyone; It is faithful and merciful; It loves people; It wishes peace for the empire; in [Heaven], there is will, law, providence and judgement.

---

98 In the ARSI manuscript (fol. 45ʳ), there is only a short conclusion here: 'From all the things which we have said in this section made of eight paragraphs, you can notice how the more recent Chinese seem to attribute the same perfections to Heaven or the Lord of Heaven as the Europeans attribute to the true God, and therefore it is correct to assume that they express with *Tian* and *Shangdi* the true God'. (*Jam vero ex iis, quae tota hac sectione per octo paragrafos deducta diximus, potes conspicere quommodo Recentiores Siniae videantur etiam easdem Caelo, Coelive Domino, quasi Europaei vero Deo, attribuere perfectiones, adeoque jure possit prosumi per ipsas voices Coelum, Coeli Dominus ac Rector, ab iis verum Deum utcumque exprimi*).

5. As for justice, they say that He examines and observes all things with utmost clarity, rewarding good people with happiness and punishing evil people with unhappiness; when meting punishments and rewards, the just ruler considers only what the heart of Heaven considers and sanctions.

6. As for life, they say that *Shangdi* had talked to an emperor in dreams, and indeed the one whom He spoke about did exist; He appoints emperors; He fosters, esteems, and guides their virtues.

7. As for immensity and eternity, they say that He reaches all things and exists everywhere, sees everything, and nothing happens that His intelligence and cleverness does not influence; He penetrates all things closely; no one can know His place; He is the immense king of human beings; the Law of Heaven always act and unfolds constantly.

8. As for simplicity or spirituality, they say that *Shangdi* is the Spirit of Heaven who cannot be seen except in His operations and spiritual way of action; the Spirit is an incomprehensible excellence by which the four seasons are controlled; Heaven is not anything corporeal or perceptible like Earth.[99]

Let us now return to our purpose. All those manners of speech clearly do not differ from the original opinion of the ancient books that we mentioned in the first chapter, and in fact explain more explicitly, efficiently, and clearly what the ancients had said in a general way.[100] All the perfections that the ancients attributed to *Tian* (Heaven) or *Shangdi* (Lord of Heaven) were also attributed to Him by the moderns. Therefore, as we have considered that the ancients in their books meant God with the words *Tian* or *Shangdi*, similarly we conclude that the moderns in their books also meant God with the same words. Consider the fact that whenever I did not cite in this chapter the interpretation of modern authors concerning the original quotes mentioned in the first chapter, this is because there was no difference between them.[101]

You may object that the modern authors frequently explain *Tian* (Heaven) as Reason, law, air, or vital breath, time or course of time, First Emptiness, perceptible body, etc., and that they confuse *Shangdi* (Lord of Heaven) with Heaven, and thus the meaning of their words would seem to disagree with the true meaning of the supreme divinity. We shall now respond to all the objections in the following questions.

---

99 This eight-point summary is not present in the ARSI manuscript and was added later by Noël.
100 For Noël, the theistic thinking of neo-Confucianism is even clearer than in ancient Confucianism.
101 This paragraph ('Let us now return … difference between them') is not present in the ARSI manuscript.

Question 2: How Do Modern Authors Explain *Tian*, and Do they Distinguish *Tian* from *Shangdi*?

Above all, I need to explain three things: first, what sort of harmony (*concordia*) can be found among all the names by which Heaven or the Lord of Heaven is called; second, whether the Spirit of Heaven is the Soul of Heaven; third, what kind of identity exists between men and Heaven according to the Chinese?[102]

§.1. [*Di* or *Shangdi* as equivalent of *Tian*]

They affirm that the word *Shangdi* means the Lord of Heaven or the Ruler of Heaven, or more precisely the Lord and Ruler of Heaven (A). The Lord of Heaven or *Shangdi* is Spirit (B). This Spirit or Lord of Heaven is the same as Heaven (C). Moreover, the Spirit is a kind of supreme perfection (D). When they explain Heaven or the Lord of Heaven with other names, they want to indicate or suggest His several perfections; otherwise they would utter contradictions. Thus, they say that Heaven or the Lord of Heaven should be understood as the supreme and first Reason for all things, both in making them exist and in making them subsist. They add that Reason in terms of substance or essence, and cause, is understood as Heaven; in terms of infusion as nature, in terms of conservation, as mind. Insofar as it is in Heaven, Reason is called Law; insofar as it is in human beings and other things, it is called nature; insofar as it is in actions, it is called the way or the norm; but it is always the same Reason (E). Does this not resemble the opinion of the ancient Platonic philosophers who posit three states of things: ideal in the divine mind, natural in the production of things with the participation and impressions of ideas, and rational in the human mind?[103] Indeed, an idea is nothing else than an exemplary reason.[104] They also say that Heaven is worshipped because Reason subsists there (F). As It is Reason, Heaven is not something perceptible and material (G). The substance or essence of Reason is called Heaven; insofar as He governs, guides, and rules, it is called the Lord and Ruler of Heaven (H). Heaven, insofar as It must be obeyed as legislator, is called Law (I). As Providence, [Heaven] is called the cycle of time (K). (His Providence, Law, etc., will be discussed below).

---

102 The manuscript does not explicitly mention the second question, and Noël rearranged the content of this section into three questions.

103 Noël establishes here an interesting parallel between the three dimensions for a thing as ideal, natural, and moral, and the three dimensions of *li* as *Tian*, *xing* and *xin*. However, this parallel is far from being perfect because neo-Confucianism does not constitute metaphysics and physics as separated from the human mind.

104 The notion of exemplary reason or archetypal ground (*ratio exemplaris*) is a development of Plato's theory of ideas by the Jewish philosopher Philo, and then by the neo-Platonists and Christian philosophers. The medieval theologian Saint Bonaventure held that God was not only the beginning and end of all things, but also their *ratio exemplaris*. Before the Creation of the world, the divine mind contains for all eternity the *ratio exemplaris* of all things, including some which will never be created. Accordingly, the three areas of metaphysics, natural philosophy, and intellective illumination all lead to the exemplary reason which is God.

Insofar as it is an immaterial, imperceptible, and most simple substance, it is called First Emptiness [*taixu*]. Emptiness here is understood neither as a perceptible and material Being, such as an immense and empty space of aether [*taikong*],[105] nor as something fictitious or non-existent, but as a truly existing Being and as Reason, with its double meaning: something immaterial and something existing before things. Hence, in the stone tablet recording the entrance of Christianity into China in AD 700,[106] God is expressed with the word *lingxu*, or spiritual and empty, with the word *xuanshu*, or mysterious ultimate of things, with the word *zaohua*, or efficient Cause, and with the word *shentian*, or Spiritual Heaven (L).[107] First Emptiness is the same as *taiji*, the First Ultimate of things (M). *Taiji* can even be understood as Heaven, but I shall deal with this in Question 6 below. Also, Emptiness is understood as something alive and not as something dead (N). Finally, Heaven or the Master of Heaven as being the Author, Founder, Creator, is called the producing and destroying Spirit [*guishen*] (O). As vital principle, it is called air, or vital breath, and the next Question shall discuss about this.

From all this, you can see that all the different names with which Heaven is called can be very well applied to the true Lord of Heaven and Earth. As matter and substance which can be perceived, it is called *Tian*; in terms of dominion and governance, it is called *Di* (Lord and Ruler) (P). They should be understood in this sense. In its proper sense, Heaven means the material and perceptible heaven, but it does not mean this when used as a figure of speech for the Lord and Ruler of Heaven. Alternatively, heaven with its vast material extension and dimension, by which it covers and encompasses everything, represents the immense essence of the Lord and Ruler of Heaven, which encompasses all things or the Lord of Heaven through the vast extension of Heaven covers and encompasses all things. Or rather as they openly say, *Tian* or *Shangdi*, are in reality the same, though things out of which these names are derived, are different. See below B.7. When the Chinese say that Heaven and the Lord of Heaven, or the Spirit of Heaven are the same thing (Q), and say that It is Reason, or something immaterial and imperceptible, their claims can only be coherent if you say that Heaven is identical in meaning to the Lord of Heaven, who should be also understood as immaterial and beyond the senses. When understood not literally but as a figure of speech, Heaven is the same as the Lord and Ruler of Heaven because the Lord and Ruler of Heaven is immaterial and imperceptible insofar as He is Spirit. But Heaven in its literal meaning is something material and perceptible.

---

105 Aether was considered by most Greek philosophers as a kind of subtle matter filling the universe and above the earth. Scholastic philosophers attributes changes of density to aether.
106 This Nestorian stele was erected in 781 and it records the entrance of Christianity into China in 635. It was discovered and unearthed in 1623 near Xi'an. The stele can be seen today in the Forest of Stone Steles Museum (Beilin bowuguan 碑林博物館) in Xi'an.
107 Noël mentions the monotheistic use of the concept of emptiness (*xu*) by the Nestorian Church in China in order to justify the use of the concept of emptiness to describe God by the neo-Confucians. Indeed, the concept of emptiness is from Daoist origin and was used also widely by Buddhists and eventually adopted by some neo-Confucian thinkers such as Zhang Zai.

NOTES

A.1 《詩經說約集解・大雅・文王》：朱熹：「上帝，天之主宰也。」

About chapter 'Wen Wang' in the volume 'Daya' in the *Book of Odes*, Zhu Xi says as follows: 'The word *Shangdi* means the Lord and Ruler of Heaven'.[108]

A.2 《周易正解・說卦・第五》：朱熹：「帝者，天之主宰。」

About chapter 5 of 'Shuogua', the *True Explanation of the Book of Changes and Productions* cites Zhu Xi as follows: '*Di* (or *Shangdi*, which is the same thing) means Lord and Ruler of Heaven'.

A.3 陳澔《禮記集說・月令・第六》：「帝者，天之主宰。」

About chapter 'Yueling', Chen Hao in volume 2 of commentary on the *Book of Rites* states as follows: '*Di* means Lord and Ruler of Heaven'.

A.4 蔡沈《書經集傳・卷四・周書・洪範》：「帝以主宰言；天以理言也。」

About chapter 'Hongfan' in the *Book of Imperial Annals*, Cai Chen in volume 4 [of the *Shujing jizhuan*] explains *Di* as follows: 'As Lord and Ruler, it is called *Di*; as Reason, it is called Heaven'.

B.5 《詩經說約集解・小雅・正月》：「朱熹曰：『上帝，天之神也；程子曰：「以其形體謂之天，以其主宰謂之帝。」』」

About the ode 'Zhengyue' in the volume 'Xiaoya' in the *Book of Odes*, Zhu Xi states as follows: '*Shangdi* is the Spirit of Heaven, and as Doctor Cheng says, in terms of its form and substance, it is called Heaven; in terms of its dominion and rule, it is called *Di*'.[109]

B.6 陳澔《禮記集說・卷五・郊特牲・第十一》：「朱熹曰：『上帝即天也。聚天之神而言之，則謂之上帝。』」

About chapter 11 'Jiaotesheng' in the *Book of Rites*, Chen Hao in volume 5 [of his commentary] cites Zhu Xi as follows: '*Shangdi* is the same as Heaven; or *Shangdi*

---

108 According to Zhu Xi, Heaven has three different meanings: blue heaven, ruling heaven, and sometimes *li* without any other implication (又側問經傳中天字。要人自看得分曉也，有說蒼蒼者也，有說主宰者也，有單訓理時; *Zhuzi yulei, juan* 1). For a discussion of the three meanings of Heaven, physical (as Nature), religious (as Master), and philosophical (as Principle) in Zhu Xi, see Ching, *The Religious Thought of Chu Hsi*, pp. 54–60. In this section, Noël addresses the religious meaning, Heaven as Lord (*Di*), and he explicitly mentions Zhu Xi eight times, stressing the religious dimension of Heaven in Zhu Xi's thought, an aspect that has been rediscovered only recently, thanks especially to Julia Ching. See also Sang Jingyu 桑靖宇, 'Zhu Xi zhexue zhong de Tian yu Shangdi' 朱熹哲學中的天與上帝, *Wuhan daxue xuebao* 武漢大學學報 [*Wuhan University Journal*], 64.2 (2011), 21–26. The concept of *zhuzai* 主宰 (Master and Guide) does not appear in the classics, until Brother Cheng 程子 interpreted Di in terms of *zhuzai* (see c.2, §.8, D.3) and this was adopted by Zhu Xi, becoming very influential and later applied also to *Tian*. *Zhuzai* appears 45 times in the First Treatise (*Rijiang, Zhijie, Zhouyi zhengjie*, etc.). In *The True Meaning of the Lord of Heaven*, Ricci uses thirteen times the concept of *zhuzai* and applies it to God.

109 The more complete sentence by Master Cheng is given above (c.2, q.1, §.8, D.3).

is Heaven. While expressing that Heaven is the Spirit of Heaven considered collectively, it is called *Shangdi*'.

B.7 《性理標題・卷三・天文》：「以形體謂之天, 以主宰謂之帝, 以至妙謂之神, 以功用謂之鬼神, 以性情謂之乾。其實一而已, 所自而名之者異也。」

Chapter 'Tianwen' in volume 3 of the *Summary of the Book of Nature and Reason* (in Chinese *Xingli biaoti*), Cheng discusses Heaven as follows: 'In terms of its sensible shape and substance, it is called Heaven; in terms of its dominion and rule, it is called *Di*, or Lord and Ruler of Heaven; in terms of its excellence, it is called Spirit; in terms of operations and effects, it is called the producing and destroying Spirit, or invisible Author; in terms of its nature and efficiency, it is called Power or active Force; *Tian* and *Shangdi* are the same thing in reality but the things from which their names are drawn are different'.[110] See also c.2, q.1, §.2, Q.9.

C.8 《詩經說約集解・周頌・我將》：朱熹：「程子曰：天即帝也。」

About chapter 'Wojiang' in the chapter 'Zhousong' of the *Book of Odes*, Zhu Xi cites Cheng[zi] as follows: 'Heaven is the same as *Di*, the Lord and Ruler of Heaven; or Heaven is the Lord and Ruler of Heaven'.

C.9 蔡虛齋《四書蒙引・卷六・論語・第七》：「天字以主宰言。」

About chapter 7 of the *Book of Sentences* [*Lunyu* 7.23], Cai Xuzhai says in volume 6 of the *Sishu mengyin*: 'The word Heaven means Lord and Ruler'.

D.10 蔡虛齋《四書蒙引・卷六・論語・第七》：「程頤曰：天與帝一也；天言其體, 帝言其主。」

The same book quotes Cheng Yi: 'Heaven (*Tian*) and the Lord of Heaven (*Di*) are the same; Heaven expresses the substance of Heaven, and *Di* expresses the Lord of Heaven'.

D.11 See above B.7.

E.12 蔡虛齋《四書蒙引・孟子・盡心上》：「此天字重在理上。天者, 理之本體也。故曰：道之大原出於天。『知性知天』, 或曰：知性是知其所當然, 又知其所以然, 乃物格知之事。至於天, 則理之所從出者也, 非惟所當然者從此出, 所以然者亦從此出也。如《論語》『五十而知天命』, 則以所以然者屬諸天, 而對那所當然者為兩項。《大學》所謂『所當然之則』與其『所以然之故』, 皆是也。」

About Chapter 7 'Jinxin shang' in the second part of the *Mencius*, Cai Xuzhai in volume 15 of his commentary *Sishu mengyin* seems to relate the opinion of others:

---

110 This quote drawn from *Ercheng cuiyan* 二程粹言 (Selected words of the Cheng Brothers) appears also in c.2, q.1, §.8, D.3. See also q.1, §.2, Q.9. refers to a quote by Zhu Xi discussing the difficulty of knowing the actions of Heaven. Longobardo mentions this quote and understands it as expressing monism: '*Shangdi* (spirit of heaven) is the same thing as heaven, and therefore by extension, or at least by analogy, the same ought to be said about the spirits of other things'. Longobardo, *A Brief Response on the Controversies*, pp. 142–43 (prelude 11, n. 7). Cheng means here that *Tian, Di, shen, guishen*, and *qian* refer to the same reality, but Noël translates this as *Tian* and *Shangdi* are the same.

'The meaning of the word Heaven chiefly concerns Reason. Heaven is the very substance or essence of Reason. Hence it is said that Heaven is the great origin of moral actions. When Mencius says, "Whoever knows nature knows Heaven", it is meant that to know nature is to know its effect, and when the cause is also known, then this is the ultimate operation and end of the intellective faculty. Indeed, Heaven is the origin of reason, and it is not only the origin of effect, but also the origin of cause. When Confucius said that he knew the Law of Heaven at fifty, the cause which is ascribed to Heaven insofar as it is opposed to its effect is something twofold.[111] This is what the *Science of Adults* calls the norm of the effect and the cause of the cause'.[112]

E.13 朱熹《孟子集注·盡心上》：「程子曰：心也，性也，天也，一理也。自理而言，謂之天；自稟受而言，謂之性；自存諸人而言，謂之心。」「張子曰：由太虛，有天之名；由氣化，有道之名；合虛與氣，有性之名；合性與知覺，有心之名。」

About Chapter 7 'Jinxin shang' in the second part of the *Mencius*, Zhu Xi cites Doctor Cheng [Hao] as follows: 'Heart [*xin*], nature [*xing*] and Heaven are all the same Reason (obviously at a generic level); in terms of Reason, it is called Heaven; insofar as it is infused and received, it is called nature; insofar as it conserves people, it is called heart or mind'. Doctor Zhang [Zai] says: 'In terms of First Emptiness [*taixu*], Reason is called Heaven; in terms of a vital and active breath [*qihua*], it is called the way or norm for action [*dao*]; in terms of Emptiness [*xu*] joined with air [*qi*], it is called nature [*xing*]; in terms of nature joined with intellective faculty, it is called heart or mind [*xin*]'.[113]

E.14 蔡虛齋《四書蒙引·卷三·中庸·第二十六》：「此理在天則為命，在人物則為性，在事物則為道，皆理也。」

About chapter 26 of the *Book of the Unalterable Mean*, Cai Xuzhai says in volume 3 of the *Sishu mengyin*: 'This reason, insofar as it is in Heaven ...' See above.

F.15 蔡沈《書經集傳·卷三·商書·太甲下》：「天謂之敬者。天者，理之所在。動靜語默，不可有一毫之慢。」

About the chapter 'Taijia' in the *Book of Imperial Annals*, Cai Chen says in volume 3 of his commentary [*Shujing jizhuan*]: 'Heaven is said to be worshipped because Reason subsists in it; it should not be despised through the slightest movement, rest, word and silence'.

---

111 Reference to *Lunyu* 2.4.
112 This last reference does not come from the *Daxue* itself but from Zhu Xi's *Daxue huowen* 大學或問.
113 While Cheng Hao and Zhu Xi distinguish three dimensions: *Tian, xing, xin,* Zhang Zai has four: *Tian, dao, xing, xin.* But Noël discusses the canonical three-fold dimension based on Cheng Hao and Zhu Xi. For a discussion of this passage, see Wang Ge's chapter.

G.16 蔡虛齋《四書蒙引・卷五・論語・八佾・第三》:「獲罪於天, 無所禱也。朱子曰:『天即理也。』愚謂天之所以為。天者, 理而已矣。此注蓋謂此天字非以形體言也。又非以生物者言也。蓋就理言也。」「蓋孔子出一天字, 特地是以壓竈與奧, 而其所主則在道理上。故《集注》云耳。」

Chapter 3 of the *Book of Sentences* [*Lunyu* 3.13] states: 'If you have sinned against Heaven, there is no one to whom you can flee to seek refuge'. Cai Xuzhai comments on this passage in volume 5 of his *Sishu mengyin* as follows: 'For Zhu Xi, "The word Heaven means Reason". I myself consider that, on the basis of this interpretation identifying Heaven with Reason, Heaven does not indicate Heaven as a perceptible and material body, nor as the producer of things, but that it consists in the word Reason alone'. A few words after, Cai Xuzhai continues: 'Confucius used the word Heaven to bring down the power of the spirits of hearth and of the South-West corner of the room; what matters the most is the guiding and teaching Reason, and thus, the interpretation [of Zhu Xi] proposed the word Reason'.[114]

H. 蔡虛齋《四書蒙引・卷五・論語・八佾・第三》:「此箇道理, 其體則謂之天。其主宰則謂之帝, 如父子有親, 君臣有義。雖是理如此, 亦須上面有箇道理教他如此始得。」

[About chapter 3 of the *Book of Sentences*, Cai Xuzhai in volume 5 of his *Sishu mengyin* states the following]: 'The substance or essence of the guiding and teaching reason is called Heaven; its Lord and Ruler [*zhuzai*] is called *Di* or *Shangdi*. It is like the love between father and son, and the justice between king and subject.[115] Even though Reason requires this, it is necessary that a guiding Reason which teaches and gives orders exists above; only then, justice and love can exist'.

I.17 蔡虛齋《四書蒙引・卷十三・孟子・萬章上》:「以主宰而言謂之天; 以當聽受而言謂之命。」

About chapter 3 'Wan Zhang shang' in the second part of the *Mencius*, Cai Xuzhai comments in volume 13 of the *Sishu mengyin*: 'To express Lord and Ruler, it is called Heaven; to express that which must be obeyed, it is called the Law'.

K.18 《日講四書・卷七・論語・子罕・第九》:「『子罕言利與命, 與仁。』命兼理氣, 其故其微而難測。」

Chapter 9 of the *Book of Sentences* [*Lunyu* 9.1] states: 'Confucius very rarely talked about profit, providence, piety or rectitude of heart'. Volume 7 of the *Daily*

---

114 Unlike Noël, the *Confucius Sinarum philosophus* implicitly criticizes Zhu Xi for identifying *Tian* with *li*, and contrasts Zhu Xi's interpretation with that of Zhang Juzheng who implicitly refers to the 'mutual interaction between Heaven and men' (*Tianren ganying* 天人感應) articulated by Dong Zhongshu (179–04 BC). See Meynard, *The Jesuit Reading of Confucius*, pp. 167–68. In fact, Zhu Xi was not opposed to the theory of 'mutual interaction' as can be seen in his interpretation of Gaozong's dream about Fuyue in the *Shujing*. See c.2, q.1, §.6, A.1.
115 Zhu Xi has very similar words: '其體, 即謂之天; 其主宰, 即謂之帝, 如父子有親, 君臣有於此理也'. *Lunyu* 7, *Zhuzi yulei*, 25 *juan*. This imagery seems almost Trinitarian; the language is evocative of Augustine's description of Holy Spirit as the expression of the mutual love of Father and Son.

Explanation on the Four Books comments on this passage as follows: 'Providence involves Reason and the cycle of time, or time; therefore it is something very subtle and difficult to understand'.[116] See c.2, q.1, §.4, P.14 and R.

L.19 蔡虛齋《四書蒙引·卷十五·孟子·盡心上》：「太虛即太極之謂。虛者不雜於氣之名。形而下者謂之氣, 則皆是寔物。惟理則虛。」「太虛：一說, 以其無聲無臭而謂之太虛；一說, 其未有物而謂之太虛。」「此太虛以理言, 他處亦有以形器言者。如此亦『浮雲之過太虛』耳, 是以太虛當太空。」「上天之載, 無聲無臭, 故曰：由太虛, 有天之名。是太虛以理言, 不以形氣言也；此說乃合張朱之意。」

About Chapter 7 'Jinxin shang' of the *Mencius*, Cai Xuzhai in volume 15 of the *Sishu mengyin* discusses Heaven as follows: 'First Emptiness [*taixu*] is that which is called *taiji*, the first ultimate of things. Emptiness is a word meaning things that has not been mixed with air [*qi*] or something material. However, that which is perceptible or material and inferior or second rate, is called air. Both of them are real and truly existing, but only Reason is empty, that is, immaterial'.[117] He continues a little further down: 'First Emptiness has two meanings: first, something without sound and smell or devoid of sensation; second, something before the existence of things'. Shortly after is added: 'First Emptiness is understood as Reason, even though in some other respects it can be understood as material, like the immense and lifeless space of aether [*taikong*]'. Further below: 'When it is said that "the reality of Supreme Heaven, or nature, is without sound and smell; and thus, Heaven is called First Emptiness", this expresses First Emptiness as Reason, and not as matter [*xing*] or air [*qi*]; it is a Being which is consisting in Reason, not matter, air or anything perceptible. This explanation is truly consistent with the opinion of Doctor Zhang [Zai] and Doctor Zhu [Xi]'.[118]

L.20 大秦景教流行中國碑：「粵若, 常然真寂, 先先而無元, 窅然靈虛, 後後而妙有, 摠玄樞而造化, 妙眾聖以元尊者, 其唯 我三一妙身無元真主阿羅訶歟？」「神天宣慶, 室女誕聖于大秦, 景宿告祥。」

An ancient stone recording the entry of Christianity in China[119] begins as follows: 'I attentively contemplate the true and perpetual Tranquility [*ji*], the Being which precedes all beginnings, itself without beginning, spiritual and empty [*lingxu*] like something very profound, the most universal, perfect, mysterious Ultimate of

---

116 Here, Noël does not translate *ming* as Law, but as Providence, and he interprets *qi* as cycle of time.
117 Cai Qing gives a special meaning to the concept of *xu*, as meaning above forms, and this is interpreted by Noël as meaning unmixed with matter, and therefore spiritual according to scholastic philosophy.
118 On Noël's interpretation of *taixu* 太虛 (*primum vacuum*), see Chapters 2.12, 3.7, and 5.5.
119 Section L.20 is not present in the Roman manuscript and was later added by Noël. The Chinese text of the Nestorian stele was published by Li Zhizao in 1625. Nicolas Trigault, Michael Boym, and Antonio de Gouvea made Latin translations. The Chinese and Syrian texts with the Latin translation was first published in Europe by Athanasius Kircher in his *China monumentis ... illustrata* (Amsterdam: Jacob van Meurs, 1667). In translating those few excerpts here, Noël does not copy other translations but proposes his own translation.

all things [*xuanshu*] and the efficient Cause [*zaohua*] which adorns and perfects all the Saints through its exemplary and grand Majesty [*yuanzun*]. Can this be that I (I am who I am),[120] Three and One, the most perfect substance [*miaoshen*] without beginning, the true Lord [*zhenzhu*], Eloho [*Aluoheyu*]?' In Chaldean language 'Eloho' means God.[121] Because the Chinese lack the vowels 'a' and 'e' at the beginning of a word, they pronounce 'e' as 'nghe'. Thus they say 'nghe loho' and can even say 'oloho'. A little further down: 'Spiritual Heaven [*shentian*] revealed the blessing (through the Archangel Gabriel) and the Virgin gave birth to a Saint in the kingdom Daqin (as Chinese call the kingdom of Judaea); a very bright star announced His propitious arrival'.

M.21 See L.19

N.22 蔡虛齋《四書蒙引·卷一·大學》：「吾儒之虛,虛得活；佛老之虛,虛得死殺也。」「虛靈二字,有動靜體用之分。玉溪云：『虛猶鑑之空；靈猶鑑之照。不昧,申言其明也。』」「虛則有以具眾理,靈則有以應萬事,能具眾理而應萬事,此所以為明德也。」

> About the *Science of Adults* (in Chinese *Daxue*), Cai Xuzhai says in volume 1 of the *Sishu mengyin*: 'By the word emptiness [*xu*], our Doctors indicate something alive, while the idolatrous schools of Buddhism and Daoism indicate something dead'. He says about the mind, which is said to be empty and intelligent [*xuling*]: 'By the two words "empty" and "intelligent", its movement is distinguished from its rest; its substance from its effect. As Yuxi says, "Emptiness is like the empty surface of a mirror; intelligence is like the reflection or representation in the mirror"'.[122] And further below: 'The mind through Emptiness can know the cause of all things, and through intelligence can deal and respond to all affairs; because of emptiness and intelligence, it is called a bright, or rational, capacity'.[123]

O.23 See B.7

P.24 蔡沈《書經集傳·卷三·商書·仲虺之誥》：「天以形體言,帝以主宰言。」

> About chapter 'Zhonghui zhi gao' in the *Book of Imperial Annals*, Cai Chen says in volume 3 of his commentary [*Shujing jizhuan*]: 'In terms of matter or body and perceptible substance, it is called *Tian* (Heaven); in terms of dominion and governance, it is called *Di* (Lord and Ruler)'.

---

120 Exodus 3:4: 'Sum qui sum'. This is the Latin version of YHWH, the name God.
121 In Hebrew, Elohim.
122 This quote is from Lu Xiaobiao 盧孝標 (1186–1257), *zi* Xiaosun 孝孫, also called Master Yuxi 玉溪先生. He obtained the grade of advanced scholar (*jinshi*) in 1202.
123 Cai Qing takes inspiration here from Zhu Xi: '明德者, 人之所得乎天, 而虛靈不昧, 以具眾理而應萬事者也'. Zhu Xi, *Sishu zhangju jizhu*. For Cai Qing, *xu* represents mostly the Confucian practice of personal cultivation (*gongfu* 工夫). He attached such importance to this that he chose Xuzhai (Empty studies) as his literary name. See Wang Suqin 王素琴, 'Cai Qing ji qi *Sishu mengyin* yanjiu' (unpublished doctoral thesis, National Taichung University of Education, 2019), p. 57.

P.25 蔡沈《書經集傳・卷五・周書・君奭》：「伊陟、臣扈之佐太戊，以賢輔賢，其治化克厭天心。自其徧覆言之謂之天，自其主宰言之謂之帝。《書》或稱天，或稱帝，各隨所指，非有重輕。」

> About the chapter 'Junshi' in the *Book of Imperial Annals*, Cai Chen says in volume 5 of his commentary [*Sishu jizhuan*]: 'When Yizhi and Chenhu served as prime ministers of Emperor Taiwu, these wise men helped the wise [emperor]. Consequently, his rule and the effects of his government could please the heart of Heaven. When expressing that it covers everything, this is called *Tian*; when expressing that it controls and rules everything, this is called *Di*. Books [i.e. *Shangshu*] use either *Tian* or *Di* according to what they want to indicate, but there is no difference of higher or minor importance'.

Q.26 陳澔《禮記集說・郊特牲・第十一》：「問：『郊祀後稷以配天，宗祀文王以配上帝，宗祭文王以配上帝』。帝只是天，天只是帝，卻分祭，何也？」

> About chapter 11 'Jiaotesheng' of the *Book of Rites*, Chen Hao in volume 5 of his commentary [*Liji jishuo*] cites Zhu Xi as follows: 'You ask about the *ji* ritual to be offered in the *jiao* suburbs to Houji together with Heaven, and the *ji* ritual to be offered in the imperial court to Wen Wang together with the Lord of Heaven. However, the Lord of Heaven [*Di*] is nothing other than Heaven [*Tian*]; and Heaven nothing other than the Lord of Heaven, so why there would be a difference of ritual?' See below the response [of Zhu Xi] in q.5.A.1.[124]

Q.27 See above C.10.

§.2. [Spirit of Heaven as Different from the World-Soul]

The Spirit of Heaven is neither the Soul of Heaven nor the substantial form of the physical heaven. The Chinese neither follow and nor know anything about the error of the ancient philosophers who affirmed that Heaven is animated and made up of a body and soul or spirit.[125] This is evident because they say that *Tian* is exactly the same as the Lord of Heaven, and the Lord of Heaven is the same as Heaven, or that Heaven is the Lord of Heaven and the Lord of Heaven is Heaven (R). It is impossible to hold that body and soul are the same. To summarize what I have said so far, they always accept the Lord of Heaven as a *suppositum*, and not as a part of the *suppositum*.[126] They never oppose Heaven to the Lord of Heaven,

---

124 This quote gives the question of a disciple of Zhu Xi about the *Xiaojing* 孝經, and not the actual answer of Zhu Xi, which is given below. See *Zhuzi yulei*, juan 82.
125 Noël refers to the ancient theory of God as the soul of world, found for example in the writings of Plato, Plotinus, and Averroes. Jesuits in China like Ricci, Longobardo, Intorcetta, and Couplet have often regarded neo-Confucianism as a world-soul theory.
126 *Suppositum* is a scholastic term which is defined as: 'That which underlies all the accidents of a thing, i.e., the individual substance of a certain kind which is the subject of existence and all accidental modifications which constitute the individual, synonym of hypostasis, *subjectum*, and *substantia*'. Roy Joseph Deferrari, *A Lexicon of St Thomas Aquinas Based on the Summa Theologica and Selected Passages of His Other Works* (Washington, DC: Catholic University of America Press, 1948). Despite the affirmation of Noël, many literati did not put *Shangdi* on par with *Tian*, and considered *Shangdi* only a part of *Tian*. In reaction to

as if one partakes in the other, but they always use Heaven when referring to one aspect, and the Lord of Heaven when referring to another aspect, while affirming that they are both the same. Clearly, the Chinese do not make out of Heaven and the Lord of Heaven a composite which would be partly material, partly spiritual. On this issue, see the following question [Question 3] near the end.

NOTES

R.28 《詩經說約集解·大雅·文王》：「上天之事, 無聲無臭, 不可得度; 惟爾祖文王與天同德, 即天載所在也。」「《大全》慶源輔氏[127]曰: 文王之詩七章, 以一章言之, 首尾只是言文王與天為一。」朱熹:「思子曰:『維天之命, 於穆不已,』蓋曰天之所以為天也。『於乎不顯, 文王之德之純,』蓋曰文王之所以文王也, 純亦不已。夫知天之所為天, 又知文王之所以為文, 則夫與天同德者, 可得而言矣。」

> About the ode 'Wen Wang' in the volume 'Daya' of the *Book of Odes*, the *Exhaustive Compilation of the Book of Odes* states as follows: 'The reality of the Supreme Heaven being without sound, smell, or sense perception cannot be sufficiently conceived and understand. Your grandfather Wen Wang had the same virtue as Heaven, and reality of Heaven consisted in this'. Little further below: 'To summarize the seven sections of this ode into one, Wen Wang is said as being one with Heaven from the beginning to the end'. Zhu Xi comments this ode as follows: 'Zisi[128] said: "How mysteriously the Law of Heaven completes its course without intermission and end!" The *Book of Odes* clearly expresses the reason why Heaven is Heaven. Is it not patently clear? "The virtue of Wen Wang was shining without any mixture of fiction and falsity". This ode also expresses the reason why Wen Wang was Wen Wang, namely because "his most sincere and pure virtue never stopped its course". This is what Zisi said. Since we know the reason why Heaven is Heaven and why Wen Wang was Wen Wang is known, it can thus be said that Wen Wang had the same virtue as Heaven'.[129]

R.29 《詩經說約集解·大雅·皇矣》: 朱熹: '呂氏曰: 此言文王, 德不形而功無迹, 與天同體而已。雖興兵以伐崇, 莫非順帝之則, 而非我也。'

> About the ode 'Huangyi' in the volume 'Daya' of the *Book of Odes*, Zhu Xi cites Lü as follows: 'This passage means that the virtue of Wen Wang was devoid of any external appearance, and his wonderful deeds emanated from the imperceptible force of his soul. He finally was of the same nature as Heaven (namely in terms of effects and origin, as it shall be explained soon). Even though he launched a military expedition against the kingdom of Chong, he did it not by himself, but by obeying the instruction of the Lord of Heaven [*Di*]'.

---

the Christian valorization on *Shangdi* in the ancient classics, Chinese literati in the late Ming and early Qing paid more attention to the term *Shangdi*.

127 Fu Guang 輔廣, *zi* Hanqing 漢卿, *hao* Qian'an 潛庵, from Zhaozhou Qingyuan 趙州慶源 (Gansu province).
128 i.e. in the *Zhongyong*.
129 Zhu Xi's quote comes from his *Shijing jizhuan*, *juan* 6. The union of Wen Wang with *Tian* is understood here as a moral union, based on virtue (*yutian tongde* 與天同德).

§.3. [Union of Man with *Tian*]

When those writers say that the wise and perfect man is made one with Heaven, is united with Him, this should be understood as referring to the virtue of the wise man which is the same as the virtue of Heaven in terms of effects, but not in terms of substance I, or that the wise man is similar to Heaven (S); or that there is a perfect union between the Reason of the wise man and the Reason of Heaven (T); or that there is union between the will of the wise man and the will of Heaven (V). This is quite close to the meaning of Saint Paul: 'Whoever is united to the Lord becomes one Spirit with Him' (First Corinthians 6:17). Though the perfect man is closely united with Heaven, they still constitute two entities (X).[130]

When they say that the Reason of man and the Reason of Heaven is one (Z), this should be understood as a generic unity, or as natural law that the Theologians sometimes associate with Divine Law, because natural law or the dictates of reason, in doing or avoiding something in conformity with nature, are materially produced and drawn from the human intellect. Since natural law and its dictates necessarily proceed from the impression of the light given by God, and since those commands are formally binding, thus they are rightly ascribed to God as Legislator. See what I said about the eternal law in c.2, q.1, §.1.

The emperor after his death is called Heaven, and this title is used as a figure of speech. Similarly, even the deeds of the emperor are called heavenly (W). This is similar to how we say 'Angelic' Doctor, a 'Divine' Orator, and 'Heavenly' Prudence. When the explanation of the modern authors is correctly understood, this does not change the true meaning of the Lord of Heaven, but their explanation envelops this meaning with other terms which are more general and slightly more difficult to understand. If you wish to see how the Lord of Heaven is sketched with the various names of Reason, Spirit, Author, and Nature, how He makes and destroys, rules and governs, and how He is the first Beginning of all things, see the following question [Question 3].

NOTES

R.30 蔡虛齋《四書蒙引・卷三・中庸・第二十六》：「『此言聖人與天地同體』，亦就用上說也；蓋亦『體用一原』之理。」

> About chapter 26 of the *Book of the Unalterable Mean*, Cai Xuzhai says in volume 3 of his commentary *Sishu mengyin*: 'When Zhu Xi says that a man perfect in wisdom and science is of the same nature as Heaven and Earth, this has to be understood about the effects, because nature and effects have the same origin'.[131]

---

130 In this section, the issue is about the Confucian claim of a union of the *Shengren* with the cosmos (聖人與天地同體) and with Heaven (與天合一). Following Zhu Xi's distinction between essence (*ti*) and function (*yong*), Noël shows that the union is not essential but functional. Jesuit Figurists like Joseph de Prémare later shifted to a theological interpretation of the *Shengren*, understanding the appearances of the *Shengren* in the Chinese classics as announcing Jesus Christ. In this sense, Jesus Christ is the one who realizes the union with the cosmos.

131 In *Zhongyong zhangju*, Zhu Xi considers that the virtue completing things (*chengwu* 成物) realizes a

R.31 《詩經說約集解・大雅・思齊》：朱熹：「文王之德如此,故其大難雖不殄絕,而光大亦無玷缺。雖事之無所前聞者,而亦不合於法度。雖無諫諍之者,而亦未嘗不入於善。《傳》所謂『性與天合』是也。」

> About the ode 'Siqi' in the volume 'Daya' in the *Book of Odes*, Zhu Xi says: 'The virtue of Wen Wang was such that, even though he could not avoid facing great difficulties and toil, his virtue was always shining without any stain; even though he had to execute things that he had not heard about before, he never deviated from honesty; and even though there was no one exhorting him, he always made progress in virtue. This is what the commentators call a nature conforming to and being united with Heaven'.

S.32 See R.28.

T.33 《性理標題・卷三・道理》：「上蔡謝氏曰：『天,理也；人,亦理也。循理則與天為一。與天為一,我非我也,理也；理非理也,天也。』」

> The chapter 'Daoli' in volume 3 of the *Summary of the Book of Nature and Reason* states: 'Xie says that Heaven is reason. Man is also the same Reason Whoever follows Reason becomes one with Heaven. United with Heaven, the self is not longer the self, but becomes Reason. Moreover, Reason is not Reason, but becomes Heaven'.[132]

T.34 《周易正解・卷二十二・說卦・第一》：「易則於天下之理,窮究而無所遺。於人物之性,全盡而無所歉,且於理性之所從來,而為天命之於穆不已者。復與之脗合而無間焉。蓋得其所當然,便契其所以然。」

> About chapter 1 of 'Shuogua', volume 22 of the *True Explanation of the Book of Changes and Productions* states as follows: 'The *Book of Changes and Productions* investigates every reason of all things and teaches that human beings and all other

---

functional union between the sage and Heaven (此言聖人與天地同用), while the virtue matching Heaven and Earth (配天地) realizes an union of substance (此言聖人與天地同體). In *The True Meaning of the Lord of Heaven*, Ricci criticized the idea that the myriad of things are forming one body, and the idea that Heaven and man are forming one single body (*yiti* 一體). See Ricci, *True Meaning of the Lord of Heaven*, pp. 177–87 (n. 221–43). Similarly, Longobardo rejected the monistic thinking of the Chinese: 'Since the Chinese believe that all things are one and the same substance (*wanwu yiti* 萬物一體), it is evident that they did not recognize two really distinct substances, namely spiritual substances, such as God, the Angels and the rational soul, as distinct from corporeal substances'. Longobardo, *A Brief Response on the Controversies*, p. 138 (prelude 10, n. 1). In response to Longobardo, Noël clarifies that, according to Zhu Xi and Cai Qing, the union is not at the level of the substance (*ti*), but at the level of the effects (*yong*). This rejects any divinization of the wise men since they are distinct in nature from God. However, a more correct translation of the passage by Cai Qing would be: 'When Zhu Xi says that a man perfect in wisdom and science is one with Heaven and earth, *this is related to what is said above about the effects*, because nature and effects have the same origin' (our italics). The following words by Cai Qing make clear that the permanent union is realized, in fact, both in function and in substance: '「此言聖人與天地同用」,非非此始與天地同用也。「此言聖人與天地同體」,亦非至此始與天地同體也。看「言」字其實博厚便載物,載物便配地,豈略有先后邪？天地,本體也；天地之覆載,用也。味此可見體用同義'.

132 This quote is from Xie Liangzuo 謝良佐 (1050–1103), alias Xie Shangcai 謝上蔡, who was a disciple of Cheng Yi. The union with *Tian* is expressed as 'following *li*'.

things achieve their full nature. Moreover, their nature finally returns to unite itself with the origin of reason and nature, namely the Law of Heaven which revolves constantly and secretly. The effect being obtained, their nature unites itself immediately to its cause'.

V.35 張居正《四書直解・論語・第十四》:「夫聖人盡性至命, 與天合一。其獨得之妙, 真有人不能知而天獨知之者。」

Commenting on chapter 14 of the *Book of Sentences* [*Lunyu* 14.37], Zhang Juzheng states in the sixth volume [of *Sishu zhijie*]: 'By fulfilling all the parts of his rational nature while adhering to and putting into practice the Law of Heaven, the perfect man reaches the unique excellence of a close union with Heaven. He surely cannot be known and examined by people, but only Heaven knows him'.[133] See c.2, q.1, §.4, G.6.

V.36 《日講四書解義・卷二・中庸・第一》:「人心即天心, 故心盡而天應; 人事即天事, 故事修而天從。」

About chapter 1 of *Book of the Unalterable Mean*, volume 2 of the *Daily Explanation on the Four Books* discusses the supremely spiritual man as follows: 'The heart of man is the heart of Heave. Therefore, when man fulfills all the parts of his heart, Heaven corresponds to him. The affairs of man are the affairs of Heaven and when man correctly settles his own affairs, Heaven is compliant with him'.[134]

X.37 《詩經說約集解・周頌・維天之命》:「輔氏曰:『此詩上四句言文王之德與天為一。』《詩緝》:[135]『凡言聖人如天者[, 以此擬彼], 天與聖人猶為二也。此詩但以天命之不已與文德之純對立而並言之, 蓋有不容擬議者。』」

About the ode 'Weitian zhi ming' in the volume 'Zhousong', the *Exhaustive Compilation of the Book of Odes* states as follows: 'The first four verses of this ode say that virtue of Wen Wang made him one with Heaven'.[136] A little further below: 'Although it is often said that a man of perfect virtue and knowledge is like Heaven, Heaven and the perfect man are still two things. This ode shows that the Law of Heaven continuously revolving was compared with the sincerest virtue of Wen Wang and also treats them separately. For us, there is no space to argue or doubt about his sincerity'.[137]

---

133 The *Confucius Sinarum philosophus* also translates this quote of Zhang Juzheng about *Lunyu* 14.37. See Meynard, *The Jesuit Reading of Confucius*, p. 450.
134 The expression of a correspondence between Heaven and human mind can be found in Zhu Xi, and it was further expressed by the Song scholar Huang Lun 黃倫 in his *Shangshu jingyi* 尚書精義 (42 *juan*) as: 'Heaven and man are not far apart; my mind is the mind of Heaven' (天人不遠, 我之心即天心). This quote of the *Rijiang* here is not found in the *Gujin*.
135 Yan Can 嚴粲 (Southern Song dynasty, fl. thirteenth century), *Shiji* 詩緝 in 36 *juan*.
136 Quote from Fu Guang 輔廣 (fl. twelfth century), author of the *Liujing jijie* 六經集解.
137 The Chinese text has a different meaning: not to discuss further about it.

Z.38 蔡虛齋《四書蒙引·卷十五·孟子·盡心下》：「按《論語》『性與天道』章，《集註》曰：『性者,人之所受之天理；天道者,天理自然之本體：其實一理也。』小註王氏曰：『此理在天,未賦於物,故曰天道；此理具於人心,未應於事,故曰性,即「元亨利貞」、「仁義禮智」是也。』」

> About chapter 7 'Jinxin xia' of the *Mencius*, Cai Xuzhai says in volume 15 of the *Sishu mengyin*: 'According to Zhu Xi, "nature is the reason received by man from Heaven; the Way of Heaven, or Heaven's Way of acting, is the essence or substance of the natural Reason of Heaven; and in reality, both are the same Reason".[138] According to the short commentary by Wang [Bai], "the Reason existing in Heaven before it was infused into things is called the Way of Heaven or Heaven's Way of acting. Being contained in the human soul before it does anything, it is called nature, and obviously it is the first, participative, directive and perfective power of Heaven, as well as the inborn goodness, justice, honesty and intelligence of man"'.[139]

W.39 陳澔《禮記集說·曾子問七》：「『唯天子稱天以誄之。』誄之為言,累舉其平生實行為誄,而定其諡以稱之也。稱天以誄之者,天子之尊無二,惟天在其上,故假天以稱之也。人君之事多稱天,不獨誄也。」

> About chapter 7 'Zengzi wen' in the *Book of Rites* ('The emperor is called Heaven in funeral orations or eulogy') Chen Hao says in the seventh volume of his commentary [*Liji jishuo*]: 'That which he did in his life is used to compose the eulogy and is decided that he be called by this name. In eulogies, the Emperor is called "Heaven" because of his supreme and matchless majesty. Only Heaven is above or superior to the emperor, and thus the name of Heaven is borrowed to call the emperor. Not only in eulogies but in other occasions, the deeds of the emperor are mostly called "Heaven" or "Heavenly"'.[140]

---

138 The quote comes from Zhu Xi's *Lunyu jizhu* 論語集註.
139 The quote come from the *Luzhai Wang Wenxian Gong wenji* 魯斋王文憲公文集 by Wang Bai 王柏 (1197–1274).
140 Most probably Noël was quoting this reference about the emperor being called heaven to refute some missionaries who pointed out the confusion of temporal and religious spheres in China. Christianity had also to deal with this issue during the Roman Empire, with some emperors being deified even in their lifetime.

Question 3: What Do Modern Commentators Recognize as First Origin of the World?

Five questions need to be investigated. First, do they recognize any First Mover or First Living Being, which is intelligent and unproduced? Second, is this first living and intelligent Being a universal cause and involved in all things or is it only the substantial form of the world? Third, is this first living and intelligent Being unique, that is, is the Spirit of Heaven and Earth unique? Fourth, whether He has a law that directs all things? Fifth, does He has a providence that watches all things?[141]

§.1. The Modern Commentators Recognize a First Mover, or First Living Being that Is Intelligent and Unproduced

This is shown from what I have said in c.2, q.1, §.1 and §.2, and elsewhere. The writer quoted below [Cai Xuzhai] says: 'There is a First Being which has no Reason apart from Air, and no Air apart from Reason (by Air, you should understand life). However, if by this term is expressed the Author of things, then Air divides itself into two (stillness *yin* and motion *yang*, or from not being active it becomes active), and Reason includes both, and it controls, rules, produces, and acts in them; it is called "the unique cause, which is Spirit".[142] Thus, Reason comes before Air and is called *taiji* or first ultimate of things. This way, it can be said that Reason is anterior, and Air, posterior'. But a little before he had said: 'Air could be said anterior, and Reason, posterior' (A).[143] You should understand this priority and posteriority through the intellect. It is clear that since Reason, or Spirit, is the unique cause, it is also living, for there is no Spirit without life, and thus, Reason includes in itself Air or vital breath as the Chinese affirm everywhere.

As they say, the inexhaustible Author of things is the vital Air (B). The word Air should be understood as a vital principle, and the word Reason, as intellectual principle. As they say, the universal substance and essence of the whole first and great principle is the Spirit of active Heaven (C). Spirit is the power of Heaven and it is not material since this power is Reason, and Reason is Spirit. The effective force is Air (life or vital principle); the Spirit is within what the effective force produces (D). Do you not realize that the infinite greatness of the way of Heaven is the whole Air or total Breath of the universal Spirit, that the void waiting for this

---

141 Question 3 is a new elaboration based on the traditional attributes of God already discussed in Question 1. The first issue develops further the analysis of the attributes of dominion, power, knowledge, and life (§.1, 2, 3 and 6); the second issue, about the relation of the First Being to the world, corresponds to the attribute of simplicity (§.8); the four and fifth issues correspond to the attributes of will and justice (§.4 and 5). The third issue about the unicity was not discussed as such above.
142 Cai Qing refers here to the words of Zhang Zai: 'A single spiritual cause' (一故神).
143 There was an important debate among Song-dynasty philosophers over whether there is any priority between *li* and *qi*. Here Cai Qing attempts to harmonize the positions of Zhu Xi (priority of *li*) and of Zhang Zai (priority of *qi*). Cai Qing also introduces the concept of Origin (*yuan* 元) that Noël understands as First Being.

Air or Breath is preserved in the midst of darkness,[144] and that before it has made anything, it already exists to produce all the species of things? (E)

Since the word *li* or Reason can be understood as intellectual principle, and *qi* or Air as vital principle, or rather since an infinite substance (*suppositum*) acting with life and intelligence is included in the universal Reason and Breath,[145] thus the recent Chinese dictionary [*Xiesheng pinzijian*][146] affirms more openly: 'The authors explain the character *Tian* or Heaven with *li* or Reason, which is always connected to *qi* or Air, and they exhaust its entire meaning with almost a single word [*li*]. But in the midst of it there must be an absolute Lord who can provide stability for people with His secret virtue'. The chapter 'Taijia' of the *Book of the Imperial Annals* says: 'Heaven does not love all people but only those who revere and love Him'.[147] The chapter 'Xianyou yide' says: 'Do not trust rashly in Heaven; Its command and providence change easily'. The chapter 'Yixun' says: 'He sends thousands of good things to people who act well, and thousands of bad things to people who act badly'.[148] If active reason (*li*) and breath (*qi*) are only found in the midst of it and if there is not a one true and extremely intelligent ruler, then when the *Book* [*of Imperial Annals*] says that he only loves these people, I am asking you who else he could be? Who else he could be when it is said 'Do not trust rashly since his command and providence changes easily'? Could he not be indeed the one called *Shangdi*, the King of kings?[149] We who live under his constant gaze not only do not know how to revere the terrible majesty of Heaven with fear and dread, but we also dare to oppose ourselves to the Lord of Heaven with our opinion and perverse heart. What greater stupidity could be conceived!' (E).[150]

The twenty-eight volume of the *Xingli daquan* states on page 37 as follows: 'According to the commentary of the *Yijing*, the producing and destroying Spirit is

---

144 The ARSI manuscript (f. 56ᵛ) has a different meaning: 'In the midst of darkness, it preserves its incorporeal intelligence and makes it progress'.
145 For the scholastic concept of *suppositum*, see above (c.2, q.2). According to Noël, the quote below connects the two attributes of intelligence (*li*) and life (*qi*) to an infinite individual substance.
146 The dictionary called by Noël *Pintsucien* corresponds to the *Xiesheng pinzijian*. For further explanation, see 2.6, 2.14 and 3.3.
147 Quoted above, 'Tractatus primus', p. 13 (c.1, q.2, §.4, I.8); this edition p. 185. Here Noël translates the title of the *Shujing* with 'fastorum', whereas elsewhere he translates as 'annalium'.
148 Quoted above, 'Tractatus primus', p. 17 (c.1, q.2, §.5, K.9); this edition p. 190.
149 The Chinese has *huanghuang zhi Shangdi* 皇皇之上帝. The title of King of kings is usually attributed to Christ, but here Noël means God.
150 The Chinese text and its Latin translation are not present in the ARSI manuscript, and the *Pinzijian* itself is not present in the ARSI collection. It is very likely that Noël copied the text directly from Bouvet's own preface, dated 1707, to *Gujin*, pp. 124–25: 「漢詁天者, 理而已矣. 又理不離氣, 顧其中必非漫無所主, 而能陰騭下民者. 《太甲》曰: 『惟天無親, 克敬惟親. 』《咸有一德》曰: 『天難諶, 命靡常. 』而《伊訓》直曰: 『作善降之百祥, 作不善降之百殃. 』使天中止此渾然行之理若氣, 而絕無至靈之真宰焉, 則所云『無親』『惟親』者誰? 所云『難諶』『靡常』而『降祥』『降殃』者又誰? 倘所謂皇皇之上帝非乎? 乃吾人日在鑒茲之下, 不知時加警惕以畏天威, 且敢以小智私心與帝天角, 弗思甚矣. 」 Accordingly, besides *li* and *qi*, Heaven is endowed with a supreme intelligence or spirit (*zhiling* 至靈) to direct the people. The Latin text is also found in the *Summarium NAT* (p. 88).

the Author of things (in Chinese *zaohua*)'. Shortly after is written: 'Air is Spirit'.[151] It perhaps would not surprise you that the Chinese could explain the word Air or vital air as *spiritus* because the Latin word *spiritus* is derived from the word *spiro*, which on its own means 'airy breathing'.[152] In the fifth book of the *Tusculan Disputations*, Cicero calls the soul a small part of 'divine breath'.[153] Even the Bible calls God a consuming fire,[154] and the Symbol of Faith talks about 'Light from light, true God from true God'.[155] Perhaps a Chinese person hearing these things will think that we Europeans believe that God is a material consuming fire, and that He is true light from material light. In fact, this should not be understood literally but symbolically.

Moreover, this Reason or unique cause, which is Spirit, is called *taiji*, and *taiji* is called First Emptiness [*taixu*], as we saw already above (F). Emptiness is the spiritual power of Heaven and Earth; Emptiness is called the supreme goodness; Heaven and Earth are born out of Emptiness (G). First Emptiness is the truth of Heaven, or the true and real existence of Heaven; all things receive from First Emptiness what they need, especially man who is born from First Emptiness (H).

As we have seen above, First Emptiness is this same Reason, that is, an incorporeal and real Being, and Reason is the same as the immaterial Heaven, and the immaterial Heaven is the same as the Ruler of Heaven, or *Shangdi*. It is clear that the Lord and Ruler of Heaven is the First Mover, the Principle, first living and intelligent Being, unproduced and unlimited since there is nothing before by which He could be produced and limited.[156]

---

151   The Chinese quote and its Latin translation are not present in the manuscript, but the Chinese text can be retrieved easily from the *Xingli daquan, juan* 28, p. 37b. The first quote corresponds to 「《易》說, 鬼神便是造化也」 and the second to 「只氣便是神」. Both these passages come from Cheng Yi. In the following question of this chapter, Noël quotes similar words from Cheng Yi, expressing *guishen* as traces of *zaohua* (造化之迹); see below (c.2, q.4, K.10 and L.11). In his translation here Noël identifies *shen* and *qi*, as a way to spiritualize *qi*. On the contrary, interpreters like Fu Xihong consider that *guishen* and *shen* are nothing but *qi*, meaning that there is no *shen* outside of *qi*, stressing the limited function of *qi* as yin-yang and the possibility to understand the invisible *shen* only by the change of *qi*: 「『鬼神只是氣』應該理解為鬼神並不是『氣』以外的東西。同樣地,『只氣便是神』說的也並不是『氣=神』, 而是說神並不是『氣』以外的東西。這兩句話實際上等同於『氣外無神』, 強調的是陰陽之氣的限定作用, 也就是僅就此氣的變化, 就足以瞭解不可見的神。」Fu Xihong 傅錫洪, 'Songdai lixue guishenlun de xingcheng' 宋代理學鬼神論的形成, *Zhongshan daxue xuebao* 中山大學學報, 5 (2018), 149–47. For discussion of this citation, see Wang Ge's chapter.
152   For this sentence, I adopt here the translation in Wong, 'The Unalterable Mean', p. 220. Besides the process of spiritualization of *qi*, Noël advances here a symbolic interpretation.
153   This citation is not found anywhere in the *Tusculan Disputations*. However, this seems an exact quote from Horace's *Satires* (*Sermones* 2.79).
154   Deuteronomy 4:24.
155   The Symbol of Faith was adopted during the First Council of Nicea (325).
156   In the *Proemium* to the Third Treatise, Noël restates his understanding of *li* as a Reason abstracted from matter: 'Quod attinet ad Metaphysicam, videntur etiam aliquid de ea insinuare, dum omnia ultimatè reducunt ad Rationem generalissime sumptam; illamque sic sumptam dicunt esse unam, esse veram, esse bonam; nempe illam generalissimam Rationem, seu illlud Ens generalissime sumptum & a materia abstractum, habere metaphysicas Entis proprietates, quae sunt unitas, veritas, bonitas transendentalis. De Ente increato, & Intelligentiis quid sentiant, jam fusè vidimus in Tract. I de Cognitione primi Entis Cap. 1 & 2'. Noël, 'Tractatus tertius', p. 2.

If someone now wants to investigate the way in which the First Being produces all things (even though the question pertains not to our topic but more properly to physics), he could commence the following reasoning.[157] When the Chinese say that Heaven and Earth are born out of emptiness, that emptiness is Reason, and that Reason is Spirit, it is possible to gather from this that Heaven and Earth were created by God, the Supreme Spirit and exemplary cause.[158] Also, when they say that the most subtle primitive Air was born at the beginning of the world and that heaven and earth were made from its division, it could be said that the primitive Air means the great abyss which was over the surface of the earth, like the great Chaos, from which the firmament, stars above, plants, fishes, birds, animals, and all the sublunary and terrestrial things were produced.[159] You may similarly understand the earth, which lies enclosed in the middle of the great abyss, together with the abyss, as their cause or material co-cause.[160]

In chapter 7 of the first book of the *Two Books on Genesis against the Manichees*, Saint Augustine says: 'The formless matter which God made from nothing is first called heaven and earth, not because it already existed, but because it could potentially do so; for the Bible also says that heaven was made later on. Similarly, when we consider the seed of a tree, we may say that it has the roots, trunk, branches and leaves, not because they already exist, but because they shall exist in the future'.[161] Gregory of Nyssa understands also heaven and earth as Chaos massed together with one universal, common and rough form, out of which the celestial bodies and all the elements are drawn out.[162] See Cornelius à Lapide in his commentary on Genesis.[163]

---

157 After the conclusion to his first point, Noël inserts here a digression on cosmogenesis, already present in the manuscript but developed further in the printed version.
158 The notion of exemplary cause is not properly Aristotelian but Platonic, holding the pre-existence of a form or idea. In the previous question (Question 2) in this same chapter, Noël mentions the neo-Platonic concept of exemplary reason. Accordingly, all the forms of the objects of the world were already contained in *taixu*.
159 Accordingly, *yuanqi* corresponds to the great abyss or chaos in the first day of Creation in *Genesis*. In the *Proemium* to the Third Treatise, Noël briefly mentions the Chinese cosmogenesis based on *yuanqi*, which he calls chaos or informed prime matter: 'Physicam per sensum allegoricorum saepe morali immiscent. Materia prima juxta quosdam illorum authores, est primigenius aer, cujus pars subtilior, purior ac levior formando terrae, seu rebus terrestribus inserviit; (Chaos nempe informe, juxta ea quae dixi in Tract. primo de Cognitione primi Entis Cap. 2 Quaest. 3). Ista igitur aeris tenuissima substantia, vel ista aera corpuscula sunt materia, ex qua rerum corpora tum animata, tum inanimata conflantur'. Noël, 'Tractatus tertius', p. 1.
160 This corresponds to the third day of Creation.
161 Augustine, *De Genesi contra Manichaeos*, 7:11.
162 Cf. Gregory of Nyssa, *Hexamaeron*, c. 11.
163 The testimonies of Augustine and Gregory of Nyssa are not in the ARSI manuscript and were added later, based on the work of Cornelius à Lapide, an influential Flemish Jesuit and exegete (1567–1637), *Commentaria in Pentateuchum Mosis*, first published in 1617 and reprinted many times in the seventeenth and eighteenth centuries.

This can be gathered with sufficient clarity from the text or ode that they sing for receiving the Spirit of *Shangdi*: 'Oh, this obscure and antique first chaos! When the five elements (water, fire, wood, metal and earth) had not yet begun their course and the two luminaries not yet shone, in the midst stood above something (that is *Shangdi*, to whom the emperor performs the sacrifice), without shape or sound. The spiritual King revealing His dominion started dividing the pure from the impure, and establishing earth and man, and from then on followed the generations of all things' (I).

It is necessary to distinguish a double First Principle: one spiritual and uncreated, that is, God, and another material and created, that is, the primordial air or aether.

The Chinese do not make a sufficiently clear distinction [between the two], and sometimes seem to conflate spirit with matter, and reason with body.[164] In my opinion, this is because of the ambiguity of the word 'air' (*qi* in Chinese), which despite meaning material air, can be used metaphorically to mean anything material and corporeal (K), as well as human life (L), the Spirit (M), time (N), action and motion, etc. (O). But now let us return to the question.

NOTES

A.1 蔡虛齋《四書蒙引・卷一・大學》：「愚意天地間元無『無氣之理』，亦無『無理之氣』。但自造化言，則氣分為二，而理兼有二，實能主宰幹運之，所謂『一故神』者也。故理尊於氣，而得太極之名。是亦可先言理、後言氣耳。」「愚謂天地間無懸空之理。此處雖先言氣，后言理亦可也。」

About the beginning of the *Science of Adults*, Cai Xuzhai in volume 1 of the *Sishu mengyin* says: 'I think there is a First Being, etc.'[165] See above. Shortly before he wrote: 'I affirm that in the world exists a Reason which is non suspended in the void, and thus it can be said that Air is anterior and Reason posterior'.[166]

B.2 The dictionary *Zhengzitong* for the character *qi* has: 'As Doctor Cheng says, the inexhaustible Author of things is the vital air'.[167]

C.3 《周易正解・卷一・乾卦》：「夫此四德之流行,乃乾之化也；一元之統體,乃乾之神也。」

About the symbol 'Qian', volume 1 of the *True Explanation of the Book of Changes and Productions* states as follows: 'The quadruple power that constantly revolves is the effective Origin of active Heaven; and the substance and essence of the first Origin is the Spirit of active Heaven'.[168]

---

164 This is a very interesting concession, which seems to negate much of Noël's argument about the compatibility of Christian theology with neo-Confucianism.
165 It seems that Noël selected this quote because of the mention of *yuan* 元 that he misunderstands as a name for Origin or First Being. In fact, *yuan* has here has adverbial force equivalent to 'originally'.
166 Zhu Xi had expressed a formal priority of *li* over *qi*. This was later criticized by Xue Xuan 薛瑄 (1389–1464).
167 There is no mention of this quote in the manuscript, but ARSI has a copy of the *Zhengzitong*, which is called *Chim tsu tu* in the printed text. The original text is:「程子曰：造化不窮,蓋生氣也」. There is another mention of the *Zhengzitong* below (c.2, q.3, Y.35). For further explanation, see Chapter 2.14.
168 For this quadruple power of Heaven (元亨利貞), see above (c.2, q.1, §.1, B.2).

D.4 《字彙・化字》：「造化,天地、寒暑、晝夜,皆造化所為也…又氣化,有形化,又神化。神,天德也。化,天道也。神,理也。化,氣也。理雖不雜於氣,而實不離於氣。故化之所運,即神之所在也。」

> The dictionary *Zihui* defines the character *hua* as follows: '*Hua* means to effect or to produce. Heaven and earth, cold and hot, as well as days and nights are made by an efficient cause. One efficient cause is the air or vital breath. Another cause is the body or a perceptible and material thing. Another cause is the Spirit. The Spirit is the virtue or power of the Heaven. To make is the way of Heaven, or Heaven's mode of action. Spirit is Reason. The effective force is air. Even though Reason should not be confused with Air, in fact it cannot be separated from Air. Therefore, the Spirit is in that which the effective force produces'.[169]

E.5 蔡虛齋《四書蒙引・卷三・中庸・第十六》：「一氣孔神兮,於中夜存；虛以待之兮,無為之先；庶彙以成兮。」

> About chapter 16 of the *Book of the Unalterable Mean*, Cai Xuzhai in volume 3 of the *Sishu mengyin* cites Qu [Yuan] as follows: 'Do you not realize that the infinite, etc.'[170] See above.

E.6 The dictionary *Pinzijian* defines the character *Tian* as follows: 'The writers explain, etc.'[171] See above.

F.7 蔡虛齋《四書蒙引・卷十五・孟子・盡心上》：「太虛即太極之謂。虛者不雜於氣之名。形而下者謂之氣,則皆是寔物。惟理則虛。」

> About chapter 7 'Jinxin shang' of the *Mencius*, Cai Xuzhai in volume 15 of the *Sishu mengyin* states the following about Heaven: 'First Emptiness [*taixu*] is called *taiji*, the first ultimate of things; Emptiness is a word meaning something unmixed with air [*qi*] or anything material; what is material and inferior, or second rate, is called air. Both of them [*taiji* and *taixu*] are something real and truly existing, but only Reason is empty, that is, immaterial'.[172]

G.8 《性理標題・卷三・天文》：「程子曰：『天地以虛為德。至善者,虛也。天地從虛中來。』」

> Chapter 'Tianwen' in volume 3 of the *Summary of the Book of Nature and Reason* cites Doctor Cheng as follows: 'Emptiness is the power of Heaven and Earth; Emptiness is called the supreme goodness; Heaven and Earth are born in the middle of Emptiness'.

---

169 As pointed out by Felix Wong, Noël understands *hua* 化 as equivalent to the Aristotelian-Thomistic concept of efficient cause. See Wong, '*The Unalterable Mean*', p. 216.
170 This is a quote from the chapter 'Yuanyou' 遠遊 in *Lisao* 離騷 by the poet Qu Yuan 屈原 (340–278 BC).
171 The Chinese text of the quote is not present in the ARSI manuscript. See note 151, above, with the Chinese text.
172 Same as above (c.2, q.2, L.19). Cai Qing is influenced here by Zhang Zai's concept of *taixu*.

H.9 《性理標題・卷三・誠忠恕》：「張子曰：『太虛者, 天之實也, 萬物取足於太虛, 人亦出於太虛。太虛者, 心之實也。』」

Chapter 'Chengzhongshu' in volume 3 of the *Summary of the Book of Nature and Reason* cites Doctor Zhang as follows: 'First Emptiness is the truth of Heaven, or the true and real existence of Heaven; all things receive from First Emptiness what they need; in fact, man himself is born from First Emptiness. First Emptiness is the true reality and existence of the heart, namely the heart of Heaven'.[173]

I.10 Volume 82 of the *Da Ming huidian* states the following about the ritual to Heaven for receiving the Spirit or the Supreme Lord *Shangdi*: 'Oh, this obscure, etc.' See above and also F.7.[174]

K.11 蔡虛齋《四書蒙引・卷十四・孟子・告子上》：「朱子曰：『生之謂氣, 生之理之謂性』。愚謂生之謂氣, 無不同也；生之理之謂性, 則有不同矣。然要之人與物, 氣有不同, 性因有異。」

About chapter 5 'Gaozi shang' in the second part of the *Mencius*, Cai Xuzhai in volume 14 of the *Sishu mengyin* cites Zhu Xi as follows: 'Life is air, and the Reason of life is nature'.[175] Then he says: 'I consider that when life is called air, this [air] is of the same kind in every (living) thing, but when Reason of life is called nature, this [nature] is not of the sort kind. Generally speaking, since the air of man and of other things is somewhat different, their nature is also different'.[176]

L.12 朱熹《孟子集注・告子上》：「生者, 人之所得於天之氣也。」

About chapter 5 'Gaozi' in the second part of the *Mencius*, Zhu Xi says as folows: 'Life is the air that man receives from Heaven'.[177]

L.13 張居正《四書直解・卷三・中庸・第三十一》：「凡有血氣者, 莫不尊親。」

About chapter 31 of the *Book of the Unalterable Mean*, Zhang Juzheng says in the third volume [of the *Sishu zhijie*]: 'Among all those who have blood and air, that is, among all living men, there is no one who does not respect and love the virtue of the wise'.[178]

M.14 《孔子家語・哀公問政・第十七》：「魂氣歸於天, 此謂神。」

Chapter 17 of the *Book of the Domestic Sayings of Confucius*: 'The Air of the soul returning to Heaven is called Spirit'.

---

173 In opposition to Buddhism which considers everything as illusory, Zhang Zai holds *taixu* as real.
174 The Chinese quote of the *Da Ming huidian* and its Latin translation are not found in the ARSI manuscript. The Chinese text corresponds to *Da Ming huidian*, juan 82, on the *jiaoshe* ritual: 「於昔洪荒之初兮, 混濛。五行未運兮, 兩曜未明。其中挺立兮, 有無容聲。神皇出御兮, 始判濁清。立天立地立人兮, 群物生生」. For the *Da Ming huidian*, see Chapter 2.15.
175 Slightly different wordings in Zhu Xi's *Mengzi zhangju*:「性者, 人之所得於天之理也；生者, 人之所得於天之氣也」.
176 Quote from *Zhuzi yulei*, juan 59.
177 From Zhu Xi's *Sishu zhangju jizhu*. For a discussion of this passage, see Wang Ge's chapter.
178 Zhang Juzheng's gloss is omitted in the ARSI manuscript:「凡有血氣者, 指人類說」.

M.15 《禮記·孔子問居·第二十九》：「地載神氣。」

> Chapter 29 'Kongzi wenju' in the *Book of rites*: 'Earth receives the air of the Spirit, or the spiritual air'.

M.16 張居正《四書直解·孟子·盡心上》：「人之氣體本同, 而居養各異, 惟其處在尊貴之地, 則神氣為所移易, 而精采自覺其發揚, 惟其奉養有豐厚之資, 則形體為所移易, 而容貌自覺其充盛。」

> About chapter 7 'Jinxin shang' in the second part of the *Mencius*, Zhang Juzheng in the twenty-fifth volume [of the *Sishu zhijie*] states as follows: 'Even though the vital breath and body are of the same sort in all men, there is a difference in station and food, and this creates difference. When there is someone of high station, the vital breath of the Spirit changes itself due to the place of station, and it reveals itself in a superior way. While someone uses more delicate and abundant food, the appearance of the body changes itself, and the external appearance knows how to satisfy its entire splendour'.

N.17 See below EE.42

O.18 《易經·繫辭傳上·第五章》；朱熹《周易本義》：「陰陽迭運者, 氣也。其理則所謂道。」

> About chapter 5 of 'Zhuan shang' in the *Book of Changes and Productions*, Zhu Xi [in *Zhouyi benyi*] says: 'The alternate motion and constant succession of stillness *yin* and motion *yang* is air, or *qi*, but it is established by Reason, which is called the way or the mode of action'.

§.2. The First Living and Intelligent Being Is the Universal Cause, Produces Everything in the World in an Invisible and Incomprehensible Way, and Is Concurrent with all Things

The first living and intelligent Being is the universal cause, makes all things in the world in an invisible and incomprehensible way, and is concurrent with all things. As they say, day and night, cold and heat, wind and clouds, action and cessation, motion and stillness, birth and death are done by the producing and destroying Spirit. Heaven, earth, sun and moon, the seasons of the year, the changes of air, as well as things which can be seen and sensed, cannot be called the producing and destroying Spirit, but are only the traces and effects of the producing and destroying Spirit. Indeed, the producing and destroying Spirit is the motive force of the vital breath, which silently and invisibly acts in them. How could it be perceived with vision or hearing? Even though the producing and destroying Spirit cannot be perceived by vision and hearing, you can see it in the effects. Indeed, that which causes things to begin or exist through the conjunction of stillness (*yin*) and motion (*yang*) is the Spirit extending itself, coming or producing, *shen* in Chinese; and that which causes thing to cease through the disjunction of stillness (*yin*) and motion (*yang*) is the Spirit gathering, returning, or destroying, *gui* in Chinese. Therefore, the beginning and end of things, or the generation and corruption, are done by the producing and destroying Spirit, penetrates completely all things and exists everywhere. Though devoid of body, it makes and destroys all the corporeal substances of the world (P). Thunder, wind, water, fire, mountain, and lake cannot be called Spirits, but that by which they move and are stirred is Spirit. That which universally and indivisibly makes all things is called Spirit (Q).

The Spirit is called intelligent insofar as It is the Lord, Ruler, and Efficient Cause. In an incomprehensible way, It itself brings about the annual changes of heaven and earth through the alternating reciprocation of stillness and motion' (R). Hence they ask as follows: 'When the way of Heaven and earth, or their mode of action, is mentioned, should we understand that it simultaneously encompasses something internal and external?' It is replied as follows: 'Heaven and earth have a nature and a natural tendency; the Lord and Ruler is present in their constant operations and actions; therefore, it can be called both Spirit and efficient cause. How would it not encompass something internal and external?' It is further replied: 'The way of heaven and earth or their mode of action, also called the Being without ultimate and the first Ultimate of all things, when it is called Spirit, is something most pure, simple and perfect' (S).[179] Reason is that by which there is the constant reciprocal action of stillness (*yin*) and motion (*yang*), and the Spirit is not something distinct from Reason or something outside that Reason, insofar as Spirit is identified with it, but Spirit is the excellence of Reason. Although Reason is found in any stillness (*yin*) and motion (*yang*), it transcends stillness and motion, despite not being separated from them. Reason is neither mixed with them nor like like something attached to a fixed subject such that it could be investigated by the senses. Hence Reason clearly exists everywhere, and thus it is praised or proclaimed as Spirit (T).

Let us recall the opinion of Plato and other ancient philosophers who had affirmed the existence of a great form and soul common to the world, or God. Virgil says the following in relation to their views: 'Infused through the limbs mind moves the entire mass and mingles with the great body'.[180] Such an opinion does not have its place here. Indeed, any substantial form which is part of a composite, attached to a fixed subject, mixing with it, and enclosed within it, cannot be the cause of the part constituting the composite, nor the effect of the part, for example the body being the cause of the soul, or matter the cause of the form. Reason or Spirit is nowhere said to be the part of the other, but on the contrary it is said to be the universal

---

179 *Zhongyong* 26 states that 'perfect sincerity is unceasing … Being far-reaching and long-lasting is how it completes things' (故至誠無息[…]悠久, 所以成物). In *Zhongyong zhangju*, Zhu Xi comments that being far-reaching and long-lasting joins internal and external and speaks of these (悠久, 即悠遠, 兼內外而言之也). In his comment of *Zhongyong* 26, Cai Qing explains this double-character word of being both internal and external (天地有性有情。化工運行皆有主宰處。故曰神、曰化). See S.23 below.
180 Virgil, *Aeneid*, 6.726. Just as in c.2, q.2, Noël rejects here the idea that Chinese believed in the soul of the world. Longobardo brought such an accusation: 'The ancient Chinese held that all things come from infinite chaos, which they imagined to be the first material principle and prime matter. They were persuaded themselves that this [first principle] is one and the same with the parts of the world and that there is nothing beyond it or outside it. Therefore, in their cosmological imaginations they fused the whole host of gods and all idolatry'. Longobardo, *A Brief Response on the Controversies*, p. 155 (prelude 13, n. 1).

substance of the whole First Principle, is neither mixed with any visible part nor enclosed in anything, is not attached to any fixed subject, but transcends all things. All visible things of the world are made by it or are its effects. Therefore, all visible things of the world are not the parts of one single composite. Reason is not the form or soul of the world, but the true, intelligent, and infinite substance (*suppositum*), as well as the intelligent and incomprehensible Spirit, that is, an incomprehensible intelligence. All this is enough to show that the Chinese recognize an invisible, living, and intelligent First Being in the world as the universal cause producing and destroying all things, and realizing the generations and corruptions of all things with the help of all the secondary causes. As I say, the Chinese recognize that there is an invisible Spirit of heaven and earth, independent from all matter. But let us see now whether the Spirit is one.[181]

NOTES

P.19 蔡虛齋《四書蒙引·卷三·中庸·第十六》：「甚矣, 鬼神之不測也！且如天地間, 忽然光亮亮的而為日, 又忽然黑窅窅的而為夜, 忽然凍膚裂指而為寒, 又忽然流金爍石而為暑。風雲雨露之屬忽然而至也, 莫知其從何而來；忽然而止也又, 莫知從何而去。人物忽然而動, 又忽然而止；忽然而生, 又忽然而死。凡此皆鬼神之為也。氣機默運自往自來, 自屈自伸, 人孰得其形迹而執之哉？」

> About chapter 16 of the *Book of the Unalterable Mean*, Cai Xuzhai states the following in volume 3 of the *Sishu mengyin*: 'Oh, how inconceivable and incomprehensible is the producing and destroying Spirit! For example, day and night, cold and heat, wind and clouds, rains and dew suddenly come and cease without knowing how. Also, men and other things suddenly act and stop, suddenly are born and die: all these things are made by the producing and destroying Spirit.[182] Can anyone possibly physically represent or apprehend the motive force of the vital breath which acts constantly in a silent way, going and coming, gathering and extending itself?'[183]

「如今天地之覆載, 日月之照臨, 四時之代序, 風雲雨露之變化, 皆可見可聞者也, 故指此以為鬼神則不可。此等乃鬼神之迹也。鬼神則是氣機之往來, 默

---

181 In the *Proemium* of the Third Treatise, Noël reformulates his interpretation of *Tian* as the universal efficient cause: 'Causa efficiens universalis est Caelum, de quo in eodem primo Tractatu; id est, vel Caelum immateriale seu Deus, si agatur de Causa prima Universali; vel potius universalis Virtus supremi Domini *Xam Ti*, (nempe Divina potentia) in caelo ac terra residens, quae per alternantem motus *Yam*, & quietis *Yn* vicissitudinem, ac perquinque elementariorum principiorum aquae, ignis, ligni, metalli, terrae (haec quinque Sinae vocant elementaria principia, eaque penè omnibus rebus etiam moralibus per tropum accommodant) producit omnes mundi res corporeas' (pp. 1–2).
182 *Zhongyong* 16 does not discuss the beginning and end of things or the role of *yin* and *yang*. Cai Qing follows here Zhu Xi who in the *Zhongyong zhangju* understands *guishen* in terms of *yin* and *yang*: 'Ghosts and spirits have neither form nor sound. Nevertheless, the ends and the beginnings of things are nothing other than what are created by the merging and dispersing of *yin* and *yang*'. Ian Johnston and Wang Ping (trans.), *Daxue & Zhongyong* (Hong Kong: Chinese University of Hong Kong, 2012), p. 437.
183 The concept of *qiji* 氣機 (cause of *qi*) developed by Cai Qing was introduced above through the *Zhouyi zhengjie* while discussing the power of *Tian* (c.2, q.1, §.2).

運於其中者,誰得而見之?誰得而聞之? 然鬼神雖不可見聞,但就物上觀之,則物之所以始者,陰陽之合也,神之伸也;物之所以終者,陰陽之散也,鬼之歸也。是物之始終,一皆鬼神之所為。鬼神固無物不體,無所不在矣。道之不可須臾離也,於此可見。」

Shortly after is added: 'The heaven covering all things, the earth sustaining all things, the sun and the moon illuminating all things, the four seasons coming one after the other, the changes of winds, clouds, rains and dew, all these things which can be perceived by the vision and hearing cannot be called the producing and destroying Spirit, but are only the traces and effects of the producing and destroying Spirit.[184] Indeed, the producing and destroying Spirit is the motive force of the vital breath, which in its coming and going acts in them in a silent and secret way. How could this be perceived with vision or hearing? Even though the producing and destroying Spirit cannot be perceived with vision and hearing, you can see it in the things themselves. Indeed, that which causes things to begin through the conjunction of stillness (*yin*) and motion (*yang*) is the Spirit extending itself. That which causes things to cease is the Spirit gathering itself or returning. Therefore, the beginning and end of things are caused by the producing and destroying Spirit in extending or gathering itself. This producing and destroying Spirit penetrates completely all things, and it occupies every place. Clearly, the guiding reason of the way cannot leave us a single moment'.

「以一歲言春夏為陽,秋冬為陰,凡一歲之始終,莫非鬼神之所為也。以一日言之,晝為陽,夜為陰,凡一日之始終,無非鬼神之所為也。又如人物之始生,草木之方榮,陰陽氣合之所為也。人物之死,草木之枯,陰陽氣散之所為也。又無非鬼神所為也。」

After a few words, he continues: 'If you consider a single year alone, spring and summer (from the winter solstice to summer) are called motion (*yang*), and autumn and winter (from the summer solstice to winter) are called stillness (*yin*); the entire course of the year, its beginning and end, are done by the producing and destroying Spirit or the generating and corrupting Spirit. If you consider a single day alone, the day is called motion (*yang*), and the night stillness (*yin*), and the full course of a day, its beginning and end, are done by the producing and destroying Spirit. Also, when man and other things are born, when the plants sprout, this is done by the conjunction of stillness (*yin*) and motion (*yang*) with vital breath. When they die and dry up, this is done by the disjunction of stillness (*yin*) and motion (*yang*) from vital breath. All those things are done by the producing and destroying Spirit'.[185]

---

184 *Zhongyong* 16 does not discuss the notion of trace, and Zhu Xi borrowed it from Chengzi in his commentary: '*Guishen* are the effective agents of Heaven and Earth and the traces of creation and transformation' (鬼神,天地之用,而造化之跡也). See below (c.2, q.4, K.10 and L.11).

185 Cai Qing insists on the actions of the *guishen* (鬼神之所為) which cannot therefore be understood as only passive mechanisms in nature. Similarly to Cai Qing, Shao Yong had insisted on the pervasive actions of the *guishen* in the 'Guanwu waipian' 觀物外篇, *Huangji jingshi shu* 皇極經世書:「若人之

「可見鬼神之無物不體。」「鬼神雖無形也，而有以形天下之形，又併其形而反之。雖無聲也，而有以聲天下之聲，又併其聲而收之。故曰：『物之終始，莫非陰陽合散之所為也。』」

A little further down: 'You see that all things are penetrated completely by the producing and destroying Spirit'. Finally, he concludes: 'Though devoid of body, the producing and destroying Spirit makes and destroys all the corporeal substances of the world'.[186]

P.20 About chapter 16 of *Zhongyong*, Zhu Xi in the second volume of the *Sishu huowen*, or *Questions on the Four Books* states as follows: 'There is no place in which the producing and destroying Spirit does not exist between heaven and earth, or in the whole world. It may not move and be almost at rest, and yet it communicates itself through motion. It may be devoid of shape and sound and be imperceptible to senses, and yet it is said to be wondrously bright and cannot be deceived'.[187]

Q.21 《周易正解・卷二十二・說卦・第六》：「朱子曰：『雷風水火山澤，自不可喚做神。其所以動、所以撓者，是神也。』」「鄭康成云：『共成萬物，[188] 不可得而分，故合而謂之神。』」

About chapter 6 of 'Shuogua', volume 22 of the *True Explanation of the Book of Changes and Productions* cites Zhu Xi as follows: 'Thunder, wind, water, fire, mountain and lake cannot be called Spirits, but that by which they are moved and stirred is Spirit'.[189] It quotes also Zheng Kangcheng as follows: 'It universally and indivisibly makes all things, and thus taken together can be called Spirit'.[190]

R.22 《易經・說卦・第一》：「昔者，聖人之作《易》也。幽贊於神明而生蓍。」《周易正解・卷二十二・說卦・第一》：「神明即指天地之化育，不曰化育而曰神明者，自其主宰運用者言，蓋一闔一闢，而運用莫測者，神明也。」

Chapter 1 of 'Shuogua' states: 'In the past the wise man helped the intelligent Spirit by devising the teaching of the *Book of Changes and Productions* (by pointing out with precepts and skills the secondary causes in the production of things) and

---

耳目鼻口手足，草木之枝葉花實顏色，皆鬼神之所為也。福善禍淫，主之者誰耶？聰明正直，有之者誰耶？不疾而速，不行而至，任之者誰耶？皆鬼神之情狀也。」．

186 In fact, the last sentence is not from Cai Qing, as Noël believes, but a quote from *Zhongyong zhangju* 16. With the term of *suowei* (所為), Zhu Xi seems to attribute to *guishen* an active role in the merging and dispersing of *yin* and *yang*.
187 The Chinese text is not present in the ARSI manuscript. I could not find a match in the *Zhongyong huowen*, but Noël is possibly translating from *Da Cheng yunfu* 答程允夫 (Questions and answers with Cheng Xun), where Zhu Xi quotes the Northern Song scholar Lü Dazhong 呂大忠：「鬼神周流天地之間，無所不在，雖寂然不動，然因感而必通，雖無形無聲而有所謂昭，昭不可欺者。」Noël selects this passage probably because it contains something similar to the action of a divine spirit interacting with human beings.
188 In the manuscript, the character *wu* 物 is missing.
189 The first part of the sentence is from a disciple of Zhu Xi, and the second part constitutes the words of Zhu Xi himself. see 'Shuogua', in *Zhuzi yulei, juan* 77.
190 Zheng Xuan 鄭玄, *zi* Kangcheng 康成 (127–200). This quote is also present in *juan* 12 of the *Yijing mengyin* by Cai Qing.

the herb *shi* was adapted for his use.' Volume 22 of the *True Explanation of the Book of Changes and Productions* comments as follows: 'That two-character word "Intelligent Spirit" indicates the constant productions and nourishments of heaven and earth. It is called "Intelligent Spirit" and not "productions and nourishments" because It is the Lord, Ruler and the efficient cause, for It itself is, etc.' See above.

S.23 蔡虛齋《四書蒙引・卷三・中庸・第二十六》：「天地之道亦兼內外言耶？曰：天地有性有情，化工運行皆有主宰處，故曰神、曰化。安得為不兼內外？」

About chapter 26 of the *Book of Unalterable Mean*, Cai Xuzhai in volume 3 of the *Sishu mengyin* states as follows: 'When it is called the way of heaven and earth, etc.' See above.

S.24 《周易正解・卷二十・繫辭傳上・第四》：「天地之道,見於氣化之聚散者,皆鬼神之所在,而其所以為情狀者,則理也。」

About chapter 4 of 'Zhuan shang', volume 20 of the *True Explanation of the Book of Changes and Productions* states as follows: 'The way of heaven and earth or their method of action insofar as it appears clearly in generations and corruptions is that in which the Spirit exists. That by which it is constituted in its essential nature is Reason'.

S.25 《周易正解・卷九・恆卦》：「天地之道,無極太極,一之而為神者,固皆純粹之精。」

About the symbol 'Hen', volume 9 of the *True Explanation of the Book of Changes and Productions*, states as follows: 'The way of heaven and earth or their mode of action, also called the Being without Ultimate, etc.' See above.

T.26 《周易正解・卷二十・繫辭傳上・第五》：「神即道之妙；非道之外,別有所謂神也。」「言道寓於陰陽之中,而超乎陰陽之外,不離於陰陽,而亦不雜於陰陽,非若物之膠於一定,而可以形求者也。」「林次崖曰：『此是就一陰一陽之道上見道之無所不在,而贊其為神。』」

About chapter 5 of 'Zhuan shang', volume 20 of the *True Explanation of the Book of Changes and Productions* states as follows: 'The Spirit is the excellence of the way or mode of action, and outside of this mode of action, there is nothing else which is called Spirit'. Little further the writer Lin Ciya says: 'These things display the way of action by which the reciprocal action of stillness *yin* and motion *yang* is constituted; clearly, the way of action or Reason exists everywhere, and thus it is proclaimed as Spirit'.[191]

---

191 Lin Xiyuan 林希元 (1481–1565), *hao* Ciya 次崖.

§.3. The First Living and Intelligent Being according to their Books is One, and the Spirit of Heaven and Earth Is One[192]

When it is said that the three first dynasties of China served the intelligent Spirit of heaven and earth always using divination to avoid despising the service of the Lord of Heaven or *Shangdi* with their own particular choice (c.1, q.2, §.1, O.15), *Shangdi* or the Lord of Heaven is clearly the Spirit of heaven and earth. It is also said that, when the rituals conducted in the ancestral hall honouring deceased kings are well conducted and observed, this may suffice for the deceased kings to be united with the intelligent Spirit of heaven and earth (V). Only the founder of the imperial dynasty or an eminent ancestor was united with *Shangdi*, the Lord of Heaven, as it can be seen elsewhere; thus, the Lord of Heaven, or *Shangdi*, is the intelligent Spirit of Heaven. Truly, *Shangdi* is one; that is to say, the Spirit of Heaven is the one Lord (X). Heaven and earth are the one producing and destroying Spirit (Z). Or it could be rather said: there is one producing and destroying Spirit on heaven and earth. Since for the Chinese the Spirit cannot be seen, it is something incorporeal and invisible, but heaven and earth can be perceived with sight and are therefore something corporeal and visible. It must be said therefore that 'heaven and earth' is not truly heaven and earth, unless if you consider heaven and earth figuratively as a metonymy, that is the container for the contained. By saying heaven and earth is Reason, the Chinese mean to say that the Spirit is Reason (W).

This Reason, as I have already said, is the one cause, which is Spirit, or rather the first Ultimate of things. Hence the Chinese clearly recognized [this Reason] as the one universal Cause in the whole world or the one Spirit of heaven and earth, namely *Shangdi*. When they say, 'the vital breath and reason of man is the vital breath and reason of heaven and earth', understand this in terms of participation, such that man only unites with the Spirit of heaven and earth in the same generic reason of life and intelligence. Evidently, the Spirit of heaven and earth has reason or intelligence and a vital breath or infinite life through its essence whereas man has these attributes in finite terms through participation. Finally, heaven, earth, and all things are governed by one Lord alone (Y), as it will now be made clearer.

NOTES

V.27 《禮記集說・二十七・哀公問》：「孔子遂有言曰：『內以治宗廟之禮, 足以配天地之神明。出以治直言之禮, 足以立上下之敬。』」

> About chapter 27 'Aigong wen' of the *Book of Rites*, volume 9 of the commentary [*Liji jishuo*] states the following: 'Confucius told the petty king Aigong: "Concerning internal things, if the rituals in the ancestral hall are well conducted and observed, then this will be surely enough for the [deceased ancestors] to unite with the intelligent Spirit of heaven and earth. Concerning external things,

---

192 This question should be placed within the context of the Rite Controversy. The Dominicans and Franciscans consider that the Chinese are polytheist because they worship ancestors.

if the rituals of the royal court are well conducted and observed, this will be surely enough to cement the respect between superiors and inferiors".

X.28 《易經大全・卷二十》：「享于上帝, 使人知天無二主。」

Chapter 20 of the *Great Commentary of the Yijing* states as follows: 'The ancient emperors sacrificed to *Di*, the Lord of Heaven, so that people know that Heaven has not two masters'.

X.29 《日講易經・卷十三・渙卦》：「故敬天尊祖, 自展仁孝之思, 而天下之心, 已知天神無二主, 不敢以下而犯上；知人物無二本, 不敢背死而忘生。」

About the symbol 'Huan', volume 13 of the *Daily Explanation of the Book of Changes and Productions*, published under Emperor Kangxi, states as follows: 'To worship Heaven and to revere deceased ancestors is to fulfill the true spirit of a pious and filial observance, and because all the habitants of the empire know that the Spirit of Heaven is the only Lord, inferiors do not dare to offend a superior; because they know that all men and other things have one origin, they do not dare to abandon the rites towards the dead and to forget their ancestors'.

X.30 《文獻通考・卷六十八・郊社考一》：「楊氏曰：『愚按程、朱二先生之言, 則天帝一也。』」

The sixty-eighth volume of the *Wenxian tongkao* cites Doctor Yang as follows: 'According to Cheng and Zhu, the words Heaven [*Tian*] and the Lord of Heaven (*Di*) have the same meaning'.[193] See the remaining part of this quote in c.3, q.1, E.6.

X.31 《文獻通考・卷七十四・郊社考七》：「王肅曰：『天惟一神。』」

Volume 74 of the *Wenxian tongkao* cites Doctor Wang Su: 'Heaven is the one Spirit'.

X.32 《文獻通考・卷七十一・郊社考四》：「對越天地, 神無二主。」

Volume 71 of the *Wenxian tongkao* states as follows: 'When the ritual is performed before Heaven and Earth, that is, a sacrifice is made to heaven and earth, the Spirit is the one Lord'.

Z.33 蔡虛齋《四書蒙引・卷四・中庸・第二十九》：「三重合乎理, 則合乎天地, 天地惟理而已矣。合乎理, 則合乎鬼神, 鬼神亦惟此理而已矣。合乎理, 則合乎三王, 三王亦惟理而已矣。」「人得天地之氣, 則具有天地之理。吾之理, 即天地之理也, 天地一鬼神也。」「人同此心, 心同此理, 萬古一理, 千聖一心。所謂『百世之上有聖人出焉, 此心同也, 此理同也；百世之下有聖人出焉, 此心同也, 此理同也。』」

About chapter 29 of the *Book of the Unalterable Mean*, in volume 4 of the *Sishu mengyin* Cai Xuzhai writes as follows: 'If the three things (rites, offices and words)[194] required by the emperor agree with Reason, then they immediately

---

193 All the quotes from the *Wenxian tongkao* are absent from the ARSI manuscript and were added later. About the *Wenxian tongkao*, see Chapter 2.14.
194 *Zhongyong* 29 discusses three important things but without explaining in what they consist. In his

agree with heaven and earth, since indeed heaven and earth is only Reason. If they agree with Reason, they agree immediately with the producing and destroying Spirit, since the producing and destroying Spirit is only Reason. Also, if they agree with Reason, they agree at the same time with the first emperors of the three dynasties since those emperors were only Reason'.[195] Shortly afterwards: 'Since man has the vital breath of heaven and earth, he also has in himself the Reason of heaven and earth. Indeed, the Reason in the vital breath is the Reason of heaven and earth. However, Heaven and earth are only a single producing and destroying Spirit'.[196] Further down is added: 'The soul or the heart of all men is the same, and the reason of the soul is the same (namely, in species and in equal individual perfection); from all eternity it is only the same unique Reason (obviously in generic or specific unity), from all eternity it is the only one soul of all perfect men (namely, in specific unity). Therefore, it is said, "This will be the same soul and the same Reason for all perfect men to come. Similarly, it was the same soul and the same Reason for all in the past"'.[197]

W.34 蔡虛齋《四書蒙引·卷四·中庸·第二十九》:「朱熹:『天地者, 道也』。猶云: 天者, 理而已矣。」

About chapter 29 of the *Book of the Unalterable Mean*, Zhu Xi says the following: 'Heaven and earth is the way or mode of action'. Doctor Cai Xuzhai explains these words in volume 4 of the *Sishu mengyin*: 'When it is said that heaven and earth is the way, this is the same as saying that Heaven is Reason'.[198]

Y.35 The dictionary *Zhengzitong* for the character *zhu*, which is written as 丶: 'When this character is added to the character *wang* 王 (by doing this is formed the composite character *zhu* 主, which means Lord), then heaven, earth and all things are ruled by the One alone'.[199]

Zhongyong zhangju, Zhu Xi adopts the interpretation of Lü Dazhong: 'The three important things are to determine the rituals, to establish standards and to verify the words' (三重, 謂議禮、制度、考文). Cai Qing explains the three important things in more detail, but Noël gives in bracket Lü Dazhong's short explanation.

195 Zhu Xi comments *Zhongyong* 29 as follows: 'To know Heaven and to know man is to know their Reasons' (知天知人, 知其理也), and Cai Qing follows this interpretation based on *li*.
196 In Zhu Xi's philosophical system, all individual *li* can be said to be identical at the level of Heaven-Earth. Cai Qing deduces that all *guishen* are also identical at that level. Noël notices in Cai Qing this emphasis on the unity of both the *li* and *guishen*.
197 Cai Qing's insistence on the unity of the heart-mind and of the *li* in all men is used as proof by Noël that the Chinese do not believe in a dyad but in a monad. The last sentence comes from Lu Jiuyuan 陸九淵.
198 Cai Qing subsumes the duality of the Way (*Tian-Di*) under the monad *Tian* or *li*.
199 This citation is not present on the manuscript. The original text is: 《正字通·丶字》:「從、配以王, 天地萬物統於一也。」Noticeable here is a very rare use of Chinese characters in a book printed in early modern Europe. A few Chinese characters were inserted in the *China illustrata* (Amsterdam, 1667) by Athanasius Kircher and in the portrait of Confucius in the *Confucius Sinarum philosophus* (p. cxvi). Noël worked with the printer Kamenicky in Prague to produce here the fonts for the two characters 王 and 主. Noël also arranged the printing of a few other Chinese characters in his *Historica notitia* (1711). For discussion, see Wang Ge's chapter in this book.

§.4. The Universal Spirit of Heaven and Earth Has a General Law for all Things and a Particular Law for Man

There is a general Law which constantly runs its course in a deep and mysterious darkness without interruption and end. It is called the quadruple power of Heaven, giving to everything its beginning, increase, direction, perfection, or the attainment of the end (AA). See above c.2, q.1, §.1 and 2, and below AA.36 and AA.37. With the particular Law, [the Spirit of Heaven and Earth] infuses in the human body a soul or intelligent Spirit that is capable of all cognition and in the soul reason, which is the faculty obeying the innate five virtues of piety, justice, honesty, intelligence, and truth. These virtues should be understood broadly and incipiently as the implanted seeds of virtues and not as habitus.[200] Therefore, whoever knows this reason also knows the origin, that is Heaven, from which it originates. A wise person recollects diligently his soul, carefully obeys reason, and faithfully serves Heaven (BB).

NOTES

AA.36 《性理標題・卷三・心》：「『維天之命, 於穆不已。』所以為生物之主者, 天之心也。人受天命而生, 因全得夫天之所以生我者, 以為一身之主, 渾然在中, 常昭昭而不昧, 生生而不可已, 是乃所謂人之心；其體即所謂『元亨利貞』之道, 具而為『仁義禮智』之性。」

> The chapter 'Xin' in volume 3 of the *Summary of the Book of Nature and Reason* states as follows: "'Oh the Law of Heaven! How secretly and mysteriously it runs its course without interruption or end!' This Law by which Heaven is the Lord producing things is the heart of Heaven. Man receives at birth the Law of Heaven, and because Heaven produces me completely, I consider Heaven as Lord of my whole body, being completely in me, constantly shining in me without darkness, constantly acting without interruption, and therefore Heaven can be called the mind or soul of man. Its substance is called the way of the great or first, communicating, guiding, and perfecting principle. In terms of Its function, It is the congenital seed of piety, justice, honesty, and intelligence'.[201]

AA.37 《日講四書解義・卷五・論語・公冶長》：「子貢曰：『夫子之文章, 可得而聞也；夫子之言性與天道, 不可得而聞也。』」「至若仁義禮智稟初生之謂性, 元亨利貞運於『於穆』之謂天道。性、天之理亦有流行發見之端, 然淵微精奧, 夫子非其人不傳。」

> Chapter 5 of the *Book of Sentences* [*Lunyu* 5.13] states: 'Any disciple can notice the unique modesty, gravity, and eloquence of our master Confucius, but he is almost not allowed to hear him discuss nature or the way of Heaven'. Volume 5 of the *Daily Explanation of the Four Books* comments on this passage as follows: 'That which

---

200 Noël is trying to distinguish these incipient virtues from the Aristotelian concept of virtue as habit: i.e. people have the potential for these virtues, but they need to be actualized through habit (Aristotelian concept of virtue).

201 This quote is found in *juan* 11 of the *Beixi daquanji* 北溪大全集 (Complete works of Beixi) by the Song dynasty scholar Chen Chun 陳淳.

pertains to the piety, justice, honesty and intelligence received inchoately at birth is called Nature; that which pertains to the first or great, communicating, guiding and perfecting principle, which acts and constantly turns amid a secret and mysterious darkness, is called the way of Heaven or Heaven's mode of action. The reason of Nature and the reason of Heaven both have their own visible course through which they are revealed, but Confucius was not used to explain to anyone its deep subtlety and most perfect mystery, unless his disciples were capable'.[202]

AA.38   蔡虛齋《四書蒙引・卷五・論語・第九》:「命在天最玄妙, 故曰理, 曰微。」「命即天道之流行而賦於物者。」

About chapter 9 of the *Book of sentences* [*Lunyu* 9.1], Cai Xuzhai in volume 5 of the *Sishu mengyin* writes as follows: 'The Law of Heaven is obviously in Heaven, being something most outstanding and excellent, and therefore is called Reason and the most subtle and simple perfection'. Shortly after is added: 'The Law of Heaven means Way of Heaven, or the Reason constantly active and grafted in things'. See above c.2, q.2, §.1 and 2.

BB.39   《日講四書解義・卷二十五・孟子・盡心上》:「人之主宰乎一身者, 惟心。心乃人之神明, 具眾理而應萬事, 其體量至為宏大, 人能充滿其量, 使全體大用無一毫之虧欠, 則心由於知性。性者, 心所具之理。即事窮究而洞然無疑, 則理明[203]而心之體全矣。夫此理在性為健順五常之德, 在天即為於穆流行之本, 非有二也。能知性, 則性所從出之原, 亦融會貫通矣, 知天何事外求哉?」

About chapter 7 'Jinxin shang' ('To know nature is to know Heaven'),[204] volume 25 of the *Daily Explanation of the Four Books* states as follows: 'The master and guide of the human body is the mind or the soul. The mind is the intelligent Spirit of man which encompasses the Reason of anything, that is to say, it can know the Reason of everything and direct and manage all actions.[205] Its intellectual ability or faculty is the greatest. Whoever fulfills it completely knows what nature is.

---

202   Translating *Lunyu* 5.13, Longobardo understood wrongly that Confucius never spoke about human nature and the natural condition of Heaven 'except towards the end of his life', suggesting that Confucius had a secret and atheistic message that he revealed only to a few disciples just before dying. See Longobardo, *A Brief Response on the Controversies*, p. 117 (prelude 3, n. 6). Instead, Noël follows the common understanding of the Confucian tradition, emphasizing that Confucius spoke only about those things to people who were able to understand.

203   In the manuscript there is the character *ze* 則 instead of *ming* 明.

204   James Legge translates the first sentence of the chapter 'Jinxin shang' as follows: 'He who has exhausted all his mental constitution knows his nature. Knowing his nature, he knows Heaven. To preserve one's mental constitution, and nourish one's nature, is the way to serve Heaven. When neither a premature death nor long life causes a man any double-mindedness, but he waits in the cultivation of his personal character for whatever issue; this is the way in which he establishes his Heaven-ordained being' (盡其心者, 知其性也。知其性, 則知天矣。存其心, 養其性, 所以事天也。殀壽不貳, 修身以俟之, 所以立命也) James Legge, *The Works of Mencius* (Hong Kong: At the author's; London: Trübner & Co., 1861), pp. 324–25. The comment which follows is the longest of the First Treatise.

205   The beginning of this quote was translated in French by Joseph de Prémare; 'Essai sur la philosophie des Chinois Canton, 10 Septembre 1728', *Annales de la Philosophie Chrétienne*, 17 (1861), 375–404 (p. 380).

Nature is the Reason contained in the soul. Whoever discerns things correctly and knows without doubt has a bright reason in him, and the ability of his mind is complete. Since reason is in nature, this faculty firmly obeys the five inborn or inchoate virtues of piety, justice, honesty, intelligence, and truth as I said. Insofar as reason is in Heaven, it is the first cause, revolving and constantly active in a secret and mysterious way, without any duality. Whoever knows what nature is also knows clearly where it comes from. What else to be searched for to know Heaven?'

「君子達天之學如此。心固當盡, 而又貴有以存之。心之出入無時, 必常操而不舍。一動一靜, 不使奪於外誘之私, 性固當知, 而又貴有以養之。性之純然不雜, 宜常順而不悖。勿忘勿助, 不使違乎自然之則。心與性, 皆天之付於我者。存養如此, 則天理常存, 即所以奉承乎天而無違也。君子事天之學如此。

'The wise person who penetrates well the science of Heaven certainly must fulfil all the parts of his soul. This consists especially in the recollection of the soul, in restricting its mobility, and not allowing that the smallest motion and stillness of the soul be diverted by evil desires for external things. Furthermore, he must know nature. This primarily consists in feeding its needs, in faithfully fulfilling its purest tendency, without never withdrawing from its natural law by failing to follow seriously and swiftly its lead. Soul and nature are infused into us by Heaven; whoever gathers and feeds them always preserves Heavenly Reason and in this way faithfully serves Heaven. Therefore, the science whim the wise man learns is for serving Heaven'.[206]

「然使知天事天, 猶不能不惑於殀壽之故, 而修身之學怠焉, 非仁智之盡也。惟盡心知性, 至於洞徹之極, 而殀壽不以貳其心, 存心養性以修其身, 而俟夫命之自至, 則天所付於我之理毫無虧欠, 而命自我立矣, 豈非知天事天之全功乎?人主繼天立極, 時與天命相陟降, 惟當格物致知以窮理。存心養性以修身, 與天地合其德, 又何天之不可知, 何天之不可事, 何命之不可立哉?故機祥禍福, 數也, 而知天不在乎是; 郊壇享祀, 文也, 而事天不盡乎是; 禱祀鬼神, 妄也, 而立命不繫乎是。夫亦求之於身心性命之實, 天人合一之理而已矣。」

'Finally, one may know and serve Heaven, but if he does not pay attention to the reasons for a short and long life, is negligent in his efforts to regulate his behaviour, and does not fulfill all the dimensions of piety and intelligence, he would not perfectly know nature to the point that his mind would be no longer be blinded by a short or long life. However, if someone gathers his soul through well-ordered behaviour and obeys Reason to the point that he waits for the disposition coming from Heaven, he alone preserves the complete Reason received from Heaven and arranges his whole life according to Heaven's one disposition. Is there not an absolute need in knowing and serving Heaven? The ruler who is entrusted with the mandate of Heaven and adheres completely to the Law of Heaven wishes to pass down by words and deeds the norm of supreme perfection. He strives with the greatest diligence in penetrating the nature of things, recollects his soul and follows

---

206 This sentence is quoted in the *Gujin*, n. 19 (p. 161).

nature to regulate his manners, and he raises the greatness of his nature to the level of heaven and earth. Could he not know Heaven then? Could he not serve Him? Could he not adjust his life to Providence? Since indeed prosperity and disaster change with time, the knowledge of Heaven does not consist in those.[207] Since the sacrifice made to Heaven is an external worship, this does not satisfy the entire service of Heaven. To pray to the producing and destroying Spirit (that is for some temporal goods) is something vain, and the foundation of one's life according to the providence of Heaven does not depend on this. It is enough to search for the truth of morality, mind, nature, and Heavenly law by seeking a true union of man with heaven'.[208]

「凡人之生, 吉凶禍福, 遭遇不同, 莫非天之所主宰, 是謂氣數之命。然其中有正命焉, 為善而獲福, 固謂之正。即為善而或蒙禍, 亦不可不謂之正。」

A little further down: 'There is nothing favourable or unfavourable to man in this life which is not directed by Heaven as Lord and Ruler, and this is called the Law of the temporal cycle.[209] But a just and correct mandate is contained in this Law. The mandate is called just and correct because it bestows good things on those acting well and correctly. Those acting badly may be punished with evil things, but the mandate cannot be said on this account unjust and evil'.[210]

---

207 Literally: 'To know heaven does not consist in making divination of good and bad fortunes' (故機祥禍福數也, 而知天不在乎是). Commenting on the chapter 'Jinxin xia' of the *Mencius*, Zhu Xi distinguishes between two fates given by *Tian* (*ming* 命): 'a fate determined by *qi*' (氣數之命) and 'a moral fate' (義理之命): '命, 謂天之付與, 所謂天令之謂命也。然命有兩般: 有以氣言者, 厚薄清濁之稟不同也, 如所謂"道之將行、將廢, 命也", "得之不得曰有命", 是也; 有以理言者, 天道流行, 付而在人, 則為仁義禮智之性, 如所謂"五十而知天命", "天命之謂性", 是也。二者皆天所付與, 故皆曰命'. Zhu Xi, *Zhuzi yulei*, *juan* 61. Though neo-Confucianism recognizes a determination of *qi*, it still places the moral fate on the highest level.
208 Noël translates here the important Mencian idea of the union between Heaven and man (*Tianren heyi* 天人合一). This idea was mentioned in the quotes about the attributes of dominion, knowledge and will of *Tian* (c.2, q.1, §.3, D.3; c.2, q.1, §.4, G.6; c.2, q.1, §.7, F) and also discussed about the distinction between Heaven and man (c.2, q.2).
209 The concept of *qishu* 氣數 had appeared once above (c.2, q.1, §.4, D) and it is developed further below (fifth point).
210 This commentary corresponds to the beginning of the second sentence of the chapter 'Jinxin shang' which James Legge translates as follows: 'There is an appointment for everything. A man should receive submissively what may be correctly ascribed thereto' (莫非命也, 順受其正). The notion of law of temporal cycle (*qishuzhiming* 氣數之命) is not mentioned in the corresponding passage of Zhu Xi's *Mengzi zhangju*, neither the idea that evil people may be punished. Mencius unified the ancient belief in serving *Tian* (*shitian*) with the inner mind. Only with the neo-Confucians in the Song dynasty, Mencius obtained an elevated status and they developed his interpretation of a moral inner law. This long quote from the *Rijiang* just shows that Noël did pay attention to the Mencian idea of a moral union between *Tian* and man, as developed by Zhu Xi and Cai Qing.

§.5. The First Living and Intelligent Being with a Providence Watching all Affairs

Moreover, the providence watching all things is considered under different aspects. First, it can be understood as the way of Heaven or Heaven's mode of action, which is secretly, mysteriously and incessantly active, and which contains the law and commandment of the Lord of Heaven (CC), almost as Boethius defines providence in Book 4 of his *Consolation of Philosophy*: 'Providence is divine Reason itself, seated in the Supreme Ruler, and disposes all things'.[211] Second, it can be understood as law of the astronomical temporal cycle through which Heaven as Lord and Ruler directs all things favourable and unfavourable, and which contains a correct and just commandment [*zhengming*] whereby those acting correctly accumulate good things (DD). Third, it can be understood as Heaven's mode of action and temporal cycle, either at the same time or as a combination of both (EE). Fourth, as Heaven's disposition which is received in the birth of each thing and cannot be changed with the result that man should not throw all his affairs against this disposition of Heaven and neglect them, or omit what should be done out of propriety and justice (FF). The shortness or longevity of life is also called the Law and providence of Heaven (GG). A wise person must know the infused Reason or the natures of things in order to know Heaven; he must recollect himself and obey Reason to serve Heaven; he must strive for moral perfection to welcome the providence of Heaven. The knowledge of Heaven does not consist in the favourable or adverse vicissitudes of time; the complete service of Heaven does not consist in the external worship of sacrifice, and the arrangement of life according to providence does not depend on praying to the Spirit (HH).[212] About the Law of Heaven and Providence, those things are clear enough, and nothing needs to be added.

NOTES

CC.40 《日講四書解義‧‧卷三‧中庸‧第二十六》：「『維天之命, 於穆不已』, 言天道運行, 其帝命所存之處, 無聲無臭, 幽深邃遠, 而無一時之止息。」

About chapter 26 of the *Book of the Unalterable Mean*, the *Daily Explanation of the Four Books* states as follows: 'The *Book of Odes* says: "Oh Law of Heaven! How secretly and mysteriously it runs its course without interruption nor end!"'[213] This means that mandate of the Lord and Ruler of Heaven resides in the way of Heaven,

---

211 Boethius, *De consolatione philosophiae*, 4.6: 'Providentia est ipsa divina ratio in summo omnium principe constituta, quae cuncta disponit'. This passage is quoted in Aquinas, *Summa theologiae*, I^a, q.22, a.1. This first meaning of *ming* is transcendental.
212 Noël suggests that the Chinese do not engage in superstitious practices attempting to manipulate human fate, but aim at a higher moral fate. In the context of the Rites Controversy, this was indeed an important point to make.
213 From chapter 'Wenwang' 文王 in 'Daya' 大雅 of the *Shijing*. This passage is quoted above (c.1, q.2, A.1; c.2, q.2, R.28 and c.2, q.3, AA.36), as well as below (c.2, q.6, D.4).

which constantly revolves and acts, cannot be perceived by voice or smell, is hidden, deep, and mysterious, and never stops its course'.²¹⁴

DD.41 See the end of BB.39.²¹⁵

EE.42 《日講四書解義·卷七·論語·子罕》:「『子罕言利與命與仁。』命兼理氣, 其故甚微而難測。」

About chapter 9 of the *Book of Sentences* [*Lunyu* 9.1] ('Confucius very rarely talked about profit, about providence, about piety or rectitude of mind'), volume 7 of the *Daily Explanation of the Four Books* states as follows: 'Providence or the Law of Heaven involves Reason and time, or the cycle of time (in Chinese *qi*), and thus it is something very subtle and difficult to understand'.²¹⁶ See also below FF.44.

FF.43 《日講四書解義·卷二十一·孟子·萬章上》:「凡人力莫之召致而自然至者, 是之謂命, 稟受於有生之初, 不可得而移也。」

About chapter 3 'Wan Zhang shang' in the second part of the *Mencius*, volume 21 of the *Daily Explanation of the Four Books* states as follows: 'Something that no human forces bring about by themselves happens is called the Law of Heaven'. Same also can be found in [the *Sishu zhijie*] by Zhang Juzheng.²¹⁷

FF.44 蔡虛齋《四書蒙引·卷六·論語·第九》:「命有以理言者, 有以氣言者。理精微而難言, 氣數又不可盡委之, 而至於廢人事。」

About chapter 9 of the *Book of Sentences* [*Lunyu* 9.1.], Cai Xuzhai in volume 6 of the *Sishu mengyin* states as follows: 'The Law of Heaven is explained as Reason, and also as time. Reason is something very perfect, subtle, and difficult to explain. As for the cycle of time, it is not possible to reject any event in this cycle and to omit or neglect the due action of man'.

GG.45 蔡虛齋《四書蒙引·卷十五·孟子·盡心上》:「下章命字以氣言, 與『命之短長』字正同。上章命字以理言, 故曰『全其天之所賦』也。」

About chapter 7 'Jinxinshang' in the second part of the *Mencius*, Cai Xuzhai in volume 15 of the *Sishu mengyin* states as follows: 'The character for Law or Law of Heaven [*ming*] in the second chapter is taken to mean time [*qi*], namely the shortness and longevity of life. In the first chapter, it means Reason. Therefore, it encompasses everything that is infused by Heaven'.

HH.46 See BB.39.²¹⁸

---

214 Quoted in the *Gujin*, n. 1 (p. 132).
215 BB.39: 'There is nothing favourable or unfavourable to man in this life which is not directed by Heaven as Lord and Ruler, and this is called the Law of temporal cycle'(凡人之生, 吉凶禍福, 遭遇不同, 莫非天之所主宰, 是謂氣數之命).
216 Same quote and similar translation in c.2, q.2, K18.
217 Quoted in the *Gujin*, n. 33 (p. 195).
218 BB.39: 'Since indeed prosperity and disaster change with time, the knowledge of Heaven does not consist in those. Because also the sacrificial ritual is done to Heaven, it is an external worship, and the entire service of Heaven is not satisfied. To ask the producing and destroying Spirit for some temporal

NOTE: Although modern commentators often seem to refer to the visible and material heaven, in fact, in their way of speaking, they always indicate something invisible and immaterial. For example: 'O very remote and blue Heaven, you have your love for the people as your own virtue! When shall you make me return home?' (II). 'O blue Heaven, you dispense such good things to good people, and bad things to evil people, and you never make mistakes, but always check and restrain the haughty, and pity and comfort the poor' (KK). You can see that to love, to dispense good and bad things, to take mercy, to comfort, refer to something invisible, vital, and intelligent.

You may point out the ambiguity of expressions such as 'the unexhausted Author is vital breath' (LL), but you should understand this as meaning either the first cause alone like the supreme vital source of things as we said above, or a first cause concurring with a secondary cause such that the same action arising from the primeval air or material Being inasmuch it is the actual exercise of its activity arises also from God inasmuch as it is the actual exercise of its potentiality. Indeed, the concurrent role of God in a secondary act is in reality the action of a secondary cause.[219]

They perhaps use ambiguous expressions because they do not wish to worship what they recognize [as God], or because they do not dare to express clearly what they do not see with the sense of vision, or because they do not find suitable words to express the supreme divinity. Therefore, the character for worship [*jing*] is not, as they say, to be further discussed, nor there is the need to examine it further (MM).

It is clear from all those quotes that they know in the visible world a Spirit which is invisible and incomprehensible, Author of things, Ruler, Planner, unproduced, eternal, unlimited, and infinite in every kind of perfection.

You may say: 'Recently I read in a European book that the Chinese do not recognize any Spirit in the world'.[220] I shall answer to you and to them that, even though all the quotes mentioned until now are more than enough, the next question will show that the Chinese have a more complete knowledge of the Spirit.

NOTES

II.47 《詩經說約集解·唐國風·鴇羽》：「『悠悠蒼天』，以愛民為德也，果何時使我釋此王事，以耕田養親而得其所也乎？」

    About the ode 'Baoyu' in the volume 'Guofeng', the *Exhaustive Compilation of the Book of Odes* states as follows: 'O very remote and blue Heaven, you have your love for the people as your own virtue! When shall you relieve me from military duty so that I cultivate the fields to feed my parents and occupy my seat at home?'

goods is something vain, and the foundation of one's life according to the providence of Heaven does not depend on this' (故機祥禍福數也，而知天不在乎是；郊壇享祀文也，而事天不盡乎是；禱祀鬼神妄也，而立命不擊乎是).

219 In scholastic philosophy, God is not the first direct and immediate cause of every action in the world, but intervenes as a secondary cause.
220 It is difficult to determine the book to which Noël is referring because such notions were quite widespread in European writings at the same.

KK.48 《詩經說約集解・小雅・巷伯》：「『蒼天蒼天』，福善禍淫。理有不爽，共『視彼驕人』，庶乎有以抑遏沮止之也。『矜此勞人』，庶乎有以扶持慰安之也。」

About the ode 'Xiangbo' in the volume 'Xiaoya', the *Exhaustive Compilation of the Book of Odes* states as follows: 'O blue, blue, etc.' See above.

LL.49 《大字彙・氣字》：「程子曰：造化不窮，蓋生氣也。」

The dictionary *Dazihui* for the character *qi* (vital breath) quotes Doctor Cheng: 'The unexhausted Author is vital breath.'[221]

MM.50 《詩經說約集解・大雅・板》：「敬字不必深求。」

About the ode 'Ban' in the volume 'Daya', the *Exhaustive Compilation of the Book of Odes* states: 'The character worship, etc.' See above.

Question 4: Definitions, Types, and Properties of the Spirits by Modern Authors

Chinese writers talk about the Spirit quite frequently, and even make all their knowledge and morality depend on the nature of the Spirit. However, there is nothing more obscure, confused, and intricate than how they explain Spirit. Being unable to express its absolute perfection and intelligence, they gave it a 'supreme name' [*zunji zhicheng* 尊極之稱] and decided to call it publicly *guishen*, that is, the producing and destroying Spirit (A). Here a few things from the Chinese writers.

NOTES

A.1 陳澔《禮記集說卷八・祭義第二十四》：「因其精靈之不可掩者，制為尊極之稱，而顯然命之曰鬼神，以為天下之法則。故民知所畏而無敢慢，知所服而無敢違。」

About chapter 24 'Jiyi' of the *Book of Rites*, Chen Hao says about the Spirit: 'Because of its absolute superiority and intelligence which cannot be concealed, a most excellent name was given to it and it was ordered to be called publicly *guishen*, that is, the producing and destroying Spirit so that it could be the standard and the norm for the whole empire. Thus, all know what to fear and don't dare to despise it; they know to what they are subject and don't dare to disobey it.'[222]

---

221 *Dazihui* designates *Zihui*, quoted a few times above.
222 By translating *guishen* as 'producing and destroying Spirit', Noël emphasizes the unity between *gui* and *shen*, which are both understood as the two functions of a same entity, the spirit. The words 'producing and destroying' seem unusual and are left unexplained, but they translate Zhu Xi's explanation that *shen* has the function of uniting (*he* 合) and *gui* has the function of dispersing (*san* 散). See K.10 in this section.

§.1. [Descriptions of the Spirit]

First: The Spirit is what cannot be comprehended by motion (*yang*) or stillness (*yin*) (B); when it moves, it rests, and while it rests, it moves; its motion is mixed with rest, and its rest, mixed with movement, and it is always in a state of motion and rest (C). Also, the Spirit is the excellence of the way, that is, the way of stillness (*yin*) and motion (*yang*) in alternation; since it cannot be comprehended, it is called Spirit (D). Finally, the Spirit is incomprehensible and ineffable (E).

Second: The Spirit transcends by far all things and makes them wonderfully perfect (F).[223] It is not separated from the sensible world, neither is it included within it; and because it transcends by far all things, it extends itself to all things. When it is said that the Five Universal Principles are both one stillness (*yin*) and one motion (*yang*), or that stillness (*yin*) and motion (*yang*) constitute the one *taiji*, the first Ultimate of all things, all this means that the Spirit is a substance transcending by far all things. When it is said that the five weather conditions of heaven (rain, brightness, heat, cold and wind) succeed each other by yielding to each other, that the four seasons of the year move in a fixed succession, or that the being without ultimate, stillness (*yin*) and motion (*yang*), and the Five Universal principles make a perfect unity, this means that the Spirit is a cause wondrously perfecting all things' (G).

Third: The producing and destroying Spirit is the natural principle of a double vital operation. As destroying Spirit, it is the intelligence of stillness (*yin*), and as producing Spirit, it is the intelligence of motion *yang*. As Spirit coming and extending itself, or communicating itself through the production of the world, it is called *shen*, the producing Spirit. As Spirit returning and gathering itself, ceasing to communicate itself through the production of the world, it is called *gui*, the destroying Spirit (H). Note: the word 'natural' should not be taken here as being opposed to voluntary, but as being opposed to violent; indeed, what is voluntary and free can be natural (I).

Fourth: The Spirit is the efficient cause of Heaven and Earth, or the Author of things, causing them to exist or cease to exist (K).[224] It is called an efficient cause because it comes and extends itself, causing something to exist, and because it returns and gathers itself, causing something to cease to exist (L). (See below quote K.10, towards the end, what the production of the world and its ceasing mean for the Chinese, and how they explain it). As a double efficient cause, it is called *guishen*, the producing and destroying Spirit; as a substance transcending by far all things, or as the unique cause which is the Spirit (in the sense of a potential cause), or as something which is spiritual, then it is called *shen*, Spirit. But, when the word *shen* is taken in opposition to the word *gui*, or when the producing Spirit is taken as distinct from the destroying Spirit, this is a partial and inadequate understanding.

---

223 Noël's translation of *miao* 妙 as 'perfecting' is correct, but to translate as 'transcending' is tenuous since *miao* refers to the efficiency of the *dao*, and not to *dao* itself.

224 The noun Author (*Effector*) serves to personify the Spirit.

However, when *shen* is taken alone, disconnected from *gui*, it can be understood as *taiji*, or first Ultimate of things (M).

From the above, it follows that the human soul when united to the body is called *shen*, spirit (N). When separated from the body, it is called *gui* (O), but very frequently it is called with the original name of *shen* (P). Furthermore, the compound word *guishen* can be applied to the Spirit of Heaven and Earth, to the spirit of human beings, and to all things in which the Spirit is present and active (Q).[225] The Chinese authors explain at length the nature of Spirit either through its sensible effects, or through its abstraction from the sensible world, or through its way of being mysteriously active. They seem to do this therefore so that they are not thought to be discussing the false spirits of the Chinese idols (R).

From all those definitions or descriptions of the Spirit, you can see that the Chinese understand Spirit as a Being, or a certain invisible and immaterial cause, removed from the sensible world and incomprehensible to the human mind.[226]

NOTES

B.2 《易經‧繫辭傳上‧第五章》：「陰陽不測之謂神。」

> Chapter 5 of the 'Zhuan shang' in the *Book of Changes and Productions*: 'The Spirit is that which cannot comprehended by stillness (*yin*) or motion (*yang*)'.[227]

C.3 《性理標題‧卷一‧動靜》：「動而無靜，靜而無動，物也；動而無動，靜而無靜，神也。動而無動，靜而無靜，非不動不靜也。物則不通，神妙萬物。」

> Chapter 'Dongjing' in volume 1 of the *Summary of the Book of Nature and Reason* states: 'Material objects either move without rest or rest without motion. But the Spirit moves by itself but rests, and moves while resting; since motion is combined with rest, and rest combined with motion, it is always in the state of rest and motion. Material things cannot extend to many other things, but the Spirit transcends and perfects everything'.[228]

D.4 《周易正解‧卷十八‧繫辭傳上‧第五》：「節節有一陰一陽之道，亦節節有陰陽不測之神。神即道之妙，非道之外別有所謂神也。」「陰陽之迭運謂之道；就其不測者而言，謂之神。」

> About chapter 5 of 'Zhuan shang', chapter 18 of the *True Explanation of the Book of Changes and Productions* states: 'In all the chapters above, as there is the Way of one stillness (*yin*) and one motion (*yang*), so there is the incomprehensible Spirit of stillness (*yin*) and motion (*yang*). The Spirit is the excellence of the Way, such

---

225 In Noël's definition of the Spirit, there is a relatively short treatment of human spirits (three quotes N-O-P) compared to the lengthy treatment of the metaphysical definition of the Spirit above (quotes from B to L).
226 What Noël retains in the definitions of the Spirit is the metaphysical definitions of neo-Confucianism and not the ancient meaning. We can notice his use of Western ontology with the word Being (*Ens*).
227 This is a direct quote from the *Xici*.
228 This comes from Zhou Dunyi's chapter 'Dongjing' 動靜章 in the *Tongshu* 通書. For Zhu Xi, see 'Xingli'er' 性理二, *Zhuzi yulei*, juan 5.

that there is nothing outside the way which is called Spirit'. A little further down: 'When the way of stillness (*yin*) and motion (*yang*) in alternation is said to be incomprehensible, it is called Spirit'.

E.5 《性理標題・卷一・神化篇》：「神，天德；化，天道。德，其體；道，其用。一於氣而已。」「形而上者，得辭斯得象矣；神為不測，故緩辭不足以盡神。化惟難知，故急辭不足以体化。」

Chapter 'Shenhua' in volume 1 of the *Summary of the Book of Nature and Reason* states: 'Spirit is the power of Heaven; the cause is the way of Heaven. Virtue is substance, but the way, its function, and both of them are one with vital breath'. 'Because a being removed from matter can be expressed in words, it has something by which it can be represented, but the Spirit, being incomprehensible, cannot have any explanation forced upon him, and words cannot explain him completely. Since the cause is difficult to know and penetrate, its explanation is pursued with great difficulty, and words are not sufficient to explain it truly'.[229]

F.6 《易經・說卦・第六》：「神也者，妙萬物而為言者也。」

Chapter 6 of 'Shuogua' in the *Book of Changes and Productions* states: 'The Spirit transcends by far all things, etc.', as above.

G.7 《性理標題・卷一・動靜》：「有形，則滯於一偏；神，則不離於形，而不囿於形矣。動中有靜，靜中有動也。物滯於一偏，則不能通；神妙於萬物，則無不通。」「所謂『神妙萬物者如此，五行一陰陽，陰陽一太極』者，以神妙萬物之體而言也；『五氣順布，四時行焉，無極、二、五，妙合而凝』者，以神妙萬物之用而言也。」

Chapter 'Dongjing' in volume 1 of the *Summary of the Book of Nature and Reason*: 'A material thing is bound to one specific area. However, the Spirit is neither detached from a material thing nor enclosed in it. In motion, it has rest, and in rest, motion. A thing which is bound to one specific area cannot generally extend itself to many other things. But because the Spirit transcends by far all things, it generally extends itself to all things. Thus, it can be called, etc.' See above.[230]

H.8 朱熹《中庸章句・第十六》：「張子曰：『鬼神者，二氣之良能也』。愚謂以二氣言，則鬼者，陰之靈也；神者，陽之靈也。以一氣言，則至而伸者為神，反而歸者為鬼。其實一物而已。」

About chapter 16 of the *Book of the Unalterable Mean*, Zhu Xi comments:[231] 'Doctor Zhang said: "The destroying and producing spirit is the natural principle [*liangneng*] of the double vital breath [*erqi*]". However, I myself think this should

---

229 Those quotes reproduce the words of Zhang Zai. See 'Shenhuapian' 神化篇, *Zhengmeng* 正蒙. They express the idea that the Spirit is beyond language, same as negative theology affirms that God cannot be expressed with words.

230 In his commentary to Zhou Dunyi's *Tongshu*, Zhu Xi explains *shen* in terms of *ti* and *yong*. See Notes on 'Tongshu' 通書注, *Zhuzi quanshu* 朱子全書, *juan* 13. The Five *qi* 五氣 (five weathers of heaven) are mentioned in 'Hongfan' 洪範, *Shujing*:「曰雨，曰暘，曰燠，曰寒，曰風」.

231 Noël seems here to quote directly from Zhu Xi, and this is quite rare.

be understood like this.²³² If the destroying and producing Spirit is expressed as the double vital breath, then the destroying spirit is the intelligence of stillness (*yin*), and the producing spirit is the intelligence of motion (*yang*). If the destroying and producing Spirit is expressed as a single breath, then the spirit coming and extending itself [*shen* 伸] is the producing Spirit [*shen* 神], and the Spirit returning and gathering itself [*gui* 歸] is the destroying Spirit [*gui* 鬼]. In reality, this is the one and same thing'.²³³

I.9 《孟子·盡心上》:「孟子曰:『人之所以不學而能者, 其良能也。所不慮而知者, 其良知也。』」

Chapter 7 'Jinxin shang' in the second part of the *Mencius*: 'That which man can do without study comes from his natural faculty of acting; that which he can understand without thinking comes from his natural faculty of understanding'.

K.10 蔡虛齋《四書蒙引·卷三·中庸·第十六》:「程子曰:『鬼神, 天地之功用, 而造化之迹也。』程子之言為恐學者求鬼神於窅冥之鄉, 故曰此乃『天地之功用, 而造化之迹也』, 說迹字略涉於見聞。蓋此章之旨, 本謂鬼神無可見聞, 而卻能體物不遺也。」「『天地之功用』, 即『造化之迹』也。『造化』指天地之作為處言。造者自無而有, 化者自有而無。」

About chapter 16 of the *Book of the Unalterable Mean*, Cai Xuzhai in volume 3 of the *Sishu mengyin*: 'Doctor Cheng says: "The destroying and producing Spirit is the operation of heaven and earth, the traces of the Author of things (here as a metonymy, namely taking the effect for the cause, as it can be seen from the text here and from the interpretation elsewhere)".²³⁴ Doctor Cheng, being afraid that the students of the literati would look for the Spirit in some obscure and secret region, mentioned "the operation of heaven and earth and the traces of the Author of things". This word "traces" is used because the Spirit does not appear at all through these things to our vision or hearing. The correct and original meaning of this passage is that the producing and destroying Spirit cannot be seen or heard, but it penetrates all things so much that it cannot be separated from them.²³⁵
The words "operation of heaven and earth" designate "the traces of the Author's things", and the words "Author of things" [*zaohua*] designate heaven and earth as something in which He himself acts.²³⁶ Indeed, He acts either by causing the

---

232 By using 'however' (*autem*), Noël's translation implies a difference between Zhu Xi and Zhang Zai. The Chinese text does not contain this insinuation, indicating only that Zhu Xi interprets the words of Zhang Zai. *Liangneng* 良能 is translated as natural principle, or natural faculty, and *erqi* 二氣 as double vital breath.
233 Zhu Xi understands *guishen* in their double mode of action in the world, extending (*yang* mode) and returning (*yin* mode). Noël interprets this double mode of action as producing and destroying.
234 Cheng Hao describes *guishen* as 'trace' in the process of transformation of Heaven (*zaohua zhi shen* 造化之神), but the word 'trace' is quite ambiguous because it may be easily understood as something visible. However, Noël correctly understands that *guishen* or trace are both invisible.
235 For analysis of this metaphoric reading, see Wang Ge's chapter.
236 For discussion of *zaohua*, see see Wang Ge's chapter.

existence of something or by causing the ceasing of something.²³⁷ He first brings something from non-existence to existence and then from existence to non-existence'.²³⁸

「清嘗合章句三說而一之曰：鬼神，天地之功用、二氣之良能也；其至而伸者為神，反而歸者為鬼。此鬼神，天地、人物而一以貫之者也。陰陽非鬼神；陰陽之能屈伸、一往而一來者，乃鬼神也。盖即氣機之動靜而已，故曰『二氣之良能』也。曰陰之靈也，曰陽之靈也，盖天地無心而成化者也。原陰陽之所以有是靈者，盖『太極動而生陽，動極而靜，靜而生陰，靜極復動，一動一靜，互為其根』此其所以一往一來、一屈一伸，而不見其有窮已也：所謂『兩故化』也。知其『兩故化』，其體物不遺矣，無餘蘊矣。」

Shortly after: The interpreter Qingchang²³⁹ combines the triple explanation of the producing and destroying Spirit, given above by Doctor Zhu Xi into a single explanation, saying: 'The producing and destroying Spirit, the operation of heaven and earth, the natural principle of the vital breath, is called producing Spirit when it comes and extends itself, and is called destroying Spirit when it returns and contracts. Thus, the producing and destroying Spirit encompasses Heaven, earth, human beings and the other things. The producing and destroying Spirit is not stillness (*yin*), nor motion (*yang*) but the principle of stillness *yin* and motion *yang*, which can contract or extend, leave and come, because it is the motive force [*qiji*] of vital breath and causes motion and rest.²⁴⁰ Thus, it is called the natural principle of the double vital breath, or of the double second life, that is, the intelligence of stillness (*yin*) and motion (*yang*).²⁴¹ Indeed, Heaven and earth make things naturally and invisibly. Stillness (*yin*) and motion (*yang*) have intelligence because "when the first ultimate of things moves, it produces the mode *yang*, completes its motion, then rests; while resting, it produces the mode *yin*;

---

237 Ricci rejected the interpretation of *guishen* as trace, but upheld the ancient meaning. See Ricci, *The True Meaning of the Lord of Heaven*, p. 147 (n. 178). Longobardo rejected the ancient meaning of *guishen*, and also criticized Cheng Hao's interpretation. See Longobardo, *A Brief Response on the Controversies*, p. 149 (prelude 12, n. 1): 'Spirits are none other than the operations of heaven and earth, and certain signs or vestiges of natural generations and corruptions. Here it must be noted that the term "operations" is to be understood as operative virtue, or its very power of operation, and by the term vestiges are also to be understood the being and essence of natural causes'. Unlike Ricci and Longobardo, Noël reads *guishen* as the transcendental causes through which God operates, since he understands trace *ji* 迹 as meaning in fact cause, according to what he calls a metonymy. For Noël's support in reading *guishen* as cause, see below M.13.
238 In scholasticism, since generation is a change from non-existence to existence, corruption is the change from existence to non-existence. However, generation does not take place from just any non-being, but from the non-being which is being in potency. See Aquinas, *De principiis naturæ*, § §6–7.
239 The Chinese text has: 'I [Qing, i.e. Cai Qing] have already (said)' (*qingchang* 清嘗), but Noël understands wrongly *qingchang* as making reference to an interpreter named Qingchang (*Cim cham*).
240 The *guishen* are not at the same level of reality that *yin* and *yang*. The *guishen* are the Spirit, intelligence, or vital breath of *yin* and *yang*. The concept of *qiji* 氣機 as developed by Cai Qing was mentioned a few times previously.
241 With the term of secondary life (*vita secunda*), Noël seems to suggest two levels of life: the spiritual life with the vital spirit or *guishen*, and the life of motions with *yin* and *yang*.

and when the rest is completed, it starts moving again".[242] The alternation of one motion and one rest is the mutual origin and principle of the modes *yin* and *yang*. This is why intelligence or Spirit goes and comes, then contracts and extends itself without end. This is what they call the double efficient cause [*liang guhua*] which penetrates all things so deeply that they are not separated from it and that nothing else is hidden'.

「小註云：『功用只是論發見者，如寒來暑往、日往月來、春生夏長皆是。』又曰：『風雨霜露、日月晝夜，此鬼神之迹也。』斯言要是借此示人以默會鬼神之所在耳。若謂此即是鬼神，則為視而可見、聽而可聞矣。且日月風雨之類，其合也，如何便為物之始？其散也，又如何便為物之終？要之日月風雲之類，亦物也，皆鬼神之所體者也。」「陰陽一合而物以之始；始者，神之伸也；陰陽一散而物以之終；終者，鬼之歸也；是其體物而不可遺矣。」

Shortly after, 'Doctor Zhu Xi makes this brief interpretative note: "When the spirit refers to the operation of heaven and earth, this refers to things in which the Spirit makes itself visible, for example with the arrival of cold weather, summer departs; with the departure of the sun, the moon arrives; things born in the spring mature in summer".[243] He also says: "Wind, rain, frost, dew, sun, moon, day, and nights are all the traces of the Spirit".[244] With those words, Zhu Xi shows that he uses these words as metaphors to show people how they can reach and know the place of the producing and destroying Spirit by meditating in their heart. If the things enumerated here are understood as representing the producing and destroying Spirit, then the Spirit could be seen and heard (and this would contradict what the text says). Finally, how can the union of sun, moon, wind, rain, and similar things, become a principle that causes things to exist, and their dispersion become a principle that causes them to end? Therefore, sun, moon, wind, rain, and similar things are things which are penetrated by the producing and destroying Spirit'.

Again, not far below: 'Through the union of stillness (*yin*) and motion (*yang*), things begin to exist; that which causes things to exist is the Spirit as it extends or communicates itself. Through the separation of stillness *yin* and motion *yang*, things cease to exist; that which makes things cease to exist is the Spirit as it contracts and returns to itself. This is what the text says: the Spirit penetrates all things so deeply that it cannot be separated from them'.

---

242 Quote from Zhou Dunyi's *Taiji tushuo* 太極圖說. Ricci had made an allusion to the thought of Zhou Dunyi concerning the production of things through the alternation of *yin* and *yang*, but Ricci criticized it as a flawed theory; Ricci, *The True Meaning of the Lord of Heaven*, p. 89 (nn. 89–90). Here Noël accepts Zhou Dunyi's thought.
243 This passage of Zhu Xi comes from *Zhuzi yulei*, juan 68.
244 This passage of Zhu Xi comes from *Zhuzi yulei*, juan 3. Longobardo translates this important quote in a similar way as: "Rain, wind, dew, hail, sun, moon, day and night are all vestiges and effects of the spirits"; *A Brief Response on the Controversies*, p. 151 (prelude 12, n. 7). But while Noël suggests that the material things are animated by a principle which is immaterial and spiritual, Longobardo holds that the material things are produced by a material principle.

NOTE: To rephrase this according to our European way of speaking, the phrase 'union and separation of stillness (*yin*) and motion (*yang*)' could to a certain extent be understood as union and separation of matter and form. However, it seems that it should be understood in more general terms as a passage from non-action or rest to action or motion. The passage from non-action to action results in something non-existent becoming existent. This is called union because matter is united with form, nature with substance, or subject with accidents. The passage from action to non-action results in something existent becoming non-existent. This could be called a separation because things are obviously disjoined. Thus, the words *yin* and *yang* in their most general meaning, as it can be gathered from here and as it will appear below, signify nothing other than rest and motion. *Yin* means rest, either positive as conservation, or negative as cessation. *Yang* means motion, or a continuing action. More precisely, the words *yin* and *yang* mean the mode resulting from rest and motion, that is, a transcendental relationship. Surely, according to the Philosophers, every continuous action allows for a brief delay or rest, such that, after the first action, there is a little delay, and after this action, another action follows; then, another little delay, etc. Thus, the Chinese mutual alternation or production of stillness (*yin*) and motion (*yang*) has some resemblance, and is perhaps even identical, to this way of action.²⁴⁵

L.11 蔡虛齋《四書蒙引‧卷四‧中庸‧第十六》：「既曰『鬼神,造化之迹也』，又曰『鬼神至幽而難知』，一也。『迹』指其屈伸往來言,非謂有迹可見聞也。」

About chapter [16] of the *Book of the Unalterable Mean*,²⁴⁶ Cai Xuzhai in volume 4 of the *Sishu mengyin*: 'Doctor Zhu Xi said: "The producing and destroying Spirit is the trace of the Author of things", and then says, "The producing and destroying Spirit is extremely secret and difficult to know". They are both the same thing. The word trace indicates that the producing and destroying Spirit extends itself and retracts, comes and goes, and this surely does not mean that it is something which can be sensed with vision or hearing'.²⁴⁷

---

245 Instead of comparing *yin* and *yang* with form and matter, Noël rightly sees that *yin* and *yang* are not static entities, but dynamic and inter-related. On the basis of the Aristotelian concepts of relation and movement, he explains that *yin* and *yang* constitute a transcendental relation, not only in the sense that *yin* and *yang* cannot exist without each other, but also that *yang* tends becoming *yin*, and vice versa.
246 Both the Chinese and Latin texts mistakenly attribute this passage to *Zhongyong* 29. However, this text is from *Zhongyong* 16. The meaning of this passage is roughly as follows: while *shen* are said to be *ji* (traces) of *zaohua* (natural transformation), the *guishen* are also said to be very hidden and imperceptible. These two statements seem to be in contradiction because *ji* with the meaning of footprints or course would seem to signify something perceptible, that is visible or tactile. However, these two statements can be reconciled by understanding *ji* as a metaphor for the motions and changes of contraction, extension, going, and coming. For Noël, the *guishen* are traces not as visible traces in the concrete world but insofar as they are invisible causes of what we see in the concrete world. The interpretation of *guishen* as causes allows for the articulation of different levels of causal relations.
247 Cai Qing interprets trace *ji* 跡 as being invisible, same as *guishen*.

L.12 《周易正解・卷十七・繫辭傳上・第四》：「蔡虛齋曰：『晝夜、上下、南北、高深, 此只是幽明之迹, 非幽明之故也。故, 則其所以然之理也。』」「死生就人物言, 鬼神就造化言。死生是人物之死生也, 鬼神是人物之所以死生者。」「幽明、死生、鬼神, 理之至難窮者也。」

> About chapter 4 of 'Zhuan shang', volume 17 of the *True Explanation of the Book of Changes and Productions* states as follows: 'Cai Xuzhai said: "Days and nights, upper and lower things, south and north, and high and low things are the traces of a dark and bright principle, but they are not causes; the cause is the reason by which things exist"'. Further below: 'The two words death and life refer to human beings and other things; *guishen*, the producing and destroying Spirit, refers to the Author of things. Life and death are the life and death of human beings and other things; *guishen* is what makes human beings and things live and die'. Further on it continues: 'The reason or essence of the dark and bright principle, of life and death, of the producing and destroying Spirit, is extremely difficult to penetrate'. See above K.10.

M.13 蔡虛齋《四書蒙引・卷三・中庸・第十六》：「以功用謂之鬼神, 兩故化也。以妙用謂之神, 一故神也。神字對鬼字而言, 則偏矣；單言神, 則當得太極。」

> About chapter 16 of the *Book of the Unalterable Mean*, Cai Xuzhai in volume 3 of the *Sishu mengyin*: 'When the Spirit refers to the operation of heaven and earth, it means the producing and destroying Spirit as a double efficient cause, i.e., of generation and destruction in the sense of actualization (*actus secundus*).[248] But when it refers to the transcendental being which is active and perfect, this is the Spirit as the unique cause, i.e., in the sense of potentiality (*actus primus*). When *shen* is taken in opposition to *gui*, or the producing Spirit in opposition to the destroying Spirit, then this is a partial and inadequate understanding. However, when *shen* is taken alone, disconnected from *gui*, it means *taiji*, first ultimate of things'.[249]

N.14 蔡虛齋《四書蒙引・卷五・孟子・盡心上》：「注：心者, 人之神明。」

> About Chapter 7 'Jinxin shang' in the second part of the *Mencius*, Cai Xuzhai in volume 5 of the *Sishu mengyin* states as follows: 'When the commentators explain what mind is, they say that it is the intelligent spirit of a human being'.[250]

---

[248] On the meaning of *actus primus* and *actus secundus* in scholastic philosophy, see the chapter by Pierre Galassi, p. XX.
[249] The explanation of Cai Qing follows closely the interpretation of Zhang Zai: 'One single thing with a double constitution, that is *qi*. As one single thing, it is spiritual; as double, it is transformation' (一物兩體, 氣也。一故神, 兩故化). 'Zhengmeng' 正蒙, in *Zhangzai ji* 張載集, ed. by Zhang Xichen 章錫琛 (Beijing: Zhonghua shuju, 1978), p. 10. Unlike Zhang Zai and Cai Qing, Noël gives a secondary role to *qi* compared to *Tian*. Noël crossed out a few lines from the manuscript (fol. 74ʳ).
[250] This is a quote from Zhu Xi's *Mengzi zhangju*.

O.15 陳澔《禮記集說·卷八·祭法·第二十三》：「大凡生於天地之間者，皆曰命；其萬物死，皆曰折；人死曰鬼。方氏曰：『人謂之鬼，言其有所歸也。』」

> About chapter 23 'Jifa' of the *Book of Rites*, [Chen Hao] in volume 8 of his commentary [*Liji jishuo*] states: 'Whatever lives in the world follows a certain law of life and condition: when all things perish, they are said to be destroyed. But when man dies, it is said that his Spirit (*gui*) returns. A commentator puns on the character *gui* [鬼] meaning returning spirit and the character *gui* [歸] meaning to return, saying: "When a person is called a spirit (*gui*), this means that he has a place to return".'

P.16 范之恒、萬經《詩經說約集解·大雅·文王》：「朱熹：『此章言文王既沒，而其神在上，昭明於天。』」

> About the ode 'Wen Wang' in the volume 'Daya' in the *Book of Odes*, Zhu Xi says [as recorded in the commentary *Shijing shuoyue jijie* by Fan Zhiheng and Wan Jing]: 'According to this strophe, the spirit (*shen*) of Wen Wang exists on high and shines brightly in heaven'.

Q.17 張居正《四書直解·論語·第八》：「鬼神，是天神、地祇、人鬼。」

> About chapter 8 of the *Analects* [*Lunyu* 8.21], Zhang Juzheng in volume 6 [of the *Sishu zhijie*]: 'The Spirit in its coming and going, contracting and extending or communicating, encompasses the spirits of heaven and earth, and the souls of the dead'.[251]

R.18 See above K.10.

§.2. [Categories of Spirits]

First, the Spirit of Heaven and Earth (S).

Second, the spirits of fields, crops, mountains, rivers and all species (T).

Third, the five spirits of the house (V).

Fourth, the spirit of the living human beings, understood sometimes as the human soul alone (X), and sometimes as the spiritual and interior man: 'Whoever excels through his inner and secret virtue or through the intelligence of his sharp mind can be called a spiritual man' (Z). The *Book of the Changes and Productions*, by the rulers Fu Xi, Wen Wang, and Zhou Gong, often refer to the Spirit as a penetrating intelligence; they found, explained, and transmitted the teaching of changes and productions, or natural causes, and illustrated it with enigmatic symbols (W). They call all those things a spiritual teaching, or Spirit, partly because of the sharp intellect, or spirit, of the people who founded and transmitted the teaching, and partly because of the Author of nature whose actions and continuous effects are shown and explained by the teaching, as the Chinese say all the time (Y). They even call spiritual the stalks of this sprawling herb *shi* with which they adjust the

---

251 For human beings, Noël uses the Western concept of soul.

symbols [hexagrams] and their parts into different arrangements to see whether their conjunction or variation shows something rational (AA). Obviously, the intelligence of a spiritual man has arranged and used this art [of the herb *shi*] to indicate through the spiritual reason of human being something to be done or avoided (BB). Anyone who calls spiritual the art of algebra which is used to find the square root certainly calls it and understands it as an art of a spiritual intelligence.[252]

Fifth, the spirits of the deceased. The ancients who have served their country and the common good and for whom are performed the *ji* ceremonies are called spirits (CC). Certainly, the five famous emperors and their five famous ministers are also spirits (DD). In the third chapter of the First Letter of Peter, chapter 3 [verse 19], the deceased in limbo are also called spirits: 'He [Christ] came and made proclamation to the spirits who were prisoners'.[253] Thus, the souls of the ancestors and deceased parents are called spirits.

However, the modern Chinese who follow the teaching of the literati always say that human soul after death perishes and is scattered (EE); also, according to the followers [of Buddha], the human soul returns to its principle and origin, but nothing can be said about this (FF).[254] Certainly, I could inquire persistently about this, but my efforts will come to nought: What qualities and properties does the human soul have after death? The soul or spirit of living people, as well as its qualities and properties, will be discussed later, in the Treatise of Chinese Ethics.[255] It remains here to investigate the qualities and properties of the spirits which never perish and are never scattered (GG).

NOTES

S.19 《禮記・卷三・王制・第五》：「天子祭天地, 諸侯祭社稷[, 大夫祭五祀]。天子祭天下名山大川, [諸侯祭名山大川之在其地者]。」

> Chapter 5 'Wangzhi' of the *Book of Rites*: 'The emperor makes the *ji* offering to Heaven and Earth, that is, to their Spirit; the petty king makes the offering to the spirits of the fields and crops. The emperor makes the *ji* offering to the famous mountains and important rivers under his dominion'.[256]

---

252 With the example of algebra, Noël suggests that the spiritual intelligence (*spiritualis intellectus*) is not mystical, but an abstract intelligence, beyond any form. Ancient Chinese used a special herb and turtle shells for divination.
253 According to the Christian teaching, Christ descended into Hell to deliver the souls imprisoned there.
254 In suggesting that the neo-Confucians do not believe in the immortality of the soul, Noël follows Ricci who had argued that, while ancient Chinese believed in the immortality of the soul and instituted ancestor rituals, the contemporary literati keep performing the rituals but have lost the belief in the immortality of the soul. See Ricci, *The True Meaning of the Lord of Heaven*, p. 133 (n. 154). Noël argues that neo-Confucians have maintained the ancient monotheism, but modified the ancient teaching on the immortality of the soul. Perhaps Noël took this awkward position in the context of the Rites Controversy: it was safer to hold that the literati did not believe in the immortality of the soul so there could not be any suspicion of idolatry.
255 This refers to the Third Treatise of the *Philosophia Sinica*.
256 Noël neglects to translate the following words: 「大夫祭五祀」and 「諸侯祭名山大川之在其地者」.

T.20 《禮記‧卷三‧王制‧第五》：「山川神祇, 有不舉者為不敬。」

Chapter 5 'Wangzhi' of the *Book of Rites*: 'If you do not make offering to the spirits of the mountains and rivers, you sin against reverence'.

T.21 《書經‧舜典》：「肆類于上帝, 禋于六宗, 望于山川, 徧于羣神。」

Chapter 'Shundian' in volume 1 of the *Book of Imperial Annals*: 'The ruler Shun made a sacrifice to the Lord and Ruler (*Shangdi*) and he made offerings to venerate the spirits of the seasons, of cold and heat, of the sun, of the moon, of the stars, of drought and humidity, and next he made a sacrifice to the mountains and rivers (i.e., to theirs spirits), and finally to the multitude of spirits'.[257]

V.22 《白虎通‧五祀》：「五祀者何謂也？謂門、戶、井、竈中、霤也。」

Chapter 'Wusi' in volume 1 of the *Baihu tong*: 'What are the five offerings? They are those which are made to the spirits of the door of the house, of the door of the inner room, of the well (Chapter 6 "Yueling" of the *Book of Rites* has road instead of well), of the center of the house, and of the hearth'.[258]

X.23 See N.14 above.

Z.24 《日講四書解義‧卷二十六‧孟子‧盡心下》：「其盛德淵微, 而莫知其所以為德。大業顯著, 而莫知其所以為業。蓋變化無方, 陰陽迭運, 有非耳目之所能窮。心思之所能測者, 是則所謂神也。」

About chapter 8 'Jinxin xia' in the second part of the *Mencius*, volume 26 of the *Daily Explanation of the Four Books* states as follows: 'Whoever excels with a virtue that is so subtle, pure, perfect and detached from all the senses that it cannot be perceived and known despite accomplishing wonderful things, is called a spiritual man'.[259]

Z.25 《周易正解‧卷十八‧繫辭傳下‧第五》：「『子曰：知幾其神乎』。
子曰：天下之事莫不有幾；能知幾者, 其惟神而明之人乎！」

Chapter 5 of 'Zhuan xia' in the *Book of Changes and Productions* states: 'Isn't it the case that a truly spiritual man knows all the inner impulses and tendencies of things?' Volume 18 of the commentary [*Zhouyi zhengjie*] includes the following remark: 'Confucius means that there is nothing in the world without a special impulse and propensity. How could anyone except a spiritual and intelligent man know it?'

---

257 There are several interpretations for the six *zong* 六宗. Here Noël follows the interpretation by Wang Su 王肅 (195–256): 'the spirits of the four seasons, of heat and cold, of the sun, of the moon, of flood, of drought' (四時、寒暑、日、月、星、水旱). Quoted in the *Gujin*, p. 190 (n. 30), in the *Ditian kao*, p. 27 (n. 1) and in the *Tianjiao he Ru*, p. 34 (n. 10).
258 Concerning the *Baihu tong*, see Chapter 2.14. This work is also quoted twice below (c.2, q.5, V.21 and Y.27).
259 For the spiritual nature of man and his ability to know all things, see for example the First Letter of Saint Paul to the Corinthians 2:15: 'The spiritual man judges everything'. However, the Confucians, unlike the Daoists, refrain from talking about a spiritual man (*shenren* 神人) since they consider that the higher level for man is a wise (*shengren* 聖人). Thus, in this passage and the following one, *shen* does not qualify a person, but it refers only to a situation.

W.26 《周易正解・卷十九・繫辭傳上・第十》：「至精、至變而至神，皆《易》之道，而聖人為之者也。」「是象變者，聖人所以研窮乎幾微之理也。變之至而能神者，此也。」

About chapter 10 of 'Zhuan shang', volume 19 of the *True Explanation of the Book of Changes and Productions* states as follows: 'The highest perfection, highest change and highest spirituality is the way of the *Book of Changes and Productions*; a wise man authored it'. Not far below: 'It is with the mobility of the symbolic figures that the wise man discusses fully the reason of the highest subtlety, undoubtedly by bestowing spirituality upon that highest mobility'.[260]

Y.27 《周易正解・卷十八・繫辭傳上・第九》：「蔡虛齋曰：『神是《易》中有理以神之，如「元亨利貞」。勿用利見之類，都是使人之作事合理處。却因數衍出來，此便是《易》有以神其德行也。』」

About chapter 9 of 'Zhuan shang', volume 18 of the *True Explanation of the Book of Changes and Productions* cites Cai Xuzhai's commentary [*Zhouyi zhengjie*] as follows: 'The teaching of the *Book of Changes and Productions* contains a method for making spiritual with expressions such as "the power of Heaven, which is first or great, participative, directive and perfective"; "Do not use"; "It is beneficial" and similar such expressions.[261] These things through their norms make people follow the correct path in their actions. This is obtained through the number of enigmatic symbols made up of numbered lines. This teaching of the *Book of Changes and Productions* has something by which spiritualizes or makes spiritual the work of virtue'.[262]

Y.28 《周易正解・卷十七・繫辭傳上・第四》：「《易》道之大如此，而聖人用之則何如。夫道一也。自其散殊於天地萬物者，言之謂之理。自其稟受於人物者，言之謂之性。自其流行於造化者，言之謂之命。而惟聖人為能體之。今以聖人用《易》窮理之事言之。」

About chapter 4 of 'Zhuan shang', volume 17 of the *True Explanation of the Book of Changes and Productions* states the following: 'Since the way of the *Book of Changes and Productions* is so great and vast, how could a wise man put it into practice? The way is one, but insofar as it is diffused and distributed in heaven, earth and all things, it is called reason [*li*]; insofar as it is endowed and received in human beings and other things, it is called nature [*xing*]; insofar as it is continuously acting in the Author of things, it can be called law [*ming*]. Only the wise man can penetrate and embrace it mentally. The wise can put the teaching of the changes and productions into practice by completely realizing and penetrating the whole breadth of reason'.

---

260 This passage and the following ones emphasize the role of the *Yijing*. Since this book is supposed to contain the Way of Heaven, the *shengren* is the one who penetrates its content and applies it to concrete realities. Through his mind, he transforms the mundane reality into something spiritual.
261 Noël connects *wuyonglijian* 勿用利見 to the preceding sentence (元亨利貞), whereas in the Chinese text this is better understood as the subject of the next sentence.
262 We can notice here the use of the verb 'to spiritualize' (*spiritualizare*).

AA.29 《周易正解・卷十九・繫辭傳上・第十一》：「『是故蓍之德圓而神。』夫《易》之用周於天下，而《易》之理實具於聖心。是故《易》之所有，蓍、卦、爻而已。」

> Chapter 11 of 'Zhuan shang' states: 'The *shi* herb becomes a spiritual force through various arrangements of stalks'. Volume 19 of the *True Explanation of the Book of Changes and Productions* comments as follows: 'The use of the teaching of the changes and productions extends to all things in the world, yet its method is really confined in the mind of the wise man who alone has the *shi* herb, the enigmatic symbols and their numbered lines'.[263]

AA.30 《周易正解・卷十九・繫辭傳上・第十一》：「『是以明於天之道，而察於民之故，是興神物以前民用。』聖人既具此理，又將此理就蓍龜上發明出來，使民亦得前知而用之也。」「民用之，則神明民德；聖人用之，則自神明其德。」

> Chapter 11 of 'Zhuan shang' states: 'Since the wise man correctly understood the way of Heaven and attends to the affairs of the people, he instituted this spiritual thing to promote the welfare of the people'. Volume 19 of the *True Explanation of the Book of Changes and Productions* comments as follows: 'When the wise man had an idea of this teaching held in his mind, he expressed it outwardly and then he adjusted it with the *shi* herb and the turtle. In this way, the people could understand the use of this teaching and put it into practice'. A little further down: 'When the people use the art of this teaching, the spirit (of the one who practices this art) introduces a clear intelligence into the natural faculty of the people. When a wise man uses it, his own spirit introduces a clear intelligence into his natural faculty'.[264]

AA.31 《周易正解・卷十九・繫辭傳上・第十》：「『《易》无思也，无為也。』朱熹曰：『《易》指蓍卦；無思無為，言其無心也。』」「蓍卦本是個無商度底物事，故曰无思无為。蔡虛齋曰：『无思无為，只是无心。』」

> Chapter 10 of 'Zhuan shang' in the *Book of Changes and Productions* states: 'The teaching of changes and productions is devoid of thought and action'. Volume 19 of the *True Explanation of the Book of Changes and Productions* comments as follows: 'Doctor Zhu Xi says: "The teaching of changes and productions" refers to the enigmatic symbols with their numbered lines and the stalks of the *shi* herb arranged in a certain order; "devoid of thought and action" means being devoid of soul, mind and intention'.[265] A little further down: 'When those symbols are arranged with the stalks of the *shi* herb, they are something devoid of deliberation and reasoning, and thus they are said to be "devoid of thought and action"'.[266] According to Doctor Cai Xuzhai, '"devoid of thought and action" only means that the teaching and enigmatic symbols are devoid of soul, mind and intention'.[267]

---

263 Following Zhu Xi, the *Zhouyi zhengjie* fully recognizes that the *Yijing* was originally a work for divination, but still contains a teaching for the wise to understand *Tian* and the mutations.
264 These two quotes come from Zhu Xi's 'Chapter 11 on the Yijing' 易十一in *Zhuzi yulei*, *juan* 75.
265 Zhu Xi, 'Xici zhuan shang' 繫辭傳上, *Zhouyi benyi* 周易本義, *juan* 3.
266 This seems borrowed from *juan* 10 of the *Yijing cunyi* 易經存疑 by Lin Xiyuan (Lin Ciya).
267 The teaching of the *Yijing* as such is devoid of soul and mind and intention, because it is only through human

BB.32 《日講易經・卷十六・繫辭傳上・第十一》：「按蓍亦植物中之一物耳。使不遇聖人，何由知為神物？使非聖人神明化裁，制而用之，則神物終屬無用之物。亦烏能自著其神耶?故神物非神，必經聖人之裁制，而後成其為神。」

About chapter 11 of 'Zhuan shang', volume 16 of the *Daily Explanation of the Book of Changes and Productions* states as follows: 'The *shi* herb is only a plant like any other. Ensure that it does not come upon a wise man. How could it be known that it is something spiritual? If the intelligent spirit of a man had not taught and used this art, this spiritual thing would remain useless forever. How could the *shi* herb become spiritual by itself? Thus, the herb is not spiritual as such, but it is made spiritual after the wise man has taught the art'.

CC.33 《禮記・卷八・祭法・第二十三》：「夫聖王之制祭祀也：法施於民則祀之，以死勤事則祀之，以勞定國則祀之，能禦大菑則祀之，能捍大患則祀之。」

About chapter 23 'Jifa' in volume 8 of the *Book of Rites*: 'The ancient emperors, famous for their knowledge and virtue, established the rites and rules of the *ji* ceremonies. They made the *ji* ceremonies, that is a ceremonial expression of gratitude, for those who had taught people the precepts of good life and government, for those who had shed their life to promote the public good, for those who had strengthened the weak state of the country through their strenuous efforts, for those who had helped the people amid great distresses, and finally for those who had prevented great evils from afflicting people'.

DD.34 《孔子家語・五帝・第二十四》：「『天有五行，水火金木土，分時化育，以成萬物，其神謂之五帝。』古之王者，易代而改號，取法五行，五行更主，終始相生，亦象其義。[…]是以太皞配木，炎帝配火，黃帝配土，少皞配金，顓頊配水」「康子曰：『吾聞勾芒為木正，祝融[為]火正，蓐收為金正，玄冥為水正，后土為土正，此五行之主而不亂，稱曰帝者，何也？』孔子曰：『凡五正者，五行之官名。[……]此五官各以其所能業為官職，生為上公，死為貴神。別稱五祀，不得稱帝。』」

Chapter 24 of the *Book of the Domestic Sayings of Confucius*: '"Heaven contains the Five First Universal Principles: water, fire, metal, wood, and earth, which serve the production of things according to the seasons of the year. Their spirits are said to be the first five emperors". Since those ancient emperors changed the name of the empire when there was a change in dynasty, they represented it with the Five Universal Principles which preside in alternation over the continuous generation and corruption of things. Thus, Emperor Taihao, or Fuxi, was represented with wood; Yandi, with fire; Huangdi with earth; Shaohao with metal; Zhuanxu with water'.[268] Shortly after: 'The Prefect Kang said, "I heard that Prince Goumang

---

virtue and intelligence that the teaching acquires soul, mind and intention. Zhu Xi expresses here his opposition to the divinatory use of the *Yijing*, as if the *Yijing* could directly express ideas and thoughts.

268 The Five *Di* are explained here as human beings, the first five emperors representing the Five Phases. Sometimes the Five *Di* are considered as Five Heavens or even Five *Shangdi* 五方上帝, as said in the 'Tianguan' 天官 of the *Zhouli* 周禮. See Wu Liwei 吳莉葦, *Zhongguo liyi zhizheng* 中國禮儀之爭 (Shanghai: Shanghai guji chubanshe, 2007), pp. 48–49. The explanation of Five *Di* as Five Heavens is rejected below (c.3, q.2, E.6).

presided over wood; Zhurong, fire, Rushou, metal; Xuanming, water; Houtu, earth. They were presiding over the Five Universal Principles. But why were they not called emperors?" Confucius answered, "Those five chief ministries were called according to the names of the men presiding over the Five First Universal Principles"'. After few other words [Confucius] adds: 'Each of those five ministers had a function according to his capacity; while alive, they were the chief ministers of the empire; after their death, they were honorary spirits and called by the name of the five *si* ceremonies, but they were not called emperors'.

DD.35 陳澔《禮記集說・卷三・月令・第六》：「聖神繼天立極,生有功德於民,故後王於春祀之。四時之帝與神,皆此義。」

About Fuxi and his prime minister Gou Mang [勾芒] in chapter 6 'Yueling' of the *Book of Rites*, Chen Hao says in volume 3 of his commentary [*Liji jishuo*]: 'Those men were perfected with learning, virtue and spiritual perfection, followed the Law of Heaven, taught by word and deed the way of perfect discipline, and served with the greatest distinction the people in their lifetime. Thus, during the spring season, later emperors began to perform for them the *ji* ceremony. This was the same method as for the emperors and spirits of the four seasons'. See above DD.34.

DD.36 陳澔《禮記集說・卷五・郊特牲・第十一》：「聖人欲報其神之有功者,故求索而享祭之也。」

About chapter 11 'Jiaotesheng' in the *Book of Rites*, Chen Hao says the following in the fifth volume of his commentary [*Liji jishuo*] when discussing the souls of Emperor Shennong and Prince Houji: 'Since the wise man wishes to give thanks to the spirits for their service to the country, he enquires where they are and performs the *ji* ceremony for them'.[269]

EE.37 蔡虛齋《四書蒙引・論語上・八佾・第三》：「如天地、山川、社稷之類,生氣萬古不化,隨祭而享,其理固真。若夫人死,則魂已歸天,魄已歸地,隨化而盡矣。」「若究竟到底,祖先之氣果是盡了。」

About chapter 3 of the *Analects* [*Lunyu* 3.12], Cai Xuzhai in volume 5 his *Sishu mengyin* states the following: 'The vital breath of heaven, earth, mountains, rivers, fields, and crops is never destroyed. Therefore it is reasonable to have and perform the *ji* thanksgiving ceremony in its honour. But when human beings die, their soul goes to heaven, and the body goes to earth and vanishes completely after its destruction'. Not far below: 'If we discuss things in depth, the breath of the deceased ancestors really finishes and perishes completely'.[270]

---

269 In fact the quote comes from Zheng Xuan 鄭玄.
270 Above Noël affirmed that for the literati the human soul perishes after death, but here his translation suggests that the three *hun* go to Heaven and only the seven *po* perish. However, the *qi* associated with the three *hun* eventually disappears. The neo-Confucian *hun-po* theory of the soul is impossible to reconcile with the Christian concept of the immortal soul. Noël may have shared the view of Pietro Pomponazzi (1462–1525) that the immortality of the soul cannot be proven by philosophy, unlike the existence of God, and therefore one should not criticize the neo-Confucian philosophers for having abandoned the ancient belief in the immortality of the soul.

FF.38 蔡虛齋《四書蒙引・卷三・中庸・第十六》：「要認得至而實, 若泥於返而歸之詞, 則異端所謂歸根還原者, 亦無得而議矣。」

> About chapter 16 of the *Book of the Unalterable Mean*, Cai Xuzhai in volume 3 of the *Sishu mengyin* states the following: 'The coming of the spirit (in human generation) must be said to be true; but as for its return, if you follow the literal meaning, this is identical to what the idolatrous sects affirm about the spirit returning to its principle and origin. However, nothing can be said about this'.[271]

GG.39 See EE.37.

§.3. [Main Properties of the Spirit][272]

The first property of the Spirit is incorporeality because the Spirit has neither body nor voice (HH).

Its second property is imperceptibility because it cannot be seen by the eyes, nor heard with the ears (II).

Its third property is intelligence because it cannot be deceived (KK).

Its fourth property is righteousness because it cannot be perverted by adulation (LL).

Its fifth property is justice because it brings good things to good people and bad things to evil people (MM).

Its sixth property is knowledge with which it knows the obscure and secret things that the human ear, eye and mind cannot reach (NN).

Its seventh property is majesty by which it is offended by human sins (OO).

Its eighth property is unreachable mystery or an invisible action by which it produces effects and makes them perceptible (PP). Therefore, it is very difficult to know it.

As they say, it is sufficient to worship the Spirit and it is not necessary to investigate in depth its nature (QQ). It is great blindness to seek through adulatory worship what cannot be known; hence, human beings should only dedicate themselves to that which is demanded of them by their status, office, and reason. As for the worship of the Spirit, it is enough to show reverence to fulfill one's obligation. One must not offend it by being too close or make an offering to obtain temporal

---

271 Cai Qing shows here his disbelief in returning spirits, and he criticizes Buddhism, Daoism, and also the ancient belief in returning spirits. The double mode of action of the *guishen* in the world, as extending and returning, are real, but this does not mean for Cai Qing that there is a reversibility from death to life.
272 Neo-Confucianism tends to interpret *guishen* as anonymous forces, while the classical texts imply that *guishen* are endowed with individuality, knowledge, justice, will, etc., like Heaven itself. Zhang Juzheng's understanding of *guishen* is based on the classical texts and on the Han interpretation insisting on the mutual interactions between *guishen* and human beings. In this section, Noël cites Zhang Juzheng's *Sishu zhijie* four times to demonstrate the personal qualities of *guishen* and their similarity to angels.

goods with inappropriate adulation and prayer (RR). As for eternal things, Chinese writers hardly ever mention them.

The entire knowledge that the [Chinese] have of the Spirit amounts to this, but we shall say something more below. Now someone may advance this objection: 'Here the Spirit of Heaven and Earth is said to be one, but I have heard that Chinese make offerings to King-Heaven and Queen-Earth. Why? How is it consistent?' As I recall, those of you who advance these objections had said earlier that the Chinese are atheist, and until now, I have been fighting against this opinion. Now you make the Chinese idolatrous because, for you, King-Heaven and Queen-Earth are idols, like [the Anatolian Mother goddess] Cybele and [the Roman god] Caelus, or Heaven. But to solve the objection, I shall proceed to the next question.[273]

NOTES

HH.40 蔡虛齋《四書蒙引·卷三·中庸·第十六》：「惟鬼神也，雖無其形，無其聲，而寔有其理也。」

> About chapter 16 of the *Book of the Unalterable Mean*, Cai Xuzhai [in volume 3 of the *Sishu mengyin*]: 'Although the spirit lacks body and voice, its reason truly exists'.

II.41 《日講四書解義·卷二·中庸·第十六》：「天下惟有形者可見，鬼神無形，雖視之而弗見；惟有聲者可聽，鬼神無聲，雖聽之而弗聞。」

> About chapter 16 of the *Book of the Unalterable Mean*, volume 2 of the *Daily Explanation of the Four Books* states as follows: 'Only corporeal things can be seen in this world. Since the spirit is incorporeal, you cannot see it even if you want to see it. Only things with voice can be heard in this world. Since the spirit lacks voice, it cannot be heard even if you want to hear it'. Another way of putting it: 'Even if you may see and hear it in its effects, you cannot see and hear it itself'.[274]

KK.42 《日講四書解義·卷四·論語上·八佾》：「嗚呼！季氏之越禮而諂求者，吾不知其何心。彼林放一魯人耳，尚悼流俗之弊而問禮之本。何況泰山五嶽之尊，其神必聰明不可欺，必正直不可諂，豈反不如林放之知禮，而享季氏非禮之祭乎？」

> About chapter 3 of the *Analects* [*Lunyu* 3.6] ('Confucius says: "Alas! The prefect Ji has transgressed the laws and rituals and has sought wealth through adulation, but I myself do not know what he thinks"'), volume 4 of the *Daily Explanation of the Four Books* states: 'The famous Lin Fang was an inhabitant of the kingdom of

---

273 The question of the sacrifice to *Tian* or Huangtian is discussed below in the first point of Question 5, and the question of the sacrifice to Houtu, discussed below in the second point of Question 5. Noël points out the contradictory stance of those opposing the Jesuits' position in the Rites and Terms controversies: following Longobardo, they consider all the Confucians to be atheist; however, in accordance with their understanding of Confucian rituals, they consider them as idolatrous.

274 Noël gives here two different interpretations of 'We look for them, but do not see them' (視之而弗見, *Zhongyong* 16) which are not mutually exclusive but complementary.

Lu and had learnt the wicked manners of the world, but he was striving to enquire about the true mode of rituals and honesty. Compared to this ordinary man Lin Fang, the spirit of Taishan, the first of the five famous mountains, could not be more deceived by tricks because of its perspicacity and intelligence, and could not be more corrupted by adulation because of its rightness and justice. How much more the spirit of Taishan knows the laws of rituals and honesty! How could it accept from the prefect Ji an offering so contrary to the *ji* ritual and to moral integrity?'²⁷⁵

LL. 張居正《四書直解・論語・第三》：「神不可欺。」「其神聰明正直，必然知禮。」

[About *Lunyu* 3.6], Zhang Juzheng says in volume 4 among other things: 'The Spirit cannot be deceived or cheated'. A little further below is added: 'The Spirit of the mountain is clever and intelligent, as well as just and fair, and surely knows the rituals and the moral laws'.²⁷⁶

MM.43 張居正《四書直解・卷二・中庸・第十六》：「惟是鬼神，則實有是理流行於天地之間，而司其福美、禍淫之柄。故其精爽靈氣，發見昭著，而不可揜也如此夫！」

About chapter 16 of the *Book of the Unalterable Mean*, Zhang Juzheng in volume 2 [of the *Sishu zhijie*] states as follows: 'The reason of the producing and destroying or coming and going Spirit is true and real. Constantly active in the world, it has the power and office of granting good things to good people and bad things to evil people. Hence its perfect beauty and intelligent breath are made visible outside, and thus it cannot be hidden'.²⁷⁷

NN.44 《性理標題・卷三・皇極》：「『思慮一萌，鬼神得而知之矣。』故君子不可不慎獨。」

The chapter 'Huangji' in volume [3] of the *Summary of the Book of Nature and Reason* states as follows: '"Once a thought emerges, immediately the producing and destroying Spirit knows it".²⁷⁸ Thus, the wise man must diligently watch over the inner loneliness of his mind'.

NN.45 張居正《四書直解・卷三・中庸・第二十四》：「蓋凡幽遠之事，耳目心思所不及者，人不能知，除是鬼神知得。」

About chapter 24 of the *Book of the Unalterable Mean*, Zhang Juzheng in volume 3 of the [*Sishu zhijie*]: 'The producing and destroying Spirit alone has to the power to know any obscure and secret affair which the ear, eye, mind and thought do

---

275 For the neo-Confucians, the spirit of Taishan, like the spirits of other mountains or rivers, is not endowed with any thought or intention, but participates in the Spirit of Heaven.
276 The *Confucius Sinarum philosophus* makes a reference to this commentary of Zhang Juzheng. See Meynard, *The Jesuit Reading of Confucius*, pp. 157–58.
277 Zhu Xi insists on the reality of the actions of the *guishen* as *yin* and *yang* (陰陽合散，無非實者), but Zhu Xi does not discuss in his commentary of *Zhongyong* 16 about the retribution of goodness and evil. On the contrary, this point is mentioned by Zhang Juzheng in this passage of *Zhongyong* and in many other passages of the Four Books.
278 This is a quote from Shao Yong's 'Guanwu waipian' 觀物外篇, *Huangji jingshi shu* 皇極經世書.

not reach and which people cannot know, with the exception of that which I have already mentioned'.[279]

OO.46 《春秋‧隱公上》：「胡安國：春秋之時，會而歃血，其載果掌於司盟，猶不以為善也。又況私相要誓，慢鬼神，犯刑政，以成傾危之習哉？」

About chapter 'Yingong' of the *Spring and Autumn [Annals]*, the commentator Hu [Anguo]: 'Those private conspiracies and plots are by far the worst, offend the producing and destroying Spirit, and break the laws of good government, such that they destroy and corrupt everything'.[280]

OO.47 陳澔《禮記集說‧卷八‧祭義‧第二十四》：「『致鬼神，以尊上也。』致鬼神，所以極鬼神尊嚴之理。」

About chapter 24 'Jiyi' of the *Book of Rites* ('The nature of the producing and destroying Spirit is investigated and penetrated by thought in order that veneration be applied to what is above'), Chen Hao in volume 8 of his commentary [*Liji jishuo*] states as follows: 'By investigating and penetrating into the nature of the producing and destroying Spirit, the highest reason [*li*] of its majesty is acknowledged'.

PP.48 蔡虛齋《四書蒙引‧卷三‧中庸‧第十六》：「甚矣！鬼神之不測也，云云。」

About chapter 16 of the *Book of the Unalterable Mean*, Cai Xuzhai in volume 3 of his *Sishu mengyin* states as follows: 'Ah! How the producing and destroying Spirit cannot be conceived and comprehended!' See c.2, q.3, P.19.

QQ.49 《日講四書解義‧卷四‧論語‧述而》：「至鬼神之不可知者，敬而遠之可也。」

About chapter 7 of the *Analects* [*Lunyu* 7.20], the *Daily Explanation [of the Four Books]* states as follows: 'Since the Spirits cannot be known, we can revere them, but refrain from investigating them deeply'.

RR.50 張居正《四書直解‧卷四‧論語‧第六》：「人生日用，自有當為的道理。若鬼神之福善禍淫，雖與人事相為感通，然其事則幽昧而難知者也。不可知諸事以求之，惑之甚矣。今惟用力於人道之所宜，凡倫理所當盡，職分所當為者，一一着實去做。至於鬼神，則惟敬以事之而已，却不去褻近，而諂瀆禱祀以求福也。」

About chapter 6 of the *Analects* [*Lunyu* 6.20], Zhang Juzheng states as follows [in the *Sishu zhijie*]: 'A man living in daily activities has by himself the correct way of action to be followed. Concerning the good and bad things that the producing and destroying Spirit assigns respectively to good and evil people, those things are mutually connected with human actions, yet are very obscure, abstruse, and very

---

279 In his commentary of *Zhongyong* 24, Zhu Xi considers that the omens of good fortune (*zhenxiang* 禎祥) are 'the first manifestation of the principle' (理之先見者), but Noël adopts here Zhang Juzheng's interpretation of *guishen* as endowed with knowledge.

280 It is unclear from what book Noël draws this quote from Hu Anguo 胡安國 (1074–1138)'s *Chunqiuzhuan* 春秋傳. It may come from the *Chunqiu zuozhuan jujie* 春秋左傳註解 by Zhong Xing 鐘惺 (1529–1624), since this book is found in ARSI, Jap. Sin. I, 29.1. See Albert Chan, *Chinese Books and Documents from the Jesuit Archives in Rome*, p. 25.

difficult to know. Therefore, the worst blindness is to serve the Spirit in order to seek that which cannot be known. Therefore, the one thing to which people must dedicate all their strength is to conform themselves to the right way of people or right reason, that is to do whatever the right reason shows to be done and to perform truly and carefully whatever is required by one's duty and station. As for the spirit (in general) or the producing and destroying Spirit, it is enough to show him a due reverence, but you should not despise it by being too close or make offering with inopportune adulation to obtain benefits'.[281]

Question 5: What does *jiaoshe* or the Sacrifice to Heaven and Earth Mean?

I should explain here four things. First, what does it mean to sacrifice to Heaven? Second, what does it mean to sacrifice to Earth? Third, whether the sacrifice to Heaven and Earth consists in sacrificing to a material heaven and earth, or their Spirits? Fourth, whether the sacrifice to Heaven and Earth consists in worshipping the unique Spirit of Heaven and Earth?[282]

§.1. The Ritual Sacrifice to Heaven

The sacrifice to Heaven has two meanings according to whether it is conducted outdoors and indoors. When the sacrifice is conducted outdoors, Heaven is worshipped according to what is required by the Way of Heaven or Its way of acting, as well as with the purpose of showing that the Spirit of Heaven and Earth has no abode, or rather that It is not confined to an abode. Mats woven from straw or twig (Chinese used to sit on mats), earthen cups or plates, and a tender calf starting to grow horns are used; after the floor has been swept, the calf is sacrificed (A). To represent Heaven, the sign of the sun is used as substitution, just as a petty king or a prefect of the first rank can represent the emperor in imperial matters. In addition to the sign of the sun, there is also the sign of the moon, which is opposed to or corresponds to the sign of the sun (obviously each word is written on the tablet, papyrus or something similar) and both represent Heaven (B). Or rather,

---

281 For Zhang Juzheng, the *guishen* influence (*gantong* 感通) many actions of human life. One should recognize the actions of the *guishen* and conform oneself to them. One should pay respect to the *guishen*, but not attempt to influence the *guishen* for one's own advantage. From the point of view of Noël, this implies that the Chinese do not engage in idolatry. In contrast, according to the Catholic teaching, the faithful may address prayers to the Holy Virgin Mary and to the saints, prayers which are then brought to Christ. Chinese Catholics were not allowed to pray the *guishen* and the wise men of the antiquity as if they could function as intercessors to God.
282 This section on ritual inside a metaphysical treatise may appear quite surprising, but Noël quite rightly does not dissociate the belief in Heaven from the ritual to Heaven and the Spirits. He wants to show that the Chinese have a knowledge of God and also worship Him. He addresses here the issue of the hierarchy between the sacrifices given to Heaven and to the Earth. This is the longest section of the First Treatise. The Second Treatise deals entirely with the rituals to the ancestors.

to represent and reveal the Way of Heaven or Its Way of action, this Way of Heaven is only visible in its effects but not in the Author Himself (C).

When the sacrifice is made to Heaven under a roof, Heaven is worshipped according to what the way of the Lord of Heaven [Di] requires. Lamb and veal, utensils made out of reed and wood, kitchen pots and trays full of food are used, and the libations are cooked (D). In the past, the emperors Wu Wang, Huangdi, and Shennong made sacrifices beneath the roof of the hall of the imperial palace, and from the most ancient times, the hall of the imperial palace was a place of sacrifice (E). Furthermore, this hall was used to conduct the *ji* ceremony for the souls of the five ancient emperors, called *Di*, and of the five imperial ministers, called *shen* (F). Their names can be found in c.2, q.4, DD.34.

Also, Heaven is none other than the Lord of Heaven [Di], and the Lord of Heaven is none other than Heaven. Therefore, the differences in ritual are based on the fact that a circular platform is built to make sacrifices to Heaven under the open sky, and thus this is called the sacrifice to Heaven because of the round shape of the platform, which represents round Heaven, and the fact that the sacrifice to the Spirit of Heaven and Earth is conducted under a roof in order to worship the Spirit of Heaven and Earth, and thus it is called the sacrifice to the Lord of Heaven (G). This explanation should be followed even though some may hold different views (H). It happens that over time four buildings adorned with their own platforms were built in the suburbs of Beijing for the four regions of the world: placed in the south was the platform dedicated to Heaven; in the north was the platform dedicated to the earth; in the east was the platform dedicated to the sun; in the west was the platform dedicated to the moon. This is explained in volumes 82 and 83 of *Da Ming huidian*.[283] If the emperor or someone else in his name makes a sacrifice or *ji* offering there, please refer to the things mentioned above and below, unless there is a new meaning or a teaching contradicting the classical books. Indeed, the *Wenxian tongkao* discusses in great detail over several volumes the offerings made to Heaven, Earth, Sun and Moon. It often attributes to these ceremonies many things, which were not part of the original teaching of the classical books but come from the errors of the sectarians or idol worshippers.[284]

Furthermore, since everything originates from Heaven, and human beings come from their ancestors, the emperors compared their ancestors and the founder of their dynasty with Heaven. When they sacrificed to Heaven on an open platform in the suburbs (this ritual is called *jiao*, which means suburb), they inscribed the name of the ancestor on the tablet, which they placed on the altar so that he could accompany the Lord of Heaven [Di] (I). Later, Zhou Gong wanted to venerate his deceased father Wen Wang through a special honour but did not dare to perform the *ji* ritual on the open platform in the suburbs in the same way as it was performed for Houji, the founder of the dynasty. Moreover, he did not dare to despise his duty towards the Spirit of Heaven or the Lord of Heaven, by ritually worshipping Him

---

283 The reference to the *Da Ming Huidian* is not present in the manuscript.
284 This reference to the *Wenxian tongkao* is not present in the manuscript.

within the confined space of the ancestor hall in a similar way to how deceased people are venerated (K). Therefore, he started to offer the *ji* ritual to his deceased father in the hall of the imperial palace and he placed him as the companion of the Lord of Heaven in this way: the symbol [*wei*] of the Lord of Heaven was in the middle and the symbol of Wen Wang was in the South-West corner, both facing east. It was the Lord of Heaven who both presided over the *ji* ceremony and to whom the ceremony was directed (L). Zhou Gong joined his father Wen Wang as partner to the Lord of Heaven because the Lord of Heaven is the first parent or first principle of everything that has been produced, just as a father produces a son (M). Since they joined the deceased parents to the Lord of Heaven as companions, they did not perform the *ji* ceremony to the Lord of Heaven and to the deceased parents in the same way, but used different rites. For the Lord of Heaven, they used a young calf which was set aside in a clean enclosure for three months, but for the ancestors, they used any calf at hand, even one that was slightly older (N). They did it this way to distinguish the ritual service for venerating the Lord of Heaven and for venerating the souls of deceased people (O). The aim of these rituals was not the same: the aim of the ancestral ceremony was only correlative and comparative. (P). I omit here other differences.

NOTES

A.1 《詩經說約集解·周頌·我將》:「濮氏曰:文王之祀,既不敢同后稷于郊。又無屈天神於宗廟之禮。故特尊其祀于明堂,斯為曲盡矣。」「問:『天即是帝,却分祭何也?』朱子曰:『為壇而祭,故謂之天;祭于屋下,而以神祇祭之,故謂之帝。』」「曹氏曰:『以天道事之,則藁秸為席,陶匏為器,繭栗之牲,掃地而祭。以帝道事之,則牛羊為牲,簠簋為器,鼎俎之寔,其薦用熟。』」

> About ode 'Wojiang' in volume 'Zhousong', the *Exhaustive Compilation of the Book of Odes* states as follows: 'Zhou Gong did not dare to perform the *ji* ceremony for his deceased father Wen Wang outdoors in the *jiao* suburbs as it was performed for Houji, the founder of his family, nor did he dare to venerate ritually the Spirit of Heaven inside the narrow confines of the ancestor hall just as the deceased are venerated. Thus, he performed the *ji* ceremony in the hall of the imperial palace, called Mingtang. This was a clever way that he devised to fulfill his filial feelings. But you may ask: Since Heaven is none other than the Lord of Heaven, why is there this difference in sacrificial rituals? Zhu Xi answered: "The *ji* ritual is performed on a circular platform built above ground, and it is thus called Heaven or the sacrifice to Heaven; however, a sacrifice made under a roof is made to the Spirit of Heaven and Earth, and thus it is called the Lord of Heaven [*Di*], or the sacrifice to the Lord of Heaven".[285] The commentator Cao says: "When it is worshipped according to that which the Way of Heaven or Its Way of acting requires, one uses a mat woven from straw or twig, earthen cups or plates, and

---

[285] The quote comes from *Zhuzi yulei, juan* 82. Concerning *jiaoshe* 郊社, Noël adopts the interpretation of Zhu Xi who distinguished two different rituals, even though Ricci had argued that there was one single ritual offered to Shangdi. See Ricci, *The True Meaning of the Lord of Heaven*, p. 97 (n. 104).

a tiny calf starting to grow horns like threads of silk or chestnut-tree; after the floor has been swept, the calf is sacrificed. When it is sacrificed according to the requirements stipulated by the Way of the Lord of Heaven, one uses lamb and veal, utensils made of reed and wood, kitchen pots and the plates full of food".'

A.2 蔡虛齋《四書蒙引・卷一・中庸・第十九》：「祭天何以謂之郊？外也，郊對廟言，廟是人鬼。人之生也，宮室而居，故其死也，以生之所養者奉之而為廟。若天地神祇，非宮室居者，故壇而不屋。」

About chapter 19 of the *Book of the Unalterable Mean*, Cai Xuzhai in volume 1 of the *Sishu mengyin* states as follows: 'Why is the sacrifice to Heaven said to be performed in an outdoor place in the suburbs? I answer that the outdoor place in the suburbs is in contrast with the ancestor hall which concerns the souls of the departed. As long as a human being is alive, he dwells in a home (obviously in a public residence if he holds office). After he passes away, this house is considered as the place for food offerings to show filial piety, and this is made into an ancestor hall, which is called *miao* in Chinese. As for the Spirit of Heaven and the Earth, It does not dwell in any house, and thus an earth platform is built, but it is not really a house'.

B.3 《禮記・郊特牲・第十一》：「郊之祭也，迎長日之至也。大報天而主日也。兆於南郊，就陽位也；掃地而祭，於其質也；器用陶匏，以象天地之性也。」「戴冕，璪十有二旒，則天數也。乘素車，貴其質也。旂十有二旒，龍章而設日月，以象天也。天垂象，聖人則之。郊所以明天道也。帝牛不吉，以為稷牛。帝牛必在滌三月，稷牛唯具。所以別事天神與人鬼也。萬物本乎天，人本乎祖，此所以配上帝也。郊之祭也，大報本反始也。」陳澔：「稷乃人鬼，其牛但得具用足矣。」

Chapter 11 'Jiaotesheng' in volume 5 of the *Book of Rites*: 'The *jiao* sacrifice is performed outdoors in the suburbs during the winter solstice when the daytime starts to increase again. This sacrifice was performed to express the greatest gratitude to Heaven, and the Sun serves as a sign of Heaven. An earthen platform in the southern suburbs is chosen because the south represents the place of increasing light. The ground is swept and the sacrifice is made; in this matter, the simplicity and form of the rites are to be respected. Clay dishes like plates are used as utensils so as to represent the nature of Heaven and Earth'. Shortly after is added: 'When preparing for the sacrifice, the emperor wears a crown adorned with twelve ribbons hanging down in reference to the twelve months of the year. He rides a simple chariot which is not decorated to show the bare virtue of the worship. Flags painted with dragons and with twelve ribbons hanging down are carried in the front. Then, the Sun and the Moon are shown to represent Heaven. Heaven reveals the stars. The wise man imitates Heaven'.

'Through the *jiao* sacrifice, the Way of Heaven or Its Way of acting is shown and known. If something unpropitious befalls the calf that is destined to be sacrificed to the Lord of Heaven, it should be offered to the deceased prince Houji instead. The calf that will be sacrificed to the Lord of Heaven should be set apart for three months in a clean enclosure, but any calf at hand can be used for the ceremonial ritual in honour of Houji. This is how the rituals offered to the Spirit of Heaven and those offered to the deceased are distinguished. However, since all things draw their origin from Heaven and because all human beings draw their origins from their ancestors, Houji (the founder of the Zhou dynasty) is united with the Lord of Heaven or is joined as His partner in this ritual of thanksgiving. The *jiao* sacrifice is made to offer the greatest gratitude to the Origin of all things and as a reminder of It'.[286] Chen Hao comments: 'Since Ji (Houji) is only a deceased person, any calf at hand can be sacrificed to him'.

B.4 陳澔《禮記集說・祭義・第二十四》:「『郊之祭,大報天而主日,配以月。』道之大原出于天,而縣象著明,莫大乎日月。故郊以報天,而日以主神,制禮之意深遠矣。方氏曰:『郊雖以報天,然天則尊而無為,可祀之以其道,不可主之以其事,故止以日為之主焉。猶之王燕飲則主之以大夫,王嫁女則主之以諸侯而已。有其祀,必有其配,故又配以月也。猶祭社則配以勾龍,祭稷則配以周棄焉。』」

> About chapter 24 'Jiyi' in volume 8 of the *Book of Rites* ('The *jiao* sacrifice is performed to give the greatest thanks to Heaven, and the Sun serves as a sign of Heaven; the Moon, as its counterpart, is joined to the Sun'), Chen Hao makes the following comment: 'The great Origin of the Way came from Heaven, and among the suspended stars which clearly reveal themselves, there is no greater than the Sun and the Moon. Therefore, greatly mysterious and hidden is the end of this established ritual, in which the *jiao* sacrifice is performed in a suburban earth platform so as to give the greatest thanks to Heaven and the Sun is designated as the sign representing [Heaven's] Spirit. The commentator Fang says, "The *jiao* sacrifice is performed to give the greatest thanks to Heaven, because Heaven excels with supreme majesty. Therefore, the reality or nature of Heaven does not appear clearly and the Way of Heaven or Heaven's Way of Action can be adopted so as to sacrifice to [Heaven]. However, the reality or nature of Heaven cannot be understood as the visible sign of the worship, and thus the Sun can be only understood as a sign representing It. For example, when the king or emperor wants to treat someone with a banquet, he entrusts this to a prefect of the first degree managing domestic affairs. Likewise, when he wants to marry off a daughter, he entrusts that to a petty king managing domestic affairs. When the *ji* ritual is performed to someone as a ceremonial expression of gratitude, there is another expression of gratitude given to the counterpart corresponding to it: when the *ji* ritual is performed for the Sun, it is also performed for the Moon. When the *ji* ritual is performed for the Earth, or to the Spirit of the Fields, it is also performed for Goulong as its counterpart. When the *ji* ritual is performed for the Spirit of the Crops, it is also performed for Ji or Houji of the Zhou dynasty as its counterpart". Those two rulers had in the past greatly promoted agriculture, and the *ji* ritual was also made to them by association.
>
> NOTE: The way in which the Moon is associated with the Sun is different from how deceased rulers are associated with the Spirit of Fields and Crops. In the *jiao* sacrifice to Heaven, the Moon is associated with the Sun with the result that each of them is a sign representing Heaven, as it has already been said. In a different way,

---

286 This long quote does not come from a commentary, but from the *Liji* itself. The last sentence was already given above (c.1, q.2, §.2, A.1).

the Sun governs the day, and the Moon governs the night. However, in the *sheji* sacrifice to fields and crops, the deceased are associated together with the Spirit or Spirits of Fields and Crops, not as signs of these spirits, but as their imitators, namely by comparing the deeds and beenfits of those people with the fruits and benefits of the Spirit of Fields and Crops.

C.5 《禮記・哀公問・第二十七》：「公曰：『敢問君子何貴乎天道也?』孔子對曰：『貴其不已，如日月東西相從而不已也，是天道也。不閉其久，是天道也。無為而物成，是天道也。已成而明，是天道也。』」

Chapter 27 'Aigong wen' in volume 9 of the *Book of Rites* states as follows: 'Wen Gong speaking to Confucius asks, "Master, I venture to ask what is it that the wise man esteems so much in the Way of Heaven?" Confucius answers, "He esteems its constant course which is never interrupted. The Sun and the Moon constantly revolve without end or intermission, each coming after the other from east and west. This is the Way of Heaven. After thousands of years, Heaven has never stopped moving and revolving. This is the Way of Heaven. When it makes things without (visible) action and effort, this is the Way of Heaven. When things clearly reveal themselves after they have been made, this is the Way of Heaven"'.

陳澔：「劉氏曰：『蓋其機緘密，運而不已者，雖若難名，而成功則昭著也。無爲而成者，不見其為之之迹，而但見有成也。此「唯天爲大，唯尭則之」。』」

Commenting on this passage, Chen Hao cites the author Liu: 'Although the force of movement which acts in secret and without intermission cannot be easily explained or expressed, it becomes very visible once its effect has been achieved. When it is said "It makes things without action and effort", this means that the traces of that which produces the effect are not seen, but only the effect is seen after it has been completed. Mencius says, "Only Heaven can be said great, and only Yao could imitate it perfectly"'.[287] See B.3 above.

D.6 See A.2

E.7 《詩經說約集解・周頌・我將》：「《樂記》曰：『武王克殷，祀于明堂。』《新論》云：『神農氏祀明堂，有蓋而無四方。』《通典》曰：『黄帝拜祀上帝于明堂』，則明堂為祭祀之所，上古已然矣。惟宗祀文王以配上帝，昉於周公，《孝經》以此贊其孝。」

About ode 'Wojiang' in the volume 'Zhousong', the *Exhaustive Compilation of the Book of Odes* states as follows: 'According to chapter "Yueji" of the *Book of Rites*, after having defeated his enemy Zhou [紂], Wu Wang made a sacrifice in the hall of the imperial palace, called Mingtang. According to the *New Explanation* [*Xinlun*], Emperor Shennong made a sacrifice in Mingtang, which had a roof and openings unto the four directions.[288] The *Tongdian* says that Huangdi lowered

---

287 Noël attributes this to Mencius, but in fact, it comes from *Lunyu* 8.19. The same mistake is already present in the manuscript (91ʳ).
288 *Xinlun* 新論 is a political and philosophical text written by Huan Tan 桓譚 (43 BC–AD 28).

his body to ground in supplication and made a sacrifice to the Lord of Heaven in Mingtang.²⁸⁹ Therefore, Mingtang was the place of sacrifice in the imperial palace, and it was like this from ancient times. Zhou Gong started displaying honour to his parents and associated his father Wen Wang with the Lord of Heaven [*Shangdi*] in the *ji* ritual as if his father were joined to [the Lord of Heaven] as a companion. The booklet *Filial Piety* publicizes his filial piety'.²⁹⁰

F.8 蔡虛齋《四書蒙引・卷九・孟子上・梁惠王下・第二》：「明堂者，……以奉《月令》之五人帝、五人神，所以配食四郊也。」

About chapter 2 'Lianghui wang xia' in the first part of the *Mencius*, Cai Xuzhai comments in volume 9 of his *Sishu mengyin*: 'The hall of the imperial palace, Mingtang, was used to venerate five ancient emperors called *Di* and five imperial ministers called *shen*, meaning spiritual men, as it is mentioned in the chapter "Yueling" of the *Book of Rites*. When the *ji* ritual was performed for the Spirit of Heaven in the four regions of the world, it was done for those people'.²⁹¹

G.9 陳澔《禮記集說・郊特牲・第十一》：「朱子曰：『父者，我所自生。帝者，生物之祖。故推以為配而祀於明堂。』此議方正。」

About chapter 11 'Jiaotesheng', Chen Hao in volume 5 of his commentary of the *Book of Rites* cites Zhu Xi as follows: 'Since a father is he by whom I was begotten, and the Lord of Heaven [*Di*] is the first parent or first Principle of things begotten, it can therefore be deduced that the father is associated with the Lord of Heaven like a partner being added, and the *ji* ritual in the Mingtang is performed for him together with the Lord of Heaven'.²⁹²

「問：『「郊祀后稷以配天, 宗祀文王以配上帝。」帝只是天, 天只是帝, 卻分祭何也？』朱子曰：『為壇而祭, 故謂之天；祭於屋下, 而以神祇祭之, 故謂之帝。』」

You may ask: the *ji* ritual is performed on an open platform in the suburbs for Houji, who is joined to Heaven as a companion, whereas the *ji* ritual in Mingtang is performed for Wen Wang, who is joined to the Lord of Heaven as a companion, but since the Lord of Heaven is none other than Heaven, and Heaven is none other than the Lord of Heaven, why is there this distinction in the *ji* rituals? Zhu Xi answers: "Since the *ji* ritual is performed on a circular platform made of earth, it is called Heaven or the sacrifice to Heaven. When the ritual sacrifice is made under a roof, it is called the Lord of Heaven or the sacrifice to the Lord of Heaven because the sacrifice is performed for the Spirit of Heaven and of Earth [*shendi*]".²⁹³
See above [q.5.]A.1.

---

289 *Tongdian* 通典 is an administrative history written by Du You 杜佑 (735–812).
290 *Filial Piety* corresponds to the *Xiaojing*. This work was translated into Latin by Noël.
291 In the *Mencius*, King Xuan is advised against destroying Mingtang. See *Mencius* 2B12.
292 This interpretation is drawn from Zhu Xi's *Zhuzi yulei, juan* 82.
293 Zhu Xi, *Zhuzi yulei, juan* 82.

H. 陳澔《禮記集說・郊特牲・第十一》：「今按郊祀一節，先儒之論不一者：有子月、寅月之異；有周禮、魯禮之分；又以郊與圜丘為二事；又有祭天與祈穀為二郊。今皆不復詳辨，而以朱說為定。」

[About chapter 11 'Jiaotesheng', Chen Hao in his commentary *Liji jishuo* states as follows]: 'Ancient writers held different opinions about the *jiao* sacrifice. Some wanted it performed in the month Zi and others in the month Yin.[294] Some distinguished the rituals of the Zhou dynasty from the rituals of the kingdom of Lu. Others considered that the *jiao* sacrifice in the suburbs was not the same as the sacrifice performed on the circular mound or platform. Others held that the sacrifice to Heaven and the sacrifice to pray for crops were performed in two different suburban places. Since all those things cannot be discussed further, the opinion of Zhu Xi should be followed'.

I.10 See B.3.

K.11 《詩經說約集解・周頌・我將》：「此宗祀文王于明堂，以配上帝也，曰明堂之祭，主之者上帝也。」

About ode 'Wojiang' in the volume 'Zhousong', the *Exhaustive Compilation of the Book of Odes* states as follows: 'This expression of piety towards one's parents, or *ji* ritual, was performed for Wen Wang in the Mingtang with the purpose of joining him as a companion to the Lord of Heaven [*Shangdi*]. Hence it is said that the Lord of Heaven presides above the *ji* ritual in the imperial hall (*Mingtang*) and is the one to whom the ritual is offered'.

L. 《詩經說約集解・周頌・我將》：「明堂之位，帝居中，文王居西南，主皆西生東向。」

Further below [about the ode 'Wojiang', the *Exhaustive Compilation of the Book of Odes* states as follows]: 'The arrangement of the images in Mingtang was like this: the symbol of the Lord of Heaven [*Di*] was in the middle, and the symbol of Wen Wang was in the south-west corner; both of them looked to the East'. See above A.1.

M.12 See above G.9.

N.13 See above B.3.

O.14 See above B.3.

P.15 See above B.3.

---

294 The month Zi corresponds to the eleventh lunar month, and the month Yin to the first lunar month.

§.2. Ritual Sacrifice to Earth

The sacrifice to Earth has a double meaning. First, the sacrifice to Earth is combined with the outdoor ritual to Heaven, that is to say, the sacrifice to Earth is encompassed within the sacrifice to Heaven. Indeed, the vases used in the sacrifice to Heaven represented the nature of Heaven and Earth, and the sacrifice to Heaven was something by which the Way of Heaven or Heaven's mode of action was revealed and understood (Q). The Earth is encompassed in the Way of Heaven since Heaven and Earth as reason is the way of Heaven, as we said above in c.2, q.3, W.34. Earth is not mentioned more often because it is already encompassed in Heaven, either understood as a perceptible body or as vital breath (R). The emperor is often said to sacrifice to Heaven and Earth, and Earth is implicitly included in the sacrifice to Heaven (S). This is different from the sacrifice of Earth performed in the northern *jiao* suburbs since this place is dedicated to the sacrifice to Earth (T). Therefore, the worship to Earth is included in the worship to Heaven.

NOTES

Q.16 《文獻通考・卷七十一・郊社考四》：「臣以此知古者祀上帝, 並祀地祇矣。何以明之?《詩》之序曰：『《昊天有成命》, 郊, 祀天地也。』終篇言天而不及地。頌以告神明也, 未有歌其所不祭, 祭其所不歌也。今祭地於北郊, 獨歌天而不歌地, 豈有此理哉?臣以知周之世祀上帝, 則地祇在焉。歌天而不歌地, 所以尊上帝, 故其序曰『郊祀天地』也。」

> Volume 71 of the *Wenxian tongkao* states as follows: 'We know that when the ancients sacrificed to the Lord of Heaven (*Shangdi*), they sacrificed the Spirit of Earth at the same time. This is proven by the prologue to the *Book of Odes*: "Highest Heaven has a perfect law; the *jiao* sacrifice consists in sacrificing to Heaven and Earth".[295] At the end of the ode, only Heaven and not Earth is named. Clearly those verses are sung to celebrate the Spirit: for he to whom no sacrifice is made is not celebrated in song; nor is a sacrifice made to him who is not celebrated in song. How can it be that only Heaven and not Earth is celebrated in song when a sacrifice is made on the platform in the northern suburb? We know for sure that under the Zhou dynasty, the Spirit of Earth was included in the sacrifice to *Shangdi*. Therefore, celebrating Heaven and not Earth in song is the way in which we venerate the highest majesty of *Shangdi*'.[296] See also B.3 above and FFF.67 below.

R.17 蔡虛齋《四書蒙引・卷一・大學》：「『天道流行, 發育萬物。』不言地者, 以形言, 則天之形包乎地之外也；以氣言, 則地之氣實亦天之氣也。生物主宰, 全是天, 只借地以發育之耳, 故地非天敵也。言天, 則地在其中矣。」

> Cai Xuzhai in volume 1 of his *Sishu mengyin* explains these words of Zhu Xi concerning the *Science of Adults*: 'The Way of Heaven, constantly active, produces

---

[295] This prologue is a reference to the Short Preface [*xiaoxu* 小序] to the *Mao shixu* 毛詩序.
[296] This Chinese quote and the Latin translation are absent from the manuscript and were added later. We have retrieved the Chinese directly from the *Wenxian tongkao*.

and preserves all things'.²⁹⁷ He states as follows: 'He does not mention Earth or the way of Earth, because if you take Heaven as a perceptible body, then Earth is already included; and if you take Heaven as vital breath, the vital breath of Earth is in reality the vital breath of Heaven. Heaven is the total and complete Producer and Lord of things, and in the production of things, Heaven receives from Earth only the support of nourishment. Therefore, Earth cannot therefore be put on par with Heaven. When we say Heaven, Earth is already included'.²⁹⁸

S.18 陳澔《禮記集說・卷二・曲禮下・第二》:「『天子祭天地, 祭四方, 祭山川。』呂氏曰: 此章泛論祭祀之法, 冬日至祭天, 夏日至祭地, 四時各祭其方以迎氣。」

Chapter 2 'Quli xia' of the *Book of Rites* states as follows: 'The emperor makes a *ji* sacrifice to Heaven and Earth, to the four regions of the world, to mountains and rivers or their spirits'. Commenting on this passage, Chen Hao in volume 2 of [*Liji jishuo*] cites the writer Lü as follows: 'This passage deals more broadly with the rules for the *ji* offerings. At the winter solstice, the emperor makes a sacrifice to Heaven whereas in summer he sacrifices to Earth (either on a platform made of earth as said below, or through a sacrifice to Heaven that encompasses Earth but under a different name). However, in each of the four seasons, he makes an offering to the four regions of the world to receive a different mixture of air, etc.' Finally, the same writer [Lü] criticizes this passage in different ways.²⁹⁹

S.19 陳澔《禮記集說・卷三・王制・第五》:「天子祭天地, 諸侯祭社稷, 大夫祭五祀。天子祭天下名山大川。」

Chapter 5 'Wangzhi' in volume 3 of the *Book of Rites* states as follows: 'The emperor makes offering to Heaven and Earth; the petty king to the Spirit of Earth or the Spirit of the Fields and Crops; the prefect of the first degree or governor to the five Spirits of the House. The emperor also makes offering to the most famous mountains and important rivers of the empire, i.e., to their Spirits'. Almost the same thing is mentioned in chapter 9 'Liyun' of volume 4 of the *Book of Rites*. See also below VV.51.

T.20 蔡虛齋《四書蒙引・卷四・中庸・第十九》:「祭天何以謂之郊?外也, 郊對廟言, 廟是人鬼。人之生也, 宮室而居; 故其死也, 以生之所養者奉之而為廟。若天神地祇, 非屋居者, 故壇而不屋。今之山川社稷, 皆壇也。」

About chapter 19 of the *Book of the Unalterable Mean*, Cai Xuzhai in volume 4 of his *Sishu mengyin* comments the following: 'Why is the sacrifice to Heaven called *jiao* performed in an outdoor suburban place? He answers that the outdoor suburban

---

297 Zhu Xi, *Zhuzi yulei*, juan 1.
298 As Felix Wong remarks, even though *Tian* and Di 'apparently play an approximately equal role in the evolution and production of everything', Noël borrowed from some commentators, such as Cai Qing, the idea that the Earth was inferior to Heaven. See Wong, '*The Unalterable Mean*', p. 219. Noël makes the same point below (WW.54) about the inferiority of Earth compared to *Tian*, still referring to Cai Qing.
299 The last sentence by Noël suggests that Master Lü (呂氏) was against broadening the category of the *ji* sacrifices. Indeed, Mr Lü limits the number of *ji* sacrifices, from the emperor down to the literati, to only five (則自天子至士, 皆祭五祀).

place is in contrast to the ancestor hall, called *miao* in Chinese. The ancestor hall is for the souls of the departed. When a person is alive, he resides in a house (an official house if he holds office). After his death, his home is used to give food offerings as acts of filial piety in the place of his past life, and it is transformed into an ancestral hall or house of representation, in Chinese *miao*. However, the Spirit of Heaven and Earth does not reside in any house. Thus, earthen platform, and not a house, is erected. In this way an earthen platform is now erected for the spirits of the mountains, rivers, region or fields, and crops'.

「天子之社便是地, 豈社外又有地哉？故朱子取五峰胡氏之說, 謂『無北郊祭地之理』, 且引《周禮》及〈郊特牲〉為證, 似無疑矣。臨川吳氏乃反之, 以為天子祭地於北郊之方澤；此只據《禮記》之說, 且曰：『胡氏以為天子之尊, 亦只祭社而已』, 蓋不知天子之社即地也。」

Also, the imperial earthen platform used to sacrifice to the Spirit of Earth, called *she* in Chinese, is the same as earth. After all, how could there be any other earth besides the earthen platform? Doctor Zhu Xi accepts the opinion of Hu Wufeng and rejects having a platform in the northern suburbs for sacrificing to Earth. Zhu Xi cites as evidence the *Book of Rites of the Zhou Dynasty* and the chapter 'Jiaotesheng' of the *Book of Rites*, and thus there cannot be any doubt about this. However, Wu Linchuan considers that the emperor had worshipped to Earth within a square trench in the platform of the northern suburbs, but Wu only relies on the words of the *Book of Rites* and then mentions the commentator Hu as saying, "Since the emperor excels in supreme majesty, he sacrifices only on the earthen platform". Clearly, Wu Linchuan did not know that the imperial earthen platform called *she* was the same as earth'. See also below RR.48.[300]

「王應韶嘗問清曰：『祭祀之禮亦有似無謂者, 今祭天地山川, 悉以人間飲食之屬, 其實天地山川之神, 豈能飲食此耶？』清謂：『此箇[301]道理, 終不可易。』」

Also, Cai Xuzhai says a little further down: 'Emperor Yingshao once asked Doctor Qing, "The *ji* rituals do not seem to accord with right reason: for those things which are offered in sacrifice to Heaven, Earth, rivers and mountains are only things used by human beings for food and drink. How could the Spirits of Heaven, Earth, mountains and rivers eat or drink them?" To this Doctor Qing answers, "This is indeed something which is absolutely unalterable".[302]

---

300 This makes reference to the long scholarly and political dispute about the *jiaoshe* ritual. As we can read here, Zhu Xi and Hu Wufeng 胡五峰 (Hu Hong 胡宏, 1105–1161) supported performing the *jiao* and *she* rituals at one place, the Altar of Heaven (southern suburbs), while Wu Linchuan (Wu Cheng 吳澄, 1249–1333) supported performing the ritual in two different places (southern suburbs for the *jiao* ritual, and northern suburbs for the *she* ritual). The choice of quotes by Noël shows clearly that he supports the view of Zhu Xi and Hu Wufeng, which coincides more closely with Christian monotheism.
301 The manuscript has *tong* 筒 instead of *ge* 箇.
302 This refers to a conversation between Cai Qing and Wang Yunfeng 王雲鳳 (1465–1518), *zi* Yingshao 應韶, *hao* Hugu 虎谷. Here Noël mistakes him for an emperor.

The second way of sacrificing to Earth is as follows: once when the emperor had set up a tract of land in the kingdom, he dedicated a special place to perform the *ji* ritual every spring and autumn to the Spirit of crops which the people needed to survive, and to the Spirit of the land or region and the fields which the crops need to grow and the people need as a place to stay. This place was within the enclosure of the ancestor hall of the deceased kings on the right hand side and between the middle and first or exterior door. The platform of piled earth which stood in the middle and in the open, was not too high, with the eastern side painted blue, the southern red, the western white and the northern black. The area on the top was covered with red earth or yellow earth in the case of an imperial platform. Indeed, the emperor had two platforms of Earth, one for the imperial city and another for the whole empire. Similarly, a petty king had two platforms, one for their royal city and one for all his people or for his fiefdom, while the officers of the first degree or governors had only one. The imperial platform was 50 cubits wide, whereas the royal platform was only 25 cubits wide. Around the platform was a flat area with a long line of trees planted on both sides. The area was enclosed by a low wall (V). Besides the mound of the southern suburbs where the emperor sacrificed to Heaven and Earth at the same time (X), there was also another place where he specifically sacrificed to Earth. This place seems to be threefold at least.

NOTES

V.21 《白虎通・社稷》：「《禮記・三正》曰：『王者二社，為天下立社曰太社，自為立社曰王社；諸侯為百姓立社曰國社，自為立社曰侯社。』」「社稷在中門之外，外門之內。」「右社稷，左宗廟。」「《禮・祭法》曰：『大夫成羣立社曰置。』」「社無屋。」「《周官》曰：『司社，而樹之各以土地所生。』」「王者自親祭社稷何？社者，土地之神也。土生萬物，天下之所主也。尊重之，故自祭也。其壇大何？如《春秋・文義》曰：『天子之社稷，廣五丈，諸侯半之。』其色如何？《春秋傳》曰：『天子有太社焉。東方青色，南方赤色，西方白色；北方黑色，上冒以黄土。』」

    The chapter 'Sheji' of the *Baihu tong*, or *Ordinary Meaning of the Royal Scholars*:³⁰³ 'According to the chapter "Sanzheng" of the *Book of Rites*, the emperor has two earthen platforms: the one which he establishes for the empire is called the great and primary platform (*taishe*); and the other which he establishes for his imperial city is called the platform of the emperor (*dishe*).³⁰⁴ Similarly, the one that the petty king establishes for his people is called the platform of the kingdom, and the other which is establishes for himself is called the platform of the petty king'. A little further down: 'The platform of the Earth and crops is situated outside the

---

303 The *Baihu tong* is mentioned above (c.2, q.4, V.22) and below (c.2, q.5, Y.27). The literal meaning is: the discussions of the white tiger, in reference to the White Tiger Pavilion in Luoyang where the discussions took place in the year 79. Ban Gu (32–92) is considered as the editor of the work, on the orders of emperor Zhang of Han. Here Noël translates the title as *Ordinary Meaning of the Royal Scholars*, reflecting the official dimension of this work.

304 The text of the *Baihu tong* has in fact *wangshe* 王社 and not *dishe* 帝社. In Y.27, Noël explicitly has *dishe* as an equivalent of *wangshe*.

middle door of the ancestor hall and inside the first exterior door'. Still below: 'The platform of Earth and crops is on the right, and the ancestor hall on the left'. Again, further below: 'According to the chapter "Jifa" of the *Book of Rites*, the primary officer, who is in charge of a multitude of people, also establishes an earthen platform, which is called the specially appointed platform'. A little further below: 'The platform of the Earth is in the open air'. Then, shortly after: 'According to the *Zhouguan*, the officer in charge of the platform planted trees according to the qualities of each region'. A few words down below is added: 'You may ask why the emperor himself sacrifices on the platform of the Earth and crops? The answer is that the Spirit of the platform of Earth is the Spirit of the region; the Earth produces all things, that is, everything pertaining to the empire, and since the emperor venerates and esteems the Spirit of the region, he himself sacrifices to It. You may further ask how large the platform of this Spirit is. According to the chapter "Wenyi" of the *Chunqiu*, the imperial platform for the region and the crops is 50 cubits whereas the royal platform is 25 cubits.[305] What colour is it? According to the commentary of the *Chunqiu*, the greatest and primary platform of the emperor is painted in blue in the east, red in the south, white in the west and black in the north, and the area above is covered with yellow earth'.

V.22 朱熹《孟子・卷七・盡心下》:「社, 土神; 稷, 穀神。建國則立壇壝以祀之。」

About chapter 7 'Jinxin xia' in the second part of the *Mencius*, Zhu Xi comments as follows: 'The character *she* (platform of Earth or of the region) means the Spirit of Earth or of the region; the character *ji* (platform of crops, which was the same, or at least in the same enclosure) means the Spirit of cereals. When some tract of land is erected in the kingdom, thereupon is built a platform of earth, which is surrounded by a small wall, to make offerings to the Spirit of Earth and crops'.[306]

X.23 《文獻通考・卷七十六・郊社考九》:「哲宗元祐七年, 帝初郊, 合祭地祇於圓丘。」

Volume 76 of the *Wenxian tongkao* states as follows: 'In the seventh year, called *Yuanyou*, Emperor Zhezong, after first making a sacrifice to Heaven, thereupon made a sacrifice to the Spirit of Earth on the circular platform in the southern suburbs'.[307]

The first place is called *she*, the platform of the Spirit of Earth, where the emperor in the summer solstice sacrificed to Earth (Z). It is wrongly called *beijiao*, that is, the mound of the northern suburbs for sacrificing to Earth since the character *jiao* indicates specifically a sacrifice to Heaven taking place in the southern suburbs (W).[308]

---

305 One *zhang* 丈 equals 3.33 metres, so 50 *zhang* amount to 166 metres. However, one cubit equals around 5 metres, so 50 cubits amount to 250 metres.
306 Drawn from Zhu Xi's *Sishu zhangju jizhu*.
307 The Chinese text for X.23 and Z.24 is not present in the manuscript, and it was retrieved directly from the *Wenxian tongkao*.
308 The text here does not match with quote W.35. Noël seems to refer here to a quote from the *Wenxian tongkao* (*juan* 68) where Chen Xiangdao 陳祥道 (1044–1116) mentions the problematic expression of

The place *she* is also called *fangze* or *fangqiu*, that is a ditch in square mound in which the offerings are buried. For many centuries, there has been a great and endless controversy about this sacrifice among Chinese scholars, specifically over whether the emperor should sacrifice to Heaven and Earth together or separately. Some emperors sacrificed together and others separately, sacrificing to Heaven in the winter solstice and Earth in the summer solstice. This controversy is discussed in several volumes of the *Wenxian tongkao*, namely volumes 70, 71, 72, 74, 75, etc. As I understand, the *Da Ming huidian* presents the sacrifice to Heaven and Earth together in *juan* 81, the individual sacrifice to Heaven in *juan* 82, and the individual sacrifice to Earth in *juan* 83.

The second place for the emperor to sacrifice to Earth is called *taishe*, that is, the great and primary platform of Earth that the emperor erected to worship the Spirit of Earth in thanksgiving on behalf of the whole empire.

The third place is called *dishe*, that is, the imperial platform of Earth that the emperor erected for the same reason on behalf of the imperial city.[309]

NOTES

Z.24 《文獻通考・卷七十六・郊社考九》：「楊氏曰：冬至一陽生，此天道之始也。」「陽一噓而萬物生，此又天道生物之始也。故《周官・大司樂》以圜鍾為宮，冬日至，於地上之圜丘奏之，六變以祀天神，所以順天道之始而報天也。」「夏至一陰生，此地道之始也；陰一噏而萬物成，又地道成物之始也。故《大司樂》以函鍾為宮，夏日至，於澤中之方丘奏之，八變以祀地示，所以順地道之始而報地也。」

> Volume 76 of the *Wenxian tongkao* cites Doctor Yang as follows: 'The winter solstice is the beginning of the Way of Heaven, which starts producing things through the unfolding of *yang*. Hence during the winter solstice, a sacrifice is offered to the Spirit of Heaven on the circular platform so as to be in conformity with the beginning of the Way of Heaven and to give thanks to Heaven. This is performed in the southern suburbs to be in conformity with the place of the increasing year'. (This means the place where the sun is found in the southern zodiac). 'The summer solstice is the beginning of the Way of Earth which starts making things complete through the return of *yin*, and thus, during the summer solstice, a sacrifice is offered to the Spirit of Earth on the square platform so as to be in conformity with the beginning of the Way of Earth and to give thanks to the Earth. This is performed in the northern suburbs so as to be in conformity with the place of the decreasing year'. (This means the place where the Sun is found in the northern zodiac).[310]

---

beijiao: '陳氏《禮書》曰：「祀天於南郊，而地上之圜丘者，南郊之丘也。丘圜而高，所以象天，此所謂'為高必因丘陵」也。祭地於北郊，而澤中之方丘者，北郊之丘也'.

309 The references to the *Da Ming Huidian* and the *Wenxian tongkao* are not found in the manuscript.
310 This passage is not present in the manuscript and the Chinese text has been retrieved directly from *Wenxian tongkao*.

W.25 蔡沈《書經集傳・卷四・商書・泰誓中》:「『郊社不修』。郊所以祭天;社所以祭地。」

> Chapter 'Taishi' of the *Book of Imperial Annals* states as follows: 'Emperor Zhou neglected the *jiaoshe* rite of sacrificing to Heaven and Earth'. Cai Chen in volume 4 [of the *Shujing jizhuan*] comments as follows: '*Jiao* is the sacrifice to Heaven, and *she* the sacrifice to Earth'.[311]

Y.26 《文獻通考・卷八十二・郊社考十五》:「魏自漢後,但太社有稷,官社無稷,故常二社一稷也。至明帝景初中,立帝社。」

> Volume 82 of the *Wenxian tongkao* states as follows: 'In the Han dynasty and at the beginning of the Wei dynasty a platform, called *she*, was erected for the Earth, and another platform, called *ji*, was erected for the crops. Later, a primary platform for the Earth (*taishe*) and the crops was added. In addition, a special platform was built for the emperor, called *dishe*'.[312]

Y.27 《白虎通・卷一・社稷》:「王者有二社:為天下立社曰太社,自為立社曰王社。」

> Volume 1 of the *Baihu tong* states as follows: 'The platform *taishe* is for giving thanks on behalf of the whole empire, while the platform *wangshe*, or *dishe*, for giving thanks on behalf of the capital of the empire'.

Y.28 《文獻通考・卷八十二・郊社考十五》:「王為群姓立社曰太社,王自為立社曰王社;諸侯為百姓立社曰國社,諸侯自為立社曰侯社;大夫以下成群立社曰置社。」

> The beginning of volume 82 of the *Wenxian tongkao* states as follows: 'The emperor builds for all the inhabitants of the empire the platform of Earth, called *taishe*, that is, the first and great platform of Earth. Then he builds for himself another platform called *wangshe*, that is, the imperial platform of the Earth. The petty kings erect for their subjects a platform called *she*, which is called the platform or mound of the kingdom. Then they build for themselves another platform or mound, which is called royal. The primary officers or governors, as well as the other lower officers who rule or manage a certain number of houses (at least one hundred), build a platform of Earth, which is called *zhishe*, that is a platform of Earth established for a singular or particular purpose'.[313]

---

311 Neither the text of the *Shujing* nor Cai Chen's comment are found on the manuscript which has instead the following comment by Chen Hao on the *Liji*, which quotes himself Hu Wufeng: 陳澔《禮記集說・郊特牲第十一》:「五峰言『無北郊,只祭社便是』;此說卻好。今按〈召誥〉『用牲于郊,牛二』,蔡氏以為祭天地,非也。牛二,帝牛、稷牛也。社于新邑,祭地也,故用太牢'.

312 This passage is not present in the manuscript and the Chinese text has been retrieved directly from *Wenxian tongkao*. This quote comes from the chapter 'Liwu' of the *Diantong* 典通 by Du You 杜佑 (735–812).

313 This passage is not present in the manuscript and the Chinese text has been retrieved directly from *Wenxian tongkao*.

Moreover, at the beginning of the Chinese monarchy, Prince Gonggong obtained or subjugated all nine provinces of China, that is the whole country as it was divided at the time. Then his own son Goulong, who had given peace to the country, contained the rushing waters and advanced agriculture, was named Houtu, that is, officer of the Earth, or ruler over the Earth (AA). When they sacrificed to the Spirit of Earth on one of those platforms, they performed the *ji* ritual to Goulong at the same time, placing him as an associate on the table with the Spirit of Earth to give thanks for ancient benefits. In a similar way, they placed Prince Houji, officer or ruler of the crops, who had greatly promoted agriculture, as associate on the table with the Spirit of crops. When they sacrificed to the Spirit of crops, they performed also the *ji* ritual to Houji (BB). Hence Prince Goulong was even called the Spirit of Earth or fields, and Prince Houji, the Spirit of crops (CC). (Evidently, the souls of those deceased people who had been officers of agriculture were not the true Spirits of fields and crops). The *ji* ritual was not performed on this platform primarily to them, but only through association. The *ji* ritual was performed primarily to the supreme Spirit of Earth and Heaven, or to a tutelar Spirit as I shall say soon. The ritual was performed to other deceased people only as associates of the table or banquet by placing their tablets next to the tablets of the true Spirits, to give thanks for the benefits which had been received (DD).

NOTES

AA.29 陳澔《禮記集說・卷八・祭法・第二十三》：「共工氏之霸九州也, 其子曰后土, 能平九州, 故祀以為社。」

    Chapter 23 'Jifa' in volume 8 of the *Book of Rites* states as follows: 'Prince Gonggong had gained power and subjugated the nine provinces of China. Later, his own son was named Houtu, that is, officer in charge of or ruling over the Earth because he had established peace in the nine provinces. The *ji* ritual was performed on the earthen platform to him as the Spirit of Earth'.[314]

BB.30 《字彙・社字》：「土神能生萬物, 以右之有大功者配之, 共工氏有子曰句龍, 為后土, 能平水土, 故祀以為社。后土, 官名, 故世人謂社為后土。」

    The dictionary *Zihui* defines the character *she* as follows: 'The character *she* means the Spirit of Earth producing all things. The ancient men who performed great service to the empire were associated with the Spirit of Earth, and joined to It as associates, and the *ji* ritual was performed for them at the same time. Goulong, the son of Prince Gonggong, was called Houtu. Since he contained the rushing waters and brought peace to the whole region, the *ji* ritual was later performed to him on the earthen platform as the Spirit of Earth. The name Houtu means officer of Earth. Worldly and foolish people have called this officer of Earth, the Spirit of the earthen platform'. See above B.4.[315]

---

314 Houtu, son of Gonggong, was the object of a *ji* ritual on the earthen platform, being associated with the Spirit of Earth. This could appear as a case of idolatry, but Noël provided an accurate translation.

315 Goulong is written either 勾龍 or 句龍, with the same pronunciation. Following Zheng Xuan 鄭玄

CC.31 蔡沈《書經集傳・卷四・周書・定武成》：「『厎商之罪, 告于皇天后土。』后土, 社也。勾龍為后土。」

> Chapter 'Wucheng' in volume 4 of the *Book of Imperial Annals* states: 'As for the sins of the Shang dynasty (that is, of Emperor Zhou), I told Great Heaven and Thick Earth, in Chinese Huangtian Houtu (according to Zhang Juzheng, the Spirit of Great Heaven and Thick Earth or Master of Heaven and Master of Earth)'. Cai Chen comments on this passage as follow: 'The two character word Houtu or Thick Earth is the earthen platform *she* or the Spirit of the earthen platform. Prince Goulong is called Houtu as officer of Earth'.

> 嚴保琭《詩經辨錯解》辨曰：「此解有兩未當。皇, 君也；后, 亦君也。君天君土, 言上帝也。天地皆上帝所造成, 豈上帝獨君天而不君土乎？豈君天屬之上帝, 君土尚有他屬乎？」

> A certain Christian bachelor [scholar] named Paul Yan[316] argues against Cai Chen, saying: 'His commentary makes two mistakes. The word *Huang* does not mean here great, but Ruler or Master, and the word *Hou* does not mean here thick but Ruler or Master (Note that a Chinese dictionary gives this meaning as the first definition for those two words). Therefore, by "Master of Heaven and Earth" should be understood *Shangdi*, the Lord and Ruler of Heaven. Indeed, Heaven and Earth are made by the Lord of Heaven, or *Shangdi*. Could the Lord of Heaven rules only over Heaven, without ruling over Earth? Since the dominion over Heaven is held by *Shangdi*, could it be that dominion over Earth be be held by another?'

DD 蔡沈《書經集傳・卷四・周書・定武成》：「注所言后土, 官名也。此本《祭法》共工之子曰后土, 能平九州, 故祀以為社。勾龍, 人名也, 此本《春秋傳》, 勾龍為后土, 蓋后土掌水土之官, 勾龍或嘗居是官。然此不過以為祭之配而已, 鄭玄云：『勾龍以有平水土之功, 配社祀, 非謂即祀以為社也。』」

> Cai Chen rejects what is said about Prince Houtu as Spirit of the earthen platform: 'What the commentators call Houtu is only the name of some officer of agriculture; in chapter 23 "Jifa" in volume 8 of the *Book of Rites* Houtu is called the son of Gonggong. Since he obtained peace for all nine provinces, the *ji* ritual was performed to him, like to the Spirit of Earth. This son was called Goulong, but it

---

(quoted already in c. 1, q.2, §.6, Q.21), the *Zihui* points out the confusion made by ordinary people between the man Goulong and the Spirit of Earth. Zheng Xuan and the *Zihui* talk only about the confusion made by ordinary people (*shiren*), but Noël stressed also their foolishness, implying the foolishness of making a man divine. In the context of the Rites Controversy, Noël was keen to show here that Chinese literati made a distinction between the official ritual to the Spirit of Earth and the popular interpretation identifying the man Goulong with the Spirit of Earth. In fact, the ancient texts are contradictory and difficult to harmonize in one sense or the other.

316 This is only one of two quotes by Chinese Christians in the first two chapters of the First Treatise. This is also the only explicit reference to the Chinese Christian Paul Yan or Yan Mo 嚴謨 in the Chinese text of the manuscript. In the *Ditian kao*, Yan Mo refers to a larger work, already lost, called the *Shishu biancuojie* 詩書辨錯解. The mention of *Shijing* 詩經 on the manuscript seems here a mistake for *Shishu* 詩書. In this quote, Yan Mo conflates Huangtian and Houtu into one, that is, Shangdi. Noël seems here to agree on this monotheistic reading of *Huangtian houtu*, though it is quite debatable.

is only a personal name, and the commentary of *Chunqiu* [*Zuozhuan*] says that Goulong was called Houtu because the Houtu was an officer in charge of water and land, and probably Goulong had once held this office. The *ji* ritual was only performed to him as an associate to the Spirit of Earth. Doctor Zheng Xuan says: "The *ji* ritual was performed on an earthen platform both to the Spirit of Earth and Prince Goulong, who was associated to the Spirit of Earth because of his merits in containing the flooding waters and in making the land peaceful, but this does not mean the *ji* ceremony was performed to him as if he he were the spirit of the earthen platform".[317]

As for the Chenghuang temple, it has no connection with this [*jiaoshe* ritual]. The origin of this temple is related as follows: during the Han dynasty, there was a general named Guan Ying who was renown for his loyalty and courage. Under the Jin dynasty, a sign was erected in his honour. After some time had passed, a temple was erected with an elaborate statue of him. He was believed to be in charge of the magistrates, cities, and city dwellers. When taking office, as well as on the first and fifteenth day of every month, magistrates would go to this temple and prostrate in front of the statue (EE). Therefore, this statue is not less an Idol than the other many Chinese idols, but it has nothing in common with the earthen platform. Indeed, the classical books and their interpreters say nothing about the word Chenghuang, which means the dry moats of the city wall. Thus this temple has no connection with the teaching of those Chinese being discussed here. It is true that volume 94 of the *Da Ming huidian* discusses Chenghuang and the *ji* sacrifice together with the souls deprived from rituals and makes some ridiculous and superstitious prescriptions, but these rituals are not supported by the authority of any classical book. Moreover, the *Da Ming huidian* itself does not adhere to classical teaching and contains many other superstitions established especially by emperor Jiajing, a supporter of idolatrous sects. The work even prescribes the common *ji* ritual to the Spirit of Chenghuang together with the Spirits of mountains and rivers. Thus this work either discusses these things in a superstitious way or takes Chenghuang as the Spirit of the city wall.[318]

I think these earthen platforms held by the emperor, petty kings, and governors within the enclosures of their ancestor hall no longer exist in the same way, but volume 85 of the *Da Ming huidian* states that *taisheji*, the imperial platform of Earth and crops, was erected outside the southern door on the right-hand side (in the

---

317 While in the Shang and Zhou dynasties the term *pei* 配 had a strong religious association of being united with the divine, starting with Zheng Xuan in the Han dynasty, the association becomes mostly moral, to be united with the virtue of the wise of the past. Such was the interpretation of Zhu Xi and other neo-Confucians. Noël seems to project the religious meaning of ancient Confucianism onto the moral meaning of neo-Confucianism.
318 The discussion about the *Da Ming huidian* is not present in the manuscript. Noël has eight mentions of the *Da Ming huidian*, which were added later, and he seems to hold a quite negative view of this work, especially in relation to the corrupting influence of emperor Jiajing 嘉靖 (1507–1567; r. 1521–1567) who published a revised edition and who was an follower of Taoism.

imperial city) and surrounded by a wall. Its design was the same that used for the *ji* ritual.[319] In the same passage it is similarly mentioned that Emperor Jiajing ordered the erection of a *disheji*, a platform of Earth and crops, in another enclosure.[320] The platform *taishijie* is on behalf of the whole empire, as I said above, but the platform *disheji* is only on behalf of the imperial city. But the same work says that the platform *disheji* and its *ji* ritual was later abrogated.

Moreover, volume 94 of the *Da Ming huidian* prescribes and describes the platform or mound for the Spirit of the region and of crops to be used in all other cities of China, as well as *ji* ritual for it.[321] I write down below the description of the platform exactly as I saw and examined it in Nanchang, the metropolitan city of Jiangxi province. Since the Chinese empire loves complete uniformity in public affairs and especially in buildings, I think that such platforms or earthen mounds are similar to the ones erected in other cities. Like the metropolitan cities of other provinces, Nanchang is divided into two towns, and has in its suburbs two earthen platforms, one located in the south and another in the north. During spring and autumn, the governors of the two towns, one in the southern platform and the other in the northern platform, perform the *ji* ritual by themselves or through a lower level officer. They offer a goat, a pig, or both, which had been slaughtered earlier by the butcher and with the whole body being stripped of hair, together with reels of silk next to a tablet on which is written the name of the Spirit or the Spirits (mountains, rivers, fields, crops of the region). I saw the platform in the north: it looks like an oblong area surrounded by a low wall. The door entrance is supported by columns, and it is always open and freely accessible. Not far away from the end of the area, a low earthen platform is erected, with the shape of a square. On the platform is fastened a stone column of around two feet high, with square pedestal and the rest round. This is because the Chinese represent earth as a square and heaven as a circle. In front of the platform there is a delapidated building supported by columns, open on both sides and without door. In this building there is nothing other than walls, columns and roof. When the *ji* ritual is performed, tables are arranged in this building which wide open from the area of the earthen platform. On each of these tables are tablets on which are written the names of the Spirits of the mountains, rivers, crops, and on other tables are placed the dishes to be offered. This building seems to be built more for making offerings than for other purpose, such as protection from wind and rain when the ritual is performed, as it is written in volume 85 the *Da Ming huidian* about the imperial platforms of earth and crops. Therefore, when there is not such a building, as it

---

319 *Da Ming huidian* (1587), *juan* 85: '洪武三年，於壇北建享殿，又北建拜殿，各五間，以備風雨行禮。十年，改建社稷壇於午門外之右。先是社主用石，高五尺，闊二尺，上微尖，立於社壇，半埋土中，近南向北'.
320 *Da Ming huidian, juan* 85: '嘉靖十年，上命於西苑空閒地，開墾為田，樹藝五穀'.
321 *Da Ming huidian, juan* 94: 《群祀四・有司祀典下》：「洪武二十六年著令：天、下府州縣合祭風、雲、雷、雨、山川、社稷、城隍、孔子及無祀鬼神等，有司務要每歲依期致祭。其壇壝廟宇制度、牲醴祭器體式具，載《洪武禮制》。」.

is often the case, a tabernacle is set up to perform the *ji* ritual. In the other cities which are not divided in two towns, I have heard that there is one earthen platform.

The founder of the dynasty Da Ming started to imitate what is contained in the *Book of Rites of the Zhou Dynasty* [*Zhouli*], and he erected both in the northern and southern suburbs a mound. The sacrifice to Heaven was performed on the day of the winter solstice above the round summit of the mound whereas the sacrifice to Earth was performed on the day of the summer solstice in the square trench of the mound. This custom lasted a long time, but after several droughts and extreme weather conditions, it was decided that the sacrifice to Heaven should be performed only in the first month of the year at the top of the southern mound (FF).

I have said enough about the sacrifice to both Heaven and Earth, and now it should be investigated what matters most, that is, the object of the sacrifice. Was it the material heaven or the Spirit of material heaven? Was it the material earth or the Spirit of material earth?

NOTES

EE.32 《醒迷篇‧論城隍》：「城隍者，原非神，亦非人，乃晉朝司馬炎所立也。因守土官治民不正，遂以漢沛公之將名灌嬰者，豎一木牌於贊政廳，名為城隍。此將極忠於沛公，故稱灌嬰為陰官，鑒察陽官為政。晉國所設城隍，其間甚其有所碍。後于衙門外另造一祠，立像祀之。世人未察其來歷，以訛傳訛。一邑之事，及人之生死、病疾、患難、皆賴城隍保祐。不論大小官員，新任必要先謁城隍，然後上任。至於朔望之日，各官行香，禱告一邑之人民，禍福疾病，求其施救減滅。」

> A famous manuscript called the *Xingmipian* written by a Chinese Christian deals with almost all the Chinese idols.[322] The chapter 'Chenghuang' states: 'The two-character word "Chenghuang" means by itself neither Spirit nor human being, but what Sima Yan, prime minister under the dynasty Jin, had built. Since the officers of the provinces were performing their duties very badly and not managing the people well, he decided to erect in the front hall of the officers some kind of wooden symbol which he called Chenghuang, in remembrance of Guan Ying, a famous general who had fought under Pei Gong [Liu Bang], first emperor of the Han dynasty. Since Guan Ying was extremely faithful to the emperor Pei Gong, Sima Yan called him the officer of the afterlife [*yinguan*] who watched over the officers in this life and examined their administration. The erection of the wooden Chenghuang by the Jin dynasty in this location brought several inconveniences. Later, a temple was built outside the official residence of the magistrates, and statues were erected for sacrifices. The ordinary people did not consider the origin of all this, and spread error after error, because they were hoping some

---

322 This anonymous work was written around 1650. There are three copies at BnF: Courant 7149, 7150 and 7151; and there is one copy at ARSI, Jap. Sin. I, 150. See Chan, *Chinese Books and Documents from the Jesuit Archives in Rome*, p. 202. Noël had probably seen the manuscript which is now kept at ARSI. Since the manuscript was never published, it is quite strange to call it famous, as Noël claims. The *Xingmipian* mentioned here and the *Shuwenpian* mentioned just below are the only two Christian writings mentioned in Chapters 1 and 2 of the First Treatise.

FF.33 《述聞篇・淫祀非禮》：「明之太祖, 礿倣周制, 築壇為南北郊, 冬³²⁴至祀天於圜丘, 夏至祀地於方澤。行之數年, 而風雨不時, 天多變異, 乃定以正月行禮, 祀天於南郊, 餘皆統於此而從祀焉。」

The chapter 'Evil sacrifices that contravene rituals' or 'Yinsi feili' of a manuscript by the Christian licentiate Qiu Zhenxin states as follows: 'The founder of the previous dynasty, etc.' See above.³²⁵

§.3. Whether the Sacrifice to Heaven and Earth Consists in Worshipping a Material Heaven and Earth, or their Spirits?³²⁶

When they sacrifice to Heaven under a roof, it is clear that they sacrifice to the Spirit of Heaven as well as to Heaven as Lord of Heaven (GG). But the Lord of Heaven or *Shangdi*, as we have often seen, is Spirit; therefore, they do not sacrifice to a material Heaven, but to its Spirit. When they sacrifice to Heaven in the open, they also sacrifice to Heaven as Spirit and not as something material. You should understand the same about the sacrifice to Earth, because it is included in the sacrifice to Heaven, as I said. Indeed, they sacrifice in the open to show that the Spirit of Heaven and Earth does not have a dwelling place, and they present edible

---

323   The anonymous author does not provide his source about Chenghuang originating wih Guan Ying, but the *Jiangcheng mingjiji* 江城名蹟記 records that the people of Nanchang worshipped Guan Ying as Chenghuang. This Christian author wants to show that Chenghuang is not idolatrous at the origin, but the people transformed it later in idolatry. Ricci advanced the theory of Aquinas that the idolatry originated from the legitimate respect due to virtuous people now deceased, but this later was turned into an illegitimate worship. See Ricci, *The True Meaning of the Lord of Heaven*, p. 327 (n. 503). This theory about the origin of idolatry is called Euhemerism, and was very popular with patristic theologians.

324   In the manuscript the character *dong* 冬 is written as *ge* 各.

325   Qiu Sheng 丘晟, *zi* Zhenxin 振新, was the son of the Christian scholar Qiu Shuliang 丘叔良. He became an advanced scholar (*jinshi*) in 1706. According to Ad Dudink (CCT-Database), the *Shuwenpian* 述聞篇 was probably written around 1701 and, according to Albert Chan (p. 49), was never published. Noël probably had in his hands the manuscript found today in ARSI, Jap. Sin. I, 40/4. Apparently, there is no other extant copy. For the reproduction of this passage, see Nicolas Standaert and Adrian Dudink, *Chinese Christian Texts from the Roman Archives of the Society of Jesus* (Taipei: Ricci Institute, 2002), X, p. 249. Qiu Sheng wrote this work in defence of the Chinese Rites, probably at the request of the Jesuits, and in explicit opposition to the Dominicans and Franciscans. In the ARSI manuscript, Noël calls Qiu Sheng a licentiate. Qiu Sheng obtained the title of doctor in 1706, but during Noël's short stay in Macao in the second half of 1707 he may not have heard about it, and the printing text has still him as a licentiate.

326   Longobardo in his *Brief Response* had famously argued that the Spirits were material, while Noël needs to argue here that the Spirits are spiritual. See Longobardo, *A Brief Response on the Controversies*, pp. 140–48 (prelude 11).

and drinkable offerings when they sacrifice to Heaven and Earth despite knowing that the Spirit of Heaven and Earth neither eats nor drinks (HH). Moreover, a special victim is used to sacrifice to Heaven in the open so that the Spirit of Heaven may be distinguished from the Spirit of a dead person (II), and the sun is brought as a sign substituting the Spirit of Heaven (KK). They say that, while sacrificing to Heaven and Earth, they warn the Spirit of Heaven and Earth (LL). Therefore, this sacrifice is performed to the Spirit, and not to material heaven and earth.

Finally, by sacrificing to Earth on the earthen platforms (*she*), they also sacrifice to the Spirit of Earth, because that to which they sacrifice is said to be Spirit of Earth (MM). Moreover, the emperor by sacrificing on the great imperial platform is said to warn the Spirit of Earth (NN). Let us not dwell too long on those matters but let us now examine the last difficulty, namely whether in sacrificing to Heaven and Earth they sacrifice to the one supreme Spirit of Heaven and Earth.

NOTES

GG.34　See above A.1.

HH.35　See above T.20.

II.36　See above B.3.

KK.37　See above B.4.

LL.38　張居正《四書直解・論語・堯曰・第二十》：「『予小子履，敢用玄牡，敢昭告於皇皇后帝。』皇是大；皇皇后帝，即皇天后土。敢昭告于皇天后土之神。」

　　　According to the interpretation of Zhang Juzheng or Zhang Gelao [in the *Sishu zhijie*], chapter 20 of the *Book of Sentences* [*Lunyu* 20.1] is to be understood as follows: 'I myself, Li (the name of Emperor Tang), I am a little child who dared to use a tender black calf for sacrificing and to warn openly the Spirit of Great Heaven and Thick Earth (*Huanghuang houtu*)'. You should understand the words *Hou* and *Huang* as above. See also c.2, q.1, §.5, B.2.[327]

MM.39　See above V.22 and B.2.

NN.40　蔡沈《書經集傳・卷四・周書・泰誓上》：「『類于上帝，宜于冢土，以爾有眾，底天之罰。』冢土，太社也。告于天神地祇，以爾有眾，致天之罰於商也。」

　　　The chapter 'Taishi' of the *Book of Imperial Annals* states as follows: 'I myself, Wu Wang, made a sacrifice to the Lord of Heaven; then, I made a sacrifice on the great earthen platform on behalf of you all so that I may carry out the punishment of Heaven'. Cai Chen explains this passage in volume 4 [of his *Shujing jizhuan*] as follows: 'I myself warned the Spirit of Heaven and Earth on behalf of you all, so that I may carry out the punishment of Heaven against the Shang imperial dynasty'.[328]

327　The explanation of Zhang Juzheng about the related passage of the *Shujing* is given above (c.1, q.5, F).
328　For the translation of the passage of the *Shujing*, see above (c.1, q.2, F.7).

§.4. Whether the Sacrifice to Heaven and Earth Consists in Worshipping the Unique Spirit of Heaven and Earth?

When the emperor makes a ritual sacrifice to Heaven in an open-air suburban mound (*a fortiori* when he worships under a roof), this includes Earth, as I said above. Hence, he clearly sacrifices to the Lord and Ruler of Heaven, and this Lord and Ruler of Heaven is one (OO). Indeed, the Spirit of Heaven and Earth is one (see c.2, q.3). When they mention the Lord of Heaven, they imply that He is also the Ruler of Earth (PP). Therefore, they sacrifice to the one supreme Spirit of Heaven and Earth. For this reason, only one victim is used in this sacrifice (QQ). A commentator [Cai Chen] made a mistake by saying that two calves were used in the sacrifice to Heaven because there was a sacrifice to Heaven and to Earth. In fact, one calf was for the sacrifice to Heaven, but the other calf was used for the deceased Prince Houji, for whom the *ji* ritual was performed, associating the founder of the Zhou dynasty with Heaven, or placing him as a companion, as I said. Therefore, only one calf was used in the sacrifice to Heaven (RR). Also, when the emperor visited the petty kings in his kingdoms, the petty king offered to the emperor one single calf. This was because the rite with which the petty king honours the emperor acting as deputy of the Lord of Heaven is the same as that with which the emperor honours Heaven or the Lord of Heaven (SS). In the sacrifice to Heaven which includes the sacrifice to Earth, the emperor uses one single calf and offers it to the Lord of Heaven, or *Shangdi*, who is the Spirit of Heaven and Earth. Clearly, the emperor sacrifices to a single supreme Spirit of Heaven and Earth. When they say *Shangdi*, this includes the Spirit of Earth (TT). But this will become clearer from the following discussion.

When the emperor once made a sacrifice on *she*, the imperial earthen platform, to the Spirit of Earth, it seems that he made a sacrifice to the one supreme Spirit of Heaven and Earth. For Confucius asserts that the open-air sacrifice on the suburban platform, called *jiao*, to Heaven and the sacrifice on the earthen platform, called *she*, to Earth is how the Lord of Heaven, or *Shangdi*, is worshipped. Therefore, to make a sacrifice on the earthen platform to Earth is also to worship the Lord of Heaven, no less than sacrificing to Heaven on the suburban platform. The commentators clearly recognize this, saying, 'When only the Lord of Heaven or Heaven is mentioned, this includes *Houtu*'. As I shortly discuss, *Houtu* means either the Thick Earth, or the One Ruling over the Earth. Therefore, the One Ruling over the Earth or Ruler of Earth is included in the Lord of Heaven, just as Thick Earth is included in material heaven, or encompassed by it. Thus, a sacrifice is made to the Lord of both since the sacrifice is made to the Spirit, as I have said. The commentators add, 'Worship is given to Heaven and Earth to express gratitude for the power by which Heaven protects and produces all things and by which Earth sustains and perfect all things'. The whole power of Heaven and Earth is brought back to the Lord of Heaven, or the Spirit acting invisibly within and Author of things (see c.2, §.2, q.1 and c.2, q.3). Hence in the same place the commentators again say that *jiao*, the sacrifice to Heaven, and *she*, the sacrifice to Earth, are sacrifices to *Shangdi*, the Lord of Heaven (VV). Moreover, they refer the two ritual sacrifices to no other Spirit but the Lord of Heaven who encompasses in Himself the dominion over Earth. They say that Heaven is the whole and complete Producer and Lord of things. When things are produced, Heaven only receives the sustenance of food offerings from Earth (XX). The reason why Earth nourishes all things is because the Lord of Heaven has dominion over the Earth and commands Earth to come and serve Him (ZZ). Whatever Earth produces it receives from Heaven communicating with it (WW). Also, there is in Heaven and Earth one single producing and destroying Spirit (YY). In other words, there is one single Reason which is the Lord of Heaven infusing the inner rectitude of rational nature and the Law of Heaven infused in nature (AAA).

Thus, it is clear that all things on Earth and the actions of the whole world are referred to a single Lord of Heaven or *Shangdi*, and to no other Spirit, and moreover there is no celestial king and terrestrial queen, or two Spirits, one husband and the other wife. The word *Hou* frequently means queen, especially when it is joined with the word *Huang*, which itself means emperor, prince, ruler, lord (BBB). But when joined with the word *Tu*, then it refers to the density of Earth, as the dictionary says (CCC), and thus it means specifically the Ruler of Earth, or the One Ruling over Earth, and not the Queen (DDD). When speaking of the souls of the departed, the Chinese deny any difference in sex (EEE). Moreover, they will also deny that *Houtu* exists among other Spirits, which indeed are never called female. It seems that the diversity of sacrifices is related to the difference of rituals, and not to different objects, because visible heaven is more excellent, while the earth is more base, and both their aspect and their mass are different. They established some rituals to sacrifice to the Principle of all things as Lord of Heaven, and other rituals to sacrifice to the same Principle of all things as Lord of Earth (FFF). The ancient emperors are said to have made sacrifices on the open-air suburban mound to the Lord of Heaven to show the rituals of Heaven-Father and Earth-Mother (GGG). Through secondary causes as Heaven-Father and Earth-Mother, the Lord of Heaven produces, preserves, and nourishes all things. Hence when a sacrifice is made to Heaven and Earth at the same time, two tablets are placed side by side: on one is inscribed *Huangdi Qi* or Spirit controlling Earth, and on the other is written *Huangtian Shangdi*, or supreme Lord ruling over Heaven. In the Manchu language, which the emperor now uses for sacrifice, the character *Qi* (Spirit) and the two-character word *Shangdi* (supreme Lord) are both translated as *Han* (supreme Lord). and This provides further evidence that in the sacrifice to Heaven and Earth only one Spirit is understood.[329] Also, as they say, the vital breath of Heaven and Earth (which, according to the Chinese, is one) is equivalent to a whole father and mother (HHH). As they call Heaven father and mother, they also call the emperor the father and mother of the people, and nowadays the governors of the cities are everywhere called the father and mother of the habitants (III). Regardless of whether the emperor sacrifices to Heaven or Earth, this always refers

---

329   This sentence referring to the Manchu language is not present in the manuscript and was added later by Noël.

to the Lord of Heaven, that is, the one Spirit of Heaven and Earth. The emperor is called only son of Heaven, but not son of Earth. The sacrifice to Earth is not lesser than the sacrifice to Heaven in how the emperor pays thanks to the Principle of all things and recollects it in his mind (KKK). The sacrifice to Earth is that by which the Way of Earth is made spiritual and known (LLL). However, the Way of Earth and the Way of Heaven is a single Way, a unique Spirit, as said above. Therefore, the emperor by making a sacrifice to Earth makes a sacrifice to the one supreme Spirit of Heaven and Earth.

You may wish to apply some of the things that I said above about the *she* sacrifice to Earth to that other sacrifice to Earth which is implicitly encompassed in the *jiao* sacrifice to Heaven. In this way, there can be further corroboration of what was said above about the *jiao* ritual, which is the chief issue being discussed here.

When the emperor made the *ji* offering on the two earthen platforms mentioned above (*taishe* and *dishe*), it is not indicated very clearly whether he was making the offering to the supreme Spirit of the whole Earth and Heaven, or only to the tutelar Spirit of the whole empire. Indeed, the formula pronounced by the Jiajing emperor during the *taisheji* offering seems to mention some lower Spirit or Spirits of Earth and crops,[330] even though the formula used for the *disheji* offering speaks in more general terms about Spirits through whose favour the goods of Earth are obtained.[331] We know how much this emperor was devoted to the followers of the sects [of Buddhism and Taoism]. Even the emperor would not disdain to make a sacrifice to the supreme Spirit of Earth and Heaven on *dishe*, the imperial platform of Earth, as we saw; and on the other platform *taishe*, he would make the *ji* offering to the tutelar Spirit of the whole empire, to the Spirit of the fields, to the Spirit of crops, just as he would make an offering to the Spirits of all the famous mountains and rivers of the whole empire. But this was done with lower-ranking rituals. In this way you should understood when they seem to insert another Spirit of Earth or fields, or another Spirit of crops. You should also understand in the same way what they say the Spirits or soul of the Prince Houji who was in charge of agriculture and crops, and of Prince Goulong who was in charge of floods and fields. As I have said, the *ji* offering was made together to both in sofar as they correlated with the true Spirits of the fields and crops.

You may first ask whether the petty kings and governors sacrificed to the one supreme Spirit of Earth and Heaven on their own earthen platforms.

I answer as follows. Since the *Book of Rites* deals only with the rituals performed by the emperor, it is not possible to know whether the petty kings and governors when adapting other rituals of inferior rank to their own social station had indeed sacrificed to the one Spirit of Earth and Heaven, or were only making an offering

---

330　*Da Ming huidian* (1587), *juan* 85: '皇帝御名敢昭告於太社之神、太稷之神：惟神贊輔皇祇, 發生嘉穀, 粒我烝民, 萬世永賴。時當仲春、秋, 禮嚴告祀、報謝, 謹以玉帛牲齊粢盛庶品, 備茲瘞祭, 以皇考仁祖淳皇帝配神'.

331　*Da Ming huidian* (1587), *juan* 85: '嗣天子御名致告祭於帝社之神、帝稷之神：春雲秋雲時, 當務農之期, 萬寶告成, 庸修恆祀。特茲告祈、報謝。惟神歆鑒。俾五穀皆登, 萬方咸永福予民, 萬世攸賴'.

to the tutelary Spirit of their fiefdom, to the Spirit of fields and to the Spirit of crops. Even though only the emperor could make sacrifice to the supreme Spirit of Heaven and Earth on the suburban mound and on the imperial platform of Earth with the ritual of highest rank, the petty kings and governors could do it in their earthen platforms with a lower and adapted ritual: the petty kings could only use a sheep or a goat, while the emperor used a cow for the offering on the earthen platform that is to be to sacrificed to this same Spirit of Heaven and Earth (MMM). Certainly, after lowering their head onto the ground and in other ways they and all others were allowed to worship the Lord of Heaven. Even now most Chinese people on New Year's Eve place food and drink on the table and then prostrate themselves to venerate Heaven, and yet they are not said to be usurping the emperor's ritual. Among Christians, even though only priests are authorized to worship God by celebrating Mass, others may worship the same God with a different ritual. But regardless of whatever happens in the case of petty kings and governors, the question we are dealing with here is whether the emperor by sacrificing to Heaven and Earth sacrifices to the one Lord of Heaven and Earth, and what we have said above is enough to prove this.

You may ask next what is the purpose of the sacrifice that the emperor makes to Heaven or the Lord of Heaven and Earth.

In this controversial matter which matters little or not at all for our question (indeed we investigate here the material object towards which the ritual is directed and not its purpose), I answer as follows. In the classical books, there are three names for this sacrifice. The first is *lei*, that is, a type of sacrifice to Heaven performed by the emperor when he was about to go to war (NNN). Was this ritual per chance aimed at obtaining something? The second is *chai*, or cremation, which the emperor Wu Wang performed by burning an entire victim after he had defeated the enemy Zhou, obtained the empire, and arranged all things (OOO). Was this perhaps a devotional sacrifice or offering? The third is the *jiao* ritual in the suburbs discussed above. The emperor performs this to give thanks to the source of all things and to recollect it mentally (PPP). Was this perhaps a sacrifice of thanksgiving?[332] In the *jiao* ritual, the deceased parents are associated with the Lord of Heaven, as I have said, but not in the *lei* sacrifice or in the *chai* sacrifice (which I suppose distinct from the *jiao* ritual, though it appears that a sacrificial offering was burnt in the *jiao* ritual). Indeed, in the sacrifice in which the emperor makes a sacrifice to the Lord of Heaven to beg for abundant crops, it is said that Prince Houji is associated to Him, meaning that the tablet of Houji is placed on the table (QQQ). But either this sacrifice is not a *jiao* sacrifice but a *she* sacrifice to Earth in which Prince Houji is associated with the Lord of Heaven or the Spirit of Earth, not as parent and founder of the Zhou dynasty, but as a benevolent officer who had been in charge of agriculture, either insofar as thanksgiving alone without any supplication for crops is directed to him, or he is even joined as an intercessor, considering that he

---

332 Noël uses here the word *eucharisticum*, which usually refers to the Mass in Christianity.

was now in a place where he could intercede to the Lord of Heaven.[333] The same can be said about other such men, who served the empire with distinction not long after the deluge or when China had not yet been perverted by evil sects.[334] The Second Treatise will deal with this in greater detail.

Finally, you should note that I do not claim that the open-air *jiao* sacrifice observed every year by the Chinese emperor is licit, since the ancient law concerning the rites, judgements and sacrifices is indeed abrogated after a sufficient proclamation of the Gospel.[335] But I wanted only to explain whether the material object towards which the ritual was directed was established according to the legitimate and true teaching of the classical books. Now someone by chance make ask whether *taiji* or the First Ultimate of things, which I have often discussed and about which the modern Chinese commentators have so many divergent views, could be called the Lord of Heaven and Earth insofar as it is the cause of all things? Please consider my answer in the following question.

NOTES

OO.41 《禮記・卷五・禮器・第十》：「祀帝於郊, 敬之至也。」

> Chapter 10 'Liqi' in volume 5 of the *Book of Rites*: 'To sacrifice to the Lord of Heaven (*Di*) in the open-air suburban mound is the supreme testimony of veneration'.[336]

OO.42 陳澔《禮記集說・卷四・禮運・第九》：「『故祭帝於郊, 所定天位也。祀社於國, 所以列地利也。』天子致尊天之禮, 則天下知尊君之禮; 故曰『定天位』。食貨所資皆出於地, 天子親祀后土, 正為表列地利, 使天下知報本之禮也。」

> Chapter 9 'Liyun' of the *Book of Rites* states as follows: 'By sacrificing on the open-air suburban mound to the Lord of Heaven (*Di*), the emperor strengthens the authority which he received from Heaven, and by sacrificing on the great earthen platform to the Spirit of Earth, the emperor shows the usefulness of the land'. Chen Hao comments on this passage in volume 4 [of the *Liji jishuo*] as follows: 'When the emperor knows how to venerate Heaven with the proper honorific ritual, then the empire knows how to venerate the emperor with the proper honorific ritual. Therefore he is said to strengthen the authority that he received from Heaven. Also, all the food and wealth for the necessity of life come from earth, and the

---

333 In this religious interpretation of the *she* ritual, Houji is considered not as an idol, but as playing a role equivalent to a saint in the Christian tradition.
334 In the *Confucius Sinarum philosophus*, the Jesuits had argued that the Chinese had maintained an authentic monotheism until the introduction of Buddhism during the Han dynasty. Noël considers the possibility that Chinese, from Fuxi down to Confucius, could have been authentic saints.
335 Noël suggests that the imperial sacrifice to *Tian* has become now illicit because Christianity has been openly proclaimed in China since the entry of the Jesuit missionaries in China in 1582. In the Second Treatise, Noël argues that the rituals in honour of Confucius and to the ancestors are still licit because there are purely civic or political.
336 Quoted in the *Gujin*, p. 152 (n. 13) and in the *Tianjiao he Ru*, p. 33 (n. 10). Quote mentioned in Noël's *Renzui zhizhong*. See Zhu Qianzhi, *Zhongguo sixiang duiyu Ouzhou wenhua yingxiang*, p. 127.

emperor himself worships *Houtu*, or the Spirit ruling the earth, and thus shows the usefulness of Earth, making the empire know the ritual of thanksgiving to the Principle of things'.

OO.43 陳澔《禮記集說・卷七・雜記下・第二十一》：「『孟獻子曰：「正月日至，可以有事於上帝。」』有事上帝，郊祭也。」

Chapter 21 'Zajixia' in volume 7 of the *Book of Rites* states as follows: 'The officer Meng Xianzi says that in the winter solstice, in the first month of the year, it is suitable to serve *Shangdi*, the Lord of Heaven'. Chen Hao explains this passage as follows: '"To serve the Lord of Heaven" means to sacrifice on the open-air suburban mound'.

OO.44 《文獻通考・卷八十三・郊社考十六》：「帝只一上帝而已，安有山而為之帝？」

Volume 83 of the *Wenxian tongkao* states as follows: 'The character *Di* means only the one *Shangdi*. Thus how could the mountain (the Spirit of the mountain Taishan) be called *Di*, the Lord of Heaven?'[337]

PP.45 《文獻通考・卷七十六・郊社考九》：「舜肆類於上帝…言『類於上帝』，則地祇之合可知矣。」

Volume 76 of the *Wenxian tongkao* states as follows: 'The emperor Shun sacrificed to *Shangdi*, and from this it can be understood that this included the Spirit of Earth'. See also VV.51 below.

QQ.46 《禮記・卷五・王制・第五》：「祭天地之牛角繭栗。」「天子社稷皆太牢，諸侯社稷皆少牢。」陳澔《禮記集說・郊特牲・第十一》：「『郊特牲，而社稷太牢。』禮有以少為貴者，故此二者皆貴特牲而賤大牢也。」

Chapter 5 'Wangzhi' in volume [5] of the *Book of Rites* states as follows: 'The little calf destined to be sacrificed to Heaven and Earth should be such that the horns start to grow like a cocoon or chestnut'. However, this little calf is not the same little calf of the earthen platform because immediately before the work states: 'The emperor in making a ritual sacrifice on his earthen platform uses a cow; a petty king on his earthen platform uses a sheep or goat'. Also, that the cow used on the earthen platform is not a tender calf is clearly shown in chapter 11 'Jiaotesheng' in volume 5 of the *Book of Rites*: 'A unique and special victim is used in the open-door sacrifice to Heaven (*jiao*), that is, a tender calf, but in the sacrifice on the platform of Earth and crops, a cow is used'. Chen Hao [in his *Liji jishuo*] comments on this passage as follows: 'Rituals more greatly value something small than something big. Therefore, among these two things, a unique and special victim, namely a small calf, has more value than a cow, that is, an older calf or a big cow'.[338]

---

337 This quote, like the others from the *Wenxian tongkao*, is not present in the manuscript and was retrieved directly from the Chinese work. This quote presents a forceful argument for Chinese monotheism.

338 For this last sentence, we follow the Latin text of the ARSI manuscript, which is clearer than the printed Latin text: 'idcirco inter haec duo, pluris fit, plurisque aestimatur unica, et singularis victima, nempe parvus vitulus, quam bos; (nempe vel maior vitulus, vel magnus bos'. ARSI, Fondo Gesuitico 724/4, fol. 95ᵛ.

RR.47 蔡沈《書經集傳・卷五・周書・召誥》：「『越三日丁巳,用牲于郊,牛二。越翼日戊午,乃社于新邑,牛一,羊一,豕一。』祭天地也,故用二牛,社祭用太牢,禮也。皆告以營洛之事。」

> Chapter 'Zhaogao' of the *Book of Imperial Annals* states as follows: 'On the following day called *dingsi*, two animals or cows were offered during the open-air *jiao* sacrifice to Heaven. On the third day called *wuwu*, a sacrifice was made to the Spirit of Earth on the earthen platform within the new city. The animals offered were one cow, one sheep or goat, and one pig'. Cai Chen in volume 5 [of the *Shujing jizhuan*] comments on this passage as follows: 'The *jiao* sacrifice consists in sacrificing to Heaven and Earth, and therefore are offered two cows. In the sacrifice to the Spirit of Earth on the earthen platform, one cow was offered (namely an older cow since the cow used in the *jiao* sacrifice to Heaven was a tender calf, as said above). The rituals are prescribed this way. The sacrifices are made to announce to the Spirit that the building of a new city is now completed'. In RR.48, Chen Hao refutes such an interpretation about using two cows in the sacrifice to Heaven and Earth.[339]

RR.48 陳澔《禮記集說・卷五・郊特牲・第十一》：「『五峰言無北郊,只祭社便是;此說卻好。』今按〈召誥〉『用牲于郊,牛二』,蔡氏以為祭天地,非也。牛二,帝牛、稷牛也。社于新邑,祭地也,故用太牢。」

> About chapter 11 'Jiaotesheng' of the *Book of Rites*, Chen Hao in volume 5 [of the *Liji jishuo*] cites Doctor Zhu Xi as follows: 'As Hu Wufeng says, there is no northern *jiao*, that is an open-air place in the northern suburbs which would have been dedicated to the sacrifice of Earth. But when there is a sacrifice on the earthen platform, this is what is called the northern *jiao*. This is the correct understanding'.[340] Chen Hao himself says: 'In explaining the chapter "Zhaogao" of the *Book of Imperial Annals* ("During the *jiao* sacrifice, that is, the open-air sacrifice to Heaven two cows were offered"), Cai Chen thinks that two cows were used in the sacrifice to Heaven and to Earth, but this is not true because one cow was offered to *Di*, the Lord of Heaven, and the other to Prince Houji (the founder of the Zhou family whom they joined as an associate in the sacrifice to Heaven, as discussed in the same passage). However, to sacrifice on the earthen platform in the new city is to sacrifice to Earth, and therefore, an (older) cow was offered'.[341]

SS.49 陳澔《禮記集說・卷五・禮器・第十》：「『天子適諸侯,諸侯膳以犢。』天子祭天惟用一牛;若巡守而過諸侯之境,則諸侯奉膳亦止牛。其尊君之禮,亦如君之尊天也。」

> Chapter 10 'Liqi' of the *Book of Rites* states as follows: 'When the emperor visits the kingdom of a petty king, the petty king offers him a tender calf'. Chen Hao in volume 5 [of his *Liji jishuo*] comments on this passage as follows: 'When the emperor makes a ritual sacrifice to Heaven, he presents only one single calf only;

---

339 This seems to be the only occurrence where Noël explicitly criticizes the interpretation of Cai Chen.
340 Zhu Xi, *Zhuzi yulei*, juan 90.
341 For Zhu Xi's comment on this same passage, see also 'Tractatus primus', p. 125 (c.2, q.5, §.2, T.20); this edition, p. 315.

similarly, when the emperor visits the fief of a petty king, the petty king presents to the emperor only a single calf. Indeed, the ritual with which a petty king honours the emperor is the same with which the emperor honours heaven'.

TT.50 See PP.45 above.

VV.51 朱熹《四書章句集註・中庸・第十九》：「『郊社之禮，所以事上帝也。』郊，祭天；社，祭地。不言后土者，省文也。」

Chapter 19 of the *Book of Unalterable Mean* states: 'The *jiaoshe* ritual of making a sacrifice to Heaven and Earth is to serve the Lord of Heaven, or *Shangdi*'. Zhu Xi comments on this passage as follows [in the *Sishu zhangju jizhu*]: '*Jiao* means to sacrifice to Heaven, and *she*, to sacrifice to Earth. It is not mentioned that *she* is to sacrifice to Houtu who rules over the Earth or Thick Earth because it is an abbreviated way of speech'.

張居正《四書直解・中庸・第十九》：「郊，是祭天；社，是祭地。上帝即是天，言上帝則后土在其中。」「郊社之禮，或行于圜丘，或行于方澤。蓋所以事奉上帝與后土，答其覆載生成之德也。」

Zhang Juzheng in volume 3 [of the *Sishu zhijie*] comments on this passage as follows: '*Jiao* is to sacrifice to Heaven, and *she* is to sacrifice to Earth. *Shangdi* is the same as Heaven. When *Shangdi* is mentioned, this includes Houtu'. Shortly after is added: 'The *jiaoshe* ritual, performed either on the round summit of a mound (*jiao*) or in a square ditch within the mound (*she*), is to serve *Shangdi* and Houtu, showing gratitude for the power by which things are controlled, sustained, produced and perfected'.

《日講四書解義・卷三・中庸・第十九》：「有郊社之禮焉。郊以祭天，冬至祭天於圜丘；社以祭地，夏至祭地於方澤。蓋所以奉事上帝與后土。答其覆載生成之德也。夫郊社之所以享帝。」

Volume 3 of the *Daily Explanation [of the Four Books]* comments on this same passage in almost the same words: '*Jiaoshe*, or the sacrifice to Heaven and Earth, is that with which a sacrifice is made to *Shangdi*, the Lord of Heaven'.[342]

XX.52 See R.17 above.

ZZ.53 《周易正解・卷二十二・說卦・第五》：「林次崖曰：『坤養萬物，乃為物所役。然坤之所養萬物者，皆帝主之，是帝致役事於坤也。』」

About chapter 5 of 'Shuogua', volume 22 of the *True Explanation of the Book of Changes and Productions* states as follows: 'Lin Ciya says, "When the power of

---

[342] Ricci had rejected Zhu Xi's explanation about the elision of Houtu in the original text of *Zhongyong* 19. See Ricci, *The True Meaning of the Lord of Heaven*, p. 97 (n. 104). Like the *Confucius Sinarum philosophus*, Noël seems to accept the elision, as we can see his translation of the quote above (c.1, q.1, §.1, R.18). Noël finds support here in Zhang Juzheng, who recognizes Zhu Xi's interpretation but tries to articulate further the two rituals, having the lower sacrifice to Earth included within the higher sacrifice to Heaven. Furthermore, the *Sishu rijiang* stresses that the *jiaoshe* is made to Shangdi.

Earth nourishes all things, it is a service because it comes to help those things.³⁴³ The reason why the power of Earth nourishes all things is because the Lord of Heaven rules over it. This Lord of Heaven orders the power of Earth to undergo and to sustain this service"'.

WW.54 蔡虛齋《四書蒙引・卷三・中庸・第一》：「程子曰：『夫天, 專言之則道也。』」「朱子註亦謂『言天而不以地對』者, 以理言也, 即所謂『上帝降衷』, 即所謂『天命之性』也。」「凡地之所生, 無非是得於天之所施。所以謂『地對天』不過也, 所以獨言天命也。」

About chapter 1 of the *Book of Unalterable Mean*, Cai Xuzhai in volume 3 of the *Sishu mengyin* states the following: 'Doctor Cheng says, "When the word *Tian* is used separately, it means the way or way of action". Shortly after is added: 'Zhu Xi's interpretation asserts that even Heaven should not be said as something opposed to or in correspondence with Earth, but Heaven should be understood as Reason since it is said, "The Lord and Ruler of Heaven infuses the inner rectitude of rational nature" and "The Law of Heaven is Reason infused in nature"'.³⁴⁴ A little further down is added: 'Whatever Earth produces it receives from Heaven communicating with It [Earth]. Therefore, it is said that Earth can in no way be compared to Heaven, or put on equal footing, and this is the reason why we only talk about the Law of Heaven'.³⁴⁵

YY.55 蔡虛齋《四書蒙引・卷四・中庸・第二十九》：「天地, 一鬼神也。」

About chapter 29 of the *Book of Unalterable Mean*, Cai Xuzhai in volume 4 of the *Sishu mengyin* states as follows: 'Heaven and Earth consist in one single producing and destroying Spirit, or there is one single producing and destroying Spirit in Heaven and Earth'. Indeed, the Spirit for the Chinese does not seem to be free from body and figure.³⁴⁶

AAA.56 See WW.54.

BBB.57 《書經・泰誓上》：「亶聰明, 作元后。」

Chapter 'Taishi' in volume 4 of the *Book of Imperial Annals* states: 'The man who excels in truth, attentiveness and intelligence acts as the ruler of the people, in Chinese *hou*'.³⁴⁷

---

343 The name of Lin Ciya 林次崖 (Lin Xiyuan) appears above (c.2, q.3, T.26).
344 This text does not seem present in the editions of the *Sishu mengyin* we have consulted. Perhaps it was a manuscript note on the *Sishu mengyin* that Noël recopied. The quote is derived from Zhu Xi's *Chuci jizhu* 楚辭集註 (Collected annotations on the *Chuci*), chapter 'Tianwen' 天問. The original text is: 「然《穀梁》言天而不以地對, 則所謂天者, 理而已矣。成湯所謂「上帝降衷」, 子思所謂「天命之性」是也」. Noël seems to be influenced by the Christian theological idea of God as reason or *logos*.
345 The same idea about the superiority of Heaven over Earth is expressed above in R.17.
346 Noël reads the Spirit as immaterial and yet being endowed with body and figure, and he seems to think here in terms of Tertullian's understanding of the soul. Tertullian is mentioned explicitly below (c.2, q.7).
347 Quoted in the *Gujin* n. 28 (p. 184).

BBB.58 《書經・舜典》:「班瑞于羣后。」

Chapter 'Shundian' in volume 1 of the *Book of Imperial Annals*: 'Emperor Shun distributed his marks to all the petty kings and princes, called *hou*'.

BBB.59 《書經・太甲中》:「乃曰:『徯我后, 后來無罰!』」

Chapter 'Taijia' in volume 3 of the *Book of Imperial Annals*: 'The neighbouring people were saying, "We are anxiously waiting for our prince (in Chinese *hou*). After our prince (*hou*) comes, shall he punish us?"'

BBB.60 蔡沈《書經集傳・卷三・商書・盤庚中》:「『予念我先神后之勞爾先。』后, 先王也。」

Chapter 'Pan Geng' of the *Book of Imperial Annals* has the emperor Pan Geng saying: 'I myself remember that the spiritual emperors coming before me (in Chinese *shenhou*) have used the work of your ancestors'. [Cai Chen comments on this passage] in volume 3 [of the *Shujing jizhuan*] as follows: 'Spiritual emperors (in Chinese *shenhou*) refer to the spiritual King of the Heaven on High'. This is also mentioned in c.1, q.2, §.8, I.9.

BBB.61 《詩經・大雅・下武》:「三后在天。」

Ode 'Xiawu' in the volume 'Daya' of the *Book of Odes*: 'Three deceased princes (in Chinese *hou*) are in Heaven'.

CCC.62 《字彙・后字》:「又后土取厚載之義。」

The Chinese dictionary *Zhengzitong* defines the character *hou* as follows: 'This character *hou* means "king", "prince", and "ruler". In the past, it also meant "royal minister". It also means "queen". It also means "thick": the Earth is called thick, or Houtu in Chinese, because it sustains things through its thickness and firmness'.[348]

DDD.63 「后字有二義。我后、元后皆是稱君。后妃是稱皇后。若后土, 則后字又作厚字看, 亦是君之土, 故又曰:『后土不是皇后, 說皇后是錯了。』」

Some twenty years ago, a Christian who was an officer of bachelors [scholars] in two small cities was once asked whether the word Houtu meant Queen of Earth.[349] He took exception to this interpretation of Houtu as Queen of Earth with a laugh and answered negatively. The next day, he brought a written explanation to me, even though I was not thinking about this at all and had not requested it. He claimed that this interpretation could be found in a great work of Zhu Xi called the *Yulei*.[350] 'This word *hou*', he said, 'had two meanings. *Wohou* and *yuanhou* mean our ruler, the ruler of the people. *Houfei* means the queen. As for Houtu, the first

---

348 The Chinese text on the manuscript indicates the *Zihui*, while the Latin text does not specify the name of the dictionary. The Latin printed text refers specifically to the *Zhengzitong*. In fact, this quote was present in the *Hongwu zhengyun* 洪武正韻 (Correct rhymes from the Hongwu reign, 1375), which was thereafter cited by the *Zihui, Zhengzitong, Kangxi zidian*, etc.
349 This may have happened while Noël was residing in the Changjiang area (1688–1691).
350 We did not find in the *Zhuzi yulei* any mention of Houtu as being the queen or Huanghou 皇后.

character *hou* means dense and also means the ruler of or over the land. Therefore, *hou* means prince, king, and master. The second character *tu* means earth. Therefore, *hou* does not mean Queen as it has been mistakenly explained'.

EEE.64 陳澔《禮記集說 · 卷八 · 祭統 · 第二十五》：「人生則形體異, 故夫婦之倫在於有別。死則精氣無間, 共設一几。」

About chapter 25 'Jitong' of the *Book of Rites*, Chen Hao comments the following in volume 8 [of the *Liji jishuo*]: 'When human beings are alive, the substance of the body is different, and therefore, the order between husband and wife consists in sexual difference. After their death, the simplest and subtlest breath is not differentiated; that is to say, the intelligent Spirit is not different. Thus, there is only one common table for the offerings during the *ji* ritual'.

FFF.65 陳澔《禮記集說 · 卷五 · 禮器 · 第十》：「『是故昔先王。』『因天事天, 因地事地。』因天之尊而制為事天之禮, 因地之卑而制為事地之禮。郊社是也。」

Chapter 10 'Liqi' of the *Book of Rites* states: 'The ancient emperors worshipped Heaven as Heaven, and worshipped Earth as Earth'. Chen Hao comments on this passage in volume 5 [of the *Liji jishuo*] as follows: 'Since Heaven is more honourable, they sanctioned rituals for the worship of Heaven in this way, and since Earth is baser, they sanctions the ritual for the worship of Earth in this way. This is called *jiaoshe*, or the sacrifice to Heaven and Earth'.

FFF.66 陳仁錫《古周禮 · 卷三 · 春官 · 宗伯 · 第三》：「以玉作六器, 以禮天地四方: 以蒼璧禮天, 以黃琮禮地, 以青圭礼東方, 以赤璋礼南方, 以白琥礼西方, 以玄璜禮北方。」陳仁錫：「璧員象天之形, 蒼[351]則象其色也；琮方象地之形, 黃則象其色也。」

Chapter 'Chunguan zongbo' of the *Zhouli* or the *Book of the Zhou Rituals* states: 'This officer should take care of making six precious vases for the rituals to Heaven and Earth, and dedicating them to the four parts of the world: one precious blue vase (*bi*) for the ritual of Heaven, one yellow *zong* for that of Earth; one violet *gui* for that of the east; one red *zhang* for that of the south; one white *hu* for that of the west; one black *huang* for that of the north'. Chen Renxi comments on this passage in volume 3 [of the *Gu Zhouli*]: 'The *bi* vase is round like the shape of Heaven, and blue like the colour of Heaven. Similarly, the *zong* vase is square like the shape of Earth, and yellow like the colour of Earth'.[352]

The other four vases in this passage correspond to the qualities or talents of the four first emperors: Fuxi, Shennong, Shaohao and Zhuanxu. As said above in F.8, the *ji* ritual was performed to the Spirit of Heaven in the four regions of the world.

---

351 In the manuscript there is the character *yi* 薋 instead of *cang* 蒼.
352 Chen Renxi 陳仁錫 (1581–1636) is listed in the catalogue of ARSI as commentator of the *Gu Zhouli* 古周禮. See Chapter 2.15.

FFF.67 《字彙·璧字》：「《白虎通》：『璧者，外圓象天，內方象地。』」《字彙·琮字》：「外八角而內圓，八角取義八方，象地之形；中虛圓以應無窮，象地之德，故以祭地。」

> The dictionary *Zihui* defines the character *bi* as follows: 'According to *Baihu tong*, the *bi* vase was spherical on the outside to represent Heaven and was square inside to represent Earth'. The same dictionary defines the character *zong* as follows: 'The *zong* vase was octagonal outside and round inside. With the eight angles, it represented the eight corners of the world and the shape of the Earth. The empty space inside was round so that the power of earth may have an infinite power to receive and sustain. Thus, this vase was used to make a sacrifice to Earth'.

GGG.68 《日講易經·卷十三·渙卦》：「『先王以享于帝，立廟。』當渙之時，郊廟之禮廢，上帝祖宗幾於無主，使無以合之，將終於渙散而不聚矣。先王享帝于郊，以明父天母地之禮，而上帝之精神散於精虛之表者，乃萃於郊祀之餘矣。立廟於國，以報祖功宗德之隆，而祖考之精神散於杳冥之中者，乃聚於廟祭之時矣。夫享帝以明有尊，而人皆知尊尊之義；立廟以明有親，而人皆知親親之義。仁孝兼至，而誠無不通，幽無不格，此治渙之大者也。按：渙之象，因人各有心，不相聯屬貫通，而天下之勢遂至乖離；必有所以鼓動感乎之，使歸於一，則渙者不求而自合。故敬天尊祖，自展仁孝之思，而天下之心，已知天神無二主，不敢以下而犯上；知人物無二本，不敢背死而忘生。」

> About the symbol 'Huan', or dispersion, the *Book of Changes and Productions* states the following: 'The ancient emperors sacrificed to *Di*, the Lord of Heaven, and erected ancestor halls'.[353] Volume 13 of the *Daily Explanation of the Book of Changes and Productions* comments on this passage as follows: 'At time of dispersion, the rituals of the *jiao* sacrifice on the suburban mound and the rituals of the ancestor hall lay so dorment that the Lord of Heaven and the deceased ancestors had no one overseeing their rituals. If the ancestors are not mentally united, if you are not united with your ancestors, then they will always remain in this state of dispersion and will not be mentally gathered. The ancient emperors sacrificed on the suburban mound to *Di*, the Lord of Heaven, to reveal the ritual of Heaven-Father and Earth-Mother. Thus, the most perfect and subtlest Spirit of the Lord of Heaven (*Shangdi*), was scattered widely through the visible space of the purest emptiness or ether and gathered in the very abundant worship of the *jiao* sacrifice. They erected ancestor halls in the imperial court to give thanks for the remarkable benefits and merits of the ancestors and to praise their virtues. The most perfect and subtlest Spirit of the deceased ancestors, which had been dispersed in the deepest darkness, was gathered at the time of the *ji* ritual (this mental gathering and lively description will be discussed in the Second Treatise). A sacrifice was made to the Lord of Heaven to reveal and make known the supreme Majesty. Thus, everyone knew how to venerate the supreme Majesty. Ancestor halls were erected to display and make known close blood ties so that everybody knew how to love their blood relatives. Therefore, to observe piety and filial obedience, to extend truth to all things, to join obscure things to oneself, this is the greatest and most

---

353 Mentioned above (c.1, q.2, R.20).

powerful duty of mastering dispersion. Regarding the figure that this dispersion takes, you should understand that human souls are not united among themselves through mental thoughts or feelings. Thus, disagreements very frequently occur due to their social condition and natural abilities. Therefore, there must be something by which people are stimulated, moved, brought together. When they return to the unity of peace and mind, then the dispersions spontaneously coalesce. To worship Heaven and to revere the ancestors is to fulfill the true spirit of a pious and filial observance. Since all the inhabitants of the empire know that the Spirit of Heaven is the one Lord, inferiors do not dare to offend their superior; since they know that all men and other things have one origin, they do not dare to abandon the rites towards the dead and forget their ancestors'.[354]

HHH.69 蔡虛齋《四書蒙引・卷三・中庸・第十六》：「今人但知為父母所生，而不知其所以生者，固自有天地之氣在，均一父母也。」

About chapter 16 of the *Book of Unalterable Mean*, Cai Xuzhai in volume 3 of the *Sishu mengyin* states as follows: 'Today people only know that they were born from a father and a mother, but they do not know that the cause by which they were born is in truth the vital breath of Heaven and Earth, like a complete father and mother'.

III.70 《詩經說約集解・小雅・巧言》「悠悠昊天，曰父母且。」

Ode 'Qiaoyan' in the volume 'Xiaoya' of the *Book of Odes*: 'Most distant, hidden and immense Heaven, you are called Father and Mother'.[355]

III.71 《書經集傳・卷四・周書・泰誓上》：「元后作民父母。」

Chapter 'Taishi' in volume 4 of the *Book of Imperial Annals* states: 'The ruler of the people is their father and mother'.[356]

KKK.72 《禮記・卷五・郊特牲・第十一》：「天子大社必受霜露風雨，以達天地之氣也 … 社，所以神地之道也。地載萬物，天垂象，取財於地，取法於天，是以尊天而親地也，故教民美報焉。家主中霤而國主社，示本也 … 唯社，丘乘共粢盛，所以報本反始也。」

Chapter 11 'Jiaotesheng' in volume 5 of the *Book of Rites* states: 'The ritual sacrifice to Earth is how the way of Earth is known and made spiritual.[357] Earth sustains all things; the stars are suspended from Heaven; wealth is received from Earth while norms are received from Heaven. Therefore, Heaven is worshipped, and Earth is loved. The people are taught the best way to give thanks. The head of family, that is, the first-rank officer, stands in the middle of the house; the king on the royal platform makes a sacrifice to the Spirit of Earth to indicate the source of things'. Shortly after is added: 'However, the reason for making a sacrifice on the earthen

---

354 The last sentence was already translated above (c.2, q.3, X.29).
355 Mentioned also above (c.1, q.2, O.13).
356 Quoted in the *Tianjiao he Ru*, p. 24 (n. 7).
357 Another occurrence here of the verb *spiritualizare*.

platform to the Spirit of Earth is that nearby counties and towns around may provide dishes full of rice, giving thanks externally to the source of things and recollecting it with the mind'.

LLL.73   See above K.72.

MMM.74   See above QQ.46.

NNN.75   《禮記・卷三・王制・第五》：「天子將出，類乎上帝。」

Chapter 5 'Wangzhi' in volume 3 of the *Book of Rites*: 'When the emperor is about to march for war, he makes a sacrifice to *Shangdi*, the Lord of Heaven, with the ritual called *lei*'.

OOO   王昌會《全史詳要・卷二・武王踐位》：「諸侯受命于周，尊武王為天子。柴于上帝。」

Volume 2 of the *Book of Universal Annals* [*Quanshi xiangyao*] states: 'When prince Wu Wang took control of the state, the petty kings of Zhou submitted themselves to him and recognized him as emperor. Then, he himself made a sacrifice to *Shangdi*, the Lord of Heaven, using the ritual called *chai*, that is by burning the entire animal offering'.

PPP.77   See above B.3.

QQQ.78   陳澔《禮記集說・月令・第六》：「『是月也，天子乃以元日祈穀于上帝。』郊祭天而配以后稷，為祈穀也。」

Chapter 6 'Yueling' of the *Book of Rites* states: 'On the first day of the month called Xin, the emperor prays to the Lord of Heaven (*Shangdi*) for harvest'. Chen Hao comments on this passage in volume 3 [of the *Liji jishuo*]: 'A sacrifice is made to Heaven on the suburban mound and the ruler Houji is joined to Heaven as an associate to pray for the harvest'.[358]

Question 6: What does the Two-Character Word *taiji* or First Ultimate of Things Mean among the Chinese?

So far, we have always translated the word *taiji* as First Ultimate of Things. Let us now see what the Chinese understand by this. Please note that [Western] philosophers understand the concept of nature in many ways.[359] First, nature may be God, or the Creator of all things, called *natura naturans*, in contrast with Creation called *natura*

---

358   The classical text is mentioned above (c.1, q.2, §.2, P.15).
359   Noël follows here the Coimbra commentary on Aristotle's *Physics* (1592), which discusses six different meanings of nature. The first three meanings given by Noël correspond to the first three in the Coimbra commentary, whereas the fourth and fifth meanings given by Noël loosely correspond to the sixth and fourth meanings respectively. Noël does not include the fifth meaning found in the Coimbra commentary perhaps because it concerned the mixing of the four elements, a theory which does not have a precise correspondence in Chinese metaphysics. *Commentarii Collegii Conimbricensis Societatis Iesu, in octo libros Physicorum Aristotelis Stagiritae*, pp. 217 –18 (II, c.2, q.1, a.1).

naturata.³⁶⁰ Second, nature may be the essence of a thing.³⁶¹ Third, it may be the total aggregate of the natural agents.³⁶² Fourth, it may be the birth or generation of life, arising from an internal principle of a thing. Fifth, it is an internal principle by which something is first moved. According to the Coimbra commentaries, this principle resides in living and non-living things.³⁶³ Aristotle adopts the fifth meaning, defining nature as the principle and cause of motion and rest, by itself and not by accident.³⁶⁴ You should understand motion as any change, successive or instantaneous, insofar as motion can be called *actio* or *passio*.³⁶⁵ You should understand rest as something positive, like the preservation of the end acquired through motion.³⁶⁶

Since Aristotle defined nature as an essential part of a complete substance, it is clear that, in this meaning, neither God nor angels can be properly called nature. However, due to a similarity with true nature, inasmuch as God and angels are the principle of operations of the whole, they can be loosely called nature. Hence we often speak of 'divine nature' or 'angelic nature', even though they lack the conditions required for nature.³⁶⁷

Now that I have finished discussing these preliminary points, I can respond to the question above. I argue that *taiji*, or the First Ultimate, can be best understood as nature explained here in various ways.

§.1. *Taiji* as God, or *natura naturans*

Taiji, or the First Ultimate, can be understood as *natura naturans*, or God as author of all things. This is proven by what the Chinese say: 'It is Heaven and Earth which produce all things; and it is *taiji* which produces Heaven and Earth; therefore, how could *taiji* be expressed with a true name? How could it be fully understood? *Taiji* is only a conventional name, and that which is called *taiji* is in fact without

---

360 The first meaning is nature as a creative power of God. In relation to this concept see Chapter 3.7.
361 The second meaning of nature is the substance or quiddity of an individual thing.
362 The third meaning of nature as the totality of Creation is mentioned by Aristotle in chapter 7 of Book 12 of the *Metaphysics*, with Aristotle having probably in mind philosophers like Pythagoras.
363 The fourth meaning expresses natural causalities which encompass both living and non-living things.
364 The fifth meaning is the proper meaning of nature according to Aristotle who defines *physis* as an inner principle of cause and movement. Aristotle, *Physics*, 2.1 (192b20–23). Following Aquinas, Coimbra adopts this Aristotelian definition of nature, and stresses that Heaven is spontaneously inclined to motion but also to rest. See *Commentarii Collegii Conimbricensis Societatis Iesu, in octo libros Physicorum Aristotelis Stagiritae*, p. 223 (I, c.2, q.2, a.3). This suggests indeed a similarity with the double principle of motion and rest in the *Yijing*.
365 Coimbra discusses nature as including both matter and form; hence, motion and rest have to be understood as forms which can be active or passive. See *Commentarii Collegii Conimbricensis Societatis Iesu, in octo libros Physicorum Aristotelis Stagiritae*, p. 226 (II, c.1, q.3, a.2).
366 See *Commentarii Collegii Conimbricensis Societatis Iesu, in octo libros Physicorum Aristotelis Stagiritae*, p. 350 (II, c.9, q.1, a.1).
367 Unlike in monism, God or angels do not enter into the nature of things as if God or angels were essential parts of the things. However, God or angels can be called nature from the standpoint of the whole. Therefore, the first definition of nature as God still holds some validity.

any name'. (A). Suárez says something similar about the ineffability of God in his work (Volume 1, Book 2, Chapter 3[1]): 'The Fathers of the Church praised Plato and Trismegistus for saying that God is difficult to understand, but impossible to name'. Further below Suárez says: 'According to John of Damascus in Chapter 4 of Part 1 of his book, it is impossible to say what God's essence or nature is'.[368]

The Chinese also say: 'The operation, or nature, of highest Heaven is without voice, smell or sensation, yet it is truly the efficient cause, or the hinge and root of all the things that have been produced. Thus, it is said, "*Wuji*, or the Being without Ultimate, and at the same time, *taiji*, or the First Ultimate". Beyond the First Ultimate, there is no such thing as the Being without Ultimate'.[369] (B) This is because the Being without Ultimate is the First Ultimate. When the First Ultimate includes motion and rest, the Way of Heaven's Law is constant, running its course without interruption (C). 'The Way of Heaven's law, which is constant and runs its course without interruption, just as when it is said "The nature of highest Heaven is without sound and smell", refers to the Lord and Ruler' (D). This means the Lord and Ruler of Heaven. Therefore, *taiji* or the First Ultimate is understood as the Lord and Ruler of Heaven. In addition, *Shangdi* or Lord of Heaven was in the past called *taiyi*, the First or Greatest Unity (E). All the doctors explain *taiyi* as *taiji* (F). Thus, *taiji* is the Supreme Lord *Shangdi*, and thus the supreme and first Author of things.

As we saw above in L.19 of Question 2 in Chapter 2, *taixu*, the First Emptiness, is also called *taiji*. *Taixu* as a real and immaterial Being, or as Reason, is called Heaven or the Lord of Heaven. Besides, as we have seen above in A.1 of Question 3 in Chapter 2, Reason is the sole cause, which is the Spirit, and is called *taiji*, or the First Ultimate. Furthermore, in M.13 of Question 4 in Chapter 2, *shen*, which means by itself Spirit, can also be understood as *taiji*. It is clear now that *taiji*, or the First Ultimate, often means Spirit, Reason, the single spiritual cause, the Lord of Heaven, God separate from things [independently from the subjective mind], the first Creator of all things, and *natura naturans*.[370]

---

368 The two citations come from Suárez, *Tractatus de divina substantia ejusque attributis*; *Opera omnia De divina substantia ejusque attributis* (2.31): 'Platonis et Trismegisti dictum celebratur à Patribus: Deum intelligere difficile est; loqui autem impossibile'; 'Damascenus libro I. caput 4 sic ait: In Deo impossibile est, quidnam essentia sua ac natura ipsa sit, dicere'. These citations are not found in the ARSI manuscript but were added later. Through Suárez, Noël invokes the negative theology, which was espoused not only by some Fathers of the Church like Saint John of Damascus (675–749), but also by Plato and by Trismegistus, the purported author of the Hermetic Corpus.
369 Quote from Zhu Xi's *Taiji tushuo jie*. Noël interprets *shuniu* 樞紐 and *gendi* 根底 as efficient cause (*causa effectiva*).
370 Noël identifies *taiji* with God as *natura naturans*, expressing its transcendence in a double sense: as the producer of all things and as the active principle within the world. This would mean that *taiji* or God is both transcendent and immanent to the world. Against the tradition of dualism between spirit and matter in Western philosophy and Christianity, Noël's interpretation of *taiji* affirms that the immanent world is not utterly separated from transcendence but can be seen as its extension and domain of activity. Despite the boldness of his analysis, Noël shows a kind of reserve about radical consequences since this would mean that God as *natura naturans* can never be conceived as distinct from the concrete world,

NOTES

A.1 《性理標題・卷二・無名公傳》:「能造萬物者,天地也;能造天地者,太極也。太極其可得而名乎?可得而知乎?故強名之曰太極。太極者,其無名之謂乎?」

The chapter 'Wuming gong zhuan' in volume 2 of the *Summary of the Book of Nature and Reason* states: 'What produces Heaven and Earth …' See above.[371]

B.2 《性理標題・卷一・太極》:「『上天之載,無聲無臭』,而實造化之樞紐,品彙之根柢也。故曰:『無極而太極。』非太極之外復有無極也。太極之有動靜,是天命之流行也。」[372]

The chapter 'Taiji' in volume 1 of the *True Explanation of the Book of Changes and Productions* states: 'The operation, or nature, of Supreme Heaven …' See above.

C.3 See P.15 below.

D.4 蔡虛齋《四書蒙引・中庸・第二十六》:「天道之至誠無息,如何?曰『維天之命,於穆不已』,此正是『上天之載、無聲無臭』處,以主宰者言也。至於『覆載生成』處,乃其功用也。」

About chapter 26 of the *Book of the Unalterable Mean*, Cai Xuzhai in volume 4 of the *Sishu mengyin* explains as follows: 'The true Way of Heaven never ceases. How can this be explained? The phrase "How secretly and mysteriously the Law of Heaven runs its course without interruption!" refers to what is said elsewhere: "The nature of highest Heaven is without sound and smell". This is understood to mean Lord and Ruler. As for the phrase "protecting and sustaining, producing and accomplishing", this refers to His effects'.[373]

E.5 《文獻通考・卷六十八・郊社考一》:「昊天上帝之名,歷代不同。漢初曰上帝,曰泰一,元始間曰皇天上帝,魏初元間曰皇皇天帝,梁曰天皇大帝。」

Volume 68 of the *Wenxian tongkao* states: 'The name "Vast-Heaven-Supreme-Lord" changed under different dynasties. In the beginning of the Han dynasty, the names *Shangdi* or the Supreme Lord and *taiyi* or the First Unity were used;

---

thus ruining the traditional idea that God has created the world at some point in history. Therefore, Noël still talks about an objective existence of God, independent from the subjective mind, and here lies a crucial difference with Song philosophy since the original mind of man unifies all reality.

371 This is a quote from Shao Yong's *Wuming gong zhuan* 無名公傳 [Biography of Mr No One].
372 This quote comes from Zhu Xi's *Taiji tushuo jie* 太極圖說解 [Commentary on the Explanation of the *taiji* Diagram]. Unlike Zhou Dunyi, the brothers Cheng same as Zhu Xi consider that *wuji* and *taiji* are identical. See P.15 below. However, Bouvet follows Zhou Dunyi and criticizes Zhu Xi for having deleted *wuji*. See note 391 below at R.17.
373 Cai Qing in this quote does not explicitly mention *taiji*; however, he had just before explicitly mentioned *taiji*, so Noël could understand this quote as discussing *taiji* according to its two complementary dimensions, one metaphysical or transcendental, and the other operative or immanent. In other words, *taiji* is both the cause of the world and its active operating principle, or in Scholastic terms, *natura naturans*. In Noël's translation, we can see a subtle semantic transformation: his Latin translation of the term *zhuzaizhe* 主宰者 as Lord and Ruler suggests a personification, similar to the idea of a personal God, while *zhuzaizhe* in its original Chinese context means 'what masters and directs' and can be understood as a non-personal entity.

under the Emperor Pingdi, they used the name Huangtian *Shangdi* or the Supreme Lord ruling Heaven. During the Wei dynasty, they used the name Huanghuang Tiandi, the Lord of Heaven ruling rulers or the Supreme Heaven-Lord. During the Liang dynasty, they used the name Tianhuang Dadi or the Great Lord Ruler of Heaven'.³⁷⁴

F.6 陳澔《禮記集說・卷四・禮運・第九》：「石梁王氏曰：『禮家見「易有太極」字，翻出一箇「太一」，仍是諸子語。』」

About chapter 9 'Liyun' of the *Book of Rites*, Chen Hao comments the following in volume 4 [of the *Liji jishuo*]: 'According to Doctor Wang Shiliang, the commentators of the *Book of Rites* saw that in the *Yijing* word *taiji* could be found, that is *taiyi* or First or Greatest Unity, and later the doctors followed this'.³⁷⁵

§.2. *Taiji* as Essence of Both Created and Uncreated Things

According to the Chinese, 'If we consider all things, each thing has its own specific nature, and at the same time all things have the same First Ultimate (*taiji*) in common. If things are taken all together, the universal essence of all things is the one common First Ultimate; if things are taken individually, each thing has its own individual First Ultimate' (G).³⁷⁶ 'The First Ultimate is the perfection of nature; no mode or form can be found to explain it, and there is no voice nor smell with which it can be perceived' (H). In other words, it does not fall under sensory organs. Thus, it is said, 'The reason why the First Ultimate can be said to be without sound and smell, or imperceptible, is because it is like the substance of nature' (I), that is to say, an essence. Also, 'each thing contains in itself one substantial principle, and all the principles come from one source; the First Ultimate is the word which collectively encompasses all the substantial principles of things' (K). From this, it is clear enough that the First Ultimate means the essence of a thing.³⁷⁷

---

374 With E.5 and F.6, Noël intents to show that *taiji* was not a recent invention by the neo-Confucians, as Ricci had said, but had ancient roots like *taiyi*, *taixu*, etc. This quote is not present in the ARSI manuscript and was directly retrieved from the *Wenxian tongkao*, which quotes here the *Chenshi lishu* 陳氏禮書 by Chen Xiangdao.

375 The quote mentioned by Wang Shiqian 王時潛 (fl. 1280), *zi* Yuanlu 源魯, *hao* Shiliang 石梁, comes from the *Xici*, and Ricci mentioned it in the *True Meaning of the Lord of Heaven* (p. 73, n. 66). It is indeed the only occurrence of *taiji* in the ancient classics. The logical conclusion is that Shangdi, *taiyi*, and *taiji* are identical, with different names given at different epochs of China to the 'highest and first Author of the universe'. Noël's logical deduction is valid only if the premise of the argument is true, but the Ricci's idea of Shangdi as an equivalent to God was precisely the object of debate among missionaries.

376 In the Chinese text (一物各具一太極), Noël reads an individual *taiji* as the essence of an individual thing, distinguished from an universal *taiji*. On the contrary, Zhu Xi claims it is the same and unique *taiji*, considered in each individual thing and in the cosmos as a whole. Noël seems struggling with a conception so different from the philosophy of Aristotle, for whom there is a clear distinction between the essence of each individual thing and the essence of the whole cosmos.

377 In fact, Zhu Xi does not understand *taiji* as an essence, but as the universal principle which unifies different dimensions of reality. See Cheng, *Histoire de la pensée chinoise*, pp. 472–81. Noël operates a reduction of the concept of *taiji*, from the ultimate reality present in each thing to the essence of a specific thing.

NOTES

G.7 《性理標題・卷一・太極》：「自萬物而觀之,則萬物各一其性,而萬物一太極也。蓋合而言之,萬物統體一太極也；分而言之,一物各具一太極也。」

The chapter 'Taiji' in volume 1 of the *Summary of the Book of Nature and Reason* states: 'If we look at all things …' See above.[378]

H.8 《性理標題・卷一・太極》：「山陽度氏曰：太極本然之妙。初無方所之可言,無聲無臭之可識。」

The chapter 'Taiji' in volume 1 of the *Summary of the Book of Nature and Reason* states: 'Du Shanyang says, "*Taiji* is the the perfection of nature …"' See above.

I.9 《性理標題・卷一・太極》：「至於所以為太極者,又初無聲臭之可言,是性之本體然也。」

The chapter 'Taiji' in volume 1 of the *Summary of the Book of Nature and Reason* states: 'Thus, it is said …' See above.

K.10 《性理標題・卷三・天文》：「西山真氏曰：萬物各具一理,萬理同出一原。太極者,乃萬物統會之名。」

The chapter 'Tianwen' in volume 3 of the *Summary of the Book of Nature and Reason* states: 'Zhen Xishan [Zhen Dexiu 真德秀] says, "Each thing contains its reason, or essence …"' See above.

§.3. *Taiji* as Total Aggregate of Natural Agents

This can be proven from these words of their authors. When it is said that 'in each enigmatic symbol [hexagram] and its six numerical lines [line statements] can always be found the principle of the First Ultimate of the First Three Principles (Heaven, Earth and human being, that is, the total aggregate of the natural agents), which are thus called the Three Ultimates', this means that, after each symbol and its numerical parts have been attached to and practically inserted into a particular thing through motion or change, each symbol contains its own First Ultimate. When it is further said that 'the doctrine of the *Book of Changes and Productions* contains in itself the First Ultimate', this means that, before each symbol and its numerical parts have been applied to a particular thing through motion or change and put into practice, their universal substance (or more exactly their universal aggregate) is this unique First Ultimate, or rather one common nature' (L).[379]

This shows that the first and second meanings of *taiji* given by Noël are not complementary aspects or dimensions of *taiji*, but different meanings which are contradicting each other. Yet, for Zhu Xi, the two meanings should not be disconnected since the *taiji* at the level of the universe is also the *taiji* at the level of each individual thing.

378 This quote comes from Zhu Xi's *Taiji tushuo jie*.
379 In this passage, already quoted above (c.1, q.2, §.2, G), Hu Yunfeng 胡雲峰 considers two aspects of *taiji*. The first aspect concerns *taiji* as present in individual things, that is, after the differentiation into the myriad things, but Noël has just explained this according to the second meaning of *taiji*. Noël's concern

Also, 'if you wish to express the complete substance and essence of the Way, it is called the First Ultimate; if you wish to express the constant action and virtue of the First Ultimate, it is called the Way' (M). All these points suffice to show that the First Ultimate can be taken as the total aggregate of natural agents.[380]

NOTES

L.11 《周易正解・卷十七・傳上・第二》：「雲峰胡氏曰：一卦六爻之間，莫不有三才太極之理，此曰『三極』，是卦爻已動之後，各具一太極。後曰『易有太極』，是卦爻未生之先，統體一太極也。」

> About chapter [2] of 'Zhuan shang', volume 17 of the *True Explanation of the Book of Changes and Productions* states as follows: 'Each enigmatic symbol …' See above.[381]

M.12 《周易正解・卷二十・傳下・第五》：「『道不離乎陰陽，而亦不離[382]乎陰陽，』乃太極之謂也。」「語道之全體，則謂之太極［…］語太極之流行，則謂之道；語道之妙，則謂之神。節齋蔡氏謂：『主太極而言，則太極在陰陽之先；主陰陽而言，則太極在陰陽之內。蓋自陰陽未生之時而言，則所謂太極者，其理已具；自陰陽既生之時而言，則所謂太極者，卽在乎陰陽之中也。』」

> About chapter 5 of 'Zhuan xia', volume 20 of the *True Explanation of the Book of Changes and Productions* states as follows: 'When it is said that "the Way of acting is neither set apart from rest (*yin*) and motion (*yang*), nor mixed with them", this refers to the First Ultimate'. Further below is added: 'The whole Way, that is substance or essence of the Way of action, is called the First Ultimate. The Way of action refers to the constant working and course of the First Ultimate; the Spirit refers to the perfection of the Way. As Cai Jiezhai says, "If you consider rest (*yin*) and motion (*yang*), then the First Ultimate is contained in them. Before the production of rest (*yin*) and motion (*yang*), that which is called the First Ultimate is their cause, mentally represented. After they are produced, what we call the First Ultimate is the same thing contained inside rest (*yin*) and motion (*yang*), that is, inside this substantial composite of rest and motion, which has Nature or the First Ultimate as substantial element"'.[383]

---

here lies in Hu's second aspect of *taiji*, by which Heaven, Earth, and humanity constitute collectively an aggregate of the natural world, also called *taiji*, that is, before the differentiation into the myriad things.

380 This aggregate should not be understood as sum of all the entities, but as a metaphysical reality existing prior to the existence of concrete things and existing after, always unchanged. This point of view is similar to the Pythagorean and Platonic theory of the world-soul.

381 Noël quotes from the *Zhouyi zhengjie*, which quotes Hu Yunfeng.

382 Mistake in the ARSI manuscript for 雜.

383 For Zhu Xi, *yin* and *yang* belong to the realm of the physical world and thus cannot mix with *taiji*; their energy (*yinyang zhi qi* 陰陽之氣) but not *yin* and *yang* themselves can be found in *taiji*. Cai Chen's elder bother, Cai Yuan 蔡淵 (1156–1236), *zi* Bojing 伯靜, *hao* Jiezhai 節齋, here seems to be influenced by Zhu Xi's rival Lu Jiuyuan 陸九淵 (1139–1193), who considered *yin* and *yang* in the realm of what is without shape, and thus held, unlike Zhu Xi, that even before the differentiation into concrete things, *taiji* contains *yin* and *yang*. By following Cai Jiezhai's interpretation, and not Zhu Xi's, Noël can show more clearly the third meaning of *taiji* as representing the totality of the cosmos, including

§.4. *Taiji* as Birth or Generation of Life

Since the fourth meaning is included in the fifth, we shall omit it and deal only with the fifth meaning.

§.5. *Taiji* Mostly as Causal Origin of Motion and Stillness

Taiji or the First Ultimate is most frequently understood as nature, insofar as nature is the causative principle of motion and rest. Thus the Chinese define the First Ultimate as 'the substance by which there is motion from *yang*, and stillness from *yin*; the motion producing *yang* is the source of *yin*, and through this, the First Ultimate acts as a cause; rest producing *yin* is the source of *yang*, and the essence of the First Ultimate subsists through this'. Zhou [Dunyi] expresses this as follows: 'When the First Ultimate moves itself, it produces *yang*, and when the motion is completed, the First Ultimate rests; when resting, it produces *yin*, and when rest is completed, it moves itself again; this alternation of motion and rest is the mutual origin and principle of *yin* and *yang*. Through this partition between *yin* and *yang*, there are Two Formalities or relations' (N).[384] From this, it follows that the First Ultimate as efficient principle of motion and rest corresponds to the concept of nature according to Aristotle.[385]

NOTE: Since the two words *yin* and *yang* have been mentioned frequently, it is necessary to discuss briefly their meaning. In their general and proper sense, as evidenced here, *yin* and *yang* mean nothing else but the two modes or transcendental relations of motion and rest: *yang* is a transcendental relation, or the essential order of motion towards rest; and *yin* is the essential order of rest towards motion. To avoid confusion, I have always translated *yin* and *yang* as rest and motion respectively, though in reality one exists only in relation to the other, and vice-versa.[386]

Since those two transcendental relations are extremely broad and general, the Chinese apply *yin* and *yang* to almost everything, saying: 'There is nothing in the world except the endless alternation of motion and rest; this alternation is the teaching of the *Book of Changes and Productions*, and the First Ultimate causes the

---

all its rational principles and physical elements. We should notice that this third meaning of *taiji* is completely different from the first meaning as transcendental cause. Here *taiji* is considered as the totality of all things brought into a single whole, and thus quite similar to the idea of a world-soul as expressed by Pythagoras or Plato, an idea which was harshly criticized by Aristotle and rejected by Christian thinkers as pantheistic. It did not come to Noël's mind that *taiji* could have been both the totality of beings and also their transcendental cause. Julia Ching precisely holds that such is the opinion of the neo-Confucians. See Ching, *The Religious Thought of Chu Hsi*, p. 46.

384 Noël had already quoted the same words of Zhou Dunyi's *Taiji tushuo* in Question 4, K.10.
385 Like the Aristotelian definition of nature as movement, *taiji* has also been defined as a principle of motion and rest by Zhou Dunyi, and Noël quotes from Wu Sunyou's *Zhouyi zhengjie* (Correct explanation of the *Yijing*). Following Zhu Xi, *taiji* is explained here in terms of an ontology (*ti* 體, or *substantia*) of movement and rest, and thus Noël considered that *taiji* fulfills the Aristotelian definition of nature.
386 Noël appreciates that *yin* and *yang* are not static entities, but always in the state of becoming something else, and so he talked in terms of two 'transcendental relationships', in the sense that the relationship tends toward an object which is not in oneself: *yang* tends to become *yin*, and vice versa.

alternation of motion and rest' (O). 'Since *yin* and *yang* are always found in the production of everything, the First Ultimate and the Two Formalities are always present' (P). From the perspective of the First Ultimate, it is prior to rest (*yin*) and motion (*yang*) since it is their efficient cause (*ratio productiva*); but from the point of view of *yin* and *yang*, the First Ultimate is contained in them insofar as it is the essential principle of the whole (Q). Since the teaching of the *Book of Changes and Productions* embraces all the changes and productions that constantly and endlessly take place in the world, it is necessary that the teaching contains a single, original, and unchangeable Reason which controls and regulates the changes and productions; this Reason is called the First Ultimate. For the First Ultimate or Reason is single, ultimate, supreme, and most perfect. It cannot be increased, is far more excellent than anything, and lacks sound and smell. It controls and directs all changes and productions (R).

From this you can see that the First Ultimate can be properly understood according to the fifth meaning of nature, insofar as it is the principle and cause of movement and rest and that this principle is in it *per se* and not by accident. But the First Ultimate can also be seen in relation to the Divine Nature operating constantly in the world, if nature is loosely understood, as I said, as being the principle of operations of everything without insisting upon the other conditions necessary to nature when understood in narrow terms.³⁸⁷

NOTES

N.13 《周易正解・太極圖說》：「太極者, 乃所以動而陽、靜而陰之本體也。動而陽者, 陰之根也, 太極之用所以行也。靜而陰者, 陽之根也, 太極之體所以立也。故周子曰：『太極動而生陽, 動極而靜, 靜而生陰, 靜極復動, 一動一靜, 互為其根。分陰分陽, 兩儀立焉。』此之謂也。」

> The *True Explanation of the Book of Changes and Productions* says in its preface: '*Taiji* is substance by which motion ...' See above [Question 4, K.10]. See also P.15 below.

O.14 《周易正解・太極圖說・太極》：「朱子：『太極只是二氣五行之理[...]天地之間, 只有動靜兩端循環不已, 更無餘事, 此之謂「易」。而其動其靜, 則必有所以動靜之理, 是則所謂太極也。』」

> The preface to the *True Explanation of the Book of Changes and Productions* cites Zhu Xi as follows: 'The First Ultimate is but the Reason of the Double Vital Breath or Life and of the Five Universal Principles. There is nothing in the world but the alternation of motion and rest without any end, and nothing else. This alternation is said to be teaching of the *Book of Changes and Productions*. As for motion and rest, there must be some Reason producing both, and this Reason is called the First Ultimate'.³⁸⁸

---

387   Though each individual thing has motion in itself and no other thing can enter into its specific nature, yet it is possible to say loosely that Nature (God or *taiji*) is the ultimate cause of motion of the whole.
388   The *Zhouyi zhengjie* quotes Zhu Xi from *juan* 94 of the *Zhuzi yulei*.

P.15 《周易正解·太極圖說》：程子《周易程氏傳·原序》：「所以《易》有太極, 是生兩儀。太極者, 道也。兩儀者, 陰陽也。陰陽, 一道也。太極, 无極也。萬物之生, 負陰而抱陽, 莫不有太極, 莫不有兩儀。絪縕交感, 變化不窮。」

> In the preface to the *True Explanation of the Book of Changes and Productions* Chengzi is cited as follows: 'The *Book of Changes and Productions* contains the First Ultimate which produces the Two Formalities. The First Ultimate is the Way, and the Two Formalities are *yin* and *yang*; the Way of *yin* and *yang* is one, that is to say, the First Ultimate. The First Ultimate [*taiji*] is the same as the Being without Ultimate [*wuji*]. Since *yin* and *yang* are found in the production of all things, the First Ultimate is always present, as well as the Two Formalities which are interconnected by a mutual and invisible link and constitute the endless principle of changes and productions'.[389]

Q.16 See M.12.

R.17 《日講易經·卷十六·上傳·第十一》：「太極, 謂至極無上, 以主宰萬化之理言。」「易固生生不已, 變化無端矣。然必有至一不變之理主宰於中, 以為生生之本, 太極是也。」「先儒周敦頤所論太極, 指無聲無臭之理言。」

> About chapter 11 of 'Zhuan shang', volume 16 of the *Daily Explanation of the Book of Changes and Productions* comments as follows: '*Taiji* means a Reason which is single, supreme, ultimate, and without anything above it. Its role is to control the productions and changes of all things and to regulate their causes'. Further below is added: 'The teaching of the *Book of Changes and Productions* contains indeed the constant and endless productions and the incessant and uninterrupted changes, but it is necessary that there is in the middle of these changes and productions a single, supreme, original and unchangeable Reason which rules and guides, and which is the source and root of all those endless productions. It is called the First Ultimate or *taiji*'. Further below: 'Doctor Zhou [Dunyi] had in the past discussed the First Ultimate, indicating that it means a single Reason without sound and smell, that is, it is imperceptible'.[390]

---

389 Brothers Cheng and Zhu Xi considered *wuji* and *taiji* to be identical, while Zhou Dunyi held a difference between the two.

390 Noël quotes here the *Yijing rijiang* which follows the orthodox interpretation set by Zhu Xi, identifying *wuji* with *taiji*. However, when commenting on this same passage of the *Yijing rijiang*, Bouvet follows Ricci in holding that *taiji* cannot be the Creator, and he also criticizes Zhu Xi for having deleted *wuji*, the true ultimate principle beyond visible objects; Bouvet, *Guijn*, pp. 132–33: '據此《日講》, 萬物本於太極, 於理而己, 其理其太極, 可為造物真主乎？考天主《聖經》, 造物主所化之類無數, 然盡於有靈無靈, 能明理、不能明理, 乃萬物萬靈二等而己。萬物萬形之妙, 一一皆合於造物主；所懷至靈至一不變當然之理, 而明顯其造者之無極而太極之能、至明至神之德, 於己像萬靈, 一看萬像, 格物窮其理。而由此可見之形像, 至於明通所無形像、無可見造物主自為無極而太極之能, 萬靈所懷至神、至靈、至一不變之理, 真為萬物萬靈根本主宰。由此觀之, 國史周濂溪等儒, 論《太極圖》, 所云無極而太極, 上原有"自""為'二字極是。朱子何刪之？"' Later, Joseph de Prémare (1666–1736) followed Bouvet and not Noël in upholding the priority of *wuji* over *taiji*. See David E. Mungello, 'The Reconciliation of Neo-Confucianism with Christianity in the Writings of Joseph de Prémare, S. J.', *Philosophy East and West*, 26.4 (1976), 389–410 (p. 400).

R.18 《周易正解・卷十九・傳上・第十一》：「劉石芝曰：『太極, 謂其理之至極而無以加也。』」

> About chapter 11 of 'Zhuan shang', volume 19 of the *True Explanation of the Book of Changes and Productions* states: 'Liu Shizhi says, "The First Ultimate means a Reason which is supreme and ultimate, and to which nothing can be added"'.

Certainly, it is unusual for the Latins to use expressions like 'God is nature', 'to worship nature', and 'to sacrifice to nature', even though nature when understood as the first Principle or Author of nature is truly God, is duly worshipped and duly offered sacrifice. Similarly, it is not common for the Chinese to say that the First Ultimate or *taiji* is 'Heaven or Lord of Heaven', 'to worship the First Ultimate', and 'to sacrifice to the First Ultimate' even though the First Ultimate when understood as the First Principle and Author of things is truly Heaven or the Lord of Heaven, is duly worshipped, and duly offered sacrifice.[391] It should not be surprising that Chinese refer to the Lord of Heaven as *taiji* or nature, since ancient Greek philosophers often spoke about divinity in this way. In *Octavius*, Minucius Felix had shown that the Greek philosophers knew the true God:

> It is well known that Xenophanes had said that God is all infinity with a mind while Antisthenes had said that there are many gods of the people, but that the God of Nature is the chief of all. What does Democritus say? Although he is the first discoverer of atoms, does he not especially speak of God as Nature, which is the basis of forms and intelligence? Even Epicurus, the man who feigns either otiose gods or none at all, still places Nature above all.[392]

In Book 1 of *On the Nature of the Gods*, Cicero also says: 'According to Antisthenes' book called the *Physicus*, there are many Gods of popular belief, but there is only God in nature'.[393] And in chapter 10 of the First Book of his *Anger of God*, Lactantius says:

> If Nature, which [the philosophers] suppose to be the mother of all things, does not have a mind, it cannot cause or produce anything, because where there is no reflection, there is neither motion nor efficacy. But if it uses its counsel to commence something, reason for arranging it, skill for producing it, virtue for completing it, and power for governing and controling it, why it should be called Nature rather than God?[394]

---

391 Noël seems here to take into account the point that Ricci made about the lack of worship of *taiji* in China. See Ricci, *True Meaning of the Lord of Heaven*, p. 81 (n. 78).
392 Minucius Felix, *Octavius*, XIX. Minucius Felix was a Christian writer from the second or third century, born in North Africa.
393 Cicero, *The Nature of the Gods*, I–XIII.32.
394 Lactantius wrote in 363 the *Anger of God* (*Ira Dei*) addressed to Donatus; *On the Anger of God*, trans. by William Fletcher, *The Works of Lactantius*, vol. 22 (Edinburgh: T. & T. Clark, 1871), p. 19.

The Platonic philosophers expressed the forms of things with numbers, and yet they designated God with the name of One, and defined the soul as a self-moving number.³⁹⁵ Just as we have observed that there is a soul from life, so we have observed that there is life from motion, especially spontaneous motion. Hence I infer that the use of this term *natura* to speak about the Divinity was once very common, just as the Chinese often use the word First Unity [*taiyi*] to denote the First Ultimate [*taiji*]. But I shall not spend more time on this. As I have proven, it is enough to understand that the First Ultimate or *taiji* can be understood not only as created but also as uncreated Nature, even though the Chinese more frequently appear to understand *taiji* according to the second and third meanings.³⁹⁶

Someone may ask now whether the Chinese books mention not only the unity of God, but also the Trinity of Persons. I answer that this mystery [of the Trinity] cannot be known by natural reason, but only through faith according to Suárez, and thus it would be vain to seek this. We can only ask whether the Chinese know through natural (not supernatural) reason the supreme and infinite Divinity in every type of essential perfection, leaving aside notional attributes.³⁹⁷ They seem to hint obscurely very few things about this mystery [of Divine Perfection] under the cloak of general vocabulary, but it is better to omit those things because this is irrelevant to the question.³⁹⁸

Question 7: Do Modern Works Give True Knowledge of the First Being or God, and Are Modern Chinese Atheists?

With all what was said above, this question may seem superfluous, but please read this brief summary so that this matter can be explained with greater clarity.

1 Please recall what I said in Question 3 of Chapter 1 about the ancient books of the Chinese. The more recent Chinese hold the same things as the ancient Chinese, with only a few changes.³⁹⁹

---

395 This expression in used by Aristotle (*De anima*, 404b30). Scholastic philosophers usually attributed this to Plato. For example, see Saint Thomas Aquinas, *Commentary on Aristotle's De Anima* (Notre Dame: Dumb Ox Books, 1994), p. 21. In fact, this originates with Pythagoras.
396 Noël rejects the two immanent meanings of *taiji* (second meaning: individual essence of a thing; and third meaning: total aggregate of things) as candidates for the notion of God, and he promotes the idea of *taiji* as creating nature (first meaning) and origin of life and motion (fourth and fifth meanings).
397 This is to ask whether the Chinese had a knowledge of the attributes of God, not as notional or conceptual attributes, but as existing realities.
398 Noël stays within the bound of reason and does not engage into finding some hidden truths beyond words, like the Jesuit Figurist Bouvet who intended to prove Trinity or Divine Perfection. However, Noël's last sentence suggests that he does not reject Figurism.
399 This conclusion goes against the position of Ricci who held that the Chinese thinkers had departed from the teaching of the ancients. While Longobardo stressed the continuity, he discards the whole of Confucian philosophy as atheistic. Noël stresses the continuity and accepts the whole of Confucian philosophy as monotheistic.

2 The modern works and authors attribute to to Heaven or the Lord of Heaven supreme dominion, supreme power, unfailing knowledge, free will, wise justice, life, immensity, simplicity, or spirituality. Thus, they have a true knowledge of the First Being, God.

3 They acknowledge a First Principle in the world, which is invisible, spiritual, uncreated, first mover, the maker of all things, coinciding with all things in an invisible way, governing everything, providing for everything, and they say that this Principle is one and spiritual. Thus, they have a true knowledge of the First Being or God.

4 Although they explain the First Principle and the First Being as Reason [*li*], Nature [*taiji*], Vital Breath [*qi*], or Law of Heaven [*Tiandao*], these names do not obstruct true knowledge of it, since our ancient wise men [in the West] explain the Divinity as Reason, Providence, Nature and Vital Breath. For example, Cicero in the Second Book of *On the Nature of the Gods* says:

> If all parts of the world have been so structured that they could not be better in terms of utility and beauty, let us consider whether this is the result of chance, or whether the parts of the world are in such a condition that they could not possibly have cohered if they were not controlled by intelligence and by divine providence. If then the products of nature are better than those of art, and if art cannot produce anything without reason, nature too cannot be deemed to be without reason.[400]

In Book 2 of *On the Nature of the Gods*, Cicero also says:

> When we see something moved by machinery, like an orrery or clock or many other such things, we do not doubt that these contrivances are the work of reason; when therefore we behold the whole compass of the heaven moving with revolutions of marvelous velocity and executing with perfect regularity the annual changes of the seasons with absolute safety and security for all things, how can we doubt that all this is done not merely by reason, but by a reason that is excellent and divine?[401]

In the fifth chapter of the *Tusculan Disputations*, Cicero calls the soul a particle of divine breath.[402] Seneca mentions the movement of the stars, saying: 'Their unhindered speed proceeds from the command of the eternal Law'.[403] Pythagoras

---

[400] Cicero, *The Nature of the Gods (De Natura Deorum)*, trans. by H. Rackham (Cambridge: Harvard University Press, 1933), p. 207 (2.34). We have slightly modified Rackham's English translation to be closer to the Latin.

[401] Cicero, *The Nature of the Gods*, p. 217 (2.38). We have slightly modified Rackham's English translation to be closer to the Latin.

[402] Noël is mistaken here. The mention is not found in Cicero's *Tusculan Disputations*, but in Horace's *Satires* 2.2.79. See also note 154 above.

[403] Seneca, *On Providence (De Providentia)*, 1.2.

said that the world stays together through harmonic Reason. Even the Christian writer Lactantius in the chapter 'About false religion' in the first book [of his *Divine Institutions*] addressed to Emperor Constantine, after having related the various testimonies and opinions of the Poets and Philosophers, says:

> The opinion of all, though uncertain, amount to his: they agree that there is one Providence, which may be called Nature, Aether, Reason, Mind, Fatal Necessity, Divine Law, or something else, yet it is always the same as what we call God. This variety of names is not a hindrance since all the names come back to the same meaning. Aristotle may sometimes contradict himself, yet he overall he affirms that there is only one Mind governing the world.[404]

Thus, I conclude that there is nothing strange about the Divinity being indicated by these and other similar names.

5 Saint Paul in the first chapter of his Letter to the Romans believes that the true God was naturally known to the ancient wise men and philosophers. According to Cornelius à Lapide, Saint Paul criticized the philosophers very harshly, and yet they were not atheists, 'for what can be known about God is manifest to them, because God has shown it to them'.[405] Cornelius explains this passage as follows:

> Saint Paul affirmed clearly that they could have and ought to have known God and the truth about Him, and indeed they truly knew Him since truth is naturally open and manifest, and nature itself teaches and orders it. Thus, God through the light of nature revealed the truth to them. The words of Saint Paul, 'what can be known about God', are expressed in Greek as *gnoston tou theou*, which means what can be naturally known about God, such as the fact that God is the one, eternal ruler and judge of the world. The phrase 'manifest to them' means that this knowledge was in their mind, intellect and consciousness.[406]

Since nature teaches and declares the truth of the One God, and this is known through natural reason, and since the wise men in antiquity knew this truth, how could it be that only the more recent Chinese who talk so much about this truth are not taught the same by nature and natural reason? Would they be alone without natural light? In the First Book of the *Laws*, Cicero says:

> Out of so many species, there is no animal besides the human being that has any notion of god, and among human beings themselves there is no

---

404 Lactantius, *Divine Institutions*, 1.5.
405 Saint Paul, Letter to the Romans, 1:19.
406 Cornelius à Lapide, *In omnes divi Pauli Epistolas commentaria* (Lyon, 1683), p. 35 (1.19). Noël was quite familiar with the works of Cornelius à Lapide since he quoted his *Commentaria in Pentateuchum Mosis* in Question 3 of Chapter 2.

nation either so tame or so wild that it does not know that it should have a god, although it may be ignorant of what sort it ought to have.[407]

In chapter 9 of the *Topica*, even Aristotle says that the one who doubts whether God has to be worshipped should be punished. And Seneca says: 'There has never been any people so far beyond the reach of laws and customs that they do not believe at least in gods of some sort'.[408] Plotinus in Chapter 1 of Book 5 of the *Sixth Ennead* says: 'A common conception of the human mind indicates that something unitary in number is present everywhere since everyone affirms with the same natural instinct that God dwells in each one of us'. And Tertullian mentions the soul as being naturally Christian.[409] I omit Minucius Felix,[410] the Platonic philosopher Maximus of Tyre,[411] as well as Orosius[412] and other ancient philosophers who have proven the same.

Could not those famous testimonies of philosophers who have denied that there is Atheism in the world prevail upon those few missionaries wishing to cast the aspersion of Atheism on the Chinese people, who are so clever and cultivated, and have discussed at length and with great clarity a supreme Being, perhaps even surpassing most of the ancient philosophers in this matter?[413] But let us set aside those general and abstract considerations and return to more concrete things.

6 Ancient and more recent Chinese all acknowledge the Spirit of the mountains and rivers, the Spirit of Heaven and Earth; they venerate them, sacrifice to them, and thus are not Atheist.

7 As we have said, the words Reason, Nature, Vital Breath, Law of Heaven, etc., with which the Chinese frequently indicate divinity, can be also applied, due to the universal presence of Divinity, to the human soul, and those words are effectively used that way. However, Divinity and human soul should be clearly distinguished from each other, especially when the Chinese compare the soul

---

407 Cicero, *De Legibus*, 1.24; *On the Republic and On the Laws*, trans. by David Fott (Cornell University Press, 2014), p. 138.
408 Seneca, *Epistles*, trans. by Richard M. Gummere (Cambridge, MA: Harvard University, 1925), p. 341 (117.6). The translation has been slightly modified.
409 Tertullian, 'De testimonio animae', *Apologeticum*, 17.6; *Patrologia Latina*, 1:377.
410 In Question 6 of Chapter 2, Noël has quoted Minucius Felix's *Octavius*.
411 Maximus of Tyre was a Greek philosopher from the second century. Nominally a Platonist, he was an Eclectic and a precursor to neo-Platonism.
412 Paulus Orosius was an Iberian priest and disciple of Saint Augustine. He wrote *Historiarum adversum paganos libri VII*. Despite this negative title, he often gives a favourable impression of 'pagan' culture. In presenting this list of authors in support of natural theology, Noël draws on a long Christian tradition starting from Minucius Felix. In the seventeenth century, the French Jesuit Denis Pétau (1583–1652) has a similar list in his *Dogmata theologica* (1644–1650), a work which Noël probably knew.
413 Noël addresses here the problem of missionaries like Navarrete and Caballero who condemn more recent Chinese as atheist. He is suggesting that the modern Chinese philosophers are better than the ancient (Western) philosophers mentioned in this paragraph.

of the wise to Heaven, and they attribute the same virtue to both [Heaven and the soul] due to their similarity. Even Cicero in chapter 9 of the *Tusculan Disputations* compared human soul to Heaven, making it almost the equivalent of God, saying:

> Know, then, that you are a god, if a god is that which lives, feels, remembers, and foresees, and which rules, governs and moves the body over which it is put in charge, just as the Supreme God above us rules the universe.[414]

8   Notice how I said above that more recent Chinese have natural knowledge of God according to Saint Paul's understanding, and thus they are not atheist. However, according to this same understanding, I consider that 'they have kept the truth of God in injustice'.[415] Indeed, they clearly acknowledge the existence of a single, supreme and true God, Creator of the world, and yet, being under the control of their wicked passions, they do not pay Him due obedience and honour. Their knowledge of God is like a gem in the mud, being obscured and immersed in their sins. Like a bat, they flee from the light of truth, and do not wish to discuss it. Even if the truth is proposed to them under the manifest and clear name of *Deus*, they would immediately reject it as being repugnant to natural light, returning to the more abstract and general names of Reason, Nature, Law of Heaven, which, as explained above, amount to the same thing. Since God cannot be known through the eyes of the body, they prefer to remove this truth from the eyes of their mind, without further scrutiny and discussion, so not to be forced to acknowledge more clearly what their conscience, through natural light, dictates to be true. Clearly, they are not atheist, but should be properly called impious instead.

Also, please make sure not to bring the notion of 'political form of worship' since we are dealing here with knowledge and not worship, whatever form it takes. I am talking here about speculative and natural knowledge, and not about a practical knowledge joined to worship.[416]

---

414   Cicero, *On the Republic*, trans. by Clinton Walker Keyes (Cambridge, MA: Harvard University Press, 1928), pp. 26–28 (6.24). This is an erroneous attribution, as the Dream of Scipio is the sixth book of *On the Republic*.
415   Saint Paul, Letter to the Romans, 1:18.
416   For Longobardo, the Chinese literati are hidden atheists. They reject the truth of God and the true religion, but they are using God and religion as tools for their own political control of the world. Couplet also makes the literati atheists and qualify them as politico-atheists. However, he moderates the accusation against the intentions of the literati: they are not positive atheists, but only negative atheists, who could lead other people towards positive atheism. See Meynard, ed., *Confucius Sinarum Philosophus*, p. 163. Noël has shown that both ancient and more recent Chinese have known God as *Tian*. However, when the contemporary Chinese are presented with the higher truth of the Christian God, they morally resist acknowledging what their conscience dictates. They know about God's existence, but they do not embrace this truth in their mind, give assent to this truth, and therefore they are impious. The issue of the assent to a truth is classical theme debated in Stoicism, in the Academy and by Cicero.

9 Finally, if all the things discussed in the two chapters are considered together, and the series of quotes of so many writers and their coherence are examined carefully, no prudent reader could consider the modern Chinese, let alone the ancient Chinese, as atheist.

But someone may ask, what's the point of all this discussion? Why does it matter whether the Chinese had and still have knowledge of God, and whether they are atheist? Where do all the things covered in those two chapters lead us? To what end and purpose? I answer that all those things would be best discussed, one by one, in the next chapter.

Chapter 3: True Name of God in China

Everything we have said so far is aimed at helping us see how to name God in China.[1] Therefore, we investigate whether God can be called *Shangdi* or the Lord and Ruler of Heaven, Heaven, the First Ultimate (*taiji*) or Nature, Reason (*li*), Vital Breath (*qi*), or something similar. *Taiji*, *li* and *qi* have been understood by the modern Chinese to explain or outline the different perfections and operations of Heaven or the Lord of Heaven. For example, *taiji* is the first cause or *natura naturans*; *li*, the ideal and exemplar cause, or supreme intelligence; *qi*, the Vital Power or operation and execution, or spirituality and excellence. Those terms are used by the Chinese in different ways, and their meaning is rather vague, undetermined, and indiscriminately used with various objects, referring sometimes to the whole and sometimes to the part, sometimes to the substance and sometimes to the accident, and sometimes to Creation and sometimes to the Creator. Thus the Fathers of the mission have always refused to use them as expressions for God and have attacked the more recent Chinese writers who make the name of Heaven and the Lord of Heaven obscure and almost unintelligible to them. Indeed, a great deal of circumlocution would be needed to express God with the words *taiji*, *li* and *qi*. Putting all those things aside, the whole discussion boils down to whether God can be expressed in China as *Shangdi* or *Tian*.[2]

Question 1: Can God be called *Shangdi*, that is the Lord and Ruler of Heaven, or Supreme Lord?

§.1. Affirmation

Since the meaning of *Shangdi* among ancient and more recent Chinese has been demonstrated abundantly above, I answer that God in China can be called *Shangdi*. This can be proven from what is written below.

---

[1] This section contradicts the instructions given after the Jesuit conference of Jiading which prohibited the terms *Tian* and *Shangdi* for God, as well as the *Mandatum* of the Apostolic Vicar Charles Maigrot (1652–1730) in 1693, and the proclamation in 1710 of the papal decree *Cur Deus Optimus*.

[2] In Question 6 of Chapter 2, Noël has explained some meanings of *taiji* which are compatible with Aristotle and Christian thought, but here he is quite cautious about using *taiji* within the Catholic Church in China. Though Noël personally seems to prefer Shangdi, he still considered *Tian* the best term as we shall see below.

From Reason

1. Words are arbitrary signs which obtain their power of signifying meaning from a decision made at the time of their institution.³ As evident from the discussion in Chapter 1, the word *Shangdi* was instituted in early antiquity to signify the true God, and its institution has been maintained until now, as shown in Question 1 of Chapter 2. Therefore, the true God can be called *Shangdi*.

2. The ancient and modern Chinese attribute to *Shangdi* the same perfections that we attribute to God, as we have seen throughout both preceding chapters, and the word *Shangdi* has the same meaning as what we signify by the word *Deus*.

3. Everyone agrees that in China God can be called *Tianzhu* or Lord of Heaven, but *Shangdi* also means Lord of Heaven, or *Shangdi* is the same thing as the Lord of Heaven, as shown in Question 2 of Chapter 2. It is also said that *Shangdi* is the spirit of Heaven, and the spirit of Heaven is the one Lord, as said in Question 3 of Chapter 2. Finally, *Shangdi* is the Spirit of Heaven and Earth, as said in Question 3 of Chapter 2. Therefore, God can be called *Shangdi*.

4. As for the reasons of the credibility of faith, it is said: even if some reasons considered separately do not convince the intellect and do not have total efficacy, when considered together, they are so convincing that it would be considered sinful not to believe in them. Let's explain this with an analogy: even if, when taken separately, the things discussed in the first two chapters do not convince and lack total efficacy, when taken together, they seem to be able to convince the intellect, or at least give sufficient reasons for the intellect to give prudently its assent. When Christ wanted to persuade the Apostles that He had risen from the dead, He said: 'Touch me and see, because a spirit has no flesh and bones' (Luke 24:39). On its own, this evidence does not efficaciously prove His Resurrection because spirits could assume bodily appearance. However, when joined with other signs and testimonies of the Resurrection, this evidence efficaciously proved that Christ had truly risen from the dead. I say also: the arguments and evidence given in the first two chapters lack efficacy when taken individually, but when considered with other evidence, they can efficaciously prove that the word *Shangdi* means God for the Chinese, and therefore, God can be called *Shangdi*.⁴

---

3 Medieval scholastic logicians such as Ockham discussed the nature of language. Ockham, *Summa totius logicae*, cap. 11. See Chapter 1, n. 163.
4 Noël expresses here his method of proofs by texts. Only an accumulation of texts pointing towards a common meaning can provide a proof that is sufficiently convincing.

From Usage

God has long been called *Tianzhu* in China.[5] In the beginning, there were some doubts whether God could be named in this way since it is also the Chinese name for an idol.[6] However, the name of *Shangdi* has also been accepted for a long time because *Shangdi* and *Tianzhu* were used to signify God throughout the book called *Tianzhu shiyi* or *Tianxue shiyi*, by Father Ricci, who was the founder of the Chinese mission, and the book called *Qike*, by his companion Father Pantoja. Both these books were printed at the beginning of the seventeenth century under the reign of Emperor Wanli and are very famous among the Chinese.[7]

This is the same for many other Christian books around this date and after, by the Jesuits and members of other religious orders. For example, the *Tian Ru yin*, which was written by the Franciscan Antonio de Santa María and published in 1664, contains the following words: '*Shangdi* is the same as the one Lord of Heaven (*Tianzhu*) and should be venerated with the highest majesty since He controls and governs all things' (A).[8] The *Chuhui wenda*, which was written by the Franciscan Pedro de la Piñuela, revised by the Franciscan Fathers Tarín and San Pascual and approved by the commissary visitor Father Navarro,[9] contains the following in Chapter 3: 'When the Imperial Palace is mentioned, this refers not only to a magnificent building, but also to the fact that there is necessarily a supreme power residing inside the palace. Therefore, when *Tian* or Heaven is mentioned, it is truly shown that in Heaven there must be a single supremely venerable and true Lord and Governor of the Spirits, human beings and all things and that we must give thanks to Him. This is why Doctor Zisi said, "The ritual of sacrificing to Heaven and Earth is how *Shangdi* or the Supreme Lord is served". Also, when the *Book of Odes* says, "Prince Wen Wang publicly served *Shangdi* with the greatest care and reverence", this shows that the ancient Chinese philosophers, who were famed for their virtue and knowledge, intended to indicate that the true Lord of Heaven and Earth, and not the material heaven, should be worshipped. But nowadays today people turn away from the intention of those ancient Chinese philosophers who were famed for their virtue and knowledge, and worship material heaven; this error directly contradicts right reason'. The host objects, 'But when Confucius said, "Whoever sins against Heaven does not have anyone to whom he can pray to escape punishment", where did Confucius mention *Tianzhu*?' I answer that the words of Confucius clearly mean that 'there is a single Lord and Ruler who watches over us and reaches us, such that we dare not in the slightest offend Him. How could Confucius possibly refer to blue and material heaven? How could the word *Tian* possibly mean the reason *li* and nothing else?' (B) In the preface

---

5   More than one hundred years had passed since the publication of Ruggieri's *Tianzhu shilu* in 1584.
6   As the Jesuits discovered after 1584, *Tianzhu* refers also to a lower divinity in the Buddhist pantheon.
7   The *Tianzhu shiyi* was published in 1603. Later, Giulio Aleni (1582–1649) gave it the name of *Tianxue shiyi*. The *Qike* by Diego de Pantoja (1571–1618) was published around 1610–1615.
8   For Antonio de Santa María Caballero (1602–1669) and his *Tian Ru yin*, see Chapter 2.16.
9   For Pedro de la Piñuela (1650–1704) and his *Chuhui wenda*, see Chapter 2.16.

of this same book, Pedro de la Piñuela calls the Christian religion *Tianjiao* [the doctrine of Heaven].[10]

Since the use of *Shangdi* to express God has been long attested, God can be called *Shangdi*, especially since this appellation for God, after having met some doubt in the beginning, was discussed, examined, and has remained in use.[11]

From Authority [by the Chinese Christians]

The Chinese themselves can contribute an authoritative judgement on this matter if these two conditions are met. First, they should know what Europeans mean by God. Second, they should be extremely well versed in Chinese literature. The Chinese affirm that the word *Shangdi* means God and they call God *Shangdi* throughout their books. The minor premise of the argument is proven.[12]

1. Doctor Xu [Guangqi], Chief Minister or *gelao* of the emperor, states in his famous booklet *Piwang* as follows: '*Shangdi* is the Lord of the living and the dead' (C).[13] In a petition presented to Emperor Wanli on behalf of Christianity, Xu Guangqi also says: 'The intention of these people (that is, the missionaries) is to make all people follow virtue and respond to the will of Highest Heaven, which loves them. They have as their first principle the public worship of *Shangdi*' (D). He calls God sometimes *Di* and sometimes *Shangdi*. See for example the postfaces of *Tianzhu jiangsheng yanxing jilüe* and the *Ershiwu yan* (E).[14]

2. The famous Christian Doctor Feng [Yingjing] says: 'What does *Tianzhu* or God mean? This means *Shangdi*, who should not be understood as something lifeless, but true and real. How can anyone consider [*Shangdi*] something lifeless and empty when our six classical books and our four doctors, Confucius, Mencius, Zisi and Zengzi, and all men of every age who are famed for their

---

10 See *Chuhui dawen*, preface (*xu*), 1a, in Pascale Girard, *Les Religieux occidentaux en Chine à l'époque moderne* (Paris: Gulbenkian, 2000), p. 411.

11 Noël makes here a discreet allusion to the Jiading conference and the decision to forbid the term of *Shangdi*. He suggests that the constant ecclesiastical usage of the term *Shangdi* overrides the prohibition.

12 Noël selected below quotes mentioning *Shangdi* and put them into a chronological order, with the three pillars, Xu Guangqi, Yang Tingyun and Li Zhizao, as well as the early supporter Feng Yingjing. Then, he mentions other Chinese Christians or supporters during the late Ming: Chen Yi, Han Lin, Zhang Geng, and Zhu Zongyuan. Finally, he mentions Chinese Christians during the early Qing, such as Li Jiugong, who continues the tradition of using *Shangdi* despite the repeated prohibitions. Yet, it is difficult to see from those excerpts the importance they gave to the name of *Shangdi*. Noël does not mention explicitly the *Ditian kao* 帝天考 by the early Qing Chinese Christian Paul Yan Mo 嚴謨. For Noël's debt to the *Ditian kao*, see Chapter 2.7.

13 The *Piwang* is an anti-Buddhist work which has been attributed for a long time to Xu Guangqi, as attested here by Noël. However, scholars have recently raised doubts about this attribution. The text can be found in Li Tiangang, *Ming Qing Tianzhujiao sanzhushi wenjianzhu* 明清天主教三柱石文箋注 [Catholic documents of Xu Guangqi, Li Zhizao, Yang Tingyun] (Hong Kong: Daofeng, 2007), pp. 121–36. The quote from Xu Guangqi can also be found in the *Summarium NAT*, p. 83.

14 Noël refutes here the dubious claim of Longobardo who interviewed Xu Guangqi through the intermediary of the Macanese Jesuit Brother Pascal Mendez (邱永良厚, 1584–1640). See Chapter 2.16.

virtue, knowledge and wisdom say, "Fear *Shangdi*, assist *Shangdi*, serve *Shangdi*, to approach *Shangdi*, and to unite with *Shangdi*'" (F)?[15]

3. The Christian doctor Yang Tingyun, who received [in 1592] the first degree [*jinshi* 進士] in his advancement [in the imperial examination] said: 'Christianity can be summarized by these two commandments: first, to worship one God (*Tianzhu*) above all things; second, to love your neighbour as yourself. Worshipping the one God is what our doctors have called "publicly serving *Shangdi*"' (G).[16] In a preface to the *Zhifang waiji*, as well in his own books, the *Tianshi mingbian* and the *Daiyi*[*pian*], Yang Tingyun refers to God in the same way (H).[17]

4. The Christian doctor Li [Zhizao] writes as follows: 'The (Christian) religion consists only in serving *Tianzhu*; and this corresponds to what our doctors say: to know Heaven, to serve Heaven, to serve *Shangdi*. He is not called *di*, but *zhu*, and this can be explained by quoting Doctor Zhu Xi: "This word *di* means *zhuzai*, or lord and ruler". Since God is the Lord who produced Heaven, Earth and all things, this single word *zhu* or lord better expresses what [God] is. Finally, if we want to penetrate more deeply what [God] is, [we can say that] He is the only great Father and Mother of all of us on earth' (I).[18] The two words Father and Mother stand for what I said above about the sacrifice to Heaven and Earth.[19] Li Zhizao often calls God *Shangdi* and *Di*. See for example his prefaces to the *Jiren shipian*, to the *Tianzhu shiyi*, etc. (K).[20]

---

15 Noël mentions Feng Yingjing (1555–1606) as a Christian, but this is incorrect. Feng was a supporter of Ricci and helped with the publication of the *Tianzhu shiyi*, but he did not receive baptism. The quote of Feng can be found in the *Summarium NAT* (p. 83).
16 Yang Tingyun collaborated with Diego de Pantoja in writing *Qike*, which was published around 1610–1615. The quote from Yang's preface can be also found in the *Summarium NAT* (p. 83).
17 Yang Tingyun's preface was published in Aleni's *Zhifang waiji* in 1623. His own *Daiyipian* was published in 1621, and his *Tianshi mingbian* in 1645. Longobardo had also interviewed Yang Tingyun: 'He replied that according to the interpretations of all interpreters there is no mystery except that after the death of Wen Wang his earthly parts were reduced to dust while his heavenly parts of Air ascended upwards and joined themselves to heaven itself and to *Shangdi* who is himself the most-high heaven insofar as he operates and manages things under heaven. And so, with this praise the Chinese poet intends no more than to extol and praise Wen Wang, feigning that the ethereal body and heavenly globe is like a supernal emperor, standing at the side [of *Shangdi*] like a faithful vassal. With these responses, the doctor excellently showed that according to the teaching of the Chinese literati there is no God or angels except by some extremely obscure conjecture, which became ever more obscure and weak in the conceptual imagination of the Chinese who consider spirits as the same thing as the places in which they reside'. Longobardo, *A Brief Response on the Controversies*, p. 189 (prelude 17, part 2, n. 6).
18 The words of Li Zhizao can also be found in the *Summarium NAT*, p. 84. The quote from Zhu Xi's *Zhouyi zhengjie* was mentioned above (c.2, q.1, F.3 and c.2, q.2, A.2).
19 Since Ruggieri and Ricci, God was also called Great Father and Mother, or *Da fumu* 大父母.
20 For Noël, Li Zhizao, like Xu Guangqi and Yang Tingyun, approved the meaning of *Shangdi* in the ancient Confucian classics as an equivalent for God. However, after interviewing Li Zhizao and other Chinese Christians, Longobardo reported: 'They say that it seems to them only that in order to accommodate ourselves to China we must follow the texts of the ancient teachings which were favourable to our purposes, caring little of the opinion of the moderns and of the explanations of the ancient interpreters'. Longobardo, *A Brief Response on the Controversies*, p. 196 (prelude 17, part 2, n. 15).

5. The Christian doctor Chen [Yi][21] in his preface to the *Xingxue cushu* says: 'Our Chinese doctors talk about *Tian* as something obscure while the Europeans talk about *Tianzhu* as something clear. When interpreting the odes "Huangyi" ("He awe-inspiringly comes down to these lower parts") and "Daming" ("He approaches you: do not stagger!") in the *Book of Songs*, both the former and the latter refer everything back to *Shangdi* that is, the Lord of Heaven'. (L).[22] See also his preface to the *Qike*.[23]

6. Han [Lin], a licentiate I believe, or maybe a doctor, from Shanxi province, is very famous for his *Duoshu*, a commentary of a short instruction ordered by the emperor to be taught monthly to the people. This book was revised by eighteen literati from different provinces, and exceptionally the provincial president of justice and another doctor of the Royal College showed it to the emperor to read; the two praised Han Lin very highly in their prefaces.[24] As Han Lin says in the beginning of the book: 'Heaven is our Great Parent according to this passage of the *Book of Odes*: "Extremely vast and high Heaven, you may be called the parent of human beings". Heaven should not be understood as the blue and visible heaven, but as the one Lord and Ruler on high who produces Heaven, Earth, spirits, human beings, and everything. He is the Supreme Lord *Shangdi*, whom our Five Classics from the time of the emperors Yao and Shun and of the three dynasties Xia, Shang, and Zhou, have successively transmitted to posterity. When the visible heaven is used to indicate Heaven, this is like using the imperial court to refer to the emperor since the supreme power resides there. However, how could a material palace contain the person of the emperor? All ancient and modern emperors were appointed to rule and teach the people because of their remarkable virtue and

---

21 Chen Yi 陳儀 (1575–1634) passed the degree of *jinshi* in 1610 and met Ricci in Nanjing in 1598–1600. He met Giulio Aleni in Beijing in 1616 and welcomed him in Fuzhou in 1625, writing around 1628 the preface to the *Xingxue cushu* which was only published around 1640. Chen Yi was a supporter of Christianity but there is no indication that he was baptized, contrary to what Noël says here. The quote of Chen Yi is found in the *Summarium NAT* (p. 84). For the English translation of the preface by Chen Yi, see Aleni, *A Brief Introduction to the Study of Human Nature*, pp. 64–69.
22 Noël's contrast between obscurity and clarity is too strong. In fact, Chen Yi contrasts the Chinese perception of Heaven as an undifferentiated whole (*hunran* 渾然) with the Western perception of the Lord of Heaven as distinctive (*biaoqi de ran* 標其的然), claiming that both perceptions are found in the *Book of Odes* with reference to *Shangdi*.
23 Noël seems to confuse Chen Yi with Chen Liangcai 陈亮采 (*jinshi* 1595) who mentioned *Shangdi* once in his *Qike pianxu* 七克篇序. See Huang Xingtao 黃興濤, *Mingqing zhiji xixue wenben* 明清之際西學文本 (Beijing: Zhonghua shuju, 2013), I, p. 43.
24 Han Lin 韓霖 (1601–1644) obtained the degree of *juren* in 1621 but did not obtain the degree of *jinshi*. He was a close collaborator to Vagnone, and around 1641 he wrote the *Duoshu* 鐸書 as a commentary of the *Shengyu* 聖諭 of Emperor Ming Taizu. The name of the prefacer belonging to the Royal College (翰林院) was deleted from the original edition, but the historian Chen Yuan had proposed the name of Li Jiantai 李建泰 (died 1649; *jinshi* 1625). The name of the prefacer who was provincial president of justice in Shanxi is Li Zhengxiu 李政修 (*jinshi* 1616). The quote of Han Lin is found in the *Summarium NAT*, pp. 84–85.

wisdom. Thus, the emperor makes a sacrifice to highest Heaven (*Shangdi*). Although he holds supreme power, he describes himself with this formula: "O Heaven, I, so and so, am the heir of your empire, your son and your servant"' (M).

7. Zhang Geng, licentiate from the province of Fujian, famous for his books, wrote in the beginning of his work called the *Tianxue zhengfu*: 'Could there be any learned or unlearned literatus who would dare to condemn the Christian teaching of serving Heaven as false or perverse? This word *Tian* does not refer to the visible and blue heaven, but to the one Lord and Ruler (*zhuzai*). However, most people do not examine this point. From ancient times to now, the holy men in the Great West, that is Europe, have called Heaven *Tianzhu* or Lord of Heaven, and this name should receive the greatest honour. Doctor Zhu Hui, also called Zhu Xi, explains in his commentary of the *Yijing*, "*Di* means the Lord and Ruler of Heaven". This agrees with the holy men in the Europe. Our Five Classics (*Wujing*) and the Four Books (*Sishu*) do not explicitly mention *Tianzhu*, but they do mention *Tian* because they prefer to use a succinct manner of speech. Similarly, when people want to mention the governor of a city or town, they use directly the name of the city or town by way of abbreviation. "The names *Di* and *Tianzhu* are different yet mean the same"' (N).²⁵ Later, Zhang Geng affirmed the same thing in many other books.

8. The Christian licentiate Zhu [Zongyuan] in his *Zhengshi lüeshuo* says: 'Among all things, Heaven-Earth is one and the greatest; therefore, there must be some Maker of Heaven and Earth and this Maker, insofar as He has supreme and incomparable power, is called *Shangdi* (*Shang* means supreme; *Di* means Lord and Ruler). Since He apprehends all things, He is called their Maker; since He governs and rules all the living, He is called *Tianzhu* or Lord of Heaven'. Throughout this book, as well as another book called *Dakewen*, Zhu uses *Shangdi* to refer to God (O).²⁶

9. The Christian bachelor [scholar] Li [Jiugong] in his book the *Shensi*[*lu*], which was revised by eighth persons outstanding for their knowledge of Chinese language, has: 'The name *Shangdi* which is always mentioned in the books of our Doctors refers clearly and without any doubt to *Tianzhu*'. He himself very

---

25 Zhang Geng 張庚 (c. 1570–1646/47) wrote the *Tianxue zhengfu* 天學證符 around 1628–1636. This book is preserved in ARSI (Jap. Sin. I, 141), and Albert Chan remarks this work is very rare. See Chan, *Chinese Books and Documents in the Jesuit Archives in Rome*, p. 186. This quote of Zhang Geng is also found in the *Summarium NAT*, p. 85.
26 Zhu Zongyuan 朱宗元 (c. 1615–1660, *jinshi* 1648) published the *Dakewen* 答客問 in 1643 and the *Zhengshi lüeshuo* 拯世略說 in 1644. ARSI has three copies of the *Zhengjiu lüeshuo* (Jap. Sin. I, 145, 145a and 166a). The quote from the *Zhengshi lüeshuo* is present in the *Summarium NAT*, p. 84.

often uses the name *Shangdi* in his work to call God (P).[27] I omit many others not to be boring. Please see the prefaces to *Qike, Shengjiao sigui* and *Piwang tiaobo he* (Q).[28]

All those Chinese knew exactly what God meant: they had embraced Christianity and were faithful and intelligent. At the same time, they knew perfectly the meaning of *Shangdi* since they had passed the degrees of the Chinese examination and even reached the highest degree. They all affirmed that *Shangdi* has the same meaning as *Tianzhu*, or God, and they further affirmed that *Shangdi* means God, and always called Him with this name. Is there any room for doubt? Should we not trust them? Or should we trust the few missionaries who raise objections instead of these doctors and teachers who are very learned in Chinese language and affirm the contrary? Would a distinguished Flemish or German who has come to Paris and absorbed some knowledge of the French language condemn the Parisians who are most skilled in French as having erroneous opinions about the meaning of French words? Would not he be expelled and condemned?[29] Please check the equally efficacious arguments in Question 2 below about the word *Tian*. But need I say more? All those proofs demonstrate more than enough the truth of the matter. But it remains now to examine the objections.

---

27 Li Jiugong 李九功 is the only Qing Christian mentioned in Chapter 3. The *Shensilu* was published after his death, in 1682. ARSI has two copies of the work (Jap. Sin. I, 34/37 and 136). The quote from the *Shensilu* is present in the *Summarium NAT*, p. 86.
28 Besides the preface to the *Qike* by Yang Tingyun and the one by Chen Liangcai mentioned above, Noël probably considered the preface by Cao Yubian 曹於汴 (1558–1634, *jinshi* 1592) which mentioned *Shangdi* twice, as well as the preface by Cui Chang 崔淐 (*jinshi* 1601) which mentioned *Shangdi* eight times. For the preface by Cao Yubian, see Zhou Zhenhe, *Ming Qing zhiji Xifang chuanjiaoshi Hanji congkan*, II, pp. 11–12; for the preface by Cui Chang, see *Juejiao tongwenji* 絕徼同文紀, in Standaert and Dudink, *Chinese Christian Texts from the National Library of France*, VI, pp. 221–27. As for the *Shengjiao sigui* 聖教四規 (c. 1662) by Francesco Brancati (1607–1671), the edition kept in ARSI (Jap. Sin. I, 106) contains a preface by Xu Erjue, the grandson of Xu Guangqi, which mentions *Shangdi* once. See Standaert and Dudink, *Chinese Christian Texts from the Roman Archives of the Society of Jesus*, V, pp. 261–64. Finally, Wang Ruohan 王若韓's *Piwang tiaobo he* 闢妄條駁合 is the most recent work, published in 1689, containing a preface by Hong Ji 洪濟 and another by the Chinese Christian Zhang Xingyao 張星曜 (1633–c. 1715), which both mention Shangdi. See Standaert and Dudink, *Chinese Christian Texts from the Roman Archives of the Society of Jesus*, IX, pp. 435–47.
29 Noël seems to say: being a Fleming he would not dare to discuss French grammar, but about the question of *Shangdi*, the Chinese should be trusted.

NOTES

A.1 泰西利安當詮義《天儒印》:「上帝者, 即主宰萬有、至尊無二之天主也。」

Father Antonio [Caballero] de Santa Maria, etc. See above.³⁰

B.2 泰西石鐸琭述《初會問答》:「譬猶有朝廷也, 言朝廷者, 不過言其宮闕而已, 朝廷之內, 必有至尊存焉。所以言天者, 正以徵上天必有一至尊真主, 為神人萬物之主宰, 吾人宜感謝欽崇之故。子思云:『郊社之禮, 所以事上帝也。』³¹ 又《詩》曰:『小心翼翼, 昭事上帝。』³² 可見中國聖賢之意, 非指敬形天, 乃是敬天地之真主也。今背上古聖賢之旨, 而拜敬形天, 不合真理, 誠謬矣。客曰:『然則孔子所云: 獲罪于天無所禱。彼何嘗說有天主?』曰:『孔子此言, 正謂明明上天之中有一主宰, 鑒我臨我, 朝夕不敢稍有獲罪也。豈謂此蒼蒼之天乎? 又豈謂天者理而已乎?』」³³

Father de la Piñuela in his *Chuhui wenda*, etc. See above.

C.3 徐光啟撰《闢釋氏諸妄·無主孤魂血湖》:「無分人鬼, 皆上帝為主。」

The *gelao* Xu Guangqi in the chapter 'Wuzhu guhun xuehu' of his book *Piwang*. See above.

D.4 徐相國《辨學奏疏》萬曆四十四年七月題:「欲使人人為善, 以稱上天愛人之意, 以昭事上帝為宗本。」

The *gelao* [Xu Guangqi] in his petition *Bianxue zoushu*, presented to Emperor Wanli in the seventh lunar month of the 44th year of his reign [August 1616]. See above.³⁴

---

30 ARSI, Fondo Gesuitico 724/4, fol. 117. See also Zhou Zhenhe, *Ming Qing zhiji xifang chuanjiaoshi Hanji congkan*, I, p. 132.
31 This Franciscan text quotes the *Zhongyong* with the mention of the *jiaoshe* ritual to serve Shangdi. For the text of the *Chuhui dawen*, chapter 4, 9b–10a; in Pascale Girard, *Les Religieux occidentaux en Chine à l'époque moderne* (Paris: Gulbenkian, 2000), pp. 436–37.
32 The quote of the *Shijing* was already mentioned above, Question 1, T.22.
33 The ARSI manuscript does not have this entire quote from the *Chuhui wenda*, but a quote coming from another work by La Piñuela, the *Moxiang shengong* 默想神功 (1695): '想已罪, 獲罪之心, 是全無畏懼, 侈然自縱, 不復知有上帝之臨汝'. ARSI, Fondo Gesuitico 724/4, fol. 117.
34 ARSI, Fondo Gesuitico 724/4, fol. 117. The work is alternatively titled the *Bianxue zhangshu* 辨學章疏. See Zhu Weizheng 朱維錚 and Li Tiangang 李天綱 (eds), *Xu Guangqi quanji* 徐光啟全集 [Complete works of Xu Guangqi] (Shanghai guji chubanshe 上海古籍出版社, 2010), vol. 9, pp. 249–54; Li Tiangang, *Ming Qing Tianzhujiao sanzhushi wenjianzhu*, pp. 62–69. For an English translation, see William Theodore De Bary, *Sources of Chinese Tradition* (New York: Columbia University Press, 2000), vol. 2, pp. 147–49. In the late Ming, 'zhaoshi Shangdi' (to serve *Shangdi*) had in fact lost most of its original religious dimension and meant for the neo-Confucians to follow the moral Law of Heaven. See Xiao Qinghe, 'Yitiangebiao: Rujia zongjiaoxing yu Ruye duihua' 一天各表: 儒家宗教性於儒耶對話 [One heaven, respective interpretations: the religiosity of Confucianism in the dialogue between Confucianism and Christianity], *Beijing xingzheng xueyuan xuebao* [Journal of Beijing Administrative Institute] 北京行政學院學報, 129.5 (2020), 118–28.

E.5 西極耶穌會士艾儒略譯述《天主降生言行紀略》；《二十五言》，大西利瑪竇述。

    Both the *Tianzhu jiangsheng yanxing jilüe* and the *Ershi wuyan* have, etc. See above.[35]

F.6 馮應京《天主實義·序》：「天主何？上帝也。『實』云者，不空也。吾國六經四子，聖聖賢賢，曰『畏上帝』，曰『助上帝』，曰『事上帝』，曰『格上帝。』」

    Doctor Feng Yingjing in the preface to *Tianzhu shiyi*. See above.[36]

G.7 《七克·篇序》：「大指不越兩端，曰欽崇一天主萬物之上；曰愛人如己。夫『欽崇天主』，即吾儒『昭事上帝』也。」「鄭圃居士楊廷筠書於明旦齋中。」

    Yang Tingyun in a preface to the *Qike*. See above.[37]

H.8 西海艾儒略增譯《職方外紀》、武林楊廷筠著《天釋明辨》、武林楊彌格子著《代疑篇》。

    The books *Zhifang waiji*, *Tianshi mingbian* and *Daiyi[pian]*. See above.

I.9 東海波臣李之藻題《聖水紀言·序》：「其教專事天主，即吾儒知天、事天、事上帝之說。不曰『帝』，曰『主』者，譯語，質朱子曰：『帝者，天之主宰。』以其為生天、生地、生萬物之主也，故名之主則更切，而極其義，則吾六合萬國人之一大父母也。」

    Doctor Li Zhizao in the preface to the *Shengshui jiyan* wrote as follows: 'That religion …, etc.' See above.[38]

K.10 泰西利瑪竇述《畸人十篇》、耶穌會利瑪竇述《天主實義》。

    The two books *Jiren shipian* and *Tianzhu shiyi*. See above.

L.11 陳儀《性學觕述·序》：「吾儒舉其渾然者則曰天，西氏標其的然者則曰天主。要明《皇矣》之『臨下有赫』，《大明》之『無貳爾心』，皆總而屬之上帝。」《七克篇序》

    Doctor Chen Yi in his preface to the *Xingxue cushu* states as follows: 'Our doctors …, etc.' See above.

---

35 Matteo Ricci's *Ershi wuyan* was published in 1604; the postface by Xu Guangqi can be found in Li Tiangang, *Ming Qing Tianzhujiao sanzhushi wenjianzhu*, pp. 76–78. Gulio Aleni's *Tianzhu jiangsheng yanxing jilüe* was published in 1635, two years after Xu Guangqi's death. Thus Noël is mistaken here about Xu's postface. In fact, the *Tianzhu jiangsheng yanxing jilüe* includes at the end one folio with the poem 'Da zan shi' 大讚詩 by Xu Guangqi.

36 For the text of the preface of 1601 by Feng Yingjing and its French translation, see Matteo Ricci, *Le sens eel de Seigneur du Ciel*, trans. Thierry Meynard (Paris: Les Belles Lettres, 2013), pp. 254–57.

37 The preface by Yang Tingyun to the *Qike* can be found in Li Tiangang, *Ming Qing Tianzhujiao sanzhushi wenjianzhu*, pp. 342–45. Same remark about *zaoshi Shangdi* as in D.4.

38 The *Shengshui jiyan* was written by Sun Xueshi 孫學詩 and published around 1616. The preface of Li Zhizao to the *Shengshui jiyan* (c. 1616) by Sun Xueshi 孫學詩 can be found in Li Tiangang, *Ming Qing Tianzhujiao sanzhushi wenjianzhu*, pp. 172–75.

M.12 [韓霖《鐸書・孝順父母》:「吾人要知,天為大父母。《詩》云:『悠悠昊天,曰父母且。』非蒼蒼之天也。上面有個主宰,生天、生地、生神、生人、生物,即唐、虞三代之時五經相傳之上帝。今指蒼蒼而言天,猶以朝廷稱天子也。中有至尊居之,豈宮闕可以當天子乎?古今帝王聖賢,皆天所生以治教下民者。天子祀昊天上帝之文曰:『嗣天子臣某。』」]

    The literatus Han Lin in his *Duoshu* says: 'When Heaven is mentioned …, etc.' See above.[39]

N.13 張賡《天學證符・引》:「或明或昧,寧敢訑以為邪?第天非蒼然色象,自有個主宰;人多習而不察;惟西方聖人古來相傳稱謂天主,是乃確當尊稱。朱晦翁注《易傳》曰『帝者,天之主宰』;實與之符矣。五經四部書只言天,不顯言天主,蓋從簡語法,如世俗稱府主、縣主,只從簡,呼其府某縣云耳,非真說天便了也。」

    The literatus Zhang Geng, etc. See above.[40]

O.14 右越朱宗元著《拯世畧說・宇宙之內真教惟一》:「既謂之物,天地亦物之大者耳。而更有造天地者,以其至尊無匹,謂之上帝;以其搏摶萬有,謂之造物;以其主宰群生,謂之天主。」《答客問》。

    The licentiate Zhu Zongyuan in the chapter 'Yuzhou zhi nei zhenjiao weiyi' of his *Zhengshi lüeshuo* states: 'Heaven and Earth …, etc.' See above. See also his *Dakewen*.

P.15 閩福唐李九功《慎思錄》:「儒書上帝之稱,固明指天主。」

    The bachelor [scholar] Li Jiugong in chapter 1 of the *Shensilu* states: 'The name *Shangdi* …, etc.' Please note that the first character is the family name, and the remaining characters are the personal name.

Q.16 《七克》、《聖教四規》、《闢妄條駁合》。

    The prefaces of the *Qike*, the *Shengjiao sigui* and the *Piwang tiaobo he* use the word *Shangdi* to express God.

---

[39] The Chinese text is missing in the Roman manuscript. For the annotated text of the *Duoshu*, see Han Lin 韓霖, annotated by Sun Shangyang 孫尚揚 and Xiao Qinghe 肖清和, *Duoshu jiaozhu* 鐸書校注 (Beijing: Huaxia chubanshe, 2008).

[40] The Chinese text is missing in the Roman manuscript but was retrieved from the printed text: Standaert and Dudink, *Chinese Christian Texts from the Roman Archives of the Society of Jesus*, VIII, pp. 43–44.

§.2. Resolution of the Objections

First Objection

You may object that the five *Di*, which are white, blue, yellow, red, and black, are mentioned in the books (A), and therefore *Di* cannot indicate God.

I answer that this conclusion needs to be discussed: I reject that *Di* when taken to mean *Shangdi* cannot indicate God, but I concede that *Di* when taken to mean emperor or another man cannot indicate God. Indeed, five *Di* are mentioned, and not five *Shangdi*.[41]

You may say that *Di* is very often taken to mean *Shangdi*, and the word *Di* is assimilated with the word *Shangdi*, as said above.

I answer that this affirmation needs to be discussed: I concede that *Di* is assimilated with *Shangdi* by antonomasia, but I deny that it happens in the ordinary way. The word Apostle is assimilated with Saint Paul by antonomasia, and Philosopher with Aristotle, but this does not happen in the ordinary way, and this is the same for *Di*.

As mentioned in c.2, q.4, DD.34 and DD.35, the five *Di* refer to the five ancient emperors, Taihao (Fuxi), Yandi (Shennong), Shaohao, Zhuanxu, and Huangdi, listed in the Dictionary under the entry for the character *Di* (B). Also, in the chapter 'Yueling' of the *Book of Rites*, people sacrificed to *Shangdi*, the Lord of Heaven, and they also performed the *ji* ritual to the five *Di*, remembering them with gratitude. See c.2, q.5, F.8. Furthermore, according to the *Book of the Zhou Rituals*, the *ji* ritual was performed for the ancient emperors four times a year (spring, summer, autumn and winter) with raw meat, aromatic wine and rice (C). The five colours are associated with the primary and universal principles (water, fire, earth, wood, and metal), with each one of the five emperors representing a specific virtue, as said in c.2, q.4, DD.34. The vessels used to perform the *ji* rituals in the four regions of the world each had their own colour (D).

Second, the sectarian idolaters certainly seized from these five emperors the occasion to fashion five other emperors called *Di*, but this is irrelevant to our question because we are dealing here only with the classical books and those five *Di* have nothing to do with the true teaching of the Chinese literati.

Some commentators like Zheng Kangcheng and others after him tried to associate the five *Di* with *Shangdi*, appointing the five *Di* according to each region of the world and each season of the year, and may sometimes called them *Shangdi*. But they were refuted by the true commentators of the ancient classical books. As a result, all the sacrifices performed in the different regions of the

---

41 The concept of the five *Di* emerged during the Qin and Han dynasties and has been interpreted in three different ways: unitary Heaven, five mythical emperors, or five divinities. See Wu Liwei, *Zhongguo liyi zhizheng*, p. 48. From the standpoint of the Jesuits' monotheistic reading of ancient China, Noël can accept the notion of unitary Heaven since this connects to *Shangdi* and can even accept the veneration of ancient emperors in show of gratitude, but he rejects the polytheistic meaning of five divinities.

world referred to the one and same *Shangdi*, who governs everywhere and in every season. This matter is discussed in great detail from volume 68 onwards of the *Wenxian tongkao* I.

Moreover, they ordinarily talk about the five *Di* and not the five *Shangdi*. In the dictionaries mentioned above, there is even the idea of 32 *Di* and many other *Di*.⁴²

NOTES

A.1 《字彙·時字》：「天地、五帝所基止,祭地。漢武帝郊見五時。先是,秦文公作鄜時祭白帝；秦宣公作密時祭青帝；秦靈公作吳陽上時祭黃帝,下時祭赤帝；漢高祖作北時祭黑帝。是五時也。」

> The dictionary *Dazihui* defines the character *zhi* as follows: '*Zhi* is the place where the *ji* ritual was performed for Heaven, Earth and the Five Emperors. Emperor Wudi of the Han dynasty himself performed the *ji* ritual in five places. Before him, a petty king [Wengong] of the Qin kingdom (Shanxi province) had built in a tract of land called Fu a *zhi* for performing the ritual to the white *Di*. Later his successor Xuangong built in a tract of land called Mi another *zhi* for performing the *ji* ritual to the blue *Di*. Next his successor Linggong built in a tract of land called Wuyang a *zhi* with two levels: on the upper level the *ji* ritual was performed for the yellow *Di*, and on the lower level for the red *Di*. Finally, Gaozu, the first emperor of Han dynasty, had erected in a northern tract of land a *zhi* for performing the *ji* ritual to the black *Di*. There were five *zhi* places'.⁴³

B.2 《正字通·帝字》：「又五人帝：太皡、炎帝、少昊、顓頊、黃帝。」

> The dictionary *Zhengzitong* for the character *Di*: 'This character *Di* means the five emperors: Taihao, Yandi, Shaohao, Zhuanxu, Huangdi'.⁴⁴

C.3 陳仁錫《古周禮禮·春官·宗伯·第三》：「以肆獻祼享先王,以饋食享先王,以祠春享先王,以禴夏享先王,以嘗秋享先王,以烝冬享先王。」

> The chapter 'Chunguan zongbo' in volume 3 of the *Book of the Zhou Rituals* states: 'When the *ji* ritual is performed for the ancient emperors, raw meat is presented; aromatic wine is poured onto the ground; rice is offered, and the *ji* ritual is performed for them in each of the four seasons of the year'.⁴⁵

---

42 The Taoist pantheon has different lists of deities, including a list of 32 *Di* or *Tiandi*.
43 The ARSI manuscript gives also an excerpt from the *Zihui* for the character *Di* 帝字: "又五天帝：青帝靈威仰、赤帝赤熛怒、黃帝含樞紐、白帝白招拒、黑帝叶光紀". This is quite redundant and was eliminated on the printed version. The *Zihui* is quite correct in tracing back the origin of the five *Di* to the Qin and Han dynasties, when the theory of the five phases became prominent. Concerning the Five *Di*, see above (c.2, q.4, DD.34), explained also as the Five Emperors.
44 The ARSI manuscript gives the same excerpt but makes reference to the *Zihui*.
45 Chen Renxi's *Gu Zhouli* was quoted above (c.2, q.5, FFF.66).

D.4 《古周礼禮‧春官‧宗伯‧第三》：「以玉作六器，以禮天、地、四方。以蒼璧禮天，以黃琮禮地，以青圭禮東方，以赤璋禮南方，以白琥禮西方，以玄璜禮北方。」陳仁錫：「東方其帝太皞，圭形銳，以象出雲；生物青，則以象木也。南方其帝炎帝，半圭曰璋，以象相見乎離；夏物豐盛，赤則以象火也。西方其帝少皞，琥琢為虎形，象虎猛蕭物；白則金之色也。北方其帝頊帝，半璧曰璜，象物藏於黃泉之宮；玄則水之色也。」

> The chapter 'Chunguan zongbo' in volume 3 of the *Book of the Zhou Rituals* states: 'May this prefect ensure that six precious vases are made for the rites to Heaven, Earth and the four parts of the world. The precious *bi* vase for Heaven is blue; the *zong* vase for Earth, yellow; the *gui* vase for the east, violet; the *zhang* vase for the south, red; the *hu* vase for west, white; the *huang* vase for the north, black'. Chen Renxi explains: 'The emperor or *Di* of the eastern region is Taihao (Fuxi), and the shape of the *gui* vase ends at its tip to represent the birth of the clouds out of which the productions of things come; its colour is violet to represent plants. The emperor of the south is Yandi (Shennong), and half of the *gui* vase is called *zhang* to represent the mutual aspect of things reaching maturity in the summer; the enigmatic symbol [hexagram] *Li*, which means clarity, represents those things, and red represents fire. The emperor of the west is Shaohao, and the *hu* vase, meaning tiger, is indeed shaped like a tiger, which is something simultaneously wild and serious; its white colour represents the metal. The emperor of the north is Zhuanxu, and half of the *bi* vase is called *huang*, representing things hidden in the deepest recesses of Earth; its black or blackisk colour represents water'.[46]

E.5 《正字通‧帝字》：「五天帝：青帝靈威仰，赤帝曰赤熛怒，黃帝曰含樞紐，白帝曰白招拒，黑帝曰叶光紀。」「一說：因五行生育之功，別之為五，其實一也。」

> The dictionary *Zhengzitong* defines the character *Di* as follows: 'The character *Di* means also the five emperors of heaven, namely the blue *Di* who is smart and solemn, the red *Di* who is passionate and angry, the white *Di* who summons and rejects, the yellow *Di* who moves the axis, the black *Di* who is synonymous with keeping the memory of things'. Another interpretation states as follows: 'Due to the effects of the five primary universal principles which produce and maintain things in the world, the *Di* are similarly divided into five, but they are in fact the one (that is, the one *Shangdi*)'.[47]

---

46 On the association of the five vessels with the five colours, see above (c.2, q.5, F.66).
47 The quote of the *Zhengzitong* is not present in the ARSI manuscript and has been partially and tentatively reconstructed here. Concerning the Five *Di*, see c.2, q.4, DD.34 and c.3, q.1, A.1.

E.6 《文獻通考・卷六十八・郊社考一》：楊氏曰：「愚按程、朱二先生之言,則天帝一也。以一字言,則祀天、饗帝之類；以二字言,則格于皇天、殷荐上帝之類；以四字言,則惟皇上帝、昊天上帝、皇天上帝之類；以氣之所主言,則隨時隨方而立名,如青帝、赤帝、黃帝、白帝、黑帝之類。其實則一天也。是以前乎鄭康成,如鄭眾、如孔安國注《書》,并無六天之說；鄭康成後出,乃分為六天,又皆以星象名之,謂昊天上帝者北辰也,謂五帝者太微宮五帝座星也。夫在天成象,在地成形,草木非地,則星象非天,天固不可以象求也。以象求天,是何異於知人之有形色、貌象,而不知其有心君之尊也？」

Volume 68 of the *Wenxian tongkao* cites Doctor Yang as follows: 'According to the words of doctors Cheng[zi] and Zhu [Xi], Heaven [*Tian*] and the Lord of Heaven [*Di*] are the same. Both Heaven and the Lord of Heaven are indicated in the books either with a single character, such as to sacrifice to *Tian* or *Di*, or with two characters, such as to reach Great Heaven (*Huangtian*), to sacrifice with reverence to the Supreme Lord (*Shangdi*), or with four words, such as One Great Supreme Lord (*Weihuang Shangdi*), Supreme Lord of Immense Heaven (*Haotian Shangdi*), Supreme Lord of Great Heaven (*Huangtian Shangdi*), etc. If explained as Lord of the air, then He has different names according to the seasons and regions of the world, for example blue *Di*, red *Di*, yellow *Di*, white *Di* and black *Di*, but all those are the one Heaven. Before Doctor Zheng Kangcheng, no commentator has never discussed six heavens, but this classification into six heavens took place after him because of the sectarian and corrupt interpretations (as mentioned in the book cited above), with each heaven being attached to the name of a constellation or celestial configuration … But since those configurations of stars are not Heaven itself, Heaven cannot be sought through those figures. If indeed you want to seek Heaven through those figures, you would be like someone who knows that man has bodily shape and external appearance but is unaware that man has a sovereign mind of venerable greatness, or rather the greatest of a sovereign mind'.[48]

Second Objection

The idol Yuhuang is not only called *Di*, but also *Shangdi*. According to the *Universal Annals*, an emperor of the Song dynasty gave this name to Yuhuang (F). Therefore, God cannot be named *Shangdi*.[49]

I answer that we must first distinguish what is called *Shangdi* by the sectarians and idolaters from that which is called *Shangdi* by the Chinese literati professing the the true teaching. That emperor, who bestowed this name on that idol, was a follower of Taoism and became crazed by the sectarian Lin Lingsu [林靈素], as explained in the *[Universal] Annals*.[50] Another emperor, of the [Tang] dynasty,

---

48 Quote from Yang Xinzhai 楊信齋 (Song dynasty). Zheng Xuan (Han dynasty), also called Zheng Kangcheng, is quoted several times above. The *Wenxian tongkao* rejects his theory of multiple heavens, not so much here on the ground of a single heaven, but on the ground of morality. See also c.2, q.4, DD.34. Already in the Tang dynasty, Xu Jingzong 許敬宗 had rejected Zheng Xuan's theory of multiple heavens. See Wu Liwei, *Zhongguo liyi zhizheng*, p. 49.
49 The name of Yuhuang dadi was mentioned above (c.2, q.1, §.6, A.1), within a quote by Zhu Xi.
50 This refers to Emperor Huizong (1082–1135, r. 1100–1126) of the Song dynasty.

had previously given to Yuhuang the title of Emperor of Heaven or *Tiandi*, and a commentator denounced both of them.[51] A commentator attributes the extreme calamities suffered by those two emperors to their crime of idolatry (G). Even the [third] emperor of the [Tang] dynasty, while visiting the temple of the idol Laojun, the founder of the [Taoist] sect conferred upon him the honorary epithet of 'most excellent and hidden Prince and greatest Ruler' (H).[52] But the Chinese who follow the texts and the true teaching of China reject all those things. This resulted in this proverb: 'the worthless words of the [Tang] dynasty'.[53] They cannot harm the true appellation of *Shangdi* that the Chinese literati use.

NOTES

F.7 王昌會《全史詳要・卷二十五・宋徽宗》：「九月，帝詣玉清和陽宮，上玉帝徽號赦，其號曰：『太上開天、執符、御歷、含真、體道、昊天玉皇上帝』。又詔天下洞天福地，修建宮觀，塑造聖像。」

> Volume 25 of the *Book of Universal Annals*, when discussing Emperor Huizong of the Song dynasty, states as follows: 'In the ninth month, the emperor came to the Yuqingheyang palace. He conferred an honorific title upon Yuhuang, or the Precious Ruler (a Chinese idol), and decreed a general amnesty throughout the whole empire. The title was: "Most excellent one, you open Heaven, know the pact, rule over time, embrace truth, penetrate the way; you are the Precious Ruler *Shangdi* of the most Hidden Heaven". Moreover, he ordered that temples should be repaired or built, and statues erected in all the places of the sect'.[54]

G 王昌會《全史詳要・卷二十五》：「丘瓊山曰：唐玄宗崇天帝位號於『天寶』，於是有漁陽之變；宋徽宗上玉皇徽號於『政和』，於是有黃龍之禍。嗚呼！可畏哉！」

> The commentator Wang Changhui [in volume 25 of the *Book of Universal Annals*] cites Qiu Qiongshan as follows: 'Emperor Xuanzong of the Tang dynasty, in the years of his reign called Tianbao, conferred upon Yuhuang the highest dignity of Ruler of Heaven, and afterwards he suffered a terrible defeat in the battle of Yuyang, when An Lushan, his chief minister, revolted against him.[55] Later, Emperor Huizong of the Song dynasty, in the years of his reign called Zhenghe, conferred upon Yuhuang an honorific title, but afterwards he suffered a terrible

---

51 This refers to Emperor Xuanzong (685–762; r. 713–56) of the Tang dynasty.
52 This refers to Emperor Gaozong (628–83; r. 649–83) of the Tang dynasty. In fact, he is not the first emperor of the Tang dynasty, as indicated mistakenly in the manuscript (fol. 118ʳ) and the print (p. 159), but the third emperor. For the dynasty, the printed text has 'Xam' (Shang) but the manuscript correctly has 'Tam' (Tang). We have corrected those two mistakes in the main text.
53 A dubious interpretation of *huangtang* 荒唐.
54 In 1113, Emperor Huizong built the Palace of the Harmony of Yang and Purity of Jade (玉清和陽宮) and in 1116 he conferred the title to the Jade emperor.
55 At the end of 755, the general An Lushan 安祿山 revolted and in July 756 he took over the capital Chang'an, forcing Xuanzong to abdicate in favour of his third son. Retracing the history of Daoism, the preface of the *Confucius Sinarum philosophus* noticed that the sixth emperor of the Tang dynasty (Xuanzong) erected a statue of Laozi at the court; see Meynard, *Confucius Sinarum philosophus*, p. 113.

defeat in the battle of Huanglong, that is, he was captured by the Western Tartars.[56] Those things are truly dreadful'.[57]

H 王昌會《全史詳要・卷十八》：「高宗乾封元年,謁老君廟,尊為『太上玄元皇帝。』」

The same commentator in the chapter 'Emperor Gaozong' in volume 18 of the [Book of] Universal Annals states the following: 'Emperor Gaozong in the first year of his reign called Qianfeng [in the year 666] visited the temple of the idol Laojun to venerate him, and he gave him the honorific title of "Most Excellent and Hidden Principle, Great Lord and Ruler"'.[58]

Third Objection

Shangdi is the name of an idol. Therefore, God cannot be called by this name, just as God cannot be called Jupiter, since this is the name of an idol.

I answer that *Shangdi* is not the proper name of the idol but rather the epithet of an idol. The proper name of the idol Yuhuang or rather the person living at the end of the Han dynasty was Zhang Yi. He lacked an honorific because he was a common man (I). However, Jupiter is a proper name which is not shared by anybody else. Surely, the true divinity can be called with the name an idol because in the Church's earliest period the same word *deus* was used to express Jupiter, Saturn, Apollo, and other idols, as well as the true divinity of the Christians.

1. It is clear that the idols were called *deus*. In Book 1 of the *Fasti*, Ovid writes: 'This land Latium is so called because *deus* was hiding there'. *Deus* here refers to Saturn. In *Epistles* 1.11, Horace writes: 'And you, whatever hour *deus* has given for your benefit'. Here *deus* refers to Jupiter. In Book 6 of *Fasti*, Ovid writes: '*Deus* is in us, and we are inflamed by his motion'. Here *deus* refers to Apollo. The same applies to other passages.

2. Around the same time (especially when these verses and names for gods were in vogue), the true divinity of the Christians was called *Deus*, or *Theós* in Greek, as is clear from the Gospels of Saint John and Saint Luke in Greek, and Saint Mark in Latin. It is also clear from the Vulgate Latin translation of the whole New Testament, which existed probably during the time of the Apostles (Saint Jerome did not make it but only corrected a few passages), and the Psalms,

---

56 In 1127, Huizong was captured by the Jin and in 1135 he died in captivity. The *Confucius sinarum philosophus* attributes to Huizong's idolatry the responsibility for the fall of the Song dynasty and for the Mongol conquest; see Meynard, ed., *Confucius Sinarum philosophus*, p. 115.
57 For the original text, see *Qiu Wenzhuang gong congshu* 丘文莊公叢書 [Collection of writings by Qiu Jun] (Taipei: Editorial and Publishing Committee for the Collective Works of Qiu Jun 丘文莊公叢書輯印委員, 1972), vol. 2, p. 370. The *Confucius Sinarum philosophus* mentioned several times the name of the Ming scholar Qiu Qiongshan 邱瓊山 or Qiu Jun 邱濬 (1420–1495) for his opposition to Buddhism and Daoism, including his harsh judgement of Emperor Huizong of the Song dynasty; see Meynard, ed., *Confucius Sinarum philosophus*, p. 115.
58 This happens during the Tang dynasty, in the year 666.

which were translated into Greek long before Saint Jerome, probably by Saint Lucian who died martyr under emperor Maximinus, and immediately after by someone else into Latin.[59] Throughout these writings, the true divinity of the Christians is called *Deus* or *Theós*. See, for example, Mark 1[.15]: 'The kingdom of *Deus* is near'; Mark 1[.24]: 'I know you are the holy one of God'; Mark 3[.12]: 'You are the son of God'; Psalm 10[.26]: 'God is not before his eyes'; Psalm 21[.21]: 'Deliver, O God, my soul from the sword'. Please note that the word *theós* is very often used in the Greek Gospels for the true divinity of the Christians, even though all the Greek idols were also called theós.

3. It is clear that *deus* is a common noun, both from the examples above, and also from the etymology of the word *theós* that the writers relate as follows: in Hebrew God is *El*, which means strong, and according to [John of] Damascus the Greek word theós is derived either from 'to burn' (*apò toū aíthein*), 'to run' (*apò toū théein*), or 'to see' (*apò toū theásthai*). This expresses that God is a consuming and perennial fire, lasting, and seeing all things. All these words have a generic meaning. Suárez in Chapter 32 of Book 2 in Part 1 says: 'Because of his providence, He foresees everything, scans and moves everything, burns and destroys every iniquity'.[60]

4. That *Shangdi* is also a common noun is clear from the quotes of Question 2 in Chapter 2, and elsewhere, and also from the etymology of the common character. Indeed, the character *shang* means supreme, and the character *di* means king, ruler, master and guide, as indicated in the Chinese dictionary (K). Cai [Xuzhai] in reference to the three emperors Fuxi, Shennong, and Huangdi, says: 'The character *di* denotes the person who governs and rules an empire. It is neither a noun proper to the three emperors nor an honorific bestowed on them after death, but an honorary name' (L). I shall conclude with one thing. Since the Latin word *deus* is a common noun and not a proper noun, the early Latin Church had called the true divinity of the Christians *Deus*, *Dominus*, *Altissimus*, etc.: '*Dominus* thundered from Heaven, and *Altissimus* spoke strongly' (Psalm 17:14), despite the idolaters calling their idols with the same name. It is even more the case that the true divinity of the Christians can be called *Shangdi* in this primitive Chinese church. Although the idolatrous sectarians call their idol or idols with this name, it is clear that this is not a proper noun because the majority of the Chinese, including the pagan literati, understand *Shangdi* as the Lord and Ruler of Heaven and not as that idol, and they explain *Shangdi* with the concepts of Heaven or Reason. In Book 1 of the *Tristia*, Ovid flattered Caesar Augustus by calling him a god, and similarly a Chinese poet criticized a living emperor for his excessive severity and rigour by calling him *Shangdi* (M).

---

59 The Psalms were already translated in Greek in the *Septuaginta*, and Noël makes here reference to a possible translation of the Hebrew Psalms into Greek by Saint Lucian of Antioch (*c.* 240–312).
60 For this third point, Noël borrows from Suárez. See Suárez, *Opera omnia* (Paris: Louis Vives, 1856), vol. 1, p. 191.

From all this it can be deduced a kind of similitude between the words *Deus* and *Shangdi*. The word *Tian* for Heaven is also a common noun and should be understood in a similar way since the words *Tian* and *Shangdi* usually mean the same thing for the Chinese, as we have said. Also, the etymology of *Tian* confirms this: according to the ancient dictionary *Shuowen*, the character *Tian* 天 is derived or formed out of the two characters one (*yi* 一) and big (*da* 大), and thus *Tian* means something one and great, the Great Oneness, or the One Greatness.[61]

NOTES

I.8　朱宗元《答客問》：「問：然則天主即道家之玉皇乎？曰：非也。玉皇乃漢末人，姓張名儀，學修煉之術。宋徽宗崇道教，因術士林靈素之請，封張儀為『昊天玉皇大帝』。」

> The *Dakewen* by Zhu Zongyuan states as follows: 'Shall God be the same as Yuhuang who is worshipped by the Dao sect? He answers: Not at all. This Yuhuang was a man named Zhang Yi, a follower of the Dao sect who lived at the end of the Han dynasty. Since Emperor Huizong of the Song dynasty followed the Dao sect, and at the request and persuasion of a sectarian called Lin Lingsu, he conferred upon Zhang Yi the honorific title of Most Secret and Precious Principle of Heaven, Great Lord and Ruler'.[62]

I.9　《醒迷篇·論玉皇》：「論張儀，乃一小民，又無至德格言傳世，止以煉丹施藥，採補養神之術，惑眾誣民耳。」

> The chapter 'Yuhuang' of the manuscript *Xingmipian* states: 'Zhang Yi was only a common man and was not commended for his virtue or teaching by posterity. Through the tricks of the perverse Dao sect, he ensnared and deceived uneducated people'.[63]

K.10　《字彙·帝字》：「君也。《呂氏春秋》：帝者，天下之所適。」

> The dictionary *Dazihui* defines the character *di* as follows: 'The character *di* means king, ruler and guide. Commenting on the *Chunqiu*, Doctor Lü says that *di* means someone who rules the empire'.

61　This last sentence about the etymology of *Tian* is not in the ARSI manuscript. We can notice that the three Chinese characters 天, 一, and 大 are the only ones printed in the entire book. The *Shuowen jiezi* 說文解字 gives indeed this explanation (天, 字形由一大构成), though this etymology is neither accepted today nor representative of Chinese mainstream tradition.
62　Zhu Zongyuan and the *Dakewen* are mentioned above (c.3, q.1, n. 8). Lin Lingsu 林靈素 (c. 1076–c. 1120) was a famous Daoist master who became engaged in court politics during the reign of Huizong. Narrating the history of Daoism, the *Confucius Sinarum philosophus* mentions that Huizong conferred upon Zhang Yi the title mentioned here. See Meynard, ed., *Confucius Sinarum Philosophus*, p. 115. For the Chinese Christians as well as the Jesuits, Huizong committed an act of blasphemy by divinizing a human being.
63　The *Xingmipian* is mentioned above (c.2, q.5, EE.32).

L.11 蔡虛齋《四書蒙引》《大學章句序》：「帝者，主宰天下之稱也。以上三帝皆是號，非謚也，亦非名也。」

> Cai Xuzhai in his commentary *Sishu mengyin* on the beginning of the *Science of Adults* states as follows: 'This character *Di*, etc.' See above.

M.12 《詩經集傳・小雅・菀柳》：「上帝甚蹈，無自瘵焉。」朱熹：「上帝，指王也。」

> Ode 'Yuanliu' in the volume 'Xiaoya' of the *Book of Odes*: '*Shangdi* is very terrifying and very clever, and it is impossible to approach him'. Zhu Xi comments as follows: '*Shangdi* means emperor'.

Fourth Objection[64]

In the past a few philosophers understood Jupiter not as a man or an ancient king who was carried to Heaven, but as Heaven itself, the air or aether, and the Christians never dared to call God with the name of Jupiter. Similarly, since *Shangdi* is understood now by Chinese philosophers and literati as Heaven, or frequently as celestial air, the Christians cannot use the name of *Shangdi* to signify the true God.

I answer first by rejecting the conclusion. We accept the fact that Jupiter was understood by philosophers and scholars as Heaven, air or aether. However, through the name of Jupiter, they have never fashioned or represented anything else but a material being, a corporeal heaven, air or material aether. As Suárez say in Chapter 3 of Book 1 in Part 1, those philosophers did not succeed in understanding anything but the material, and they did not propose or conceive a one, true and supreme spirit, which is Master, Omnipotent, Providential, and invisible Author that is separated from all sensation, such as what the Chinese literati understood *Shangdi* to be as we saw above.[65] Next, Jupiter is thought by the people to have been a man or an ancient king who was raised or elevated to divinity, and indeed he was venerated as such. But no one in China thinks or conceives that the *Shangdi* described in the Chinese classics was ever a human being. Rather, everybody knows and worships *Shangdi* as a Spirit which was not begotten of any human being. Moreover, all the ancient pagans, including the philosophers, adored Jupiter as dwelling in a statue or idol because they believed that something divine, special, or mysterious dwelt within the statue. Even if a few philosophers and others did not believe this, they still adored the idol in which the entire people had placed a false divinity and thus were at least on the surface idolaters. Moreover, the temple of Jupiter was erected with this idolatrous statue. But no Chinese, either a commoner or a literatus, has ever erected a statue to *Shangdi*. However, the emperor presents only a tablet on

---

64 This entire fourth objection is absent from the ARSI manuscript.
65 Suárez refers in fact to an opinion of Aristotle in *De physica* IV.6. See Suárez, *Tractatus de divina substantia ejusque attributis*; *Opera omnia*, I, p. 10. Aristotle criticized the philosophers who 'hold that everything which is in body is body and say that what has nothing in it at all is void' (212a30). Scholastic philosophers understood Aristotle as criticizing the materialist philosophy of his predecessors. For Noël, the Chinese philosophers like Aristotle understood the existence of a spiritual realm detached from the material world.

which is written *Shangdi*'s name, and he does not acknowledge or believe that there is anything divine or mysterious in this tablet. No temple with a statue has ever been built for *Shangdi*, but only an earthen mound in which the emperor makes an open-air sacrifice, not to a man raised to divinity, but to a supreme Spirit. Whenever the emperor makes a sacrifice indoors, the sacrifice is performed before the name written on the tablet, and not before a statue. If a building is erected, it is only to house the tablet or rather the name of *Shangdi*, and to ensure that the sacrifice is conducted in a dignified and comfortable environment. Even if the building were made for the worship of *Shangdi*, its true meaning would not be corrupted. Therefore, there is no comparison whatsoever between *Shangdi* and Jupiter. Please review the precedent chapters.[66]

Fifth Objection[67]

The Chinese literati understand the word *Shangdi* as something lifeless, indefinite, and empty, as well as an adscititious term.

I answer by rejecting the assumption. They understand the word *Shangdi* as something real, which they do not wish or are unable to express with sufficient clarity, as they themselves recognize. When they try to explain it, they often have recourse to terms Reason of Heaven, or Law of Heaven. But they consider Heaven, Reason, Law of Heaven as real, physical, true and not as lifeless, empty and indefinite, especially because they establish the entire teaching on a real truth. Therefore, they do not understand *Shangdi* as lifeless, empty, and indefinite, and neither is the term *Shangdi* adscititious as if it were empty, lifeless, and passive, but it is adscititious insofar as it was was chosen to address with respect the first and supreme Being, which is God.

It is clear from all this that God can be called with the name of *Shangdi*, especially since the name of *Shangdi* appears much more elegant to the Chinese than the word *Tianzhu* used by the Chinese Christians to address God since *Tianzhu* is absent from the Chinese classics.[68]

---

66 While Noël considers the rituals to ancestors and Confucius as only civic or political, and thus devoid of any religious meaning, the sacrifice to *Shangdi* or *Tian* performed by the emperor alone has a high religious meaning, but unlike the ancient sacrifice to Jupiter, is not idolatrous.
67 In the ARSI manuscript this corresponds to the fourth objection. For the *jingtian* tablet, see below (c.3, q.2).
68 Noël considers *Shangdi* as better than *Tianzhu*, but he does not advocate rejecting *Tianzhu* for *Shangdi* as it can be seen below.

Question 2: Can God be Called *Tian* (Heaven)?

§.1. General Affirmation about the Word *Tian*

Having presupposed the meaning of *Tian* among ancient and contemporary Chinese that I explained in detail above, I answer by affirming that, just as the Latins call God *Caelum*, so the Chinese can call God *Tian*.

First, it is proven from the manner of speech used by the Latins: 'Father, I have sinned against Heaven and against you' (Luke 15:[21]), 'My sins have reached Heaven', where the four sins are said to be calling to Heaven since their voice have reached God as said in the scriptures (Apocalypse 18:5). Here as everywhere the word *Caelum* is understood as God. The Chinese use expressions such as 'to serve, sacrifice to and obey *Tian*', and 'to revere, fear and pray to *Tian*'. Here, as we have seen above, *Tian* should be understood as God.

Second, it is proven from all the texts quoted in the whole Chapter 1 and in Questions 1 and 2 of Chapter 2. Remember or re-read these texts, and you shall see clearly that *Tian* means God.

Third, it is proven from long usage. Since the foundation of the Chinese mission more than one hundred years ago, the character *Tian* has always been understood as meaning God, as it is shown in all the Christian writings, and never any controversy has raised among missionaries about the meaning of the word *Tian*, except only very few years ago when one or two stirred up the controversy, and I shall soon say something about the reason and the occasion for this controversy;[69] however, there was a controversy about *Shangdi*. This is especially proven by the tombstone of the Most Illustrious and Reverend Doctor Gregory Lopez, first bishop of Nanjing, where he died in 1691. On the tombstone, it is written *Tianxue zhujiao* [天學主教], that is, bishop of the Teaching of Heaven, and *Tianxue siduo* [天學司鐸], that is priest of the Teaching of Heaven, that is, of God. It said that he *du Tianxue shu* [讀天學書], that is, he read the books of the Teaching of Heaven. This meant he read books about God and not about mathematical forms or material heaven. Therefore, the character *Tian* often means God or Lord of Heaven. If you take it as meaning the material heaven or its material virtue, then wrong inscription on the tombstone would be false and thus should be removed, or rather the tombstone should be taken away, though the Chinese Christian literati would object.[70]

---

69 Noël does not seem completely honest here. Even though he acknowledges the controversy about *Shangdi*, he overlooks the rejection of *Tian* by most missionaries.

70 The epitaph of Gregory Luo Wenzhao 羅文炤 (1617–1691) in ARSI was recently examined by Song Liming. See Song Liming 宋黎明, 'Luo Wenzhao haishi Luo Wenzao? Wei Zhongguo shou wei guoji zhujiao Luo zhujiao zhengming' 羅文炤還是羅文藻?: 為中國首位國籍主教羅主教正名 [Luo Wenzhao or Luo Wenzao?: A study on the Chinese name of the first Chinese bishop Gregorio Lopez (1617–1691)], *Haijiaoshi yanjiu* 海交史研究 [Journal of Maritime History Studies], 3 (2019), 40–51. In a letter dated 25 May 1709 to Clement XI, Noël accused Giovanni Francesco Nicolai a Leonessa OFM (1656–1737), who opposed the use of the Chinese terms *Tian* and *Shangdi*, of having written the epitaph of Luo Wenzao in 1691, with mention of the character *Tian*. On 4 August 1709, the Franciscans in Rome

Fourth, it is proven from the authority of the Chinese Christians who were mentioned in the previous question. Throughout their books, they understand *Tian* as meaning God. Indeed, they prefer *Tian* to *Tianzhu* for denoting God because *Tian* is more elegant. Moreover, the Chinese pagans do not understand well the word *Tianzhu* unless we explain it to them because this two-character word is not present in their classical books and they consider the word not elegant enough. Even Emperor Kangxi once asked why we could not call God with a more elegant name. With *Tian* understood as the Lord of Heaven, they understand far more easily what we want to say, that is, the supreme and incomprehensible excellence of a First Being and a supreme divinity.[71]

Fifth, it is proven from the authority of the Muslims residing in China.[72] It is certain that the Muslims do not consider the material and visible heaven, or a material virtue innate to heaven, as the object of their worship, but the supreme and most intelligent Lord of Heaven and all created things. But in China they explain and express this with the words *Tian* and *Shangdi*. Therefore, those words do not mean for them a material heaven.

The minor [premise] is proven from their dogmatic works printed in Chinese. I cite only three of them. The first is the *True Exposition of the Correct Religion* (*Zhengjiao zhenquan*) in which the character *Tian* is used for God nine times, *Shangdi* for God ten times, *Tianjing* for the Bible of Heaven five times, *Tianli* for the Reason of Heaven once, and *Tianming* for the Mandate of Heaven seven times.[73] The second book, the *Examination of the Pure and True Religion* (*Qingzhenjiao kao*), uses the single character *Tian* for God twenty-two times, and the word *Shangdi* for God once, *Tianjing* for Bible of Heaven three times, *jingtian* for revering Heaven seven times, *shitian* for serving Heaven twice, and *baitian* for worshipping Heaven three times.[74] The third work, the *Explanation of the Teaching of Four Chapters, Necessary for the Understanding of the Uneducated* (*Sipian yaodao buzhu bianmeng qianshuo*), where the word *Tian* is used for God once, *Tianzhi* for the Decree of Heaven once, *Tianming* for the Mandate of Heaven twelve times, *Tianli* for the Reason of Heaven once, and *Tianjing* for the Bible of Heaven three times.[75] As you can see the Muslims in China use the words *Tian* and *Shangdi* to mean the supreme

---

sent a note of explanation to Clement XI. See 'Adnotationes in epigramma Illmi D. Gregorii Lopez, Clementi Papae XI communicatae', in *Sinica franciscana*, ed. by G. Mensaert, vol. 6.1, p. 331.

71 In Question 1 of Chapter 3, Noël argued that the best translation for God should be Shangdi, but here he expresses the preference of the Chinese for *Tian*. However, Yan Mo considers *Shangdi* as better than *Tian* or *Tianzhu* for expressing the idea of God as a person. See Xiao Qinghe, *Tian Ru yitong: Qingchu Rujia Jidutu yanjiu*, p. 148.

72 The proofs based on the testimony of the Muslims, the Jews, and the Chinese pagans, are not found in the ARSI manuscript.

73 Wang Daiyu 王岱輿 (c. 1570–1660) published the *Zhengjiao zhenquan* 正教真詮 in 1642. The three works by Muslims mentioned here are not found in the ARSI collections.

74 Zhan Yingpeng 詹應鵬 (*jinshi* in 1616) and Sun Ke'an 孫可庵 (dates unknown) published the *Qingzhenjiao kao* 清真教考 in the early years of the Kangxi reign.

75 Zhang Zhong 張中 (c. 1598–1698) translated into Chinese the *Sipian yaodao buzhu bianmeng qianshuo* 四篇要道補注便蒙淺說, which was published sometime between 1653–1660.

and living Lord of all things. You can see many Muslims who are distinguished by their degrees in Chinese letters and offices, and who become senior officers of the literati.

Sixth, it can be proven from the authority of the Jews. Many of them live in Beijing and in Henan province. The Jesuit Father Gianpaolo Gozani,[76] who resides in Henan, the metropolitan city of Kaifeng province, testifies the following in a letter of 30 June 1705: 'I testify that the head of the Jewish synagogue (indeed the Jews have a synagogue in this city), or *zhangjiao* in Chinese, with the Chinese surname Gao and the Hebrew name Phineas,[77] stands today in front of me in my room and has written the Hebrew names of Adam, Abraham, Hodoi (Shaddai), Elohim and Adonai, the last one which he pronounces as Ngetonoi. Second, he said that the three names for God — Hodoi, Elohim, and Adonai — are explained by him and his fellow Jews in Chinese with the word *Tian* or Heaven, and with the word *Tianye* [天爺] or Lord of Heaven (the Chinese words *Tianye* and *Tianzhu* have the same meaning except that *Tianye* is more colloquial). Third, the Jews do not understand *Tian* or *Tianye* as the material heaven, but as the Creator of Heaven and Earth, who created the first man Adam, prescribed circumcision to Abraham through the angels, gave the Law to Moses on Mount Sinai, etc.'[78]

These things are confirmed by three big stone monuments which were erected in their synagogue under different emperors and contain a compendium and acclamation of the Mosaic Law.[79] The first monument was erected under Emperor Hongzhi around 1487. On this monument, the word *Tian* for God occurs six times, and the expression *jing Tian* or 'revere Heaven' four times.[80] On the second monument, erected under Emperor Zhengde around 1511, the word *Tian* for God occurs once, and *Tianming* for the Mandate of Heaven twice.[81] On the third monument, erected under Emperor Kangxi in 1663, the word *Shangdi* for God appears once, the word

---

76 In the context of the Rites Controversy, the Italian Jesuit Gianpaolo Gozani (1659–1732), who resided in Kaifeng from 1698 to 1724, was asked to report on the use of Chinese names for God among the Jewish community.

77 Rabbi is translated as *zhangjiao* 掌教. His family name is Gao 高.

78 This document is found in ARSI, Jap. Sin. 150, fol. 267. For a translation of this document, see Joseph Dehergne and Donald Leslie, *Juifs de Chine* (Rome: Institutum Historicum Societatis Iesu, 1984), p. 72. We have slightly modified Dehergne's translation. The three comments in parenthesis were added by Noël. In the second comment, Noël proposes that Hodoi does not mean Jehova as Gozani suggested, but rather Shaddai.

79 As Dehergne suggests, Noël drew this passage about the three monuments and the *Mingjiao xu* from another document, BNCVE, Fondo Gesuitico, MS 1383. For a transcription and English translation of this document, see Dehergne, *Juifs de Chine*, pp. 70–72.

80 The *Chongjian Qingzhensi beiwen* 重建清真寺碑文 [Stone Inscription for the Reconstruction of the Temple of Purity and Truth] dates from the second year of Hongzhi's reign, that is 1489. All the occurrences were counted by Gozani. For the names of the stone monuments and the number of occurrences, see ARSI, Jap. Sin. 168, fol. 449. This document is dated 8 November 1705, only five months after the letter mentioned just above, and is reproduced in Dehergne, *Juifs de Chine*, p. 253.

81 The *Zunchong Daojingsi beiwen* 尊崇道經寺碑文 [Stone inscription for the Temple of the Venerable Classic of the Way] dates from the seventh year of Zhengde's reign, that is 1513.

Tian for God seven times, and the expression *jing Tian* for 'revere Heaven' twice.⁸² Finally the Jews of Beijing gave to the Fathers of the Society of Jesus a book about their Law, written in Chinese for domestic instruction and entitled *Brief Instruction of the Bright Religion* (*Mingjiao xu*); in this book there is one mention of *Shangdi* for God, and eight mentions of *Tian* for God.⁸³ It is thus clear that the Jews, some of whom are bachelors [scholars], licentiates, or doctors and well-versed in Chinese literature, use the words *Tian* and *Shangdi* to express God.⁸⁴

Seventh, it is proven by the authority of Chinese pagans. Besides the Jews and Muslims using the words *Tian* and *Shangdi* to refer to the supreme divinity, even the Chinese who are zealous followers of the literati sect do the same. I cite only one book, which opposed our religion. This book was published a few years ago in Songjiang, a city in the province of Nanjing, and is entitled *Refutation of the Evil Religion of the Europeans* (*Pi xiyang xiejiao lun*). It states as follows: 'Is there anyone who is unaware that there is one supreme Lord called *Tian* and *Shangdi* in our [Four Books and Five] classics (*Sishu wujing*)? But it is uncouth and stupid to say that he was incarnated. He is the Most High. Since He produces Heaven, Earth, and human beings, thunders in the heavens, brings up the winds from the ends of the world, how could He become a man and suffer shame?'⁸⁵

This is also proved by a certificate in favour of the Christian religion. This certificate was given to Father Alfonso Vagnone of the Society of Jesus, by the governor of the city of Jiangzhou in Shanxi province in 1633, when there was not yet any controversy about the word *Tian*, as said above.⁸⁶ In his certificate, the governor uses the words of *Tian* and *Shangdi* to refer to the God of our religion.⁸⁷ Please recall all what was said in the previous chapter about modern authors (especially c.2, q.3, E.6).

---

82 There is another monument entitled *Chongjian Qingzhensi beiwen* 重建清真寺碑文 [Stone Inscription for the Reconstruction of the Temple of Purity and Truth] which dates back to the second year of Kangxi's reign, that is 1563.
83 Gozani mentions the *Mingjiao xu* 明教序, a book which has been lost. See Dehergne, *Juifs de Chine*, p. 62.
84 Noël places the use for *Tian* and *Shangdi* on the same level, an indication that he is personally promoting *Shangdi*, but this term is, in fact, mentioned only twice in the Jewish texts quoted here. See also documents written by Gozani, ARSI, Jap. Sin. 168, fol. 446ʳ–449ᵛ.
85 In the printed text the title is indicated as *Pie Si Yam Sie Kiao Lun*, and this should be: *Pi xiyang xiejiao lun* 闢西洋邪教論 or 辟西洋邪教論. However, we have not yet identified the author of this work, which was published in Songjiang, probably around 1700.
86 Again, Noël ignores the Jiading conference of 1628.
87 Lei Chong, *Jiangzhou zhengtang Lei wei zuntian quxie* 絳州正堂雷為尊天袪邪 [Proclamation Issued by Prefect Lei of Jiangzhou Regarding the Worship of Heaven and the Elimination of Heterodoxy], 1635; punctuated text in: Han Qi 韩琦 and Wu Min 吴旻, *Xichao chongzheng ji, Xichao ding'an* 熙朝崇正集, 熙朝定案 (Beijing: Zhonghua shuju, 2006), p. 235: 「照得開闢一天,萬古所尊,正道惟一而已。自堯舜禹湯文武周孔以來,相傳所謂事天,事上帝者是也。先儒解曰:『上帝,天之主宰。』今人以所見之蒼蒼者,言天是猶稱帝王,曰朝廷也。即至愚之人,不識不知,未嘗不曰『天爺』,曰『天命』,曰『天理』,曰『天報』,曰『天罰』。可見性中帶來,非因勉強。」Noël does not provide a translation for the text and he may not have the document in his hands. Also, the indication of 1633 is a mistake.

Eighth and finally, God can be called *Shangdi* as we have proven and examined in the previous question, and he can also be called *Tian* because the Chinese very frequently use these terms interchangeably. Please note that, as I say that God can be called *Tian*, I understand it as a way of speaking. When the word *Tian* is mentioned, the Chinese as well as the Europeans can understand and signify God by this.[88]

All those things are enough to prove that the use of *Tian* and *Shangdi* indicate the true and supreme Lord of Heaven, or God, that such a use has flourished in China until now, and that the [Han] Chinese and the other inhabitants of the country truly signify God through those words. Why cannot the Chinese Christians continue to use the same words to express and signify God, especially taking into account their usefulness, convenience, as well as necessity?[89]

First objection: All the books and commentaries of the modern commentators are full of atheism. They refer everything to the material heaven or its inborn material property as a primary cause. Those commentaries of the classical books printed by Emperor Kangxi have the same aim. For example, volume 2 of *Shujing rijiang*, when commenting on the chapter 'Yaodian' in the *Imperial Annals* states: 'There is nothing more important in worshipping Heaven than creating the calendar and knowing the reason for the cycles of Heaven'.[90] Since this word *Tian* is now commonly understood by the Chinese literati as a material thing, it cannot be used to express God.

I answer by refuting the premise.[91] The books and commentaries that we examined in the second chapter recognize a Spiritual Being or Spirit for the first origin of things, which they explain either as universal cause, Reason, Excellence, First Ultimate, or something invisible and incomprehensible. They do not refer everything to a material heaven, or its material property, as the first cause. They recognize one supreme divinity which produces, controls and plans everything, while remunerating virtue and punishing vice. The commentaries published by the emperor Kangxi, just like the others, tend to the same interpretation. There is not a single text or passage teaching atheism; rather, in various passages it is often taught with clear words that there is one true and supreme Lord of all things, especially throughout the commentary *Shujing rijiang*. This is also clear from various passages of those commentaries which I have very often quoted and will cite further on.[92]

As for the quote mentioned in the objection, here are the words of the commentary: 'In the wise man, the worship of Heaven and the governance of the people proceed not merely from an interior disposition of the mind, but his soul,

---

88 This corresponds to the fifth proof in the ARSI manuscript.
89 This concluding paragraph is not present in the manuscript.
90 This passage is not in *juan* 2 but *juan* 1. The ARSI manuscript does not have the Chinese text and we have retrieved it directly from the *Rijiang shujing*: 「帝堯以事之最大、最先莫過治曆明時。乃總命羲氏、和氏二人,以為日月星辰運于昊天有常數。」
91 The ARSI document does not provide further explanation, but only refers to c.2.§.1, 2 and 3.
92 Noël states here his break-through opinion about the philosophy of the Song, Ming, and Qing dynasties, not being atheistic as held by the Jesuits before him, but as monotheistic.

with which he reveres Heaven, takes special care that calendars and instruments are made for knowing celestial motions; furthermore, his soul, with which he provides for the people, takes special care that there is a division of time for the people, that is, a calendar'.[93] Hence nothing is said there other than that the worship of Heaven and the governance of the people consists not in the interior disposition of the mind alone, but that the wise man should also pursue external things, like taking care of the calendar and celestial motions, and giving people a distribution of time.

Second objection.[94] When the Chinese pagans discuss *Tian*, they understand nothing other than the blue and material heaven, or its material property.

I answer by negating the assumption. They understand *Shangdi*, Reason, and other terms discussed as immaterial things.

Third objection. According to their understanding, the words *Shangdi*, Reason and other terms are empty and concern a self-negating subject (*subjectum non supponens*).[95]

I answer by refuting the assumption. Those terms suppose a subject which is invisible, spiritual, incomprehensible, existing everywhere and active in all things. Please see c.2, q.3 and elsewhere. More recently, the Chinese went through every mental effort and turned to various methods to explain Reason, *Shangdi*, Heaven, and similar words. In the end, however, they always end up understanding that these words signify some hidden First Principle, which constantly acts in an obscure and mysterious darkness. Is this the true God or does it concern a self-negating subject? Indeed, a material heaven is not obscure, secret, occult, or invisible, and there is no need of such circumlocution to explain it. Thus, it is clear that they understand as the true Spirit of Heaven or indeed as the Lord of Heaven. Thus, God can be called *Tian*, or *Tian* can be understood as God.

§.2. Particular Declaration about Revering Heaven (*jing Tian*)

This was the origin of the controversy about this two-word expression.[96] In 1675, that is in the fourth year of his reign, Emperor Kangxi visited out of special benevolence the residence of the Fathers of the Society of Jesus in Beijing. When he was inside the room of Father Ludovico Buglio, he himself wrote with a brush

---

93 This corresponds to a passage of the chapter 'Yaodian' in the *Shujing rijiang*, *juan* 1: '蓋聖人事天治民, 不出欽敬之心而已。敬天之心, 嚴于曆象; 勤民之心, 嚴于授時'. The commentary emphasizes that the veneration and respect of the mind for Heaven finds concrete application in the observance of the celestial motions and the establishment of the calendar. For the missionaries who opposed Song philosophy, this means that the wise man follows a materialistic law of the universe. For Noël, the veneration and respect for God implies understanding the natural world and making use of it for the people.
94 This objection is not present in the ARSI manuscript.
95 The expression *subjectum non supponens* seems to have been used in seventeenth century to indicate a meaningless subject: 'Subjectum non supponens est cum quo aliqua particula conjungitur quae subjectum ipsum destruit, v.g. *homo qui non est animal est Doctus*'. Pierre Mounyer and Honoré Fabri, *Philosophiae tomus primus* (Lyon: Sumptibus Ioannis Champion, 1646), p. 144.
96 The expression *jing Tian* 敬天 appeared in a passage of the *Shijing* quoted above (see c.1, q.2, §.7, B.2)

the two characters *jing Tian* (revere Heaven). In accordance with Chinese custom, the word was exhibited outside on a tablet. The Beijing Fathers immediately ordered that the word be placed in the Beijing church to reveal Emperor's attitude and esteem towards our religion.[97] Other missionary Fathers residing in the other provinces took care to hang similar tablets they had received from Beijing. Some hung the tablets in the entrance hall of the church, or rather in the reception hall for guests, and others hung them inside the church.[98] After some time, when new missionaries arriving in China noticed the tablet, as is often the case, they first expressed their astonishment and then their disdain, criticizing the fact that the tablet which had been given to Ferdinand Verbiest alone was hung in other Jesuit residences.[99] Then they denounced and rejected the meaning of the word. In the end, they came to say that idolatry should not be tolerated and the imperial tablet should be removed, even if only the risk [of idolatry] was suspected, lest there be placed 'the abomination of desolation in a holy place'.[100] Thus a small spark lit a great fire. My investigation does not consider the motivation, method of inquiry, deliberation, and obstacles [that led them to this conclusion], but let us examine only whether this *jing Tian* tablet or inscription is idolatrous.

I answer that this tablet is no more idolatrous than Heaven is an idol. Since Heaven is not an idol, the tablet is not idolatrous. I prove the minor premise. In the commentary by Cornelius à Lapide on Chapter 8 of the First Letter to the Corinthians, it is said that אֱלִילִים (*elilim*) means vanity, or something vain and empty, while others understand it as little god or a little strong man. However,

---

and in the *Shijing shuoyue jijie* (see c.2, q.1, §.7, B.2). Noël cites on two occasions a passage containing this expression in the *Rijiang Yijing* 日講易經, the Kangxi commentary of the *Yijing* (see c.2, q.3, X.29 and c.2, q.5, GGG.68). Noël also cites the use of this expression in the *Chuhui wenda* by the Franciscan Pedro de la Piñuela (see c.3, q.1, B.2). The idea of *jing Tian* became more important in late Ming and reached prominence in Zhang Juzheng's *Sishu zhijie*. This was probably one of the reasons why the Jesuits chose Zhang Juzheng's commentaries as their principal reference. Chinese Christians like Yan Mo also promoted the idea of *jing Tian*. The Christian emphasis on *jing Tian* reinforced an early Qing trend which was already present since the late Ming. See Thierry Meynard, *The Jesuit Reading of Confucius*, pp. 35–37.

97 The visit happened on 12 July 1675. Two months after the visit, Gabriel de Magalhães (1609–1677) reported it in a letter dated 6 September 1675. See ARSI, Jap. Sin. 124, fol. 100^{r-v}. See also João de Deus Ramos, 'Tomás Pereira, *Jing Tian* and Nerchinsk', in *In the Light and Shadow of an Emperor*, ed. by Artur Wardega and António Vasconcelos de Saldanha (Newcastle upon Tyne: Cambridge Scholars, 2012), pp. 518–29 (p. 521). In 1687, Couplet mentioned the visit of Kangxi. See Meynard, ed., *Confucius Sinarum Philosophus*, p. 231.

98 This is also reported in that same letter of Magalhães. See Noël Golvers, *François de Rougemont, S. J., Missionary in Ch'ang-Shu* (Leuven: Leuven University Press, 1999), p. 483.

99 Though Kangxi wrote *jing Tian* in Buglio's room, it was intended as a personal gift to Verbiest. See Claudia von Collani, 'Jing Tian: The Kangxi Emperor's Gift to Ferdinand Verbiest in the Rites Controversy', in *Ferdinand Verbiest, 1623–1688*, ed. by John W. Witek (Nettetal: Steyler Verlag, 1994), pp. 453–70.

100 Noël is paraphrasing the words of Jesus in Matthew 24:15, in reference to the prophet Daniel. Noël alludes here to Charles Maigrot who arrived China in 1684 and became Apostolic Vicar for Fujian in 1687. His *Mandatum* of 1693 orders seven interdictions. The first order was to forbid the use of *Tian* and *Shangdi* and use only *Tianzhu*. The second order was to remove from Catholic churches the *jing Tian* tablet, which he considered as idolatrous and as the 'abomination of desolation'. Since Noël mentions this same expression a few times, it is clear that he refers here to the *Mandatum* of 1693 by Maigrot.

when Heaven is understood as Ruler and Lord of Heaven, it is not vanity, or something vain and empty, as we have often seen. Nor is Heaven a little strong man or a little god, since the Chinese acknowledge nothing greater, more excellent, and honourable than Heaven. Therefore, Heaven is not an idol. In the same passage, Cornelius explains the Greek word εἴδωλον which on its own means appearance, saying that Scripture and ecclesiastical writers associated the name of idol with an image of God, which is taken for God while in reality it is not.[101] But what, I ask, is Heaven the image of? It is not the image of material heaven. Otherwise, Heaven would be simultaneously the image and the very thing represented by the image. This is impossible because an image is distinct in reality from the thing which it represents. Therefore, Heaven is not the image of material heaven. If you say that Heaven is the image of immaterial heaven or something immaterial, then this would be the image of the Lord and Ruler of Heaven, the invisible Author, Reason causing and ruling everything. Indeed, there is no immaterial Heaven or immaterial things, but the Lord, Ruler and Author of Heaven is in reality the true God. Therefore, Heaven is not understood as an idol. Since *Tian* is the reason why the *jing Tian* tablet was reproved and condemned and this word does not signify an idol at all, the tablet is therefore free from this mark of ignominy, and there is no danger of placing an 'abomination of desolation in a holy place'.

Also, this sort of Chinese tablet or inscription serves as only some words of praise which the emperor and the mandarins customarily grant on special occasions as an expression of their benevolence and esteem towards people. Afterwards, as it can be seen throughout China, the tablets are hung in private houses or temples for public display, without any ceremony or honour being performed. As the intention is to show the benevolence and esteem of the benefactor; they are only honorary gifts. But is there any prohibition on hanging an honorary gift, either at home as an ornament or in a temple for glory (unless for worship)? Would anyone prohibit hanging in a church the banners captured from the Turks, or fixing other gifts to the dome?[102] Or would anyone reprove the hanging of Saint Ignatius' sword, which was once a profane object, in the holy temple of Montserrat?[103] I remember seeing in the holy house of the Blessed Virgin in Namur a small ancient idol of Namen, from which the name of Namur is believed to have originated, left as a memory within the cavity of the stone pillars.[104] Would anyone shout out 'abomination of

---

101 See Cornelius à Lapide, *Commentarius in Pentatheucum Mosis* (1627), caput 5, p. 940.
102 The Great Turkish War between the Holy League and Turkey lasted from 1683 to 1699. In 1697, the Holy League won the decisive battle of Zenta (today in Serbia).
103 The founder of the Jesuits, Saint Ignatius of Loyola (1491–1556), had visited the monastery of Montserrat in 1522, and hung his sword and dagger at the Virgin's altar during an overnight vigil at the shrine.
104 Around 1340, Jean d'Outremeuse wrote *La Geste de Liège*, and without much historical evidence, he mentioned the legend that in the year 123, Saint Materne, disciple of Saint Peter and bishop of Treves, made the local idol Nam mute (Nam mutum), giving the name of Namur. The legend of Saint Materne became increasingly popular in the seventeenth century, and in the Collégiale of Notre Dame (destroyed in the nineteenth century and replaced today by a new church), people were shown a small statue of Nam. Being Flemish, Noël probably visited the place and saw the statue before his departure for China in 1684. See Jacques Poucet, 'Autour du Materne de Jean d'Outremeuse ou l'évolution d'un personnage

desolation in a holy place'? I may be overstating my point. On the contrary, the *jing Tian* tablet or inscription is only an honorary gift as it is known by everybody who knows the Chinese, and it is hung publicly without any indication of religious worship, but only as an expression of esteem for the gift. As we understand, this tablet even contains a very safe meaning, which is very compatible with our religion.

It is not at all improper to place the tablet in a church, and it seems rather more suitable than anywhere else because a church is more public. This position shows on its own that the inscription hanging there concerns the Christian God being made well known in China, especially in the absence of a statue of Christ the Saviour. From any perspective you take this inscription, there is no hint or danger of idolatry. Finally, to make truth even clearer, let us bring the public and authentic testimony of the person who gave the tablet. Through his words *Tian* and *Shangdi* were efficaciously proven and confirmed.

§.3. Public and Authentic Testimony of the Sino-Tartar Emperor Kangxi Declaring the Authentic Meaning of *Tian* and *Shangdi*, as Well as the Disputed Rituals in Honour of Deceased Ancestors

When the Fathers of the Society of Jesus living in Beijing saw how ardently Europeans in China and Europe disputed the true and legitimate meaning of certain Chinese rituals and terms, then they unanimously decided to write a petition about these controversies and to present it to the emperor, as the legislator and supreme interpreter of the Chinese laws and rites, in the hope that he would deign to declare their true and legitimate meaning. On 30 November 1700, they publicly presented their petition:

> 治理曆法遠臣閔明我、徐日昇、安多、張誠等奏為恭請睿鑒，以求訓誨事，遠臣等看得西洋學者聞中國有拜孔子及祭天祀祖先之禮，必有其故，願聞其詳等語。
>
> 臣等管見，以為拜孔子敬其為人師範，並非求福、祈聰明爵祿而拜也。祭祀祖先出於愛親之義，依儒禮亦無求佑之說，惟盡孝思之念而已。雖設立祖先之牌位，非謂祖先之魂在木牌位之上，不過抒子孫「報本追遠」、「如在」之義耳。至於郊天之禮典，非祭蒼蒼有形之天，乃祭天地萬物根原主宰，即孔子云「郊社之禮，所以事上帝也」。有時不稱「上帝」而稱「天」者，猶如主上不曰「主上」，而曰「陛下」、曰「朝廷」之類，雖名稱不同，其實一也。前蒙皇上所賜匾額，親書「敬天」之字，正是此意。遠臣等鄙見，以此答之。但緣關係中國風俗，不敢私寄，恭請睿鑒訓誨。遠臣不勝惶悚，待命之至。[105]

---

dans l'hagiographie médiévale', *Folia Electronica Classica*, 37 (January-June 2019) <http://bcs.fltr.ucl.ac.be/FE/37/VALER/COMM06_TOURNEE.pdf> (accessed 29 October 2021).

105 The request was addressed in Manchu, and Kangxi also replied in Manchu. Later, the request and the answer were translated into Chinese and Latin, and the document was published in the three languages: *Brevis relatio eorum quae spectant ad declarationem Sinarum Imperatoris Kam Hi circa caeli Confucii et*

A petition which Filippo Grimaldi, president of the Bureau of Mathematics, Tomas Pereira, Antoine Thomas, François Gerbillon and other honourable Europeans present to the emperor, humbly asking to be instructed by him.[106]

We, the foreign subjects of Your Majesty, have learnt that some erudite European men heard that there are rites in China for honouring Confucius, for making sacrifices to Heaven [*jitian*], and for performing the ceremony in honour of deceased ancestors [*si zuxian*]. They say that there is undoubtedly a reason and cause for these rituals, but we are longing to learn more in detail about it, etc.[107]

We, the subjects of Your Majesty, according to our very limited mental capacity, consider that honour is displayed to Confucius not to seek wealth, intelligence, or offices, but only because of the famous teachings that the Master has left people. Also, the *ji* ritual which is performed for deceased ancestors originates from the intention of professing love for one's parents. According to the rituals of the Chinese professing the teaching of the literati, this ceremony is not to be explained or understood as a request for help of any kind, but it is performed only to fulfill intention of filial piety by which descendants remember their deceased parents. Even though they erect tablets for their deceased parents, this does not mean that the souls of the parents reside in the wooden tablets, but they only display them as an external expression of their gratitude to their ancestors and keep them as a lasting memory, as if they were present. As for the ritual of sacrifice performed on the suburban earthen mound, we consider that it is not performed for the blue or material heaven, but offered to the Principle, Lord and Ruler of Heaven, Earth and all things, as Confucius says: 'The sacrificial ritual to Heaven and Earth is how the Lord and Ruler of Heaven (*Shangdi*) is served'.[108] Sometimes He is called Lord of Heaven (*Shangdi*) and sometimes, Heaven (*Tian*). This is like how Your Majesty

---

avorum cultum (Peking, 1701). See also ARSI, Jap. Sin I, 206 and ARSI, Jap. Sin. 165, fols 188–89. The ARSI manuscript of the *Philosophia Sinica* contains the Latin and Chinese versions, with the Latin translated from the Chinese, and therefore, the wording is somehow different from the Latin translation from the Manchu contained in the *Brevis relatio*.

106 The petition to Kangxi is called in Latin the *Libellus supplex*, and four Jesuits are named: Filippo Grimaldi (1638–1712), Tomás Pereira (1645–1708), Antoine Thomas (1644–1709), and Jean-François Gerbillon (1654–1707). Among the others not listed is Joachim Bouvet.

107 The text suggests that the Beijing Jesuits needed to answer a query, and Kangxi would have already guessed that the Jesuits were not completely free in this matter.

108 The Jesuits purposely introduced in their petition to Kangxi this quote from the *Zhongyong* which mentions the religious worship of *Shangdi*. The quote of the *Zhongyong* is mentioned in c.1, q.2, §.1, R.18, and also in Zhu Xi's commentary cited in c.2, q.5, VV.51. Also, the text of their petition offers an interesting parallel with the *Chuhui wenda* by the Franciscan La Piñuela, an excerpt of which is translated above in c.3, q.1, B.2. The Jesuits seemingly use a Franciscan text to destroy the argument of their enemies, including the Franciscans. This is also the case for the idea here of Imperial Palace as relating to the emperor himself, also mentioned in the same excerpt by La Piñuela.

is sometimes called 'Beneath the steps' (that is the usual expression of the servants standing beneath the steps of the imperial hall) or sometimes 'Imperial Hall'.¹⁰⁹ Although the expressions are different, they signify the same thing. We consider that this is true meaning of the word *jing Tian* (to revere and worship Heaven) which Your Majesty a few years ago deigned to write with his own hand on a tablet and bestow upon us for public display.¹¹⁰ We the foreign subjects of Your Majesty respond to them in this way according to our weak understanding, but since those things relate to Chinese customs, we do not dare to rely upon and trust in our own judgement. Thus we ask with every reverence Your Majesty not to disdain to teach us. We, the foreign subjects of Your Majesty, await his order with supreme veneration and humility.¹¹¹

The 20th day of the 10th month of the 39th year of Kangxi's reign,¹¹² the memorial was delivered into the hands of the emperor and the same day he answered as follows:

> 康熙三十九年十月二十日奏。是日奉旨：「這所寫甚好，有合大道，敬天及事君親、敬師長者，係天下通義。這就是無可改處。」

> The things you have written are well written, and fully agree with the Great Way (the True Teaching common to all mankind). The whole world has the common custom and notion of worshipping Heaven, serving rulers and parents, and respecting teachers and superiors. All the things contained in this writing are completely true and there is nothing that should be changed or corrected.¹¹³

From the emperor's explicit declaration which was promulgated throughout the empire it is clear that Europeans have no need for controversy or scruple in adopting the meaning of the Chinese Rites and Terms explained by the best commentator of all and by Chinese men of prime importance.¹¹⁴ Indeed, besides the emperor's

---

109 While the first two parts of the petition deal with the rites to Confucius and the ancestors, only the third part deals specifically with the Chinese Terms.
110 This refers to the visit of Kangxi on 12 July 1675 mentioned in the second paragraph above. In 1675, Emperor Kangxi offered to the Jesuits of Beijing an inscription with the two characters *jing Tian*. The preface of the *Confucius Sinarum philosophus* mentions the *jing Tian* inscription by Kangxi. See Meynard, ed., *Confucius Sinarum Philosophus*, p. 231. The papal bull *Ex illa die* (1715) forbade the inscription *jing tian* in all the churches of China.
111 We have translated from the Latin text provided by Noël in his book. For an English translation based on the Manchu text, see Stumpf, *The Acta Pekinensia*, pp. lxxxi–lxxxiii.
112 This corresponds to 30 November 1700.
113 Again, Noël provided a translation not from the Manchu but from the Chinese. The text in parenthesis is an addition by Noël. In the ARSI manuscript, the quote from Kangxi is followed by an alternative translation which is not present in the book: 'Others understand this way: The words you have written are well said. This coheres with the great way of human action, of reverence towards Heaven, of the service to king and parents, to the honour towards teachers and magistrates. This is the common opinion of men all over the earth, and this is as well the opinion of men in this whole empire, or *tianxia*. All the things are true, etc., same as above'.
114 When Antoine Thomas assumed the office of vice-provincial in June 1701, he planned to send a full set

declaration there are also testimonies of the nobility and top-rank scholars in Beijing, especially the elder brother of the emperor who dedicated himself to studies and scholarship;[115] Prince Sosan who was for 10 years Chief Minister, or *gelao*;[116] Prince Ming, Chief Minister for 15 years;[117] Prince Yisange, Chief Minister for 14 years;[118] men remarkable for their learning in Chinese letters;[119] doctor and *gelao* Zhang Ying, teacher of the emperor and of his sons for many years, and president of the Royal College of the Doctors, or *Hanlinyuan*;[120] I omit others.[121] They all not only approved what the emperor had approved in the petition, but also testified with greater detail and clarity that *Tian* and *Shangdi* can be used for God, and that the Chinese ritual towards the deceased contains nothing but political observance. Their testimonies, including the declaration of the emperor, are preserved in the archive of the Jesuits' residence in Beijing, and I think it would be useless to name them one after one because they have already been printed and it is easy for anyone to see them.[122]

But let us move now to even other testimonies which are even clearer about the meaning of *Tian* or *Shangdi*, since *Tian* and *Shangdi* are usually understood as interchangeable by the Chinese. The testimonies in Rome are sealed, and the ones in Beijing are kept in the archive of the emperor.[123]

---

of documents to Rome, including the Kangxi's *Brevis relatio* of 1700. In November 1701, he wrote a letter to Noël in Jiangxi asking him to prepare himself to return to Europe to bring documents; Standaert, *Chinese Voices*, p. 20.

115　Chang Ning 常寧 (1657–1703) was a younger brother of Kangxi. See Chan, *Chinese Books and Documents from the Jesuit Archives in Rome*, p. 268. The *Brevis relatio* (21ab) indicates Chang Ning correctly as younger brother of Kangxi, but our book has him as elder brother. The list of names which follows is not present in the ARSI manuscript. Noël follows the list of ten testimonies given in the *Brevis relatio*, but he mentions only five persons out of the ten.

116　Prince Sosan 索三 (died 1703?) or Songgotu 索額圖 in Manchu was the third son of Soni 索尼, and the chief negotiator for the Nerchinsk treaty of 1689, on which occasion he became a good friend of the Jesuits. His testimony is listed second and one of the longest in the *Brevis relatio* (22b–25a). See also Chan, *Chinese Books and Documents from the Jesuit Archives in Rome*, p. 268; Stumpf, *The Acta Pekinensia*, p. 157.

117　Mingzhu 明珠 (1675–1708), listed third in the *Brevis relatio* (25a–28a). As Chan remarks, he did not serve fifteen years as Grand Secretary or *gelao* but only twelve years. See Chan, *Chinese Books and Documents from the Jesuit Archives in Rome*, p. 269.

118　Isangga 伊桑阿 (1638–1723), listed fourth in the *Brevis relatio* (28a–29b).

119　Noël skips here the names of Kong Yuqi 孔毓圻 and Wang Xi 王熙; *Brevis relatio* (29b–30b).

120　Zhang Ying 張英 (1638–1708) was a member of the Hanlin Academy 翰林院 and was promoted in 1677 as Nanshufang 南書坊. He is mentioned seventh in the *Brevis relatio* (30b–31b). It is not clear why Noël mentions Zhang Ying and not Wang Xi since both held the position of Grand Secretary in 1701. See Standaert, *Chinese Voices*, p. 147.

121　Noël omits three other names. See *Brevis relatio* (31b–35a).

122　Among the ten names of the *Brevis relatio*, Noël and Castner in their *Summarium NAT* only mentioned six, curiously leaving out the four Manchu princes but including the six Han officers. See Standaert, *Chinese Voices*, p. 146.

123　The text from this paragraph onwards is not present in the ARSI manuscript (1703) but was added by Noël in 1708–1709 and was drawn from the first part of the *Acta Pekinensia*, the official documents related to the delegation of Charles-Thomas Maillard de Tournon (1668–1710) in China.

On 22 July 1706, the emperor sent two court servants, He-shi-heng [Henkama] and Zhao Chang 趙昌 to the most illustrious patriarch of Antioch who was then in Beijing (now a very eminent cardinal of the Holy Roman Church).[124] Through them the emperor told him: 'The people of your Christian Law say, "to worship the Master of Heaven" (*jing Tianzhu*) and the Chinese say, "to worship Heaven" (*jing Tian*). The expressions are different, but the meaning the same'.[125] Moreover, he ordered them to tell Lord Appiani,[126] the interpreter of our Very Illustrious Lord Patriarch: 'You, Bi Tianxiang (that is Lord Appiani's name in Chinese) have taken a name which sounds like "likeness of Heaven". Why did you not want to be called Bi Tianzhuxiang (This indicates that Lord Appiani himself understood the word *Tian* as the Lord of Heaven, not the material heaven since he would not want to be called likeness of material heaven but of the Lord of Heaven or God). Every country has its own customs for naming things, and it cannot be said that the reason and the teaching are different because of names and words'. When the Very Illustrious Patriarch had answered through his interpreter that Europeans in China did not use *Tianzhu* unless it had first been well explained, they told him: 'We ourselves did not use *Tian* unless it had first been well explained during many centuries. However, our mode of speech is much broader than yours because you only say Lord of Heaven, whereas we say Lord of Heaven, Earth, animals, plants, and all the living and non-living things'.[127]

Later, on 2 August 1706, the emperor summoned the Most Illustrious Bishop of Conon to Tartary for a meeting.[128] The emperor testified once more as follows to the bishop of Conon in presence of the court officers and many missionaries, including both secular priests and priests of the Society of Jesus: 'Have I not told you before that *Tian* means the Lord of Heaven, and that this a far more beautiful name for God than *Tianzhu* or *Tiandi wanwu zhi zhu* which is how you address God in China? For *Tianzhu* means only the Lord of Heaven, whereas *Tiandi wanwu zhi zhu* means the Lord of Heaven, Earth and the ten thousand things; but *Tian* means the Lord of Heaven, Earth and the universe. Tell me why people address me with *Wansui*, ten thousand years. According to your religion, this cannot be done because I am not ten thousand years old'. The Bishop of Conon answered: 'This is done to express the wish that Your Majesty live as long as possible'. The emperor told him: 'You have answered correctly, and you should learn from this that the terms and rites in China should not be understood merely as they sound or according to their external appearance'. Finally, towards the end of their conversation, he told him: 'As I said before, *Tian* and *Tianzhu* have the same meaning'.[129]

---

124 Tournon was created cardinal on 1 August 1707. Noël seems here ironic.
125 See Kilian Stumpf, *The Acta Pekinensia*, pp. 522–24.
126 Luigi Antonio Appiani (1663–1732) in Chinese Bi Leisi 畢類思 or Bi Tianxiang 畢天祥, a priest of the Congregation of the Mission (CM).
127 Those words of Kangxi on 22 July 1706 are recorded in Stumpf, *The Acta Pekinensia*, pp. 523–24.
128 This refers to Charles Maigrot, bishop of Conon.
129 This famous conversation between Kangxi and Maigrot on 2 August 1706 is recorded in Stumpf, *The Acta Pekinensia*, pp. 693–94.

The emperor thought that his public oral declaration on the authentic meaning of *Tian* was not sufficient. On 2 August, he ordered two court servants He-shi-heng and Zhao Chang to tell officially the Bishop of Conon in writing: 'I, the emperor, sought to open a path to you, by telling you that *jing Tian* is the same as when in your law you say *jing Tianzhu*'.[130] He also ordered that this text may be officially proclaimed and handed to the Most Illustrious Patriarch of Antioch, and on 11 August, the court servant He-shi-heng handed it to him.[131]

What, I ask, can be more clearly declared, more authoritatively affirmed, or more officially ordered? Can there remain any room for doubt about the meaning of *Tian*? Do judges have more powerful, efficacious, and clearer proofs when they bring judgement in civil and criminal cases? Could any malevolent person or an obstinate opponent of the China Mission say that the testimonies were extorted from the emperor and given to please the Society of Jesus? Would the emperor want to give discordant, absurd and false responses before his whole court, proclaim them in writing, and keep them in his inner archive, such that he may appear ignorant, fawning, and ridiculous to the Chinese today and in the future? What a remarkable objection! Please bring the same judgement about the emperor's other answers and testimonies. It seems impossible to add anything clearer to prove and demonstrate what we have affirmed: the terms *Tian* and *Shangdi* have the meaning of God in China.[132]

Finally, the testimony of the emperor and others about the petition mentioned above also encompasses the rituals and ceremonies performed by the Chinese to honour their deceased ancestors and teacher Confucius and publicly declares that they are performed in such a way that they are clearly a pure civil observance without any underlying superstition. Thus, it would seem that the following Treatise about the Chinese Rites to the deceased could be omitted and that I could stop my pen here. However, since people may be eager to know what the Chinese books themselves say about those things, what they prescribe, what ambiguities and obscurities they contain, what difficulties they create, I now proceed to discuss it.[133]

---

130   Those words of Kangxi to Maigrot on 2 August 1706 are recorded in Stumpf, *The Acta Pekinensia*, p. 578. The imperial decree to Maigrot is dated 2 August 1706 but delivered on 11 August 1706.
131   On 11 August 1706, Kangxi sent also a decree to Tournon. See Stumpf, *The Acta Pekinensia*, p. 579.
132   The words of Noël present on the printed text were written after August 1706 (interview between Kangxi and Maigrot). Since Noël expresses his hope of a decision of Rome in favour of the Chinese Rites and Terms, those passages were written before 25 September 1710, when Pope Clement XI published the decree *Cum Deus Optimus* (which had been secretly signed in 1704) condemning the Chinese Rites. This indicates that the final text should be dated 1709 or early 1710.
133   The Second Treatise on the Chinese Rites is not included in this translation. For the text, the reader may consult the *Philosophia Sinica* of 1711.

About the Authors

Daniel Canaris is a DECRA Fellow and lecturer in the Department of Italian Studies at the University of Sydney. His research focuses on Sino-Western exchange in the early modern period. After receiving his PhD from the University of Sydney in 2017, he has held fellowships in Germany, England, China and the United States. His first monograph, *Vico and China*, was published in the *Oxford University Studies in the Enlightenment* series.

Pierre Galassi, O.P., obtained his PhD in Systematic Theology from the Theological Faculty of Emilia Romagna (Bologna), with a particular focus on the theology of religions and evangelization in China. He is currently a BA student in Chinese Studies at Ca' Foscari University in Venice, and an adjunct professor of Sacramental Theology at the Theological Faculty of Emilia Romagna. His current research focuses on the role of metaphysics and theology in the study of the sacred, inculturation, and in particular the evangelization of China. His work has been published in journals such as *Divus Thomas* and *Sacra Doctrina*.

Thierry Meynard, S.J., is professor in the Department of Philosophy and director of the Archive for the Introduction of Western Knowledge at Sun Yat-sen University, Guangzhou. Prior book publications in English include: *The Jesuit Reading of Confucius* (2015), *The Religious Philosophy of Liang Shuming* (2011), *Confucius Sinarum Philosophus* (2011), and co-authored with Daniel Canaris, *A Brief Response on the Controversies over Shangdi, Tianshen and Linghun by Niccolò Longobardo* (2021); Dawei Pan, *A Brief Introduction to the Study of Human Nature by Giulio Aleni* (2020), and with Sher-shiueh Li, *Jesuit Chreia in Late Ming China* (2014).

Yves Vendé is currently a research fellow at the Université Catholique de Lille and an adjunct professor at the Centre Sèvres in Paris. After receiving his PhD from Sun Yat-sen University in 2018, where he was supervised by Chen Shaoming, he was a postdoctoral fellow at Loyola Marymount University. His current research focuses on cross-cultural Virtue Ethics and philosophical hermeneutics.

Wang Ge is an associate professor in the Department of Philosophy at Shanghai University of Finance and Economics. His research focuses on neo-Confucianism and Sino-Western exchange in the early modern period. After receiving his PhD from Sun Yat-sen University (Guangzhou) in 2014, he has held fellowships at Peking University, Beijing (2014–2016) and Sun Yat-sen University, Guangzhou (2016–2020). He has also been a Visiting Scholar at The Chinese University of Hong Kong, Hong Kong (2017), the Confucius Academy, Guiyang (2019), and Zhejiang University, Hangzhou (2019–2020).

Bibliography

Published Writings of Noël (Listed Chronologically)

1698

Noël, François [Wei Fangji 衛方濟], *Renzui zhizhong* 人罪至重 (Shanghai: Cimutang 慈母堂, 1698)

1704

Noël, François, and Kaspar Castner, *Memoriale, et summarium novissimorum testimoniorum Sinensium in prosecutione causae Sinen* (Rome, 1704)

Noël, François, and Kaspar Castner, *Responsio ad libros nuper editos sub nomine Illustriss. DD. Episcoporum Rosaliensis & Cononensis super controversiis Sinensibus* (Rome, 1704)

Noël, François, and Kaspar Castner, *Summarium novorum authenticorum testimoniorum tam Europaeorum quam Sinensium novissime e China allatorum circa veritatem et subsistentiam facti* [*Summarium NAT*] (Rome, 1704)

1706

Noël, François, 'Mémoire sur l'état des missions de la Chine, présenté en Latin à Rome, au Révérend Père Général de la Compagnie de Jésus, l'an 1703, par le Père François Noël, missionnaire de la même Compagnie, et depuis traduit en Français', in *Lettres édifiantes et curieuses* (Paris: Nicolas Le Clerc 1706), vol. 6, pp. 68–106; original document: ARSI, Fondo Gesuitico 730, 'Registro Lettere 1702–1703'; translations: German (1726), Spanish (1754), Italian (1827), Japanese (1970), Chinese (2005)

1710

Noël, François, *Observationes mathematicæ et physicæ in India et China factæ ab anno 1684 usque ad annum 1708* (Prague: Kamenicky, 1710)

1711

Noël, François, *Historica notitia rituum ac ceremoniarum Sinicarum in colendis parentibus ac benefactoribus defunctis* (Prague: Kamenicky, 1711)

Noël, François, *Philosophia Sinica tribus tractatibus* (Prague: Kamenicky, 1711)

Noël, François, *Sinensis imperii libri classici sex, nimirum Adultorum schola, Immutabile medium, Liber sententiarum, Memcius, Filialis observantia, Parvulorum schola* [*Libri sex*] (Prague: Kamenicky, 1711); French translations: 'Siao hio, ou l'école des enfans, sixième Livre classique, divisé en plusieurs chapitres & paragraphes', Jean-Baptiste Du Halde, *Description géographique, historique, chronologique, politique et physique de l'empire de la Chine et de la Tartarie Chinoise* (Paris: P. G. Le Mercier, 1735); Abbé Pluquet, *Les Livres classiques de l'empire de Chine recueillis par le Père Noël*, 7 vols (Paris: De Bures, 1784–1786)

1717

Noël, François, *Opuscula poetica* (Frankfurt: Thomas Fritsch, 1717)

1729

Noël, François, *Elegiae Marianae: sodalibus latinae Congregationis Minoris B. V. Mariae Elisabetham Visitantis oblatae Friburgi Helvetiorum* (Luzern: Henrici Ignatii Nicomedis Hautt, 1729)

Noël, François, *Serenissimi Delphini genethliacum carmen* (Lille: J.-B. de Moitemont, 1729), French translation: *Vers sur la naissance de Monseigneur le Dauphin*, trans. by Sr. Thiroux (Lille: G.-E. Vroye, s.d.)

1732

Noël, François, *Theologiae R.P. doctoris eximii Francisci Suarez, e Societate Jesu, summa* (Madrid: Antonio Sanz, 1732); other editions: *Theologiae R.P. doctoris eximii Francisci Suarez, e Societate Jesu, summa* (Cologne: Sumptibus Fratrum de Tournes, 1732); *Theologiae R.P. doctoris eximii Francisci Suarez, e Societate Jesu, summa* (Venice: Apud Nicolaum Pezzana, 1733)

1975

Noël, François, Letters to Duchess of Aveiro (facsimile), in Tenri University Library, ed., *The Far Eastern Catholic Missions 1663–1711: The Original Papers of the Duchess d'Aveiro*, vol. 2 (Tokyo: Yushodo, 1975), letter dated 23 December 1685 from Macao, p. 31; letter dated 27 September 1687 from Macao, p. 49; letter dated 27 August 1689 from Huai'an, p. 55; letter dated 18 August 1690 from Huai'an, p. 61; letter dated 5 November 1702 from Paris, p. 85; letter dated October 1709 from Rome, p. 99

Manuscripts of Noël

Archives françaises de la Compagnie de Jésus, Vanves, Autograph, 6 pages: 'Abrégé de l'histoire des guerres civiles de 1674 à 1686'

Archivum Romanum Societatis Iesu, Rome [ARSI], 'Doctrinae Sinicae brevis indagatio'; Fondo Gesuitico 724/4

—, 'Index Scriptorum et Librorum in Causa Sinensi'; Fondo Gesuitico 722/2

—, 'Relatio de statu Sinicae ecclesiae et progressu S. Fidei in Imperio Sinarum, ab anno 1692 quo data est per edictum Imperatoris Sinarum, praedicandae Legis Divinae libertas ad annum saecularem 1700'; Jap. Sin. 125, fols 200^r–231^v

—, 'Relatio P. Francisci Noël à Chinâ Romam missi cum P. Casparo Castner, de suo itinere'; Fondo Gesuitico 724/6

—, Letter dated 10 August 1690 from Huai'an to 'his dear brother'; Jap. Sin. 164, fols 283^r–284^v

—, Letter dated 4 October 1702 from London to the Superior General; Jap. Sin. 167, fols 50^r–51^v

—, Letter dated 23 October 1702 from Calais to the Superior General; Jap. Sin. 167, fol. 68

—, Letter dated 5 November 1702 from Paris to the Superior General; Jap. Sin. 167, fol. 77
—, Letter dated 30 December 1707 from Macao to the Superior General, Macao; Jap. Sin. 171, fols 200^r–211^v
—, Letter dated 1 July 1708 to Pope Clement XI from Bahia; Fondo Gesuitico 723/3
—, Letter dated 3 July 1708 from Bahia to the Superior General; Jap. Sin. 173, fol. 46
—, Letter dated 1 February 1709 from Genoa to the Superior General; Jap. Sin. 173, fol. 12
—, Memorandum to Pope Clement; Fondo Gesuitico 724/6
—, 'Testimonium Patris Francisci Noel …', dated 26 February 1710, Rome; Jap. Sin. 199, I, fol. 166
Bibliothèque municipale d'Arras 1103–1167, Fonds d'Advielle 1170 (1341–1342): *Doctrinae Sinicae brevis indagatio*, vol. 1 (394 pages), vol. 2 (416 pages plus supplement 9 pages)
BnF, collection Bréquigny 15 and 16: *Doctrinae Sinicae brevis indagatio, ex ipsis Sinarum libris eruta in qua dilucidantur pene omnes controversiae Sinenses*
—, collection Bréquigny 17: 2–70: *Historica notitia rituum*; 71–140: *De ethica Sinensi*
—, Manuscrits Français, Mélanges sur la Chine, 17239: fols 132–68: *Copie d'une lettre du P. François Noël, Jésuite, de Xamhay en la Chine, le 22 Juin 1688, à son frère le P. Nicolas Noël, Jésuite en la province Gallo-Belgique*. Digital copy available on Gallica. Joseph Dehergne transcribed the letter using the BnF document; see folder Noël, Archives of the French Jesuit Province, Vanves
Royal Library of Belgium, Brussels KBR 19.930: *Immutabile Medium ex sinico in latinum idioma traductum a P. Francisco Noël Societatis Jesu, Missionario Sinensi, Nancham in China, 1700*
—, Brussels KBR 19.931: *Mencius ex sinico in latinum idioma traductus a P. Francisco Noël Societatis Jesu, Missionario Sinensi, Nancham in China, 1700*
Saint Petersburg Library; Cordier *Bibl. sin.* p. 1395: *Liber Sententiarum ex sinico in latinum idioma traducta a P. Francisco Noël Societatis Jesu, Missionario Sinensi, Nancham in China, 1700*

Secondary Sources about Noël

Acta eruditorum (Leipzig: Typis Joh. Casp. Mulleri, 1711–12)
Abel-Rémusat, Jean-Pierre, 'François Noël', *Biographie universelle, ancienne et moderne*, vol. 31 (Paris: Michaud, 1822), pp. 335–38
—, 'François Noël, missionnaire à la Chine', *Nouveaux mélanges asiatiques*, 2 vols (Paris: Schubart & Heideloff, 1829), II, pp. 252–57
Alvin, Frédéric, 'Noël, François', in *Biographie nationale de Belgique*, 44 vols (Brussels: Académie royale de Belgique, 1866–1986), V (1899), pp. 765–69
Collani, Claudia von, 'François Noël and his Treatise on God in China', in *History of the Catholic Church in China: From its Beginning to the Scheut Fathers and 20th Century*, ed. by Ferdinand Verbiest Institute (Leuven: Ferdinand Verbiest Institute, 2015), pp. 23–64
Dehergne, Joseph, *Répertoire des Jésuites de Chine de 1552 à 1800* (Rome: Institutum Historicum Societatis Iesu, 1973), pp. 185–86
Igawa Yoshitsugu 井川義次, *Sōgaku no seisen: Kindai keimō e no michi* 宋學の西遷——近代啓蒙への道 (Kyōto: Jimbunshoin, 2009)
Jäger, Henrik, 'Mit Aristoteles die *Sishu* lesen: Das sinologische Werk von François Noël SJ', in *Leibniz and the European Encounter with China: 300 Years of Discours sur*

la théologie naturelle des Chinois, ed. by Li Wenchao (Stuttgart: Franz Steiner, 2017), pp. 129–47

—, 'Reading the Four Books with Aristotle: A Hermeneutical Approach to the Translation of the Confucian Classics by François Noël SJ (1651–1729)', *International Comparative Literature*, 1.3 (2018), 367–76

Kern, Iso, 'Die Vermittlung chinesischer Philosophie in Europa', in *Grundriss der Geschichte der Philosophie. Die Philosophie des 17. Jahrhunderts*, ed. by Jean-Pierre Schobinger (Basel: Schwabe, 1998), I, pp. 225–95

Kolmaš, Josef, 'François Noël (Franciscus Natalis) "Philosophia Sinica"', *Pojednání o věcech čínských* [Treatises on Chinese Matters] (Prague: Vyšehrad, 2015), pp. 143–62

Ledieu, Alcius, *Catalogue général des manuscrits des bibliothèques publiques de France: Tome 40, Supplêment – tome 1: Abbeville – Brest* (Paris: Plon, 1902)

Liščák, Vladimír, 'François Noël (1651–1729) and his Latin Translations of Confucian Classical Books Published in Prague in 1711', *Anthropologia Integra*, 6.2 (2015), 45–52; Chinese translation: Li Shijia 李世佳, 'Wei Fangji he 1711 nian zai Bulage chuban de Rujia jingdian Ladingyu fanyi' 衛方濟和1711年在布拉格出版的儒家經典拉丁語翻譯, *Shijiehanxue* 世界漢學 [World Sinology], 16 (2016), 103–12

Liu Yong 劉勇, 'Zhong wan Ming Lixue xueshuo de hudong yu diyuxing Lixue chuantong de xipuhua jincheng: yi Minxue wei zhongxin' 中晚明理學學說的互動與地域性理學傳統的系譜化進程——以「閩學」為中心, *Xinshixue* 新史學 [New History], 21.2 (2010), 1–6

Luo Ying 羅瑩, 'Qingchao lai Hua Yesuhuishi Wei Fangji jiqi Ruxue yishu yanjiu' 清朝來華耶穌會士衛方濟及其儒學譯述研究, *Beijing xingzheng xueyuan xuebao* 北京行政學院學報 [Journal of Beijing Administrative Institute], 1 (2015), 120–28

—, 'Yesuhuishi Wei Fangji jiqi Zhongyong Ladingwen yiben' 耶穌會士衛方濟及其《中庸》拉丁文譯本, *Revista do Instituto Politécnico de Macau*, 57 (2015), 132–42

Meynard, Thierry [Mei Qianli 梅謙立], *Confucius Sinarum Philosophus (1687): The First Translation of the Confucian Classics* (Rome: Institutum Historicum Societatis Iesu, 2011)

—, 'François Noël's Contribution to the Western Understanding of Chinese Thought: Taiji sive natura in the *Philosophia Sinica* (1711)', *DAO: A Journal of Comparative Philosophy*, 17.2 (2018), 219–30

—, *The Jesuit Reading of Confucius* (Boston: Brill, 2015)

—, 'Wei Fangji Zhongguo zhexue yinzheng zhongwen wenxiankao' 衛方濟《中國哲學》征引中文文獻考, *Xixue dongjian yanjiu* 西學東漸研究 [Research on the Introduction of Western Learning to the East], 10 (2021), 270–302

—, 'Yesuhuishi Wei Fangji dui guishen de lijie' 耶穌會士衛方濟對鬼神的理解, *Beijing xingzheng xueyuan xuebao* 北京行政學院學報 [Journal of Beijing Administrative Institute], 5 (2018), 110–15

—, 'Yesuhuishi Wei Fangji dui Tianren heyi de jieshou: Zhongguo zhexue dui Tian de shuxing' 耶穌會士衛方濟對「天人合一」的接受：《中國哲學》對「天」的屬性, *Zongjiao yu Lishi* 宗教與歷史 [Religion and History], 13 (2020), 25–57

Meynard, Thierry [Mei Qianli 梅謙立] and Wang Ge 王格, 'Chaoyue eryuan maixiang tongyi: Yesuhuishi Wei Fangji Zhongguo zhexue (1711) jiqi Rujia quanshixue de chutan' 超越二元，邁向統一：耶穌會士衛方濟《中國哲學》（1711年）及其儒家詮釋學的初探, *Zhexue yu wenhua* 哲學與文化 [Universitas], 522 (2017), 45–61

Mungello, David E., 'The First Complete Translation of the Confucian Books in the West', in *Collected Essays of the International Symposium on Chinese-Western Cultural Interchange in Commemoration of the 400th Anniversary of the Arrival of Matteo Ricci, S. J. in China*, ed. by Lo Kuang 羅光 (Taipei: Furen daxue chubanshe, 1983), pp. 515–41

Novotný, Daniel, 'François Noël, S. J. (1651–1729): Byli starověcí Číňané ateisté?' [François Noël, S. J. (1651–1729): Were the Ancient Chinese Atheists?], *Studia Theologica*, 16.3 (2014), 111–32

—, 2020, 'Suárez on Beings of Reason', *Conimbricenses.org Encyclopedia*, ed. by Mário Santiago de Carvalho and Simone Guidi, < www.conimbricenses.org/encyclopedia/suarez-on-beings-of-reason/>

Pan Feng-chuan 潘鳳娟, 'God, Sinner, and Saintly Governance: François Noël and *Ren zui zhi zhong*', in *Light a Candle: Encounters and Friendship with China: Festschrift in Honour of Angelo Lazzarotto P.I.M.E.*, ed. by Roman Malek and Gianni Criveller (Sankt Augustin: Monumenta Serica, 2010), pp. 159–98; Chinese translation: 'Qingchu Yesuhuishi Wei Fangji de renzuishuo yu shengzhilun' 清初耶穌會士衛方濟的人罪說與聖治論, *Xinshixue* 新史學, 23.1 (2012), 9–53

—, 'Wei Fangji de jingdian fanyi yu Zhongguo shuxie' 衛方濟的經典翻譯與中國書寫, *Bianyi luncong* 編譯論叢, 1 (2010), 189–212

—, 'Zhongguo liyi zhi zheng mailuo zhong de Xiaodao: Wei Fangji yu Xiaojing fanyi chutan' 中國禮儀之爭脈絡中的孝道：衛方濟與《孝經》翻譯初探 [Filial piety in the context of the Chinese Rites Controversy: François Noël's translation of *Xiaojing*], *Daofeng: Jidujiao wenhua pinglun* 道風：基督教文化評論 [Logos and Pneuma: Chinese Journal of Theology], 33 (2010), 67–95

Pfister, Louis, *Notices biographiques et bibliographiques sur les jésuites de l'ancienne mission de Chine, 1552–1773*, 2 vols (Shanghai: Imprimerie de la Mission catholique, 1932)

Rule, Paul, 'François Noël, SJ and the Chinese Rites Controversy', in *The History of the Relations between the Low Countries and China in the Qing Era (1644–1911)*, ed. by Willy Vande Walle and Noël Golvers (Leuven: Leuven University Press, 2003), pp. 137–65

Standaert, Nicolas, *Chinese Voices in the Rites Controversy* (Rome: Institutum Historicum Societatis Iesu, 2012)

Wesselius, Carel, 'The *Ethica Politica*: François Noël's (1651–1729) Description of Confucian Political Thought in his *Philosophia Sinica Tribus Tractatibus*' (unpublished MA thesis, Leiden University, 2020)

Witek, J. W., 'François Noël', in *Diccionario histórico de la Compañia de Jesús*, 4 vols (Rome, Institutum Historicum Societatis Iesu, 2001), III, pp. 2827–2828

Wong Ching Him 黃正謙 [Felix Wong], 'Lun Yesuhuishi Wei Fangji de Ladingwen Mengzi fanyi' 論耶穌會士衛方濟的拉丁文《孟子》翻譯, *Zhongguo wenhua yanjiusuo xuebao* 中國文化研究所學報 [Journal of Chinese Studies], 57 (2013), 133–72

—, '*The Unalterable Mean*: Some Observations on the Presentation and Interpretation of *Zhongyong* of François Noël, SJ', *Zhongguo wenhua yanjiusuo xuebao* 中國文化研究所學報 [Journal of Chinese Studies], 60 (2015), 197–224

Zhu Qianzhi 朱謙之, *Zhongguo sixiang duiyu Ouzhou wenhua zhi yingxiang* 中國思想對於歐洲文化之影響 (Taiyuan: Shanxi chuban chuanmei jituan, 2014)

Other Sources

Aleni, Giulio, *A Brief Introduction to the Study of Human Nature*, ed. and trans. by Thierry Meynard and Dawei Pan (Boston: Brill, 2020)

Aquinas, Thomas, *Commentary on the Gospel of John*, trans. by Fabian Larcher and James A. Wiesheipl, 3 vols (Washington: The Catholic University of America Press, 2010)

—, *The Summa Theologica of Saint Thomas Aquinas*, trans. by Fathers of the English Dominican Province, rev. by Daniel J. Sullivan, 2 vols (Chicago: Encyclopaedia Britannica Inc., 1952)

—, *Super Evangelium S. Ioannis lectura*, c. 6, lectio 3, § VII; *Commentary on the Gospel of John*, trans. by Fabian Larcher and James A. Wiesheipl, 3 vols (Washington: The Catholic University of America Press, 2010)

—, *Truth: Questions I–XXIX*, trans. by Robert W. Mulligan, 3 vols (Eugene: Wipf and Stock Publishers, 2008)

Aristotle, *De Anima*, trans. and ed. by Mark Shiffman (Newburyport: Focus Publishing R. Pullins Co., 2011)

—, *Metaphysics: Book Λ*, trans. and ed. by Lindsay Judson (Oxford: Clarendon Press, 2019)

Atti imperiali autentici, di vari trattati, passati nella regia corte di Pekino, tra l'imperatore della Cina, e M. Patriarca Antiocheno, al presente Sig. Cardinale di Tournon negli anni 1705, e 1706 (Cologne, 1710)

Bary, William Theodore de, 'The Uses of Neo-Confucianism: A Response to Professor Tillman', *Philosophy East and West*, 43.3 (1993), 541–55

—, *Sources of Chinese Tradition* (New York: Columbia University Press, 2000)

'Extracta ex monumentis Judaeorum (nella Cina)' BNCVE, Fondo Gesuitico, MS 1383/3

Bodnar, Istvan, and Pierre Pellegrin, 'Aristotle's Physics and Cosmology', in *A Companion to Ancient Philosophy*, ed. by Mary Louise Gill and Pierre Pellegrin (Malden, MA: Blackwell, 2006), pp. 270–91

Bouvet, Joachim, *Gujin jing Tian jian* 古今敬天鑑 [Examination of 'revere Heaven' in past and present]; facsimile: Nicolas Standaert and Ad Dudink, eds, *Chinese Christian Texts from the National Library of France*, 26 vols (Taipei: Ricci Institute, 2009), XXVI, pp. 25–160 (BnF, MS Chinois 7161); XXVI, pp. 161–330 (BnF, MS Chinois 7162); punctuated edition (based on a comparison between BnF, MS Chinois 7161 and BnF, MS Chinois 7162): Zhou Zhenhe 周振鶴, *Ming Qing zhiji xifang chuanjiaoshi Hanji congkan* 明清之際西方傳教士漢籍叢刊, 6 vols (Nanjing: Fenghuang chubanshe, 2013), III, pp. 113–319

Brancati, Francesco, *De sinensium ritibus politicis acta. seu R. P. Francisci Brancati, Societatis Jesu, apud Sinas per annos 34. missionarii, responsio apologetica ad R. P. Dominicum Navarette Ordinis Praedicatorum* (Paris: Nicolas Pepié, 1700)

Brockey, Liam Matthew, *Journey to the East* (Cambridge, MA: Harvard University Press, 2007)

Busquets Alemany, Ana, 'Más allá de la *Querella de los Ritos*: el testimonio sobre China de Fernández de Navarrete', *Anuario Historia de la Iglesia*, 24 (2015), 229–50

Caballero, Antonio de Santa María [Antoine de Sainte Marie], *Traité sur quelques points importants de la mission de la Chine* (Paris: Guérin, 1701)

Canaris, Daniel, 'Mediating Humanism and Scholasticism in Longobardo's "Resposta Breve" and Ricci's Reading of Confucianism', *Renaissance Quarterly*, 74.2 (2021), 498–527

Chan, Albert, *Chinese Books and Documents in the Jesuit Archives in Rome: A Descriptive Catalogue, Japonica-Sinica I–IV* (Armonk: M. E. Sharpe, 2002)

Chan Wing-Tsit 陳榮捷, ed., *A Sourcebook in Chinese Philosophy* (Princeton: Princeton University Press, 1963)

Chen chun 陳淳, *Beixi ziyi* 北溪字義 (Beijing: Zhonghua shuju, 1983)

Chen Lai 陳來, 'Songdai lixue huayu de xingcheng' 宋代理學話語的形成, *Hebei xuekan* 河北學刊, 1 (2008), 32–35

—, *Song Ming lixue* 宋明理學 (Shanghai: Huadong shifan daxue chubanshe, 2004)

Chen Lisheng 陳立勝, 'Lixuejia yu yulu ti' 理學家與語錄體, *Shehui kexue* 社會科學, 1 (2015), 129–42

—, 'Zhuzi dushufa: quanshi yu quanshi zhi wai' 朱子讀書法：詮釋與詮釋之外, in *Song Ming ruxue zhong de 'shenti' yu 'quanshi' zhi wei* 宋明儒學中的「身體」與「詮釋」之維 (Beijing: The Commercial Press, 2019), pp. 193–96

Chen Shaoming 陳少明, 'Jingdian shijie zhong de ren, shi, wu––dui Zhongguo zhexue shuxie fangshi de yi zhong sikao' 經典世界中的人、事、物——對中國哲學書寫方式的一種思考, *Zhongguo shehui kexue* 中國社會科學, 5 (2005), 57–67

Chen Yun 陳贇, 'Zifa de zhixu yu wuwei de zhengzhi: Zhongguo gudian sixiang zhong de zhengzhi zhengdangxing wenti' 自發的秩序與無為的政治———中國古典思想中的政治正當性問題, *Shehui kexue* 社會科學, 1 (2003), 79–86

Cheng, Anne, *Histoire de la pensée chinoise* (Paris: Seuil, 1997)

Cheng Liaoyuan 程燎原, 'Xingfa, Tianfa, Ziranfa: Qing mo de yilun lüeshu'「性法」、「天法」、「自然法」：清末的譯論略述, *Jindai fa yanjiu* 近代法研究 (Beijing: Beijing daxue chubanshe, 2007), vol. 1, pp. 95–106

Cheu king, trans. by Séraphin Couvreur (Taipei: Éditions Kuangchi Press, 1966)

Ching, Julia 秦家懿, *The Religious Thought of Chu Hsi* (Oxford: Oxford University Press, 2000)

Churchill, Awnsham, and John Churchill, eds, *A Collection of Voyages and Travels*, 6 vols (London: John Walthoe, 1732)

Cicero, *The Nature of the Gods (De Natura Deorum)*, trans. by H. Rackham (Cambridge, MA: Harvard University Press, 1933)

—, *On the Republic*, trans. by Clinton Walker Keyes (Cambridge, MA: Harvard University Press, 1928)

—, *On the Republic and On the Laws*, trans. by David Fott (New York: Cornell University Press, 2014)

Clooney, Francis, *Western Jesuit Scholars in India* (Boston: Brill, 2020)

Cobo, Juan, *Beng Sim Po Cam o Espejo rico del claro corazón*, Biblioteca Nacional de Madrid, MS 6040; Madrid: Librería General, 1959

Collani, Claudia von, *Die Figuristen in der Chinamission* (Frankfurt: Lang, 1981)

—, 'Jing Tian: The Kangxi Emperor's Gift to Ferdinand Verbiest in the Rites Controversy', in *Ferdinand Verbiest, 1623–1688*, ed. by John W. Witek (Nettetal: Steyler Verlag, 1994), pp. 453–70

—, *P. Joachim Bouvet S. J., Sein Leben und sein Werk* (Nettetal: Steyler, 1985)

Commentarii Collegii Conimbricensis Societatis Iesu, in octo libros Physicorum Aristotelis Stagiritae (Coimbra: Antonius à Mariz, 1592)

Copleston, Frederick, *A History of Philosophy. Volume 3: Late Medieval and Renaissance Philosophy* (New York: Doubleday, 1993)

Cornelius à Lapide, *Commentaria in Epistulam ad Romanos* (Lyon, 1664)

—, *Commentarius in Pentatheucum Mosis* (Antwerp: Martin Nuyts, 1627)

—, *In omnes divi Pauli Epistolas commentaria* (Lyon, 1683)

Couplet, Philippe, Prospero Intorcetta, François de Rougemont, and Christian Herdtrich, *Confucius Sinarum philosophus, sive, Scientia sinensis latine exposita* (Paris: Apud Danielem Horthemels, 1687)

Daxue & Zhongyong, trans. and ed. by Ian Johnston and Wang Ping (Hong Kong: Chinese University of Hong Kong Press, 2012)

Deferrari, Joseph, *A Lexicon of St Thomas Aquinas Based on the Summa Theologica and Selected Passages of His Other Works* (Washington, DC: Catholic University of America Press, 1948)

Dehergne, Joseph, and Donald Leslie, *Juifs de Chine* (Rome: Institutum Historicum Societatis Iesu, 1984)

Delattre, Pierre, ed., *Les Établissements des jésuites en France depuis quatre siècles*, vol. 2 (Enghien, Belgium: Institut supérieur de théologie, 1953)

Deus Ramos, João de, 'Tomás Pereira, *Jing Tian* and Nerchinsk', *In the Light and Shadow of an Emperor*, ed. by Artur Wardega and António Vasconcelos de Saldanha (Newcastle upon Tyne: Cambridge Scholars, 2012)

Dudink, Ad [Adrian], 'The Image of Xu Guangqi as Author of Christian Texts', in *Statecraft and Intellectual Renewal in Late Ming China*, ed. by Catherine Jami, Peter Engelfriet, and Gregory Blue (Leiden: Brill, 2001), pp. 99–152

—, 'The Inventories of the Jesuit House at Nanking, Made Up during the Persecution of 1616–1617 (Shen Que, "Nan gong shu du", 1620)', in *Western Humanistic Culture Presented to China by Jesuit Missionaries (XVII–XVIII Centuries)*, ed. by Federico Massini (Rome: Institutum Historicum Societatis Iesu, 1996), pp. 119–57

Fastiggi, Robert, 'Francisco Suárez and the Non-Believers', *Pensamiento: Revista de Investigación e Información Filosófica*, 74.279 (2018), 263–70

Filippucci, Francesco Saviero, 'Tractatus P.is Francisci Xaverij Philippucci de Ritibus Sinicis', Rome, Biblioteca nazionale centrale Vittorio Emmanuele [BNCVE], Ges., 1248/3

Finnis, John, *Natural Law and Natural Rights* (Oxford: Clarendon Press, 1980)

Fung Yu-lan 馮友蘭, *A History of Chinese Philosophy*, 2 vols (Princeton: Princeton University Press, 1983)

—, *A Short History of Chinese Philosophy*, ed. by Derk Bodde (New York: Free Press, 1976)

Fu Xihong 傅錫洪, Songdai lixue guishenlun de xingcheng 宋代理學鬼神論的形成, *Zhongshan daxue xuebao* 中山大學學報, 5 (2018), 149–47

Gaubil, Antoine, *Correspondance de Pékin, 1722–1759*, ed. by Renée Simon (Geneva: Librairie Droz, 1970)

Gernet, Jacques, *Chine et christianisme: action et réaction* (Paris: Gallimard, 1982)

Golvers, Noël, *François de Rougemont, S. J., Missionary in Ch'ang-shu (Chiang-nan)* (Leuven: Leuven University Press, 1999)

Grendler, Paul, 'Jesuit Schools and Universities in Europe 1548–1773', *Brill Research Perspectives in Jesuit Studies*, 1 (2019), 1–118

Gu Yanwu 顧炎武, 'Yu Shi Yushan shu' 與施愚山書, in *Gu Tinglin Shiwen ji* 顧亭林詩文集 (Beijing: Zhonghua shuju, 1983)

Guzzo, Augusto, Vittorio Mathieu, and Virgilio Melchiorre, 'NATURA (nature; Natur; nature; naturaleza)', in *Enciclopedia filosofica*, ed. by Centro di Studi Filosofici di Gallarate, 12 vols (Milan: Bompiani, 2008), VIII, pp. 7729–48

Hadot, Pierre, *Le voile d'Isis: Essai sur l'histoire de l'idée de Nature* (Paris: Gallimard, 2008)

Han Lin 韓霖, annotated by Sun Shangyang 孫尚揚 and Xiao Qinghe 肖清和, *Duoshu jiaozhu* 鐸書校注 (Beijing: Huaxia chubanshe, 2008)

Han Qi 韩琦 and Wu Min 吴旻, *Xichao chongzheng ji, Xichao ding'an* 熙朝崇正集, 熙朝定案 (Beijing: Zhonghua shuju, 2006)

Huang Xingtao 黃興濤, *Mingqing zhiji xixue wenben* 明清之際西學文本 (Beijing: Zhonghua shuju, 2013)

Huang Zhongxi 黃宗羲, *Ming Ru xue'an* 明儒學案 (Beijing: Zhonghua shuju, 2008)

Imago primi saeculi Societatis Jesu (Antwerp: Officina Plantiniana, 1640)

Intorcetta, Prospero, *Sapientia Sinica* (Jianchang, 1662)

—, *Testimonium de cultu sinensi, 1668* (Paris: Nicolas Pepié, 1700)

Jensen, Lionel, *Manufacturing Confucianism* (Durham, NC: Duke University Press, 1997)

Jingyin Wenyuange Siku quanshu 景印文淵閣四庫全書 (Taipei: Taiwan shangwu yinshuguan, 1986)

Julien, Stanislaus, *Meng tseu vel Mencium inter sinenses philosophos, ingenio, doctrina, nominisque claritate Confucio proximum* (Paris: Societatis Asiaticae et Comitis de Lasteyrie impensis, 1824)

Kircher, Athanasius, *China monumentis … illustrata* (Amsterdam: Jacob van Meurs, 1667)

Knebel, Sven K., 'Entre logique mentaliste et métaphysique conceptualiste: la distinctio rationis ratiocinantis', *Les Études philosophiques*, 61.2 (2002), 145–68

Lactantius, *On the Anger of God*, trans. by William Fletcher, *The Works of Lactantius*, vol. 22 (Edinburgh: T. & T. Clark, 1871)

Larrimore, Mark, 'Orientalism and Antivoluntarism in the History of Ethics: On Christian Wolff's "Oratio de Sinarum Philosophia Practica"', *The Journal of Religious Ethics*, 28.2 (2000), 189–219.

Legge, James, *The Sacred Books of China: The Texts of Confucianism*, vol. 1 (Oxford: Clarendon Press, 1879)

—, *The Works of Mencius* (Hong Kong: At the author's; London: Trübner & Co., 1861)

Leibniz, Gottfried, *Discourse on the Natural Theology of the Chinese*, trans. and ed. by Daniel Cook and Henry Rosemont (Hawaii: University of Hawaii Press, 1977)

Li Tiangang, *Ming Qing Tianzhujiao sanzhushi wenjianzhu* 明清天主教三柱石文箋注 [Catholic documents of Xu Guangqi, Li Zhizao, Yang Tingyun] (Hong Kong: Daofeng, 2007)

Liu Yu, *Harmonious Disagreement: Matteo Ricci and his closest Chinese friends* (New York: Peter Lang, 2015)

Lonergan, Bernard J. F., *Verbum: Word and Idea in Aquinas*, ed. by Frederick E. Crowe and Robert M. Doran (Toronto: Lonergan Research Institute – University of Toronto Press, 2005)

Longobardo, Niccolò, *A Brief Response on the Controversies over Shangdi, Tianshen and Linghun*, ed. by Thierry Meynard and Daniel Canaris (Singapore: Palgrave Macmillan, 2021)

Loyola, Ignatius of, *Spiritual Exercises and Selected Works*, ed. by George E. Ganns (New York: Paulist Press, 1991)

Lukács, Ladislaus, ed., *Monumenta paedagogica Societatis Jesu*, 7 vols (Rome: Institutum Historicum Societatis Jesu, 1986)

Lundbaek, Knud, 'Notes sur l'image du Néo-Confucianisme dans la littérature européenne du XVIIe siècle à la fin du XIXe siècle', in *Actes du 3e Colloque International de Sinologie* (Paris: Les Belles Lettres, Cathasia, 1983), pp. 131–76

Malebranche, Nicolas, *Œuvres complètes* (Paris: Vrin, 1958)

Mao Heng 毛亨 zhuan, Zheng Xuan 鄭玄 jian, Kong Yingda 孔穎達 shu: *Mao shi zhengyi* 毛詩正義 (Beijing: Beijing daxue chubanshe, 2000)

Meng Qingnan 孟慶楠, 'Deyi zhi fu: *Shi* de jingdianhua ji qi yiyi' 德義之府：《詩》的經典化及其意義, *Zhongguo ruxue* 中國儒學, 13 (Beijing: Zhongguo shehui kexue chubanshe, 2019)

Meynard, Thierry, 'Conflicting Interpretations on the *Collected Statutes of the Ming Dynasty*: the Debate between Navarrete and Brancati on the Ritual to Confucius in Canton in 1668', in *Crossing Borders: Sinology in Translation Studies*, edited by T. H. Barrett and Lawrence Wang-chi Wong (Hong Kong: Chinese University Press, 2022), pp. 1–36

—, ed., *Confucius Sinarum Philosophus (1687): The First Translation of the Confucian Classics* (Leiden: Brill, 2011)

—, 'Fan Shouyi, a Bridge between China and the West under the Rites Controversy', *Annales Missiologici Posnanienses*, 22 (2017), 21–31

—, *The Jesuit Reading of Confucius The First Complete Translation of the Lunyu (1687) Published in the West* (Leiden: Brill, 2015)

—, 'Leibniz as Proponent of Neo-Confucianism in Europe', *Studia Leibnitiana Sonderhefte*, 52 (2017), 179–95

—, 'La première traduction des Entretiens de Confucius en Europe: entre le li néo-confucéen et la ratio classique', *Études chinoises*, 30 (2011), 173–92

—, 'Review of *Harmonious Disagreement* by Liu', in *Archivum Historicum Societatis Iesu*, 85.169 (2016), 245–48

Meynard, Thierry, and Roberto Villasante, *La filosofía moral de Confucio por Michele Ruggieri SJ: La primera traducción de las obras de Confucio al español en 1590* (Madrid: Mensajero – Sal Terrae, 2018)

Mittelstrass, Jürgen, 'Nature and Science in the Renaissance', *Metaphysics and Philosophy of Science in the Seventeenth and Eighteenth Centuries: Essays in Honour of Gerd Buchdahl*, ed. by R. S. Woolhouse (Dordrecht: Kluwer Academic Publishers, 1988), pp. 17–43

Morali, Ilaria, '*Religioni ac boni artibus*: l' "apostolato scientifico" dei Gesuiti in Cina', in *Pianeta Galileo 2009*, ed. by Alberto Peruzzi (Florence: Regione Toscana – Consiglio Regionale, 2009), pp. 399–415

Mou Zongsan 牟宗三, *Shengming de xuewen* 生命的學問 (Guilin: Guangxi shifan daxue chubanshe, 2005)

—, *Zhongguo zhexue de tezhi* 中國哲學的特質, in *Mou Zongsan xiansheng quan ji* 牟宗三先生全集 (Taipei: Lianjing chuban shiye youxian gongsi, 2003), vol. 28

Mungello, David E., *Curious Land: Jesuit Accommodation and the Origins of Sinology* (Honolulu: University of Hawaii Press, 1985)

—, *The Forgotten Christians of Hangzhou* (Honolulu: University of Hawaii Press, 1994)

—, 'The Reconciliation of Neo-Confucianism with Christianity in the Writings of Joseph de Prémare, S. J.', *Philosophy East and West*, 26.4 (1976), 389–410

—, *The Silencing of Jesuit Figurist Joseph de Prémare in Eighteenth-Century China* (Lanham: Lexington Books, 2019)

—, 'Unearthing the Manuscripts of Bouvet's *Gujin* after Nearly Three Centuries', *China Mission Studies*, 10 (1988), 34–61

Murray, Chris, 'Coleridge's Daoism? Joseph Needham, Dominican Sinology, and Romantic Pantheism', *The Wordsworth Circle*, 51.2 (2020), 205–20

Navarette, Domingo, *Controversias antiguas y modernas entre los missionarios de la gran China* (Madrid, 1679)

—, *Tratados históricos, políticos, ethicos, y religiosos de la monarchia de China* (Madrid, 1676)

Needham, Joseph, *Science and Civilization in China. Volume 2: History of Scientific Thought* (Cambridge: Cambridge University Press, 1959)

Ockham, *Summa totius logicæ*, ed. by Ph. Boehner, G. Gal, and S. Brown (Saint Bonaventure, N.Y.: Franciscan Institute of St. Bonaventure, 1974)

Olmi, Antonio, *P. Matteo Ricci e san Tommaso d'Aquino* (Bologna: Edizioni Studio Domenicano, 2020)

O'Malley, John W., *The First Jesuits* (Cambridge, MA: Harvard University Press, 1993)

Padberg, John W., ed., *The Constitutions of the Society of Jesus and Their Complementary Norms: A Complete English Translation of the Official Latin Texts* (Saint Louis: The Institute of Jesuit Sources, 1996)

Perkins, Franklin, *Leibniz and China: A Commerce of Light* (Cambridge: Cambridge University Press, 2014)

Pidel, Aaron, 'Francisco Suárez on Religion and Religious Pluralism', in *Francisco Suárez (1548–1617): Jesuits and the Complexities of Modernity*, ed. by Robert Alexander Maryks and Juan Antonio Senent de Frutos (Leiden: Brill, 2019), pp. 128–53

Prémare, Joseph de, 'Essai sur la philosophie des Chinois Canton, 10 Septembre 1728', *Annales de la Philosophie Chrétienne*, 17 (1861), 375–404

Pseudo-Dionysius the Areopagite, *The Divine Names and the Mystical Theology*, trans. and ed. by John D. Jones (Milwaukee: Marquette University Press, 1999)

Qiu Wenzhuang gong congshu 丘文莊公叢書 [Collection of writings by Qiu Jun] (Taipei: Editorial and Publishing Committee for the Collective Works of Qiu Jun 丘文莊公叢書輯印委員, 1972)

Ratio atque institutio studiorum Societatis Iesu (1586, 1591, 1599), ed. by Ladislaus Lukàcs, vol. 5 of *Monumenta paedagogica Societatis Iesu*, 7 vols (Rome: Institutum Historicum Societatis Iesu, 1986)

Ricci, Matteo, *Lettere (1580–1609)*, ed. by Francesco D'Arelli (Macerata: Quodlibet, 2001)

—, *Le sens réel de Seigneur du Ciel*, trans. Thierry Meynard (Paris: Les Belles Lettres, 2013)

—, *The True Meaning of the Lord of Heaven*, ed. by Thierry Meynard (Boston: Jesuit Sources, 2016)

Rivière, Jean, 'Quelques antécédents patristiques de la formule "Facienti quod in se est"', *Revue des Sciences Religieuses*, 7.1 (1927), 93–97

Rosso, Antonio Sisto, *Apostolic Legations to China of the Eighteenth Century* (South Passadena, California: P. D. and Ione Perkins, 1948)

Ruggieri, Michele, *Disciplina de los varones*, San Lorenzo de El Escorial, MS c.III-2

—, 'Diversorum autorum sententiae ex diversis codicibus collectae, e Sinensi lingua in Latinam translatae' NCVE, Fondo Gesuitico, MS [3314] 1185, fols 78ʳ–93ᵛ

—, *Michele Ruggieri's* Tianzhu shilu *(The True Record of the Lord of Heaven, 1584)*, ed. and trans. by Daniel Canaris (Leiden: Brill, 2022)

Rule, Paul, *K'ung-tzu or Confucius?* (Sydney: Allen and Unwin, 1986)

Sang Jingyu 桑靖宇 'Zhu Xi zhexue zhong de Tian yu Shangdi' 朱熹哲學中的天與上帝, *Wuhan daxue xuebao* 武漢大學學報 [Wuhan University Journal], 64.2 (2011), 21–26

Seneca, *Epistles*, trans. by Richard M. Gummere (Cambridge, MA: Harvard University, 1925)

Schloesser, Stephen, 'Accommodation as a Rhetorical Principle. Twenty Years after John O'Malley's The First Jesuits (1993)', *Journal of Jesuit Studies*, 1 (2014), 347–72

Smith, Kurt, *Matter Matters: Metaphysics and Methodology in the Early Modern Period* (Oxford: Oxford University Press, 2010)

Solution de la question soy-disant curieuse [ARSI, Jap. Sin. 197 II, fols 227–30], 1719

Song Liming 宋黎明, 'Luo Wenzhao haishi Luo Wenzao? Wei Zhongguo shou wei guoji zhujiao Luo zhujiao zhengming' 羅文炤還是羅文藻?:為中國首位國籍主教羅主教正名 [Luo Wenzhao or Luo Wenzao?: A study on the Chinese name of the first Chinese bishop Gregorio Lopez (1617–1691)], *Haijiaoshi yanjiu* 海交史研究 [Journal of Maritime History Studies], 3 (2019), 40–51

Song Yecao 宋野草, *Cai Qing Yixue sixiang yanjiu* 蔡清易學思想研究 (Beijing: Zhongguo shehui kexue chubanshe, 2015)

Spinoza, Baruch, *Ethics*, trans. by Edwin Curley (London: Penguin, 1996)

Spruit, Leen, *Species intelligibilis*, 2 vols (Leiden: Brill, 1995)

Standaert, Nicolas [Zhong Mingdan 鐘鳴旦], *Keqin de Tianzhu: Qing chu jidujiaotu lun 'di' tan 'tian'* 可親的天主：清初基督教徒論「帝」談「天」(Taipei: Guangqi chubanshe, 1998)

Standaert, Nicolas, and Ad [Adrian] Dudink, eds, Chinese Christian Texts Database (CCT-Database) <http://www.arts.kuleuven.be/sinology/cct>

—, *Chinese Christian Texts from the National Library of France*, 26 vols (Taipei: Ricci Institute, 2009)

—, *Chinese Christian Texts from the Roman Archives of the Society of Jesus* (Taipei: Ricci Institute, 2002)

Stumpf, Kilian, *The Acta Pekinensia or Historical Records of the Maillard de Tournon Legation: Volume I, December 1705 – August 1706*, ed. by Paul Rule and Claudia von Collani (Rome: Institutum Historicum Societatis Iesu, 2015)

Suárez, Francisco, *Opera omnia*, 28 vols (Paris: Vivès, 1856–1878)

Su Dechao 蘇德超, 'Zai lun "luoji zaixian"' 再論「邏輯在先」, *Jiangsu shehui kexue* 江蘇社會科學, 4 (2011)

Tang Yijie 湯一介, *Rudaoshi yu neizaichaoyue wenti* 儒道釋與內在超越問題 (Nanchang: Jiangxi renmin chubanshe, 1991)

'Testimonium de iuramento a quattuor iesuitis emisso, Cantone 5 Octobris 1687', in *Sinica Franciscana*, vol. 6.1, ed. by G. Mensaert (Rome: Collegii S. Bonaventurae, 1961), pp. 489–90

Thomas, Antoine, *Brevis relatio eorum quae spectant ad declarationem Sinarum Imperatoris Kam Hi circa caeli Confucii et avorum cultum* (Peking, 1701; Augsburg and Dillingen: Johann Kaspar Bencard, 1703)

Tillman, Hoyt Cleveland, 'A New Direction in Confucian Scholarship: Approaches to Examining the Differences between Neo-Confucianism and Tao-Hsüeh', *Philosophy East and West*, 43.3 (1993), 455–74

Tranquillus, Thomas Albert, *Theses ex Universa Philosophia* (Prague: Literis Danielis Michalek, 1682)

Vendé, Yves, 'Hermeneutical Conflicts on Zhu Xi — Some Remarks about Late 19th Century Debate De Harlez and Le Gall', *Lumen: A Journal of Catholic Studies*, 5.2 (2017), 23–54

Wang Bi 王弼 *zhu*, Kong Yingda 孔穎達 *shu*, *Zhouyi zhengyi* 周易正義 (Beijing: Beijing daxue chubanshe, 2000)

Wang Ge 王格, *Cong Tian dao Tianzhu de Ruye huitong quanshi: Fandigang suocang Lun Rujia zhi Tian, Taiji yu Tianzhu* 從「天」到「天主」的儒耶會通詮釋——梵蒂岡所藏《論儒家之天、太極與天主》析論 [Confucian-Christian Comprehensive Hermeneutic from Heaven to the Lord of Heaven; Analysis of the Discourse on the Confucian Notions of Heaven, *taiji* and on the Lord of Heaven], *Guoji hanxue* 國際漢學, 19.2 (2019), 78–85

—, '"Gewu qiongli": wan Ming Xiyang zhexue yu Song Ming lixue zhi jian de huayu jingzheng' 「格物窮理」：晚明西洋哲學與宋明理學之間的話語競爭, *Shijie zhexue* 世界哲學, 4 (2021), 123–31

—, 'Yesuhuishi *Lunyu* fanyi (1687 nian) zhong de "guxue" qingxiang' 耶穌會士《論語》翻譯（1687年）中的「古學」傾向, *Xixue dongjian yanjiu* 西學東漸研究, vol. 6 (Beijing: The Commercial Press, 2017), pp. 109–23

—, 'Wang Yangming "Zhixing heyi" yili zaitan' 王陽明「知行合一」義理再探, *Daode yu wenming* 道德與文明, 5 (2015), 137–42

—, '"Zhongguo zhexue" heyi zhengdang de zui zao lunshuo–– Ming Qing zhi ji Xiren zhi zhengyan' 「中國哲學」何以正當的最早論說——明清之際西人之證言, *Zhexue yanjiu* 哲學研究, 7 (2019), 57–66

—, 'Zhou Rudeng de jingdian quanshi: yi qi sishuxue yu shixue wei zhu de tantao' 周汝登的經典詮釋——以其四書學與詩學為主的探討, *Kongzi yanjiu* 孔子研究, 4 (2015), 103–10

Wang, Robin, 'Zhou Dunyi's Diagram of the Supreme Ultimate Explained (*Taijitu shuo*): A Construction of the Confucian Metaphysics', *Journal of the History of Ideas*, 66.3 (2005), 307–23

Wang Shouren 王守仁, *Wang Yangming quanji* 王陽明全集 (Hangzhou: Zhejiang guji chubanshe, 2010)

Wang Suqin 王素琴, 'Cai Qing jiqi Sishu mengyin yanjiu' 蔡清及其《四書蒙引》研究 (unpublished doctoral thesis, National Taichung University of Education, 2019)

Weststeijn, Thijs, 'Spinoza sinicus: An Asian Paragraph in the History of the Radical Enlightenment', *Journal of the History of Ideas*, 68.4 (2007), 537–61

Witeck, John, *Controversial Ideas in China and in Europe: A Biography of Jean-François Foucquet* (Rome: Institutum Historicum Societatis Iesu, 1982)

Wu Liwei 吳莉葦, *Zhongguo liyi zhizheng* 中國禮儀之爭 (Shanghai: Shanghai guji chubanshe, 2007)

Wu Zhen 吳震, 'Shen xin jifa "jingzuo":Shi xi zhuzixue de xiuyang lun' 身心技法：靜坐——試析朱子學的修養論, in *Zhuzi xuekan* 朱子學刊 (Hefei: Huangshan shushe, 2000)

Xiao Qinghe 消清和, *Tian Ru tong yi kao: Qingchu Rujia jidutu Zhang Xingyao wenji* 天儒同異考：清初儒家基督徒張星曜文集 (Taipei: Ganlan chubanshe, 2015)

—, *Tian Ru yitong: Qingchu Rujia jidutu yanjiu* 天儒異同：清初儒家基督徒研究 (Shanghai: Shanghai daxue chubanshe, 2019)

—, 'Yitiangebiao: Rujia zongjiaoxing yu Ruye duihua' 一天各表：儒家宗教性於儒耶對話 [One heaven, respective interpretations: the religiosity of Confucianism in the dialogue between Confucianism and Christianity], *Beijing xingzheng xueyuan xuebao* [Journal of Beijing Administrative Institute] 北京行政學院學報, 129.5 (2020), 118–28

Xiong Shili 熊十力, *Dujing shiyao* 讀經示要, in *Xiong Shili quanji* 熊十力全集, vol. 3 (Wuhan: Hubei jiaoyu chubanshe, 2001)

Xin Yamin 辛亞民, '"Shuogua zhuan" "Di chu hu zhen" zhang xilun' 〈說卦傳〉「帝出乎震」章析論, *Zhongguo zhexue shi* 中國哲學史, 4 (2015), 66–70

Xu Zongze 徐宗澤, *Ming Qing jian Yesuhuishi yizhu tiyao* 明清間耶穌會士譯著提要 (Shanghai: Shanghai guji chubanshe, 2006)

Yan Mo 嚴謨, *Ditian kao* 帝天考 [Study on *Tian* and *Di*]; copies in the Vatican Library: BAV, R.G Oriente III 248 and Borgia Cinese 316.9; punctuated version: Nicolas Standaert [Zhong Mingdan 鐘鳴旦], *Qing chu jidujiaotu lun 'di' tan 'tian'* 可親的天主：清初基督教徒論「帝」談「天」(Taipei: Guangqi chubanshe, 1998), pp. 27–56

Yu Yingshi 余英時, *Lun Tianren zhi ji: Zhongguo gudai sixiang qiyuan shitan* 論天人之際：中國古代思想起源試探 (Beijing: Zhonghua shuju, 2014)

Zhang Dongsun 張東蓀, *Lixing yu Liangzhi: Zhang Dongsun wenxuan* 理性與良知：張東蓀文選 (Shanghai: Yuandong chubanshe, 1995)

Zhang Juzheng 張居正, *Zhang Juzheng jiangping Lunyu* 張居正講評論語, ed. by Chen Shengxi 陳生璽 (Shanghai: Shanghai cishu chubanshe, 2007)

Zhangzai ji 張載集, ed. by Zhang Xichen 章錫琛 (Beijing: Zhonghua shuju, 1978)

Zhang Zhidong 張之洞, *Shumu dawen buzheng* 書目答問補正, ed. by Fan Xizeng 范希曾 (Shanghai: Shanghai guji chubanshe, 2001)

Zhou Zhenhe 周振鶴, *Ming Qing zhiji xifang chuanjiaoshi Hanji congkan* 明清之際西方傳教士漢籍叢刊, 6 vols (Nanjing: Fenghuang chubanshe, 2013)

Zhu Weizheng 朱维铮 and Li Tiangang 李天纲 (eds), *Xu Guangqi quanji* 徐光啟全集 [Complete works of Xu Guangqi] (Shanghai guji chubanshe 上海古籍出版社, 2010)

Zhu Xi 朱熹, *Sishu zhangju ji* 四書章句集注 (Beijing: Zhonghua shuju, 1983)

Concordance List of Titles and Names

Ancient Classics

Pinyin	Characters	Noël's Romanization	Noël's Latin gloss	English translation of Noël's Latin gloss
Wujing	五經	V Kim	Quinque libri Classici	Five Classics
Shijing	詩經	Xi Kim	Liber Carminum	Book of Odes
Shujing	書經	Xu Kim	Liber Annalium Imperialium	Book of Imperial Annals
Yijing	易經	Ye Kim	Liber mutationum et productionum	Book of Changes and Productions
Liji	禮記	Li Ki	Liber Rituum	Book of Rites
Daxue	大學	Ta hio	Doctrina Adultorum	Teaching of Adults
Zhongyong	中庸	Chum yum	Liber immutabilis medii	Book of the Unalterable Mean
Lunyu	論語	Lun yu	Liber Sententiarum	Book of Sentences
Mengzi	孟子	N/A	Memcius	Mencius
[Chongding Gu] Zhouli	[重訂古]周禮	Cheu li	Liber rituum Imperium Cheu	Book of the Zhou Rituals

Commentaries

Pinyin	Characters	Noël's Romanization	Noël's Latin gloss	English translation of Noël's Latin gloss
Sishu huowen	四書或問	Su xu hoe ven	Quaestiones in 4 libros classicos	Questions on the Four Books
Sishu mengyin	四書蒙引	Su xu mum yn	Quatuor librorum classicorum facilis explanatio	Easy Explanation of the Four Books
Sishu zhijie	四書直解	N/A	N/A	N/A
Sishu rijiang jieyi	四書日講解義	Si xu ge kiang	Quotidania quatuor librorum explicatio	Daily Explanation of the Four Books
Zhouyi zhengjie	周易正解	Cheu ye chin kiay	Vera libri mutationum et productionum explicatio	True Explanation of the Book of Changes and Productions
Xingli biaoti	性理標題	Sim ly piao ti	Naturae et rationis brevis expositio	Summary of the Book of Nature and Reason
Xingli daquan	性理大全	Sim li ta ciuen	De Natura et Ratione magnus Commentarius	Great Commentary on Nature and Reason

Pinyin	Characters	Noël's Romanization	Noël's Latin gloss	English translation of Noël's Latin gloss
Daming huidian	大明會典	Ta mim hoei tien	Collectio Rituum ac Satutorum Imperialis Familiae Ta mim	Collection of Rites and Statutes of the Da Ming Dynasty
Liji jishuo	禮記集說	N/A	Liber Rituum	Book of Rites
Shijing shuoyue jijie	詩經說約集解	N/A	Compendiosa explicatio libri Carminum interpretum compilatio	Exhaustive Compilation of the Book of Odes
Quanshi xiangyao	全史詳要	N/A	Liber Annalium Universalium	Book of Universal Annals
Shujing rijiang	書經日講	Ge kiam xu kim	Quotidiana libri Annalium Imperialium explicatio	Daily Explanation of the Book of Imperial Annals
Shujing jizhuan	書經集傳	N/A	Liber Annalium Imperialium	Book of Imperial Annals
Shujing daquan	書經大全	Xu kim ta ciuen	Magnus libri annalium imperialium commentarius	Great Commentary on the Book of Imperial Annals
Baihu tong	白虎通	Pe hu tum	Communis Regiorum Professorum sensus	Ordinary Meaning of the Royal Scholars

Dictionaries

Pinyin	Characters	Noël's Romanization	Noël's Latin gloss	English translation of Noël's Latin gloss
Wenxian tongkao	文獻通考	Ven hien tum kao[cao]	Universalis inquisitio priscorum tum librorum tum Sapientum	Universal Investigation of Ancient Books and Sages
Zhengzitong	正字通	Chim tsu tum	N/A	N/A
Dazihui	大字彙	Ta tsu guei	N/A	N/A
Zihui	字彙	Tsu Guey	N/A	N/A
(Xiesheng) pinzijian	諧聲品字箋	Pin tsu cien	N/A	N/A

Catholic Writings

Pinyin	Characters	Noël's Romanization	Noël's Latin gloss	English translation of Noël's Latin gloss
Tianzhu shiyi/ Tianxue shiyi	天主實義/ 天學實義	Tien Chu Xe y/ Tien hio Xe y	N/A	N/A
Qike	七克	Cie Ke	N/A	N/A
Tian Ru yin	天儒印	Tien yu yn	N/A	N/A
Chuhui wenda	初會問答	Tso hoei Ven ta	N/A	N/A
Piwang	闢妄	Pie Vam	N/A	N/A
Tianzhu jiangsheng yanxing jilüe	天主降生言行記略	Tien Chu Kiam sem yen him ki lio	N/A	N/A
Ershiwu yan	二十五言	Lh xe u yen	N/A	N/A
Jiren shipian	畸人十篇	Ki gin xe pien	N/A	N/A
Duoshu	鐸書	To xu	Instructoris liber	The Teacher's Book
Tianxue zhengfu	天學證符	Tien hio chim fu	N/A	N/A
Zhengshi lüeshuo	拯世略說	Chim xi lio xue	N/A	N/A
Dakewen	答客問	Ta ka uen	N/A	N/A
Shensilu	慎思錄	Xin Su	N/A	N/A
Shengjiao sigui	聖教四規	Xim kiao su quei	N/A	N/A
Piwang tiaobo he	闢妄條駁合	Pie vam tiao po ho	N/A	N/A
Bianxue zoushu	辨學奏疏	Pien hio tseu su	N/A	N/A
Zhifang waiji	職方外紀	Che fam vay ki	N/A	N/A
Tianshi mingbian	天釋明辨	Tien xe mim pien	N/A	N/A
Daiyi pian	代疑篇	Tay y	N/A	N/A
Shengshui jiyan	聖水紀言	Xim xui ki yen	N/A	N/A
Xingmi pian	醒迷篇	Sim my pien	N/A	N/A

Other Writings

Pinyin	Characters	Noël's Romanization	Noël's Latin gloss	English translation of Noël's Latin gloss
Mingxin baojian	明心寶鑒	Mim sin pao kien	Cordis speculum	Mirror of the heart
Zhengjiao zhenquan	正教真詮	Chim Kiao chin chuen	Rectae Religionis vera expositio	True Exposition of the Orthodox Religion
Qingzhenjiao kao	清真教考	Cim chin Kiao Kao	Purae ac verae Religionis examen	Examination of the Pure and True Religion
Sipian yaodao buzhu bianmeng qianshuo	四篇要道補注便蒙淺說	Su pien yao tao pien mum cien xue	Quatuor capitulorum doctrinae valde necessarie ad rudiorum captum explicatio	Explanation of the Teaching of the Four Chapters Necessary for the Understanding of the Uneducated
Mingjiao xu	明教序	Min Kiao Siu	Clarae Religionis brevis instructio	Brief Instruction of the Bright Religion
Pi xiyang xiejiao lun	闢西洋邪教論	Pie Si Yam Sie Kiao Lun	Pravae Religionis Europaeorum refutatio	Refutation of the Evil Religion of the Europeans

Personal Names

Xia, Shang, Zhou, and Han Dynasties

Pinyin	Characters	Noël's Romanization
Yao	堯	Yao
Shun	舜	Xun
Tang	湯	Tam
Cheng	成	Chim
Kang	康	Kam
Wen Wang	文王	Ven Vam
Gaozong	高宗	Kao Tsum
Wu Wang	武王	Vu Vam
[Shang Wang] Shou/Zhou [Wang]	[商王]受/周王	Xeu/Cheu
Wan Zhang	萬章	Van Chan
Cheng Tang	成湯	Chim Tam
Zisi	子思	Tsu Su
Dong Zhongshu	董仲舒	N/A
[Han] Wudi	[漢]武帝	Vu ti

Song Dynasty

Pinyin	Characters	Noël's Romanization
Hu Anguo	胡安國	Hu
Zhouzi/Zhou Dunyi	周子/周敦頤	Doctor Cheu
Cheng Hao	程顥	Chin hao
Zhu Xi	朱熹	Chu hi
Huizong	宋徽宗	Hoei Tsum
Cai Chen	蔡沈	Tsai Xin
Zhang Zai	張載	N/A

Ming Dynasty

Pinyin	Characters	Noël's Romanization
Cai Xuzhai [Cai Qing]	蔡虛齋[蔡清]	Tsay hiu chay
Qiu Qiongshan [Qiu Jun]	邱瓊山	Kieu Kiun Xan
Zhang Juzheng/ Zhang Gelao	張居正/張閣老	Cham kiu chim/Cham ko lao
Feng Yingjing	馮應京	Fum yim kim
Wanli	萬曆	Van Lie
Li Zhizao	李之藻	Ly chi tsao
Yang Tingyun	楊廷筠	Yam tim yun
Xu Guangqi	徐光啟	Siu quam ki
Han Lin	韓霖	Han lin
Chen Yi	陳儀	Chin y
Li Jiugong	李九功	Ly kieu kum
Zhang Geng	張庚	Cham kem
Chen Renxi	陳仁錫	Chin gin sie
Wang Changhui	王昌會	Vam cham hoei

Qing Dynasty

Pinyin	Characters	Noël's Romanization
Kangxi	康熙	Kam hi
Zhu Zongyuan	朱宗元	Chu tsum yuen
Qiu Zhenxin	丘振新	Kieu xim chin
Zheng Kangcheng	鄭康成	Chim kam chim
Zhao Chang	趙昌	Chao cham
He Shiheng	赫世亨	Hescken/Hen Kama

Concepts

Pinyin	Characters	Noël's Romanization	Noël's Latin gloss	English translation of Noël's Latin gloss
Shangdi	上帝	Xam Ti	Coeli Dominus/Rector	Lord/Ruler of Heaven
di	帝	Ti	N/A	Emperor
Tian	天	Tien	Coelum	Heaven/sky
jiao	郊	Kiao	Litamen	Sacrifice
qi	氣	Ki	Aer/vitalis aura	Air, vital breath
qiji	氣機	N/A	Vis motrix	Motive force
guishen	鬼神	Quey Xin	Producens et destruens spiritus	Producing and destroying spirit
li	理	Ly	Ratio	Reason
taiji	太極	Tay Kie	Primus terminus	First Ultimate
Tianzhu	天主	Tien Chu	Caeli Dominus	Lord of Heaven
Tianming	天命	Tien mim	Caeli lex	Law of Heaven
jingtian	敬天	Kim Tien	Colere Caelum	Worship Heaven
shitian	侍天	Su Tien	Servire Caelo	Serve Heaven
baitian	拜天	Pay Tien	Revereri Caelum	Revere Heaven
liangneng	良能	N/A	Naturale principium	Natural principle
erqi	二氣	N/A	Duplex aura vitalis	Double vital breath

Charts

Chart 1: Quotes of ancient classics common to *Ditian kao*, *Gujin*, and/or *Tianjiao he Ru*

Philosophia Sinica c. 1		*Ditian kao*	*Gujin juan* 1	*Tianjiao he Ru*
Meanings	C.3 *Shujing*	~	n. 40	n. 19
	D.4 *Lunyu*	~	n. 33	n. 15
	F.6 *Shujing*	n. 21	n. 27	n. 11
§.1 Dominion	A.1 *Shujing*	n. 23	n. 28	n. 7 & 11
	B.2 *Shujing*	n. 33	n. 32	n. 7
	E.4 *Shujing*	n. 15	n. 19 & 42	n. 9
	E.5 *Zhongyong*	~	~	n. 3 & 6
	E.6 *Shijing*	~	n. 14	n. 2
	F.7 *Shujing*	n. 24 & 25	n. 32	n. 8
	H.8 *Shujing*	n. 30	~	n. 7
	I.9 *Liji*	~	~	n. 7
	K.10 *Liji*	~	~	n. 6 & 8
	M.12 *Shujing*	n. 22	n. 27	n. 8
	N.13 *Lunyu*	n. 60	n. 9	n. 2
	P.16 *Liji*	~	~	n. 1 & 10
	Q.17 *Liji*	~	n. 13	n. 10
	R.18 *Zhongyong*	n. 62	n. 9	n. 2
	R.19 *Mencius*	n. 65	n. 11	n. 13
	R.20 *Mencius*	~	n. 9	~
	S.21 *Yijing*	~	n. 9	n. 10
	T.22 *Shijing*	n. 45	~	n. 19
§.2 Power	A.1 *Liji*	~	~	n. 3 & 10
	D.4 *Yijing*	~	~	n. 1
	E.5 *Shijing*	n. 57	n. 4	n. 3
	F.6 *Shujing*	n. 11	n. 5	n. 6
	H.8 *Shujing*	n. 9	n. 28	~
	K.11 *Yijing*	~	~	n. 11
	L.12 *Shijing*	n. 56	~	n. 1
	M.13 *Shijing*	n. 59	~	~
	P.15 *Liji*	~	~	n. 14
	Q.16 *Shujing*	n. 28	n. 2	~
	R.17 *Mencius*	~	n. 33	n. 15
§.3 Knowledge	A.1 *Shijing*	n. 35 & 36	n. 14	n. 5
	B *Shijing*	n. 37	~	~
	C *Shijing*	n. 38	~	n. 6
	D.2 *Shijing*	n. 50	n. 10	n. 2, 4 & 8
	E.3 *Lunyu*	~	n. 14 & 33	n. 8 & 12
	F.4 *Lunyu*	~	n. 20	n. 8

Philosophia Sinica c. 1		Ditian kao	Gujin juan 1	Tianjiao he Ru
§.4 Will	C.2 *Shujing*	n. 17	n. 19 & 32	n. 9 & 17
	D.3 *Shijing*	~	~	n. 1 & 6
	F.5 *Shujing*	~	n. 28	n. 7
	H.7 *Shujing*	~	n. 24	n. 11 & 17
	I.8 *Shujing*	n. 16	n. 22	n. 12
	K.9 *Shijing*	n. 34	n. 28	n. 9
	M.11 *Mencius*	~	~	n. 3
	N.12 *Shijing*	~	~	n. 11
	O.13 *Shijing*	n. 58	n. 38	n. 11
	P.14 *Shijing*	~	~	n. 16
	Q.15 *Lunyu*	~	n. 34	n. 11
§.5 Justice	B.2 *Shujing*	n. 17	n. 22	~
	C.3 *Shujing*	n. 8	n. 32	~
	D.4 *Shujing*	n. 10	n. 32	~
	E.5 *Shujing*	n. 12	~	n. 12 & 17
	F *Shujing*	n. 13	n. 14	~
	F *Lunyu*	~	~	n. 1 & 12
	I.8 *Shujing*	~	~	n. 18
	K.9 *Shujing*	n. 14	~	n. 1 & 12
	M.11 *Shujing*	~	n. 24	n. 13, 16, 17, 18
	O.13 *Shijing*	~	~	n. 6 & 8
	P.14 *Shujing*	~	~	n. 11
§.6 Life	A.1 *Shujing*	~	n. 16	~
	C.3 *Shujing*	n. 29	n. 27	n. 11
	E.5 *Shijing*	~	n. 28	~
	F.6 *Shijing*	n. 48	~	~
	G.7 *Shijing*	n. 49	~	~
	H.8 *Shijing*	n. 40	~	n. 5
	K.10 *Shujing*	~	n. 14	n. 5
§.7 Immensity-eternity	A.1 *Shijing*	~	n. 1	~
	B.2 *Shijing*	n. 54	n. 14	n. 4 & 16
	C.3 *Shijing*	n. 47	n. 13	n. 10
	D.4 *Shijing*	n. 55	n. 2	n. 4 & 6
	F.6 *Shijing*	~	~	n. 4
§.8 Simplicity	A.1 *Shijing*	~	~	n. 1
	G.7 *Shijing*	n. 49	~	n. 5

Chart 2: Distribution of the quotes of the classics in relation to *Tian* or *Shangdi*

	Tianzhu shiyi c. 2	*Ditian kao*	*Gujin*	*Tianjiao he Ru*	*Philosophia Sinica* First Treatise, c. 1.
Shujing	3	33	73	104	42
Shijing	4	26	31	63	29
Liji	2	~	16	27	11
Yijing	1	~	20	7	10
Lunyu		2	29	13	5
Zhongyong	1	1	11	5	3
Mencius	~	3	25	7	6
Daxue	~	~	~	1	~
Xiaojing	~	~	~	2	~
Quanshi	~	~	~	~	1
Total	11	65	205	229	110

Chart 3: Attributes of *Tian* or *Shangdi* according to classical works, c. 1, pp. 1–27

	Dominion	Power	Knowledge	Will	Justice	Life	Immensity-eternity	Simplicity	Total by works
Shujing	12	4		4	13	7		2	42
Shijing	1	5	4	5	3	4	5	2	29
Yijing	2	6					1	1	10
Liji	5	2				1		3	11
Zhongyong	2	1							3
Lunyu	1		2	1	1				5
Memcius	1	1		4					6
Quanshi	3							1	4
Total by attribute	27	19	6	14	17	12	6	9	110

Chart 4: Attributes of *Tian* or *Shangdi* according to commentaries, c. 2, pp. 27–146

Works	Dominion	Power	Knowledge	Will	Justice	Life	Immensity-eternity	Simplicity	Tian Shangdi	*li*	*guishen*	*jiaoshe*	*taiji*	
Sishu zhijie	1	2	2	4	1				1	2	5	2		20
Sishu mengyin	1	3		4	1				9	14	10	11	3	56
Sishu rijiang	4	3	1	5		1	1		2	6	6	2		31
Zhouyi zhengjie	2	10					3	4	2	6	11	1	8	47
Liji jishuo									3	1	5	28	1	38
Shijing shuoyue		2	3	5	1	3	3	1	7	3	1	7		36
Shujijng jizhuan	1	1		1	1			2	4	1	1	10		22
Xingli biaoti							2	2	4	4			6	18
Quanshi											1			1
	9	21	6	19	4	4	7	9	30	36	42	62	18	268

Chart 5: Different dimensions of *shen* and *guishen*

		Heaven-earth 天地	Spirit 神	Maker of things 造化	Unique cause 一故
Invisible 无形		Operation of Heaven-earth 天地之功用	Spirit destroying and producing 鬼神 造化之迹	Trace Natural principle of the double vital breath 二氣之良能 (first life level)	Double cause 两故
Visible 有形	*yin-yang* 阴阳	Trace of Spirit destroying and producing (second life level) 鬼神之迹			Union and Separation 合散

Chart 6: Distribution of the commentaries according to the Four Books

	Daxue	*Zhongyong*	*Lunyu*	*Mencius*
Sishu zhijie	0	4	9	7
Sishu menyin	6	22	8	9
Rijiang sishu	1	6	11	10

Chart 7: References of works by missionaries and Chinese Christians (c.3, q.1, §.1, pp. 150–57)

Author	Title	ARSI
Caballero 利安當	*Tian Ru yin* 天儒印 (1664)	
La Piñuela 石铎琭	*Chuhui wenda* 初會問答 (1680) *Moxiang shengong* 默想神功 (1695)	I, 119 I, 118
Xu Guangqi 徐光啓	*Pi shishi zhuwang* 闢釋氏諸妄 *Bianxue zhangshu* 辨學章疏 (1616) Preface to Ricci's *Ershiwuyan* 二十五言 (1604) Preface to Aleni's *Tianzhu jiangsheng yanxing jilüe* 天主降生言行紀略 (1635)	I, 132 — I, 53.1 I, 58
Feng Yingjing 馮應京	Preface to the *Tianzhu shiyi* 天主實義 (1603)	I, 44
Yang Tingyun 楊廷筠	Preface to Pantoja's *Qike* 七克 (early 1610) Preface to Aleni's *Zhifang waiji* 職方外紀 (1623) *Daiyipian* 代疑篇 (1621) *Tianshi mingbian* 天釋明辨 (1645)	I, 84 II, 19 I, 165b I, 165a
Li Zhizao 李之藻	Preface to Sun Xueshi's *Shengshui jiyan* 聖水紀言 Preface to Ricci's *Jiren shipian* 畸人十篇 (1608) Preface to the second edition (1607) of the *Tianzhu shiyi*	I, 131 I, 52 I, 44
Chen Yi 陳儀	Preface to Aleni's *Xingxue cushu* 性學觕述序 (1646)	II, 16
Han Lin 韓霖	*Duoshu* 鐸書 (c. 1641)	I, 144
Zhang Geng 張賡	*Tianxue zhengfu* 天學證符 (1628–1636)	I, 141
Zhu Zongyuan 朱宗元	*Zhengshi lüeshuo* 拯世略說 (1644) *Dakewen* 答客問 (1643)	I, 145 I, 146
Li Jiugong 李九功	*Shensilu* 慎思錄 (1682)	I, 34
Xu Erjue 徐爾覺 Qiu Yuezhi 丘曰知	Preface to Brancati's *Shengjiao sigui* 聖教四規	I, 106
Wang Ruohan 王若韓	*Piwang tiaobo he* 闢妄條駁合 (1689)	I, 132

Index

accommodation: 9, 14, 35, 111, 130
Acta Pekinensia: 27, 47, 65
Aleni, Giulio: 71, 73
Altar of Earth *see ditan*
Altar of Heaven *see tiantan*
Analects see Lunyu
Appiani, Luigi Antonio: 390
Aquinas, Thomas, St.:
  and faith: 149–50
  and Great Ultimate: 146
  and *natura naturans*: 96
  and natural law: 121–22, 125, 139
  and nature: 140
  and Noël's studies and use of: 14, 18, 85, 126, 144
  and proof for God: 145
  and *relationes transcendentales*: 143
  and *religio*: 151
  and *Summa theologiae*: 81, 131, 133–37
  and theology: 129–32
Aristotle, Aristotelian:
  and divine knowledge: 136
  and efficient cause: 97
  and essence: 101, 144
  and First Being: 164
  and generation and corruption: 92
  and God: 142
  and nature: 104, 141, 143, 341, 347
  and Noël's studies and use of: 10, 18
  and one Mind: 353
  and *Physics*: 18, 96
  and *Topica*: 354
  and world-soul: 103
  as conceptualist: 137
  as philosopher: 368

Atheism, atheist, or atheistic:
  and Ancient Confucianism: 12, 33, 37, 48, 116, 132, 165, 169, 200, 203–04, 354–56
  and Buddhism: 99
  and European sympathies: 9, 38
  and Kangxi: 62, 382
  and materialism: 57, 90
  and Neo-Confucianism: 12, 79, 106, 205–06, 354–56, 382
  and Spinoza: 99
  and Zhu Xi: 54–55, 57, 84, 90, 235, 351
Atheo-politician or *atheo-politicus*: 54–55, 84, 90
Attributes of *Tian*, or *Shangdi*, or God, or Heaven:
  dominion: 39, 46, 48, 80–81, 138, 171–72, 206, 246, 249, 266, 328, 352
  eternity: 36, 45–46, 80, 84–85, 95, 194, 197, 234, 237–38, 247
  immensity: 45–46, 80, 84, 145, 194, 197, 234, 237–38, 247, 352
  justice: 46, 80, 83, 137–38, 185, 189–90, 207, 209, 227, 232–33, 247, 352
  knowledge: 45–46, 80, 82, 84, 183–85, 223–25, 246
  life: 80, 84, 193–95, 234–35, 247, 262, 352
  power: 39, 45–46, 80–81, 85, 136, 138, 178–79, 212–24, 246, 264, 278, 352
  simplicity: 45–46, 49, 80, 85, 135, 198–99, 240, 242, 247, 352
  will: 46, 71, 80, 82–83, 185–88, 225–32, 246, 258, 352
Augustine, St.: 34, 37, 96, 119–20, 151, 202, 265

Baihu tong 白虎通: 63, 66, 296, 316, 319, 338
baitian 拜天: 76, 379
Ban Gu 班固: 66
Bayle, Pierre: 9, 99–100
Beijing 北京: 21, 23–24, 26, 29, 40–41, 76, 105, 306, , 383–84, 386, 389–90
Being, First:
   and Chinese classics: 200
   and Chinese conception of God: 10, 29, 36, 48, 109, 116, 164–65, 169
   and Greco-Roman understanding of it: 110
   and neo-Confucianism: 205–06, 262, 271, 351–52, 354, 379
   and *Tian*, or *Shangdi*: 133
   as Rational Being: 61
   as *taiji*: 89
   as the Producer of all things: 265
Being, Rational: 61, 85–86, 148, 241
Being, Real: 85, 147–48, 241, 264
Being, Spiritual: 59, 382
belief *see* faith
Benavente, Álvaro de: 25, 42, 65
Bianxue zhangshu 辨學章疏: 71, 365
Book of Changes see Yijing
Book of Documents see Shujing
Book of Odes see Shijing
Book of Rites see Liji
Bouvet, Joachim: 18, 20, 23–24, 36, 41–46, 50, 55, 61, 65, 79, 81, 84, 86, 88, 120
Brancati, Francesco: 52, 56, 64, 67
Brevis relatio: 25, 40–41, 76
Brief Response on the Controversies: 37, 54, 62, 90, 100
Buddha, Buddhism: 21, 36, 61, 68, 71, 99, 110, 113, 147, 168, 204, 255, 295, 329
Buglio, Ludovico: 383
Bureau of Sacrifices *see Sijiqinglisi*

Caballero, Antonio de Santa María: 40, 64, 365
Cai Chen 蔡沈: 45, 54, 106, 327
   see also *Shujing jizhuan*
Cai Jiezhai 蔡節齋: 103, 346

Cai Qing 蔡清 or Cai Xuzhai 蔡虛齋:
   and Cheng Hao 程顥: 91
   and *guishen* 鬼神: 91–95, 119
   and *qi* 氣: 212–13
   and *qiji* 氣機: 82, 219
   and *taiji* 太極: 98–99
   and *taixu* 太虛: 98
   and Zhang Zai 張載: 50, 89
   and Zhu Xi 朱熹: 51, 89
   Noël's use of: 22–23, 50, 83, 84, 114, 126
   see also *Sishu mengyin* 四書蒙引; *Yijing mengyin* 易經蒙引
Canton Conference: 70
Canton 廣州: 19, 24–25, 47, 58, 64–65, 67, 70–71
Cartesianism: 35
Castner, Kaspar: 25–26, 33, 65, 71
cause:
   efficient: 93–94, 97, 135, 142, 144, 147, 249, 270, 286, 342, 348
   immanent: 87
   formal: 87, 97
   material: 87
   transcendental: 93, 97–98, 103
Chan, Albert 陳綸緒: 51–52, 56, 68, 74
Chen Dayou 陳大猷: 46
Chen Hao 陳澔: 52–53, 98
   see also *liji jizhu*
Chen Liangcai 陳亮采: 74
Chen Renxi 陳仁錫: 68, 337, 370
Chen Yi 陳儀: 40, 73–74, 366
Cheng Hao 程顥: 91, 93, 125
Cheng Tang 成湯: 180, 185–87, 189–91, 196, 198, 200, 203, 226, 229, 236, 233, 326
Cheng Yi 程頤: 63, 88, 102, 123, 125, 251
Chenghuang 城隍: 67, 322, 324
Chinese Christian(s):
   and accommodation of Christianity to Confucianism: 14, 75, 77
   and rejection of neo-Confucianism: 14, 20, 79
   and testimonies about the Terms and Rites Controversy: 25–26, 44–47, 68–71, 360, 377–79, 382
   and their conception of God: 105

Chinese dictionary(ies): 63–66, 88, 263, 321, 336, 374
Chinese Rites Controversy: 9–10, 12, 19, 23, 34, 110
Ching, Julia 秦家懿, 14, 103, 146
Christ: 150, 152–53, 165, 167, 204, 295, 358, 386
Christian works in Chinese: 68–75
Chuhui wenda 初會問答: 40, 70, 359, 365
Chunqiu 春秋: 21, 50, 317, 322, 375
Cicero: 264, 350, 352–53, 355
Civil examinations 科舉: 51
Classical Studies or *jingxue* 經學: 111–12, 120–21, 126
Cobo, Juan: 68
Coleridge, Samuel Taylor: 100
Collani, Claudia von: 12, 23, 26, 33
Confucianism:
    Jesuit interpretation: 9, 36, 43
    Monotheism: 12
    Accommodation: 14, 110
    Neo-Confucianism:
        Noël's studies and use of: 12–14, 20–24, 55, 57, 61, 79–107, 109–27
        Rejection of the early Jesuits: 11–12, 45, 57
        Rejection of the Chinese Christians: 45, 75, 79
Confucius:
    Monotheism of Confucius: 40
    Rites to Confucius: 9, 34, 67
    Temple of Confucius: 60
    and Longobardo: 37
    and Mencius: 112
    as Chinese philosopher: 35
    as teacher: 167
    see also Lunyu
Confucius Sinarum philosophus: 9, 22, 35–36, 50, 54–55, 57–59, 63, 84, 87, 90, 96, 99
Controversy:
    Rites: 9–10, 12, 19, 23, 26, 31, 33–34, 38, 40, 53, 57, 71, 106, 110
    Terms: 10, 33–34, 40–41, 49, 63, 69, 71, 106
    Rites and Terms: 10, 41, 49, 63

about Chinese philosophy: 38, 168
Cornelius à Lapide: 265, 353, 384
Corruption: 36, 46, 92, 269, 271, 274, 299
Costa, Inácio Da: 56
Couplet, Philippe: 21, 43, 83–84, 93
Creation, Creationism: 72, 81–82, 87, 116, 125, 137, 141, 145, 201, 340, 357
Creator:
    and Chinese philosophy: 153,
    and cult or obedience of Creator: 151, 355
    and dualism between creator and creature: 100, 105, 106, 151, 357
    as *natura naturans*: 96, 99, 141, 340, 342
    as *Tian*, or Heaven: 81, 147, 240, 249
    of all things: 72, 130, 141, 240
    of Heaven and Earth: 380

Da Ming huidian 大明會典: 47, 66–67, 268, 306, 318, 322–23
Daiyipian 代疑篇: 73
Dakewen 答客問: 74, 363, 367, 375
Daoism, or daoist(s): 21, 61, 67–68, 124, 147, 235, 255
daotong 道統: 12, 36, 44, 106, 112
Daxue 大學 / *Rijiang* 日講 / *Zhijie* 直解 / *Mengyin* 蒙引: 56–58, 61–62, 210, 231, 255
[*Da*] *Zihui* [大]字彙 *see Zihui*
De cultu coelesti Sinarum veterum et modernorum: 42
De divina substantia ejusque attributis: 18, 47
De doctrina Christiana: 37, 202
De sinensium ritibus politicis actis acta: 67
di 帝:
    and creation: 81
    and Lord of Heaven: 170, 185, 212–13, 223, 248–49, 306
    and sacrifice: 53, 117
    and *Shangdi*: 360–61, 368–69
    and its lexical meaning: 44, 46, 64–65, 360–63, 374
    and *Tian, Tiandi*: 55, 82, 118, 125
    and *Yuhuang* 玉皇, 371
    and *zhuzai*: 73
Ding Keting 丁柯亭: 51
Dionysius, the Areopagite: 142

ditan 地壇: 53
Ditian kao 帝天考: 44–46, 48–49, 54
divine attributes: 45, 133, 136–37
divine names: 133–34, 147
Doctrinae Sinicae brevis indagatio, or *Brief investigation of Chinese Teaching*: 27, 33–34, 40–41, 43, 155–56, 158
Dominican(s): 34, 52, 68–69, 129, 152
Dong Zhongshu 董仲舒: 95
Douai: 18
Duoshu 鐸書: 74, 362, 367

emptiness *see* void
enigmatic symbol, or hexagram: 81, 82, 85, 102, 123, 178, 201, 241, 294, 295, 345
erqi 二氣: 93, 288, 290, 348, 412
Ershiwu yan 二十五言: 71, 360
essence:
    as act of being: 144
    as *ti* 體: 83,
    divine: 133, 135, 240
    of a thing: 96, 101–02, 104–05, 140–41, 145, 344
    of all things: 344
    of God: 85, 134, 136, 141, 148, 165, 342
    of the Lord of Heaven: 249
    of the First Ultimate: 347
    of Reason: 248, 252, 253, 261
    eternal and infinite essence: 99
evidential learning *see kaozheng* 考證

faith: 14, 36, 59, 70–71, 75, 95, 130, 149–53, 166, 264, 351, 358
Fan Liben 范立本: 68
Fan Zhiheng 范之恆: 53, 294
Feng Yingjing 馮應京: 40, 72, 366
Feng Youlan 馮友蘭: 102, 142
figurism, figurist(s): 79, 81, 120, 147, 153
Filippucci, Francesco Saverio: 19, 25, 47, 52–54, 65, 71
Form, Substantial: 148, 256, 262, 270
Franciscan(s): 19, 34, 40, 69–70, 359
    Chinese writings of: 40, 70
Fuyue 傅說: 44, 54, 84, 235

Gaozong 高宗: 44, 54 , 84, 193–94, 234–35, 373
Gaozu 高祖: 369
Gemona, Basilio Brollo da: 65
generation: 82, 88, 92, 122–23, 125, 140–41, 266, 269, 271, 341, 347
God
    attribute(s) of/for: 36, 80, 86, 116, 171, 199, 202, 206
    name of: 134, 357
Gospel(s): 139, 150, 208, 331, 373–74
Gozani, Gianpaolo: 76, 380
grace: 131, 149, 151–52
Gu Zhouli 古周禮: 68
Gu Yanwu 顧炎武: 113, 126
guishen (spirit) 鬼神:
    as angel: 90,
    as idol: 287, 302
    as producing and destroying spirit: 91, 93–94, 285–86, 288–93, 303–05
    as *qi, yin* and *yang*: 89–93, 285–92
    as spiritual substance: 89–90, 92–94, 286, 294–300
    as traces: 93, 289, 291–93
Gujin jing Tian jian 古今敬天鑑: 23–25, 41–46, 48–49, 61–62, 65, 88

Han Lin 韓霖: 40, 74 , 362, 367
Han Tan 韓菼: 41–42
Han 漢 dynasty: 36, 39, 46, 66, 83, 98, 133, 319, 322, 324, 343, 369, 373, 375
He Shiheng 赫世亨, or Henkama: 24, 47, 390–91
hermeneutic(s):
    Christological explanations: 43
    continuity of Neo Confucianism and Ancient Confucianism: 12, 36, 44, 106, 112
    critical exegesis of the Bible: 36, 38
    hermeneutic of suspicion: 37
    literal interpretation: 37–38, 66, 115–16, 118–20, 124, 126, 166, 202, 249, 301
    Mencius' exegetic principles: 38, 167

metaphorical interpretation of texts: 37–38, 46, 74, 82, 105, 126, 119–20, 126, 196, 202–03, 266, 291
    theistic reading of Chinese classics: 38, 75, 105
Hervieu, Julien-Placide: 42
Histoire critique du Vieux Testament: 36
Hongwu 洪武 emperor: 67
Hongwu zhengyun 洪武正韻: 64
Houtu 后土: 44, 300, 320–22, 326–28, 332, 334, 336
Hu Anguo 胡安國: 304
Hu Guang 胡廣: 52, 54, 62
Huang Hongxian 黃洪憲: 63
Huangdi 黃帝: 172, 178, 203, 299, 306, 310, 328, 368–69, 374
Huangtian 皇天: 44, 173, 176, 321, 328, 344, 371
Huangtian houtu 皇天后土: 44, 321
Huizong 徽宗: 372, 375

Idol:
    and Bible: 36
    and Buddhism: 110, 168, 204, 255
    and *Chenghuang*: 322, 324
    and Daoism: 168, 235, 255, 371–74
    and *Laojun*: 373
    and name of it: 373
    and natural things: 306
    and *Shangdi*, or *Di*, or *Tian*: 133, 302, 359, 368, 374, 384
    and spirits: 287
    and Virgin Mary: 385
    and western paganism: 302, 373, 376
    and *yuhuang*: 371–72
Ignatius of Loyola, St.: 129–31, 385
immortality of the soul: 59, 90, 94–95
incarnation: 76, 130
inculturation: 129, 153
Intorcetta, Prospero: 21, 83–84
Islamic Chinese writings: 75–76

Jerome, St.: 373–74
Jesuit(s): 110–12, 114–16, 120
    China Mission of: 12–13, 18, 25, 49, 110, 129
    translation(s): 15, 56, 58
    Superior General of: 29
Jew(s): 39–40, 47, 69, 75–76, 204, 380–81
    Jewish use of *Tian* and *Shangdi*: 76
Jiading 嘉定 conference: 69, 75
Jiajing 嘉靖 emperor: 67, 322–23, 329
Jiangzhou 絳州: 76, 381
jiaoshe 郊社 rituals: 53–54, 66–67, 79, 95, 106, 133, 305, 319, 322, 334, 337
jiding 祭丁 rituals: 67
Jie 桀: 185–87, 189–91, 233, 244
Jili paozhi 祭禮泡製: 52
jing tian 敬天: 40–42, 44, 71, 76, 83, 379, 380–81, 383–86, 388, 390–91
jing tian tablet: 40, 383–86
Jiren shipian 畸人十篇: 73, 361, 366
John of Damascus: 97, 141, 342
Jupiter: 133, 373, 376–77

Kaifeng 開封 synagogue: 76, 380
Kang 康: 194, 196, 234, 236, 299
Kangxi 康熙 emperor: 27, 39–42, 44, 47, 49, 52, 61–62, 69, 75–76, 133, 379–80, 382–83, 386, 388
    see also Kangxi zidian; *Relatio brevis*; *Sishu rijiang*; Summarium NAT
Kangxi zidian 康熙字典: 64
kaozheng 考證: 49, 50
Kong Yingda 孔穎達: 117–18
Kongzi jiayu 孔子家語: 48, 83, 192
Kongzi 孔子 *see* Confucius
Kulena 庫勒納 or Kurene: 52, 61

La Piñuela, Pedro de: 40, 70, 359–60, 365
Legge, James: 11, 28, 50, 195, 199, 279
Lei Chong 雷翀: 76
Leibniz, Gottfried Wilhelm: 9, 14, 107
Li Dongyang 李東陽: 66
Li Jiugong 李九功: 74, 367
Li Zhizao 李之藻: 71, 73, 361, 366

li 理:
    and early Jesuits' rejection: 21–22, 37, 43, 46, 55, 86–87, 90
    and Noël's acceptance: 23, 50, 79, 88, 106, 121
    and *qi*: 60–61, 79, 82, 88–89, 111, 122, 123–24, 352
    and *taiji*: 101, 206, 352
    as active reason: 88, 263
    as form, formal cause: 87
    as Heaven, *Tian*, or *Shangdi*: 22, 66, 75, 77, 81, 84, 86, 125
    as reason: 88, 121, 165, 263, 352, 357, 359
liangneng 良能: 93, 288
Libri sex: 10–11, 22–23, 28, 30, 59, 61–62, 160
Libu 禮部: 41, 67
Liji 禮記: 48–49, 174, 176, 179, 182, 199
Liji jishuo 禮記集說: 52–53, 106
    Aigong wen 哀公問: 275
    Biaoji 表記: 210
    Jiaotesheng 郊特牲: 250, 256, 300, 308, 311–12, 315, 332–33, 339
    Jifa 祭法: 294, 299, 316, 320
    Jitong 祭統: 337
    Jiyi 祭義: 285, 304, 309
    Liqi 禮器: 331, 333, 337
    Liyun 禮運: 331, 344
    Quli 曲禮: 314
    Wangzhi 王制: 295, 296, 314, 332, 340
    Yueling 月令: 250, 300, 311, 340
    Zengzi wen 曾子問: 261
Lille: 30
Lionne, Artus de: 65
Liubu 六部: 67
Lixue 理學: 36, 43, 44, 60, 61
Longobardo, Niccolò: 37, 43, 54, 62, 71, 72, 111, 126
Lunyu 論語: 39, 49, 56, 58, 59, 61, 82, 84–85, 89–90
Lunyu 論語 / *Rijiang* 日講 / *Zhijie* 直解 / *Mengyin* 蒙引:
    Lunyu 3.6: 302, 303
    Lunyu 3.12: 300
    Lunyu 3.13: 90, 175, 210, 253
    Lunyu 5.13: 278
    Lunyu 6.20: 304
    Lunyu 7.20: 304
    Lunyu 6.26: 188, 230
    Lunyu 7.22: 231
    Lunyu 7.23: 251
    Lunyu 8.21: 294
    Lunyu 9.1: 253, 279, 283
    Lunyu 9.11: 184, 225
    Lunyu 12.5: 171
    Lunyu 14.37: 184, 224, 260
    Lunyu 14.43: 90
    Lunyu 16.8: 240
    Lunyu 20.1: 233, 326
Luo Wenzao 羅文藻, or Luo Wenzhao 羅文炤: 75, 378
Luo Ying 羅瑩: 12, 22–23, 61

Ma Duanlin 馬端臨: 66
Macao: 19, 25–26, 47, 65
Maigrot, Charles: 27, 47
Maillard de Tournon, Charles-Thomas: 26, 42
Malebranche, Nicolas: 9, 100
material heaven: 41, 201–02, 206, 284, 305, 324–27, 359, 378–80, 382–83, 385, 387, 390
Mei Yingzuo 梅膺祚: 64
Mencius (Mengzi) 孟子 / *Rijiang* 日講 / *Zhijie* 直解 / *Mengyin* 蒙引: 11, 21–22, 28, 38–39, 48–49, 57, 59, 61–62, 72, 80, 112, 118, 124, 167
    Gaozi shang 告子上: 220, 268
    Gong Shun Chou xia 公孫丑下: 232
    Jin xin shang 盡心上: 251–52, 254, 267, 269, 279, 283, 289, 293
    Jin xin xia 盡心下: 232, 261, 296, 317
    Li Lou shang 離婁上: 177, 231
    Li Lou xia 離婁下: 210
    Liang Hui Wang xia 梁惠王下: 209, 311
    Teng Wen Gong shang 滕文公上: 171
    Wan Zhang shang 萬章上: 182, 186–88, 222, 227–29, 253, 283
    metaphorical meaning: 37–38, 46, 74, 82, 105, 126, 119–20, 126, 196, 202–03, 266, 291
    and the Bible: 203
    and Mexico: 126

and *qi*: 266
and *Shangdi* and *Tian*: 37–38, 46, 74, 82, 120
and *taiji*: 105
and the reading of Chinese classics: 36, 119, 202
Meynard, Thierry: 12–13
Min Qiji 閔齊伋: 52–53
mingjiao 明教: 76, 381
Mingxin baojian 明心寶鑑: 68, 234
ming 命: 121–22, 260, 283, 297
Ministry of Rites see *Libu*
monotheism, monotheistic: 12, 40, 45, 53–54, 71, 75–76, 80, 106, 132
Mou Zongsan 牟宗三: 121–23
Mungello, D.E.: 42–43
Muslim(s) or Islamic: 39, 47, 69, 75, 379–81
mutual interaction: 80, 83–84, 95

Nanchang 南昌: 19–20, 24, 52, 323
natural law: 81, 121–22, 125, 138–39, 152, 207, 258, 280
nature see *xing* 性
Navarrete, Domingo: 52, 67–68
Noël, François 衛方濟:
    and Chinese books quoted by him: 40–77
    and the distinction between ancient Confucianism and neo-Confucianism: 111–15
    and *guishen*: 89–95
    and hermeneutics: 36–38
    and his acceptance of neo-Confucianism: 12, 13, 22–25, 79, 81, 110–11
    and his biography: 10, 17–20
    and the end of his life: 30–31
    and his scholarly work in Rome: 25–28
    and his translation of Chinese classics: 11
    and interpretation of Confucian classics: 115–21
    and *li* and *qi*: 86–89
    and *Philosophia Sinica*: 28–30, 33–36
    and rapprochement between Confucianism and scholasticism: 13–14, 80, 121–27
    and *taiji*: 95–107
    and *Tian* and *Shangdi*: 80–86
Noël, Nicolas: 19

Observata de vocibus sinicis Tien et Chang-ti: 41
Ockhamist conception of language: 69
Olmi, Antonio: 129
Ovid: 373–74

pagan virtue: 34
pantheism, or pantheistic: 12, 96, 103, 106
Pantoja, Diego de: 72, 359
Paris: 29, 34, 364
Paul, St.: 258, 321, 353, 355, 368
Philip II of Spain: 56
Philosophia Sinica
    and Chinese testimonies about the Terms and Rites Controversy: 25–27
    and the Coimbra Commentary: 18
    and cross-cultural dialogue: 110, 126
    and different versions of this book: 43
    and emphasis on neo-Confucianism: 13, 22–23, 106, 109–11, 114
    and its publication and suppression: 10–11, 28–31, 127
    and its relations to early Jesuits and Chinese Christian works: 45–46, 48, 50–54, 57, 59, 61, 65
    and its scholastic background: 136, 151
    and Noël's self-identity: 17
    and structure of this book: 33–39
    and theology: 14, 132, 140, 149
Pi Xiyang xiejiao lun 闢西洋邪教論: 76, 381
Pinzijian see *Xiesheng pinzijian*
Piwang 闢妄: 71, 360, 365
Piwang tiaobo he 闢妄條駁合: 75, 364, 367
Plato, Platonist, or Platonic: 81–82, 87, 97, 103, 141–42, 165, 248, 270, 342, 351, 354
Prémare, Joseph de: 42, 107
principle see *li* 理
Provana, Antonio: 26, 47
Pythagoras: 103, 166, 352

Qianlong 乾隆 emperor: 67
Qike 七克: 72–74, 359, 362, 364, 366–67
Qingzhen jiaokao 清真教考: 75
Qiu Qiongshan [Qiu Jun] 邱瓊山: 372
Qiu Sheng 丘晟: 40
Qiu Zhenxin 丘振新: 325
qi 氣:
    and early Jesuits' understanding: 79, 86, 90
    and li: 60–63, 79, 89, 111, 122–24
    and Noël's acceptance: 79, 89, 93, 103, 120
    and taiji: 23
    and yin and yang: 90, 103
    as air: 82, 87, 213
    as life: 89, 93, 124, 213, 263, 266, 352
    as matter or material cause: 87, 90, 93
    as spirit: 88, 89, 266
    as vital breath: 12, 88, 123, 212–13, 263, 357
qiji 氣機, force of movement: 52, 82, 290
Quanshi xiangyao 全史詳要: 48–49, 200, 340

reason:
    reasoned: 86, 148, 242
    transcendental: 86
retribution: 68, 83, 201, 210
Ricci, Matteo 利瑪竇:
    and accommodation of Christianity to Confucianism: 14, 24, 45, 90
    and distinction of ancient and Song Confucianism: 36, 49, 69, 106, 111, 115, 147
    and his Chinese works see Ershiwu yan, True Meaning of the
    and influence upon Noël: 86, 94
    and qi: 93
    and rejection of neo-Confucianism: 11–12, 21, 36, 43, 45, 57, 63, 77, 79, 84, 95, 114
    and sapiential realism: 130
    and Shangdi and Tianzhu: 74, 98
    and taiji: 95
    and utilization of scholasticism: 80, 129
    Lord of Heaven, Jiren shipian
rites (rituals, ceremonies, sacrifices):
    Chinese: 9–10, 12, 19, 23, 34, 110

Rites Controversy: 9–10, 12, 19, 23, 26, 31, 33–34, 38, 40, 53, 57, 71, 106, 110
    to ancestors: 35
    to Confucius: 34
    to Heaven see jiaoshe
Rome: 23–27, 29–31, 33, 35, 41, 47–48, 58, 65, 69, 71, 95, 168, 389
Ruggieri, Michele: 14, 21, 56, 68, 87, 89–90

sage see shengren
Salian, Jacques: 81, 201
Sapientia sinica: 50, 56, 58
Sapiential Realism: 13, 129–32, 150
Scholasticism, or scholastic:
    and ancient philosophy: 10
    and Confucianism: 13–14, 24, 36, 50, 61, 88, 106, 115, 118, 126, 132–34, 136, 153
    and definition of natura: 13, 98, 122
    and sapiential wisdom: 13
    and Noël's utilization of it: 14, 61, 69, 89, 94, 97, 116, 121
    and natural philosophy: 35
    and Second Scholasticism: 129
    and attributes of God: 45, 83, 85–86, 116
    and Ricci's utilization: 80
    and Philosophia Sinica: 11, 14, 39
School of Mind: 14, 112–13
School of Principle: 14, 24, 36, 43–44, 60–62, 105–06, 111–16, 119–24, 126
Shangdi 上帝:
    and its literal meaning: 38
    and its metaphorical meaning: 37, 46
    and li and qi: 88, 90
    and testimonies by non-Christians: 75–76
    as concrete entity: 148–49
    as God: 21, 25, 34, 36, 40–41, 65, 69–72, 98, 118, 133, 153
    as spirit: 89, 118
    as Tianzhu: 44, 74–75
    in ancient Confucian classics: 47, 49, 54, 116
    in neo-Confucianism: 79, 87, 106, 121
    see also Attributes of Tian, or Shangdi, or God, or Heaven; God, name of; jiaoshe; Terms Controversy

Shangshu 商書 see Shujing
Shaohao 少昊: 299, 337, 368–70
shen 神:
    and qi: 88, 123
    and taiji: 99, 287, 342
    and yin and yang: 90, 93
    as immaterial cause: 94
    as spirits: 123, 241, 269, 286–87
    as substance and function: 93
    as undifferentiated: 51
    of the dead: 306
Shengjiao sigui 聖教四規: 74–75, 364, 367
shengren 聖人: 51
Shengshui jiyan 聖水紀言: 73, 366
Shensilu 慎思錄: 74, 367
Shijing 詩經 / Shuoyue 說約 / Jizhuan 詩經
    集傳: 21, 23, 44–45, 48–49, 51, 53–54, 69,
    82–84, 90, 97, 118, 122
    Daya 大雅: 170, 173, 177, 180–81, 183–84,
        195–200, 221–23, 236, 238, 250, 257,
        259, 285, 294, 336
    Guofeng 國風: 170, 244, 284
    Lusong 魯頌: 181–82, 188
    Shangsong 商頌: 187, 229
    Xiaoya 小雅: 170, 188, 193, 198, 229–30,
        234, 250, 285, 339, 376
    Zhousong 周頌: 184, 196–97, 224,
        235–36, 251, 260, 307, 310, 312
Shishu biancuojie 詩書辨錯解: 44
shitian 侍天: 76, 367
Shujing 書經 (Shangshu 尚書) / Rijiang
    日講 / Jizhuan 集傳 / Daquan 大全:
    21, 37, 44–45, 47–49, 51, 54–55, 62, 80,
    83–84, 90, 94, 106, 116
    Duofang 多方: 37, 195, 200, 242
    Duoshi 多士: 244
    Hongfan 洪範: 182, 194, 222, 250
    Lizheng 立政: 177, 192, 211
    Pan Geng 盤庚: 336
    Taijia 太甲: 173, 187, 252, 263, 336
    Taishi 泰誓: 116, 171–72, 174–75, 187, 193,
        196, 236, 319, 326, 335, 339
    Yueming 說命: 194, 235
    Zhaogao 召誥: 170, 173, 196, 231, 333

Zhonghui zhi gao 仲虺之誥: 181, 191,
    233, 255
Shun 舜: 37, 185–86, 222, 225, 227–28, 296,
    332, 336, 362
Shuowen jiezi 說文解字: 64
sijiqinglisi 祠祭清吏司: 67
Siku quanshu 四庫全書: 60, 67
Simon, Richard: 36
Sipian yaodao buzhu bianmeng qianshuo
    四篇要道補注便蒙淺說: 75, 379
Sishu daquan 四書大全: 44, 58, 62
Sishu huowen 四書或問: 273
Sishu jizhu 四書集註: 55–58, 60
Sishu mengyin 四書蒙引: 22, 44, 50, 60–61,
    91, 98, 106
    Daxue 大學: 210, 231, 255, 266, 313, 376
    Lunyu 論語: 231, 251, 253, 279, 283, 300
    Mencius 孟子: 232, 251, 253–54, 261,
        267–68, 283, 293, 311
    Zhongyong 中庸: 222–23, 252, 258, 267,
        271, 274, 276,–77, 289, 292–93, 302,
        304, 308, 314, 335, 339, 343
Sishu rijiang 四書日講: 36, 42–45, 50, 55, 57,
    61–62, 69, 79–81, 85
    Daxue 大學: 210
    Lunyu 論語: 210, 224, 230, 233, 240, 253,
        278, 283, 302, 304
    Mencius 孟子: 209, 220, 222, 228–29,
        231–32, 279, 283, 296, 334
    Zhongyong 中庸: 209, 236, 260, 282, 302
Sishu zhijie 四書直解: 22, 36, 44, 55, 57–62, 83
    Lunyu 論語: 225, 231, 260, 294, 303–04, 326
    Mencius 孟子: 210, 222, 227–28, 232, 269
    Zhongyong 中庸: 223, 268, 303, 334
Six Ministries see Liubu
Song Yecao 宋野草: 60
Song Zhaoyue 宋兆禬: 61
Song 宋 dynasty: 9, 11, 13, 21–22, 36, 39, 46,
    80, 113, 371–72, 375
soul:
    common to world, world-soul: 87, 89,
        103, 256, 270
    of the dead: 34, 94, 169–70, 180, 268,
        294–95, 300, 307–08, 315, 320, 328
    of Heaven: 148, 248, 256

human: 94, 167, 261, 287, 294–95, 339, 354–55
immortality of: 59, 94–95
Spinoza, Baruch: 13, 99–100, 140
Spiritual Exercises: 131
Standaert, Nicolas: 33, 45, 65
Suárez, Francisco:
    and Being of reason: 85
    and divine names and divine attributes: 133–34, 374, 376
    and faith: 150, 351
    and infidels: 152
    and influence upon Noël: 14, 30, 131
    and reasoned reason: 86
    and religion: 151
    and sapiential realism: 132,
    and transcendental relations: 143–44
    and *via negationis*: 97, 141, 342
    see also *De divina substantia ejusque attributis*
Summarium NAT: 25, 27, 40–41, 53, 55, 62, 65, 68, 70–74, 159
Sun Ke'an 孫可庵: 75
Sun Xueshi 孫學詩: 73
superstition, or superstitious: 9, 34–35, 67, 166–68, 322, 391
supreme intelligence: 89, 357

Tai Wang 太王: 170, 183, 223–24
Taihao 太皞: 299, 368–70
taiji 太極:
    and neo-Confucianism: 14, 23, 50, 63, 75, 79, 87, 90
    and *taixu*: 61, 264
    as creating nature (*natura naturans*) : 13, 23, 44, 96–101, 105–06, 141–47, 206, 340–42
    as essence of a thing: 101–02, 105–06, 344
    as God: 37, 75, 77, 89, 96, 105–06, 133, 249, 262, 342, 351–52
    as matter: 95
    as principle of motion and rest: 104–05, 105–06, 140–44, 286, 347
    as spirit: 121, 126, 147, 262, 286
    as *taiyi* 太一: 98
    as totality: 102–03, 105–06

Taiji tushuo jie 太極圖說解: 97, 101
taixu 太虛: 60–61, 125–26
    and Buddhism, Daoism: 61, 99, 147
    and creation: 125
    as Being of Reason: 61, 89, 99, 249, 342
    as empty: 99, 147, 264
    as *li*: 61
    as *qi*: 61, 89
    as *taiji*: 61, 89, 98, 126, 264, 342
Terms Controversy: 10, 33–34, 40–41, 49, 63, 69, 71, 106
theism, or theistic: 23, 38, 79, 87, 105, 133–34
Thomas, Antoine: 18, 23–24, 26, 41, 387
Thomistic: 10, 82, 129–31, 133, 136, 142, 144
tian 天:
    and Chinese Christians' understanding of it: 44–47, 74
    and early Jesuits understanding: 41–44, 68, 70–71, 80
    and its metaphorical and literal meanings: 37–38, 40, 116, 120, 169
    and *li* and *qi*: 21–22, 79, 86, 124–25
    and mutual interaction of Tian and mankind: 80
    and non-Christians understanding: 75–77
    and Zhang Juzheng's interpretation: 58–59, 62
    as abstract entity: 148–49
    as God: 24, 28, 66, 71, 118–19, 165
    as name of God: 25, 34, 40–41, 69, 105, 169
    as *natura naturans*: 101
    as spirit: 66, 89
    in ancient Confucian classics: 24, 38, 45, 48–50, 54, 132–34
    in neo-Confucianism: 36, 50, 79, 87, 89, 106, 120, 123, 125–26
    see also Attributes of *Tian*, or *Shangdi*, or God, or Heaven; God, name of; *jiaoshe*; *jing Tian*; Material Heaven; Terms Controversy; Union, of man and Heaven
Tian Ru tong yi kao 天儒同異考: 46

Tian Ru yin 天儒印: 40, 70, 359
tiandi 天帝: 44, 55, 84, 118, 125, 235, 344, 372, 390
Tianjiao he Ru 天教合儒: 46–49, 79
Tianjing 天經: 76, 379
tianli 天理: 55, 59, 76, 116, 121, 126, 206, 235, 379
tianming 天命: 76, 121, 139, 210, 222, 379–80
Tianshi mingbian 天釋明辨: 73, 361, 366
tiantan 天壇: 53
tianxue 天學: 23–25, 41–42, 74–75, 359, 363, 378
Tianxue benyi 天學本意
 see *Gujin jing Tian jian*
Tianxue zhengfu 天學證符: 74
tianzhi 天志: 76, 379
Tianzhu 天主: 24, 44, 70–75, 358–64, 366, 377, 379–80, 390–91
Tianzhu jiangsheng yanxing jilüe 天主降生言行記略: 71, 360, 366
Tianzhu shiyi 天主實義 or *Tianxue shiyi* 天學實義: 45, 57, 72–73, 83, 90, 95, 258, 359, 361, 366
Tournon, Maillard de: 26, 42
transcendental: 86, 92–93, 96–99, 102–04, 140, 142–43, 292–93, 347
Tratados históricos, políticos, éticos y religiosos de la monarchia de China: 68
Trinity: 152–53, 160, 205, 351
Trismegistus: 97, 141, 342
True Meaning of the Lord of Heaven see *Tianzhu shiyi*

union:
 of man and God: 83
 of man and Heaven: 82–83, 86, 258–61
 of soul and body: 278–79, 287

Vagnone, Alfonso: 381
Valignano, Alessandro: 130
Verbiest, Ferdinand: 384
void: 91, 127, 147–48, 166, 262, 266

Wan Jing 萬經: 53, 294
Wan Zhang 萬章: 182, 186–88, 222, 227, 253, 283
Wang Bi 王弼: 117

Wang Changhui 王昌會: 48, 372
Wang Daiyu 王岱輿: 75
Wang Ji 王季: 82, 170, 183–84
Wang Qi 王圻: 66
Wang Suqin 王素琴: 60
Wang Yangming 王陽明, 110, 112
Wanli 萬曆 emperor: 57–58, 62, 67, 83, 359–60, 365
Wen Wang 文王: 37, 83–84, 172, 194, 201, 203, 234, 240, 294, 306–07, 359
Wenxian tongkao 文獻通考: 47, 63, 66, 98, 276, 306, 313, 317–19, 332, 343, 369, 371
Wesselius, Carel: 12, 29, 35, 66
Wong, Felix: 12, 22, 28, 59, 61, 91, 93
words, as arbitrary signs: 69, 358
Wu Nanzou 吳南驥: 51
Wu Sunyou, 吳蓀右: 51, 213, 219–20
Wu Wang 武王: 172, 174–75, 177–78, 193–94, 196, 203, 234, 236, 240, 242, 306, 310, 326, 330, 340
Wudi 武帝: 369
wuji 無極: 44, 97, 141–42, 342, 349
Wujing 五經: 52, 54, 62, 363, 381
Wujing daquan 五經大全: 52, 54, 62

Xia Dachang 夏大常 (Matthias): 52
Xiao Qinghe 肖清和: 46
Xici 繫辭: 51, 63, 92, 94, 98, 102, 221
Xiesheng pinzijian 諧聲品字箋: 43, 63, 65–66, 88–89, 263, 267
xing 性: 23, 87, 121, 124–25, 165, 210, 252, 297
Xingli biaoti 性理標題: 63, 87, 243, 251
Xingli daquan 性理大全: 62–63, 87, 95, 123, 263
Xingmipian 醒迷篇: 324, 375
Xingxue cushu 性學觕述: 73, 362, 366
Xiong Shili 熊十力: 123
Xu Guangqi 徐光啓: 40, 71–72, 360, 365
Xu Pu 徐溥: 66

Yan Mo 嚴謨, or Paul Yan 嚴保祿: 40, 44–46, 53, 54, 86, 321
Yandi 炎帝: 299, 368–70
yang 陽: 23, 85, 90–93, 95, 103–05, 140, 142–45, 237, 262, 269–70, 347–48
Yang Tingyun 楊廷筠: 40, 71–73, 83, 361, 366

Yao 堯: 37, 171, 185–86, 222, 225, 227, 241, 310, 362
Yijing 易經 or Zhouyi 周易: 44, 50, 51–52, 69, 118, 122–23, 125
   Mengyin 易經蒙引: 51, 217, 245
   Rijiang 易經日講: 52, 276, 299, 338, 349
   Zhouyi Benyi 周易本義: 51, 102, 106, 269
   Zhouyi Daquan 周易大全: 52, 102
   Zhouyi Zhengjie 周易正解: 44, 51, 69, 81–82, 85, 94, 102–04, 106, 211, 296–97
yin 陰: 23, 85, 90–93, 95, 103–05, 140, 142–45, 237, 262, 269–70, 347–48
yin and yang 陰陽:
   and guishen 鬼神: 287–92
   and taiji 太極: 104, 141–42, 146, 347–49
   as matter and form: 92, 143
   as transcendental relations: 92–93, 140–46, 292, 347
Yishuo 易說: 51
Yongle 永樂 emperor: 52, 54
Yu Desheng 虞德升: 65
Yu Xianxi 虞咸熙: 65

Zhan Yingpeng 詹應鵬: 75
Zhang Geng 張庚: 40, 74, 363, 367
Zhang Juzheng/ Zhang Gelao 張居正/張閣老: 22, 40, 46, 57–59, 61–62, 74, 82–84, 95, 191, 363, 367
   see also Sishuzhijie四書直解
Zhang of Han 漢章帝: 66
Zhang Xingyao 張星曜: 46, 75, 77, 79
Zhang Yi 張儀: 133, 373, 375
Zhang Zai 張載: 51–52, 60–62, 84, 89, 93, 98
Zhang Zhidong 張之洞: 120
Zhang Zhong 張中: 75
Zhao Chang 趙昌: 47, 390–91
Zhen Dexiu 真德秀: 101, 345
Zheng Kangcheng 鄭康成: 273, 368, 371
Zhengde 正德 emperor: 67, 380
Zhengjiao zhenquan 正教真詮: 75, 379
Zhengshi lüeshuo 拯世略說: 74, 363, 367
Zhengzitong 正字通: 47, 63–65, 69, 120, 266, 277, 336, 369–70
Zhifang waiji 職方外紀: 73, 361, 366

Zhongyong 中庸 / Zhangju 章句 / Rijiang 日講 / Zhijie 直解 / Mengyin 蒙引:
   Zhongyong 1: 81, 173, 209, 260, 334
   Zhongyong 13: 222, 223
   Zhongyong 16: 23, 90–91, 267, 271, 288, 289, 292–93, 301–03, 339
   Zhongyong 19: 176, 308, 314, 334
   Zhongyong 23: 124
   Zhongyong 24: 303
   Zhongyong 26: 98, 252, 258, 274, 282, 343
   Zhongyong 29: 90, 276, 277
   Zhongyong 30: 49, 182
   Zhongyong 31: 268
   Zhongyong 33: 236
Zhou Wang 周王, or Princes of Zhou Dynasty: 37, 194–95, 198, 200
Zhou 紂: 175, 179, 181, 185, 187, 189, 192, 234, 310, 319, 321, 330
Zhouyi 周易 see Yijing
Zhou Dunyi 周敦頤/Zhouzi 周子: 92, 97, 104, 347–48, 349
Zhu Xi 朱熹:
   and atheism: 54–55, 57, 84
   and guishen: 90–93
   and his commentaries: 49, 51, 53–54, 56, 82
   and influence from Daoism: 124
   and li: 45, 55, 58–59, 61, 84, 89
   and method of reading: 116
   and monotheistic interpretation: 53–54
   and Noël's acceptance: 44, 57
   and Noël's translation of Xiaoxue: 22, 28
   and qi: 60–61, 89, 124
   and religious thought: 14
   and School of Principle: 111, 126
   and taiji 太極: 44, 59, 60–61, 79, 97–98, 101–06, 143–46
   and Tian, Di, Shangdi: 45, 55, 58, 73–74, 82–84
Zhu Zongyuan 朱宗元: 40, 74, 367, 375
Zhuangzi 莊子: 124
Zhuanxu 顓頊: 172, 178, 203, 299, 337, 368–70
zhuzai 主宰: 73, 98, 253, 361, 363
Zhuzi yulei 朱子語類: 85, 87, 106
Zihui 字彙: 63–66, 196, 267, 320, 338
Zisi 子思: 72, 257, 359–60

GLOBAL PERSPECTIVES ON MEDIEVAL AND EARLY MODERN HISTORIOGRAPHY

All volumes in this series are evaluated by an Editorial Board, strictly on academic grounds, based on reports prepared by referees who have been commissioned by virtue of their specialism in the appropriate field. The Board ensures that the screening is done independently and without conflicts of interest. The definitive texts supplied by authors are also subject to review by the Board before being approved for publication. Further, the volumes are copyedited to conform to the publisher's stylebook and to the best international academic standards in the field.

In Preparation

François-Xavier Fauvelle, Benoît Grévin, and Ingrid Houssaye Michienzi, *Malfante l'Africain : Relectures de la «Lettre du Touat»* (1447)